Shooter's Bible®

ABOUT OUR COVER

The three single trigger shotguns displayed on our front cover, all made by the great British gunmaker, Boss & Company, rank among the world's rarest and most valuable firearms of their kind. The gun pictured at the top in our cover photo is the rarest of them all—a Boss .410 gauge over and under, said to be the only one in existence. In the middle is a 28 gauge over/under, which is also quite rare; and the bottom gun pictured is a 28 gauge side-by-side. All three guns were made in the 1950s and cost between $2000 and $3000. Their value today is incalculable, but certainly it ranges into the hundreds of thousands of dollars.

The story of the Boss shotgun began in 1830, when founder Thomas Boss went into the gunmaking business. Boss's father had been among the select few who served their apprenticeships under Joseph Manton, generally considered to be the greatest gunmaker of his day. The elder Boss had, in turn, taught young Tom everything he knew.

Over the years, the Boss name became synonymous with "the best" in shotgun making, helped no little by the inventive genius of John Robertson, who developed for Boss the first intercepting safety for the hammerless double, and who later came up with the first functional single trigger shotgun. Around 1905, the first Boss over and under model was introduced, featuring Boss's now standard ejector system, which Robertson had also perfected several years earlier.

Today, Boss & Company remains in the hands of John Robertson's family. The rarity of the guns they continue to produce may be judged best by the fact that only about 9,400 guns bearing the name, "Boss & Co.," now exist throughout the world. Readers who are interested in learning more about classic British shotguns are invited to read the article on that subject by Dr. Jim Casada, which begins on p. 74.

ASK YOUR BOOKSELLER OR SPORTING GOODS DEALER FOR THESE OTHER FINE PUBLICATIONS FROM STOEGER

THE ACCURATE RIFLE by Warren Page
ADVANCED BOWHUNTING by Roger Maynard
ADVANCED MUZZLELOADER'S GUIDE by Toby Bridges
ANTIQUE GUNS: THE COLLECTOR'S GUIDE by John Traister
BLACK POWDER GUIDE, 2nd Edition, by George C. Nonte Jr.
THE COMPLETE BOOK OF DEER HUNTING by Byron W. Dalrymple
DRESS 'EM OUT by Captain James A. Smith
THE DUCK HUNTER'S HANDBOOK by Bob Hinman
THE FLYTIER'S MANUAL by Mike Dawes
GAME COOKBOOK, New Revised Edition, by Geraldine Steindler
GOOSE HUNTING by Charles L. Cadieux
GUNSMITHING AT HOME by John E. Traister
GUN TRADER'S GUIDE, 13th Edition, by Paul Wahl
HANDLOADER'S GUIDE by Stanley W. Trzoniec
HANDLOADER'S MANUAL OF CARTRIDGE CONVERSION by John J.
    Donnelly
THE HANDY SPORTSMAN by Loring D. Wilson
HOW TO BUY AND SELL USED GUNS by John Traister
HUNTING PREDATORS FOR HIDES & PROFIT by Wilf E. Pyle
INTERNATIONAL GUIDE TO TROUT FLIES by Bob Church
LAW ENFORCEMENT BIBLE, No. 2, Edited by Robert A. Scanlon
MODERN WATERFOWL GUNS & GUNNING by Don Zutz
OUTDOORSMAN'S EMERGENCY MANUAL by Anthony J. Acerrano
PISTOL GUIDE by George C. Nonte Jr.
THE PRACTICAL BOOK OF KNIVES by Ken Warner
PRECISION HANDLOADING by John Withers
REALISTIC DECOYS: CARVING, TEXTURING, PAINTING & FINISHING by
    Keith Bridenhagen & Patrick Spielman
RELOADER'S GUIDE, 3rd Edition, by R.A. Steindler
REVOLVER GUIDE by George C. Nonte Jr.
RIFLE GUIDE by R.A. Steindler
TAXIDERMY GUIDE, 2nd Edition, by Russell Tinsley

Shooter's Bible

NO. 80
1989 EDITION

EDITOR:
William S. Jarrett

PRODUCTION EDITOR:
Charlene Cruson

FIREARMS CONSULTANTS:
Jim Lagiss, Bill Meade,
Vincent A. Pestilli, Frank Petrini,
Robert A. Scanlon, Nick Sisley
and Jon Sundra

COVER PHOTOGRAPHER:
Ray Wells

DESIGN AND PRODUCTION:
Publishers Graphics
Bethel, Connecticut

PUBLISHER:
Robert E. Weise

STOEGER PUBLISHING COMPANY

Published by Stoeger Publishing Company
55 Ruta Court
South Hackensack, New Jersey 07606

Library of Congress Catalog Card No.: 63-6200

International Standard Book No.: 0080-9365

Manufactured in the United States of America

Distributed to the book trade and to the sporting goods trade by Stoeger Industries, 55 Ruta Court, South Hackensack, New Jersey 07606

In Canada, distributed to the book trade and to the sporting goods trade by Stoeger Trading Company, 169 Idema Road, Markham, Ontario, L3R 1A9.

OLIVER F. WINCHESTER
A LEGEND IN HIS OWN TIME

This 80th edition of *Shooter's Bible* is dedicated to the memory of Oliver F. Winchester, founder of the renowned Winchester Repeating Arms Company. Born in 1810 to a poor family in Boston, Winchester went to work early on as an apprentice carpenter, becoming a master builder at 21. The lure of business and a better life led the young man to Baltimore, where he owned and operated a men's clothing store.

By 1848, Winchester, by now a large man with a commanding presence, had acquired enough capital to open the nation's first shirt factory in New Haven, Connecticut, where he continued to prosper. Ten years later he made his first move into the gun business, buying out the Volcanic Repeating Arms Company, located in nearby Norwich, Connecticut. His immediate goal was to develop and market the first successful repeating rifle. To do this, Winchester hired a genius of a gunmaker, Benjamin Tyler Henry, who soon perfected the first of many famous Henry Rifles. It wasn't until the Civil War, though, that the repeating rifle was able to prove its su-

periority and became accepted. By 1866, Winchester had incorporated his company as the Winchester Repeating Arms Company, with headquarters in New Haven.

The first rifle to bear the Winchester name was the breech-loading Winchester 66, which, along with the Winchester 77, revolutionized the arms industry. These successes underscored Oliver Winchester's genius as an organizer, manufacturer and marketer. His introduction of new, mass-production methods and equipment, combined with a passion for research and development, enabled the company to grow rapidly. Perhaps the highlight of this growth was the introduction in 1873 of the legendary "Gun that won the West," also called "The Boss" by an admiring fan, "Buffalo Bill" Cody.

Winchester died in 1880 at the age of 70. He left behind a prosperous company and a rich tradition, not to mention a name that has endured and become synonymous with fine gunmaking. We at *Shooter's Bible* salute him.

Contents

FOREWORD

This year's edition of Shooter's Bible—our 80th—is dedicated to Oliver Winchester, founder of the famous gun company that continues to produce fine rifles and shotguns in its New Haven (CT) plant.

Once again, we've added a color section to the book, this time featuring a 16-page reprint of Stoeger's 1939 catalog. Last year, the subject was *rifles*; this year we've chosen *shotguns*, and we highly recommend that you turn to p. 8 and see what was going on half a century ago in the shotgun field.

Immediately following that is another interesting departure from our norm: a 10-page treat for all those who admire and perhaps even collect sporting art. Our thanks to Dr. Steve Irwin for letting us borrow from his extensive and very impressive collection. And if you crave still more lively gun history, there are Jim Cobb's fascinating story about the Baker shotgun and John Malloy's nostalgic piece on the Zouave rifle.

We haven't forgotten the present and future, not by a long shot. Stan Trzoniec ("Custom Gun Shops"), Wilf Pyle ("Up-To-Date Computers") and Ralph Quinn ("Cartridges: The Quick, The Dead & The Revived") have turned in up-to-the-minute articles on contemporary subjects.

Our catalog section, as always, contains illustrations and descriptions of as many guns and accessories as we can cram into one book of this size. Two new developments are well worth commenting on: one is the series of introductory essays on "What's New" in handguns, rifles and shotguns written by three highly respected experts in these areas, namely Frank Petrini on handguns, Jon Sundra on rifles, and Nick Sisely on shotguns. We welcome them aboard, not only for this edition of Shooter's Bible, but hopefully for many more to come.

The other development has to do with the continuing effect of the falling dollar on imported guns. You'll note some familiar names are missing from our catalog section this year as a result, but as always there are notable replacements—Varner, Ultra Light, SKB, New England Firearms, Classic Doubles, Victory Arms, Modern Muzzleloading and Erma, to name a few.

So the beat goes on. We hope you enjoy wandering through our pages once again and, as ever, we welcome your comments and suggestions.

William S. Jarrett
Editor

Articles

FIFTY YEARS AGO IN SHOOTER'S BIBLE

EDITOR'S NOTE

In last year's edition (Volume 79, 1988), we introduced a new series to lead off our article section: a sampling of rifle photos and specifications taken from the pages of A.F. Stoeger's 1938 catalog (which later evolved into what is now *Shooter's Bible*).

This year, we've decided to treat our readers to more of the same, only this time the subject is *shotguns*. We hope you'll enjoy browsing through these old but well preserved pages from our 1939 catalog, and that you'll perhaps gain some new perspectives and appreciation for the advances made in shotgun design and production over the past 50 years by the world's leading shotgun makers. Those old guns had plenty going for them, of course, but modern technology has added more to shotgun accuracy and durability than most of us have ever stopped to realize. So enjoy.

NEW YORK WORLD'S FAIR 1939
☆☆ JUBILEE ISSUE ☆☆

COPYRIGHT
N.Y.W.F.

STOEGER'S
CATALOG & HANDBOOK

ARMS & AMMUNITION
GUN ACCESSORIES & PARTS
GUNSMITH TOOLS

STOEGER ARMS CORP
AMERICA'S GREAT GUN HOUSE
507 FIFTH AVENUE at 42 ST NEW YORK N.Y.

PARKER SHOTGUNS

PARKER TROJAN

BARRELS—Finest Steel. STOCK—American Walnut, neatly checkered, 2½ inches drop at heel, 1⅝ inches drop at comb, length 14 inches, full pistol grip, no cap, hard rubber butt plate. Made to the following specifications only:

  12 ga. 26, 28 or 30 inch barrels, weights, 7 to 7¾ pounds.
  16 ga. 26 or 28 inch barrels, weights, 6½ to 7 pounds.
  20 ga. 26 or 28 inch barrels, weights, 6¼ to 6¾ pounds.

The 30 inch barrels are bored both barrels full choke; 26 and 28 inch barrels bored right modified, left full choke. Barrels will be bored as above unless otherwise ordered.

Price $72.50
Parker Trojan with single trigger 101.10
Positively no other deviation will be made from above specifications.

12, 16, and 20 GAUGE

PARKER V. H. E.

With automatic ejector.................................$125.00
With selective single trigger..........................153.60

The finest gun of its grade ever produced. Built for service and durability. Parker workmanship throughout.

BARRELS—Finest steel. STOCK—American Walnut, neatly checkered. ENGRAVING—Line engraving simple but perfectly executed.

SPECIFICATIONS—Straight or half pistol grip, gauges 12, 16, 20, 28, .410. Various weights, lengths, drops and measurements.

12, 16, 20, 28 and .410 GAUGE

Beaver tail forearm, Extra $14.85

PARKER G. H. E.

With automatic ejector.................................$150.00
With selective single trigger..........................178.60

A hard shooting moderately priced gun that is fast gaining in popularity.

BARRELS—Finest Steel. STOCK—Figured American Walnut, checkering of high grade, hard rubber butt plate. ENGRAVING—Tastefully engraved.

SPECIFICATIONS—Option of straight or half pistol grip, gauges 10, 12, 16, 20, 28, .410. Various weights, lengths, drops and measurements.

10, 12, 16, 20, 28 and .410 GAUGE

Beaver tail forearm, Extra $14.85

10, 12, 16, 20, 28 and .410 GAUGE

Beaver tail forearm, Extra $19.00

PARKER D. H. E.

With automatic ejector.................................$195.00
With selective single trigger..........................227.00

There is no gun which can compare with this Parker at the price.

BARRELS—Finest steel. STOCK—Selected figured stock, fine checkering, silver shield, skeleton butt plate or rubber recoil pad. ENGRAVING—Game scenes set off with scroll.

SPECIFICATIONS—Any style of grip, gauges 10, 12, 16, 20, 28, .410. Various weights, lengths, drops and measurements.

PARKER C. H. E.

The combined fine qualities of design and workmanship insure lifetime service.

BARRELS—Finest steel.

STOCK—Selected high grade Walnut, beautifully checkered, silver shield, skeleton butt plate or rubber recoil pad. Monte Carlo or cheek piece, if desired.

SPECIFICATIONS—Any style of grip, gauges 10, 12, 16, 20, 28, .410. Various weights, lengths, measurements.

With automatic ejector................$275.00
With selective single trigger..........307.00

10, 12, 16, 20, 28, and .410 GAUGE

Beaver tail forearm, Extra $25.00

10, 12, 16, 20, 28, and .410 GAUGE

Beaver tail forearm, Extra $29.00

PARKER B. H. E.

Many features of the most costly guns are found in this popular model.

BARRELS—Finest steel.

STOCK—Imported Walnut, fine checkering, gold shield, skeleton butt plate or rubber recoil pad. Monte Carlo or cheek piece if desired.

ENGRAVING—Game scenes handsomely engraved.

SPECIFICATIONS—Any style of grip, gauges 10, 12, 16, 20, 28, .410. Various weights, lengths, drops and measurements.

With automatic ejector................$375.00
With selective single trigger..........407.00

PARKER SHOTGUNS

10, 12, 16, 20, 28 and .410 GAUGE

Beaver tail forearm, Extra $31.00

PARKER A. H. E.

Without a peer in the realm of fine quality guns offered at an attractive price.

BARRELS—Finest grade steel.

STOCK—Selected imported Walnut, highly checkered, gold shield, skeleton butt plate or rubber recoil pad. Monte Carlo or cheek piece, if desired.

ENGRAVING—Richly engraved with scroll and game scenes, beautifully wrought.

SPECIFICATIONS—Any stock measurements, including any style of grip, gauges 10, 12, 16, 20, 28, .410. Various weights, lengths, drops and measurements.

With automatic ejector..................$515.00
With single trigger...................... 547.00

PARKER A. A. H. E.

Beautiful lines, fast handling and hard shooting qualities have made this gun a favorite.

BARRELS—Finest steel, a material of great strength and durability.

STOCK—Fine imported Circassian Walnut, handsomely checkered, gold name plate, skeleton butt plate or rubber recoil pad. Monte Carlo or cheek piece if desired.

ENGRAVING—Beautiful designs in scroll or scroll and game.

SPECIFICATIONS—Any stock dimensions, including any style of grip, gauges 10, 12, 16, 20, 28, .410. Various weights, lengths, drops and measurements.

With automatic ejector...............$735.00
With single trigger.................... 776.50

10, 12, 16, 20, 28 and .410 GAUGE

Beaver tail forearm, Extra $38.00

PARKER A-1 SPECIAL

For the discriminating sportsman who appreciates the ownership of a gun of the highest quality of workmanship.

BARRELS—Best quality steel with high tensile strength.

STOCK—Finest imported Circassian Walnut obtainable, beautifully checkered, solid gold name plate, triggers heavily gold plated, skeleton butt plate or rubber recoil pad.

ENGRAVING — Individually designed, chosen for its simple richness, gold inlaying, engraved to customer's taste if desired.

SPECIFICATIONS—Made to order, individually. Any style of grip desired, gauges 10, 12, 16, 20, 28, .410. Various weights, lengths, drops and measurements.

With automatic ejector..................$890.00
With single trigger..................... 942.00

10, 12, 16, 20, 28 and .410 GAUGE

Beaver tail forearm, Extra $46.00

PARKER SKEET GUNS

All double barrel PARKER guns from the "V. H. E." Grade up are furnished in Skeet models. These guns are built to the customer's individual specifications. They are thoroughly tested to insure the finest shooting qualities at Skeet ranges.

Made in 12, 16, 20, 28, and .410 gauges, 26-inch barrels. Bored for Skeet shooting. Right barrel marked "SKEET-OUT" for first shot at outgoing target. Left barrel marked "SKEET-IN" for incoming target. Option of any other barrel length and boring. Automatic ejectors. Non-automatic safety. Option of automatic safety. Selective single trigger. Ivory bead front and rear sights. Red bead front sight if desired. Beavertail fore-end. Stock dimensions, unless otherwise specified, 14 inches long, 2¼ inches drop at heel, 1½ inches drop at comb. Checkered butt on "V. H. E." and "G. H. E." grades. Skeleton steel butt on "D. H. E." to "A. 1. SPECIAL" grades. Straight grip. Option of full pistol grip with cap or half pistol grip. Stock measurements and other specifications will be varied in accordance with descriptions and prices given under separate grades. Quality of walnut, type of engraving, and other features correspond with respective

This Illustration Shows The

"V. H. E." Grade Skeet Gun

grades. Also supplied with raised ventilated rib at the extra charge.

"V. H. E." Grade Speet Gun............................	$168.45
"G. H. E." Grade Skeet Gun............................	193.45
"D. H. E." Grade Skeet Gun............................	246.00
"C. H. E." Grade Skeet Gun............................	332.00
"B. H. E." Grade Skeet Gun............................	436.00
"A. H. E." Grade Skeet Gun............................	578.00
"A. A. H. E." Grade Skeet Gun.........................	814.50
"A. 1. SPECIAL" Grade Skeet Gun......................	988.00

L. C. SMITH SHOTGUNS

"FIELD GRADE"

This gun is especially designed for those desiring a gun for field and marsh where rough usage is required. The shooting powers of this gun can be relied upon to fully equal those of the higher grades.

Non-Ejector $43.20
With Automatic Ejector 57.20
Field Grade with Automatic Ejector and Selective Hunter Single Trigger 82.20
Field Grade with Non-Selective Hunter Single Trigger 54.10
Field Grade Long Range Wild Fowl Gun 12 gauge only (3 inch chamber) 46.35
Field Special with Recoil Pad and 2 Sights.... 46.35

12, 16, 20 and .410 Gauge

SPECIFICATIONS
Grip: Full pistol regular, half or straight to order. Barrels, 26, 28, 30 and 32-inch Armor steel only; bored any way you choose from a cylinder to a full choke. Gauge: 12, 16, 20 and .410. Weights: 12 gauge, 6¼ to 8¼ pounds; 16 gauge, 6¼ to 7 pounds; 20 gauge, 5¾ to 6½ pounds; .410, 5½ to 6 lbs.

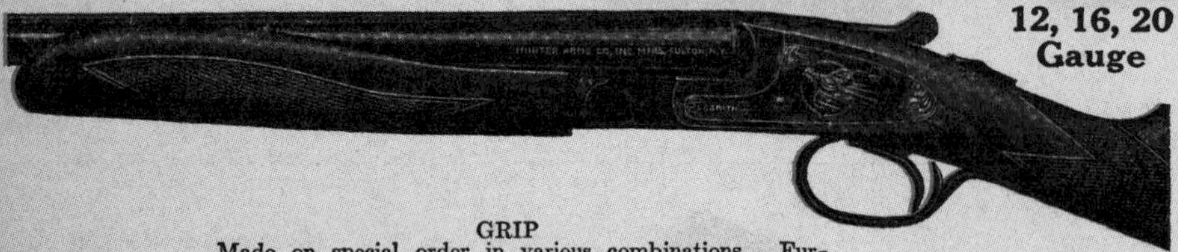

12, 16, 20 Gauge

GRIP
Made on special order in various combinations. Furnished with straight, full or half pistol grip.

GAUGE	BARRELS	WEIGHTS
12, 16 or 20	26, 27 or 28-inch London	12-gauge ....6¾ to 8 lbs.
.410-caliber	Steel, *proof tested.*	16-gauge ....6¾ to 7⅛ lbs.
	Right barrel Skeet Choke No. 1	20-gauge ....6¾ to 6¾ lbs.
	Left barrel Skeet Choke No. 2	.410-caliber .....6⅛ to 6½ lbs.

"SKEET SPECIAL"

A new gun for a new sport. An all season gun for an all season sport. 26-inch, 27-inch or 28-inch barrels. Straight grip stock, checkered wood butt, Streamline Beaver Tail Forend, Selective or Non-Selective Hunter One Trigger, Automatic Ejector. Light in weight, fast, easy to handle. Perfect balance that makes the gun point where you want it to point with the least possible effort on the part of the shooter. Right barrel has L. S. Smith Skeet Choke No. 1, and the left barrel L. C. Smith Skeet Choke No. 2, or you may have both barrels Skeet Choke No. 1 or Skeet Choke No. 2 if you choose.

Non-Ejector $54.10
With Non-Selective Single Trigger....... 65.00
With Automatic Ejector 68.10
With Non-Selective Single Trigger and Beaver Tail Forend 91.80

"IDEAL GRADE"

This gun is a "General Purpose" weapon, a sound, reliable and thoroughly serviceable gun and with just enough engraving to make it attractive, as the illustration shows. The barrels are bored and finished with extreme accuracy and care. For general purposes it is far superior to any other gun offered at a similar price.

Ideal Grade Non-Ejector $60.25
Ideal Grade with Automatic Ejector.... 74.25
Ideal Grade with Automatic Ejector and Selective Hunter Single Trigger........... 99.25
Ideal Grade Long Range Wild Fowl Gun (12 gauge only, 3 inch chamber) 63.40

12, 16, 20, and .410 Gauge

SPECIFICATIONS
Grip: Full pistol regular, half or straight to order. Barrels: 26, 28, 30 and 32-inch London steel, bored any way you choose from a cylinder to a full choke. Gauge: 12, 16, 20, and .410. Weights: 12 gauge, 6¼ to 8¼ pounds; 16 gauge, 6¼ to 7 pounds; 20 gauge, 5¾ to 6½ pounds.

12, 16, 20, and .410 Gauge

SPECIFICATIONS
Grip: Full pistol regular, half or straight to order. Barrels: 26, 28, 30 and 32-inch Crown steel bored any way you choose. Gauge: 12, 16, 20 and .410. Weights: 12 gauge, 6¼ to 8½ pounds; 16 gauge, 6¼ to 7 pounds; 20 gauge, 5¾ to 6½ pounds; .410 gauge, 5½ to 6 pounds.

"TRAP GRADE"

In this grade particular attention has been paid to the requirements of sportsmen desirous of a gun for trap shooting, as well as for field, with all the latest attachments—Hunter One Trigger and Auto Ejector especially—and at a very low price. Both lock-plates engraved with trap shooting scene. We can confidently recommend this grade as entirely satisfactory, especially for the purpose the name implies.

Trap Grade with Automatic Ejector........$95.85
Trap Grade with Automatic Ejector and Selective Hunter Single Trigger................126.55
Trap Grade with Automatic Ejector and Selective Hunter, Single Trigger, Beaver Tail Fore-end, Ventilated Rib, Recoil Pad and 2 Sights......175.65

"SPECIALTY GRADE"

A fine gun in all details, built to last a lifetime. Handsomely engraved as shown in the illustration, with fine lines of the best weapon and at a most moderate price. A thoroughly sound, serviceable gun, well fitted.

Specialty Grade, Non-Ejector.................$100.00
Specialty Grade with Automatic Ejector...... 118.50
Specialty Grade with Automatic Ejector and Selective Hunter Single Trigger............ 149.20
Specialty Grade with Automatic Ejector and Selective Hunter Single Trigger, Beaver Tail Fore-end, Ventilated Rib, Recoil Pad and 2 Sights 198.30

12, 16, 20, and .410 Gauge

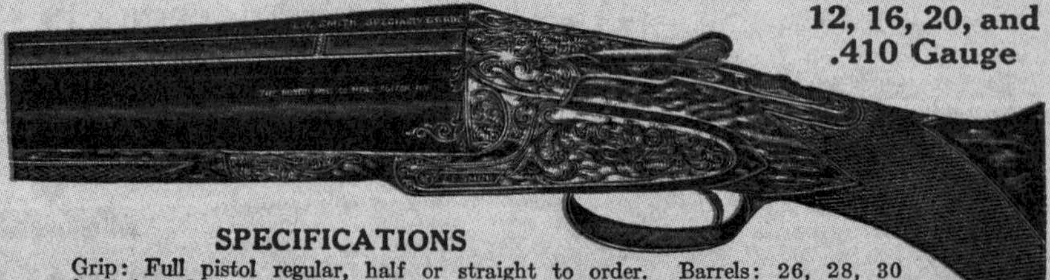

SPECIFICATIONS
Grip: Full pistol regular, half or straight to order. Barrels: 26, 28, 30 and 32-inch Nitro steel, bored any way you choose. Gauge: 12, 16, 20 and .410. Weights: 12 gauge, 6¼ to 8¼ pounds; 16 gauge, 6¼ to 7 pounds; 20 gauge, 5¾ to 6½ pounds; .410 gauge, 5½ to 6 pounds.

IMPORTANT NOTICE

If the combination you want is not listed on these pages, it may be made up from the prices shown below of the two trigger gun without ejector, the extra price of the features desired. Price combinations must be on the same grade. To obtain the price of any type combination on any L. C. Smith gun, add to the base price.

AUTOMATIC EJECTOR
Field, Skeet and Ideal—E...........................$14.00
Trap, Specialty and Crown—E....................... 18.50
Monogram, Premier and De Luxe—E................. 21.00

SELECTIVE HUNTER ONE-TRIGGER
Field Skeet and Ideal—O..........................$25.00
Trap and Specialty—O............................. 30.70
Crown, Monogram, Premier and De Luxe—O......... 33.00

NON-SELECTIVE HUNTER ONE-TRIGGER
Field, Skeet and Ideal—N......................... 10.90
Trap—N.. 13.90
Specialty—N..................................... 15.35
Crown, Monogram, Premier and De Luxe—N......... 18.00

BEAVER TAIL FORE-END
Skeet—B... 12.80
Ideal—B... 15.60

L. C. SMITH SHOTGUNS

OLYMPIC GRADE

The Olympic is especially built for trap shooting. Feel, balance and shooting qualities are featured in this model. Furnished with beaver tailed fore-end, recoil pad and Lyman ivory sights and ventilated rib.

Grip: Full-pistol is standard. All guns will be furnished with stock measurements taken from rear position of trigger.

Equipped with Automatic Ejector and Hunter Selective Single Trigger................$119.35

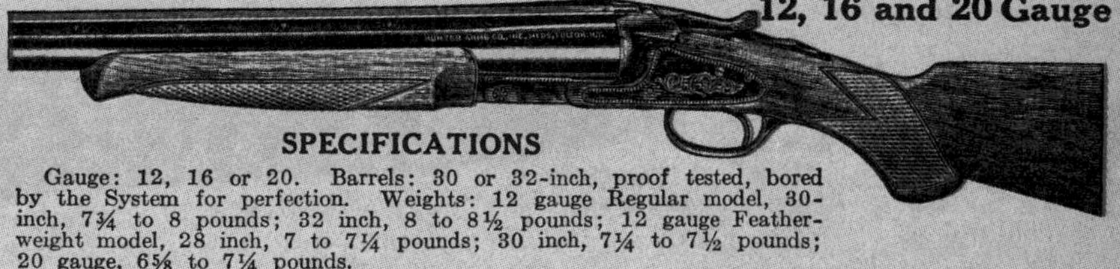

12, 16 and 20 Gauge

SPECIFICATIONS

Gauge: 12, 16 or 20. Barrels: 30 or 32-inch, proof tested, bored by the System for perfection. Weights: 12 gauge Regular model, 30-inch, 7¾ to 8 pounds; 32 inch, 8 to 8½ pounds; 12 gauge Featherweight model, 28 inch, 7 to 7¼ pounds; 30 inch, 7¼ to 7½ pounds; 20 gauge, 6⅝ to 7¼ pounds.

12, 16 and 20 Gauge

SPECIFICATIONS

Grip: Full pistol regular, half or straight to order. Barrels: 26, 28, 30 and 32-inch. Selected Nitro steel, bored to order from full choke to cylinder. Gauge: 12, 16 and 20. Weights: 12 gauge, 6¼ to 8¼ pounds, 16 gauge, 6¼ to 7 pounds; 20 gauge, 5¾ to 6½ pounds.

"CROWN GRADE"

A choice gun, with unsurpassed shooting qualities, pleasing the most critical. For hard and accurate shooting, in a class by itself. It will give unqualified satisfaction under the strain of continuous shooting at the traps and the rough usage in the field. Pleasing gold inlay and delicate engraving.

Crown Grade with Automatic Ejector and Hunter Single Selective Trigger...........$292.50
Crown Grade with Automatic Ejector, Hunter Selective Single Trigger, Beaver Tail Fore-end, Ventilated Rib, Recoil Pad and 2 Ivory Bead Sights 355.50

"MONOGRAM GRADE"

A serviceable gun of exceptionally high quality and more than usual beauty. The mechanisms of the lock and automatic ejector as well as other parts are exceedingly well finished. The engraving, embodying scroll and relief work. The stock is imported walnut, carefully finished. Sir Joseph Whitworth fluid steel barrel.

Monogram Grade with Automatic Ejector and Hunter Selective Single Trigger............$525.00
Monogram Grade with Automatic Ejector and Hunter Selective Single Trigger, Beaver Tail Fore-end, Ventilated Rib, Recoil Pad and 2 Ivory Sights 607.00

12, 16 and 20 Gauge

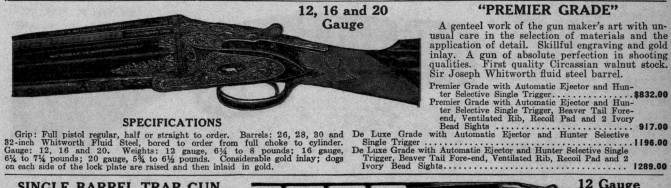

SPECIFICATIONS

Grip: Full pistol regular, half or straight to order. Barrels: 26, 28, 30 and 32-inch Whitworth fluid steel, bored to order from full choke to cylinder. Gauge: 12, 16 and 20. Weights: 12 gauge, 6¼ to 8¼ pounds; 16 gauge, 6¼ to 7 pounds; 20 gauge, 5¾ to 6½ pounds. Furnished with three block letters inlaid in gold on the trigger guard.

12, 16 and 20 Gauge

SPECIFICATIONS

Grip: Full pistol regular, half or straight to order. Barrels: 26, 28, 30 and 32-inch Whitworth Fluid Steel, bored to order from full choke to cylinder. Gauge: 12, 16 and 20. Weights: 12 gauge, 6¼ to 8 pounds; 16 gauge, 6¼ to 7¼ pounds; 20 gauge, 5¾ to 6½ pounds. Considerable gold inlay; dogs on each side of the lock plate are raised and then inlaid in gold.

"PREMIER GRADE"

A genteel work of the gun maker's art with unusual care in the selection of materials and the application of detail. Skillful engraving and gold inlay. A gun of absolute perfection in shooting qualities. First quality Circassian walnut stock. Sir Joseph Whitworth fluid steel barrel.

Premier Grade with Automatic Ejector and Hunter Selective Single Trigger...............$832.00
Premier Grade with Automatic Ejector and Hunter Selective Single Trigger, Beaver Tail Fore-end, Ventilated Rib, Recoil Pad and 2 Ivory Bead Sights 917.00
De Luxe Grade with Automatic Ejector and Hunter Selective Single Trigger 1196.00
De Luxe Grade with Automatic Ejector and Hunter Selective Single Trigger, Beaver Tail Fore-end, Ventilated Rib, Recoil Pad and 2 Ivory Bead Sights.....................................1289.00

SINGLE BARREL TRAP GUN

It has the famous L. C. Smith bolt that never shoots loose, the Smith cocking mechanism, the Smith automatic ejector and a quick action hammer that fits the firing pin dead on the head and not on an angle as in most single barrel guns. The sides of the rib are made parallel and make for quick and accurate sighting. The barrel itself is of extra fine grade steel, tough and strong, and is especially adapted to trap shooting. We furnish it in 30, 32 and 34 inch lengths. The stock is of fine quality walnut. This gun is thoroughly well made with the strongest bolting mechanism ever put into a gun, is beautifully engraved, nicely finished and well balanced. Olympic grade is made in 32 inch only. All other grades are made in 30 inch, 32 inch and 34 inch.

12 Gauge

OLYMPIC GRADE

SPECIFICATIONS

Stock and fore-end from especially selected walnut. Grip: Full pistol, half pistol or straight. Barrels: 12 gauge, 30, 32 and 34 inches, Nitro steel, bored by the Smith system for perfection in trap shooting. Trigger Position: Rear, unless otherwise specified. The Olympic single-barrel is manufactured and sold only in the one standard stock dimension, 14½—1½—1⅞, full pistol grip, while the Specialty and better grades can be had in any reasonable stock dimensions and in the different style pistol grips. Recoil pad and Lyman sights included as regular equipment on all Smith single barrel trap guns.

Olympic	..$108.45
Specialty	.. 145.50
Crown	.. 271.40
Monogram	.. 448.90
Premier	.. 748.20
De Luxe	..1122.30

Trap and Specialty—B.................................	$21.50
Crown—B	30.00
Monogram—B	49.00
Premier—B	52.00
De Luxe—B	60.00

LONG RANGE WILD FOWL GUN
12 Gauge Only

All Grade—L	3.15

VENTILATED RIB
Including Recoil Pad and Two Ivory Sights

Skeet—V	23.40
Trap and Specialty—V...............................	27.60

Crown, Monogram, Premier and De Luxe—V.................	$33.00

All grades of L. C. Smith double barrel, 12 gauge guns are made in both regular and featherweight models. This makes it possible to furnish a perfectly balanced gun in weights ranging from 6 pounds, 6 ounces, to 8¼ pounds.

The frame of the featherweight model is shorter than the regular frame and the lug is narrower; thus eliminating weight and giving the same perfect proportions in the light weight guns, which the regular frame gives in the heavier weights. This all-important feature is unique with the L. C. Smith.

ITHACA SHOTGUNS

10, 12, 16, 20, 28 AND .410–3" GAUGE

FIELD GRADE

The Ithaca Field Gun. For skeet, trap or game shooting, it's the least expensive Ithaca we can build. It will last a lifetime.

BARRELS—Smokeless Powder steel, proof tested with a double powder load.

STOCK AND FOREND—Black walnut, hand checkered, solid where stock joins the frame to prevent splitting, full pistol grip.

LOCKS—Same mechanical construction as in higher grade Ithacas and this lightning lock will improve any man's shooting.

PRICE—Field grade, $43.00. Ejector, if wanted, costs $12.95 extra. Ventilated rib, if wanted, $16.25. Beaver tail forearm, if wanted, $10.90. Ithaca Selective Single

NEW ITHACA FIELD GRADE DOUBLE

Trigger, if wanted, $21.60. Non-selective Single Trigger, if wanted, $8.50, on new or used Ithaca. Ithaca soft rubber recoil pad, if wanted, $2.25. Ivory Sights, if wanted, $1.10. Add $10.80 for the Magnum 10 gauge.

ITHACA SKEET MODEL FIELD GRADE

ITHACA SKEET GUNS

Available in all grades, Field, No. 2, No. 4, No. 5, No. 7, and $1,000.00 Grade. Special specifications best suited to skeet and upland game shooting as well: Beavertail forend, Selective Single Trigger, Automatic Ejectors, and Ivory Sights. Skeet Boring (excellent for field shooting, being an open type of boring) .26" barrels are standard. 14"x2½" are standard stock specifications.

Reasonable variations at no extra charge. Furnished in .410, 28, 20, 16, and 12 gauge.

Prices of Skeet guns with extras as described: Field Grade—$89.55, No. 2—$108.70, No. 4—$166.25, No. 5—$233.95, No. 7—$423.55, $1000.00 Grade—$1022.75.

A ventilated rib is sometimes desired on a Skeet gun. If so, add to above prices: $16.25 for Field and No. 2 Grades and $21.65 for No. 4, 5, 7, or $1000.00 Grades.

ITHACA NO. 2
10, 12, 16, 20, 28 AND .410–3" GAUGE

The Ithaca No. 2, thoroughly well-made and reliable for skeet, game or trap, at a moderate price.

BARRELS—Fluid steel of extra grade.

STOCK AND FOREND—Black walnut with nice color and finish, neatly hand checkered full pistol grip.

LOCKS—Lightning fast locks that will stand use and misuse. You do not have to strain your wrist to cock an Ithaca.

ENGRAVING—Frame, top lever, foreend iron, trigger plate and guard engraved by hand. Bird scene and leaf design on each side of the frame, leaf design on trigger plate and guard.

PRICE—No. 2, $62.15. Ejector, if wanted, $12.95 extra. Ventilated rib, if wanted, $16.25. Beaver tail forearm, if

wanted, $10.90. Selective single trigger, if wanted, $21.60. Non-selective single trigger if wanted, $8.50. Soft rubber recoil pad, if wanted, $2.25. Ivory sights, if wanted, $1.10. Beaver tail forend, if wanted, $10.90. Raised ventilated rib, if wanted, $16.25. Add $10.80 for the Magnum 10 gauge.

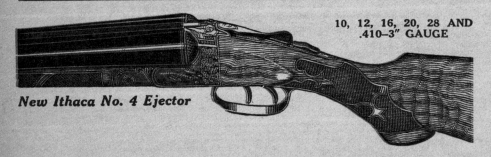

10, 12, 16, 20, 28 AND .410–3" GAUGE

New Ithaca No. 4 Ejector

ITHACA NO. 4 EJECTOR

Best Fluid steel. Stock nicely figured, carefully fitted, handsomely checkered walnut made with full pistol grip unless otherwise ordered. Locks carefully adjusted to get a quick and smooth working lock. Engraving: Frame, top lever, guard and trigger plate hand engraved in an artistic manner. Duck scene on one side of frame; pheasant scene on other side; leaf and flower design on the guard and made in .410, 28, 20, 16, 12 and 10 gauge magnum.

No. 4 Ejector $130.00

IMPORTANT NOTICE

Ithaca Doubles may be had for Trap, Skeet and Field Use with any or all of the following extras:

Ivory Sights both front and rear on any gun above..............	$1.10
Ithaca Recoil Pad* (when sold separately no tax applies)	2.25
Ithaca Non-Selective Single Trigger.......................	8.50
Ithaca Selective Single Trigger.........................	21.60
Beaver tail forearm on Field, No. 2........................	10.90
Beaver tail forearm on No. 4 Ejector......................	13.55

Beaver tail forearm on No. 5, 7 or $1000.00 Grades............. $21.65
Ventilated rib on Field, No. 2.............................. 16.25
Ventilated rib on No. 4, 5, 7 and $1000.00 Grades.............. 21.65

Standard chamber lengths are now—.410 cal. 3 inches, 20, 16 and 12 gauge, 2¾ inches, 28 gauge, 2⅞ inches, Super 10 gauge, 2⅞ inches, Magnum 10 gauge, 3½ inches.

WINCHESTER DOUBLE and SINGLE BARREL SHOTGUNS

MODEL 21
STANDARD GRADE

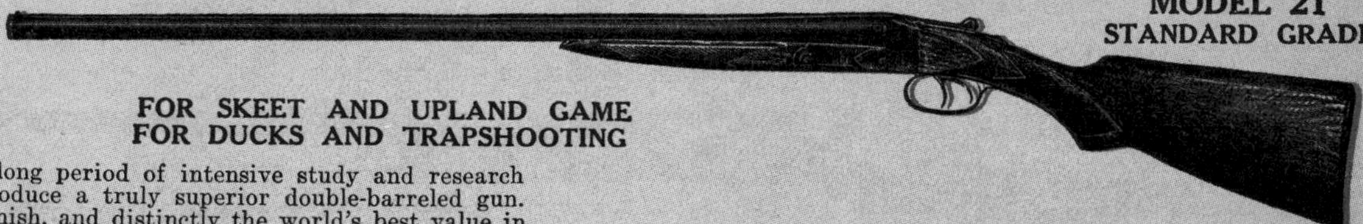

Made in 12, 16 and 20 Gauges

FOR SKEET AND UPLAND GAME
FOR DUCKS AND TRAPSHOOTING

The product of a long period of intensive study and research by Winchester to produce a truly superior double-barreled gun. New from start to finish, and distinctly the world's best value in all-around design, handling ease, operation, strength, safety and shooting ability. Barrels interlock mechanically—no brazing; no extension rib—the gun locks properly without need of one. Result, better shooting. Because barrel chambers are not warped by brazing, they retain true concentricity and alignment. Breech is built scientifically to precision fitting, instead of by obsolete cut-and-try, rule-of-thumb methods.

New Winchester method of choke reaming improves pattern. New steel give barrels of double usual strength, frame of triple strength. Will not shoot loose. Remarkably easy to open and close. An exceptionally hard-shooting gun, giving the finest uniformity of pattern. Single or double trigger with or without selective ejection. Choice in barrel lengths: 12 gauge—32, 30, 28 or 26 inches; 16 and 20 gauges—30, 28 or 26 inches. All barrels furnished in full, improved modified or modified choke, improved cylinder or cylinder bore; usual combinations. Other combinations to special order at no extra charge. Winchester special Skeet chokes, No. 1 or No. 2, introduced on Winchester Model 21 Skeet Gun, can be furnished on special order at no extra charge. Walnut stock with fluted, well-rounded comb and checkered pistol grip; hard rubber butt plate. Walnut checkered fore-end. Standard dimensions—12 gauge—length 14 inches, drop at comb 1 9/16 inches, drop at heel 2½ inches, pitch for 30-inch barrels 2½ inches. In 16 and 20 gauge, same except drop at comb is 1½ inches and at heel on 16 gauge is 2⅞ inches and on 20 gauge drop at heel is 2⅜ inches. Winchester 81A front sight with option of 81D with 94B middle sight. Extra set of barrels and fore-end can be furnished. Weight with 30-inch barrels; 12 gauge—approximately 7½ pounds; 16 and 20 gauges—approximately 6½ pounds.

MODEL 21 STANDARD GRADE, 12, 16 and 20 GAUGES

12 Gauge, 32, 30, 28, 26-inch Barrels. Usual Choke Combinations:

Double Trigger, Non-Selective Ejection	$72.45
Double Trigger, Selective Ejection	86.10
Single Trigger, Non-Selective Ejection	86.10
Single Trigger, Selective Ejection	99.75

EXTRAS add to price STANDARD GRADE

Stock to customer's dimensions	15.00
Extra set of Barrels without fore-end, purchased with a new gun:	
Non-Selective Ejection	44.00
Selective Ejection	55.00
Extra fore-end—purchased with new gun:	
Regular shape—Non-Selective	10.00
Selective	14.50
Beaver-tail—Non-Selective	18.80
Selective	23.30
Chambering for 3-inch Shell	5.50
Beavertail fore-end instead of regular fore-end, add	8.20

MODEL 21
TRAP GRADE

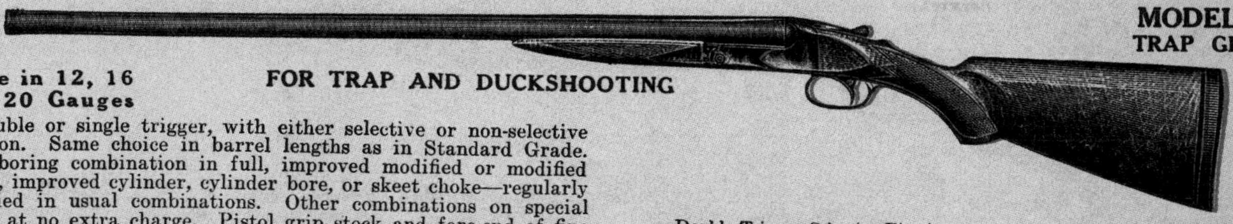

Made in 12, 16 and 20 Gauges

FOR TRAP AND DUCKSHOOTING

Double or single trigger, with either selective or non-selective ejection. Same choice in barrel lengths as in Standard Grade. Any boring combination in full, improved modified or modified choke, improved cylinder, cylinder bore, or skeet choke—regularly supplied in usual combinations. Other combinations on special order at no extra charge. Pistol grip stock and fore-end of fine figured grain walnut; stock to customer's dimensions. Straight grip or pistol grip with or without cap, Monte Carlo or offset stock, made to purchaser's specifications without extra charge. Beavertail fore-end can be furnished, as an extra. Fitted with choice of any recoil pad listed by Winchester. Weights approximately the same as Standard grade.

MODEL 21 TRAP GRADE, 12, 16 and 20 GAUGES

12 Ga., 32-in. barrels, full and full; 16 and 20 Ga., 28-in. barrels, Choke modified and full:

Single Trigger, Selective Ejection	$135.25
Single Trigger, Non-Selective Ejection	121.60
Double Trigger, Non-Selective Ejection	107.95

Double Trigger, Selective Ejection	$121.60
For Ventilated Rib add to above prices (Selective Ejection only)	33.00

(Ventilated Rib furnished in 12 ga., 30″ or 32″ barrels only)

EXTRAS add to price of TRAP GRADE

Extra set of Barrels without fore-end, purchased with a new gun:	
Non-Selective Ejection	$44.00
Selective Ejection	55.00
Extra fore-end—purchased with new gun:	
Regular shape—Non-Selective	15.50
Selective	20.00
Beaver-tail—Non-Selective	30.90
Selective	35.40
Chambering for 3-inch Shell	5.50
Extra for Cheek Piece	18.00
Beavertail fore-end instead of regular fore-end, add	13.65

MODEL 37 "STEELBILT"
SINGLE SHOT SHOTGUN

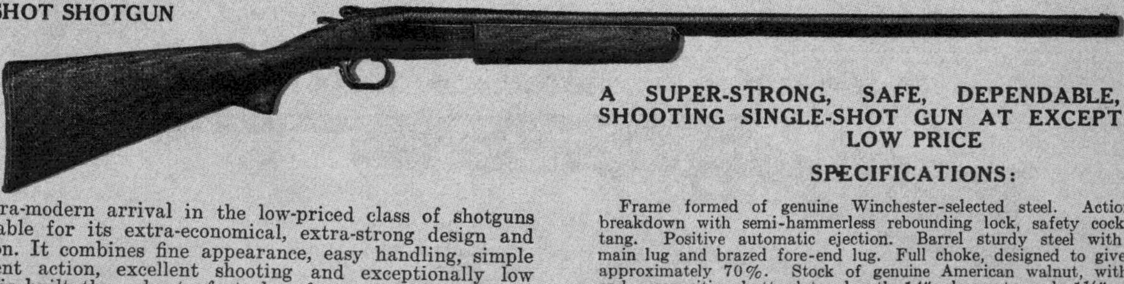

This ultra-modern arrival in the low-priced class of shotguns is remarkable for its extra-economical, extra-strong design and construction. It combines fine appearance, easy handling, simple and efficient action, excellent shooting and exceptionally low price. It is built throughout of steel, a feature which makes it outstanding in its class. Has few parts and is in every way super-sturdy. Shoots all standard shotgun loads with complete dependability and safety. Will kill cleanly at all usual hunting ranges with the usual loads, from the least expensive rabbit, squirrel, quail or crow shells to the most powerful high-speed shells for pheasants, wild-fowl, turkeys, foxes or deer. Here are its most outstanding superiorities:

A SUPER-STRONG, SAFE, DEPENDABLE, HARD SHOOTING SINGLE-SHOT GUN AT EXCEPTIONALLY LOW PRICE

SPECIFICATIONS:

Frame formed of genuine Winchester-selected steel. Action, top lever breakdown with semi-hammerless rebounding lock, safety cocking lever on tang. Positive automatic ejection. Barrel sturdy steel with extra large main lug and brazed fore-end lug. Full choke, designed to give patterns of approximately 70%. Stock of genuine American walnut, with pistol grip and composition butt plate; length 14″, drop at comb 1½″, drop at heel 2¼″. Fore-end of walnut, of new design to furnish full-hand fitting grip, diameter 2″ throughout its entire length of 8½″. Weight, 12 gauge, about 6½ lbs.

Made in 12, 16, 20 and 28 gauges, also .410 bore. Chambered in 12, 16 and 20 gauges for 2¾ inch shells; in 28 gauge for 2⅞″ shells, in .410 bore for 3″ shells. Shoots all standard shotgun loads. Barrel lengths furnished: 12 ga.—28, 30 and 32 in. 16, 20 and 28 ga.—28, 30 and 32 in. In .410 bore with 26 or 28 in. barrel.

Price	$9.35

SEE PAGE 8, "HOW TO ORDER"

SAVAGE AUTOMATIC SHOTGUNS

SAVAGE "UPLAND SPORTER"
12 and 16 Gauge—3 Shots

MODEL 726

FOR SKEET AND FIELD SHOOTING
FOR TRAPS AND DUCK SHOOTING

The Upland Sporter is a new three-shot automatic especially designed for field shooting. It is light to carry, fast in action and easy to point. The receiver is artistically decorated and this with the special checkering on stock and forearm combine to make an attractive arm for field use. It excels in ease of operation, shooting qualities and all-around dependability.

MODEL 726

Plain round barrel.

BARRELS—12 gauge, 28, 30 and 32-inch lengths; 16 gauge, 26, 28 and 30-inch lengths. Full, modified or cylinder bore.

STOCK—Selected American walnut. Full pistol grip checkered on grip and forestock. Push-button type safety in rear of trigger guard. Magazine capacity two shells, with one in chamber, giving three shots. Receiver channeled and matted in line of sight. Friction ring adjustment for light and heavy loads. Receiver artistically decorated. Weight, 16 gauge, about 7 pounds; 12 gauge, about 7¼ pounds.

Price $43.50

(Model 720, similar to Model 726 but 5 shot capacity available at same price.)

MODEL 727

With solid raised matted rib. Same specifications as Model 726. Raised rib on barrel gives a flat line of sight from receiver to end of barrel.

Price $51.25

(Model 721, similar to Model 727 but 5 shot capacity, available at same price.)

MODEL 728

With ventilated raised rib. Same specifications as Model 726.

Price $57.25

(Model 722, similar to Model 728 but 5 shot capacity, available at same price.)

EXTRA BARRELS FOR AUTOMATIC SHOTGUNS

Plain round barrel. $18.50
With raised matted rib. 26.25
With ventilated raised rib. 32.25

SAVAGE AUTOMATIC SHOTGUN WITH CUTTS COMPENSATOR

MODEL 720-C—5 shot
MODEL 726-C—3 shot

Model 720-C. .$57.75
Model 726-C. . 57.75

Same specifications as Models 720 and 726 as described above except as follows: 20-inch Special Barrel with Cutts Compensator

attached furnished with two choke tubes. Spreader tube making barrel length overall 24⅝ inches. No. 705 Full Choke Tube making barrel length overall 26¼ inches. Modified choke tube will be substituted if specified.

MODEL 740-C—3 shot Skeet Model

With Cutts Compensator and two tubes as above. With special large Beavertail forearm and selected American walnut stock both elaborately checkered and oil finished. Receiver artistically decorated on sides, channeled and matted in line of sight. Friction ring adjustment for light and heavy loads. Weight about 8½ pounds.

Price $63.50

SAVAGE AUTOMATIC SHOTGUNS WITH POLY CHOKE

MODEL 720-P—5 shot
MODEL 726-P—3 shot

Model 720-P. .$55.50
Model 726-P. . 55.50

Same specifications as Models 720 and 726 except as follows: Barrel equipped with Poly Choke—26-inch standard length. Any standard barrel length for this model on special order.

MODEL 740-P—3 shot
(not illustrated)

Price $61.00

Skeet Model. Of the same specifications and finish as Model 740-C except with Poly choke. Special barrel equipped with Poly choke. Barrel length 26 inches overall. Weight about 8½ pounds.

© **A NEW GUN CARRIES A FACTORY GUARANTEE**

REMINGTON AUTOLOADING SHOTGUNS
3-SHOT—12, 16 AND 20 GAUGES

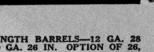

"SPORTSMAN" TAKEDOWN

For Skeet and Field Shooting
For Traps and Duck Shooting

STANDARD LENGTH BARRELS—12 GA. 28 IN., 16 AND 20 GA. 26 IN. OPTION OF 26, 28, 30 OR 32 IN. CYLINDER, MODIFIED, FULL CHOKE, OR REMINGTON SPECIAL SKEET BORING

Like most Remingtons, the "Sportsman" is of the takedown type, hammerless, with solid breech. It has what is admitted to be the most effective, positive safety feature of any gun—the Cross Bolt Safety, which is conveniently located in rear of the trigger guard for quick operation.

Beyond any shadow of doubt the "Sportsman" has the fastest action of any shotgun ever built.

The strong action and recoil springs prolong the life of the gun and reduce recoil.

There is a special friction ring device to reduce recoil of heavy loads to the very minimum; a fibre cushion is located at the back of the receiver to absorb the shock of recoiling parts. Additional features that further endear this "aristocrat of shotguns" to gun connoisseurs in particular, are the reinforced fore-end, locked breech to give maximum shooting qualities, barrel guide ring with long bearing surface to prevent buckling, loading or unloading of magazine without removing shell from the chamber—or removal of loaded shell from the chamber without disturbing those in the magazine.

The Sportsman A—"Standard" Grade........................$49.95
   Extra barrel 19.80

*Standard dimensions of stock, 14 inches long, 2½ inches drop at heel, 1⅝ inches drop at comb. Half pistol grip. Any other length or stock made to order subject to additional charge of........... 15.00

The Sportsman B—"Special" Grade........................ 80.70
   Extra barrel 19.80

*Stock dimensions same as 11A.
*Standard dimensions of stock, 14⅜ inches long, 2¼ inches drop

at heel, 1½ inches drop at comb. Straight grip option of half pistol grip. Any other length or drop of stock made to order subject to additional charge of $15.00

The Sportsman D—"Tournament" Grade......................144.50
   Extra barrel 26.40
The Sportsman E—"Expert" Grade..........................210.50
   Extra barrel 35.20
The Sportsman F—"Premier" Grade.........................276.50
   Extra barrel 41.80

Grades D, E and F also supplied with any grip, length or drop desired without additional charge.

Raised solid matted rib, extra.......................... 8.00
Raised ventilated rib, extra............................ 14.30

Remington special long range choke boring (12 ga. only 30 or 32 ins.) extra... 4.40

SPECIFICATIONS

The Sportsman. Take-down, hammerless, solid breech; 12, 16 and 20 gauges, 3 shots (2 in the magazine and 1 in the chamber). Cross bolt safety (reversed for left-handed shooters at no extra charge) 26, 28, 30 or 32-inch barrel; cylinder, modified or full choke. Top of receiver matted and both sides handsomely decorated. American walnut pistol grip stock and fore-end, both finely checkered. Barrel and receiver in rich, glossy black finish. Stock dimensions, 14 inches long, 2½ inches drop at heel, 1⅝ inches at comb. Weight, 20 gauge, about 6¾ pounds; 16 gauge, about 7 pounds; 12 gauge, about 7¾ pounds.

5-SHOT—12, 16 AND 20 GAUGES

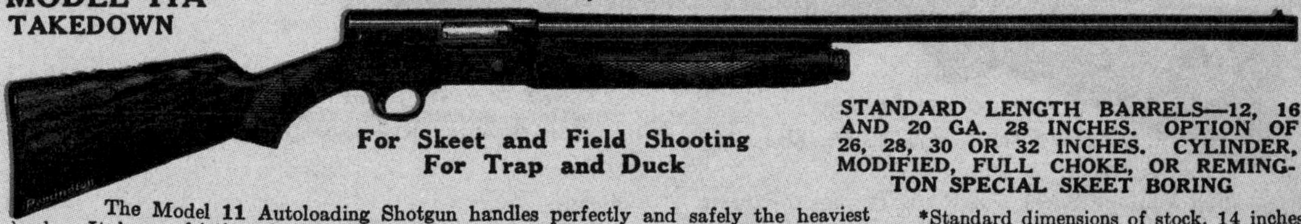

MODEL 11A TAKEDOWN

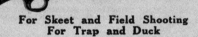

For Skeet and Field Shooting
For Trap and Duck

STANDARD LENGTH BARRELS—12, 16 AND 20 GA. 28 INCHES. OPTION OF 26, 28, 30 OR 32 INCHES. CYLINDER, MODIFIED, FULL CHOKE, OR REMINGTON SPECIAL SKEET BORING

The Model 11 Autoloading Shotgun handles perfectly and safely the heaviest long range loads. It has a friction ring device to reduce the recoil of the heavy loads, after the fashion of the shock absorbers on automobiles. A fibre cushion at the back of the receiver still further takes up the shock and makes for durability and long life in the gun.

A decided advantage in this Remington Autoloader is the fact that a loaded shell may be removed from the chamber without disturbing shells in the magazine. Furthermore, the magazine may be filled or unloaded without removing shell from the chamber.

In the Model 11 there is no loss of power of the shot charge in the operation of the mechanism. The barrel and the breech bolt are locked together until after the shot leaves the muzzle; the gun being full recoil operated.

Heavy action and recoil springs materially prolong gun life and reduce recoil. The fore-end is reinforced; the solid breech provides added protection. The barrel guide ring has long bearing surface to prevent buckling.

The Remington Model 11 and "Sportsman" are the only autoloaders, made in 16 gauge to take the Kleanbore Auto Express load in 2¾-inch shell. This splendid 16-gauge load gives 12 gauge results because it exceeds 3¼ drams of progressive burning powder and 1⅛ ounces of shot.

*Standard dimensions of stock, 14 inches long, 2½ inches drop at heel, 1⅝ inches at comb. Half pistol grip. Any other length or drop of stock made to order subject to additional charge of $15.00

No. 11B—"Special" Grade................. 80.70
   Extra barrel 19.80

*Stock dimensions same as 11A.
*Standard dimensions of stock, 14⅜ inches long, 2¼ inches drop at heel, 1½ inches drop at comb. Straight grip, option of half pistol grip. Any other length or drop of stock made to order subject to additional charge of.............. 15.00

No. 11D—"Tournament" Grade...............144.50
   Extra barrel 26.40
No. 11E—"Expert" Grade................. 210.50
   Extra barrel 35.20
No. 11F—"Premier" Grade................ 276.50
   Extra barrel 41.80

Nos. 11D, E and F also supplied with any grip, length or drop desired without additional charge.

Raised solid matted rib, extra............... 8.00
Raised ventilated rib, extra................ 14.30

Remington special long range choke boring, (12 ga. only 30 or 32 ins.) extra........... 4.40

*Note—Only Regular dimensions carried in stock. Special stocks require from five to eight weeks to make and orders for such are POSITIVELY NOT SUBJECT TO CANCELLATION.

SPECIFICATIONS

No. 11A "Standard" Grade. Chambered for 2¾-inch shells. Take-down, hammerless, solid breech; 12, 16 and 20 gauges, 5 shots. Cross bolt safety; 26, 28, 30 or 32-inch barrel, cylinder, modified or full choke. Top of receiver matted. American walnut pistol grip stock, and fore-end, both finely checkered. Regular stock dimensions 14 inches long, 2½ inches drop at heel, 1⅝ inches drop at comb. Weight, 12 gauge, about 7¾ pounds; 16 gauge, about 7 pounds; 20 gauge, about 6¾ pounds.

No. 11R—"Riot" Grade, 20-inch barrel....$49.95
No. 11A—"Standard" Grade................ 49.95
   Extra barrel 19.80

"SPORTSMAN" SKEET GUN 3-SHOT—12, 16, AND 20 GAUGES

The "Sportsman" is the ideal gun for Skeet. Nothing so attests the fine performance of the "Sportsman" as its popularity in the hands of the great army of Skeet shooters. The "Sportsman" is the main reliance of a great many expert Skeet shots. Easy to load, easy to operate, light in weight, perfectly balanced, this three-shot autoloader combines greater accuracy with faster handling, less recoil. Remington special skeet boring assures well distributed shot patterns at all skeet ranges. The shot spreads sufficiently for the close incoming targets and holds together uniformly for the speedy outgoers.

SPECIFICATIONS: Sportsman "Skeet" Grade, Takedown, hammerless, solid breech. Chambered for 2¾ inch shells. Cross bolt safety. Top of receiver

matted and both sides decorated. Raised ventilated rib. American walnut stock and fore-end, both finely checkered. Full pistol grip with rubber cap. Walnut colored Bakelite butt plate. Lyman ivory bead front sight. White metal rear sight on ribbed barrels only. Beaver Tail fore-end. Weight, 20 gauge, about 7 pounds; 16 gauge, about 7½ pounds; 12 gauge, about 8¼ pounds. Standard length barrel, 26 inches. Option of 28, 30, or 32 inches. Remington Special Skeet Boring. Option of any other boring desired.

The Sportsman "Skeet" Grade, with ventilated rib (standard) $71.50
The Sportsman "Skeet" Grade, with raised solid rib 65.20
The Sportsman "Skeet" Grade, with plain barrel. 57.20

REMINGTON OVER AND UNDER SHOTGUNS

MODEL 32A 12 GAUGE

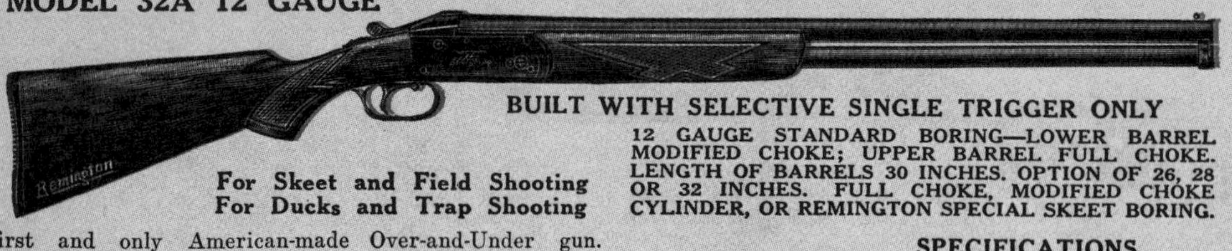

BUILT WITH SELECTIVE SINGLE TRIGGER ONLY

12 GAUGE STANDARD BORING—LOWER BARREL MODIFIED CHOKE; UPPER BARREL FULL CHOKE. LENGTH OF BARRELS 30 INCHES. OPTION OF 26, 28 OR 32 INCHES. FULL CHOKE, MODIFIED CHOKE CYLINDER, OR REMINGTON SPECIAL SKEET BORING.

For Skeet and Field Shooting
For Ducks and Trap Shooting

The first and only American-made Over-and-Under gun. No finer or stronger gun of this type available. Has exclusive features not found in other Over-and-Under guns at considerably higher prices. Its attractive appearance, smooth graceful lines and superb balance will appeal to discriminating sportsmen. Smaller, stronger and better looking frame. Simple but sturdy construction. Upper and lower tangs made in one piece with frame. Special mounting of barrels to allow for uneven expansion and to insure shooting on center. Absence of side ribs eliminates heat waves and permits better pointing. Mechanism readily accessible. Automatic ejectors. Selective three-way safety—automatic, manual or inoperative. Heat treated frame for greater strength. Both sides of frame handsomely decorated. Grip and fore-end beautifully checkered.

One barrel above the other gives the advantage of a single sighting plane; straight line recoil reduces recoil and whip of gun. Simple take-down. Narrow-grip—more natural. Ideal for Trap and Skeet shooting, especially on doubles.

Can be supplied with or without single trigger.

SPECIFICATIONS

No. 32A Standard Grade. Take-down, hammerless, automatic ejectors, 12 gauge only. Standard length barrels 30 inches; also furnished in 26, 28, inches or 32 inches. Full choke, modified choke, improved cylinder or true cylinder bore. Standard boring—upper barrel full choke; lower barrel modified choke—furnished unless otherwise specified. Option of any other choking desired. Front trigger fires lower barrel. Walnut pistol-grip stock and fore-end, both handsomely checkered. Top of main bolt is matted and both sides of frame are decorated. Regular stock dimensions 14 inches long from front trigger, 2½ inches drop at heel, and 1⅝ inches drop at comb. Bakelite butt plate. Weight about 7½ lbs.

No. 32A—"Standard" Grade	$126.00
Extra pair of barrels	60.00
*Standard stock dimensions, 14 inches long, 2½ inches drop at heel, 1⅝ inches drop at comb. Half pistol grip. Any other dimensions, subject to extra charge of	15.00
No. 32D—"Tournament" Grade	276.50
No. 32E—"Expert" Grade	326.50
No. 32F—"Premier" Grade	411.50

Nos. 32D, E, F also supplied with any grip, length or drop desired without additional charge.

Raised solid matted rib, extra.......... 8.00

MODEL 32 SKEET GUN

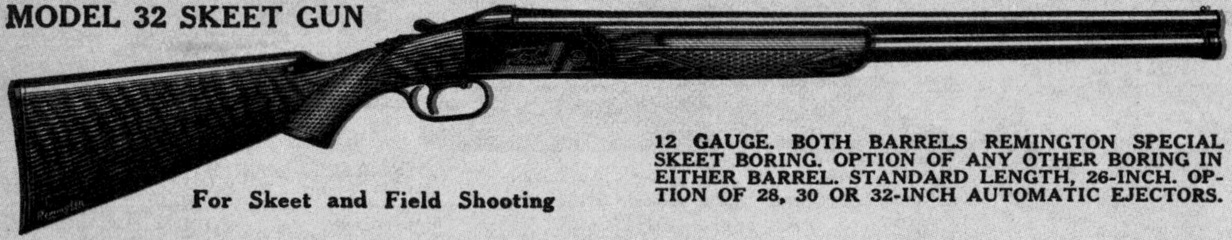

For Skeet and Field Shooting

12 GAUGE. BOTH BARRELS REMINGTON SPECIAL SKEET BORING. OPTION OF ANY OTHER BORING IN EITHER BARREL. STANDARD LENGTH, 26-INCH. OPTION OF 28, 30 OR 32-INCH AUTOMATIC EJECTORS.

This is the coming gun for Skeet shooting. Its popularity is rapidly increasing. Particularly fine on Skeet "doubles" shots. Straight line recoil of lower barrel leaves the shooter ready without disturbance for his second shot immediately after breaking the first target. Single sighting plane permits the most accurate pointing. Perfect balance. Remington Selective Single Trigger absolutely dependable. Remington Special Skeet Boring in both barrels assures well distributed shot patterns at all Skeet ranges. Lower barrel is marked "out" for use on outgoing target. Upper barrel is marked "in" for use on incoming target.

No. 32. "Skeet" Grade with plain barrel	$129.00
No. 32. "Skeet" Grade with raised solid rib	137.00
No. 32. "Skeet" Grade with ventilated rib	149.40
Shortening regular stock up to 1 inch, extra	3.00
Special drop or greater length of stock, extra	15.00

SPECIFICATIONS

No. 32 Skeet Grade (26-inch barrels). Take-down, hammerless, automatic ejectors, 12 gauge only. Standard length barrels 26 inches; also furnished in 28, 30 or 32 inches. Standard boring, both barrels Remington Special Skeet Boring. Lower barrel marked "out" for use on outgoing target, upper barrel marked "in" for incoming target. Option of any other combination of borings desired. Single trigger. Selected, high-grade walnut pistol-grip stock and fore-end, both handsomely checkered. Top of main bolt is matted and both sides of frame are decorated. Regular stock dimensions 14 inches long from front trigger, 2½ inches drop at heel, and 1⅝ inches drop at comb. Bakelite butt plate. Weight about 7½ pounds. Half pistol grip. Beaver tail fore-end.

MODEL 32TC 12 GAUGE
WITH VENTILATED RIB

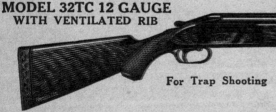

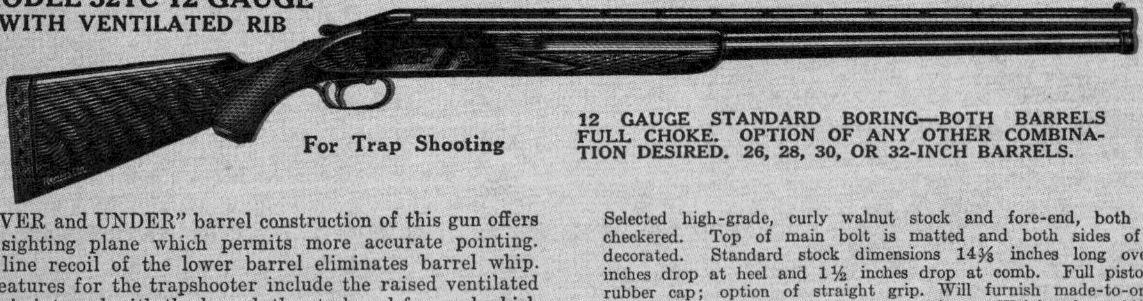

For Trap Shooting

12 GAUGE STANDARD BORING—BOTH BARRELS FULL CHOKE. OPTION OF ANY OTHER COMBINATION DESIRED. 26, 28, 30, OR 32-INCH BARRELS.

The "OVER and UNDER" barrel construction of this gun offers a single sighting plane which permits more accurate pointing. Straight line recoil of the lower barrel eliminates barrel whip. Special features for the trapshooter include the raised ventilated rib which is integral with the barrel, the stock and fore-end which are especially designed for trapshooting, the full pistol grip, soft rubber recoil pad, and Remington Selective Single Trigger.

SPECIFICATIONS

Model 32TC Target Grade with raised ventilated matted rib. Take-down, hammerless, automatic ejectors, 12 gauge only. Choice of 26, 28, 30 or 32-inch barrels. Standard boring—both barrels full choke. Option of any other combination desired. Front and rear sights. Hawkins recoil pad.

Selected high-grade, curly walnut stock and fore-end, both handsomely checkered. Top of main bolt is matted and both sides of frame are decorated. Standard stock dimensions 14⅜ inches long over all, 1⅞ inches drop at heel and 1½ inches drop at comb. Full pistol grip with rubber cap; option of straight grip. Will furnish made-to-order lengths from 13½ to 15 inches without extra charge. Weight about 8¼ pounds.

No. 32TC—"Target" Grade with Ventilated rib, Selective Single Trigger and Beaver Tail Fore-end (as illustrated).. $154.90

Stock with dimensions outside of prescribed limits, No. 32T, extra.. 15.00

NOTE—Only Regular dimensions carried in stock. Special stocks require from five to eight weeks to make and orders for such are POSITIVELY NOT SUBJECT TO CANCELLATION.

IVER JOHNSON SHOTGUNS

SKEET-ER MODEL

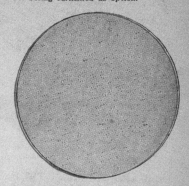

Actual photograph of pattern made with SKEET-ER, using 3 inch .410 long shells, No. 9 C shot. Reverse barrel boring furnished as option.

(Showing Straight Grip)

DOUBLE BARREL HAMMERLESS

This is a Championship Gun specially built with an advanced system of boring which gives amazing results at Skeet Shooting.

SPECIFICATIONS

Stocks are of selected fancy figured walnut beautifully hand-checkered. 14⅛ in. in length with drop of 2¾ in. at heel. The 12, 16, 20 and 28 gauges have forged steel frame, full pistol grip rubber capped with option of straight grip; the .410 straight grip with option of full pistol grip. The .410 is chambered to take the long 3 in. shells. Regular boring right barrel choked and left barrel open. Large hand-protecting forend with D. & E. fastener. Blued frame and parts. Lyman No. 10 Ivory front sight. Hard rubber butt plate.

We can supply, at no extra cost but subject to delay, variations in stock dimensions and barrel borings. We can also equip with the Miller Single Trigger, either Non-Selective or Selective type and Jostam Anti-Flinch Recoil Pad at extra charge listed below.

PLAIN EXTRACTOR			AUTOMATIC EJECTOR		
No. 512	12 Ga.		No. 612	12 Ga.	
No. 516	16 Ga.	} $45.00	No. 616	16 Ga.	} $55.00
No. 520	20 Ga.		No. 620	20 Ga.	
No. 528	28 Ga.		No. 628	28 Ga.	
No. 541	.410 Bore $43.00		No. 641	.410 Bore $53.00	
28 inch Barrels. (Option 26 inch)			28 inch Barrels. (Option 26 inch)		

Extras: Miller Single Trigger Non-Selective, $14.00; Miller Single Trigger Selective, $17.50; Jostam Anti-Flinch Recoil Pad, $1.50. Additional Ivory Sight, $ .50.

Right barrel, 338 shot in 30 inch circle at 30 yards.

Left barrel, 347 shot in 30 inch circle at 20 yards.

FOR TRAP SHOOTING   SPECIAL TRAP

A brand new trap gun of exceptional merit, correctly designed and beautifully finished. New and improved straightline ventilated rib breaks up heat waves and makes clear vision for accurate shooting.

SINGLE BARREL   12 GAUGE ONLY

SPECIFICATIONS

No. 26—12 gauge, 32 inch barrel with ventilated matted top rib, fitted with two Lyman Ivory Sights. Automatic ejector. Length of stock 14½ inches; drop at comb 1½ inches, drop at heel 2 inches. Weight, approximately 7 pounds, 6 ounces. (Jostam Anti-Flinch Recoil Pad $1.50 extra) ....Price, $18.00

HERCULES GRADE

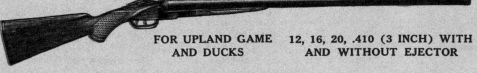

Stock and forend of selected black walnut finely hand checkered with flexible hard rubber butt plate. Lightning locks. Easy cocking. The automatic ejector mechanism is housed in the forend (D. & E. fastener) and will eject either one or both shells at option. Both barrels on the 12 gauge 32 inch and the .410 are full choke, and the .410 has straight grip. With these exceptions all others have full pistol grip capped with right barrel modified and left full choke. Both models beautifully finished and of high quality.

FOR UPLAND GAME AND DUCKS   12, 16, 20, .410 (3 INCH) WITH AND WITHOUT EJECTOR

SPECIFICATIONS—HAMMERLESS DOUBLE BARREL

PLAIN EXTRACTOR				AUTOMATIC EJECTOR			
NO.				NO.			
812	12	26, 28, 30, 32 (Reg. 30)	} $35.00	912	12	26, 28, 30, 32 (Reg. 30)	} $42.00
816	16	26, 28, 30 (Reg. 28)		916	16	26, 28, 30 (Reg. 28)	
820	20	26, 28 (Reg. 28)		920	20	26, 28 (Reg. 28)	
841	.410	26, 28 (Reg. 26) $32.00		941	.410	26, 28 (Reg. 26) $39.00	

The weight of Plain Extractor Guns 5¾ to 7½ pounds, and the Automatic Ejector 6 to 7¾ pounds, according to gauge and barrel length.

EXTRAS, BOTH MODELS

Jostam Anti-Flinch Recoil Pad........ $1.50
Lyman Ivory Sights, each............ .50
Swivels 1.00
Miller Single Trigger Non-selective......14.00
Miller Single Trigger Selective......... 17.50

SPECIFICATIONS

Has improved straightline ventilated rib. Stock and forend of handsome selected walnut hand checkered. Made only in 12 gauge, 32 inch barrels, both full choke. Two Lyman Ivory Sights and Jostam Anti-Flinch Recoil Pad. Full pistol grip, rubber capped. Beaver tail forend with D. & E. fastener. Drop at comb 1½ inches, and at heel 2 inches. Automatic Safety, with option of Independent Safety. Weight about 8½ pounds. This gun is designed for trap shooting, and is also unequaled for game.

12 GAUGE ONLY   SUPERTRAP DOUBLE BARREL

FOR TRAP SHOOTING

Price $49.50

EXTRAS

Miller Single Trigger Non-selective.....$14.00
Miller Single Trigger Selective.........17.50

©   **A NEW GUN CARRIES A FACTORY GUARANTEE**

BROWNING AUTOMATIC SHOTGUNS

The shooting advantage of the Automatic shotgun as compared to other types are well known. After loading it is necessary only to pull the trigger for each shot. The operation of the smooth action of the Genuine Browning Automatic ejects the empty shell and reloads automatically. There are many reasons for Browning superiority which we know are deciding factors with sportsmen all over the world. A few of these outstanding reasons are: Browning's long and successful experience in gun building; perfectly balanced guns; the recoil operation which absorbs the "kick" because of the ingenious Browning Shock Absorber; the Browning system of chocking which evenly distributes the shot pattern, etc. The Browning automatic has stood the test of time—almost a generation—and because of constant research and improvements, based on experience, it is the leading and most popular Automatic Shotgun.

NOTE: Available also in a 3-shot model. The 3-shot model has a more compact magazine assembly, with shorter forearm.

STANDARD GRADE 1, 5 SHOT MODEL
12 AND 16 GAUGE

STANDARD SPECIFICATIONS—3 and 5 shot Model

In design, material quality of workmanship and hand engraving, the 12 and 16 gauge Browning Automatics are identical—both have walnut stocks and forearms, hand finished and hand checkered—both have the same specially prepared steel barrel and hand-fitted action parts. The only differences are in size and weight. The 16 gauge is chambered for shells up to 2⅝ inches. Weight about 7¼ lbs. The 12 gauge is chambered for shells up to 2¾ inches. Weight about 8 lbs. Stock specifications both 12 and 16 gauge are—half pistol grip—drop at comb 1⅝ inches—drop at heel 2½ inches—length 14¼ inches.

Barrel Lengths: 12 gauge, full choke, 30 inches standard, optional, 28 and 32 inches. Modified choke, 28 or 30 inches. Improved cylinder, 26 or 28 inches. Special skeet boring, 26 or 28 inches. Cylinder bore, 26 or 28 inches.

Barrel Lengths: 16 gauge, full choke, 28 inches standard, optional, 30 inches. Modified choke, 26 or 28 inches. Improved cylinder, 26 or 28 inches. Special skeet boring, 26 inches. Cylinder bore, 26 or 28 inches.

When ordering be sure to give the Grade, Gauge, Barrel Length, Choke or Bore and whether 5 or 3 shot desired. Standard length, choke and 5 shot supplied unless otherwise specified. Extra charges for changes that differ from standard specifications. Read specifications when ordering.

The difference in prices of Standard Grade 1, Browning Special, Grades 3 and 4 (both 12 and 16 gauge) is due to extra finish, selected wood, extra hand fitting, extra hand engraving and Green and Yellow Gold inlay.

Prices for the Browning Automatic Shotgun are:

STANDARD GRADE 1—Hand engraved, either gauge 5 or 3 shot without rib $49.75

BROWNING SPECIAL—Either gauge, 5 or 3 shot with raised matted hollow rib.................................... 57.75

BROWNING SPECIAL—Either gauge, 5 or 3 shot, with ventilated rib 63.85

GRADE NO. 3—Either gauge, 5 or 3 shot, without rib.......148.50

GRADE NO. 4—Either gauge, 5 or 3 shot, without rib.......235.25

EXTRA barrel without rib:

    STANDARD GRADE 1.................................. 19.85

    BROWNING SPECIAL 19.85

    GRADE NO. 3.................................... 32.70

    GRADE NO. 4.................................... 43.25

EXTRA	
for raised matted hollow rib, any grade	$8.00
For ventilated rib, any grade	14.10
For Beavertail forearm on new gun	6.35
For Standard Grade American Walnut stock made to special dimensions on new gun, in any grade	15.65
For high grade curly selected American Walnut stock made to special dimensions on new gun, any grade	23.30
For Circassian Walnut stock made to special dimensions on new gun, any grade	35.65

THE BROWNING "SWEET 16" GAUGE
(Not Illustrated)

Special lightweight Automatic Shotgun about 6¾ lbs. The "Sweet 16" has been produced to meet the demand of skeet and field shooters who want a lighter weight, finely finished gun—outstanding and attractive—at a moderate price. All seven exclusive Browning features in regular weight guns are in this gun, plus the additional distinctive features of lighter weight; gold-plating on trigger, safety and safety latch; special conventional foliage design, hand engraving and neat, narrower raised matted hollow and ventilated ribs. Guns without rib have striped matting on barrels.

STANDARD SPECIFICATIONS
5 and 3 shot "Sweet 16" Gauge

Barrel lengths, full choke, 28 inches, modified choke, 26 or 28 inches. Cylinder bore, 26 inches, Improved cylinder, 26 or 28 inches. Special Skeet boring, 26 inches. Matted receiver. Good quality Walnut stock and forearm, all hand-finished and hand-checkered. Specially prepared steel barrel and action parts. Stock Specifications: Half pistol grip, length 14¼ inches, drop at comb 1⅝ inches, drop at heel 2½ inches. Chambered for shells up to 2-9/16 inches. Weight about 6¾ lbs. without rib. Raised matted hollow and ventilated rib guns weight slightly more.

Price Sweet 16 without rib but with striped matting...........$65.75

Price Sweet 16 with raised matted hollow rib................. 69.75

Price Sweet 16 with ventilated rib.......................... 75.85

EXTRA barrel without rib but with striped matting on barrel.. 24.60

    For raised matted hollow rib....................... 8.00

    For ventilated rib 14.10

BROWNING OVERUNDER SHOTGUNS

MIDAS GRADE

The Midas Overunder startles even the connoisseur of fine arms with the richness and artistry of its embellishments. The subjects are gold pigeons with spreading wings in relief, one on trigger guard and on each side of receiver. Heavy lines of gold form a conventional foliage design around birds and receiver, extending on to trigger guard and continuing on top of barrel. The receiver is rich blue-black, furnishing a fitting on top of barrel, contrast for the gold. Stocks of choice selected walnut, finely hand checkered. Metal polishing and blueing are of the highest quality. Firing pins, ejector hammers and trip rods are gold plated.

Price with level matted rib.........................$285.00

Price with ventilated rib........................... 305.00

12 GAUGE ONLY

©   WRITE US ABOUT YOUR "GUNNING" PROBLEMS

BROWNING OVERUNDER SHOTGUNS

The Browning Overunder shotguns are today the favorite of the hunter and skeetshooter. Their fine construction, under the exclusive Browning patents, excellent workmanship are recognized as a standard feature with all Browning guns. The Browning Overunder is all hand fitted and all hand finished. All Browning Overunder guns are equipped with single selective trigger and automatic selective ejectors and are hand engraved.

GRADE 1. "LIGHTNING MODEL"

12 GAUGE ONLY

The new "Lightning Model" Browning Overunder shotgun weighs only 6¾ lbs. The upper barrel has matted line and gun can be had with 26, 28 and 30 inch barrels and with the following standard choke combinations.
(c) Under barrel modified choke, over barrel full choke (d)

Under barrel improved cylinder, over barrel modified choke (e) Special skeet boring both barrels. Extra charge will be made for changes that differ from the standard specifications. All guns come with nice selected walnut stocks with pistol grip and full forend checkered. Standard dimensions are 1⅝ x 2½ x 14⅛ inches.
Price $75.80

Grade 1 Lightning Model equipped with ventilated rib, specially recommended for Skeet shooting. Weight 6⅞ lbs.
Price $89.90

GRADE 1. "STANDARD MODEL"

12 GAUGE ONLY

This particular model weighs about 7½ lbs. with 28" barrels. Same can be had with 28, 30 and 32 inch barrels with level Matted Rib. Field stock with pistol grip and forearm checkered. Not available without rib. Standard choke combinations are (a) Both barrels full choke (b) Under barrel modified, over barrel full choke. All frames on Browning guns are hand engraved.
Price $79.80

Grade 1 Standard Model with ventilated rib recommended for Trapshooting comes only with 30 and 32 inch barrels. Standard choke combinations are (a) Both barrels full choke (b) Under barrel improved modified choke, over barrel full choke. Weight about 7¾ lbs.
Price $89.90

PIGEON GRADE

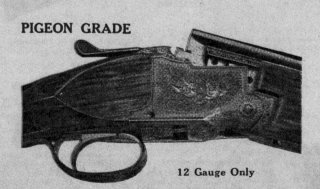

12 Gauge Only

A finely engraved and distinctive high grade gun. The receiver is finished in a rich light steel gray color, thus bringing out the finest lines of the hand engraved design of lifelike pigeons surrounded by scroll work and covering the sides and bottom of receiver. Oak leaves are artistically carved in bold relief on the top curves of the receiver. Fine line conventional designs and borders cover joints, screws and pins. Selected walnut stocks, finely hand checkered with high lustre finish.

Price with level matted rib............................$143.00
Price with ventilated rib............................. 158.00

NOTE: Available in Lightning and Standard Models, Specifications same as Grade 1 Guns.

DIANA GRADE

12 Gauge Only

The receiver of the Diana Grade is also finished in a rich ligh steel gray color, accentuating the elaborate though fine artisti hand engraved scenes of deer on one side and wild boars on tl other with appropriate scenic backgrounds; pheasant subjects o both sides of receiver available, if desired, without extra charg Flowers, etc., are hand carved in bold relief on the curves of th standing breech. We believe sportsmen will enjoy this departure in engraving from more conventional designs. Special subjects and designs supplied on special orders at additional price quoted upon request. The firing pins, ejector hammers and trip rods are gold plated. High quality selected walnut stocks, fine hand checkering.

Price with level matted rib............................$200.00
Price with ventilated rib............................. 218.00

NOTE: Available in Lightning and Standard Models, Specifications same as Grade 1 Guns.

HOLLAND & HOLLAND SHOTGUNS

The firm was founded in 1835 by Mr. Harris Holland who made sporting guns and rifles as a hobby and was persuaded by friends to take up the trade of gunmaking. In its earlier days the firm was celebrated chiefly for its rifles and was patronized by many well-known sportsmen in those days.

Mr. Henry W. Holland joined the firm in 1860 and carried on the business after the death of Mr. Harris Holland. Mr. Henry W. Holland in conjunction with other inventors introduced the "Try-Gun" for ascertaining stock measurements, the "Paradox" Ball and Shotgun, and the Holland Single Trigger.

Amongst other features which he brought out was an ingenious arrangement for making gun locks detachable by hand, and a very simple form of ejector mechanism, (Holland's Patent A.B. Ejector).

The firm's many innovations included a new system of boring for 16 bore guns, and their Special Treble Grip for Pigeon Guns shooting heavy charges. Best known, however, is the patent self-opening action, combining speedy opening with easy closing.

In 1883 all the "Field" Rifle Trials were won by Holland & Holland, and the weapons tested included 8, 10, 12 and 16 bore big game Hammer Rifles weighing from 12 pounds upwards, and rook and rabbit rifles of .250, .295 and .360 bore. Since then Holland & Holland guns have been awarded the highest prizes in international exhibits throughout the world.

"MODELE DE LUXE"

Price in London.......£157/10/0
Price in U.S.A...........$1150

This weapon, whilst containing all the points of H. & H. very best guns, has specially-selected stocks, and in addition is finished in an exceedingly artistic manner, combining a best gun with a work of art. Selected workmen of great skill are employed on this gun, and extra time is spent on it in every department in order to secure the desired effects.
"Modele de Luxe" Guns with Patent Self-Opening Action represent the highest standard of modern gunmaking yet reached in any country.

THE "ROYAL" HAMMERLESS EJECTOR PIGEON OR WILDFOWL GUN

Specification same as "Royal Brevis" except that this Model is fitted with Holland's Special Treble Grip Action for guns chambered for 2¾-inch or 3-inch shells, side-clips to action, hinged front trigger, etc. Weight 7 pounds 2 ounces. Especially suitable for "Skeet" or other Trap Shooting.
Delivery of either the above Models can usually be made

Price in London........£131/5/0
Price in U.S.A..............$950

within a few weeks from receipt of order provided nothing abnormal in the way of stock measurements, etc., is required.

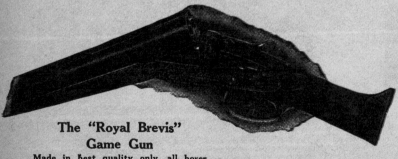

The "Royal Brevis" Game Gun

Made in best quality only, all bores

Price in London..................£126
Price in U.S.A...................$925

SPECIFICATION: Hammerless Ejector Side-lock, Patent Self-Opening Mechanism, hand-detachable locks, two triggers, English walnut stock of specially selected well-figured dark wood. Boring is required.
Barrels of Vickers' finest Nickel Chrome Steel.
Stock measurements to suit individual requirements.
Perfect balance and finish, including fine engraving on locks plates, back of action, etc. and gold oval inlaid flush in stock for initials.
Holland's Patent SELF-OPENING mechanism consists of three strong limbs only, and the ROYAL BREVIS GUN fitted as it is with this latest development makes it the last word in the art of gunmaking. The principle of "self-opening" is by no means new, but the method employed by Holland & Holland, Ltd. is decidedly simple and ingenious—there is nothing to get out of order and nothing which is in the least likely to go wrong. It is a refinement which brings the Royal Brevis a step nearer to the goal of absolute mechanical perfection.

CENTENARY MODELS—12 Gauge—2" Chamber

Holland & Holland has now placed on the market a new choice for sportsmen, their "Centenary" Hammerless Ejector Gun, weighing only 5 pounds 6 ounces, chambered for the 2-inch shell.
The killing power of this gun is quite extraordinary. It is particularly suitable for driven grouse and partridges, and pheasants, also for "walking-up." Owing to its extreme lightness it can be carried on a long day's shoot with a minimum of fatigue. The "Centenary" Gun is of special utility to those sportsmen suffering from any form of physical disability, for the young and not so very young, and for ladies.
The "Centenary" is made in three models, the illustration and description of which will be found on these pages. The price of any of these models in the "Centenary" Grade remains the same, as indicated for the respective guns.

© **A FINE GUN IS ALWAYS A GOOD INVESTMENT**

W. W. GREENER'S HAMMERLESS EJECTOR GUNS

There are few manufactured articles which call for greater experience in their production than high-grade Sporting Shot Guns.

There are few firms with greater experience than the firm of W. W. Greener, Ltd.

Established in the year 1829, the firm has remained continuously under the ægis of members of the family in direct line from father to son, grandsons and great-grandsons, until the present day. Not only have successive members of the firm served their apprenticeships to some vital branch of gunmaking, but they have, from time to time, visited the four corners of the earth and have submitted their workmanship and theories to the actual test of shooting at all classes of Game, from Snipe to Hippo.

The Greener Gun today embodies a Century's experience of Craftsmanship, and this, with 50 years' Shooting experience, is at the sportsman's service.

All prices are for delivery in London or Birmingham, England. For price in U. S. A. duty and shipping will be added which amount to about 50% extra.

W. W. GREENER'S HAMMERLESS GUNS
"FAR-KILLER" MODEL

DESCRIPTION.—As its name implies, the gun has been specially designed to fire heavy charges of both powder and shot with the maximum killing effect at long ranges. It is a Hammerless Non-ejector, fitted with the "Greener" Cross Bolt. The barrels are bored upon the "Field" Cup Winning System, with which "Greener" Guns beat all comers in the great London Trials of 1874, 1875, etc. Special attention is given to the shooting with large shot for ducks, geese and buck; and while we do not make the foolishly extravagant claims so frequently advertised by some makers, we confidently assert that this gun will consistently give the best results obtainable from any weapon of its class.

Built to order in 12 bore with 28 in., 30 in., or 32 in. barrels, chambered for 2¾ in. or 3 in. brass or paper case, firing 52 grains of smokeless powder and 1½ oz. of shot No. 4 to S.S.G. Weights recommended for 12-bore, 7½ to 9 lbs.

This gun is made as an Ejector Gun at..£52 10 0

A "wild duck" in flight is engraved on the rib of all "Far-killer" Guns.

GRADE F35. PRICE £36 15 0
PRICE IN U.S.A. $288.00

10-bore, price	£47 5 0
10-bore Ejector Gun, price	£70 17 6
8-bore, price	£57 15 0
8-bore Ejector Gun, price	£86 12 6

W. W. GREENER'S EJECTOR GUNS

GRADE DH40. PRICE £42 0 0
PRICE IN U.S.A. $325.00

The 12-bore gun with 2 in. chambers is enjoying a certain vogue with those sportsmen who want an ultra light gun firing from ¾ oz. to ⅞ oz. of shot. The tendency of shooters today is towards light guns firing light loads.

To obtain the best results the gun is not an exact 12-bore and consequently the barrels are smaller, this tending to reduce weight in all parts when the gun is proportionate.

The gun as at present made is in our opinion too light, weighing as little as 5¼ lbs. It has considerable recoil and with shorter than 26 in. barrels appreciable muzzle blast, conducive to gun headache, and is clumsy for its weight. Owing to the small charge used it gives good patterns, although apart from the spread it does not equal in handiness the 24-bore firing the same load. It should weigh 5¾ lbs. with 26 in. barrels and normal stock measures.

No light gun can stand up to overloads.

W. W. GREENER'S EJECTOR GUNS
"CROWN" MODEL

DESCRIPTION.—A new model Hammerless Ejector gun, specially designed for the sportsman requiring a well-finished weapon at a moderate price. This is not a cheap grade gun, elaborately engraved, but is well-made of superior material throughout, and is the general purpose gun of the average sportsman, suitable for all purposes in all climes, and is practically the "Standard" Greener Gun. Greener Wrought Steel Barrels, Independent Side Safety, which can be made to work automatically if desired, or automatic Top Safety to order.

This grade can be supplied in any calibre from 12 to 28 at list price. Greener's Selective Single Trigger can be fitted at an additional cost of £10 10s. Non-Selective Single Trigger, £5 5s. extra. Made in 10-bore at 90 guineas, 8-bore at £110 5s.

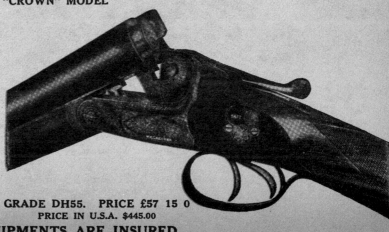

GRADE DH55. PRICE £57 15 0
PRICE IN U.S.A. $445.00

ALL SHIPMENTS ARE INSURED

A. F. STOEGER GUNS

MODEL 297
Price $425

HAND BUILT DOUBLE RIFLE AND SHOTGUN

MUZZLE VIEW

A. F. S. Model, Anson & Deeley system Hammerless combination 3-barreled Rifle and Shot Gun. Two rifle barrels side by side, for any rifle cartridges with or without rim, one shot barrel underneath for 12, 16 or 20 Gauge, double Greener cross bolt and extra strong double underbolts. Krupp steel barrels, suitable for nitro powder, doll's head or straight extension rib, sighted for 100 to 500 yards as required, Greener side safety and safety on neck of stock, finest figured walnut stock, horn heel plate, patent snap fore-end, half or full pistol grip, finest English style or hunting scenes engraving. Highest grade finish of all parts. Length of barrels, 27 to 28 inches. Weight, 8 to 9 pounds.

MODEL 256
Price $350

MODEL 256L
With Lightweight
Dural Action
$385.00

HAND BUILT OVER & UNDER RIFLE AND SHOTGUN

MUZZLE VIEW

Barrels genuine Krupp steel, suitable for nitro powder, double locking extension ribs, Greener cross bolt and double underbolt, side clips, safety on neck of stock, signal pins to show if gun is cocked; checkered patent snap fore-end, checkered pistol grip, dark walnut stock, horn heel plate, very handsome engraving, high grade finish. Shooting qualities, fitting and balance are perfect. Shot barrel full or modified choke or cylinder bore, 12, 16 or 20 Gauge, rifle barrel underneath with express boring for .30-30, .25-35, .22 Hornet, or other calibers; length of barrels, 26, 28 or 30 inches.

MODEL 259
Price $485

MODEL 259L
With Lightweight
Dural Action
$535.00

HAND BUILT OVER & UNDER DOUBLE RIFLE AND SHOTGUN

MUZZLE VIEW

This model has all the advantages of the ordinary combination Over and Under rifle and shotgun with the added advantage of a third small bore barrel which may be chambered for the .22 L. R. or even the .22 Hornet.

ADDITIONAL CHARGES FOR SPECIAL STEELS

	Rifle	Double Barrel Shotgun	Over & Under Shotgun	Drilling (3 barrels)	Combination Over & Under	Double Rifle
Krupp 3 Ring, Boehler Special, Electro Special	$35.00	$40.00	$50.00	$60.00	$55.00	$60.00
Boehler Antinit	60.00	60.00	70.00	100.00	80.00	100.00
Poldi Anticorro	100.00	115.00	140.00	175.00	150.00	175.00
Krupp Nirosta	220.00	250.00	300.00	375.00	325.00	375.00

A. F. STOEGER SHOTGUNS

ON imported firearms the name A. F. STOEGER is the mark of quality. No gun bears this name unless it is thoroughly sound, and a distinctive value of its type. As is proper in fine firearms, quality and perfection in all details is the primary consideration. A. F. STOEGER GUNS are not built to fit into a certain price bracket, on the contrary, each gun is built to represent the very finest of its class. To assure this, we have selected several of the finest makers in Europe, all master gunsmiths in centers where gunmaking is an honored tradition, handed down from father to son, craftsmen who place their professional reputation above material gain, and whose greatest pride and satisfaction is in turning out a weapon truly representative of their ability.

In gunmaking, as in every other profession, there are specialists; some are renowned for double barrel shotguns, other for the over and under type, some for the three barrel guns, and again another for double barrel rifles, and so on. It has been our object to have A. F. STOEGER GUNS built by the maker best suited for the particular arm in question, and because of our personal acquaintance with all the principal European gun makers, we have succeeded in this undertaking.

An important feature of A. F. STOEGER GUNS is that they combine the acme of European gun art, with distinctive American style, something seldom found in any other imported guns.

In many makes of guns, a higher grade means often only a higher grade stock and engraving. In A. F. STOEGER GUNS the more expensive models are mechanically different, involving much added labor and hand work, but resulting in very decided improvements. Many people are of the impression that in buying an expensive gun they pay principally for the fancy wood and engraving, but they are badly misinformed. The old adage "beauty is only skin deep" was never more inappropriate than in this case, for it is unusual whenever on an elaborately finished gun the special walnut and engraving run over 10 per cent of the total cost.

We have always taken great pride in our A. F. STOEGER GUNS, and are most conscientious in giving our customers an arm that will give lifelong satisfaction.

On the following pages we illustrate some of the most popular guns we offer, and give general specifications. While we carry a variety of these on hand, any gun can be made to practically any specifications at no added cost.

If the type gun wanted varies radically, we shall be glad to make special quotations, as we are prepared to build any type of sporting firearm whatsoever to any specifications desired at the lowest possible price.

MODEL 230E $350.00

MODEL 230EL
With Lightweight
Dural Action
$385.00

**HIGH GRADE
HAND BUILT
EJECTOR
OVER & UNDER**

AVAILABLE IN
ALL GAUGES

Double Greener crossbolts and under lugs. Quadruple lock. Raised matted rib; non-automatic safety; straight firing pins. Fine walnut stock; checkered pistol grip and forearm. Excellent finish throughout, rugged construction; with divided automatic Holland & Holland ejectors and light English Scroll engraving

and selected figured walnut. Supplied with double trigger only. Krupp or Boehler fluid steel. Can be furnished in any gauge, barrel length, choke, and specifications at no extra charge.

Extra for Ventilated Rib....................................**$50.00**

MODEL 232E $450.00

**MODEL 232EL with Light-
weight Dural Action $485.00**

**SUPERIOR QUALITY
HAND BUILT
EJECTOR
OVER & UNDER**

AVAILABLE IN
ALL GAUGES

Built of finest materials on the well-known Anson and Deeley box lock action with double Greener extension rib and crossbolts. Barrels of Krupp or Boehler fluid steel. Matted raised rib; straight firing pins; non-automatic safety; with or without lateral signal pins; patent snap forend. Beautifully figured Circassian walnut stock; jointed front trigger, buffalo horn inlay on forend, stock sides, and base of pistol grip. Very fine and artistic Arabesque and scroll engraving, executed in the best of taste.

Automatic ejector standard in this model. This is a gun which will satisfy the most discriminating of shooters who are accustomed to only the best. Can be furnished with any stock specifications at no extra charge.

Extra for ventilated rib..**$50.00**
Extra for selective single trigger................................ **75.00**

© **A FINE GUN IS ALWAYS A GOOD INVESTMENT**

THE GOLDEN AGE OF SPORTING ART

BY R. STEPHEN IRWIN, M.D.

Around the turn of the century, receiving mail in this country was still considered somewhat of a novelty, which meant that a letter carried considerable impact. Once it had been removed from the mailbox, a letter was not torn open immediately, but rather carried back to the house. Only after all the family members had gathered together was the top crease carefully slit, the letter removed, and its message read.

It was probably inevitable that some sharp minds in the advertising world would hit upon a way to use the mail as an effective promotional outlet. Radio and motion pictures had not yet become the awesome influences on consumer spending as we know them today, and struggling young companies were eager to extol the virtues of their products to a growing population any way they could. And so, in addition to posters, books, magazines, calendars and other commercial works, many of the top artists of the day began designing—anonymously—for envelopes. Rather than be dubbed "illustrators" and otherwise degraded by the art community, these fine talents refused to attach their names to this work. In any event, their output paved the way for what might be called the golden age of sporting art, a period extending from about 1890 to 1930.

No one knows exactly when or where the idea of illustrated envelopes arose, but it may have started as early as the Civil War as a vehicle for conveying patriotic messages. Soon manufacturers of firearms, ammunition and gun powder became prolific users of promotional envelopes, along with such diverse products as bicycles, seed corn, buggy tops and sewing thread. Among the major gun companies that took advantage of this new advertising media were Winchester, Remington, Ithaca, Hunter Arms, Stevens, Savage, Colt, Parker, Marlin, Lefever and Iver Johnson. Ammunition and powder companies included Remington, UMC, Peters, U.S. Cartridge, Hercules, Laflin and Rand, DuPont, E. C. Schultze, Atlas, Hazard and Sycamore.

DR. STEPHEN IRWIN, an avid big game hunter and sport fisherman, has been writing for many years on the history of hunting and fishing, including such specialized areas as antique fishing lures, duck decoys and firearms. His articles have appeared in most of the major outdoor publications. He is also the author of a book, *The Providers: Hunting and Fishing Methods of the Indians and Eskimos*.

The Art of Gun Covers

In philatelic jargon, envelopes are called *covers*, and the early gun covers featured exquisite artwork that stirred the imagination and kindled the fires of adventure within the minds of shooters all over the world. These jewels of turn-of-the-century firearms

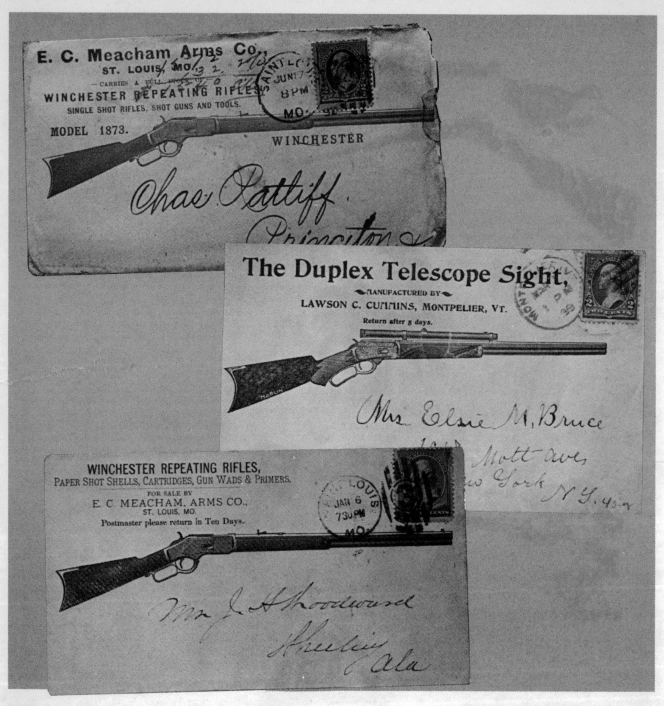

advertising depicted everything from big game, upland birds, waterfowl and hunting dogs to Indian chiefs in full ceremonial dress. There were also dramatic scenes of a north woods trapper confronting a wolf pack with his Winchester lever action, a hunter stalking Dall sheep in the mountains, and hunting camp scenes designed to elicit the wanderlust fever in even the most passive nimrod.

The space on the back side of these covers was not wasted either. Both text and illustrations were used there to promote the finer points of each product. The back side of a 1903 Peters envelope, for example, is covered with full color illustrations of the company's cartridges and shot shells.

The earliest gun covers date back to the 1880's and typically bore monochrome illustrations of rifles or

shotguns, and they were usually printed in red, black, blue or brown. As the art of lithography improved, two-color covers were produced, and eventually the stunning multi-color examples of the early 1900's evolved. Some companies, though, retained their basic color schemes; for example, "Winchester" was almost always printed in red along with the company's large red "W" trademark.

Although the artist was never credited on these envelopes, at his own request, the lithographer's name was usually found in small print in one corner of the illustration. A list of prominent lithographers known to have produced many of these gun covers includes the following: Strobridge Litho Co. (Cincinatti, Ohio), Steinbach (New Haven, Ct.), Faatz (Lestershire, N.Y.), Knapp Co. Lithographers (New York,

N.Y.), Bartlett & Co. (New York, N.Y.), and Dietzer-Sale Litho Co. (Buffalo, N.Y.).

Interestingly, advertising covers did not always come directly from the manufacturing companies; a good percentage were first distributed in bulk to jobbers and retailers all over the country, eventually with the return addresses of the retail establishments preprinted on the envelopes for business (or personal) use.

Rare—and Valuable—Commodities

With advertising covers ranking among the rarest of firearm collectibles, it is indeed fortunate that so many covers, despite their small size and fragility, have survived the years. No doubt people of that era were more inclined to save their correspondence, or perhaps they found these fascinating and colorful envelopes just as attractive as we do today. Some covers

are more rare than others, of course, but all from that era are scarce and in high demand.

The value of a gun cover is determined essentially by the same guidelines that affect the price of most other types of sporting memorabilia, including age, physical condition, aesthetic appeal, and scarcity. Used covers that were actually sent through the mail have more value than those that were never addressed and mailed. It is not the stamp itself that sets the price, moreover; these were typically regular postal issues of low denomination, hence quite common. What lends historical significance to a cover and adds to its value is the stamp in tandem with other important trappings, such as the address, postmark, and cancelation. Such information helps to authenticate the cover and establishes its point of origin, destination, and date. If the letter happens to be addressed to a famous hunter, sportsman, show-

man, exhibition shooter, or some other person of note, so much the better in terms of its value.

Stamp brokers and philatelic auctions represent the most dependable sources of firearm advertising covers. Most serious collectors willingly pay $200 or more for a moderately scarce cover in good condition. As with high quality firearms, good philatelic material continues to escalate in value over time.

The scarcity of old gun covers today belies the fact that they were once printed in large quantities. Many were no doubt destroyed upon receipt or have otherwise succumbed to the ravages of time. Still, there must exist numerous examples not yet in the hands of dealers or collectors, all waiting to be discovered. The hidden sources are endless: consider those long forgotten trunks stored away in countless attics; the

correspondence bins of old hardware stores; the drawers of abandoned rolltop desks; and musty old safes stashed in back storerooms. Many other good examples probably remain tucked away in the discarded ledger books of now defunct businesses.

Each day brings a modern blitzkrieg of junk mail that has been mass-printed on cheap, glossy paper and deposited in millions of postal boxes across our land. We hastily discard reams of this unwanted material each year, angered by the waste of time and effort they have caused. How much nicer it would be if we could return to these beautiful envelopes of a century ago, with their hunting scenes and firearms depicting our love of outdoor sports, and rekindling a lifetime of fond memories of pleasant days spent afield.

THE CUSTOM GUN SHOP: A FINE AMERICAN TRADITION

BY STANLEY W. TRZONIEC

For true gun fanciers, including those fortunate few for whom price is no object, the custom gun shop represents the epitome of fine craftsmanship and devotion to detail. This article covers the day-to-day operations of four of the top custom gun shops in the U.S. While they all share much in common, each one has its special approach to this time-honored practice. So, in an effort to sort out the differences, let's take a mini-tour of America's premier gun shops.

COLT

This shop, located in Hartford (CT.), is among the last strongholds of true craftsmanship—a place where the dyed-in-the-wool enthusiast can acquire almost anything he wants in a special order handgun. Beginning with a tradition that started way back when Colonel Samuel Colt gave away his finely engraved firearms to state and military leaders, the

STANLEY TRZONIEC is a veteran firearms writer and photographer who has long specialized in the reporting of all modern weapons. An accomplished handloader, he has written on this subject for virtually every major firearms journal. Currently Special Projects Editor of Guns Magazine, he is also the author of several books, including a major work on the .22 Rimfire to be published in late 1988.

shop still flourishes, primarily because it understands and accommodates the wishes of its most discriminating customers.

In all probability, Colt's biggest drawing card is its famous Single Action Army model, which has been in production since the 1870s. The Peacemaker, as it was called then (and still is), remains at the top of the list for customized add-on features. A few years ago, this gun was an uncertain proposition for Colt and

A typical example of a custom Colt Single Action Army revolver is shown here, with its "A" engraving, walnut grips, and blued finish.

Colt handguns are shown here in different barrel lengths and engraving patterns. Note extra cylinder on the three-inch Sheriff's Model.

consumer alike. Outdated machinery was kicking out too many rejects, creating instability in production and added costs for the consumer. As a result, the gun was discontinued; but apparently the company had second thoughts, for it soon reintroduced the model (with some modifications) to the joy of many in the shooting world. You can now purchase the SAA through Colt's Custom Shop, but you must be willing to spend at least $1000 for the gun and assorted extras. Since the gun in simple dress retails for almost $800, this outlay should not be that difficult for serious buyers, however.

Calibers in this old line gun range from the reliable .45 Colt to the popular 44-40 Winchester. Barrel lengths are available from 3" to 12", but if you're looking for something different in overall length, Colt can probably help you. Sights are fixed, just as they were on the frontier guns of yesteryear.

A nickel finish and full coverage on this Colt make the weapon even more pleasing to the eye.

Colt also offers engravings for this, and any other, gun in the company's line. Factory hand engravings are available in A, B, C, and D coverages—which, in simpler terms, relate to $^1/_4$, $^1/_2$, $^3/_4$ and Full coverage. Considering the price, and the fact that the work is performed by journeymen, this hand engraving option represents a truly remarkable value. On the other hand, custom engraving, which is yet another facet of the metal cutting art, involves artisans working with precious inlayed metals, special designs, and several different scroll patterns. Because such work is original, price quotes must be obtained before any work can even begin.

Colt's custom pistol grips are unparalleled in the industry. From the Single Action Army to the .380 Automatic, Python, and even the 3rd Model Dragoon, the choices are many. You can can select from rosewood, walnut, bacote, or ivory (when available).

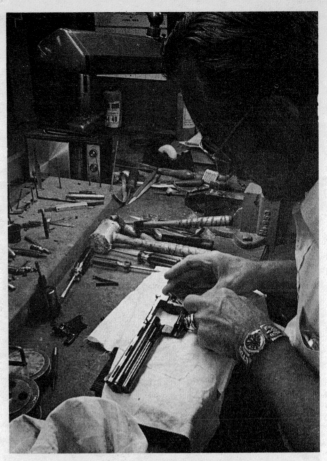

The Python, long considered by many to be the top revolver, is further enhanced by some custom action work. Here a gunsmith is shown at work on a six-inch model.

Smooth, standard or fleur-de-lis checkering patterns can update your pistol to modern standards.

To complete the picture, your gun can be housed in a custom presentation case, with special serial numbers, or your pet Python can be treated to a factory action job. With a single action pull trimmed down to about 2½ pounds, or a double action pull of 7 pounds, this has to be the best investment of $150 or so you'll ever make. Write to Colt Custom Gun Shop, Colt Industries Firearms Division, 150 Huyshope Avenue, Box 1868, Hartford, CT. 06102.

REMINGTON ARMS CUSTOM SHOP

Up in the quiet town of Ilion, New York, on foundations laid by Eliphalet Remington himself, rests the main facility of Remington Arms. And tucked

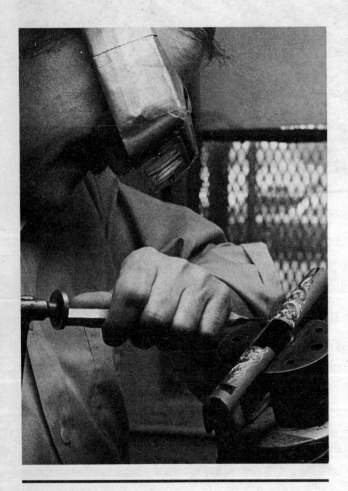

Custom engraving is a big part of most customers' requests. Here an engraver works on a Colt automatic pistol's top slide.

From top to bottom, Remington shotguns Model 700 Grade I, Model 870, and Model 1100.
Note the differences in wood, engraving, and gold inlays.

away in a small corner of the plant there is the Custom Shop, run by Tim McCormack and his staff, all busily running machines, engraving, inletting stocks, applying finish, and checking orders. This particular shop dates back to the late 1940s, when Mike Walker, then a noted benchrest shooter, first got the shop going primarily for target shooters. It still caters to the paper punchers, but most of the shop's business is in custom-built hunting rifles. While the popular 700 bolt action remains the bread and butter gun of the operation, a fair number of Model Four autoloaders and Model Six pump guns are turned out—not to mention the 870 and 1100 shotgun models. Remington also makes a single shot handgun-type weapon, called the XP-100. All decked out in fancy wood, this gun is gaining popularity as the sport of big-bore handgun hunting continues to bloom.

Another Remington single shot favorite is the 40XR Rimfire Sporter, which was introduced to American shooters in 1986. It has now been trimmed down, fancied up, and placed into a custom stock. For the rimfire buff, this has to rank among the top premium longarms chambered in this widespread cartridge.

Going down the Specifications-Options worksheet at the Remington shop, the first choice one has to make concerns what *grade* is desired, from I through IV. The difference in grades—aside from price—lies in the manner of checkering, engraving and wood selection. Using Model 700 as a prime example, Grade I features checkering with a point-to-point pattern similar to that found in a production rifle design. There is no engraving—the wood is either Claro or American walnut in a select grade. Grade II will heighten the excitement level of any connoisseur be-

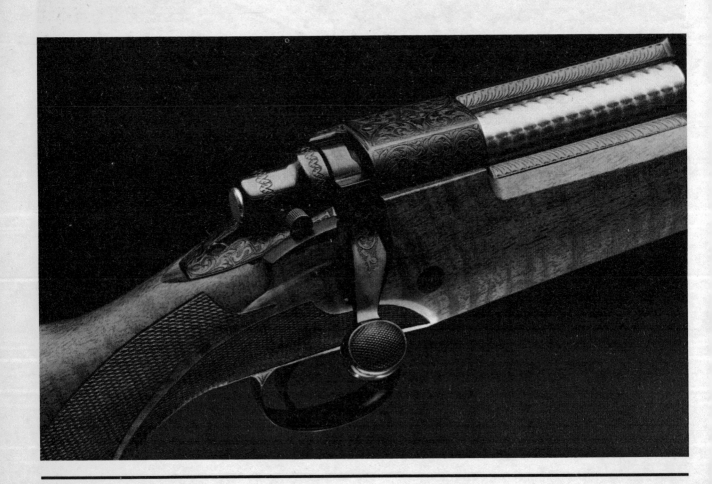

This is Remington's Model 700 Grade IV. Extra care and details are evident in both stock and engraving.

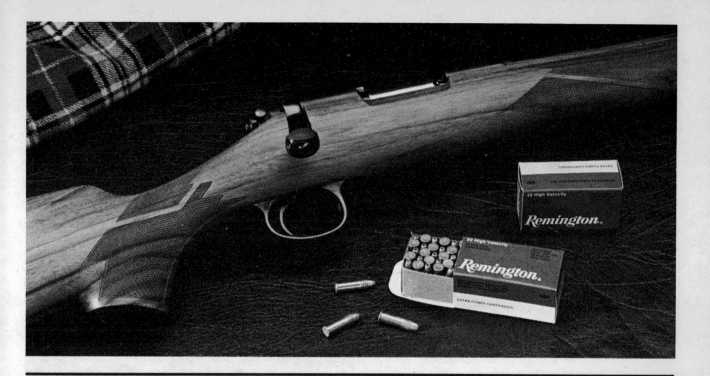

A Grade II 40XR Rimfire Sporter in .22 rimfire is shown above. Note the blind magazine.

cause of its special ribbon pattern of cut checkering. There is still no engraving, but a fancier grade of California Claro, English or American walnut is used.

The next step up, Grade III, features a truly superior wood finished in your choice of oil, satin, or grain-revealing RKW (high gloss). This grade carries engraving on the receiver, bolt handle, barrel, trigger guard, and floorplate. And finally, there is the beautiful Grade IV. The Model 700 example (p. 40) in this top grade combines the best of everything, in-

One of the stock makers at Remington's shop in Ilion, N.Y., works on a Rimfire Sporter.

Remington's only handgun—the XP-100 (above)—is available as a full custom gun. Here a stockmaker is shown "roughing in" a walnut stock.

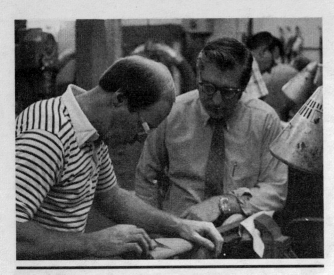

The author watches John Remington at work on a Model 700 stock.

cluding a special fleur-de-lis checkering pattern, extra high quality premium wood, and custom engraving, all done to suit the customer's own individual taste and ideas. Game animals, symbols, or any design one could wish is done in total harmony with one of America's finest big game rifles. In addition, some 26 cartridge choices include the 6.5 Remington Magnum, 7mm Mauser, .264 Winchester Magnum, 25-06, and 30-338. Lefthanded models are also available in most calibers on special request from Remington's Custom Shop.

Many more options are available—too many to list here, actually. For a complete rundown, readers are urged to send a check for $5 to cover the cost of Remington's beautifully illustrated color catalog, which tells all you ever wanted to know about custom rifles and more. The address is: Remington Arms, Eden Park Building, GCD, Wilmington, Delaware 19898.

Here are featured a production Model 70 (top) with a select stock, and the author's custom-built .300 Winchester (bottom) with its AAA fancy grade stock.

The receiver tang on this full custom Model 70 has been worked so that it is full out against the stock. Note the extra sharp checkering.

UNITED STATES REPEATING ARMS COMPANY

Just a few miles down I-91 from Colt's operation in Hartford is Winchester's facility in New Haven. Housed in old buildings rich in New England tradition, the USRAC/Winchester Custom Gun Shop turns

out quality work that's as contemporary as today. A half century ago, Winchester's catalog offered "Specials," such as a Model 54 with optional extras like stainless barrels, fancy wood, engravings, and even full plating. That same tradition carries on today.

While Winchester's shop closely parallels that of Remington in many ways, there are a few differences worth noting. For one, Winchester's facility is the only one that produces a true American side-by-side shotgun. Made almost entirely by hand, Model 21 is still available in three ascending grades—Standard Custom, Custom Grade, and Grand American. Depending upon choice of options, including extra barrels and engraving, prices begin at $7500, then rise to $10,260 for the Custom and more than $21,000 for the Grand. Extra gauge sets in 28 and .410 bore can start at $32,000 or more. Winchester will even run a special set of eight small bore combinations in the $55,000 range. Of course, that includes personal fitting of the gun to the owner's body by a Winchester representative.

While $55,000 may be out of reach for most shotgun lovers, Winchester does offer an extra that most shooters can enjoy as well as afford: a production Winchester Model 70, 94 or 9422 (.22 rimfire lever action). Priced to sell between $100 and $500, these rifles offer select, semi-fancy or fancy wood (installed).

For full custom Model 70s, three choices are available, starting with a Standard Custom Built with optional fancy AAA wood and all-metal work. The

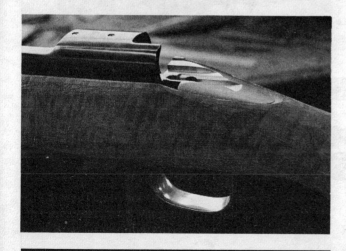

The author's gun is shown here in the building stage. Note how the Winchester shop molds the receiver into the woodwork.

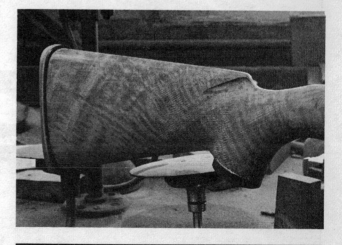

The author's Model 70 is shown here "in the rough." Datum lines have been drawn to insure that length of pull, recoil pad, and drop at the comb are all within the customer's specifications.

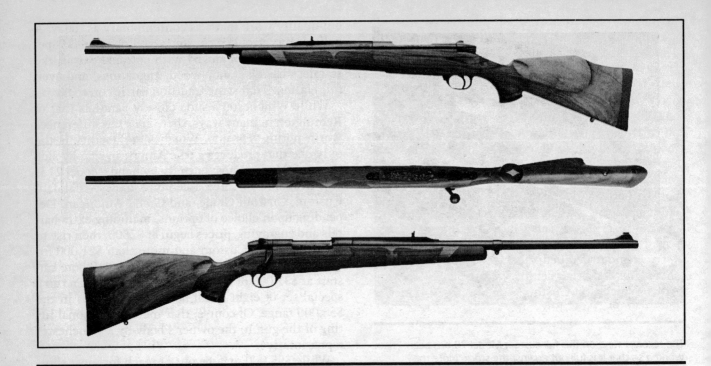

Weatherby's Crown Custom (above) is a ''Production Custom,'' which means its cost will be lower (because all options are included).

Weatherby's custom Safari Rifle includes a quarter rib on the barrel, forward, extra fancy stock, and checkering.

Exhibition Grade features premium wood with engraving on the barrel, receiver, floorplate and guard. The highest grade—called Collector—sports extra fancy wood and customized engraving patterns. Calibers for any of these guns range from the petite 22/250 to the thundering .375 and .458 Magnum. Short or Long actions are furnished (depending, of course, on cartridge length). Barrel lengths are 20, 22 or 24 inches, and there's a choice in style between Featherweight, Lightweight Carbine, Sporter and Sporter Magnum. Metal finish can be ordered in extra high polish, matte, XTR and rust bluing. Other options include pistol or straight grip, cheekpiece, forend tips or grip caps. Recoil pads can be standard or leather covered.

For a more detailed prospectus of Winchester's shop, guns and other details, write to U.S. Repeating Arms/Winchester Custom Gun Shop, 275 Winchester Avenue, P.O. Box 30-300, New Haven, CT. 06511.

WEATHERBY CUSTOM RIFLES

When it comes to promotion and eye-appealing graphics, Weatherby Custom Rifles lead the pack. The company publishes a gorgeous 120-page catalog every year or so describing in full detail its production, semi-production and custom rifle choices. In it, the prospective buyer will find any option available from the Weatherby shop with sample rifles as subjects, all in beautiful four-color reproduction. No matter what your budget restrictions may be, you'll find here at least one custom feature you can apply to your production grade rifle.

For example, even if you should order a straight off-the-shelf production grade Mark V Weatherby, you can (at small extra cost) ask the shop to add little extras, such as extending the rear of the checkering pattern into the pistol grip area. They can also damascene the bolt and follower, hone the action by hand, fully checker the bolt knob, or custom engrave the floorplate. You can also increase (or decrease) the stock length, add your initials, install iron sights, or attach a full-blown quarter rib to the barrel.

Among Weatherby's semi-production custom rifles, Safari Grade offers a fancy European walnut stock, ebony tip and cap, black recoil pad (with no white spacers), all chambered in .300 Weatherby

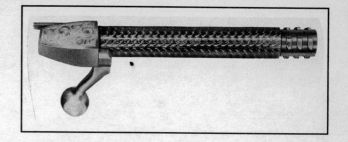

This Weatherby Mark V bolt assembly is in the "white," meaning it has been engraved and is ready for the bluing tanks.

Magnum. The Crown Model, which is built along the same lines, contains a super fancy walnut stock, some inlays (with initials), and a carved pattern in the stock. Prices on these two models tend to be somewhat lower, because they are built as "production" custom rifles. In other words, their features are all built in.

The top of the Weatherby heap, however, remains the full status custom rifle built to your own specifications. From extra fancy wood to top flight engraving, the byword here is *personal*. After you've selected the custom barreled action chambered in Weatherby calibers (plus 22/250 and 30/06), you can take your choice of 15 different ways to dress up your rifle. From engraving the barrel and adding a gold inlayed animal to plating the floorplate in gold or silver, the sky is virtually the limit.

As for custom stocks, you can have tigertail or birdseye maple, myrtlewood, fancy or super fancy walnut, plus European walnut. Moreover, there are 42 different stock inlay patterns and 22 checkering patterns. Take those figures and multiply them out, and the number of different ways to customize your Weatherby rifle becomes a staggering statistic.

To acquire Weatherby's price list and latest edition of their Weatherby Guide, write to them at: 2781 Firestone Boulevard, South Gate, California 90280.

In this day of high prices, custom guns still represent a good value for the dollar spent. Their average starting price of $1000 or so is not out of line. By sending for their catalogs, you can start making a list of all those great options you've always wanted for your very own.

UP-TO-DATE COMPUTER SOFTWARE FOR TODAY'S SHOOTERS

BY WILF E. PYLE

As everyone knows by now, computers influence nearly every part of our lives in some way. Scarcely a day passes when we do not interact directly with the computer-machine or one of its many by-products. Until recently, however, hardly any computer products had evolved to help shooters improve their performance in the field. Happily, new software designed specifically for shooters, reloaders and hunters is fast becoming commonplace. For example, several ballistic programs now give shooters an opportunity to develop and test load information, determine internal ballistics, establish downrange performance, and produce other data which would normally require laborious calculations, endless range time, and heavy costs. Finally, we have in hand

WILF E. PYLE has worked in the computer systems field since 1983. An enthusiastic reloader and ballistician, he has hunted nearly all species of big and small game. Pyle is the author of two books, *Hunter's Book of the Pronghorn Antelope* (New Century Publishers) and *Hunting Predators for Hides and Profits* (Stoeger Publishing Co.). His third book, on small game hunting, will soon be released by Stoeger Publishing Company.

programs that give us a chance to test, develop and compare various combinations without leaving our chairs.

The advantages of these programs to hunter, shooter and reloader are many. First, they provide

This shooter is learning how to benefit from new computer technology by using ballistic software designed especially to solve his special problems.

Many shooters, including the one pictured here, have already compiled a mass of data. Any of the new software programs described in this article can help in interpreting and understanding this information properly.

ready sources of information quite apart from traditional sources, such as reloading manuals and the innumerable charts that accompany them. Distances and individual firearm characteristics can be entered into these programs and retrieved instantly. Downrange information on a custom load can be obtained far more accurately than with anything you might find in a reloading manual. That's not meant to be an indictment of the manuals, but rather hard evidence of the benefits to be derived from electronic processing.

The second and perhaps single most important advantage is that new ballistic programs add another dimension to the shooting experience. Suddenly, reloading has become an integral part of the shooting sports, and along with that has come increased scrutiny of what loads to use and what performance to expect. This has led, in turn, to more familiarity with firearms and greater knowledge about individual firearm performance. It has also opened the door to comparisons among rifles of similar caliber but differing design. Moreover, because they create better understanding of cartridge capabilities, ballistic programs automatically advance the cause of firearms safety. Ballistic tinkering gets hunters thinking more about shooting during off-season, too, and thus encourages more shooting, not less. The result is a shooter who is more at home with his rifle/load combo.

Further advantages of this modern software in-

Computer-generated information on old cartridges is readily available. Both the ancient .32-20 and .38-55 shown here proved to have interesting external ballistics.

clude the instant ability it offers to compare performances among different cartridges, and to test the functional characteristics of different loads. For most shooters, these features alone would justify outright purchase of a computer and the kind of software described on the following pages.

Still another useful advantage is the information these programs provide on cartridges not always listed in reloading manuals. A good example is the .284 Winchester. Nowhere can you find good, readily available ballistic data for this long defunct cartridge; and yet, the ballistic programs tested for this article provided up-to-date loadings for the .284 Winchester. For shooters who prefer older or semi-obsolete cartridges, that's a real plus.

Until the arrival of these new ballistic software programs, the only remotely comparable product was the Powley Powder Computer. The now familiar Exterior Ballistic Charts also provided information, along with the oft-quoted Ingall's Ballistic Tables. These products still have their advocates, and no

doubt they've all served the shooting public well over the years. Even now, a shooter armed with a good calculator can determine accurate ballistic performance from these tables with little difficulty. Still, ballistic software offers as much as those now outmoded products and more. It puts the shooter in a position to take full advantage of fine-tuning his rifle and load quickly and accurately.

A Look at the Leading Software Producers

Shortly after IBM brought out the first personal computers, countless entrepreneurial types jumped on the bandwagon and designed software products that could operate on IBM machinery. Software companies flourished, some becoming giants in the field, while others fell by the wayside. The survivors quickly recognized the benefits of working closely with other hardware manufacturers, and together they produced a steady flow of new software products. This blossoming of software tools, however, never reached into the shooting sports. While dozens of obvious applications existed, no company bothered to pursue them, and the result was a market void. It was filled partially by shooters trained in computer science who saw an opportunity to develop software for their market. Some of their initial efforts were cumbersome and unsuccessful, true, but in the end several shooter-oriented software publishers emerged who now provide efficient computer-based solutions to all manner of ballistic problems. None boasts the high profile of corporate software producers, however, and you will not read about their products in the computer or data trade magazines. That's partly because marketing and selling software are the most expensive elements of the publishing process. For most companies, marketing costs represent at least one-third of the package price, while operating costs for disks and manuals total about 20 percent. That leaves shooters with a small group of publishers who are struggling to meet the needs of a growing number of computer-smart shooters.

The main purpose of the following review is to outline for modern shooters and hunters what is available in the field of ballistic software, and to provide a brief summary of their products. No attempt has been made to evaluate the products in terms of mathematical theory or the efficiency with which they utilize computer codes. The aim is simply to provide informed commentary on the products' usefulness from the shooter's point of view. For a sum-

Computer programs make comparisons between cartridges of the same caliber relatively simple. The group of .25 caliber cartridges pictured above includes (left to right): .25-20, .25-35, .250 Savage, .257 Roberts, .25-06 and .257 Weatherby Magnum. The performance range of these and other cartridges, as revealed by the various software programs, often raises the question of why some were ever invented in the first place.

mary of all programs to follow, including addresses, costs and equipment requirements, see p. TK.

INTERNAL AND EXTERNAL BALLISTICS PROGRAM VERSION 4.31
Produced by John R. Clarke: The Ballistic Program Company

In a nutshell, this program computes ballistic variables, including breech pressure, velocity, charge weights, appropriate powder, wind effects, range tables, trajectory, time of flight, and port pressure (for automatic arms only). Point blank range and rifle recoil are also available.

The program is contained in two disks—a program disk and a utility disk. The former includes the interior, exterior, ballistic and operating programs for the application, while the second disk carries documentation and sample data files for both the exterior and interior programs. The program is designed to run on any IBM PC, PC-XT or pc-compatible using MS or PC-DOS 2.00 or later operating system. Hardware requirements include two 360K floppy disk drives or a hard disk and one 360K drive. The program will run on color as well as black and white monitors. The ballistics program is written in Borlands Turbobasic with several Assembly language sub-routines for disk access.

Slight changes in powder capacity can vary performance greatly. A good software program can point out the downrange advantages of various sizes.

The program, which is reasonably easy to use, takes only 30 minutes to learn. When cross-referenced with reloading manuals and previous field experience, it proved to be accurate and reliable. The program is accessed by booting the system with DOS and typing the word "GO" at the DOS prompt. The main program menu offers three selections: Interior, Exterior and Exit. A numerical choice is made and the appropriate program is loaded (it takes about ten seconds for the program to load). First time users are well advised to print out the documentation available on the utility disk. In order to function, the program requires 11 input variables, none of which are strangers to shooters and reloaders. Included in the list are bullet weight, case capacity, barrel length, cartridge length, bullet diameter, bullet type, case length, seating depth, and loading density. Port pressure and port distance are optional.

After data is input (or retrieved from disk via main menu command), one key stroke provides the recommended powder and charge weights. Since it expresses powder in terms of its similarity to IMR powders, this program allows the shooter to pick powders of similar character, knowing that final test results are the real arbiters in powder selection for any given firearm. The load data can then be printed or sent to an ASCII file.

Fortunately, the program does not stop there. Should the user wish to modify the projected loading in any way, the next menu provides an opportunity to increase or decrease charge weight, select a different powder index and charge weight, or allow the user to go back and input a new set of ballistic data. Other important options include that of saving established data to file or retrieving other previously stored data.

Changing or modifying the loading components is what reloading is all about, and users can now do this quickly and easily. Instead of hours spent at the loading and shooting benches, four or five loadings can be compared instantly. Having viewed several loadings, modifying bullet weights and powder burning weights, and then settling on a particular load, the user can then move back into the exterior ballistic program to determine how a load will perform in any given rifle.

Shooters who are fortunate enough to own a computer have at their fingertips all the data
needed to fine-tune a load to a rifle and make accurate comparisons of several different rifles
similar to the ones pictured above.

BALLISTIC TABLE

Cartridge Name--					.30-06		0 Range Selected-- 200 Yards.		

Ballistic Coefficient-- 0.3590   Bullet Weight-- 150.0 Grains.
Alt.--   0 Ft.   Filename--   Temperature--   59 Degrees F.

Flight Time	Range Yards	Remaining Velocity	Remaining Energy	Total Drop	Bullet Path	Angle +/- 0	Deflection In 10 Mph Wind
0.00	0	3000	2997	0.00	-1.50	-1.50	0.00
0.10	100	2737	2495	2.05	1.58	1.58	0.84
0.22	200	2489	2064	8.77	0.00	0.00	3.48
0.35	300	2254	1693	21.09	-7.19	-7.19	8.15
0.49	400	2032	1376	40.30	-21.26	-21.26	15.23
0.64	500	1823	1107	67.82	-43.64	-43.64	24.94

Sample printout of Ballistic Table generated by Proware

BALLISTIC PROGRAM
Produced by Proware Inc.

This program, which addresses ballistic information only, is excellent for studying old chronograph data. Prepared on one disk, it takes only about 20 minutes to read the documentation, perform disk copy, and begin walking through the program. Written in Turbo Pascal code, its operation is smooth and response time is good. The program consumes just over 60K of memory, so it can be used on most smaller systems without difficulty. It's compatible with color as well as black and white monitors.

The system goes on line by booting in the usual manner and entering BP at the DOS prompt and hitting return. It is not necessary to retain the boot disk in the system, thereby allowing the user to record ballistic information on another disk when desired.

Following a sign-on or identification panel, the main menu appears with a list of nine options available to the user. Option 1, which represents the core of the program, displays more than 20 inputs needed to arrive at the cartridge description, ballistic table, and maximum point-blank range portions of the program. The ballistic table provides almost anything the shooter could ever want to know. Time of flight, range, remaining velocity, energy, total drop, bullet path, angle and deflection under a 10 mph wind are all printed on demand. It's also possible to modify cartridge data with different bullet weights and muzzle velocities, as well as save the data to disk, assign the names and retrieve previous data from disk. A directory display function allows the user to look at an index of previously created cartridge files—a handy device for those who wish to study many different cartridge and bullet combinations.

Maximum point-blank range data is particularly useful for hunters and long-range big game shooters. As all hunters know, point-blank range is the distance a shooter can hold dead on the vital internal organ area of a big game animal. Even though the bullet will drop over the intervening distance, it will still strike within the animal's heart-lung zone. This program feature eliminates the need for holding over at unknown ranges and reduces the chances for short and mid-range misses common to hunters who have overestimated the distance between them and the target. The accompanying documentation also gives advice on how to decide on the right distance for your rifle.

Standard deviation—which is defined as a measurement of dispersion about the mean—is available as well. For experimenters with older chronographs that lack built-in standard deviation capability, this is a very handy feature. It stands apart from the rest of the program and must be selected from the main menu and data elements entered. Other features include recoil calculations and the ability to reset sights to new ranges. Interestingly, though, the program does not allow the shooter to reduce his zero. Thus, a load recorded as sighting in at 200 yards can't be changed to 100 yards; you must re-define the distance from the ballistic table. This minor inconvenience points up the need for developers to recognize the variety of field conditions that can affect the usefulness of ballistic information. Hunting a black bear over baits often requires changing sight zero to 50 yards or less. Hunters need this kind of information, and there's no reason why it shouldn't be made available in this program, which, by the way, is undergoing revision. New features will include sight

```
** CARTRIDGE LOAD DEVELOPMENT **
-----------------------------
CARTRIDGE TYPE= .30-06
CALIBER= .308 IN BULLET WEIGHT=   150 GR
BARREL LENGTH=   20 IN
CASE CAPACITY=   68 GR OF WATER (ACTUAL)
BULLET DIAM=  .308 IN
SECTIONAL DENSITY=   .226
VOLUMETRIC RATIO=  6.4
CHARGE/BULLET WT=   .39
POWDER CLASS: MEDIUM SLOW POWDERS
POWDER TYPE: RX-21, H-414, H380
POWDER CHARGE=   58.5  GR
ESTIMATED MUZZLE VELOCITY=  2750  FT/SEC
ESTIMATED PEAK PRESSURE=  47900   PSI
SUGGESTED STARTING LOAD:  52.7  GR
```

Sample printout of Cartridge Load Development
generated by Blackwell

resetting and full metric support, plus standard deviation and the ability to output data to disk files.

LOAD FROM A DISK
Produced by W. W. Blackwell

This excellent reloading-type software offers easy access to correct powder type, powder charge, estimated muzzle velocity, and chamber pressure for any rifle cartridge, commercial or wildcat. Complete ballistics for any cartridge, including downrange muzzle velocity, time of bullet flight, wind drift, and bullet drop over any range, are also provided. The program includes a complete trajectory table, and it can determine point-blank range along with up/down hill effects.

A special feature of this program is its large resident data base of 82 cartridges, which allows the shooter to determine effective case capacity with a minimum of input data. Designed for use with another product, called Load From Disk Two, the program can stand alone in providing shooters with everything they ever wanted to know.

The application runs on the IBM, plus any compatibles and the Apple II+, IIc, IIe, Laser 128, or Commodore 64/128. The program is written in Basic but is sold in protected format to prevent user modification. It consumes about 35K of memory and runs on either color or black-white monitors. On the IBM, it is loaded the standard way. Place the application disk in drive B, enter BASCIA B:IBM160, and hit re-

turn. Because all data is entered with capital letters, it's necessary to lock the caps. It can also be loaded directly from DOS 2.1 (or a later version).

To use this program properly, you'll need to provide certain basic data. Among them are caliber, bullet weight, and barrel length. The last refers to the actual length traveled by the bullet; it's determined by chambering a dummy cartridge, inserting a cleaning rod down the barrel until it bumps the cartridge, then extracting and measuring the rod length.

Effective case capacity is also required. It's determined by weighing an empty case and bullet, then reweighing a bulleted case filled with water and subtracting the values, thereby yielding effective case capacity in grains of water. On start up, the main menu in this program displays five major sub-systems that are available to the shooter: cartridge loading, ballistic and trajectory calculations, trajectory and energy table, recoil, and ballistic coefficient correction (plus an exit facility). The cartridge loading portions give the actual weight of the powder type selected by the computer. Blackwell recommends using the starting load and working up to maximum slowly, all the while checking for pressure signs. This is good advice when using any technology.

This long range shooter found the wind drift tables and trajectories in his software program especially useful in developing new loads and testing factory loads.

```
        SIERRA   BULLETS
|=======================================================================|
|BULLET 30-06  :  taken from manual                                     |
|BULLET WEIGHT 150 GRS : MUZZLE VEL 3000 FPS                            |
|BALLISTIC COEFS. .359  .000  .000   : CHANGE POINTS OF    0 AND    0 FPS|
|WIND SPEED=  0.0 MPH FROM  0.00 O'CLOCK : ELEVATION ANGLE OF  0 DEGS    |
|ALTITUDE=  1800 FT : ZERO RANGE=  200YARDS : SIGHT HT=  1.5 INCHES      |
|PT BLNK RANGE =  450 YDS FOR ZERO AT  380 YDS AND VITAL ZONE =  18 INCH |
|=======================================================================|
|RANGE  VELOCITY   ENERGY   BULLET    DROP      DRIFT     TIME OF        |
|YARDS   (FPS)    (FT-LB)  PATH(IN)   (IN)      (IN)     FLIGHT(SEC)     |
|-----------------------------------------------------------------------|
|   0   3000.0     2997    -1.50     +0.00     +0.00    0.000000        |
| 100   2751.7     2521    +1.54     -1.95     +0.00    0.104426        |
| 200   2516.8     2109    +0.00     -8.48     +0.00    0.218431        |
| 300   2293.7     1752    -7.03    -20.51     +0.00    0.343298        |
| 400   2082.1     1444   -20.67    -39.14     +0.00    0.480585        |
| 500   1882.1     1180   -42.33    -65.79     +0.00    0.632151        |
|=======================================================================|
```

Sample printout of Ballistics Table generated by Sierra.

EXTERIOR BALLISTICS PROGRAM FOR PERSONAL COMPUTERS
Produced by Sierra

This program, developed by one of the few corporate entries in ballistic software, addresses exterior ballistics only. It does not provide reloading information or interior ballistics. Sierra's program operates in what it calls three modes. The first is a determination of the maximum point-blank range against targets of all sizes. The second is a calculation of bullet trajectory, and the third mode provides trajectory variations arising from changed shooting conditions. All are fast and powerful—it takes barely 30 minutes to read the documentation and begin using the program.

Start up is simple. The program requires 128K of computer memory and is contained on a single disk for use with either single-sided or double-sided disk drives. It needs PC-DOS 2.0 operating system or later. Start up with IBM or compatibles is completed by typing "sierra" at the prompt. Other computers use instructions common to their respective operating systems.

The program runs on Commodore, IBM (and clones), and Apple II, IIe, or IIc computer systems. It is programmed and compiled in BASIC. Once start up is completed, the menu-driven program requests required inputs. Fourteen inputs, beginning with bullet identification, are needed to drive the ballistic information. Requests follow for range calculations (either metric or yards), muzzle velocity, ballistic coefficient, coefficient change points, bullet weight, sight height, wind speed and direction. Up/down hill correction, altitude, maximum range, range increment and zero range are also required.

Once information has been entered and verified, the shooter can begin working through the three modes. A feature of this program is its ability to handle changes in bullet ballistic coefficient resulting from alternating velocities. It also allows a shooter to compute ballistics for smokeless and black powder firearms, including round ball and lead bullets. The program, which can handle bullet velocities from 0 to 4400 fps, is an easy one to learn and use.

PEJSA BALLISTICS
Produced by Pejsa Inc.

This program was developed by Arthur Pejsa, a college professor, engineer, and veteran firearms writer. In it, he provides shooters with a wide choice of external ballistic information. Its major advantage over other programs lies in its ability to change air drag coefficients, which are calculated explicitly (as opposed to series or tables). The result is a more accurate description of bullet performance at intermediate ranges. The program also provides remaining velocity, energy, flight path, sight elevation, wind deflection and flight duration at any given range increment. It is quick running and easy to learn. Available too are the effects of temperature, altitude and incline. Trajectory and wind deflection curves are also plotted.

Inputs required are bullet weight, muzzle velocity, sight height and range intervals, followed by trajectory height and sight-in range. Depending on the information desired, inputting the ballistic coefficient follows.

COMPAIR
Produced by Geo Brothers

This program requires that users have some basic knowledge of the spread sheet application Lotus 1-2-3 or comparable product. As such, Compair demands a computer capable of running Lotus 1-2-3, meaning at least 256K and a graphics board. These may be stiff requirements for most operators, but for users already configured this application offers extra mileage from most spreadsheet products. It comes on two disks—one for regular use and the other for backup.

Compair is descended from a long line of well tested and popular software programs designed by George V. V. Brothers, inventor of GB Lin-Speed Gunstock Oil. It replaces "Windbag" as the flagship program in Brothers' line, which has also included "Wind" and "UpDn." It's really two programs in one, allowing shooters to juxtapose two sets of data and thereby enabling users to see the immediate effects of changing a single input component.

The application requires the usual inputs: bullet weight, wind deflection, hill angle, muzzle velocity, ballistic coefficient, humidity, temperature and elevation. From this basic information shooters can calculate trajectory, feet per second, flight time, energy, and cross wind deflection. A small table includes minute changes, allowing the shooter to adjust sights for other ranges. Point-blank range is also available, and foot-pounds of recoil can be calculated here as well. Finally, there's a lead-determining sequence—for game that is moving at various estimated speeds.

In conclusion, it should be obvious by now that plenty of good, dependable software programs are available to shooters. All programs reviewed here

Along with gun cases and other equipment designed to enhance his sport, this hunter's computer and software have become accepted members of his arsenal.

were relatively easy to learn, and all had sufficient documentation for beginners to get started. Familiarity with your pc is vital if you are to benefit from any of these programs, however. Compair also requires advance knowledge of Lotus 1-2-3. Choice of software is determined, of course, by the user's experience, hardware availability, and the ultimate purpose for obtaining the information. It's impossible to pick an overall favorite program, but, in general, reloading programs offer greater versatility for most shooters, while those who have compiled a lot of old chronograph data will find the exterior ballistic programs useful.

The question remains: should a place be found for these software products on the shooting benches and next to the gun racks of contemporary shooters? The answer is a resounding *yes*. There is indeed a well deserved place, one that shooters everywhere will appreciate increasingly as they develop product knowledge and become more adept at translating ballistic data into practical field information.

Software products similar to the ones pictured here have improved upon traditional sources of information. While they cannot replace field testing of live ammo, they do help shooters narrow the choices considerably.

A DIRECTORY OF SOFTWARE PROGRAMS FOR SHOOTERS

TITLE: The Ballistic Program Version 4.1

PRODUCER: Ballistics Program Co.
John R. Clarke
2417 N. Patterson St.
Thomasville, GA 31792

PURPOSE: Cartridge reloading; internal & external ballistics

EQUIPMENT REQUIRED: IBM-pc or compatible using DOS 2.10, Apple, Commodore 64

DOCUMENTATION: Excellent 18-page small format booklet

LANGUAGE: Version 4.1, Version 4.31 in Turbobasic

COST: $49.95

TRAINING: Not necessary; operation can be learned in less than one hour from documentation. New Version 4.31 is in the works

TITLE: Ballistic Data Program

PRODUCER: Craig Chamberlin/Proware Inc.
1023 SE 36 Avenue
Portland, Oregon 97214

PURPOSE: External Ballistics

EQUIPMENT REQUIRED: IBM-pc or any
compatible, Apple,
Commodore 64

DOCUMENTATION: Excellent 14-page
photocopy

LANGUAGE: Turbo Pascal

COST: $49.95

TRAINING: Not necessary; operation can be
learned in less than one hour. New
version to be released soon with
improvements

TITLE: Load From A Disk

PRODUCER: W. W. Blackwell
9826 Sagedale
Houston, Texas 77089

PURPOSE: Cartridge reloading; internal and
external ballistics

EQUIPMENT REQUIRED: IBM-pc or any
compatible, Apple,
Commodore 64

DOCUMENTATION: Excellent dust-covered
mimeo (25 pages)

LANGUAGE: Basic

COST: $49.95

TRAINING: Not necessary; operation can be
learned in less than one hour from
documentation

TITLE: Exterior Ballistics Program For Personal
Computers

PRODUCER: Sierra Bullets
10532 S. Painter Avenue
Santa Fe Springs, CA 90670

PURPOSE: External ballistics

EQUIPMENT REQUIRED: IBM-pc or any
compatible, Apple,
Commodore 64

DOCUMENTATION: Excellent 44-page looseleaf
binder

LANGUAGE: Basic

COST: $199.00

TRAINING: Not necessary; operation can be
learned in less than one hour from
documentation

TITLE: Pejsa Computer Program

PRODUCER: Art Pejsa/Pejsa Ballistics
2120 Kenwood Parkway
Minneapolis, Minnesota 55405

PURPOSE: Improved external ballistics

EQUIPMENT REQUIRED: IBM-pc or any
compatible, Apple,
Commodore 64

DOCUMENTATION: One folded page

LANGUAGE: Basic

COST: $29.95

TRAINING: Not necessary; operation can be
learned in less than one hour from
documentation

TITLE: Compair

PRODUCER: Geo Brothers
Route 1, Box 42A
Great Barrington, Massachusetts
01230

PURPOSE: External ballistics

EQUIPMENT REQUIRED: IBM-pc or any
compatible (hardware
must support Lotus 1-
2-3)

DOCUMENTATION: Six-page printed booklet

LANGUAGE: Designed to run on the spread sheet
Lotus

COST: $39.95

TRAINING: Necessary to know fundamentals of
Lotus product

THE BAKER SHOTGUN

BY JIM. C. COBB

Among the early pioneers in the production of breech loading shotguns, few men were more influential than William H. Baker. Although he may not have possessed the inventive mind of a Dan Lefever or the corporate genius of Charles Parker, Baker had the unquestioned ability to see the need for a product and then gather together the people who could best bring it to market. In other words, he had the ability to get things organized. Without that ability, he could not have helped form the L. C. Smith Gun Company, the Ithaca Gun Company, the Syracuse Gun company, and the company that later bore his name, the Baker Gun and Forging Company.

One of seven children, Baker was born in 1835 and grew up in upstate New York. His youngest brother, Ellis, later played an important role in William's gunmaking career, for it was Ellis who first became associated with George Livermore and L. H. Smith, who subsequently founded the L. C. Smith Gun

---

JIM COBB is a bird hunter, waterfowl shooter, and avid collector (and user) of fine American-made shotguns. The author of numerous articles on guns and hunting, including a regular feature for "North American Hunter", he has been published in "Fins and Feathers", "Gun Dog", "American Shotgunner" and many others. He has also co-authored a book on Dan Lefever ("Lefever: Guns of Lasting Fame"), which was published in 1986.

A CARD.

——:0:——

Having many inquiries as to what distinguishes the "ITHACA GUN" from the original "Baker Gun," of which I was the inventor, and for a time the manufacturer, I will say: The "ITHACA GUN" has the top lever, instead of the trigger action, an entirely new arrangement of locks, and construction, making it more desirable in every respect; for which reason it was thought best not to have it conflict in name with the old gun.

Sincerely thanking my numerous friends for their liberal appreciation of my efforts to produce such work as our progressive shooting demands, and trusting that the "ITHACA GUN" will continue to merit their patronage and that the pleasant business relations formerly existing, may be continued with the Ithaca Gun Co. I am

Very Truly,

W. H. BAKER.

Ithaca, N. Y., May, 1885.

William Baker distributed this notice to his customers and dealers in 1885; its purpose was to explain the differences between his original "Baker Gun" and the new "Ithaca" patented model.

THE BAKER GUNNER

No. 4   1909

A CATALOGUE OF
BAKER AND BATAVIA GUNS

Front cover of "The Baker Gunner" catalog of 1909.

THE ITHACA GUN COMPLETE.

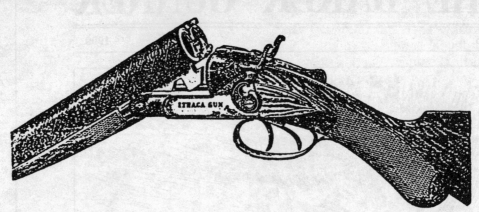

Baker's Latest and Best Invention.

TOP LEVER INSTEAD OF TRIGGER ACTION. STRONGEST, SIMPLEST AND BEST BALANCED GUN MADE, LOW HAMMERS, REBOUNDING LOCKS, INTERCHANGEABLE PARTS, SELF-FASTENING FORE END AND CHOKE BORED TO SUIT ANY KIND OF WORK.

Baker's patented Ithaca gun featured box lock action and lever opening mechanism.

An artist's rendition (c. 1885) of the Baker Gun and Forging Company factory in Batavia, N.Y.

Company. By 1878, all four men had gravitated to Syracuse, N.Y., where they came in contact with L. H. Smith's brother, Lyman Cornelius (L.C.), and persuaded him to join their new firm, called W. H. Baker and Sons Company. There, for the next two years, they produced double barrel and combination rifle and shotgun drillings under W. H. Baker's patent. Dated 1875, it documented Baker's unique trigger break, action-type cocking lever, which was then located in the trigger guard. In 1880, Lyman Cornelius bought out his brother and the two Baker brothers. The guns he made were of the same design and were marked, "L. C. Smith and Company," on the rib. The Baker patent dates also appeared on the lock.

The Ithaca Gun Company

In 1883, L. H. Smith and William Baker moved to Ithaca, N.Y., to start up a new gun factory, called the Ithaca Gun Company. The guns they made there, all under the Baker patent, were hammer boxlock guns, rather than the now familiar sidelock models. Instead of the hammer being mounted on a detachable side plate, the Baker design featured a boxlock with the hammers located in the rear of the assembly. They were available in what became known as quality grades A, B, C, D, E and F. All guns were fitted with Damascus barrels and were made in 10 and 12 gauges only. Prices ranged from $35 for the quality grade A to $200 for the F grade. By way of comparison, Lefever offered his guns around this same time period for $60 to $300.

In 1887, after William Baker had again been bought out, he returned to Syracuse. There he rejoined Ellis and they formed the Syracuse Forging Company. Two new hammer models were produced and later a new hammerless gun. When their plant was destroyed by fire in the spring of 1889, however, the Baker brothers were forced to sell what was left and start up a new company, called Syracuse Arms, which continued to produce guns under F. A. Hollenbeck's patents until about 1908. Hallenbeck had once managed his own company, which later became the 3-Barrel Drilling Company. He then joined Syracuse Arms and eventually bought it from the Bakers.

Meanwhile, never a man to sit still for long, Baker again moved his company, this time to Batavia, N.Y. The year was 1889, but in October of that same year this inveterate gunmaker died at the age of 54. Brother Ellis, who was by then practicing medicine nearby, began devoting himself full-time to the man-

The Montgomery Ward catalog of 1895 included this ad for Baker's new box lock gun along with the Ithaca model. Note the similarities between the three models shown.

ufacturing of guns. On February 13, 1890, the company was again reorganized and given a new title: Baker Gun and Forging Company.

A New Line of Shotguns

Two different hammer guns were soon in production—Models 1896 and 1897. The former utilized the old Baker patent boxlock hammer, while the 1897 model was a sidelock-type hammer gun. By 1899, the

This ad for Baker's Paragon Standard model appeared in the company's 1909 catalog.

Baker's Grade "R" hammerless shotgun, as described in the 1909 catalog.

The Paragon Model Nineteen-Nine, as featured in the 1909 Baker catalog.

company was producing its first hammerless side-lock gun, which strongly resembled the L. C. Smith guns of that same vintage. The chief difference in the two grades offered—A and B—was that the former had Damascus barrels, while the B grade featured London-Twist barrels (a different type of Damascus steel). In addition, both grades sported handsome en-gravings of hunting scenes with birds and dogs. About the only way one could distinguish A from B, in fact, was on the barrel lug, where the letter "D" (for *Damascus*) indicated the A grade gun, and the letter "T" (for *Twist*) denoted the B grade. Both models met with success, enabling the company to begin marketing a Paragon grade, priced at $78 with-out auto ejectors.

OUR NEW MODEL THREE BARREL GUN.

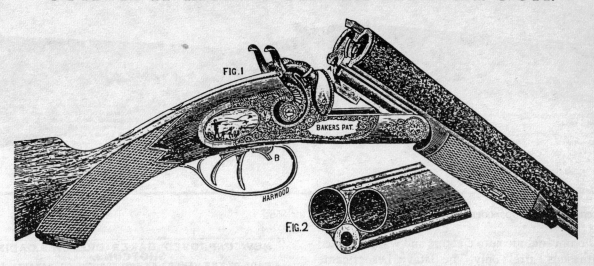

The Gun of the World for Hunting Purposes. The owner of one of these Three Barrel Guns when out Hunting has a Good Double Barrel Shot Gun and a Good Sporting Rifle with him and both combined in one Gun which does not weigh more than a Double Shot Gun.

Baker's "Three Barrel Gun;" first produced under the name of W.H. Baker & Sons, it later appeared, as shown here, in the L.C. Smith catalog. Note the trigger break action.

By 1909, the company was carrying two Paragon models: Standard and Nineteen Nine, plus two other high grades, Expert and Deluxe. The Standard, which sold that year for $82.50 (with automatic ejectors), featured fine Damascus or Krupp fluid compressed steel. The stock and forend were of fancy European walnut, beautifully finished and available in three gauges—10, 12 and 20—with full, half pistol, or straight grips. These models were all nicely engraved with scroll and pictorial designs, the latter usually consisting of pointing bird dogs.

The Paragon Nineteen-Nine model, which was more richly furnished than the Standard grade, sold for $95 with automatic ejectors. The next highest grade was the Expert, priced at $150 (also with automatic ejectors). Buyers had the option of either Damascus barrels or Holland fluid steel barrels. The next grade up was the Deluxe model, priced at $300 and furnished with barrels made of either Damascus steel or Sir Joseph Whitworth fluid compressed steel, supposedly the highest quality barrels then obtainable. Both the Krupp and Whitworth fluid steel barrels were, incidentally, used by several different gunmak-

ers, among them Lefever, L. C. Smith, Ithaca and Parker. The Whitworth fluid steel barrels were used only in top-of-the-line models, including Lefever's Optimus grade, L. C. Smith's Deluxe model, Ithaca's grade 7, and Parker's A-1 Special.

The most popular choice in Paragon's mid-range was grade R. It was available in 12 and 16 gauge only and offered a choice between Damascus barrels and Krupp fluid steel barrels. In 1909, it was priced at $58.75 with automatic ejectors. Grade S was the next lower grade. Furnished with flue-tempered steel only, and with scroll-type engravings on the lock, it came in 10, 12 and 16 gauge in semi-pistol grip only.

The lower end of the Baker gun grades consisted of the Batavia Ejector, Batavia Damascus, Batavia Leader, and Batavia Special. All were similar in appearance, the only difference being the type of barrel; i.e., with or without automatic ejectors and their steel content. The Batavia Ejector model, for example, was sold either with Damascus steel or Homotensile fluid blue steel. With steel barrels, it sold for $35, and with Damascus barrels the price was $37. The Batavia Damascus model, which was priced at

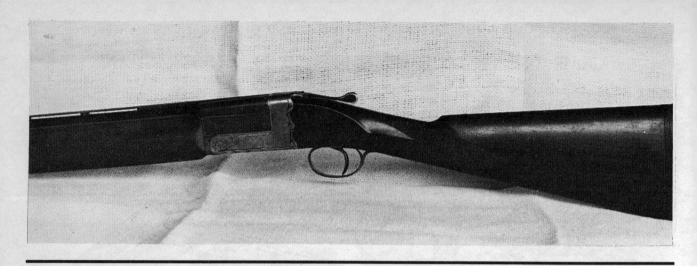

This Sterling Grade Trap model was introduced in 1909 and sold for $65.

$28, did not include auto ejectors and was furnished in Damascus barrels only. The Batavia Leader came with London-Twist barrels and was priced at $25. Later, the company replaced its Leader grade with the Black Beauty, a steel-barreled gun with blue-black frame and sidelocks. It sold for $19.95 in 1918. Still another steel-barreled model, the Black Beauty Special, was produced at $35 with automatic ejectors, safety locks, a single trigger and other niceties. And finally, at the bottom end of the scale, there was the Batavia Special. Fitted with Homo-tensile brown steel barrels, it was, in 1909, the lowest-priced hammerless gun in the Baker line.

That same year, Baker Gun and Forging Company introduced a trap model, single barrel shotgun in three grades: Sterling, Elite, and Superba. These guns, which ranged in price between $65 and $160, were produced in limited numbers and are rarely seen now. Later, between 1910 and 1915, Baker introduced a new boxlock grade gun, available with either Krupp fluid steel barrels or Nitro rolled barrels. Similar in design to the early C grade and Syracuse boxlock guns, these models are seldom available in used gun shops.

In 1919, the gun division of Baker Gun and Forging Company sold out to H & D Folsom Company of New York. Folsom, which manufactured and imported dozens of brands of firearms, continued selling Baker-made guns left in its inventory and for several years made parts for these leftover models. Later, the company introduced the Folsom Batavia ' Leader in 12, 16, 20 and the rather rare .410 gauges. All Baker guns produced by Folsom have the letter "F" added to their serial numbers.

Sears & Roebuck ran these ads for the improved Baker Breech loading shotgun and the improved Baker hammerless shotgun in its 1902 catalog.

End of the Line

The last guns made by Folsom under the Baker name probably came off the line around 1930. Their present values are difficult to determine because, having been machine-made rather than drop-forged, they are now generally undervalued by collectors. The high grade Bakers are not seen too often and command a much higher price, of course, than do the low or common grade guns. The Paragons are seen infrequently, although one Ninety-Nine grade was priced recently at $1,450. The S and R grades are usually priced between $700 and $850, while lower grade Batavia Ejectors and Batavia Leaders sell for anywhere between $300 and $400. The 20 gauge guns produced by Folsom command a higher value; and the .410 gauge model, which has become quite rare, is worth even more. Baker single barrel trap models in excellent condition will bring $700 for the lowest grade up to $1800 for the highest grade. All prices, by the way, relate to guns with steel barrels (Damascus barrels are worth about 50 percent less).

In all the annals of American gun making, it would be difficult to find any one person who had more influence over double barrel shotgun production than did W. H. Baker. And while the rich legacy of guns that he left behind may never be as highly valued among collectors as the Parkers, Lefevers or L. C. Smiths, the truth remains much the same as the Baker gun catalog of 1909 proclaimed: "You cannot get more for your money.... " Perhaps that same motto rings more true today than it did some 80 years ago.

THE ZOUAVE RIFLE

BY JOHN MALLOY

Zouave. The word is common enough now so that both shooters and nonshooters alike recognize it as the name of a replica firearm. Some also know that the name originally applied to a special sort of old-fashioned fighting man. Few, however, know the full history of the modern black powder rifles that bear this unusual name today.

The Zouave story should be better known. It is a proud and interesting history. The rifles themselves have contributed greatly to the recent growth of muzzleloaders; moreover, the modern Zouave may well be the most important replica rifle ever produced. It deserves recognition of its own, beyond its resemblance to the original weapon.

The original—after which the Zouave was patterned—was a Remington-built contract rifle of the Civil War era. Famed for its fine workmanship and handsome appearance, the Remington was not without historical significance of its own. In addition to being well made and attractive, it was the last muzzleloading rifle developed by the Remington firm. It was also, in a way, the last official U.S. muzzleloading military rifle.

How the Zouave Rifle Evolved

The history of rifles in the U.S. service began in 1803, six full decades before production of the Remington contract rifle. Prior to that, rifles had been in use, of course, but they were the personal arms of frontiersmen and militiamen, and they were all different to some degree. The accuracy of the rifle was considered such an advantage that an official U.S. rifle was created to supplement—but not replace—the .69 caliber smoothbore musket, which remained the standard military longarm.

The first U.S. Rifle—the 1803 model—was a .54 caliber flintlock with a barrel length of about 32 inches. Manufactured just in time to be used on the famous Lewis and Clark Expedition of 1804, it remained in use (in several variations) for almost 40 years before it was made obsolete by the more reliable percussion ignition system, which was adopted in 1841. The 1841 model came to be called the "Mississippi Rifle" because of its fine performance during the Mexican War by the First Mississippi Regiment

JOHN MOLLOY, while a teenager in the 1950s, took advantage of various Junior shooting programs to learn about firearms. A rusty old 1863 Springfield, which he acquired for $5, launched his career as a black powder enthusiast and authority. Although most of his serious shooting now involves cartridge arms, Malloy still enjoys shooting muzzleloading replicas—Zouaves included. He has contributed many articles to *American Rifleman, Gun Digest, Guns & Ammo, Gun Week* and other outdoor publications.

This woodcut of the 53rd New York Infantry shows a soldier (left) in full Zouave dress. The rifle shown is similar in style to the Remington contract rifle.

under the command of Jefferson Davis. The .54 caliber "Mississippi" used a 215 grain patched round ball, which was propelled by 75 grains of powder. In its day, this combination was considered both accurate and powerful.

That remarkable 1841 rifle was manufactured at Harpers Ferry Arsenal and also by several contractors, one of them being Remington. In 1854, the company took over a contract awarded earlier to a Cincinnati gunmaker who had been unable to make deliveries on time. Remington completed the transferred contract of 5,000 rifles and later produced 15,000 more. These 1841 rifles featured steel barrels; indeed, Remington was the first to use steel for military rifle barrels.

The great accuracy of these rifles gradually made the smoothbore musket obsolete. The only disadvantage of rifled arms had been their slow loading with tight patched bullets; but around 1850 that problem was solved with the appearance of a new projectile called the Minie ball. Named for the French army officer who created it, the Minie's design reached its final form in America. It was a hollow-base bullet that loaded easily and expanded on firing to fit the bore. Thus, for the first time the rapid loading of the musket could now be combined with the accuracy of the rifle. The effect of this new projectile on U.S. military arms was dramatic. In 1855, the practice of using two different calibers was eliminated, the musket itself was discontinued, and the .58 caliber was adopted as standard. From then on, all arms were rifled. In addition to the rifle, the U.S. military adopted a pistol that could be stocked for use as

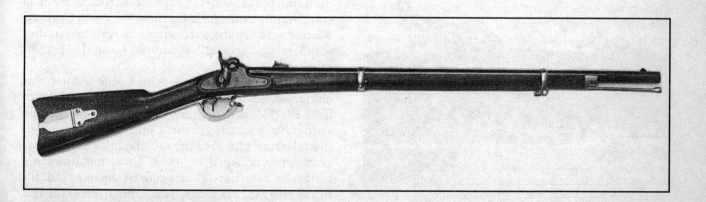

The 1862 Remington contract rifle (above) was well made and widely considered as the most handsome rifle of the Civil War period.

Remington contract rifles featured high-grade barrels made of steel. Remington was the first manufacturer to produce steel barrels for military rifles.

a carbine, and a new weapon, called the rifle-musket. It was the same caliber as the rifle, but its long barrel (40 inches) was of musket length.

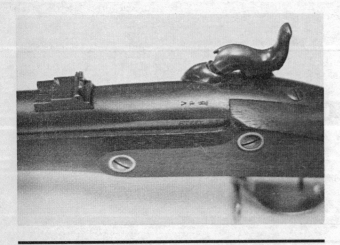

The steel barrels of Remington's contract rifles were proof-tested and dated, as shown here.

The outbreak of the Civil War in 1861 forced certain decisions in order to speed production. Such nonessentials as the tape primer system and patchbox were eliminated, and only the rifle-musket version was produced. The newly simplified arm was then adopted as Model 1861. Because federal arsenals could not meet the need for these weapons, Colt and others were awarded contracts to produce either standard or "special" versions of the 1861 rifle-musket.

Meanwhile, Remington, which still had its machinery intact for making the Model 1841 rifle, modified the "Mississippi" into a new rifle compatible with other arms then in use. Contracts were taken to manufacture 12,500 of the modified rifles and deliveries began on April 18, 1863. There remains some confusion as to the official designation, but "U.S. Rifle, Model 1862" is generally accepted. It was the last muzzleloading rifle used by the U.S. (rifled arms were designed and made by Springfield in 1863 and 1864, but they had 40-inch barrels and were thus

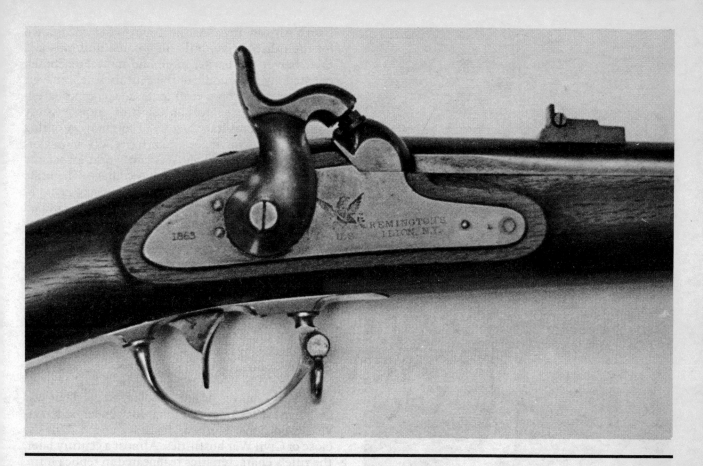

Identical with earlier 1841 lock plates made at Herkimer, N.Y., those of the Civil War Remingtons are easily identified by the Ilion stamping and appropriate date (above).

classified as rifle-muskets, not rifles). In designing its special contract rifle, Remington combined the main features of both the 1841 and 1855 models. The lock and trigger arrangement came without change from the 1841; and the lock plate mated with a nipple seat of the 1841 type on the new barrel.

Following the Mississippi pattern, the heavy 33-inch barrel was rifled with seven narrow grooves, and the caliber was changed from .54 to the then-standard .58. To stabilize the Minie balls, the twist was increased from the round ball rate of one turn in six feet to a quicker one turn in five. Still, the seven-groove bore looked much like that of the Mississippi, leading some to conclude that the Remington bore was "too tight" for the standard .58 projectile. Later production methods employed three wide grooves of the Springfield type.

A three-leaf rear sight—calibrated at 100, 200 and 300 yards for the standard military load—was adopted. A stud for a sword bayonet was mounted on the right of the barrel, near the muzzle; and the stock was similar to the 1855 rifle, with its curved butt-plate and small hinged patchbox cover. The 33-inch barrel gave it an overall length of only 49 inches, considerably shorter than rifle-musket length. Still, with its thicker barrel, this solidly built rifle tipped the scales at over nine pounds. The steel barrel was a deep blue-black, and small parts—such as the trigger, band springs and screws—were polished and heat blued. The lock plate and hammer were case hardened, and the cup-tipped ramrod, sling swivels and blade of the saber bayonet were polished bright.

Because Remington wanted to complete the contracts quickly, it used brass, which was expensive but easily cast, extensively. The barrel bands, stock tip, butt plate, trigger guard and patchbox cover were all polished brass. Stocks were of black walnut treated with linseed oil and hand-rubbed to a high polish. In the patchbox hollow nestled a spare nipple and a bullet-pulling worm. The result was an exceptionally fine rifle of distinctive appearance. It seems fitting that such a handsome arm was to be the last

A Zouave rifle and its accessories (above), most of which are available in replica form, make an interesting display of Civil War items.

North African dress. As the Zouaves became known for their distinctive, brilliant-colored uniforms and their bravery in battle, more and more Frenchmen enlisted. By the middle of the century, the Zouaves, now grown to three regiments and composed entirely of Europeans, had an esprit de corps possibly unmatched in military history. Their bravery during the Crimean War made them especially newsworthy, and soon the whole Western world associated the colorful dress with valor and courage. The basic Zouave uniforms consisted of loose baggy pants of red wool, a short blue jacket trimmed with colored braid, white canvas leggings, and a turban or fez for the head. Strange as such gaudy outfits might seem to us now, their association with bravery captured the imagination of many Federal (and some Confederate) volunteer units at the beginning of America's Civil War.

Handsome rifles would have complimented the dashing uniforms, to be sure, but the use of the 1862 Remingtons by these self-proclaimed "American Zouave" units is highly questionable. Still, this handsome rifle would have suited the flair of these Civil War Zouaves. It not only looked good but was designed for accuracy and reliability under harsh service conditions. Nor was its story ended with the close of Civil War hostilities. Almost a century later, the rifle's characteristics reappeared in replica form. The same qualities that made the original rifle so highly regarded caused the replicas to become equally popular with a much later generation of black powder shooters.

A New Wave of Muzzleloaders

As the Civil War Centennial approached in the early 1960s, interest grew concerning the weapons that had been used. Imported cap-and-ball revolver replicas had been accepted in the late 1950s, and now the Civil War buffs opened the door for introduction of an appropriate muzzleloading rifle. The one that appeared was the 1862 Remington replica, and it was called the *Zouave*.

The Remington replica was an instant hit. Civil War fans, eager to participate in demonstrations and reenactments, demanded authentic arms, and "shootable" original rifles were becoming scarce. The first waves of Zouave rifles were made in Italy and imported in the early 1960s, first by Navy Arms, then by Hy Hunter. Their initial popularity caused an increase in demand, and the Zouave came to be one of the best known and most widely used replicas.

muzzleloading rifle ever designed by Remington. Many surviving specimens are in excellent condition, causing speculation as to their issue. They may have spent the war in storage, waiting for a call to action that never came. There seems to be no clear record of Remingtons being used by any of the military groups known as the Zouaves, and they certainly were not standard issue to such units.

The Zouaves

The first men to bear the name *Zouave* were soldiers of certain infantry units of the French Army in Algeria. Organized as a native unit in 1830 from members of the local Zouaoua tribe, the Zouave Corps began to attract French volunteers, who adopted the

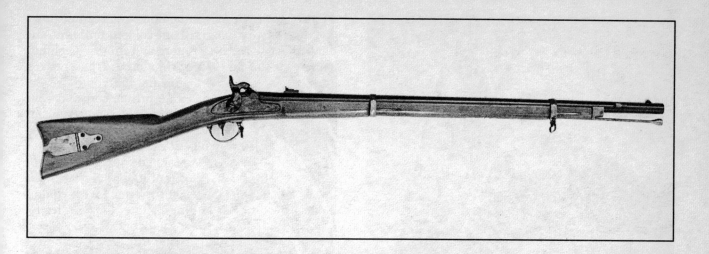

A modern Zouave rifle is similar in looks to the Remington contract rifle, but there are some differences in dimension and finish. This specimen was made by the Italian firm of Antonio Zoli.

The modern Zouave rifle is a strong and dependable rifle for black powder shooting of all types.

The Zouave's 49-inch length offers a convenient loading height for most shooters.

The Zouave rifle has proven popular for Civil War reenactments and is considered authentic for battles following April 18, 1863.

At least 17 American companies imported them, including Navy Arms, Dixie Gun Works, and Lyman. Quality of workmanship and finish may vary considerably, but all use modern steels and are strong and safe.

Some of the variations were designed that way. To prevent any chance of the replicas being represented as originals, most manufacturers made slight changes that affected neither looks nor performance. These modern Zouaves have the same general appearance as Remington's original .58 caliber rifle. The heavy barrels (about 33 inches in length) are three-grooved, as were the later Remingtons. Cheaper woods have been substituted for walnut on many Zouaves, and the swivels are blued instead of bright. Most come with two nipples; but as an ac-

commodation to the modern shooter, only one is for the large winged musket caps (the other takes the more common #11 or #12 percussion caps).

The importance of the Zouave's introduction has been generally overlooked. It was for a time not only the sole Civil War replica rifle available, it was the only muzzleloading rifle of any kind marketed in the quantities necessary to appeal to large numbers of people. Replica Kentucky-style rifles have been available since the late 1950s, but they were sold to a relatively small number of established enthusiasts.

The Zouave, on the other hand, was first noticed by people with no previous interest in black powder guns. Many were bought only because of their Civil War authenticity, nice lines, and reasonable price. But it was only natural that people would soon begin to wonder what it would be like to shoot one. Zouaves began to appear in the woods and at shooting ranges; even non-shooters with no interest in modern guns were tempted to try a few shots. The result was a growing demand for modern black powder rifles of all types.

For beginners, the muzzleloading rifle is ideal. It does not cost too much; it looks good hanging over a fireplace; and it's a comfortable rifle to use. It has enough weight to absorb recoil, yet it balances well for carrying through the woods. Most shooters also find its 49 inches a convenient loading height.

For hunting, a Zouave allows participation in special or extended hunting seasons in many states. Although not well suited for "barking" squirrels, it has adequate power and accuracy for most medium and big game hunting.

Besides the traditional Minie ball, more modern designs also shoot well in the Zouave. Round balls ranging in diameter from the recommended .570" down to .550" have been used with patches of appropriate thickness. Its shallow rifling and a bore diameter halfway been 20 gauge and 28 gauge even allow fairly effective use of shot charges at short range. Newspaper wadding works just fine.

As equipment for the target range, the Zouave is hindered by crude sights and a heavy trigger pull. The latter can be easily improved, though, and most Zouaves shoot well enough "as is" to keep their owners interested in informal target matches and shoots associated with Civil War gatherings.

Although there appears to be no record of the 1862 Remington's use in any particular military action,

Traditional Minie balls, along with more modern designs (center) and round balls (right), can all be used in the Zouave. The rifle's large bore even allows the use of shot charges.

the Zouave is a genuine Civil War design and as such is appropriate for Civil War festivities and reenactments of battles which took place after April of 1863.

Remington's 1862 rifle was a good choice for reproduction. The modern Zouave has the same traits that made the original so desirable. It has an attractive appearance and is a strong, reliable shooter. Its widespread availability and relatively low price have encouraged ownership by people who might not otherwise have developed an interest in muzzleloading firearms. Thus it has played a significant role in the growth of black powder shooting and has thereby benefitted the shooting sports in general. Quite apart from the historic arm it resembles, the modern Zouave has clearly earned its own place in gun history.

CLASSIC BRITISH SHOTGUNS—AND THE MEN WHO MAKE THEM

BY JIM CASADA

Mention the subject of fine shotguns to the average American sportsman, and his eyes will light up with thoughts of such magical names as Parker, L. C. Smith, A. H. Fox, Ithaca, Winchester and Ruger. These and other manufacturers of classic two-barreled guns have, over the decades, produced doubles and over-and-unders that are both functional and visual joys to behold. Yet these fine classic weapons, for all their appeal and considerable value, hardly compare with England's finest—or "Best"—shotguns. In this wonderful world of shotguns, the names that stand out are Boss, Churchill, Holland & Holland, Purdey and W & C Scott. "The great English guns, doubles made between the advent of breechloading and the present," wrote one gun expert recently, "are not only the best shotguns ever made but perhaps the most expensive."

These are strong words, but if anything they understate the case. Even now, England continues to produce shotguns beyond compare. And while these

DR. JIM CASADA is a college history professor who also freelances regularly on a variety of outdoor subjects. He is Editor-at-Large for *Sporting Classics* magazine and Contributing Editor/History for *Fly Fishing Heritage*. He also is a regular columnist for *The Flyfisher* and *FlyFishing News & Reviews* as well as contributing two weekly newspaper columns. He is presently in the final stages of a book manuscript on *Africa's Great Hunters*.

magnificently crafted products may lie well beyond the means of all but the wealthiest sportsmen and collectors, there is no reason not to admire them and treasure the proud gunmaking traditions they represent. The fact is, the high prices associated with the finest British shotguns are justified. They have nothing to do with snobbishness or the greedy desire of manufacturers to soak their affluent American customers. These British weapons are so costly for the simple reason that they are all hand-made. The craftsmen who create "London's Best" work painstakingly, as they have for generations, under conditions that the rest of the gunmaking fraternity could not possibly duplicate.

For one thing, each classic British shotgun is "prooftested" long before it becomes available for purchase. As a result, you can trust completely any British-made shotgun—even those made of vintage Damascus steel barrels—to perform safely *with the loads it was designed to handle.* More remarkable still is the manner in which these shotguns are created. Beginning with the basic raw materials and on through the finished product, no effort is spared to achieve the best quality possible. In today's world, with its preoccupation for fast-paced technology, this kind of respect—even reverence—for tradition has become virtually unknown. As MacDonald Hastings, a leading British gun authority, once put it so well, "Not since the fifth century B. C. has anything

This is the splendid showroom at Holland & Holland's shop on Bruton Street, London.

been made functionally better than a London Best gun." Indeed, no effort or expense is spared to make a "Best" gun precisely what the word implies.

The House of Scott

This writer once had the great pleasure and privilege of visiting W & C Scott's Premier Works in Birmingham, England. My host and the firm's managing director, Pat Whatley, struck me immediately as a man who took great and obvious pride in everything that went on under his supervision. He suggested that I spend some time observing at close hand each of the 20 or so gunmakers who were employed there. This approach would enable me to observe each of the dozens of steps involved in the process of creating a classic shotgun. First, I was shown the raw materials with which the gunmakers work. Stacks of chopper lump and round bar tubes in different lengths, cali-

bers and chokings stood like silent sentinels. Elsewhere, block after block of priceless French walnut awaited the delicate touch of a carver whose loving caress would transform the raw wood into the warm, lustrous stocks that are part and parcel of fine guns. In the delicate curls and irregular whorls of the wood, one began to comprehend how this one component would become part of the finished product.

The foreman at W & C Scott next introduced me to the Premier Works gunmakers in precisely the same order they stood in the overall process of creating a gun. We moved in unhurried fashion from bench to bench, with an introduction to each craftsman followed by an opportunity to discuss briefly the role he played in the overall process. The miracles these quiet, soft-spoken men wrought with their hands were more eloquent than any words could have described. One sensed these artisans *knew* they were offering a sportsman's gift to the ages.

The home of W & C Scott's Premier Works in Birmingham, England.

Each employee, including a young apprentice who had been at the trade for only a few months (as a group, the gunmakers at W & C Scott average close to two decades) showed me, each in turn, precisely what work he performed. The foreman then described to me how each of these components fit into the overall process leading to a finished gun. All that mattered, whether the gunmaker dealt with some aspect of a double's inner workings or its engraving or checkering, was that each step be done to perfection. If this required the removal of another one-thousandth of an inch of steel to get a perfect fit, or meant reworking a stock because it wasn't quite right, then so be it.

Fittingly, the day ended with a look at several finished doubles. The results of a very complex process, they symbolized the kind of precision and tender care that have typified Britain's finest shotguns for more than a century. This passion for perfection, I now realized, was truly the hallmark of British gun-

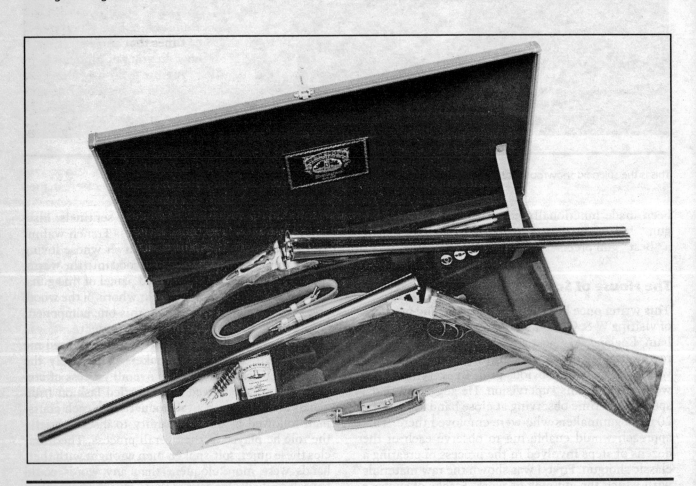

These Chatworth guns were made at W & C Scott's Premier works.

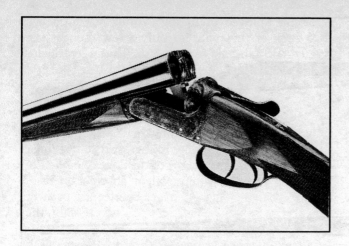

This close-up view of a modern W & C Scott shotgun reveals the fine skill of the company's engravers.

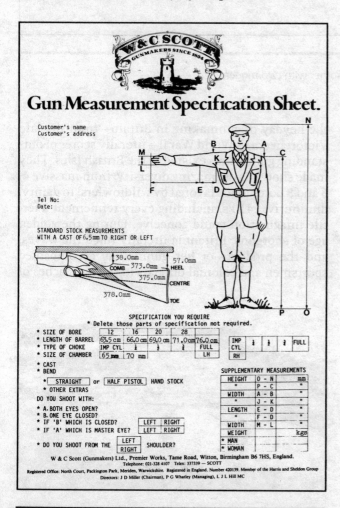

A sample form used by W & C Scott to tailor-make their guns to each customer's individual requirements.

making. The human hand and eye, strange as it may seem, can indeed reach a degree of precision far beyond the capability of sophisticated machinery. The same care that demands precision of one-thousandth of an inch from the actioner goes as well into engraving, checkering and stock shaping. Mass or standard production is unknown; virtually every weapon is tailor-made for a specific individual. The buyer is measured for his gun the same way a clothier would size him up for a fine suit; and the owner can rest assured that the finished product (which might be two years or more in the making) will be an extension of his personality as well as his body. The mystique that surrounds classic English shotguns defies description, but certainly graceful lines, superb craftsmanship and proud traditions are integral parts of that mystique.

The Best of the Finest

The fact that a simple W & C Scott boxlock costs anywhere from $4,000 up, while Best-quality guns start at more than three times that amount, is really incidental. After all, how do you put a price tag on the ultimate in quality? A vintage Boss over-and-under is probably worth $35,000 or more in fine condition, and the same is true of Purdey's best products. Perhaps the most famous of all shotgun makers, Purdey's has an unbroken tradition that dates from the firm's beginning in 1814. One immediately senses this rich past upon entering the Long Room at Purdey's Audley House offices. Portraits of great men from the gunmaking past line the walls, and precious sporting memorabilia fill the shelves of glassfronted display cases.

Lord Ripon, whom some rank as the greatest shot who over lived, once commented that, when sportsmen no longer shoot with English guns, "The England of whom the poets have sung will have ceased to exist." Indeed, England's gunmaking industry is a thriving one, thanks in no small part to American and other foreign enthusiasts who make up a good portion of today's market for classic guns. Another reason for ongoing optimism is that Britain's surviving gunmakers have, along with their constant emphasis on quality, taken some aggressive marketing steps. Holland & Holland, for example, has branched out into virtually all areas associated with shooting sports, from clothing and accessories to its recent acquisition of the long-established and well known publisher and bookseller, Rowland Ward's. In 1987, Holland & Holland joined other British organiza-

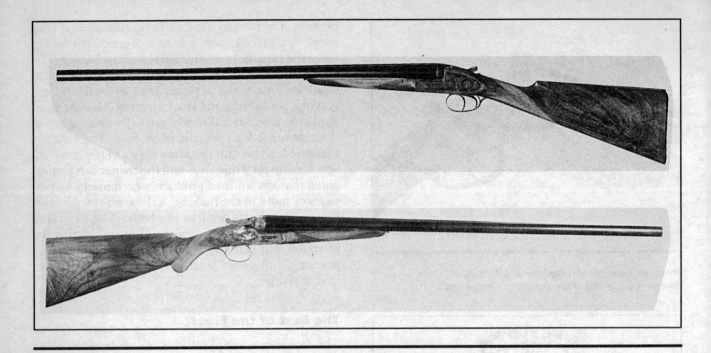

Shown here are a Purdey double with single trigger (above) and another with two triggers.

tions and the British-American Chamber of Commerce in sponsoring the first annual Sporting Clay Challenge at the Mashomack (N.Y.) Fish & Game Preserve.

Used Guns: A Boom Market

While many Americans prefer to buy new shotguns made and fitted especially to their tastes, the market for second-hand classics is also a booming one. Weapons dating back to what some consider the golden years of BRITISH shotguns—from the early breechloaders down to around 1950—are in great demand. So much so, in fact, that it is difficult to find anything of decent quality for much less than $3,500. A "Best" will sell for ten times that amount; and if it has some singular features, or is in exceptional condition, it can go even higher. The Boss shotguns shown on the front cover of this book (and described on the opening page inside) offer dramatic testimony to this fact.

Actually, the term *classic* should be extended to include lesser, but still splendid, English shotguns. Many of the firms which have produced classics in the past are no longer operating, having fallen prey to some of the same economic forces that have driven several American gunmakers out of business. During

the heyday of gunmaking in Britain—from the late Victorian era to World War II—literally scores of outstanding gunmakers existed in the British Isles. They made shotguns of amazing diversity, from massive 4, 6 and 8 bores (once favored by wildfowlers) to dainty, diminutive .410's, including every refinement a fertile imagination could conceive. During the golden age of shotguns, Britannia literally ruled the waves, and the products of her gunmakers accompanied sportsmen and colonial officials to the far reaches of

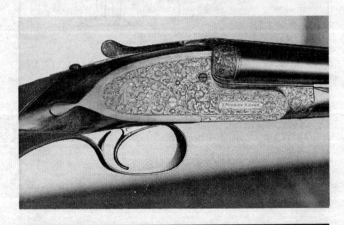

Purdey's devotion to exquisite craftsmanship is evident in this close-up view.

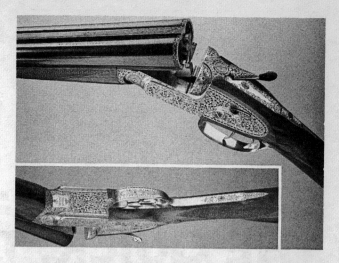

An interesting top view of Holland & Holland's 1987 set of four British field sports guns.

Two views of a Holland & Holland "Royal," a name that has been used for the company's best quality doubles since 1895.

her Empire. These shotguns also varied greatly in design. There were sidelocks made by Holland & Holland, Powell, Purdey and others, while boxlocks were available from Churchill and Westley Richards, which offered its patented hand-detachable boxlocks. You could even acquire the now extremely rare round actions created by the gunmakers at Dickson and McKay Brown. When Boss offered its special ejector action, it rightly anticipated a feature that has since become commonplace. The list of such special characteristics and innovations could go on almost without end.

In the final analysis, one conclusion is inescapable: when one speaks of "classic" shotguns, whether in the past or present tense, those made in Britain hold pride of place. Most European guns are little more than copies built and based on English patents, and the American gunmaking tradition likewise owes much to Britain. British "Bests" are just that—the best shotguns ever made. If you are among the fortunate few who possess such a weapon, or merely one of many who aspire to ownership, you know full well that these classic British shotguns truly belong to the ages.

A Listing of Recommended Reading on Classic British Shotguns

Beaumont, Richard. *Purdey's: The Guns and the Family* (1984)

Bodio, Stephen. *Good Guns* (1986)

Boothroyd, Geoffrey. *The Shotgun: History and Development* (1985)

Burrard, Major Sir Gerald. *The Modern Shotgun* (3 vols.; first published in 1931)

Greener, W. W. *The Gun and its Development* (9th ed., published 1910)

Churchill, Robert. *Shotgun Book* (1955).

Hastings, MacDonald. *The Shotgun* (1981)

King, Peter. *The Shooting Fields: One Hundred and Fifty Years with Holland & Holland* (1985)

Neal, W. Keith and Back, D. H. L. *The Mantons: Gunmakers* (1967)

Scott, W & C Gunmakers. *The History of W & C Scott* (1985)

Teasdale-Buckell, G. T. *The Complete Shot* (1986; originally published in 1900)

Zutz, Don. *The Double Shotgun* (1978) and *The Double Shotgun* (revised and expanded edition, 1985)

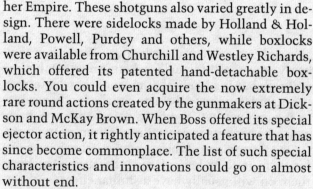

CARTRIDGES: THE QUICK, THE DEAD, AND THE REVIVED

BY RALPH F. QUINN

Since the advent of metallic cartridges and smokeless powders, dedicated shooters have struggled to drive bullets faster, farther and more accurately than ever before. From time to time, some of this so-called "wildcatting" has caught the fancy of centerfire devotees. One thing has led to another and, assuming demand was strong enough, a sharp rifle manufacturer would eventually pick up on the news and chamber the round. If the gun sold well, the cartridge became part of the American shooting scene—at least, until the next hot number came along to take its place.

Unfortunately, many of these fine loads have died premature deaths, simply because of the whims and fancies of the gun buying public. In recent years, a number of adventuresome riflemakers have managed to revive once popular cartridges by producing limited runs. Other, more astute entrepreneurs in the business have elected to "damn the torpedos" and tool up for cartridges that previously were available only as custom chamberings. Were they foolhardy or were they sound marketing men? Only time will tell, but it's likely that most of these enterprising manufacturers will create a niche for themselves in the gun market; and in so doing, they will bring welcome benefits to centerfire admirers everywhere.

One thing many of these entrepreneurs have going for them is their love of guns, because what turns them on will usually have a similar effect on shooters wherever they are. Who would have guessed, back in 1958, that Vern O'Brien, a Nevada-based riflemaker and gun fancier, could turn the head of the shooting public with his miniature .17 calibers built on SAKO's short A1 action—but he did. It took some Hollywood-style promotion to do it, though, such as bowling over brown bear and moose with well constructed, heavy jacketed 20 and 25 grain bullets. By loading the .17 Javelina—a shortened and necked down .222 case—this diminutive round produced an impressive muzzle velocity in excess of 4,000 fps (feet per second).

A few years later, Harrington & Richardson got wind of O'Brien's quick, accurate rifles and, in 1968, bought him out. Shortly after that, H&R began mass production of its Model 317 Ultra Wildcat "Bomb," the first factory rifle chambered for the .17/.223. Remington picked up on this development in 1971 and started chambering its 700 series bolt for the new

RALPH QUINN has been writing articles and books for the shooting and outdoor markets for more than a decade. As a lecturer, video/film producer and book author, he travels regularly throughout the U.S. and Canada in search of new material. A longtime "wildcatter," handloader and silhouette shooter, he enthusiastically supports the revived cartridges described in this article for both hunting and benchrest shooting.

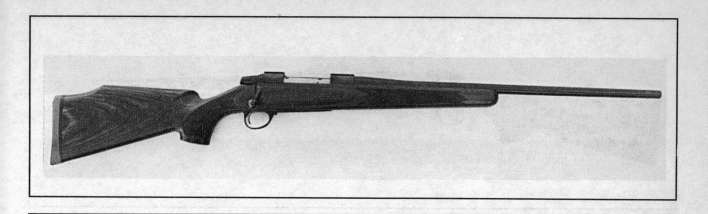

SAKO's Laminated Stock rifle is chambered in .17 Remington, .222 Remington and .22/250.

round. Today, SAKO, Remington, Winslow and Tikka all offer bolt action rifles for the ultra-high velocity load. Since its introduction, the small world of the .17 has shown a steady growth, and understandably so. It's fun to shoot, it's mild in both report and recoil, and it's one of the most accurate, out-of-the-box production cartridges offered today.

The .220 Swift

Not all quick, high-stepping cartridges enjoy the same success, however. Back in 1935, Winchester introduced the .220 Swift and touted it as the ninth wonder of the centerfire world. Loaded with either 45 or 48 grain bullets, the Swift was (and still is) the fastest commercial cartridge available with its muzzle velocity of 4100-plus fps. Enthusiasm for the .220 was overwhelming at first, but when excessive pressure began to build up in the tapered cartridge things soon turned sour. Corporate gurus, convinced that speed was the Swift's main selling point, loaded the cartridge to drive the 48 grain bullet up to 4140 fps. Somehow the story got around handloader circles that the .220 wouldn't perform unless it was loaded to the maximum, so in went the powder. Soon, barrels began developing serious throat erosion and accuracy fell off. Much to their dismay, riflers discovered that the high pressures were lengthening and thickening the case necks. Constant reaming and trimming, plus blown primers, quickly put the .220 Swift on the ropes.

Winchester tried to solve the erosion problem by using chrome-moly and stainless barrels, but the damage was done. Within three years, the bad publicity had killed the .220. When the Model 70 Win-

chester bolt was first issued in 1936, the .220 Swift was one of its standard chamberings and continued so until 1964, when it was dropped. Some months later, the .225 was issued to replace the Swift, but within eight years it had also suffered a similar fate.

This lineup of popular "quick" cartridges includes (from left): .17 Remington, .220 Swift, .22/250 and .222 Remington.

With the introduction of SAKO's PPC's, .22 and 6mm, this Finland-based manufacturer has made a bold move forward.

Shortly after its introduction in 1950, the .222 went on to dominate benchrest circles, supplanting the .220 Swift and 22/250 as preferred loads.

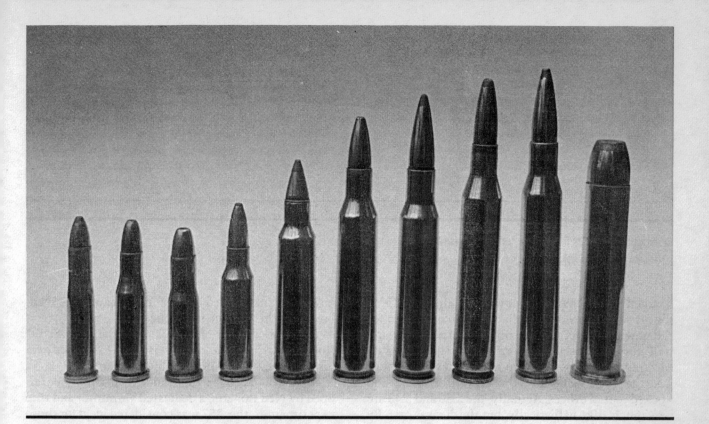

Pictured above is the current crop of revived cartridges (from left): .22 Hornet, .218 Bee, .25/20, .221 Remington, 250/3000, .257 Roberts, 7 × 57 Mauser, .280 Remington, .25/06 and .45/70.

Nearly a decade later, in 1973, the .220 Swift returned to the marketplace, thanks to the forward looking minds at Sturm, Ruger, who adapted it to the company's Model 70 bolt action. Apparently, Ruger recognized the fallacy behind the hoax placed on the Swift 30 years before—that the .220 was not accurate when operating at less than full bore, with pressures in the 55,000 psi range. By loading down to 3,600-3,700 fps, it was discovered, both barrel life and case problems were solved; moreover, these reduced loads actually delivered better accuracy. At long range, the .220 Swift surpassed a host of hot .22 centerfires, including .222 Magnum, .223, .22-250, and others.

Actually, the .220 ran into trouble soon after Grosvenor Wotkyns necked down the .250/3000 to .22 and called it the .22 Swift. The combination of accuracy, light recoil and mild muzzle blast made it a natural; thus, when the Swift .220 began to slip, riflers welcomed the .22 Swift or .22 Varminter (22-250) with open arms. Following World War II, the 22-250 continued its popularity in benchrest circles, but since then paper shooters have shifted to the .222

Remington or SAKO's .22 and 6mm PPC. Remington adopted the 22-250 cartridge in 1965 by chambering it in their bullbarreled 700 Series rifle. Today, nearly all major American, European and British rifle makers turn out rifles chambered for the 22-250.

The .250/3000 and .257 Roberts

Just as the .22 Winchester Centerfire, .219 Zipper, .22 HiPower, .220 Swift and .225 Winchester suffered at the hands of the .222 and .22/250, so did the excellent .250/3000 and .257 through the introduction of two 6mm's—the .244 Remington and .243 Winchester. Originally developed as a high intensity load for the 100 grain bullet, Savage Arms decided to lighten the bullet to 87 grains, thereby stepping up velocities to 3,000 fps, hence the name .250/3000. Its clean, efficient burning of powder, combined with outstanding accuracy and devastating knockdown power, made the .250 a winner from the start. It was so easy to shoot that countless record-book animals fell to hunters who used this sweet little cartridge.

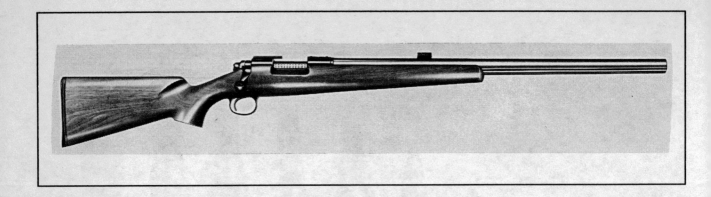

Remington's 40-XBR is the only centerfire chambered for 6mm/47 Benchrest.

When the .243 Winchester was introduced in 1955, the air was charged immediately with accolades for the new entry. Its light recoil, superb accuracy and trajectory surpassed the imagination, so claimed its admirers. Shooters were convinced that the cartridge was the 10th wonder of the centerfire world and flocked to it in droves. Actually, the .250 and .243 are very much alike ballistically, but the die was cast. By the mid-1960s, the .250 was practically dead, and shortly thereafter Savage discontinued its popular Model 99 in that caliber.

Ironically, Remington's .244 was also shot down by the .243. Conceived as a varmint cartridge with a 90 grain bullet, its barrel twist was a slow 1-in-12. When shooters discovered that the steel wouldn't stabilize the 100 grain slug, which most of them preferred, they sided with the .243 and its faster 1-in-10 twist. To stem the tide, Remington renamed it the

6mm and substituted a 1-in-9 twist barrel. By then, however, the damage was done.

The same doleful hand was dealt the superb .257 Roberts, perhaps the most versatile .25 caliber ever issued. The .257 is nothing more than the 7 × 57 Mauser necked to .25 thousandth. Originally developed by Ned Roberts, a dedicated varminter and rifle experimenter, the .257 was considered ideal for those who hunted both big game and varmints. Recoil and muzzle blast were mild, and most shooters found they could handle the Roberts better than the hard-pounding magnums.

Unfortunately, the .257 was also doomed from the start. Both Remington and Winchester standardized their loads for the caliber, but the cartridges were under-loaded, and as a result the ballistics looked "ordinary." The bullets then in use were the round-nose variety—they were good for the short magazines

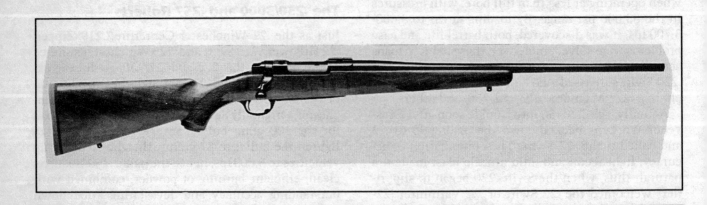

Ruger's M77R Bolt (above) is chambered for several revised cartridges, among them .25/06, .250/3000, .257 Roberts, 7 × 57 6mm, and .280 Remington.

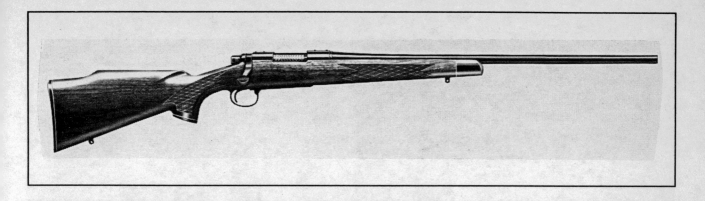

Remington's BDL 700 is produced in a number of revised cartridges, including .280 Remington, .25/06 Remington, and 6mm Remington. Also available are the .22/250, .17 Remington, and .222.

found in Remington's 722 and Winchester's Model 70 but were not suited to the handloaders' needs.

With the introduction of the 6mms, the .257 practically died. But recently, it has been given a new lease on life. In 1985, Winchester chambered its XTR Featherweight in the caliber, and Remington also made a limited run in its Classic 700. Today, Ruger lists the .257 as standard in its highly successful Models M 77R, RL, and No. 1S single shot, as does Browning with its Model 81 BLR. Additionally, the .250/3000 and 6mm are showing new life again thanks to some shrewd marketing strategy by both Ruger and Remington.

More Revived Cartridges

Other cartridges enjoying renewed interest include a collection of old favorites, such as the .218 Bee, which Winchester introduced in 1938 for its Model 65 lever rifle (and later the Model 43 bolt); and Kimber of Oregon is presently chambering its Model 82 LR Sporter as a single shot in .218 and the 25-20 WCF. The LR is also chambered for the .22 Hornet, the first small bore, high velocity cartridge marketed in the U.S. for varmints and small game. Savage is in the Hornet business too with its 340 Bolt; and SAKO's fine Model 78 Sporter has been around for several years as a top performer.

Additionally, the 25/06, 280 Remington-7mm Remington Express, 7 × 57 Mauser and the venerable 45/70 are gathering momentum as shooters take a nostalgic look backward. Since Remington picked up the 25/06 in 1969, the hot-shot .25 has rolled along at road speed; and now SAKO, Savage, Ruger, Colt Sauer, Parker-Hale, Weatherby and numerous other manufacturers of bolt action rifles are offering 25-06's as well.

When Remington introduced the .280 in 1957, it was chambered for the company's Model 740 autoloader, generating mean pressures around 47,000 psi. Round-nose bullets and lower velocity produced less than spectacular performance, though; and yet, when chambered in a strong bolt action rifle and loaded to maximum pressures, the .280 proved capable of giving .270 results. Now included among Winchester's Win-Tuff Model 70 Lightweight rifle and Remington's 700 Bolt chambering, the .280 enjoys renewed interest among 7mm fans.

Another 7mm currently experiencing a rebirth is the world-famous 7 × 57 Mauser. Long favored by custom rifle makers for lightweight rifles with moderate recoil, the 7mm has proven itself among the best all-around cartridges ever developed. American-made rifles for the 7 × 57 were discontinued about 1940, but the cartridge has been on a steady rise ever since. Ruger now chambers its No. 1A and M 77 bolts in the round, and in 1986 Winchester offered the chambering in its XTR Featherweight Model 70. In addition, Heym, K.D.F., Steyr-Mannlicher, Whitworth and Winslow all offer the 7 × 57.

Very much alive is the .45/70 Government. Adopted by the U.S. military in 1873 for the single shot ''Trap Door'' Springfield, the round continues its role as the ''Old Horse'' that refuses to die. As a short range brush or woods cartridge, it ranks right up there with other timber busters, such as the Marlin 444. With the introduction of Ruger's Model 3, Marlin's 1895SS, Brownings 1885 Single Shot, Navy Arm's #2 Creedmoor, and H&R's Officer (1963), the 45/70 has indeed staged a dramatic comeback.

Among the dead or dying cartridges are (left to right): 6.5 Remington Magnum, .264 Winchester Magnum (8mm Remington Magnum and .338 Winchester Magnum, which follow, are included for comparison only), .350 Remington Magnum, .348 Winchester, .358 Winchester and .300 Savage. The 6.5 was dead in 1966, the .264 has largely been replaced by the 7mm Remington Magnum, and the rest are either dead or dying.

And the Dead . . .

For every cartridge resurrected from the ranks of the dead or dying, there is unfortunately another side of the coin. During the late 1960's, a number of fine belted magnums hit the market based on the venerable .375 H&H; i.e., 7mm Remington Magnum, 338 Winchester, .257 Weatherby, .264 Winchester Magnum, and 6.5 Remington Magnum, among others. Most made the grade simply because they were swimming with the current demand for flat-shooting cartridges with excellent accuracy and knockdown power. Yet, for one reason or another, the latter pair of 6.5s didn't pan out.

When Winchester introduced the .264 Mag back in 1958-9, it received wide publicity as the *el primo* of long range cartridges. Initially, riflers accepted the propaganda, until accuracy began falling off. The small bore and large case capacity brought on pre-mature barrel erosion. Some reports said as few as 500 rounds caused velocities to deteriorate to .270 levels. That, combined with the lack of bullet versatility, put the hex on the .264 and to this day the cartridge, although not dead, remains very sick indeed.

The 6.5 Remington Magnum was introduced in 1966 as a companion load to the .350 Magnum and was offered in the now discontinued Model 600 and 660 carbines. The 6.5 is nothing more than the .350 necked to .264.

In the 700 bolt with a 22- or 24-inch barrel, the cartridge gave .270 performance; but in the short carbine barrel its accuracy was mediocre. The magazine length of Model 600 limited overall cartridge length to 2.790 inches, which caused case capacity to suffer. The fact that Remington did not offer a variety of heavier bullets in factory loads no doubt hastened the 6.5 to its premature death.

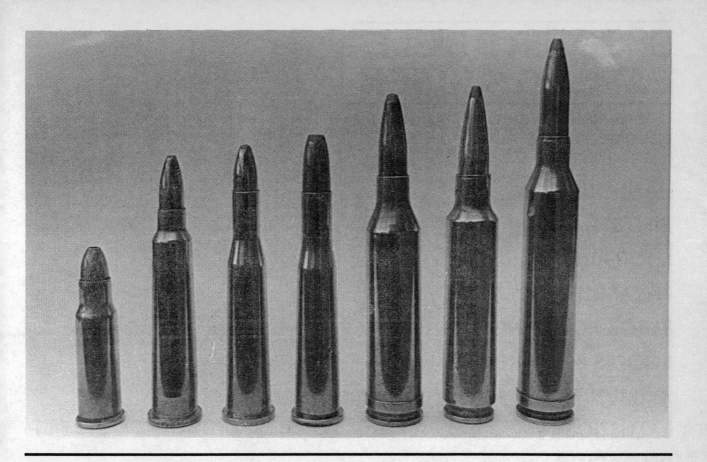

These cartridges suffer from what might be called "lack-of-rifle" syndrome (left to right): .256 Winchester Magnum, .225 Winchester, .219 Zipper, .22 Savage Hi-Power, 6.5 Remington Magnum, .284 Winchester, and 8mm Remington Magnum.

Another pair of good cartridges that failed to catch on were the .350 Remington Magnum and .358 Winchester. Both rounds were too short and stubby; and they simply didn't look powerful enough. Trying to convince Joe Hunter that both cartridges packed as much wallop as the .35 Whelen only sent him away laughing. Also, most riflers of that era were looking for high velocity. Although most deer hunters east of the Mississippi rarely, if ever, shoot over 150 yards, it was tough for them to kick the preference for flat-shooting cartridges. Since neither the .350 nor the .358 had that appeal, they were left hanging on the ropes from the very outset. At one time, Winchester chambered its lightweight Models 70 and 88 in the .358. Savage also offered its Model 99, but now nothing is manufactured in the U.S. for that cartridge. Other centerfires that suffer from this same "lack-of-rifle" syndrome are the .256, .284, .348 and .33 Winchesters, plus the .300 Savage. In simple terms, this means that any cartridge for which no rifle is available won't last very long.

Currently, cartridge lists may well have been trimmed, deleted and revised, but they have also been expanded. New entries include the 7mm-08, 7-30 Waters, .307 Winchester, .35 Whelen and 8mm Remington Magnum. Feelings among riflers and dealers alike are mixed. The new products may well bring in increased sales and profits; conversely, they could also mean more calibers and dollars tied up in inventory. The coming years will probably see renewed interest in many previously defunct or obsolete cartridges, plus a number of the so-called wildcats. With the recent chambering of SAKO's Varminter in the hot 22 and 6mm PPC's, plus Kimber's limited run of 6mm-45 and 47s, .17 Remington and .17 Mach IV, a bold entreprenurial spirit seems alive and well in the shooting trades. All good shooters should welcome that development.

SHOOTER'S BIBLE CATALOG SECTION

Complete Illustrated Listing of Guns, Specifications & Accessories

HANDGUNS

RIFLES

SHOTGUNS

PARAMILITARY

BLACK POWDER

SCOPES & SIGHTS

AMMUNITION

BALLISTICS

RELOADING

Handguns

FOR ADDRESSES AND PHONE
NUMBERS OF MANUFACTURERS AND
DISTRIBUTORS INCLUDED IN THIS
SECTION, SEE *DIRECTORY OF
MANUFACTURERS AND SUPPLIERS*

WHAT'S NEW IN HANDGUNS AND HANDGUN PRODUCTS

BY FRANK PETRINI: Shooter's Bible Handgun Consultant

According to the BATF (Bureau of Alcohol, Tobacco and Firearms), U.S. firearms sales have dropped in recent years. At the same time, large caliber handgun sales have increased. The U.S. Fish and Wildlife Service reports, moreover, that while the number of hunters is down, the fraternity of active handgun hunters has actually grown during the 1980s. Interest has also increased noticeably in spectator-competitive handgun sports, practical pistol shooting, action shooting, and metal silhouette competition, among others.

FREEDOM ARMS

Such statistics and observations have not been wasted on U.S. gun manufacturers and importers. They are evident in recent announcements coming from such up-and-coming manufacturers as Freedom Arms, located in the beautiful mountain country of western Wyoming. This firm has established itself solidly in the handgun hunting field with one of the biggest revolvers ever to achieve mass production: the .454 Casull single action. This brute of a revolver fires a 260 grain jacketed .454-inch bullet with a muzzle velocity of 1800 fps from a 7^1/$_2$-inch barrel. It generates 1870 foot-pounds of energy, more than enough to put the potent .44 Magnum to shame.

The Casull has been around in reasonable quantities for a few years now at better than $1,000 a copy, but a new Field Grade version is on the market today retailing for $300 less than the standard Premier Grade—$795 versus $1,075 for the adjustable sight models. It features a matte stainless finish for reduced glare and Pachmayr Presentation grips for positive gripping under adverse conditions. Except for the finish, which lacks the care and attention put into the more expensive models, this new economy model boasts the same good looks and performance of the Premier Grade. Besides, the utilitarian finish in the Field grade is probably a better choice for those who use their guns hard and under inclement conditions.

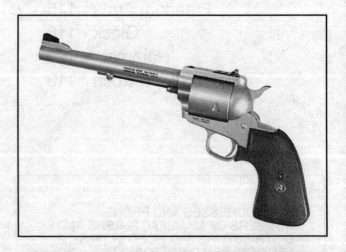

Freedom Arms' Field Grade .454 Casull single action revolver: a good choice among many good big game hunting handguns available today.

In any event, this is not a handgun for the squeamish, for its recoil is severe. If handgunning big game or knocking over metal silhouettes is your objective, though, the .454 Casull has to be top choice for the job. New ammunition for the Casull caliber is available from Freedom Arms as well in 240, 260 and 300 grain jacketed hollowpoint and soft point loadings. For those who stuff their own, components and dies are also sold; and handloaders can also choose from bullets designed for the .45 ACP and .45 Colt.

MAGNUM RESEARCH

For those who prefer the semiautomatic pistol for their game shooting, some new announcements from Magnum Research, the Desert Eagle people, are worthy of note. The Desert Eagle has been called the first major advancement in semiauto pistol design since the early years of this century—and for good reason. Weighing in at 48 ounces to more than 60 ounces empty (depending on whether the gripframe is steel or aluminum), this Israeli-made pistol was the first successful, gas-operated autoloader chambered for the .357 and .44 Magnum revolver rounds. Shooters may now expect to find a ready supply of 14-inch barrels in both the .357-inch and .429-inch bore sizes. The increased accuracy (using open sights) and muzzle velocities over the standard six-inch tube are significant. A .41 Magnum version is also available and should please those who prefer the somewhat lighter kick and flatter trajectories of the .410-inch magnum revolver round. This model ought to find a good following among the long-range metal silhouette competitors.

L.A.R. GRIZZLY

According to the L.A.R. Manufacturing Company's brochure, "When a Grizzly Win Mag roars—everything listens!" Chambered for the big .45 Win Mag round, this hunting handgun is making itself known in hunting circles. Recent announcements include chambering for the .357/.45 GWM and 10mm rounds. The former can reportedly drive a 140 grain .357-inch bullet to 2000 fps from a ten-inch barrel, placing it in a class with the .357 Remington Maximum, and definitely overshadowing the regular .357 Magnum. Compared to the .45 ACP and 9mm Luger, the 10mm chambering is also impressive, but it is not a top choice in the large Grizzly Win Mag when calibers like the .45 GWM and .357/45GWM are available.

On the other hand, the multi-caliber conversion units that are available for L.A.R.'s pistol give the shooter the option of using the lighter .45 ACP, 9mm Luger or 10mm for practice purposes. There's little doubt, though, that the hot-performing Win Mag calibers—or at the very least the regular .357 Magnum—are better choices when serious big game hunting is the sport at hand.

STURM, RUGER

Ruger's relatively new Super Redhawk is top-of-the-line among the new GP-100 design handguns being produced by Ruger to revolutionize the company's double action lineup. This product rivals the Desert Eagle and Dan Wesson 44s for weight (with an overall length of 15 inches and a $9^{1}/_{2}$-inch barrel, the Super Redhawk tips the scales at 58 ounces empty). There's an optional $7^{1}/_{2}$-inch barrel, but it hardly seems worth it. If you're going to cart that much iron around, you may as well go for the $9^{1}/_{2}$-inch tube for the greatest muzzle velocity possible. Available only in .44 Magnum, the Super Redhawk may be a hit simply because of its advanced design, massive frame, unique rubber cushioned grip, exceptional engineering, and comparatively low cost. Those are formidable qualities in anyone's handgun.

AMT

For the small game hunter, the biggest news probably comes from Arcadia Machine & Tool, Inc. (AMT). Known for its line of stainless semiautomatic firearms, AMT has announced its Automag II sports pistol, which was chambered in 1987 for the .22 rimfire magnum cartridge. This super-slim, gas-assisted magazine pistol weighs 32 ounces and carries Millett adjustable sights. With a six-inch barrel, it may well be the top choice in rimfire hunting pistols and the only one chambered for the rimfire magnum round.

Even more important is AMT's introduction of the Automag II in 9mm Luger and .30 Carbine. While the 9mm is a so-so cartridge for small game use, the .30 Carbine is a blistering handgun round—much like having a hot-loaded .32-20 Winchester in a medium-sized automatic pistol. Factory 110 grain JSP loads in .30 Carbine exit the $7^{1}/_{2}$-inch tube of a Ruger Blackhawk at velocities approaching 1400 fps. If they reach only 1200 or 1300 fps from the six-inch AMT pistol, they should prove devastating on small game and larger varmints at normal handgun ranges.

LLAMA

A number of new developments merit attention in the field of action/combat and related self-defense/ police/military handguns. Most come under the category of new semiautomatic pistol offerings aimed at combat shooters who've been smitten with large capacity, DA autoloaders made popular by Beretta's Model 92. A top example of this class of pistol is the new Llama Model M82 double action pistol. This sturdy piece shares many of the design points of the discontinued Llama Omni, a gun that was ahead of its time when it was introduced in the early 1980s. The M82 sports a knobbed hammer, smooth DA pull, and ambidextrous safety. The magazine holds 15 rounds (plus one in the chamber) and weighs 39 ounces empty (for those who prefer a lighter pistol, a 31-ounce alloy frame model is also available). With an overall length of $8^{1}/_{4}$ inches and a $1^{3}/_{8}$-inch grip, this new Llama is relatively compact for a medium-heavy gun.

ACTION ARMS

Another new 9mm DA entry is Action Arms' AT-84, a Swiss copy of the popular Czech CZ75 pistol that has been imported sporadically over the years. A major feature of this well made, all-steel pistol is its right-hand safety, which allows "cocked and locked" use. Also available is the AT-84P model, with its slightly shorter barrel and 16-round capacity. There's also an AT-84 produced in the .41 Action Express chambering. This new cartridge boasts a .41 caliber 170 grain jacketed hollowpoint with a reported muzzle velocity of 1250 fps with 590 foot pounds (factory ammunition is marketed by Action Ammo Ltd., a subsidiary of Action Arms). In addition, a 200 grain full metal case offering produces muzzle velocity of 1100 fps with 537 foot pounds of energy.

EXCAM

Excam's Tanarmi TA90 is also a copy of the Czech CZ75. This 9mm pistol sports the more common drop-hammer safety along with a 15-round magazine capacity. It's available in matte blue and matte chrome finishes with neoprene rubber grips. Fighting weight is 35 ounces (empty), placing it in the

Llama's M82 is a prime example of the new breed of 9mm double action pistols now on the market.

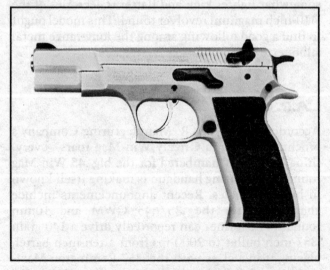

Excam's Tanarmi TA90 pistol: still another good example of high quality 9mm double action pistols available today.

medium-weight class for this type of pistol. Compact versions—dubbed the BTA90C and BTA90B—are also available. These shorties weigh in at 30 ounces and feature four-inch barrels compared to the 4.75-inch tubes on the standard pistols.

VICTORY ARMS

Magnum Research markets a unique semiautomatic produced by Victory Arms of Northampton, England, for $459.00 retail. Known as Model MC5, it's almost as intriguing as the Desert Eagle, except that the MC5 is more conventional in size, configuration and calibers. Its main claim to fame, however, is its interchangeable barrel system, which allows the use of different calibers on the same frame and slide. Barrels are available in 9mm, .38 Super, .45 ACP and the new .41 AE in barrel lengths of four, six and 7¹/₂ inches. Another good feature is a simple field-stripping procedure by which the pistol is disassembled in a few seconds to its frame, slide and barrel modules.

HANDGUN SIGHT MOUNTS

Another area of growing activity involves clamp type telescopic sight mounts for handguns. Weaver led the way some years back, but the king of the clamp mount these days is B-Square, which supplies easily attached and detached scope mounts for a wide variety of popular handguns. The mounts either clamp onto the barrel or make use of tapped holes accessible when adjustable sights are removed.

Other contenders for this market include the Millett Sight Company, which produces a limited number of "Scope-Site" mount rings using Weaver-style bases to mount on the barrel ribs of Ruger, Colt and

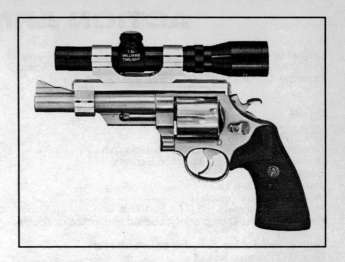

Williams' new "Guideline" scope mount fits nicely on an S&W Model 29 .44 Magnum.

Dan Wesson revolvers. These rings are unique because they carry Millett's adjustable open sights above the scope. Thus, depending upon the field situation, shooters can now choose between telescopic sights and open sights.

Williams has also jumped into the fray with a series of clamp mounts for Ruger and Smith & Wesson handguns. Ruger versions are supplied for the Blackhawk, Super Blackhawk and Redhawk revolvers. For small game hunters, there's a Williams Guideline model that attaches to the Ruger MKII bull barrel .22 pistol. It clamps on two places along the barrel without having to remove the rear sight. Obviously, the number of handgun models which these and other scope mount systems can accommodate is growing constantly. If your favorite handgun isn't covered yet, be patient and wait until next year.

ACTION ARMS PISTOLS

Crafted by the Swiss, this new double action handgun is available in two sizes and calibers (9mm and the new .41 Action Express). Can also be used cocked and locked.

AT-84

SPECIFICATIONS
Operation: Locked breech, inertial firing pin
Ammunition: 9mm or .41 Action Express
Barrel length: 4.72″
Overall length: 8.10″
Weight: 35.3 oz. (empty)
Magazines: 9mm-15 rds./41 A.E.-10 rds.
Safety system: Thumb safety; cocked and locked or double action
Sights: Fixed blade front; drift adjustable rear
Stock: Checkered walnut
Finish: Blued metal
Price: $525.00

AT-84P

SPECIFICATIONS
Operation: Locked breech; inertial firing pin
Ammunition: 9mm or .41 Action Express
Barrel length: 3.66″

AT-84 and AT-84P

Overall length: 7.24″
Weight: 32.1 oz. (empty)
Magazines: 9mm-13 rds./41 A.E.-8 rds.
Safety system : Thumb safety; cocked & locked or double action
Sights: Fixed blade front; drift adjustable rear
Stock: Checkered walnut
Finish: Blued metal
Price: $525.00

AMERICAN DERRINGER PISTOLS

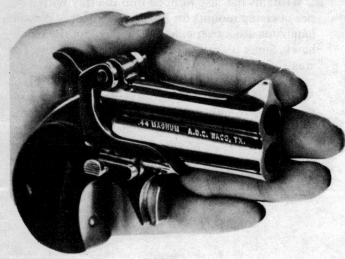

MODEL 1

SPECIFICATIONS
Calibers: 38 Super, 38 Special, 380 Auto, 9mm Luger, 32 Mag., 30-30 Win., 30 Luger, 223 Rem. Commercial Ammo, 22 LR, 22 Rimfire Mag., 22 Hornet, 45 Colt, 45 Auto, 45 Win. Mag., 45-70 (single shot), 44 Mag., 44-40 Win., 44 Special, 41 Mag., 410, 357 Maximum, 357 Magnum
Overall length: 4.82″
Barrel length: 3″
Weight: 15 oz. (in 45 Auto cal)
Action: Single action w/automatic barrel selection
Number of shots: 2

Calibers	Prices
9mm Federal, 32 Magnum, 32 S&W Long, 32-20, 30 Luger, 38 Special	$187.50
22 LR, 22 Rimfire Magnum, 45 Auto, 45 Auto Shot Shell, 357 Magnum	218.00
30 Mauser (7.62 Tokarev)	200.00
38 Special Shot Shell, 38 Super	199.95
357 Maximum	250.00
380 Auto, 9mm Luger	172.50
41 Action Auto, 9mm x 21mm	225.00
45 Colt, 44-40, 44 Special	295.00
45 Colt (2½″ .410), .410 x 2½″ (45 Colt)	297.50
45 Win. Mag., 45-70 (single shot), 50 Saunders, 44 Magnum, 41 Magnum, 30-30 Winchester, 223 Rem. Comm. Ammo only, 22 Hornet	369.00

Also available: **Ultra Lightweight (7½ oz.) Model 7**

Calibers	Prices
22 LR	$187.50
32 Magnum, 32 S&W Long	137.50
38 S&W	157.50
38 Special	187.50
380 Auto	157.50
44 Special	500.00

Light Weight (11 oz.) Double Derringer Model 11
Available in 38 Special	$159.95

Model 10 (10 oz.)
45 Colt	$237.50
45 Auto	218.00

AMERICAN DERRINGER PISTOLS

MODEL 3 (Stainless Steel Single Shot Derringer)

SPECIFICATIONS
Caliber: 38 Special
Overall length: 4.9″
Barrel length: 2¹/₂″
Weight: 8.5 oz.
Safety: Manual "Hammer-Block"
Grips: Rosewood
Price: $95.00

MODEL 4 (Stainless Steel Double Derringer)

SPECIFICATIONS
Calibers: 3″ .410 or 45 Colt lower barrel
Overall length: 6″
Barrel length: 4.1″
Weight: 16¹/₂ oz.
Price: $337.50
Alaskan Survival Model with 45-70 upper barrel,
   3″ .410/45 Colt lower barrel 369.00

MODEL 6 (Stainless Steel Double Derringer)

SPECIFICATIONS
Calibers: .410 and 45 Colt
Overall length: 8.2″
Barrel length: 6″
Weight: 21 oz.
Price: Satin finish $357.00
        Grey matte finish 337.50
        High polish finish 375.00

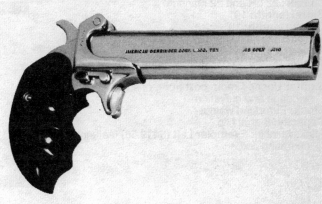

SEMMERLING LM-4 VEST-POCKET .45

SPECIFICATIONS
Caliber: 45 ACP or 9mm
Action: Double action
Capacity: 5 rounds
Overall length: 5″
Price: Blue finish $1250.00
       Stainless steel 1500.00

AMT PISTOLS

22 AUTOMAG II RIMFIRE MAGNUM
$329.00

The only production semiautomatic handgun in this caliber, the Automag II is ideal for the small-game hunter or shooting enthusiast who wants more power and accuracy in a light, trim handgun. The pistol features a bold open slide design and employs a unique gas-channeling system for smooth, trouble-free action.

SPECIFICATIONS
Caliber: 22 Rimfire Magnum
Barrel lengths: 3³/₈″, 4¹/₂″, 6″
Magazine capacity: 9 shots
Weight: 32 oz.
Sights: Millett adjustable (white outline rear; red ramp)
Features: Squared trigger guard; grooved carbon fiber grips

ANSCHUTZ PISTOL

EXEMPLAR
$395.00

SPECIFICATIONS
Caliber: 22 LR and 22 Magnum
Barrel length: 10″
Overall length: 19″
Weight: 3¹/₃ lbs.
Action: Match 64 left
Trigger pull: 9.85 oz., 2-stage adjustable
Safety: Slide
Sights: Hooded ramp post front; open notched rear; adj.for windage and elevation
Stock: European walnut
Capacity: 5-shot clip
Also available: **Exemplar Left ($419.50)** featuring right-hand operating bolt.

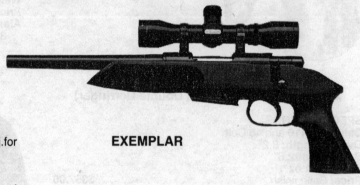

EXEMPLAR

EXEMPLAR XIV

EXEMPLAR XIV
$405.00

SPECIFICATIONS
Caliber: 22 LR and 22 Magnum
Barrel length: 14″
Overall length: 23″
Weight: 4.15 lbs.
Action: Match 64
Trigger pull: 9.85 oz., 2-stage
Safety: Slide
Also available: **EXEMPLAR HORNET ($758.00)**. A new centerfire version with Match 54 action. **Trigger pull:** 19.6 oz. **Barrel:** 10″. **Overall length:** 20″. **Weight:** 4.35 lbs. Tapped and grooved for scope mounting. Wing safety.

EXEMPLAR HORNET

ASTRA PISTOLS & REVOLVERS

357 MAGNUM

MODEL A-90

ASTRA 357 MAG. (shown above in 4″ barrel)

Potent, powerful and smooth as silk: the Astra 357. Chambered for the hot 357 Magnum cartridge, this large-frame revolver also handles the popular 38 Special, making it equally suitable for the serious target shooter and for the sportsman.

All forged steel and highly polished to a rich blue, the Astra 357 has a heavyweight barrel with integral rib and ejector shroud. The rear sight is click-adjustable for windage and elevation. The hammer is of the wide-spur target type, and the trigger is grooved. The grips are of checkered hardwood. The cylinder is recessed, and the gun utilizes a spring-loaded, floating firing pin for additional safety.

The internal lockwork of the Astra 357 is as finely fitted and finished as the exterior, giving it a smoothness second to none. There's even a four-stage adjustment to control spring tension on the hammer.

The Astra 357 is available with 4-inch, 6-inch or 8½-inch barrel. The 4-inch and longer-barreled models have square butts and are supplied with comfortable, hand-filling oversized grips. Length overall with 6-inch barrel is 11½ inches.

Barrel Length	Finish	Caliber	Weight	Price
4″ & 6″	Blue	357 Mag.	37 oz.	$295.00
8½″	Blue	357 Mag.	44 oz.	305.00

ASTRA CONSTABLE 22 L.R. & 380 ACP

The Astra Constable is a double-action, all-steel, small-frame auto, so you can safely carry it fully loaded with a round in the chamber and the safety off. A single pull of the trigger then cocks and fires the pistol without the necessity of cocking the hammer manually, as is necessary with most autos. The thumb safety completely blocks the hammer and actually locks the firing pin in place until released. The barrel is rigidly mounted in the frame for greater accuracy and the gun features quick, no-tool takedown, integral non-glare rib on the slide, push-button magazine release and a round, non-snagging hammer spur. **Barrel length:** 3½″. **Weight:** 37 oz. (380 ACP) and 28 oz. (22 LR). **Capacity:** 10 rds. (22 LR) and 7 rds. (380 ACP).

22 LR Blue	$325.00
22 LR Chrome	330.00
22 LR Chrome Engraved	410.00
380 ACP Blue	305.00
380 ACP Blue Engraved	375.00
380 ACP A-60 (13 rds.)	400.00

ASTRA MODEL A-90

Double-action, semiautomatic pistol in 9mm Parabellum and 45 ACP.

Features include an advanced, smooth double-action mechanism, increased magazine capacity (15 rounds in 9mm, 9 rounds in 45 ACP), all-steel construction, compact size, loaded chamber indicator, combat-style trigger guard, optional right-side slide release. **Barrel length:** 3¾″. **Weight:** 36 oz. (37 oz. in 45 ACP). **Price:** $450.00.

Also available: **Model A-80 ($395.00).**

ASTRA SPORT & SERVICE REVOLVER MODEL 44

Designed around the popular lines of its forerunner, the Astra 357, this revolver features wide-spur target hammers and a four-position main spring adjustment device that allows for custom tuning of trigger pull. Includes oversized, beefed-up frame and target-style grips to provide balanced weight distribution and minimize recoil.

The revolver, finished in deep astral blue, is available with 6-inch barrel that features integral sight ribs and shrouds for the ejector rods. Grooved trigger, ramp front sight and fully adjustable rear sight are standard. **Caliber:** 44. **Price:** $425.00.

CONSTABLE

BEEMAN PISTOLS AND REVOLVERS

**BEEMAN/UNIQUE 2000-U
5-SHOT SEMIAUTOMATIC
$1198.00 (Right) $1260.00 (Left)**

This improved version of the 823-U includes a reshaped grip, a redesigned firing mechanism, a faster falling hammer, and a dry firing mechanism that is easier to use. Trigger weight is only 3.5 oz. Features special light alloy frame and solid steel slide and shock absorber. Five vents reduce recoil; three removable vent screws adjust for jump control and velocity. Counter-weights available. **Caliber:** 22 Short. **Weight:** 2.7 lbs. Also available: **Beeman/Unique DES/32** (32 LG) **$1235.00.**

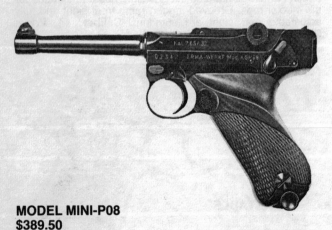

**BEEMAN/UNIQUE 69 TARGET PISTOL
$1065.00 (Right) $1090.00 (Left)**

**BEEMAN/KORTH
$2420.00—$4200.00**

SPECIFICATIONS
Caliber: 22 LR. **Capacity:** 5-shot magazine. **Sight radius:** 8.7". **Weight:** 2.2 lbs. **Grips:** Adjustable, anatomically shaped. **Features:** Trigger adjusts for position and pull weight; several barrel counterweights available; dry firing device; meets all U.I.T. requirements.

The metal parts of this revolver are hammer-forged steel super-hardened to high tensile strength. Cylinder gap of .002" eliminates stretching of the frame while firing, reduces flash, and increases velocity. **Caliber:** 357 Mag. or 22 LR w/interchangeable combo cylinders of 357 Mag./9mm Para or 22 LR/22 WMR. **Grips:** Walnut. **Barrel lengths:** 4"; 6" (Combat or Target).

**MODEL MINI-P08
$389.50**

SPECIFICATIONS
Caliber: 380 ACP. **Barrel length:** 3.5". **Overall length:** 7.4". **Weight:** I.4 lbs. **Grips:** Checkered hardwood.

**MODEL PO8
$389.50**

SPECIFICATIONS
Caliber: 22 LR. **Barrel length:** 3.8". **Overall length:** 7.8". **Weight:** 1.9 lbs. **Grips:** Checkered hardwood. Also features toggle-joint mechanism and magazine safety device.

BERETTA PISTOLS

MODEL 21 DA SEMIAUTOMATIC
$215.00 ($238.00 Nickel)

A safe, dependable, accurate small-bore pistol in 22 LR or 25 Auto. Easy to load with its unique barrel tip-up system.

SPECIFICATIONS
Caliber: 22 LR or 25 Auto. **Magazine capacity:** 7 rounds (22 LR); 8 rounds (25 Auto). **Overall length:** 4.8″. **Barrel length:** 2.4″. **Weight:** 12 oz. **Sights:** Blade front, V-notch rear. **Safety:** Thumb operated. **Grips:** Walnut. **Frame:** Special alloy.
Also available:
Model 21 Engraved $250.00

MODEL 21

MODEL 950 BS-4″ (22 Short)

MODEL 950 BS
Single Action Semiautomatic

SPECIFICATIONS
Calibers: 25 ACP and 22 Short. **Barrel length:** 2¹/₂″. **Overall length:** 4¹/₂″. **Overall height:** 3.4″. **Safety:** External, thumb-operated. **Magazine:** 8 rounds (25 cal.); 6 rounds (22 Short). **Sights:** Blade front; V-notch rear. **Weight:** 10.2 oz. in 22 cal.; 9.9 oz. in 25 cal. **Frame:** Special alloy.

Model 950 BS	$152.00
Model 950 BS Nickel	174.00
Model 950 EL Engraved	217.00

MODEL 92F (9mm)

This 9mm Parabellum semiautomatic pistol is specifically designed for use by law enforcement agencies. It has also been adopted as the official sidearm of the U.S. Armed Forces. Its 15-round firepower combines with flawless reliability and safety to make it the ideal police and military sidearm. Its firing mechanism will handle thousands of rounds without malfunction. And the ambidextrous triple-safety mechanism features a passive firing pin catch, a slide safety that acts as a decocking lever, plus a unique firing pin to insure that a falling hammer can never break safety and discharge accidentally.

SPECIFICATIONS
Caliber: 9mm Parabellum. **Overall length:** 8.54″. **Height:** 5.4″. **Barrel length:** 4.9″. **Weight** (empty): 34 oz. **Magazine:** 15 rounds, removable floorplate. **Sights:** Front, blade integral with slide; rear, square-notched bar, dovetailed to slide. **Slide stop:** Holds slide open after last round, manually operable.

Model 92F $595.00
(Wood grips **$20.00** additional)

MODEL 92F (9mm)

BERETTA PISTOLS

MODEL 84

MODEL 85

MODEL 84

This pistol is pocket size with a large magazine capacity. The lockwork is of double-action type. The first shot (with hammer down, chamber loaded) can be fired by a double-action pull on the trigger without cocking the hammer manually.

The pistol also features a favorable grip angle for natural pointing, positive thumb safety (uniquely designed for both right- and left-handed operation), quick takedown (by means of special takedown button) and a conveniently located magazine release. Black plastic grips. Wood grips available at extra cost.

SPECIFICATIONS
Caliber: 380 Auto (9mm Short). **Weight:** 1 lb. 7 oz. (approx.). **Barrel length:** 3³/₄". (approx.) **Overall length:** 6¹/₂". (approx.) **Sights:** Fixed front and rear. **Magazine capacity:** 13 rounds. **Height overall:** 4¹/₄" (approx.).

MODEL 85

This double action semiautomatic pistol features walnut grips, blued steel slide, ambidextrous safety, and anodized alloy frame with a single line 8-round magazine.

SPECIFICATIONS
Caliber: 380 Auto. **Barrel length:** 3.82". **Weight** (empty): 21.8 oz. **Overall length:** 6.8". **Overall height:** 4.8". **Capacity:** 8 rounds. **Sights:** Blade integral with slide (front); Square notched bar, dovetailed to slide (rear).

BERETTA MEDIUM FRAME PISTOLS
Calibers 22 LR and 380

BERETTA MEDIUM FRAME PISTOLS

Models	Prices
Model 84 Plastic (13 rounds)	$456.00
Model 84 Wood	485.00
Model 84 Nickel	515.00
Model 85 Plastic (8 rounds)	378.00
Model 85 Wood	392.00
Model 85 Nickel	406.00
Model 87 Wood (22 LR)	412.00
Model 87 (Long barrel, SA)	427.00
Model 87 Sport Wood (10 rds.)	525.00

MODEL 87

BERSA AUTOMATIC PISTOLS

MODEL 383 DA
$239.00

SPECIFICATIONS
Caliber: 380 Auto
Barrel length: 3¹/₂″
Action: Blow back
Sights: Front blade sight integral on slide; rear sight square notched adjustable for windage
Capacity: 7 + 1 in chamber
Grips: Custom wood
Model 223 DA: Same specifications but in 22 LR. Magazine capacity = 10 + 1. **$239.00**
Also available in Satin Nickel finish: **$279.00**

MODEL 383 DA

MODEL 226 DA
$239.00

Specifications same as **Model 224** but with 6″ barrel.

MODEL 224 DA
$239.00

SPECIFICATIONS
Caliber: 22 LR
Barrel length: 4″
Action: Blow back
Sights: Front blade sight on barrel; rear sight square notched adjustable for windage
Capacity: 10 + 1 in chamber
Grips: Custom wood
Finish: Blue

MODEL 226 DA

BRNO PISTOLS

MODEL CZ 75
$599.00

This 9mm double action service pistol features an all-steel frame, 15-shot magazine, and two integral locking lugs on top of barrel which fit into matching recesses in the slide. When slide is pulled forward, the barrel is forced downward and unlocked from the slide stop pin (which fits through the slotted barrel tang.) A pivot type extractor is pinned on the right side of the slide behind the ejection port. Trigger pull is 9 lbs.

SPECIFICATIONS
Caliber: 9mm Parabellum. **Barrel length:** 4.7″. **Overall length:** 8.1″. **Height:** 5.4″. **Weight:** 35 oz.

BROWNING AUTOMATIC PISTOLS

BUCK MARK .22 PISTOL
$182.95

Magazine capacity: 10 rounds. **Overall length:** 9 1/2". **Barrel length:** 5 1/2". **Height:** 5 3/8". **Weight:** 35 oz. **Grips:** Black molded. **Rear sights:** Screw adjusts for vertical correction; drift adjustable for windage.

Prices:

Standard	$182.95
Plus (w/contoured, laminated wood grips)	219.95
Silhouette	309.95
Varmint	279.95

BUCK MARK SILHOUETTE

MODEL BDA-380.

MODEL BDA-380. A high-powered, double-action pistol with fixed sights in 380 caliber.

BDA-380 Nickel . **$452.95**   BDA-380 Std. . . . **$429.95**

SEMIAUTOMATIC PISTOL SPECIFICATIONS

	BUCK MARK 22	BDA-380 (DOUBLE ACTION)
Capacity of Magazine	10	13
Overall length	9 1/2"	6 3/4"
Barrel Length	5 1/2"	3 13/16"
Height	5 3/8"	4 3/4"
Weight (Empty)	32 oz.	23 oz.
Sight radius	8"	4 15/16"
Ammunition	22LR	380 Auto
Grips	Black, Molded	Walnut
Front Sights	1/8" wide	1/16" wide
Rear Sights	Screw adjustable for windage and elevation.	Square notch. Drift adjustable for windage.
Grades Available	Standard	Standard, Nickel

BROWNING AUTOMATIC PISTOLS

**9mm HI-POWER
SINGLE ACTION 9mm**

The Browning 9mm Parabellum, also known as the 9mm Browning Hi-Power, has a 14-cartridge capacity and weighs 2 pounds. The push-button magazine release permits swift, convenient withdrawal of the magazine.

The 9mm is available with either a fixed-blade front sight and a windage-adjustable rear sight or a non-glare rear sight, screw adjustable for both windage and elevation. The front sight is a $1/8$-inch wide blade mounted on a ramp. The rear surface of the blade is serrated to prevent glare.

In addition to the manual safety, the firing mechanism includes an external hammer, making it easy to ascertain whether the pistol is cocked.

Prices:

Standard	**$428.50**
Polished blue with adjustable sights	**468.50**
Matte blue, ambidextrous safety	**394.50**

9MM SEMIAUTOMATIC PISTOL (SINGLE AND DOUBLE ACTION)

	SINGLE ACTION FIXED SIGHTS	SINGLE ACTION ADJUSTABLE SIGHTS
Finish	Polished Blue, Matte, or Nickel	Polished Blue or Nickel
Capacity of Magazine	13	13
Overall Length	$7^{3}/_{4}''$	$7^{3}/_{4}''$
Barrel Length	$4^{21}/_{32}''$	$4^{21}/_{32}''$
Height	$5''$	$5''$
Weight (Empty)	32 oz.	32 oz.
Sight Radius	$6^{5}/_{16}''$	$6^{3}/_{8}''$
Ammunition	9mm Luger, (Parabellum)	9mm Luger, (Parabellum)
Grips	Checkered Walnut	Checkered Walnut
Front Sights	$1/8''$	$1/8''$ wide on ramp
Rear Sights	Drift adjustable for windage.	Screw adjustable for windage and elevation.

CHARTER ARMS REVOLVERS

BULLDOG 44 SPECIAL

SPECIFICATIONS
Caliber: 44 Special. **Type of action:** 5-shot, single- and double-action. **Barrel length:** 3″. **Overall length:** 7³/₄″. **Height:** 5″. **Weight:** 19 oz. **Grips:** Neoprene or American walnut hand-checkered bulldog grips. **Sights:** Patridge-type, ⁹/₆₄″ wide front; square-notched rear. **Finish:** High-luster Service Blue or Stainless Steel.

Also available: new **44SPL Bulldog Pug Model** with 2¹/₂″ barrel and ramp front sight. **Overall length:** 7¹/₄″.

Prices:
Blue finish (2¹/₂″ Bull or 3″) $216.00
Blue finish (Pug) 234.00
Stainless Steel (2¹/₂″ Bull or 3″) 270.00
Stainless Steel (Pug) 280.00

BULLDOG PUG 44 SPECIAL 5-SHOT

357 MAGNUM REVOLVER BULLDOG "TRACKER"

SPECIFICATIONS
Caliber: 357 Magnum. **Type of action:** 5-shot. **Barrel length:** 2¹/₂″. **Overall length:** 7¹/₂″ (2¹/₂ bbl.). **Height:** 5¹/₈″. **Weight:** 21 oz. **Grips:** Hand-checkered walnut, square butt design. **Sights:** Ramp front sight; adjustable square-notched rear; elevation reference lines; definite click indicator. **Finish:** Service blue.

Price:
Blue finish and Neoprene or Bulldog grips $214.00

357 MAGNUM REVOLVER BULLDOG "TRACKER"

POLICE BULLDOG 6-SHOT REVOLVER

SPECIFICATIONS
Caliber: 38 Special and 32 H&R Magnum. **Type of action:** 6-shot single and double action. **Barrel length:** 4″. **Overall length:** 9″. **Height:** 5″. **Weight:** 20 to 23¹/₂ oz. **Grips:** square butt, American walnut hand-checkered. **Sights:** Full-length ramp front; square notch rear (adjustable rear sight on 32 H&R Mag.). **Finish:** High-luster service blue.
Price $217.17
Stainless steel 263.00

POLICE BULLDOG 6-SHOT REVOLVER

POLICE UNDERCOVER

SPECIFICATIONS
Caliber: 32 H&R Magnum and 38 Special. **Type of action:** 6-shot single and double action. **Barrel length:** 2″. **Height:** 4¹/₂″. **Weight:** 17¹/₂ oz. (2″ barrel) and 19 oz. (4″ barrel.) **Grips:** Checkered walnut panel. **Sights:** Patridge-type ramp front sight, square-notch rear sight. **Finish:** Blue.

Price $217.74
Stainless steel and checkered walnut panel 252.00

POLICE UNDERCOVER

CHARTER ARMS REVOLVERS

UNDERCOVER
32 S&W Long

SPECIFICATIONS
Caliber: 32 S&W Long. **Type of Action:** 6-shot, single- and double-action. **Barrel length:** 2″. **Overall length:** 6¼″. **Height:** 4⅛″. **Weight:** 16 oz. **Grips:** Checkered walnut panel. **Sights:** Wide Patridge-type front; notch rear 9/64″. **Rifling:** One turn in 17″, right hand twist. **Finish:** High-luster Service Blue.

Price:
Blue finish with regular grips $198.87

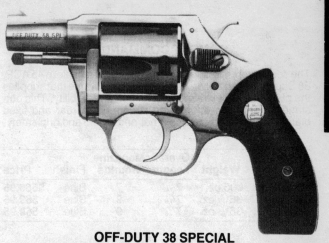

OFF-DUTY 38 SPECIAL

SPECIFICATIONS
Caliber: 38 Special. **Type of action:** 5-shot single- and double-action. **Barrel length:** 2″. **Overall length:** 6¼″. **Height:** 4¼″. **Weight:** 16 oz. (mat-black), 17 oz. (stainless steel). **Grips:** Select-a-grip (9 colors) or neoprene. **Sights:** Patridge-type ramp front sight (with new "red dot" feature); square notch rear sight on stainless.

Prices:
Mat-black finish $167.30
Stainless steel 230.42

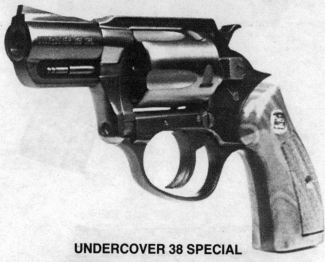

UNDERCOVER 38 SPECIAL

SPECIFICATIONS
Caliber: 38 Special (Mid-Range & Standard). **Type of Action:** 5 shots, single- and double-action. **Barrel length** (with shroud): 2″ or 3″. **Overall length:** 6¼″ (2″ bbl.), 8″ (3″ bbl.). **Height:** 4¼″ (2″ bbl.), 4¾″ (3″ bbl.). **Weight:** 16 oz. (2″ bbl.), 17½ oz. (3″ bbl.). **Grips:** American walnut hand-checkered. **Sights:** Patridge-type or standard ramp front, square-notched rear. **Finish:** High-luster Service Blue or Stainless Steel.

Prices:
2″ barrel blue finish with checkered panel grips **$198.87**
2″ barrel stainless steel with checkered panel grips . . 252.00
3″ barrel blue finish with checkered panel grips 198.87

PATHFINDER
22 L.R.

SPECIFICATIONS
Caliber: 22 LR. **Type of action:** 6-shot, single and double action. **Barrel length:** 2″, 3″ or 6″. **Overall length:** 7¾″ (3″ bbl.); 10⅝″ (6″ bbl.). **Height:** 4¾″ (3″ bbl.); 5″ (6″ bbl.). **Weight:** 20 oz. (3″ bbl.); 22½ oz. (6″ bbl.). **Grips:** Hand-checkered square butt or checkered walnut panel. **Sights:** Patridge-type ramp front sight; fully adjustable notch rear sight. **Finish:** High luster service blue.

Prices:
With 2″ or 3″ barrel $210.65
With 6″ barrel 222.11
With 3″ barrel in stainless steel 255.20
NEW: 22 LR Off-Duty (2″ matte black) 167.00

COLT AUTOMATIC PISTOLS

COMBAT COMMANDER

The semiautomatic Combat Commander, available in 45 ACP, 38 Super or 9mm Luger, boasts an all-steel frame that supplies the pistol with an extra measure of heft and stability. This outstanding Colt also offers fixed square-notch rear and fixed blade front, lanyard-style hammer and thumb and grip safety.

Caliber	Weight	Overall Length	Magazine Rounds	Finish	Price
45 ACP	36 oz.	7⅞″	7	Blue	$565.95
38 Super	36½ oz.	7⅞″	9	Blue	569.95
9mm Luger	36½ oz.	7⅞″	9	Blue	569.95

COMBAT COMMANDER
4¼″ barrel only

LIGHTWEIGHT COMMANDER

This lightweight, shorter version of the Government Model offers increased ease of carrying with the firepower of the 45 ACP. The Lightweight Commander features alloy frame, fixed-style sights, grooved trigger, lanyard-style hammer and walnut stocks; also thumb and grip safety, and firing pin safety.

SPECIFICATIONS
Weight: 27 oz.
Barrel length: 4¼″
Overall length: 7⅞″
Magazine rounds: 7
Finish: Blue
Price: $565.95

LIGHTWEIGHT COMMANDER
4¼″ barrel only

GOLD CUP NATIONAL MATCH

SPECIFICATIONS
Caliber: 45 ACP
Capacity: 7 rounds
Barrel length: 5″
Weight: 38½ oz.
Overall length: 8⅜″
Sights: Undercut front; adjustable rear
Hammer: Serrated target hammer
Stock: Checkered walnut
Finish: Colt blue or stainless
Price: $729.95 (blue)
         783.95 (stainless steel)
         835.95 (bright stainless)
Also available: **COMBAT ELITE** 45 ACP; features 3 dot front and rear combat sights, extended grip safety. **Price: $689.95**

GOLD CUP NATIONAL MATCH

COLT AUTOMATIC PISTOLS

GOVERNMENT MODEL

GOVERNMENT MODEL 380 AUTOMATIC

This scaled-down version of the 1911 A1 Colt Government Model does not include a grip safety. It incorporates the use of a firing pin safety to provide for a safe method to carry a round in the chamber in a "cocked and locked" mode. This provides for a consistent trigger pull rather than the double-action style of a heavy first pull.

SPECIFICATIONS
Caliber: 380 ACP
Barrel length: 3.29″
Height: 4.4″
Weight (empty): 21.8 oz.
Overall length: 6.15″
Magazine capacity: 7 rounds
Sights: Fixed ramp blade in front; fixed square notch in rear
Grip: Composition stocks
Finish: Blue
Price: $365.95 Blue
　　　406.95 Satin Nickel
　　　386.95 Coltguard

DELTA ELITE

The proven design and reliability of Colt's Government Model has been combined with the new powerful 10mm auto cartridge to produce a highly effective shooting system for hunting, law enforcement and personal protection. The velocity and energy of the 10mm cartridge make this pistol ideal for the serious handgun hunter and the law enforcement professional who insist on down-range stopping power.

SPECIFICATIONS
Caliber: 10mm
Type: 0 Frame, semiautomatic pistol
Barrel length: 5″
Weight (empty): 39 oz.
Overall length: 8¹/₂″
Cylinder capacity: 7 rds.
Sights: 3-dot, high-profile front and rear combat sights
Sight radius: 6¹/₂″
Grip: Rubber combat stocks with Delta medallion
Safety: Trigger safety lock (thumb safety) is located on left-hand side of receiver; grip safety is located on backstrap
Rifling: 6 groove, left-hand twist, one turn in 16″
Finish: Blue
Price: $626.95

GOVERNMENT MODEL

These full-size automatic pistols, available exclusively with 5-inch barrels, may be had in 45 ACP, 9mm Luger, 38 Super and 22 LR. The Government Model's special features include fixed military sights, grip and thumb safeties, grooved trigger, walnut stocks and Accurizor barrel and bushing.

Caliber	Weight	Overall Length	Magazine Rounds	Finish	Price
45 ACP	38 oz.	8³/₈″	7	Blue	$565.95
				Stainless	599.95
38 Super	39 oz.	8³/₈″	9	Blue	569.95
9mm Luger	39 oz.	8³/₈″	9	Blue	569.95

**GOVERNMENT MODEL
380 AUTOMATIC**

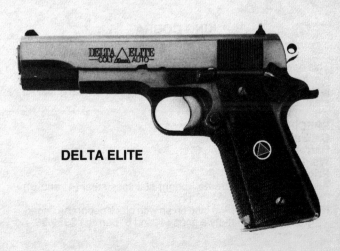

DELTA ELITE

COLT PISTOLS

COLT MUSTANG .380

This new backup automatic has four times the knockdown power of most 25 ACP automatics.

SPECIFICATIONS
Caliber: 380 ACP
Capacity: 5 rounds
Weight: 18.5 oz.
Overall length: 5.65″
Height: 3.9″
Price: $365.95 ($406.95 in nickel)
Also available: **MUSTANG POCKET LITE 380** with aluminum alloy receiver; 1/2″ shorter than standard 380; weighs only 12.5 oz. **$365.95.**
NEW: MUSTANG PLUS II features full grip length with shorter compact barrel and slide. **$365.95.**

COLT OFFICER'S ACP

SPECIFICATIONS
Caliber: 45 ACP
Barrel length: 3 5/8″
Overall length: 7 1/4″
Weight: 34 oz.
Price: $549.95 (matte finish)
     599.95 (stainless steel)
     565.95 (lightweight, 3″ barrel)
     565.95 (standard blue)

MUSTANG POCKET LITE

COLT REVOLVERS

KING COBRA 357 MAGNUM

This new "snake" revolver features a solid barrel rib, full length ejector rod housing, red ramp front sight, white outline adjustable rear sight, and new "gripper" rubber combat grips. All stainless steel.

SPECIFICATIONS
Caliber: 357 Magnum
Barrel lengths: 2 1/2″, 4″, 6″
Weight: 42 oz.
Price: $414.95
Also available: **"Ultimate"** bright stainless steel (4″ and 6″) $449.95
NEW: KING COBRA in blue finish with black neoprene finger-grooved, combat-style grips (4″ and 6″ barrels) **$389.95.**

COLT REVOLVERS

PYTHON
357 MAGNUM (shown with 6″ barrel)

The Colt Python revolver, suitable for hunting, target shooting and police use, is chambered for the powerful 357 Magnum cartridge. Python features include ventilated rib, fast cocking, wide-spur hammer, trigger and grips, adjustable rear and ramp-type front sights, ¹/₈″ wide.

SPECIFICATIONS
Caliber: 357 Mag.
Barrel length: 2¹/₂″, 4″, 6″, 8″ (357 Mag.)
Overall length: 11¹/₄″
Weight: 43¹/₂ oz.
Stock: Checkered walnut
Finish: Colt royal blue, stainless and bright steel (not in 8″)

Caliber	Barrel	Finish	Price
357 Mag.	2¹/₂″, 4″, 6″, 8″	Blue	$729.95
357 Mag.	2¹/₂″, 4″, 6″	St.S.	835.95

Now available: **Python Ultimate Bright Polished Stainless Steel,** in 2¹/₂″, 4″ and 6″ barrels. **$859.95.**

COONAN ARMS

MODEL B 357 MAGNUM
$650.00

Caliber: 357 Magnum
Magazine capacity: 7 rounds
Barrel length: 5″
Overall length: 8.3″
Weight (empty): 42 oz.
Height: 5.6″
Sights: Ramp interchangeable (front); fixed, adjustable for windage only (rear)
Grips: Smooth black walnut
Safety features: Hammer lock; half-notch lock; grip lock; inertia firing pin

DAKOTA SINGLE ACTION REVOLVERS

MODEL 1873 (With Extra Cylinder)
$595.00

SPECIFICATIONS
Calibers: 22 LR, 22 Mag., 357 Mag., 45 Long Colt, 30 M1 Carbine, 38-40 cal., 32-20 cal., 44-40 cal. **Barrel lengths:** 3¹/₂", 4³/₄", 5¹/₂", 7¹/₂". **Finish:** Engraved models, blue or nickel. **Special feature:** Each gun is fitted with second caliber.

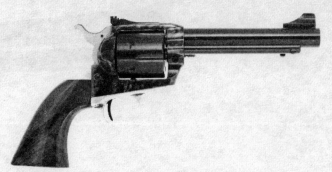

DAKOTA TARGET
$500.00

SPECIFICATIONS
Calibers: 45 Long Colt, 357 Magnum, 22 LR. **Barrel lengths:** 5¹/₂" and 7¹/₂". **Finish:** Polished blue. **Special features:** Case-hardened frame, one-piece walnut grips, brass back strap, ramp front blade target sight and adjustable rear sight.

MODEL 1875 "OUTLAW"
$485.00 ($520.00 Nickel)

SPECIFICATIONS
Calibers: 45 Long Colt, 357 Magnum, 44-40 cal. **Barrel length:** 7¹/₂". **Finish:** Blue. **Special features:** Case-hardened frame, walnut grips; an exact replica of Remington #3 revolver produced from 1875 to 1889. Factory Engraved Model: $600.00

DAKOTA 1894 BISLEY
$540.00

SPECIFICATIONS
Calibers: 22, 44-40, 45 Long Colt, 357 Magnum. **Barrel lengths:** 4⁵/₈", 5¹/₂" and 7¹/₂". Also available: **Dakota Bisley Engraved Model** with same barrel lengths and calibers. $700.00
Nickel finish 760.00

DAVIS PISTOLS

MODEL D-22 DERRINGER
$87.50

SPECIFICATIONS
Calibers: 25 Auto, 22 LR, 32 Auto, 22 Mag.
Barrel length: 2.4″
Overall length: 4″
Height: 2.8″
Weight: 9.5 oz.
Capacity: 2 shot
Grips: Laminated wood
Finish: Black teflon or chrome (32 Auto in chrome only)

MODEL P-32
$87.50

SPECIFICATIONS
Caliber: 32 Auto
Barrel length: 2.8″
Overall length: 5.4″
Height: 4″
Magazine capacity: 6 rounds
Weight (empty): 22 oz.
Grips: Laminated wood
Finish: Black teflon or chrome

DETONICS PISTOLS

**COMBAT MASTER
45 ACP**

COMBAT MASTER™ 45 ACP (Stainless Steel)

Calibers: 45 ACP, 6-shot clip; 38S and 9mm available on special order.
Barrel length: 3¹/₂″
Weight: 29 oz. (empty)
Overall length: 6³/₄″
Stock: Checkered walnut
Sights: Combat-type, fixed; adj. sights available
Features: Self-adjusting cone barrel centering system, beveled magazine inlet, "full clip" indicator in base of magazine; throated barrel and polished feed ramp.
Prices:
MK I, matte stainless, fixed sights $725.00
MK VI, polished stainless, adj. sights 795.95

SERVICEMASTER II
(not shown)

A new, shortened version of the Scoremaster, this model features coned barrel and recoil systems.

Caliber: 45 ACP
Barrel: 4¹/₄″
Weight: 39 oz.
Capacity: 7 rds. plus I chambered
Sights: Millett CCLP adj. rear; black serrated ramp front
Price: $975.00

DETONICS PISTOLS

SCOREMASTER (Stainless Steel)

Calibers: 45 ACP; 451 Detonics Magnum; 7- or 8-shot clip
Barrel length: 5″ or 6″ heavyweight match barrel
Overall length: 8³/₈″ w/5″ barrel
Weight: 42 oz. w/5″ barrel
Stock: Pachmayr grips and M.S. housing
Sights: Millett CCLP adj. rear; interchangeable front—black, orange or white
Features: Stainless steel construction; self-centering barrel system; patented Detonics recoil system; combat tuned; extended grip safety; extended magazine release
Prices: 45 ACP and 451 Detonics Magnum $1110.00
With 6″ barrel **1150.00**

THE JANUS SCOREMASTER

The Janus Scoremaster is two pistols in one: a stock 5″ barrel and slide-mounted front sight convertible (in five minutes with a ¹/₁₆″ punch) into a 5¹/₂″ comp. gun with front sight mounted on the Specialist comp.

SPECIFICATIONS
Caliber: 45 ACP
Barrel length: 5.2″ w/stock barrel; 5.6″ w/comp barrel
Overall length: 8³/₈″ w/stock barrel; 10″ w/comp. barrel
Weight: 42 oz. w/stock barrel; 46 oz. w/comp. barrel
Sights: Adj. rear sight, Millet on slide, hand serrated; custom front sight on compensator
Capacity: 7 rds. plus 1 chambered; 3 rds. plus 1 chambered w/8-rd. magazine
Rifling: 1 turn in 16″; left-hand turn, 6 grooves
Finish: Polished side of slide with matte satin surfaces
Price: $1650.00

ERMA TARGET ARMS

MODEL 777 SPORTING REVOLVER

SPECIFICATIONS
Caliber: 357 Magnum
Capacity: 6 cartridges
Barrel length: 5¹/₂″ and 4″
Overall length: 11.3″ and 9.7″
Weight: 43.7 oz.; 39.2 oz. w/4″ barrel
Sight radius: 8″ and 6.4″
Grip: Checkered walnut
Price: On request

Also available:
MODEL 773 MATCH (32 S&W Wadcutter). Same specifications as Model 777 (5¹/₂″ barrel only), but with adjustable match grip and 6″ barrel. **Weight:** 45.8 oz. **Price on request.**
MODEL 772 MATCH (22 LR). Same specifications as Model 773, except weight is 47¹/₄ oz. **Price on request.**

F.I.E. HANDGUNS

DERRINGER D-86 SINGLE SHOT
$89.95 ($109.95 DELUXE)

SPECIFICATIONS
Caliber: 38 Special
Barrel length: 3″
Weight: 11 oz.
Sights: Fixed
Safety: Transfer bar
Finish: Dyna-chrome hard matte or bright blue
Grips: Black nylon (Standard) and walnut (Deluxe)
Also available: $ 94.95 Dyna-Chrome
                  114.95 Dyna-Chrome Deluxe
                  134.95 Misty Gold
                  149.95 Misty Gold Deluxe

TITAN 25 SEMIAUTOMATIC
$72.95

SPECIFICATIONS
Caliber: 25 ACP
Barrel length: 2¹/₂″
Weight: 12 oz.
Sights: Ramp front, fixed rear
Hammer: Serrated external
Grips: European walnut
Trigger lock: Thumb operated
Also available: $ 79.95 Dyna-Chrome
                  89.95 Gold Trim
                  134.95 Misty Gold

TITAN TIGER DOUBLE ACTION REVOLVER
$154.95

SPECIFICATIONS
Caliber: 38 Special
Barrel length: 2″ or 4″
Sights: Ramp front, fixed rear
Grips: Composite, checkered
Features: Swing-out cylinder with thumb latch release

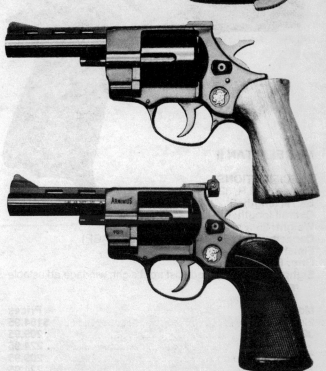

ARMINIUS DOUBLE ACTION REVOLVERS

SPECIFICATIONS
Calibers: 22S/L/LR, 22 WMR, 22 Combo w/interchangeable
   cylinders, 32 S&W Long, 38 Special, 357 Magnum
Barrel lengths: 2″, 3″, 4″ and 6″
Sights: Fixed or micro-adjustable
Weight: 26 oz. - 30 oz.
Capacity: 8 rds. (22), 7 rds. (32 S&W), 6 rds. (all others)
Prices: $169.95 (22 LR and 32 S&W snub nose)
          139.95 (22 LR 4″ and 6″; 32 S&W 6″ blue)
          214.95 (22 Magnum Convertible)
          169.95 (38 Special 4″ and 6″)
          224.95 (357 Magnum 3″, 4″ and 6″)

F.I.E. PISTOLS

MODEL TZ75
$424.95

SPECIFICATIONS
Caliber: 9mm double action, 41 A.E.
Capacity: 15 + 1
Barrel length: 4¹/₂″
Overall length: 8¹/₄″
Height: 5¹/₂″
Weight: 35 oz.
Sights: D/T ramp front (white insert); rear (white outline) adjustable for windage
Grips: European walnut, black rubber (optional)
Available in Satin Chrome: **$444.95**

MODEL A27BW "THE BEST" 25 ACP SEMIAUTOMATIC
$154.95

Once known as the "Astra Cub" and later as the "Colt Junior," this classic is now known as "The Best" pistol.

SPECIFICATIONS
Capacity: 6 shots
Barrel length: 2¹/₂″
Overall length: 6³/₄″
Weight: 12 oz.
Stock: Checkered walnut
Sights: Fixed

MODEL TITAN II

SPECIFICATIONS
Caliber: 22 LR, 32 ACP, 380 ACP
Barrel length: 3¹/₄″
Overall length: 6¹/₂″
Weight: 25¹/₂ oz.
Capacity: 10 + 1 (6 in 32 ACP and 380 ACP)
Finish: Blue
Grip: European walnut
Sights: Integral tapered post front sight; windage adjustable rear sight

SUPER TITAN II (not shown)
$249.95

SPECIFICATIONS
Calibers: 32 ACP, 380 ACP
Weight: 28 oz.
Barrel length: 3¹/₄″
Finish: Blue

Models	Prices
22 LR Blue	$154.95
32 ACP Blue	209.95
Chrome	224.95
380 ACP Blue	209.95
Chrome	224.95

FREEDOM ARMS

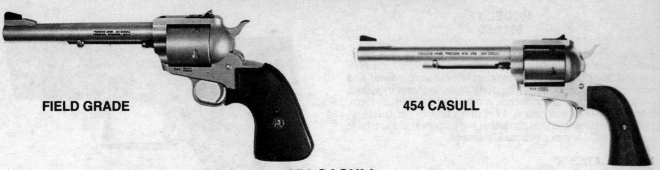

FIELD GRADE

454 CASULL

Model No.	454 CASULL	Price
FA-454AS	Adjustable sight 454 Casull, 45 Colt and 44 Rem. Mag. with 4³/₄″, 6″, 7¹/₂″ or 10″ barrel, stainless steel, brush finish, impregnated hardwood grips.	$1095.00
FA-454FS	Same as above with fixed sight	995.00

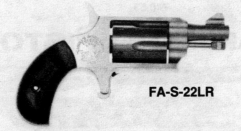

FA-S-22LR

Model	22 LONG RIFLE REVOLVERS	Prices
FA-S-22LR	Stainless Steel Mini-Revolver with 1-inch contoured barrel, partial high gloss finish. Caliber 22 Long Rifle.	$139.20
FA-S-22LR with FA/B	Same as above, with polished brass belt buckle.	178.70
	Above prices include soft zipper pouch.	

NEW 22 PERCUSSION REVOLVERS

Model		Prices
FA-S-22P	Stainless Steel Percussion Mini-Revolver with 1-inch contoured barrel, partial high gloss finish.	$184.56
FA-S-22P with FA/B	Same as above, with polished brass belt buckle.	224.10
	All Percussion Revolver prices include the following: powder measure, bullet setting tool, twenty bullets and soft zipper pouch.	

22 WIN. MAGNUM REVOLVERS

Model		Prices
FA-S-22M	Stainless Steel Mini-Revolver with 1-inch contoured barrel, partial high gloss finish.	$160.45
FA-S-22M with FA/BM	Same as above, with polished brass belt buckle.	199.95
FA-BG-22M	Stainless Steel Mini-Revolver with 3-inch tapered barrel, partial high gloss finish and custom oversized grips.	199.95
	Prices include soft zipper pouch.	

GLOCK PISTOLS

MODEL 17
$511.60

First launched in 1983, the Glock handgun represents a trend-setting development. The company's trial weapons have now passed 300,000 rounds of testfiring without visible wear and with continuing accuracy. The guns' main features include a limited number of components, a new "safe-action" system, low weight with soft recoil, 17-round capacity, and use of space-age polymers that can withstand extreme cold and heat (up to 200°C.) without structural damage.

MODEL 19 COMPACT

SPECIFICATIONS
Caliber: 9mm Parabellum
Magazine capacity: 17 rounds
Barrel length: 4¹/₂″ (hexagonal profile with right-hand twist
Overall length: 7¹/₂″
Weight: 23 oz. (without magazine)
Sights: Fixed or adjustable rear sights
Also available:
MODEL 19 COMPACT (4″ barrel) $511.60
MODEL 17L COMPETITION (6″ compensated
 barrel/slide) 740.53

HÄMMERLI PISTOLS

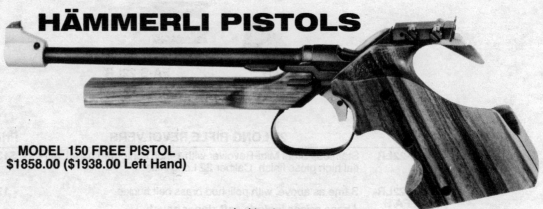

MODEL 150 FREE PISTOL
$1858.00 ($1938.00 Left Hand)

SPECIFICATIONS
Caliber: 22 LR
Overall length: 17.2″
Weight: 45.6 oz.
Trigger action: Infinitely variable set trigger weight; cocking lever located on left of receiver; trigger length variable along weapon axis
Sights: Sight radius 14.8″; micrometer rear sight adj. for windage and elevation
Locking action: Martini-type locking action w/side-mounted locking lever
Barrel: Free floating, cold swaged precision barrel w/low axis relative to the hand
Ignition: Horizontal firing pin (hammerless) in line w/barrel axis; firing pin travel 0.15″
Grips: Selected walnut w/adj. hand rest for direct arm to barrel extension
MODEL 150L: Same as above but w/left hand adjustable grips

MODEL 152 ELECTRONIC PISTOL
$1979.00 ($2059.00 Left Hand)

SPECIFICATIONS:
Same as **Model 150** except trigger action is electronic. Features short lock time (1.7 milliseconds between trigger actuation and firing pin impact), light trigger pull, and extended battery life.

HÄMMERLI PISTOLS

MODEL 208 TARGET PISTOL
$1555.00 ($1595.00 Left Hand)

SPECIFICATIONS:
Caliber: 22LR
Barrel length: 6″
Overall length: 10.2″
Weight: 37.3 oz. (w/accessories)
Capacity: 8 rounds
Sight radius: 8.3″
Sights: Micrometer rear sight w/notch width; standard front blade
DELUXE MODEL (Right Hand only): **$3250.00**

MODEL 215 TARGET PISTOL
$1226.00 ($1266.00 Left Hand)

SPECIFICATIONS
Same as **Model 208** except it has fewer "luxury" features. Also available: **MODEL 212 Hunter's Pistol** featuring safety catch, nonslip slide and optimal balance. **Price: $1359.00.**

MODEL 232 RAPID FIRE PISTOL
$1425.00 ($1465.00 Left Hand)

SPECIFICATIONS:
Caliber: 22 Short
Barrel length: 5.2″
Overall length: 10.5″
Weight: 44 oz.
Sight radius: 9.6″
Capacity: 5 rounds
Grips: Adjustable (add **$40** for wraparound grips)

HECKLER & KOCH PISTOLS

MODEL P7M13

MODEL P7 PISTOL

Features the Continuous Motion Principle in the form of a unique cocking lever. The gun can be drawn, cocked and fired with single-action accuracy in one continuous motion with either hand. Also featured are a low profile slide, polygonal rifling and rugged forged, machined steel construction.

SPECIFICATIONS
Caliber: 9mm x 19 (Luger)
Capacity: 8 rounds
Barrel length: 4.13″
Overall length: 6.73″
Weight: 1.75 lbs. (empty)
Sight radius: 5.83″
Sights: Adjustable rear
MODEL P7 with 2 magazines $881.00
Also available: **MODEL P7M13** with same barrel length, but slightly longer overall, heavier and 13-round capacity $1099.00

MODEL P7K3

Model P7K3 uses a unique oil-filled buffer to decrease recoil and increase control. An easy-to-install conversion kit in 22 LR is available as an accessory.

SPECIFICATIONS
Caliber: 380 (+ 22 LR Conversion Kit)
Capacity: 8 rounds
Barrel length: 3.8″
Overall length: 6.3″
Weight: 1.65 lbs. (empty)
Sight radius: 5.5″
Sights: Adjustable rear
MODEL P7K3 . . . . $881.00
   22 LR Conversion Kit 428.00

MODEL P7K3

HECKLER & KOCH PISTOLS

MODEL P9S 9mm AUTOMATIC PISTOL

Originally designed for West German police, the HKP9S is a light, fast-handling double-action automatic pistol. It features a cocking-decocking lever, delayed roller-locked bolt system and polygonal rifling.

SPECIFICATIONS
Calibers: 9mm x 19 (Luger); 45 ACP
Capacity: 9 rounds (9mm); 7 rounds (45 ACP)
Barrel length: 4″
Overall length: 7.55″
Weight: (empty) 1.87 lbs. (9mm); 1.74 lbs. (45 ACP)
Sight radius: 5.77″
Sights: Adjustable (Target Model); fixed (Combat Model)
MODEL P9S
   9mm w/combat sights, 2 magazines $1046.00
   45 ACP w/combat sights, 2 magazines 1299.00

MODEL P9S 9mm

MODEL VP70Z

SPECIFICATIONS
Caliber: 9mm x 19
Capacity: 18 rounds
Barrel length: 4.55″
Overall length: 8.01″
Weight: 1.80 lbs. (empty)
Sight radius: 6.90″
Sights: Movable rear; shadow front
MODEL VP70Z $399.00

MODEL VP70Z

IVER JOHNSON

POCKET PISTOL
TP22 (22LR) & TP25 (25ACP)

These 22- and 25-caliber pocket pistols offer a maximum of convenience when carried. The 7-shot capacity, small size and light weight are enhanced by the hammer safety and fast-handling double-action design.
Barrel length: 3″. **Overall length:** 5.5″. **Weight:** 12 oz. (empty). **Grips:** Black plastic. **Finish:** Blue or nickel.

TP22 and TP25 Blue $191.65
Nickel 206.12

KIMBER

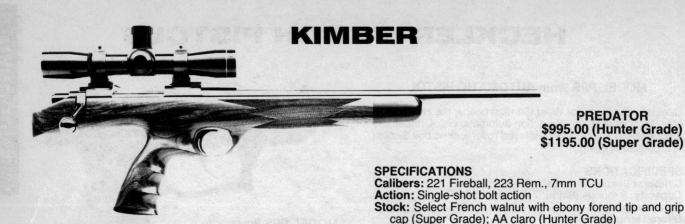

PREDATOR
$995.00 (Hunter Grade)
$1195.00 (Super Grade)

SPECIFICATIONS
Calibers: 221 Fireball, 223 Rem., 7mm TCU
Action: Single-shot bolt action
Stock: Select French walnut with ebony forend tip and grip cap (Super Grade); AA claro (Hunter Grade)

L.A.R. GRIZZLY

MARK I
GRIZZLY WIN MAG
$675.00

This semiautomatic pistol is a direct descendant of the tried and trusted 1911-type .45 automatic, but with the added advantage of increased caliber capacity.

SPECIFICATIONS
Calibers: 45 Win. Mag., 45 ACP, 357 Mag.
Barrel length: 6½"
Overall length: 10½"
Weight (empty): 48 oz.
Height: 5¾"
Sights: Fixed, ramped blade (front); fully adjustable for elevation and windage (rear)
Magazine capacity: 7 rounds
Grips: Checkered rubber, nonslip, combat-type
Safeties: Grip depressor, manual thumb, slide-out-of-battery disconnect
Materials: Mil spec 4140 steel slide and receiver with noncorrosive, heat-treated, special alloy sttels for other parts

Same model in 357 Magnum **$699.00**
Also available: **Win Mag Compensator** 60.00

Also available: **Grizzly Win Mag with 8″ and 10″ Barrels** in 45 Win Mag, 357 Magnum, 45 ACP and 357/45 Grizzly Win Mag.
Model G-WM8 (8″ barrel in 45 Win Mag, 45 ACP, or 357/45 Grizzly Win Mag **$1250.00**
Model G357M8 (8″ barrel in 357 Magnum) 1275.00
Model G-WM10 (10″ barrel in 45 Win Mag, 45 ACP, or 357/45 Grizzly Win Mag 1313.00
Model G357M10 (10″ barrel in 357 Magnum) 1337.50

6½″ BARREL

8 ″ BARREL

10 ″ BARREL

LLAMA REVOLVERS

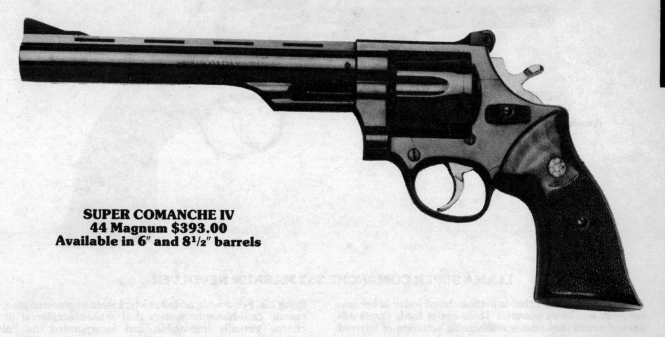

SUPER COMANCHE IV
44 Magnum $393.00
Available in 6″ and 8¹/₂″ barrels

LLAMA SUPER COMANCHE 357 MAGNUM REVOLVER

Built on a massive, heat-forged, high tensile strength steel frame. Specifically designed to absorb the maximum amount of recoil. This feature greatly reduces muzzle jump, provides greater balance, control and accuracy, and a longer firing life. Llama's .357 Magnum is a perfect blend of power and precision.

Up front there's a target-quality, precision-bored, heavyweight barrel with a solid shroud to protect the ejector rod. The frame forestrap and the integral ventilated rib are matte finished to reduce glare.

Adjustable square-notch rear sight with a ramp front sight.

The hammer and trigger are serrated for greater comfort and control.

Internally, every part is finely fitted and polished for a slick, smooth operation and a trigger pull that's crisp and clean. Like all Comanches, the .357 Magnum has a floating firing pin for greater safety and dependability.

The walnut grips are generously oversized with deep checkering.

LLAMA SUPER COMANCHE 44 MAGNUM

If ever a handgun was conceived, designed and built to fit the requirements of big bore handgunners, this one is it. The frame, for example, is massive. The weight and balance are such that the heavy recoil generated by the powerful .44 Magnum cartridge is easily and comfortably controlled.

Instead of a single cylinder latch, the Llama has two. In addition to the conventional center pin at the rear of the ratchet, there's a second latch up front that locks the crane to the frame, resulting in a safer, more secure lockup.

To minimize leading and to enhance accuracy, Llama has perfected a new honing process that imparts a mirror-smooth finish to the bore.

Additional features include a precision-lapped, heavyweight bull barrel with target accuracy. A matte finish, ventilated rib for more efficient heat dissipation, less glare and less target mirage. Oversized grips that soak up recoil for better control and a faster recovery for a second shot. A super-wide trigger for a more comfortable, controlled pull.

A three-point crane/cylinder provides support for a stronger, more rigid lockup.

The finish is highly polished and deeply blued with genuine walnut grips.

LLAMA REVOLVERS

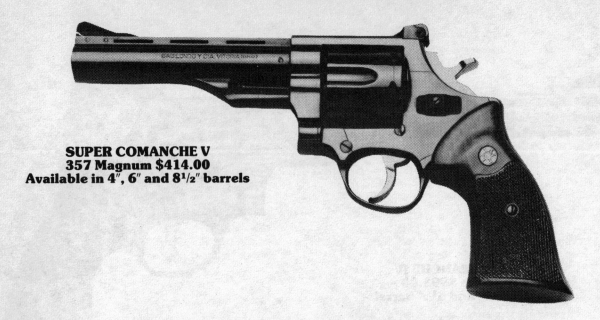

SUPER COMANCHE V
357 Magnum $414.00
Available in 4″, 6″ and 8¹/₂″ barrels

LLAMA SUPER COMANCHE 357 MAGNUM REVOLVER

The 357 ammunition that is manufactured today is becoming more and more powerful. These hotter loads create additional recoil that causes undesirable battering of internal parts and excessive stretching of the frame. As a result, shooting accuracy as well as the average firing life of the traditional 357 has been decreased.

Llama engineers built this all new 357 on the big, brawny Super Comanche frame. This frame, forged for strength, absorbs the maximum amount of recoil, reduces muzzle jump, provides greater balance, control and accuracy, and a longer firing life. For double added safety, Llama engineered an eccentric cam-hammer system that makes accidental discharge virtually impossible, and incorporated the "old reliable" triple lock crane cylinder support for additional locking strength.

And to satisfy those shooters who prefer a lighter, more compact gun, Llama engineers designed a second all-new 357, built on a medium weight frame, which also features the eccentric cam-hammer system, perfect balance and true accuracy.

	Super Comanche .44 Mag.		Super Comanche .357 Mag.		
TYPE:	Double action		Double action		
CALIBERS:	.44 Magnum		.357 Magnum		
BARREL LENGTH:	6″	8¹/₂″	4″	6″	8¹/₂″
NUMBER OF SHOTS:	6		6		
FRAME:	Forged high tensile strength steel.		Forged high tensile strength steel.		
ACTION:	Double action		Double action		
TRIGGER:	Smooth extra wide		Smooth extra wide		
HAMMER:	Wide spur, deep positive serrations.		Wide spur, deep positive serrations.		
SIGHTS:	Rear-click adjustable for windage and elevation, leaf serrated to cut down on glare. Front-ramped blade.		Rear-click adjustable for windage and elevation, leaf serrated to cut down on glare. Front-ramped blade.		
SIGHT RADIUS:	8″	10³/₈″	6″	8″	10³/₈″
GRIPS:	Oversized target, walnut. Checkered.		Oversized target, walnut. Checkered.		
WEIGHT:	3 lbs., 2 ozs.	3 lbs., 8 ozs.	3 lbs.	3 lbs., 6 ozs.	3 lbs., 12 ozs.
OVER-ALL LENGTH:	11³/₄″	14¹/₂″	9⁷/₈″	11⁷/₈″	14¹/₂″
FINISH:	High polished, deep blue		High polished, deep blue		
SAFETY FEATURE:	The hammer is mounted on an eccentric cam, the position of which is controlled by the trigger. Only when the latter is fully depressed can the firing pin contact the primer.				

LLAMA REVOLVERS

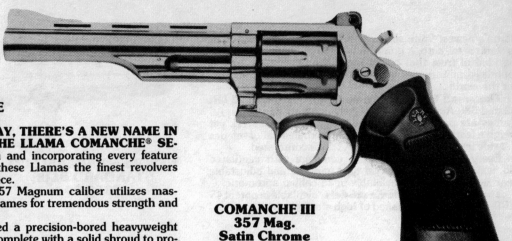

LLAMA COMANCHE

IN REVOLVERS TODAY, THERE'S A NEW NAME IN EXCELLENCE, IT'S THE LLAMA COMANCHE® SERIES. Designed for you and incorporating every feature worth having to make these Llamas the finest revolvers made today . . . at any price.

The sledgehammer 357 Magnum caliber utilizes massively forged solid-steel frames for tremendous strength and enduring reliability.

Up front, Llama added a precision-bored heavyweight barrel of target quality, complete with a solid shroud to protect the ejector rod, and a raised ventilated-rib that dissipates heat from the barrel to give you a clear, sharp sight image even when the action gets hot.

On the inside, everything is finely fitted and polished, for a double action that's slick and smooth, and a single-action trigger pull that's light, crisp and clean. Llama gave all Comanches a floating firing pin for greater safety and dependability.

COMANCHE III
357 Mag.
Satin Chrome
4″ and 6″ barrels

357 Mag. Standard Blue 4″, 6″. $301.00
357 Mag. Satin Chrome 4″, 6″ 357.00

SPECIFICATIONS COMANCHE III

CALIBERS:	**357 Magnum**
BARREL LENGTH:	4 and 6-inch
NUMBER OF SHOTS:	6 shots
FRAME:	Forged high hensile strength steel. Serrated front and back strap.
ACTION:	Double-action.
TRIGGER:	Wide grooved target trigger
HAMMER:	Wide spur target hammer with serrated gripping surface.
SIGHTS:	Square notch rear sight with windage and elevation adjustments; serrated quick-draw front sight on ramp.
SIGHT RADIUS:	With 4-inch barrel—5³/₄″; with 6-inch barrel—7³/₄″.
GRIPS:	Oversized target, walnut. Checkered.
WEIGHT:	w/4″ bbl.—2 lbs., 4ozs. w/6″ bbl.—2 lbs., 7 ozs.
OVER-ALL LENGTH:	With 4-inch barrel—9¹/₄″; with 6-inch barrel—11″.
FINISH:	High-polished, deep blue. Deluxe models; satin chrome (.357 w/4″ & 6″ bbl.)
SAFETY FEATURE:	The hammer is mounted on an eccentric cam, the position of which is controlled by the trigger. Only when the latter is fully depressed can the firing pin contact the primer.

LLAMA AUTOMATIC PISTOLS

Llama's newest 9mm single action is a compact version of its 9mm semi-auto, a gun which over the years has earned the kind of trust that has made it the issued side arm of countless military and law enforcement agencies throughout the world

The small-frame Llama models, available in 22 LR, 32 and 380 Auto., are impressively compact handguns. All frames are precision machined of high strength steel, yet weigh a featherlight 23 ounces. A full complement of safeties . . . side lever, half-cock and grip . . . is incorporated.

Every small-frame Llama is complete with ventilated rib, wide-spur serrated target-type hammer and adjustable rear sight. NEW. Also available in 45 caliber automatic.

The large-frame Llama models, available in potent 45 ACP, are completely crafted of high strength steel.

**NEW 9mm PARABELLUM
STANDARD BLUE
$352.00**

**LLAMA COMPACT 45
$352.00**

**380 Caliber Double Action
$385.00**

**LLAMA SMALL-FRAME
AUTOMATIC WITH
DEEP BLUE FINISH
22 Caliber and 380 Caliber
$299.00**

LLAMA AUTOMATIC PISTOLS

**LLAMA SMALL-FRAME
AUTOMATIC PISTOL IN
SATIN CHROME FINISH
22 and 380 Caliber
$377.00**

LLAMA Automatic Pistol Specifications

TYPE:	Small Frame Auto Pistols		Compact Frame Auto Pistols		Large Frame Auto Pistols
CALIBERS:	22 LR	380 Auto.	9mm Parabellum	45 Auto	45 Auto.
FRAME:	Precision machined form high strength steel. Serrated front strap, checkered (curved) backstrap.		Precision machined form high strength steel. Serrated front strap, checkered (curved) backstrap.		Precision machined from high strength steel. Plain front strap, checkered (curved) backstrap.
TRIGGER:	Serrated		Serrated		Serrated
HAMMER:	External. Wide spur, serrated.		External. Wide spur, serrated.		External. Wide spur, serrated.
OPERATION:	Straight blow-back.		Locked breech.		Locked breech.
LOADED CHAMBER INDICATOR:	No	Yes	No	No	Yes
SAFETIES:	Side lever thumb safety, grip safety.		Side lever thumb safety, grip safety.		Side lever thumb safety, grip safety.
GRIPS:	Modified thumbrest black plastic grips.		Genuine walnut on blue models. Genuine teakwood on satin chrome.		Genuine walnut on blue models. Genuine teakwood on satin chrome.
SIGHTS:	Square notch rear, and Patridge-type front, screw adjustable rear sight for windage		Square notch rear, and Patridge-type front, screw adjustable rear sight for windage.		Square notch rear, and Patridge-type front, screw adjustable rear sight for windage.
SIGHT RADIUS:	4 1/4"		6 1/4"		6 1/4"
MAGAZINE CAPACITY:	8-shot	7-shot	9-shot	7-shot	7-shot
WEIGHT:	23 ounces		34 ounces		36 ounces
BARREL LENGTH:	3 11/16"		5"		5"
OVERALL LENGTH:	6 1/2"		7 7/8"		8 1/2"
HEIGHT:	4 3/8"		5 7/16"		5 1/3"
FINISH:	Std. models; High-polished, deep blue. Deluxe models; satin chrome (22, 380, 45)		Std. models; High-polished, deep blue. Deluxe models; satin chrome (22, 380, 45)		Std. models; High-polished, deep blue. Deluxe models; satin chrome (22, 380, 45)

LLAMA AUTOMATIC PISTOLS

Machined and polished to perfection. These truly magnificent firearms come complete with ventilated rib for maximum heat dissipation, wide-spur checkered target-type hammer, adjustable rear sight and genuine walnut grips.

In addition to High Polished Deep Blue, the following superb handguns are available in handsome Satin Chrome 22 LR, 32, 380 Auto., 45 ACP.

**LLAMA LARGE-FRAME
AUTOMATIC PISTOL IN
SATIN CHROME FINISH**
45 Auto Caliber
$471.00

**LLAMA LARGE-FRAME
AUTOMATIC WITH
DEEP BLUE FINISH**
45 Auto Caliber
$352.00
NEW: 38 SUPER $352.00

LLAMA PISTOLS

MODEL M-82 (9mm) DOUBLE ACTION
$751.00

SPECIFICATIONS

Caliber: 9mm Parabellum
Magazine: 15 cartridges (15 + 1 shot)
Barrel length: 4¼″
No. of barreling grooves: 6
Overall length: 8″
Height: 5⁵/₁₆″
Maximum width: 1³/₈″
Weight: 39 oz. (empty)
Sights: High visibility, 3-dot sights; rear sight drift adjustable
Sight radius: 6″
Grips: Matte black polymer
Stocks: Plastic
Finish: Blued satin

After nearly a decade of research, development and testing, the new Llama M-82 is being offered to the gun buying public. Representing the state-of-the-art in double action, semiauto pistol design, this handgun offers a unique blend of highly innovative technical features, combined with the kind of ergonomic design and practical performance that are so important in day-to-day use. It's the kind demanded by military and law enforcement personnel, as well as by competitive combat shooters and otherwise knowledgeable handgunners.

Whatever criteria are used in judging a DA semiauto—whether accuracy, reliability, simplicity of design, looks, compactness, quality of fit, or finish—all are effectively combined in the M-82. The following features indicate why pistol experts are already hailing this new Llama as the world's finest production combat handgun.

1. MINIMAL BARREL/SLIDE DISPLACEMENT: As the slide moves rearward during the firing cycle, the lineal displacement required to unlock the action is but a fraction of that in other double action designs. This translates into less wear and tear on the mechanism, as well as allowing tighter tolerances. That, in turn, means greater accuracy, greater durability.

2. POSITIVE SAFETY MECHANISM: Even when at rest and with the safety disengaged, the hammer does not contact the firing pin, making this gun one of the safest handguns available today.

3. TWIN LUG LOCK-UP: Unlike other DA's, which rely on a single locking lug engagement in the ceiling of the slide, the M-82 has two lugs in the "three and nine o'clock" position. This unique system provides greater strength, greater rigidity. . . . and greater accuracy.

4. FULL-LENGTH GUIDE RAILS: For more positive, accurate alignment of barrel, slide and frame, the Llama's slide is engaged by guide rails the entire length of its movement (some autos allow as much as two inches of unsupported slide movement).

5. MAXIMUM FIREPOWER: The M-82's staggered magazine holds 15 rounds, plus one in the chamber. This potent firepower is made possible by an overall grip dimension small enough to fit comfortably in the average hand.

6. RECESSED BREECH FACE: Unlike other guns featuring flat breech faces, the Llama's is recessed, much like most modern high-powered rifles. This additional support in the critical case head area means greater safety.

7. AMBIDEXTROUS SAFETY: Allows the M-82 to be used with equal speed and convenience by both right- and left-handed shooters.

8. CHANGEABLE MAGAZINE RELEASE: Normally positioned on the left side of the grip for right-handed shooters, the clip release button on the M-82 can be changed easily to the other side for southpaw use.

9. ARTICULATED FIRING PIN: Another excellent Llama feature is its virtually unbreakable firing pin. In fact, it's guaranteed not to break—for life.

10. COMPACT SIZE: Despite its 16-shot capability, the M-82 is neither heavy nor bulky. Its overall dimensions are short—8¼″ in length, 5⁵/₆″ in height, and 1³/₈″ in extreme width. Empty weight is 39 ounces.

11. ENLARGED EJECTION PORT: To preclude any sort of ejection problems brought about by variation in loads or in slide velocity, the ejection port is slightly oversize.

12. MODULAR GRIP DESIGN: The hammer strut and main spring are housed in a separate sub-assembly which easily detaches from the frame for routine cleaning and maintenance.

13. INSTANT DISASSEMBLY: The M-82 can be field stripped in less than five seconds—without tools.

MAGNUM RESEARCH
DESERT EAGLE PISTOL
.357/.44 MAGNUM

SPECIFICATIONS	.357 MAGNUM	.44 MAGNUM
Length, with 6 inch barrel	10.6 inches	10.6 inches
Height	5.6 inches	5.7 inches
Width	1.25 inches	1.25 inches
Trigger reach	2.75 inches	2.75 inches
Sight radius (with 6 inch barrel)	8.5 inches	8.5 inches
Additional available barrels	14 inch	14 inch & 10 inch
Weight	See below	See below
Bore rifling — Six rib	Polygonal: 1 turn in 14 inches	Polygonal: 1 turn in 18 inches
Method of operation	Gas operated	Gas operated
Method of locking	Rotating bolt	Rotating bolt
Magazine capacity	9 rounds (plus one in chamber)	8 rounds (plus one in chamber)

DESERT EAGLE — WEIGHT TABLES
.357 Magnum

Frame	Without Magazine		With Empty Magazine	
	6" Barrel	14" Barrel	6" Barrel	14" Barrel
	ounces	ounces	ounces	ounces
Aluminum	47.8	55.0	51.9	59.1
Steel	58.3	65.5	62.4	96.6
Stainless	58.3	65.5	62.4	69.6

.44 Magnum

Frame	Without Magazine		With Empty Magazine	
	6" Barrel	14" Barrel	6" Barrel	14" Barrel
	ounces	ounces	ounces	ounces
Aluminum	52.3	61.0	56.4	65.1
Steel	62.8	71.5	66.9	75.6
Stainless	62.8	71.5	66.9	75.6

357 MAGNUM $589.00
(Alloy Frame Optional)
$589.00 w/Alloy Frame
$629.00 w/Stainless Steel
$803.00 w/14" barrel

DESERT EAGLE
44 MAGNUM SEMIAUTO PISTOL
(Standard Parkerized Finish)
$717.00 w/Alloy Frame
$750.00 w/Stainless Steel
$717.00 w/6" barrel
$931.00 w/10" barrel
$941.00 w/14" barrel

DESERT EAGLE
44 MAGNUM (14" Barrel)

MITCHELL ARMS

SINGLE ACTION ARMY REVOLVERS

The Mitchell Arms Single Action Army Model Revolver is a modern version of the original "gun that won the West," adopted by the U.S. Army in 1873. Faithful to the original design, these revolvers are made of modern materials and use up-to-date technology; for example, a special safety device is built into the hammer assembly as a backstop to the traditional safety.

SPECIFICATIONS

Calibers: 22 LR, 357 Mag., 44 Mag., 45 Colt
Barrel lengths: 4³/₄″, 5¹/₂″, 6¹/₂″, (7¹/₂″ in 357 Mag., 44 Mag. and 45 Colt)
Frame: Forged steel, fully machined with traditional color casehardening. Two-piece style backstrap made of solid brass.
Action: Traditional single action with safety position and half-cock position for loading and unloading.
Sights: Rear sight is fully adjustable for windage and elevation. Front sight is two-step ramp style with non-glare serrations. Fixed sight models feature deep notch with fixed blade front sight.

Grip: One-piece solid walnut grip built in the style of the old black powder revolvers.
Accuracy: High-grade steel barrel honed for accuracy with smooth lands and grooves; precise alignment between cylinder and barrel. Fully qualified for big game hunting or silhouette shooting.
Prices:
Fixed Sight Models . . . . $265.21—308.75
Target (Adjust.) Sight Models . . . . 282.20—331.01
Dual Cylinder Models (Target Sights) . . . . 303.52—335.36
Also available: **SPECIAL SILHOUETTE MODELS** 44 Magnum/44-40 caliber; 10″, 12″ and 18″ barrel lengths. **$399.95**

MOA MAXIMUM PISTOL

MAXIMUM

This new single shot pistol with its unique falling block action performs like a finely tuned rifle. The single piece receiver of chromoly steel is mated to a Douglas barrel for optimum accuracy and strength.

SPECIFICATIONS

Calibers: 22 Hornet to 358 Win.
Barrel lengths: 10″ and 14″
Weight: 3 lb. 13 oz. (10″); 4 lb. 3 oz. (14″)
Price: $499.00
Also available: **Maximum Carbine** w/18″ barrel: **$575.00**

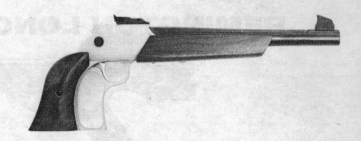

NEW ENGLAND FIREARMS

DOUBLE ACTION REVOLVERS
$110.00

SPECIFICATIONS

Calibers: 22 LR, 32 H&R Magnum or 32 S&W
Capacity: 9 rounds (22 LR); 5 rounds (32 H&R Mag.)
Barrel lengths: 2¹/₂″ or 4″
Overall length: 7″ with 2¹/₂″ barrel
Weight: 23 oz. (32 H&R Mag., 2¹/₂″ bbl.), 25 oz. (22 LR, 2¹/₂″ bbl.), 26 oz. (4″ bbl., either caliber)
Sights: Blade front; fixed rear sight (2¹/₂″ models) and fully adjustable (4″ models)
Finish: Blue or nickel
Grips: American walnut w/NEF medallion

NORTH AMERICAN ARMS REVOLVERS
MINI-REVOLVERS

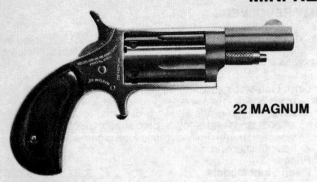

22 MAGNUM

22 LR STAINLESS STEEL

5-SHOT MINI-REVOLVERS
SPECIFICATIONS
Caliber: 22 Short, 22 LR, 22 WMR
Barrel length: 1¹/₈″, 1⁵/₈″ and 2¹/₂″
Grips: Laminated wood
Sights: Blade front, notched rear
Safety: Hammer rests in "half-way notches" to insure safety with all chambers loaded; gun fires only when cylinder is aligned

Prices: **$135.00** 22 Short w/1¹/₈″ barrel; **$136.00** 22 LR w/ 1¹/₈″ barrel; **$137.00** 22 LR w/1⁵/₈″ barrel; **$156.00** 22 Mag. w/1⁵/₈″ barrel; **$171.00** 22 Mag. w/2¹/₂″ barrel
Also available: Collector Set—three-gun set with matching serial numbers, walnut display case, high polish finish w/ matte contours **$570.00.**
Deluxe Collector Set includes high polish finish over entire gun **$622.00**

REMINGTON LONG RANGE PISTOL

**MODEL XP-100 BOLT
ACTION PISTOL**

MODEL XP-100 BOLT ACTION PISTOLS

This unique single-shot centerfire, bolt-action pistol has become a legend for its strength, precision, balance and accuracy. Now chambered for the 35 Remington and 223 Remington with a 14¹/₂-inch barrel, it's also available in 7mm BR Rem. Many consider this latter configuration to be the ideal factory-made metallic silhouette handgun for "unlimited" events.

All three "XP-100" handguns have one-piece DuPont "Zytel" nylon stocks with universal grips, two-position thumb safety switches, receivers drilled and tapped for scope mounts or receiver sights, and match-type grooved triggers.

Calibers: 35 Remington, 223 Remington, 7mm BR. **Barrel length:** 14¹/₂″. **Overall length:** 21¹/₄″. **Weight:** 4¹/₈ lbs.
Prices:

7mm BR	$380.00
223 Remington	373.00
35 Remington	393.00
Custom Long Range Model (223 Rem.-HB, 7mm-08 Rem., 35 Rem.)	907.00

MODEL XP-100 SILHOUETTE TARGET PISTOL & "VARMINT SPECIAL"

This unique single-shot centerfire, bolt-action pistol has become a legend for its strength, precision, balance and accuracy. Now chambered for the 35 Remington and 223 Remington with a 14¹/₂-inch barrel, it's also available in 7mm BR Rem. Many consider this latter configuration to be the ideal factory-made metallic silhouette handgun for "unlimited" events.

All three "XP-100" handguns have one-piece DuPont "Zytel" nylon stocks with universal grips, two-position thumb safety switches, receivers drilled and tapped for scope mounts or receiver sights, and match-type grooved triggers.

Caliber: 35 Remington, 223 Remington, 7mm BR. **Barrel length:** 14¹/₂″. **Overall length:** 21¹/₄″. **Weight:** 4¹/₈ lbs. **Price:** **$367.00** (7mm BR); **$359.00** (223 Rem.); **$380.00** (35 Rem.). Also available: **Custom Long Range** model. **Price: $887.00.**

ROSSI REVOLVERS

MODEL 68
$183.00

SPECIFICATIONS
Caliber: 38 Special
Barrel length: 2″ and 3″
Overall length: 6¹/₂″ (2″ barrel); 7¹/₂″ (3″ barrel)
Weight: 21 oz. (2″ barrel); 23 oz. (3″ barrel)
Capacity: 5 rounds
Finish: Blue
Also available in nickel (3″ barrel only) **$193.00**

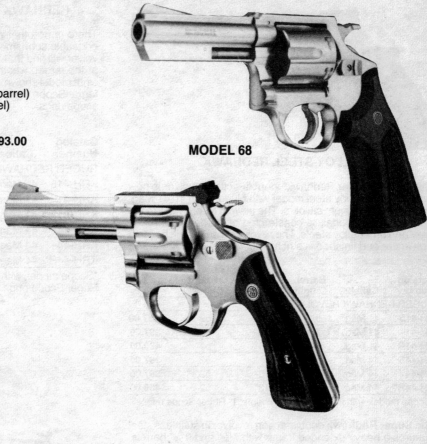

MODEL 68

MODEL 511 SPORTSMAN'S 22
$235.00

SPECIFICATIONS
Caliber: 22 LR
Barrel length: 4″
Overall length: 9″
Weight: 30 oz.
Capacity: 6 rounds
Finish: Stainless steel

MODEL M951 (not shown)
$235.00

SPECIFICATIONS
Caliber: 38 Special
Capacity: 6 rounds
Barrel length: 3″ and 4″
Overall length: 8″ and 9″
Weight: 27¹/₂ oz. and 30 oz.
Also available: **Model 971** (4″ barrel) 357 Magnum **$249.00**

MODEL M88
$210.00

SPECIFICATIONS
Caliber: 38 Special
Barrel length: 2″, 3″
Capacity: 5 rounds, swing-out cylinder
Weight: 21 oz.
Sights: Ramp front, square notch rear adjustable for windage
Finish: Stainless steel

MODEL 851
$249.00

SPECIFICATIONS
Capacity: 6 rounds
Barrel length: 3″ and 4″
Overall length: 8″ and 9″
Weight: 27¹/₂ oz. and 30 oz.
Frame: Medium

RUGER REVOLVERS

ALLOY STEEL REDHAWK

The popular Ruger Redhawk® double-action revolver is now available in an alloy steel model with blued finish in .41 Magnum and .44 Magnum calibers. The newest Redhawk, like the stainless steel model, is constructed of hardened chrome-moly and other alloy steels. The revolver is satin polished to a high lustre and finished in a rich blue.

Catalog Number	Caliber	Barrel Length	Overall Length	Approx. Weight (Ounces)	Price
RUGER REDHAWK REVOLVER					
RH-415	41 Mag.	5¹/₂″	11″	52	$397.00
RH-41	41 Mag.	7¹/₂″	13″	52	397.00
RH-41R*	41 Mag.	7¹/₂″	13″	52	430.00
RH-445	44 Mag.	5¹/₂″	11″	52	397.00
RH-44	44 Mag.	7¹/₂″	13″	52	397.00
RH-44R*	44 Mag.	7¹/₂″	13″	52	430.00

*Scope model, with Integral Scope Mounts, 1″ Ruger Scope rings.

The **Super Redhawk** double-action revolver in stainless steel features a heavy extended frame with 7¹/₂″ and 9¹/₂″ barrels. Cushioned grip panels contain Goncalo Alves wood grip panel inserts to provide comfortable, nonslip hold.

REDHAWK DOUBLE-ACTION REVOLVER

There is no other revolver like the Ruger Redhawk. Knowledgeable sportsmen reaching for perfection in a big bore revolver will find that the Redhawk demonstrates its superiority at the target, whether silhouette shooting or hunting. Scope sight model shown above incorporates the patented Ruger integral Scope Mounting System with 1″ stainless steel Ruger scope rings.

Catalog Number	Caliber	Barrel Length	Overall Length	Approx. Weight (Ounces)	Price
RUGER REDHAWK REVOLVER					
KRH-415	41 Mag.	5¹/₂″	11″	52	$447.50
KRH-41	41 Mag.	7¹/₂″	13″	52	447.50
KRH-41R*	41 Mag.	7¹/₂″	13″	52	482.50
KRH-445	44 Mag.	5¹/₂″	11″	52	447.50
KRH-44	44 Mag.	7¹/₂″	13″	52	447.50
KRH-44R*	44 Mag.	7¹/₂″	13″	52	482.50

*Scope model, with Integral Scope Mounts, 1″ Stainless Steel Ruger Scope rings.

SUPER REDHAWK
DOUBLE ACTION REVOLVER

SPECIFICATIONS
Caliber: 44 Magnum
Barrel length: 7¹/₂″ and 9¹/₂″
Overall length: 13″ w/7¹/₂″ bbl.; 15″ w/9¹/₂″ bbl.
Weight (empty): 3 lbs. 5 oz. (7¹/₂″ bbl.); 3 lbs. 10 oz. (9¹/₂″ bbl.)
Sight radius: 9¹/₂″ (7¹/₂″ bbl.); 11¹/₄″ (9¹/₂″ bbl.)
Finish: Stainless steel; satin polished

KSRH-7 (7¹/₂″ barrel) $510.00
KSRH-9 (9¹/₂″ barrel) 510.00

RUGER REVOLVERS

BLACKHAWK SINGLE-ACTION REVOLVER

SPECIFICATIONS

Caliber: 357 Magnum (interchangeable with 38 Special); 41 Magnum

Barrel lengths: $4^5/_8''$ and $6^1/_2''$

Frame: Chrome molybdenum steel with bridge reinforcement and rear-sight guard

Springs: Music wire springs throughout

Weight: 40 oz. with $4^5/_8''$ barrel and 42 oz. with $6^1/_2''$ barrel (in 357 Mag.); 38 oz. with $4^5/_8''$ barrel and 40 oz. with $6^1/_2''$ barrel (41 Mag.)

Sights: Patridge style, ramp front matted blade $1/_8''$ wide; rear sight click adjustable for windage and elevation

Grips: Genuine walnut

Finish: Polished and blued or stainless steel (357 Mag. only)

Catalog No.	Specifications	Prices
BN-34	357 Mag.; 38 Special interchangeably; $4^5/_8''$ barrel	$286.10
KBN-34	Same as above in stainless steel	352.43
BN-36	357 Mag.; 38 Special interchangeably; $6^1/_2''$ barrel	286.10
KBN-36	Same as above in stainless steel	352.43
BN-34X/36X	Same as BN34/BN36 fitted with 9mm Parabellum extra cylinder (not available in stainless steel).	299.70
BN-41	41 Magnum; $4^5/_8''$ barrel	286.10
BN-42	41 Magnum; $6^1/_2''$	286.10
BN-44	45 Long Colt; $4^5/_8''$	286.10
BN-45	45 Long Colt; $7^1/_2''$ barrel	286.10
S-45N	44 Magnum; $5^1/_2''$ barrel	330.23

SUPER BLACKHAWK SINGLE-ACTION REVOLVER

SPECIFICATIONS

Caliber: 44 Magnum; interchangeable with 44 Special

Barrel: $5^1/_2''$, $7^1/_2''$, $10^1/_2''$

Frame: Chrome molybdenum steel with bridge reinforcement and rear sight guard

Springs: Music wire springs throughout

Weight: 48 oz. ($7^1/_2''$ bbl.) and 51 oz. ($10^1/_2''$ bbl.)

Sights: Patridge style, ramp front matted blade $1/_8''$ wide; rear sight click and adjustable for windage and elevation

Grip frame: Chrome molybdenum steel enlarged and contoured to minimize recoil effect

Trigger: Wide spur, low contour, sharply serrated for convenient cocking with minimum disturbance of grip

Overall length: $13^3/_8''$

Finish: Stainless steel

KS47N—$7^1/_2''$ barrel with steel grip frame $360.75
KS411N—$10^1/_2''$ barrel with steel grip frame 360.75
S47N—$7^1/_2''$ barrel, with steel grip frame 330.23
S411N—$10^1/_2''$ barrel, with steel grip frame 330.23

RUGER REVOLVERS

NEW MODEL SINGLE-SIX REVOLVER

Caliber: 22 LR, 22 Short, 22 Long, 22 Win. Mag. Rimfire (fitted with WMR cylinder). **Barrel lengths:** 4⅝″, 5½″, 6½″, 9½″ (stainless steel model in 5½″ and 6½″ lengths only). **Weight** (approx.): 33 oz. (with 5½″ barrel). **Sights:** Patridge-type ramp front sight; rear sight click adjustable for elevation and windage; protected by integral frame ribs. **Finish:** Blue or stainless steel. **Price:** $245.03 ($308.58 in stainless steel).

NEW MODEL SINGLE-SIX SSM™ REVOLVER
$235.32

Caliber: 32 H&R Magnum; also handles 32 S&W and 32 S&W Long. **Barrel lengths:** 4⅝″, 5½″, 6½″, 9½″. **Weight** (approx.): 34 oz. with 6½″ barrel.

NEW MODEL BISLEY REVOLVER
$340.77 (not shown)

Calibers: 357 Mag., 41 Mag., 44 Mag., 45 Long Colt. **Barrel length:** 7½″. **Weight** (approx.): 48 oz. **Sights:** Adjustable rear sight, ramp-style front sight. **Special features:** Unfluted cylinder rollmarked with classic foliate engraving pattern (or fluted cylinder without engraving); hammer is low with smoothly curved, deeply checkered wide spur positioned for easy cocking.

Also available in 22LR and 32 Mag. **Weight:** 41 oz. **Barrel length:** 6½″. **Sights:** Adjustable or fixed. **Price:** $286.38.

MODEL BN-31
BLACKHAWK SINGLE-ACTION REVOLVER
(In 30 Carbine Caliber) $275.00

Caliber: 30 Carbine. **Barrel length:** 7½″; 6-groove rifling; 20-inch twist. **Overall length:** 13⅛″. **Weight:** 44 oz. **Springs:** Unbreakable music wire springs used throughout; no leaf springs. **Screws:** For security, Nylok® screws are used at all five locations that might be affected by recoil. **Sights:** Patridge-style, ramp front sight with ⅛″ wide blade, matted to eliminate glare; rear sight adjustable for windage and elevation. **Ignition system:** Independent alloy steel firing pin, mounted in frame, transfer bar. **Frame:** Same cylinder frame as 44 Mag. Super Blackhawk. **Grips:** Genuine walnut. **Finish:** Polished, blued and anodized.

RUGER 22 AUTOMATIC PISTOLS

**RUGER MARK II
TARGET MODEL**

SPECIFICATIONS
Same as for Mark II Model with the following exceptions. **Barrel:** 6⁷/₈" tapered, button rifled. **Weight:** Approx. 2⁵/₈ lbs. **Overall length:** 11¹/₈". **Sights:** Patridge-type front blade, .125" wide, undercut to prevent glare; rear sight with click adjustments for windage and elevation. **Sight radius:** 9¹/₄" for 6⁷/₈" barrel. Catalog No. MK-678 blued finish and KMK-678 Stainless Steel.

MK-678. . . . . $249.75
KMK-678 . . . . 316.35

**RUGER MARK II
STANDARD MODEL**

SPECIFICATIONS
Caliber: 22 Long Rifle only, standard or high velocity. **Barrel:** 4³/₄" or 6" length; medium weight; 6-groove rifling; 14" twist. **Weight:** 2¹/₄ lbs. with 4³/₄" barrel. **Overall length:** 8⁵/₁₆" with 4³/₄" barrel; 10⁵/₁₆" with 6" barrel. **Sights:** Front sight is fixed, .093" wide blade Patridge-type; square notch rear sight is dovetail mounted and can be adjusted for windage. **Sight radius:** 7¹/₂" with 4³/₄" barrel. Catalog No. MK-4 (4³/₄" barrel) blued finish, MK-6 (6" barrel) blued finish, KMK-4 (4³/₄" barrel) Stainless Steel; KMK-6 (6" barrel) Stainless Steel.

MK-4, MK-6 . . . . $199.80
KMK-4, KMK-6 . . . . 266.40

**RUGER MARK II
BULL BARREL MODEL**

The Mark II Bull barrel pistol is identical to the Mark II Target Model except that it is equipped with a heavier Bull barrel offered in two lengths, 5¹/₂ inches/10 inches. The Bull barrel configuration was developed to meet the needs of those shooters who prefer a greater concentration of weight at the muzzle. The longer barrel model meets all IHMSA regulations.

SPECIFICATIONS
Same as for Mark II model with the following exceptions: **Barrel:** 5¹/₂" or 10"; button rifled; shorter barrel untapered, longer barrel has slight taper. **Weight:** Approx. 2⁵/₇ lbs. with 5¹/₂" barrel; 3¹/₄ lbs. with 10" barrel. **Sights:** Patridge-type front sight. Rear sight with click adjustments for windage and elevation. **Sight radius:** 7⁷/₈" for 5¹/₂" barrel, 12³/₈" for 10" barrel; blued finish. Catalog No. MK-512 5¹/₂" barrel and MK-10 10" barrel.

MK-512 and MK-10 Blued $249.75
KMK-512 and KMK-10 Stainless steel $316.35

RUGER AUTOMATIC PISTOLS

MODEL P-85 AUTO PISTOL

SPECIFICATIONS
Caliber: 9mm. **Action:** Double action. **Capacity:** 15 rounds.
Weight: 2.38 lbs. (loaded). **Barrel length:** 4¹/₂″. **Overall length:** 7.84″. **Sight radius:** 6.12″. **Mechanism type:** Recoil-operated, semiautomatic. **Breech locking mode:** Tilting barrel, link actuated.

P-85 . . . . $295.00
With plastic case and extra magazine 325.00

MARK II GOVERNMENT
TARGET MODEL (not shown)

SPECIFICATIONS
Caliber: 22 Rimfire. **Capacity:** 10-shot magazine. **Barrel length:** 6⁷/₈″ bull barrel. **Overall length:** 11¹/₈″. **Weight:** 47¹/₂ oz. (loaded). **Sight radius:** 9¹/₄″; laser sighting device.

MODEL MK678G $288.60

GP-100 357 MAGNUM

The first in an entirely new Ruger design series, the GP-100 is presented as a complete family of double action models in three basic frame sizes handling all popular caliber handgun ammunition, from 22 rimfire to 44 Magnum. The GP-100 is designed for the unlimited use of 357 Magnum ammunition in all factory loadings; it combines strength and reliability with accuracy and shooting comfort.

SPECIFICATIONS

BLUED FINISH GP-100 $360.40		STAINLESS STEEL GP-100 $392.20	
CAT. NO.	BARREL	CAT. NO.	BARREL
GP-141	4″ Heavy	KGP-141	4″ Heavy
GP-160	6″	KGP-160	6″
GP-161	6″ Heavy	KGP-161	6″ Heavy

SAKO OLYMPIC PISTOL

Three different pistols on the same frame. Take your choice of three conversion units in 22 Short, 22LR and 32 S&W Long. No need to adjust sights when you change caliber. Free travel resistance is adjustable per conversion unit. Each caliber has its own magazine. Carrying case and tool set standard equipment.

A choice of three conversion units for the frame of Sako's 22-32 and **Triace** conversion pistols in calibers 22 Short, 22 LR and 32 S&W Long. Each conversion unit is equipped with its own sights—no need to adjust the sights when you change the caliber. The free travel resistance is adjustable per conversion unit. Each caliber has its own magazines.

To change caliber, simply remove the magazine, release mounting screw, and pull the conversion unit forward. Mount the other unit and tighten the mounting screw, then insert the magazine of the caliber selected.

SAKO TRIACE: Grip angle 65°; frame made from investment casting steel; magazines of spring steel, lips flexible; standard equipment carrying case with tool set and cleaning set.

SAKO 22-32: Grip angle 60°; frame made from machined steel; grip anatomically designed in ABS plastic; hard wearing magazines are heat treated; carrying case and tool set are standard equipment.

Additional features: Click adjustment for sights and sear engagement; sear spring adjustment; free travel length adjustment; weight of trigger pull adjustable for each caliber; action parts made of hardened and tempered steel; non-reflecting matte black upper surface and chromium-plated slide. **Triace** has adjustable wooden grip, bolt hold open lever, and magazine for six cartridges on centerfire pistol.

Price: $3995.00 for 3 barrel set
2325.00 for pistol only

SAKO TRIACE
SPECIFICATIONS

International Standard		Rimfire	Centerfire
Caliber	22LR	22 Short	32 S&W Long
Barrel length	6 inches	6 inches	6 inches
Sight distance	8.25 inches	8.25-8.85 inches	8.25 inches
Capacity	5 rounds	5 rounds	6 rounds
Weight	46 oz.	44 oz.	48 oz.
Grip angle	65°	65°	65°

SAKO 22-32
SPECIFICATIONS

International Standard		Rimfire	Centerfire
Caliber	22LR	22 Short	32 S&W Long
Barrel length	6 inches	8.85 inches	6 inches
Sight distance	8.25 inches	8.85 inches	8.25 inches
Capacity	5 rounds	5 rounds	5 rounds
Weight	45.8 oz.	44 oz.	47.6 oz.
Grip angle	60°	60°	60°

SIG SAUER DOUBLE ACTION PISTOLS

MODEL 220 "EUROPEAN"

MODEL 220 "EUROPEAN"

SPECIFICATIONS
Caliber: 38 Super, 9mm Parabellum, 45ACP
Capacity: 9 rounds (7 rounds in 45ACP)
Barrel length: 4.4"
Overall length: 8"
Weight: 26 1/2 oz.
Finish: Blue
Price: $665.00
   45 ACP Electroless Nickel with "Siglite" night sights: **$890.00**
"AMERICAN" Model (in 45 ACP): **$720.00**
   With "Siglite" night sights: **$820.00**

MODEL 225 (not shown)

SPECIFICATIONS
Caliber: 9mm Parabellum
Capacity: 8 rounds
Barrel length: 3.85"
Overall length: 7"
Weight: 26 1/2 oz.
Finish: Blue
Price: $750.00
   With "Siglite" night sights: **$850.00**

MODEL 226

SPECIFICATIONS
Caliber: 9mm Parabellum
Capacity: 15 rounds
Barrel length: 4.4"
Overall length: 7 3/4"
Weight: 30 oz.
Finish: Blue
Price: $780.00
   With "Siglite night sights: **$880.00**
   With K-Kote: **$815.00**

MODEL 226

SINGLE ACTION MODEL P210 (not shown)

SPECIFICATIONS
Caliber: 9mm
Overall length: 8 1/2"
Barrel length: 4.7"
Weight: 31.6 oz.
Capacity: 8 rounds
Price: $1,350.00

Also available: **MODEL P210-5: $1,795.00**
                  MODEL P210-6: 1,595.00

MODEL 230

MODEL 230

SPECIFICATIONS
Caliber: 380ACP
Capacity: 7 rounds
Barrel length: 3.6"
Overall length: 6.6"
Weight: 16 1/4 oz. (23 oz. in stainless steel)
Finish: Blue and stainless steel
Price: $495.00 in blue
          575.00 in stainless steel

SMITH & WESSON AUTO PISTOLS

MODEL 422
22 SINGLE ACTION
$198.00 (Fixed Sight)
$234.50 (Adjustable Sight)

Caliber: 22 LR
Capacity: 10 round (magazine furnished)
Barrel length: 4¹/₂″ and 6″
Overall length: 7¹/₂″ (4¹/₂″ barrel) and 9″ (6″ barrel)
Weight: 22 oz. (4¹/₂″ barrel) and 23 oz. (6″ barrel)
Stock: Plastic (field version) and checkered walnut w/S&W monogram (target version)
Front sight: Serrated ramp w/.125″ blade (field version); Patridge w/.125″ blade (target version)
Rear sight: Fixed sight w/.125″ blade (field version): adjustable sight w/.125″ blade (target version)
Hammer: .250″ internal
Trigger: .312″ serrated

22 CAL. AUTOMATIC PISTOL
MODEL NO. 41
$536.00 Blue Only

Caliber: 22 Long Rifle
Magazine capacity: 10 rounds
Barrel length: 5¹/₂″ and 7³/₈″
Overall length: 12″ with 7³/₈″ barrel
Sight radius: 9⁵/₁₆″ with 7³/₈″ barrel
Weight: 43¹/₂ oz. with 7³/₈″ barrel
Sights: Front, ¹/₈″ Patridge undercut; rear, S&W micrometer click sight adjustable for windage and elevation
Stocks: Checkered walnut with modified thumb rest, equally adaptable to right- or left-handed shooters
Finish: S&W Bright Blue
Trigger: ³/₈″ width, with S&W grooving and an adjustable trigger stop

38 MASTER MODEL NO. 52
$694.00 Bright Blue Only

Caliber: 38 S&W Special (for Mid-Range Wad Cutter only)
Magazine capacity: 5 rounds (2 five-round magazines furnished)
Barrel length: 5″
Overall length: 8⁵/₈″
Sight radius: 6¹⁵/₁₆″
Weight: 41 oz. with empty magazine
Sights: Front, ¹/₈″ Patridge on ramp base; rear, new S&W micrometer click sight with wide ⁷/₈″ sight slide
Stocks: Checkered walnut with S&W monograms
Finish: S&W Bright Blue with sandblast stippling around sighting area to break up light reflection
Trigger: ³/₈″ width with S&W grooving and an adjustable trigger stop

SMITH & WESSON AUTO PISTOLS

9MM AUTOMATIC PISTOL
DOUBLE ACTION
MODEL 459
Blue $528.00 ($501.50 w/Fixed Sight)

Caliber: 9mm Luger
Magazine capacity: Two 14-round magazines, furnished
Barrel length: 4″
Overall length: 7⁷/₁₆″
Weight: 28 oz.
Sights: Front, square ¹/₈″ serrated ramp; rear, square notch rear sight blade fully micrometer click adjustable
Stocks: Checkered high-impact molded nylon grips
Finish: Blue or nickel

9MM AUTOMATIC PISTOL
DOUBLE ACTION
MODEL 439 $498.50
$472.00 w/Fixed Sight

Caliber: 9mm Luger
Magazine capacity: Two 8-round magazines, furnished
Barrel length: 4″
Overall length: 7⁷/₁₆″
Weight: 30 oz.
Sights: Front, square ¹/₈″ serrated ramp; rear, square notch rear sight blade fully micrometer click adjustable
Stocks: Checkered walnut grips with S&W monograms
Finish: Blue

9MM AUTOMATIC PISTOL
DOUBLE ACTION
MODEL 469 $478.50

Caliber: 9mm Luger
Magazine capacity: Two 12-round magazines furnished
Barrel length: 3¹/₂″
Overall length: 6⁷/₈″
Weight: 26 oz.
Sights: Front, yellow ramp; rear, dovetail mounted square-notch white inline
Finish: Sandblasted blue

MODEL 639 STAINLESS
$550.50
($523.50 w/Fixed Sight)

Caliber: 9mm Luger (Parabellum)
Capacity: 2 12-round magazines
Barrel length: 3¹/₂″
Overall length: 6¹³/₁₆″
Weight: 26 oz.
Finish: Non-glare stainless

SMITH & WESSON AUTO PISTOLS

MODEL 645 AUTOMATIC
$649.00 ($622.00 w/Fixed Sight)

Caliber: 45 Auto
Action: Double action
Capacity: 8 rounds
Barrel length: 5″
Overall length: 8.7″
Weight: 37.6 oz.
Sights: Red ramp front, fixed rear (drift adjustable for windage)
Safety features: Manual with magazine interlock; internal firing pin safety
Finish: Stainless steel

MODEL 659 STAINLESS
$580.00
($553.00 w/Fixed Sight)

Caliber: 9mm Luger (Parabellum)
Magazine capacity: 2 14-round magazines
Barrel length: 4″
Overall length: 7⁵/₈″
Weight: 39¹/₂ oz.
Finish: Satin

MODEL 669
STAINLESS STEEL
$522.50

Caliber: 9mm
Magazine capacity: 12-shot
Barrel length: 3¹/₂″
Overall length: 6¹³/₁₆″
Weight empty: 26 oz.
Sights: Serrated ramp w/red bar (front); fixed sight/white outline (rear)
Finish: Non-glare stainless

MODEL 745
$699.00

Caliber: 45 ACP
Capacity: 8 rounds
Barrel length: 5″
Overall length: 8⁵/₈″
Weight: 38³/₄ oz. (empty)
Stocks: Checkered walnut
Hammer: .260″ serrated
Frame: Stainless steel
Trigger: .365″ serrated w/upper lockout screw and adjustable trigger stop

SMITH & WESSON REVOLVERS

1953 22/32 KIT GUN
MODEL NO. 34
$338.50 Blue

Caliber: 22 Long Rifle
Number of shots: 6
Barrel length: 2″, 4″
Overall length: 8″ with 4″ barrel and round butt
Weight: 22¼ oz. with 4″ barrel and round butt
Sights: Front, 1/10″ serrated ramp; rear, S&W micrometer click sight adjustable for windage and elevation
Stocks: Checked walnut Service with S&W monograms, round or square butt
Finish: S&W blue

STAINLESS STEEL MODELS
1977 22/32 KIT GUN
MODEL NO. 63 $371.50

Caliber: 22 Long Rifle
Number of shots: 6
Barrel length: 4″
Weight: 24½ oz. (empty)
Sights: 1/8″ red ramp front sight; rear sight is black stainless steel S&W micrometer click square-notch, adjustable for windage and elevation
Stocks: Square butt
Finish: Satin

MODEL 650 & 651 22 M.R.F.
$345.00 (4″ barrel)
$305.00 (3″ barrel)

Caliber: 22 Magnum Rimfire (22 LR Auxiliary Cylinder optional) and 22 Winchester Rimfire
Capacity: 6-shot cylinder
Barrel length: 3″ (Model 650); 4″ (Model 651)
Length overall: 7″ (Model 650); 8⅝″ (Model 651)
Weight (empty): 23½ oz. (Model 650); 24½ oz. (Model 651)
Sights: Front: serrated ramp; rear: fixed square notch (Model 650); Model 651 has adjustable micrometer click sight
Stocks: Checkered walnut Service with S&W monograms; square butt (**Model 650** has round butt)
Finish: Stainless steel

SMITH & WESSON REVOLVERS

K-22 MASTERPIECE
MODEL NO. 17
$347.50 w/4″ or 6″ barrel
$391.00 w/8³/₈″ barrel

Caliber: 22 Long Rifle
Number of shots: 6
Barrel length: 4″, 6″, 8³/₈″
Overall length: 9⁵/₁₆″ (4″ barrel); 11¹/₈″ (6″ barrel); 13¹/₂″ (8³/₈″ barrel)
Weight loaded: 38¹/₂ oz. with 6″ barrel; 42¹/₂ oz. with 8³/₈″ barrel
Sights: Front, ¹/₈″ plain Patridge; rear, S&W micrometer click sight adjustable for windage and elevation
Stocks: Checkered walnut Service with S&W monograms
Finish: S&W blue

32 REGULATION POLICE
MODEL NO. 31
$337.00

Caliber: 32 S&W Long
Number of shots: 6
Barrel length: 2″, 3″
Overall length: 8¹/₂″ with 4″ barrel
Weight: 18³/₄ oz. with 4″ barrel
Sights: Front, fixed, ¹/₁₀″ serrated ramp; rear square notch
Stocks: Checked walnut Service with S&W monograms
Finish: S&W blue

38 CHIEFS SPECIAL
MODEL 36
$312.00 Blue
$322.50 Nickel

Caliber: 38 S&W Special
Number of shots: 5
Barrel length: 2″ or 3″
Overall length: 6¹/₂″ with 2″ barrel and round butt
Weight: 19 oz. with 2″ barrel and round butt
Sights: Front, fixed, ¹/₁₀″ serrated ramp; rear square notch
Stocks: Checked walnut Service with S&W monograms, round or square butt
Finish: S&W blue or nickel
MODEL 37: Same as Model 36 except weight 14 oz. **$331.00;** with nickel finish **$344.00.**

SMITH & WESSON REVOLVERS

38 CHIEFS SPECIAL STAINLESS
MODEL NO. 60
$357.00

Caliber: 38 S&W Special
Number of shots: 5
Barrel length: 2″
Overall length: 6¹/₂″
Weight: 19 oz.
Sights: Front fixed, ¹/₁₀″ serrated ramp; rear square notch
Stocks: Checked walnut Service with S&W monograms
Finish: Satin

38 BODYGUARD "AIRWEIGHT"
MODEL NO. 38
$350.50 Blue
$363.00 Nickel

Caliber: 38 S&W Special
Number of shots: 5
Barrel length: 2″
Overall length: 6³/₈″
Weight: 14¹/₂ oz.
Sights: Front, fixed ¹/₁₀″ serrated ramp; rear square notch
Stocks: Checked walnut Service with S&W monograms
Finish: S&W blue or nickel

MODEL 49 .38 BODYGUARD
$331.50

Caliber: 38 S&W Special
Capacity: 5-shot cylinder
Barrel length: 2″
Overall length: 6¹/₄″
Weight (empty): 20 oz.
Sights: Serrated ramp (front); fixed square notch (rear)
Finish: S&W blue

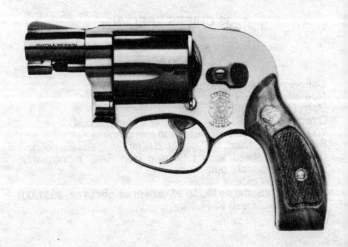

SMITH & WESSON REVOLVERS

MODEL 649 BODYGUARD
$377.50

Caliber: 38 Special
Capacity: 5 shots
Barrel length: 2″
Overall length: 6¼″
Sights: Serrated ramp front, fixed square notch rear
Weight: 20 oz.
Grips: Round butt; checkered walnut service
Finish: Stainless steel

38 MILITARY & POLICE
MODEL NO. 10
$305.00 Blue
$315.50 Nickel (4″ barrel only)

Caliber: 38 S&W Special
Capacity: 6 shots
Barrel length: 2″, (also 3″ heavy barrel), 4″ (also 4″ heavy barrel)
Weight: 30½ oz. with 4″ barrel
Sights: Front, fixed ⅛″ serrated ramp; rear square notch
Stocks: Checkered walnut Service with S&W monograms, round or square butt
Finish: S&W blue or nickel

38 MILITARY & POLICE STAINLESS
MODEL NO. 64
$331.50

Caliber: 38 S&W Special
Capacity: 6 shots
Barrel length: 4″ heavy barrel, square butt; 3″ heavy barrel, round butt; 2″ regular barrel, round butt
Overall length: 9¼″ w/4″ barrel; 7⅞″ w/3″ barrel; 6⅞″ w/2″ barrel
Weight: With 4″ barrel, 34 oz.; with 3″ barrel, 30½ oz.; with 2″ barrel, 28 oz.
Sights: Fixed, ⅛″ serrated ramp front; square notch rear
Stocks: Checked walnut Service with S&W monograms
Finish: Satin
Ammunition: 38 S&W Special, 38 S&W Special Mid Range

SMITH & WESSON REVOLVERS

38 COMBAT MASTERPIECE
MODEL NO. 15
$330.50 ($340.50 w/8³/₈″ bbl.)

Caliber: 38 S&W Special
Number of shots: 6
Barrel length: 2″, 4″, 6″, 8³/₈″
Overall length: 7¹/₄″ (2″ barrel); 9⁵/₁₆″ (4″ barrel); 11¹/₈″ (6″ barrel); 13¹/₂″ (8³/₈″ barrel)
Weight loaded: 34 oz. with 4″ barrel
Sights: Front, ¹/₈″ Baughman Quick Draw on plain ramp; rear, S&W micrometer click sight adjustable for windage and elevation
Stocks: Checkered walnut Service with S&W monograms
Finish: S&W blue or nickel

38 COMBAT MASTERPIECE
MODEL NO. 67
$360.00 Stainless Steel

Caliber: 38 S&W Special
Number of shots: 6
Barrel length: 4″
Length overall: 9¹/₈″
Weight loaded: 34 oz.
Sights: Front: ¹/₈″ Rear: S&W Red Ramp on ramp base, S&W Micrometer Click Sights, adjustable for windage and elevation
Stocks: Checked walnut Service with S&W Monograms, square butt
Finish: Satin
Trigger: S&W grooving with an adjustable trigger stop
Ammunition: 38 S&W Special, 38 S&W Special Mid Range

357 COMBAT MAGNUM
MODEL NO. 66
$363.00—$412.50 Stainless Steel

Caliber: 357 Magnum (actual bullet dia. 38 S&W Spec.)
Number of shots: 6
Barrel length: 6″ or 4″ with square butt; 2¹/₂″ with round butt
Length overall: 9¹/₂″ with 4″ barrel; 7¹/₂″ with 2¹/₂″ barrel; 11³/₈″ with 6″ barrel
Weight: 35 oz. with 4″ barrel; 30¹/₂ oz. with 2¹/₂″ barrel; 39 oz. with 6″ barrel
Sights: Front: ¹/₈″. Rear: S&W Red Ramp on ramp base, S&W Micrometer Click Sight, adjustable for windage and elevation
Stocks: Checked Goncalo Alves target with square butt with S&W monograms
Finish: Satin
Trigger: S&W grooving with an adjustable trigger stop
Ammunition: 357 S&W Magnum, 38 S&W Special Hi-Speed, 38 S&W Special, 38 S&W Special Mid Range

SMITH & WESSON REVOLVERS

357 COMBAT MAGNUM
MODEL NO. 19
$319.50—-$386.50 Bright Blue or Nickel

Caliber: 357 Magnum (actual bullet dia. 38 S&W Spec.)
Number of shots: 6
Barrel length: 2½″, 4″ and 6″
Overall length: 9½″ with 4″ barrel; 7½″ with 2½″ barrel; 11½″ with 6″ barrel
Weight: 35 oz. (2½″ model weighs 31 oz.)
Sights: Front, ⅛″ Baughman Quick Draw on 2½″ or 4″ barrel, ⅛″ Patridge on 6″ barrel; rear, S&W micrometer click sight adjustable for windage and elevation
Stocks: Checkered Goncalo Alves Target with S&W monograms
Finish: S&W bright blue or nickel

357 MILITARY & POLICE STAINLESS
HEAVY BARREL MODEL NO. 65
$337.00

Caliber: 357 Magnum and 38 S&W Special
Rounds: 6-shot cylinder capacity
Barrel length: 4″ heavy barrel, square butt; 3″ heavy barrel, round butt
Length overall: With 4″ barrel, 9¼″; with 3″ barrel, 7⁵/₁₆″
Weight: With 4″ barrel, 34 oz.; with 3″ barrel, 31 oz.
Sights: Fixed, ⅛″ serrated ramp front; square notch rear
Stocks: Checked walnut Service with S&W monograms, square butt
Finish: Satin

357 MILITARY & POLICE (HEAVY BARREL)
MODEL NO. 13
$310.00

Caliber: 357 Magnum and 38 S&W Special
Rounds: 6-shot cylinder capacity
Barrel length: 3″ and 4″
Overall length: 9¼″
Weight: 34 oz.
Sights: Front, ⅛″ serrated ramp; rear square notch
Stocks: Checkered walnut Service with S&W monograms, square butt (3″ barrel has round butt)
Finish: S&W blue

SMITH & WESSON REVOLVERS

MODEL 586
DISTINGUISHED COMBAT MAGNUM
$367.00—$423.50 (Blue or Nickel)

Caliber: 357 Magnum
Capacity: 6 shots
Barrel length: 4″, 6″, 8³/₈″
Overall length: 9³/₄″ with 4″ barrel; 11¹/₂″ with 6″ barrel; 13¹³/₁₆″ with 8³/₈″ barrel
Weight: 42 oz. with 4″ barrel; 46 oz. with 6″ barrel; 53 oz. with 8³/₈″ barrel
Sights: Front is S&W Red Ramp; rear is S&W Micrometer Click adjustable for windage and elevation; White outline notch. Option with 6″ barrel only—plain Patridge front with black outline notch.
Stocks: Checkered Goncalo Alves with speedloader cutaway
Finish: S&W Blue or Nickel
Model 686: Same as Model 586 except finish is stainless steel, **$394.00—$447.00.**

357 MAGNUM MODEL NO. 27
$429.50 (4″) $403.00 (6″)
$410.00 (8³/₈″)

Caliber: 357 Magnum (actual bullet dia. 38 S&W Spec.)
Number of shots: 6
Barrel length: 4″, 6″ and 8³/₈″
Weight: 44 oz. with 4″ barrel; 45¹/₂ oz. with 6″; 49 oz. with 8³/₈″
Sights: Front, S&W Red Ramp (4″ barrel) and Patridge (6″ and 8³/₈″ barrels); rear, S&W micrometer click sight adjustable for windage and elevation
Stocks: Checkered walnut Service with S&W monograms
Frame: Finely checked top strap and barrel rib
Finish: S&W bright blue or nickel

41 MAGNUM MODEL NO. 57
$406.50 (4″ and 6″)
$421.00 (8³/₈″)

Caliber: 41 Magnum
Number of shots: 6
Barrel length: 4″, 6″ and 8³/₈″
Overall length: 11³/₈″ with 6″ barrel
Weight: 48 oz. with 6″ barrel
Sights: Front, ¹/₈″ S&W Red Ramp; rear, S&W micrometer click sight adjustable for windage and elevation; white outline notch
Stocks: Special oversize Target type of checkered Goncalo Alves, with S&W monograms
Hammer: Checked target type
Trigger: Grooved target type
Finish: S&W bright blue

SMITH & WESSON REVOLVERS

MODEL 657 STAINLESS $433.00 (4″ and 6″)
$448.00 (8³/₈″)

Caliber: 41 Magnum
Magazine capacity: 6-shot cylinder
Barrel length: 4″, 6″, 8³/₈″
Overall length: 9⁵/₈″ (4″ barrel); 11³/₈″ (6″ barrel); 13¹⁵/₁₆″ (8³/₈″ barrel)
Weight empty: 44.2 oz. (4″ barrel); 48 oz. (6″ barrel); 52¹/₂ oz. (8³/₈″ barrel)
Sights: Serrated black ramp on ramp base (front); Blue S&W micrometer click sight adj. for windage and elevation (rear)
Finish: Satin

44 MAGNUM MODEL NO. 29
$458.50 (4″ and 6″)
$468.50 (8³/₈″)
$510.00 (10⁵/₈″ Blue only)

Caliber: 44 Magnum
Number of shots: 6
Barrel length: 4″, 6″, 8³/₈″ and 10⁵/₈″ (blue only)
Overall length: 11⁷/₈″ with 6¹/₂″ barrel
Weight: 43 oz. with 4″ barrel; 47 oz. with 6″ barrel; 51¹/₂ oz. with 8³/₈″ barrel
Sights: Front, ¹/₈″ S&W Red Ramp; rear, S&W micrometer click sight adjustable for windage and elevation; white outline notch
Stocks: Special oversize target type of checked Goncalo Alves; with S&W monograms
Hammer: Checkered target type
Trigger: Grooved target type
Finish: S&W bright blue or nickel
Also available in nickel: **$469.00** (4″ and 6″) and **$479.00** (8³/₈″).

MODEL 25
$408.00 (4″ and 6″)
$415.50 (8³/₈″)

Caliber: 45 Colt
Capacity: 6-shot cylinder
Barrel length: 4″, 6″, 8³/₈″
Overall length: 9⁹/₁₆″ (4″ barrel); 11³/₈″ (6″ barrel); 13⁷/₈″ (8³/₈″ barrel)
Weight (empty): 44 oz. (4″ barrel); 46 oz. (6″ barrel); 50 oz. (8³/₈″ barrel)
Sights: S&W red ramp on ramp base (front); S&W micrometer click sight w/white outline notch (rear), adj. for windage and elevation
Finish: S&W Bright blue or nickel

SPRINGFIELD ARMORY

MODEL 1911-A1 STANDARD

An exact duplicate of the M1911-A1 pistol that served the U.S. Armed Forces for more than 70 years, this model has been precision manufactured from forged parts, including a forged frame, then hand assembled. *See* also Springfield Armory in the Paramilitary Section.

SPECIFICATIONS
Calibers: 9mm Parabellum and 45 ACP
Capacity: 8 in mag. 1 in chamber (9mm); 7 in mag. 1 in chamber (45 ACP)
Barrel length: 5.04″
Overall length: 8.59″
Weight: 35.62 oz.
Trigger pull: 5 to 6.5 lbs.
Sight radius: 6.481″
Rifling: 1 turn in 16; left-hand, 4-groove (9mm); right-hand, 6-groove (45 ACP)
Model 1911-A1
  Blued $383.00
  Same model with Parkerized finish 362.00
1911-A1 DEFENDER w/fixed combat sights,
  bobbed hammer, walnut grips, beveled magazine
  well, extended thumb safety, in 45 ACP 434.00
  Same as above w/blued finish 454.00
1911-A1 COMBAT COMMANDER with 1/2″ short-
  ened slide and barrel, in 45 ACP 447.00
  Same as above w/blued finish 467.00

**MODEL 1911-A1
COMBAT COMMANDER**

OMEGA

Springfield's new Omega model is the first practical 10mm multi-caliber system available. Includes a ported slide with adjustable rear sight and interchangeable front sights; a hammer forged polygon barrel (with or without stabilizing ports); special lockup system for greater safety with high velocity loads; and a dual extractor system for fast barrel changes.

SPECIFICATIONS
Calibers: 10mm, 38 Super, 45 ACP (interchangeable)
Barrel length: 5″ or 6″
Overall length: 8.53″ (5″ barrel); 9.53″ (6″ barrel)
Weight: 42.88 oz. (5″ barrel); 45.36 oz. (6″ barrel)
Rifling: 6 grooves, right-hand; 1 turn in 14 (38 Spec.); 1 turn in 16 (10mm); 1 turn in 18 (45 ACP)
Grips: Pachmayr wraparound
Finish: Blue
OMEGA (5″ or 6″) $849.00
Note: in 6″ model, 38 Special is available unported only; 5″ available ported or unported in all 3 calibers.

OMEGA

STAR AUTOMATIC PISTOLS

STAR BKM & BM
9mm PARABELLUM

The Model BM offers all-steel construction, and the BKM offers a high strength, weight-saving duraluminum frame. An improved thumb safety locks both the slide and hammer with hammer cocked or uncocked; further, an automatic magazine safety locks the sear when the magazine is removed.

Overall length: 7.17". **Barrel length:** 3.9". **Magazine capacity:** 8 rounds. **Weight:** 34.06 oz. (BM); 25.59 oz. (BKM)

Model BM Blue	$360.00
Model BM Chrome	375.00
Model BKM Blue	360.00

MODEL BM

STAR MODELS 30M & 30PK
9mm PARABELLUM

The Model 30 features a staggered 15-round button release magazine, square notch rear sight (click-adjustable for windage) and square front sight (notched to diffuse light). Removable backstrap houses complete firing mechanism. All-steel frame (Model 30/PK = alloy frame).

Overall length: 8.07". **Height:** 5.32". **Barrel length:** 4.33" (Model 30PK = 3.86") **Weight:** 40.24 oz. (Model 30/Pk = 30.36 oz.) **Price:** ....$510.00.

MODEL 30PK

STAR MODEL PD
45 ACP

Chambered for the sledgehammer 45 ACP, the PD is one of the smallest .45 caliber production pistols in the world.

Overall length: 7". **Barrel length:** 4". **Weight:** 25.5 oz. **Finish:** Blue. **Capacity:** 6 rounds. **Price:** ....$395.00.

MODEL PD

TANARMI

MODEL BTA90C
$390.00

SPECIFICATIONS
Caliber: 9mm Para
Barrel length: 4″
Weight: 30 oz
Capacity: 12 shots
Finish: Matte chrome
Frame: Steel
Grips: Neoprene

MODEL TA76M
"BUFFALO SCOUT" REVOLVER
$95.00

SPECIFICATIONS
Calibers: 22 LR and 22 WRM
Barrel length: 4³/₄″
Capacity: 6 shots
Finish: Satin blue
Frame: Alloy
Grips: Walnut

MODEL TA90B
$350.00 Blue
$379.00 Chrome

SPECIFICATIONS
Caliber: 9mm Para
Barrel length: 4³/₄″
Capacity: 15 shots
Finish: Matte blue or chrome
Grips: Black Neoprene

TARGA SEMIAUTOMATIC PISTOLS

MODEL GT26S
$115.00

SPECIFICATIONS
Caliber: 25 ACP
Capacity: 6 shots
Barrel length: 2¹/₂″
Weight: 15 oz.
Frame: Steel
Finish: Satin blue
Grips: Walnut

MODEL GT22T
$200.00

SPECIFICATIONS
Caliber: 22 LR
Capacity: 12 shots
Barrel length: 6″
Weight: 28 oz.
Frame: Steel
Finish: Satin blue
Grips: Walnut

TARGA SEMIAUTOMATIC PISTOLS

MODEL GT380XE
$235.00

SPECIFICATIONS
Caliber: 380 ACP
Capacity: 11 shots
Barrel length: 3.88″
Weight: 26 oz.
Finish: Satin blue
Frame: Steel
Grips: Walnut

TAURUS PISTOLS

MODEL PT 92

Caliber: 9mm Parabellum
Action: Semiautomatic double action
Hammer: Exposed
Barrel length: 4.92″
Overall length: 8.54″
Height: 5.39″
Width: 1.45″
Weight: 34 oz. (empty)
Rifling: R.H., 6 grooves
Front sight: Blade integral with slide
Rear sight: Notched bar dovetailed to slide
Safeties: (a) Ambidextrous manual safety locking trigger mechanism and slide in locked position; (b) half-cock position; (c) inertia operated firing pin; (d) chamber loaded indicator
Magazine: Staggered 15-shot capacity
Slide: Hold open upon firing last cartridge
Finish: Blue or satin nickel
Grips: Smooth Brazilian walnut

MODEL PT 92
$381.50 (Blue)
$393.38 (Nickel)

MODEL PT 99

Caliber: 9mm Parabellum
Action: Semiautomatic double action
Hammer: Exposed
Barrel length: 4.92″
Overall length: 8.54″
Height: 5.39″
Width: 1.45″
Weight: 34 oz. (empty)
Rifling: R.H., 6 grooves
Front sight: Blade Integral with slide
Rear sight: Micrometer click adjustable for elevation and windage
Safeties: (a) Ambidextrous manual safety locking trigger mechanism and slide in locked position; (b) half-cock position; (c) inertia operated firing pin; (d) chamber loaded indicator. **Magazine:** Staggered, 15-shot capacity
Slide: Hold open upon firing last cartridge
Finish: Blue or satin nickel
Grips: Smooth Brazilian walnut

MODEL PT 99
$408.74 (Blue)
$422.43 (Nickel)

TAURUS PISTOLS

MODEL PT 58 (not shown)
$359.90 (Blue)
$366.45 (Nickel)

SPECIFICATIONS
Caliber: 380 ACP
Action: Semiautomatic double action
Capacity: Staggered 13 shot

Barrel length: 4″
Overall length: 7.1″
Weight: 30 oz.
Hammer: Exposed
Sights: Front, blade integral w/slide; rear, notched bar dove-tailed to slide
Finish: Blue or satin nickel
Grips: Smooth Brazilian walnut

TAURUS REVOLVERS

MODEL 73
$193.92 (Blue)
$211.10 (Nickel)

SPECIFICATIONS
Caliber: 32 Long
Capacity: 6 shot
Barrel length: 3″ heavy barrel
Weight: 20 oz.
Sights: Rear, square notch
Action: Double
Stock: Standard checkered
Finish: Blue or satin nickel

MODEL 83
$197.82 (Blue)
$208.15 (Nickel)

SPECIFICATIONS
Caliber: 38 Special
Action: Double
Number of shots: 6
Barrel length: 4″
Weight: 34½ oz.
Sights: Ramp, front; rear micrometer click adjustable for windage and elevation
Finish: Blue or satin nickel
Stocks: Checkered walnut target

MODEL 86 TARGET MASTER

SPECIFICATIONS
Caliber: 38 Special
Capacity: 6 shot
Barrel length: 6″
Weight: 34 oz.
Sights: Patridge-type front; micrometer click adjustable rear for windage and elevation
Action: Double
Stock: Checkered walnut target
Finish: Bright royal blue

Model 96 Target Scout: Same as Model 86 Target Master except 22 LR caliber. Blue.

MODEL 669
$241.85 (Blue)
$304.80 (Stainless Steel)

SPECIFICATIONS
Calibers: 357 Magnum, 38 Special
Capacity: 6 shots
Barrel length: 4″ and 6″
Weight: 36 oz.
Action: Double
Sights: Serrated ramp front; rear micrometer click adjustable for windage and elevation
Finish: Royal blue or stainless
Stock: Checkered walnut target

TAURUS REVOLVERS

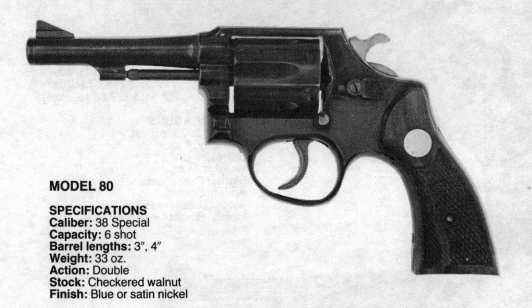

MODEL 80

SPECIFICATIONS
Caliber: 38 Special
Capacity: 6 shot
Barrel lengths: 3″, 4″
Weight: 33 oz.
Action: Double
Stock: Checkered walnut
Finish: Blue or satin nickel

MODEL 82

SPECIFICATIONS
Caliber: 38 Special
Capacity: 6 shot
Barrel lengths: 3″, 4″
Weight: 34 oz.
Action: Double
Stock: Checkered walnut
Finish: Blue or satin nickel

TAURUS REVOLVERS

MODEL 65
$216.47 (Blue)
$227.60 (Nickel)

SPECIFICATIONS
Caliber: 357 Magnum
Capacity: 6 shot
Barrel length: 3″, 4″
Weight: 34 oz.
Sights: Rear square notch; front ramp
Action: Double
Stock: Checkered walnut target
Finish: Royal blue or satin nickel

MODEL 66
$237.45 (Blue) $243.92 (Nickel)
$296.41 (Stainless Steel)

SPECIFICATIONS
Caliber: 357 Magnum, 38 Special
Capacity: 6 shot
Barrel length: 3″, 4″, 6″
Weight: 35 oz.
Sights: Serrated ramp front; rear micrometer click adjustable
  for windage and elevation
Action: Double
Stock: Checkered walnut magna grips (3″); checkered walnut
  target grips (4″ & 6″)
Finish: Royal blue, satin nickel or stainless steel

MODEL 85
$199.88 (Blue) $214.43 (Nickel)
$253.09 (Stainless Steel)

SPECIFICATIONS
Caliber: 38 Special
Capacity: 5 shot
Barrel length: 2″ and 3″
Weight: 21 oz.
Sights: Notch rear sight, fixed sight
Action: Double
Stock: Brazilian checkered walnut
Finish: Blue, satin nickel or stainless steel

THOMPSON/CENTER

CONTENDER BULL BARREL

CONTENDER
OCTAGON BARREL MODELS

This standard barrel is interchangeable with any model listed here. Available in 10-inch length, it is supplied with iron sights. Octagon barrel is available in 22 LR. No external choke in this model **$335.00**

CONTENDER SUPER "14"

CONTENDER
SUPER "14" MODELS

Chambered in 10 calibers (22 LR, 222 Remington and 223 Remington, 6mm T.C.U., 7-30 Waters, 7mm T.C.U., 30/30 Winchester, 357 Rem. Max., 35 Remington and 44 Mag.), this gun is equipped with a 14-inch bull barrel, fully adjustable target rear sight and ramped front sight (Patridge-style). It offers a sight radius of 13½ inches. **Overall length: 18¼". Weight: 3½ lbs.** **$345.00**

CONTENDER
BULL BARREL MODELS

This pistol with 10-inch barrel features fully adjustable Patridge-style iron sights.

Standard and Custom calibers available:
22 Long Rifle, 22 Hornet, 22 Win. Mag., 7-30 Waters, 223 Rem., 32 H&R Mag., 32/20 Win., 7mm T.C.U., 30/30 Win., 357 Mag., 44 Mag., 357 Rem. Max., 30 M1 Carbine, and 9mm Luger.
Bull Barrel)less internal choke) **$335.00**
Standard calibers available w/internal choke:
45 Colt/.410 . . . . **340.00**

T/C ALLOY II CONTENDER

T/C Alloy II is a permanent, electroplated surface that will not separate from the base metal. It is harder than stainless steel and improves lubricity, causing actions to function smoother and enabling parts to move with less frictional drag. As a result, it provides 30% longer barrel life than stainless steel, reduces wear on moving parts, and shrugs off the effects of corrosion or erosion. It also reduces fouling to produce a more constant velocity shot after shot. All metal surfaces of this Contender Series, internal and external (excluding sights and springs) are finished in T/C Alloy II.
    Calibers: 22 LR, 223 Rem., 357 Magnum, 357 Rem. Max., 44 Magnum, 7mm TCU, 30/30 Win. (10" Bull Barrel Model); 45 Colt/.410 (Vent rib/Internal Choke Model).
Prices:
Contender 10" Bull Barrel Model. **$405.00**
Contender Vent Rib/Internal Choke Model. **425.00**
Contender Super "14" Model (22LR, 223 Rem., 30/30 Win., 35 Rem., 7mm T.C.U., 7-30 Waters, 44 Mag.) **415.00**

CONTENDER
VENTILATED RIB/INTERNAL CHOKE MODELS
(not shown)

Featuring a raised ventilated (7/16-inch wide) rib, this Contender model is available in 45 Colt/.410 caliber. Its rear leaf sight folds down to provide an unobstructed sighting plane when the pistol is used with .410 ga. shot shells. A patented detachable choke (1⅞ inches long) screws into the muzzle internally. **Barrel length:** 10 inches **$355.00**

A. UBERTI REPLICA REVOLVERS

1873 STALLION QUICK DRAW SINGLE ACTION
$425.00

SPECIFICATIONS
Caliber: 22 LR, 22 Magnum (w/2 interchangeable cylinders)
Barrel length: 5¹/₂ round (also avail. w/4 ³/₄″ or 6¹/₂″ barrel)
Overall length: 10³/₄″
Weight: 2.42 lbs.
Sights: Fully adj. rear; ramp front
Capacity: 6 shots
Grip: One piece walnut
Frame: Stainless steel + all metal parts

Also available:
Target Model Stainless $450.00
    Casehardened and blued steel 399.00

1873 CATTLEMAN QUICK DRAW
$345.00 (Brass)
$375.00 (Steel)

SPECIFICATIONS
Calibers: 22 LR, 22 Magnum, 357 Magnum, 38 Special, 38-
    40, 44 Special, 44-40, 45 L.C.
Barrel lengths: 4³/₄ ″, 5¹/₂″, 7¹/₂″; round tapered
Overall length: 10³/₄″ w/5¹/₂″ barrel
Weight: 2.42 lbs.
Capacity: 6 shots
Grip: One-piece walnut
Frame: Color casehardened steel

Also available:
Cattleman S.A. Target Brass $375.00
    Steel. 399.00

1875 REMINGTON ARMY "OUTLAW"
$355.00

SPECIFICATIONS
Calibers: 357 Magnum, 45 Long Colt, 44-40
Barrel length: 7¹/₂ ″ round tapered
Overall length: 13³/₄″
Weight: 2.75 lbs.
Grips: Two-piece walnut
Frame: Color casehardened steel

Also available in nickel plate: **$396.00**

VICTORY ARMS

MODEL MC5
$459.00

SPECIFICATIONS
Calibers: 9mm Parabellum, 38 Super, 41 Action Express, 45 ACP (interchangeable)
Capacity: 10 + 1 (45 ACP); 12 + 1 (41 AE); 17 + 1 (9mm Para, 38 Super)
Barrel lengths: 4³/₈″, 5⁷/₈″, 7¹/₂″
Overall length: 8¹/₂″
Weight: 45 oz. (empty)
Sight radius: 6¹/₂″ (w/standard 4³/₈″ barrel)
Automatic safeties: Firing pin lock; disconnector; hammer blocked unless slide is fully forward and locked
Finish: Service matte black; custom high-luster blue
Extra barrels $100.00
Magazines (each) 25.00

WALTHER TARGET PISTOLS

MODEL P-5 DA
$999.00

Caliber: 9mm Para.
Capacity: 8 rounds
Barrel length: 3¹/₂″
Overall length: 7″
Weight: 28 oz.
Finish: Blue
Features: Four automatic built-in safety functions; lightweight alloy frame; supplied with two magazines

MODEL FP FREE PISTOL
$1750.00

Caliber: 22 LR
Barrel length: 11.7″
Overall length: 17.2″
Weight: 48 oz.
Trigger: Electronic

MODEL P-88 DA (not shown)
$1165.00

Caliber: 9mm Para.
Capacity: 15 rounds
Barrel length: 4″
Overall length: 7³/₈″
Weight: 31¹/₂ oz.
Finish: Blue
Sights: Rear adj. for windage and elevation
Features: Internal safeties; ambidextrous de-cocking lever and magazine release button; lightweight alloy frame; loaded chamber indicator

U.I.T.-BV UNIVERSAL
(not shown)

Caliber: 22 LR
Barrel length: 25¹/₂″
Overall length: 44³/₄″
Weight: 9 lbs.
Bolt action: Single shot; falling block
Prices:
U.I.T.-BV $1625.00
U.I.T. Match 1500.00

WALTHER TARGET PISTOLS

WALTHER OSP

Walther match pistols are built to conform to ISU and NRA match target pistol regulations. The model GSP, caliber 22 LR is available with either 2.2 lb. (1000 gm) or 3.0 lbs. (1360 gm) trigger, and comes with 4¹/₂-inch barrel and special hand-fitting designed walnut stock. Sights consist of fixed front and adjustable rear sight. The GSP-C 32 S&W wadcutter centerfire pistol is factory tested with a 3.0 lb. trigger. The 22 LR conversion unit for the model GSP-C consists of an interchangeable barrel, a slide assembly and two magazines. **Weight:** 22-caliber model 44.8 oz.; 32 S&W 49.4 oz. **Overall length:** 11.8". **Magazine capacity:** 5 shot.

Prices:
GSP—22 Long Rifle w/carrying case **$1300.00**
GSP-C—32 S&W wadcutter w/carrying case. 1500.00
22 LR conversion unit for GSP-C 800.00
22 Short only 1475.00
22 Short conversion unit for GSP-C 825.00
32 S&W wadcutter conversion unit for GSP-C 975.00

WALTHER GSP MATCH PISTOL
22 LR & 32 S&W Wadcutter

GSP JR. SEMIAUTOMATIC (not shown)
$1300.00 (w/Carrying Case)

Caliber: 22 LR
Capacity: 5 rounds
Barrel length: 4¹/₂"
Overall length: 11.8"
Weight: 40.1 oz.

WALTHER PISTOLS

DOUBLE-ACTION AUTOMATIC PISTOLS

The Walther double-action system combines the principles of the double-action revolver with the advantages of the modern pistol . . . without the disadvantages inherent in either design.

Models PP and PPK/S differ only in the overall length of the barrel and slide. Both models offer the same features, including compact form, light weight, easy handling and absolute safety. Both models can be carried with a loaded chamber and closed hammer, but ready to fire either single- or double-action. Both models in calibers 32 ACP and 380 ACP are provided with a live round indicator pin to signal a loaded chamber. An automatic internal safety blocks the hammer to prevent accidental striking of the firing pin, except with a deliberate pull of the trigger. Sights are provided with white markings for high visibility in poor light. Rich Walther blue/black finish is standard and each pistol is complete with extra magazine with finger rest extension. Available in calibers 22 LR, 32 ACP and 380 ACP.

The Walther P-38 is a double-action, locked breech, semi-automatic pistol with an external hammer. Its compact form, light weight and easy handling are combined with the superb performance of the 9mm Luger Parabellum cartridge. The P-38 is equipped with both a manual and automatic safety, which allows it to be carried safely while the chamber is loaded. Available in calibers 9mm Luger Parabellum, 30 Luger and 22 LR with either a rugged non-reflective black finish or a polished blue finish.

SPECIFICATIONS
Overall length: Model PP 6.7"; PPK/S 6.1"; P-38 8½"; P-38 IV 8"; TPH 5³/8"
Height: Models PP, PPK/S 4.28"; P-38 5.39"; P-38 IV 5.39"; P-38K 5.39"
Weight: Model PP 23.5 oz; PPK/S 23 oz; P-38 28 oz.; P-38 IV (29 oz); TPH 14 oz.

MODEL PPK/S "AMERICAN" 7-shot Automatic

MODEL TPH DOUBLE ACTION

Considered by government agents and professional lawmen to be one of the top undercover/back-up guns available. A scaled-down version of Walther's PP-PPK series chambered for 22 LR.

Barrel length: 2¼". **Overall length:** 5³/8". **Weight:** 14 oz. **Finish:** stainless steel. **Price:** . . . .$350.00.

Caliber: 380 ACP
Barrel length: 3.27"
Finish: Walther blue or stainless steel
Price . . . . $ 499.00
Deluxe Engraved Blue 1550.00
   Silver 1700.00
   Chrome 1600.00

MODEL P-38 DOUBLE ACTION

Calibers: 22 LR, 9mm Parabellum
Barrel length: 5"
Weight: 28 oz. (alloy); 34 oz. (steel)
Finish: Blue
Prices: 22 Long Rifle . . . . $ 995.00
9mm Parabellum 895.00
Deluxe Engraved (9mm Para. only) Blue 1750.00
   Silver 1950.00
   Chrome 1850.00
Now available: custom **all steel** classic (34 oz.) . . . 1100.00

DAN WESSON REVOLVERS

**357 MAGNUM
w/6" BARREL**

357 MAGNUM REVOLVERS

Introduced in 1935, the 357 Magnum is still the top selling handgun caliber. It makes an excellent hunting sidearm, and many law enforcement agencies have adopted it as a duty caliber. Take your pick of Dan Wesson 357's; then, add to it's versatility with an additional barrel assembly option to alter it to your other needs.

SPECIFICATIONS
Action: Six-shot double and single action. **Ammunition:** 357 Magnum, 38 Special Hi-speed, 38 Special Mid-range. **Typical dimension:** 4" barrel revolver, 9 1/4" × 5 3/4". **Trigger:** Smooth, wide tang (3/8") with overtravel adjustment. **Hammer:** Wide spur (3/8") with short double-action travel. **Sights: Models 14 and 714,** 1/8" fixed serrated front; fixed rear integral with frame. **Models 15 and 715,** 1/8" serrated interchangeable front blade; red insert standard, yellow and white available; rear notch (.125, .080, or white outline) adjustable for windage and elevation; graduated click. 10", 12," 15" barrel assemblies have special front sights and instructions. **Rifling:** Six lands and grooves, right-hand twist, 1 turn in 18.75 inches (2 1/2" thru 8" lengths); six lands & grooves, right-hand twist, 1 turn in 14 inches (10", 12", 15" lengths). **Note:** All 2 1/2" guns shipped with undercover grips. 4" guns are shipped with service grips and the balance have oversized target grips.

Price:
Pistol Pac Models 14-2S thru 715-VH . . . . $455.80 to
$887.81

MODEL	CALIBER	TYPE	BARREL LENGTHS & WEIGHT IN OUNCES							FINISH
			2½"	4"	6"	8"	10"	12"	15"	
14-2	.357 Magnum	Service	30	34	38	NA	NA	NA	NA	Satin Blue
14-2B	.357 Magnum	Service	30	34	38	NA	NA	NA	NA	Brite Blue
15-2	.357 Magnum	Target	32	36	40	44	50	54	59	Brite Blue
15-2V	.357 Magnum	Target	32	35	39	43	49	54	59	Brite Blue
15-2VH	.357 Magnum	Target	32	37	42	47	55	61	70	Brite Blue
714	.357 Magnum	Service	30	34	40	NA	NA	NA	NA	Satin Stainless Steel
715	.357 Magnum	Target	32	36	40	45	50	54	59	Satin Stainless Steel
715-V	.357 Magnum	Target	32	35	40	43	49	54	59	Satin Stainless Steel
715-VH	.357 Magnum	Target	32	37	42	49	55	61	70	Satin Stainless Steel

38 SPECIAL REVOLVER

For decades a favorite of security and law enforcement agencies, the 38 special still maintains it's reputation as a fine caliber for sportsmen and target shooters. Dan Wesson offers a choice of many barrel lengths in either the service or target configuration.

SPECIFICATIONS
Action: Six-shot double and single action. **Ammunition:** 38 Special Hi-speed, 38 Special Mid-range. **Typical dimension:** 4" barrel revolver, 9 1/4" × 5 3/4". **Trigger:** Smooth, wide tang (3/8") with overtravel adjustment. **Hammer:** Wide spur (3/8") with short double travel. **Sights:** Models 8 and 708, 1/8" fixed serrated front; fixed rear integral with frame. Models 9 and 709, 1/8" serrated interchangeable front blade; red insert standard, yellow and white available; rear, standard notch (.125, .080, or white outline) adjustable for windage and elevation; graduated click. **Rifling:** Six lands and grooves, right-hand twist, 1 turn in 18.75 inches. **Note:** All 2 1/2" guns shipped with undercover grips. 4" guns are shipped with service grips and the balance have oversized target grips.

Price:
38 Special Pistol Pacs . . . . $455.80—-804.85
Stainless Steel. . . . . 516.68—-887.81

MODEL	CALIBER	TYPE	BARREL LENGTHS & WEIGHT IN OUNCES				FINISH
			2½"	4"	6"	8"	
8-2	.38 Special	Service	30	34	38	N/A	Satin Blue
8-2B	.38 Special	Service	30	34	38	N/A	Brite Blue
9-2	.38 Special	Target	32	36	40	44	Brite Blue
9-2V	.39 Special	Target	32	35	39	43	Brite Blue
9-2VH	.38 Special	Target	32	37	42	47	Brite Blue
708	.38 Special	Service	30	34	38	N/A	Satin Stainless Steel
709	.38 Special	Target	32	36	40	44	Satin Stainless Steel
709-V	.38 Special	Target	32	35	39	43	Satin Stainless Steel
709-VH	.38 Special	Target	32	37	42	47	Satin Stainless Steel

DAN WESSON REVOLVERS

41 AND 44 MAGNUM REVOLVERS

The Dan Wesson 41 and 44 Magnum revolvers are available with a patented "Power Control" to reduce muzzle flip. Both the 41 and the 44 have a one-piece frame and patented gain bolt for maximum strength.

SPECIFICATIONS
Action: Six-shot double- and single-action. **Ammunition:** Models 41 and 741, 41 Magnum; Models 44 and 744, 44 Magnum and 44 Special. **Typical dimension:** 6″ barrel revolver, 12″ × 6.″ **Trigger:** Smooth, wide tang (3/8″) with overtravel adjustment. **Hammer:** Wide checkered spur with short double-action travel. **Sights:** Front, 1/8″ serrated interchangeable blade; red insert standard, yellow and white available; rear, standard notch (.125, .080, or white outline) adjustable for windage and elevation; click graduated. **Rifling:** Eight lands and grooves, right-hand twist, 1 turn in 18.75 inches. **Note:** 4″, 6″, and 8″ 44 Magnum guns will be shipped with unported and Power Control barrels. 10″ 44 Magnum guns available only without Power Control. Only jacketed bullets should be used with the 44 Mag. Power Control or excessive leading will result.

Price:
Pistol Pac Model 41	$623.60—672.27
Stainless Steel....................	690.40—739.20
Pistol Pac Model 44	707.52—757.80
Stainless Steel....................	814.38—867.03

MODEL 44-V 44 MAGNUM w/8″ BARREL

MODEL	CALIBER	TYPE	BARREL LENGTHS & WEIGHT IN OUNCES				FINISH
			4″	6″	8″	10″*	
41-V	.41 Magnum	Target	48	53	58	64	Brite Blue
41-VH	.41 Magnum	Target	49	56	64	69	Brite Blue
44-V	.44 Magnum	Target	48	53	58	64	Brite Blue
44-VH	.44 Magnum	Target	49	56	64	69	Brite Blue
741-V	.41 Magnum	Target	48	53	58	64	Satin Stainless Steel
741-VH	.41 Magnum	Target	49	56	64	69	Satin Stainless Steel
744-V	.44 Magnum	Target	48	53	58	64	Satin Stainless Steel
744-VH	.44 Magnum	Target	49	56	64	69	Satin Stainless Steel

22 RIMFIRE and 22 WIN. MAGNUM REVOLVERS

Built on the same frames as the Dan Wesson 357 Magnum, these 22 rimfires offer the heft and balance of fine target revolvers. Affordable fun for the beginner or the expert.

SPECIFICATIONS
Action: Six-shot double and single action. **Ammunition:** Models 22 & 722, 22 Long Rifle; Models 22M & 722M, 22 Win. Mag. **Typical dimension:** 4″ barrel revolver, 9 1/4″ × 5 3/4″. **Trigger:** Smooth, wide tang (3/8″) with overtravel adjustment. **Hammer:** Wide spur (3/8″) with short double-action travel. **Sights:** Front, 1/8″ serrated, interchangeable blade; red insert standard, yellow and white available; rear, standard wide notch (.125, .080, or white outline) adjustable for windage and elevation; graduated click. **Rifling:** Models 22 and 722, six lands and grooves, right-hand twist, 1 turn in 12 inches; Models 22M and 722M, six lands and grooves, right-hand twist, 1 turn in 16 inches. **Note:** All 2 1/2″ guns are shipped with undercover grips. 4″ guns are shipped with service grips and the balance have oversized target grips.

Price:
Pistol Pac Models 22 thru 722M	$614.73 to $922.52

MODEL	CALIBER	TYPE	BARREL LENGTHS & WEIGHT IN OUNCES				FINISH
			2 1/4″	4″	6″	8″	
22	.22 L.R.	Target	36	40	44	49	Brite Blue
22-V	.22 L.R.	Target	36	40	44	49	Brite Blue
22-VH	.22 L.R.	Target	36	41	47	54	Brite Blue
22-M	.22 Win Mag	Target	36	40	44	49	Brite Blue
22M-V	.22 Win Mag	Target	36	40	44	49	Brite Blue
22M-VH	.22 Win Mag	Target	36	41	47	54	Brite Blue
722	.22 L.R.	Target	36	40	44	49	Satin Stainless Steel
722-V	.22 L.R.	Target	36	40	44	49	Satin Stainless Steel
722-VH	.22 L.R.	Target	36	41	47	54	Satin Stainless Steel
722M	.22 Win Mag	Target	36	40	44	49	Satin Stainless Steel
722M-V	.22 Win Mag	Target	36	40	44	49	Satin Stainless Steel
722M-VH	.22 Win Mag	Target	36	41	47	54	Satin Stainless Steel

HUNTER PACS

Offered in all magnum calibers with the following:
1. Complete gun in choice of caliber (22, 32, 357, 41, 44, 357 Supermag and 375 Supermag) with 8″ vent-heavy shroud.
2. 8″ vent shroud only, equipped with Burris scope mounts and scope (1 1/2× -4× variable or fixed 2×).
3. Barrel changing tool and Dan Wesson emblem packed in attractive case.

Prices: $663.77 (357 Magnum w/2×) to $988.04 (357 Supermag Stainless w/1 1/2× -4×)

DAN WESSON REVOLVERS

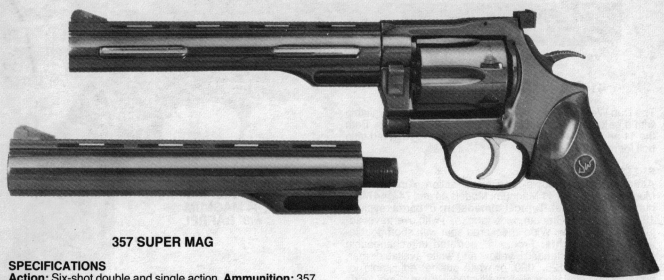

357 SUPER MAG

SPECIFICATIONS
Action: Six-shot double and single action. **Ammunition:** 357 Maximum. **Overall length:** 14.375" with 8" barrel. **Height:** 6.5". **Trigger:** Clean let-off, wide tang with overtravel adjustment. **Hammer:** Wide spur with short double-action travel. **Sights:** 1/8" serrated interchangeable front blade; red insert standard, yellow and white available; rear, new interchangeable blade (.125 or optional .080); screwdriver adjustable for windage and elevation. **Rifling:** Six lands and grooves, right-hand twist, 1 in 18 3/4 inches.

SPECIFICATIONS

Model	Caliber	Type	Barrel lengths & Weight (oz.)			Finish	Price
			6"	8"	10"		
740-V	357 Max	Target	59.5	65	62	Stainless	
740-VH	357 Max	Target	62	72	76	Stainless	$568.97—641.89
740-V8S	357 Max	Target		64		Stainless	

32 MAGNUM SIX SHOT

This target and small game gun offers a high muzzle velocity and a flat trajectory for better accuracy. Available in blue and stainless steel.

SPECIFICATIONS

Model	Caliber	Type	Barrel lengths & Weight in ounces				Finish	Prices*
			2 1/2"	4"	6"	8"		
32	.32 Magnum	Target	35	39	43	48	Brite Blue	
32V	.32 Magnum	Target	35	39	43	48	Brite Blue	$337.64—
32VH	.32 Magnum	Target	35	40	46	53	Brite Blue	$415.32
732	.32 Magnum	Target	35	39	43	48	Satin Stainless Steel	
732V	.32 Magnum	Target	35	39	43	48	Satin Stainless Steel	$366.07—
732VH	.32 Magnum	Target	35	40	46	53	Satin Stainless Steel	$451.43

*Pistol Pacs: $614.73 to $887.81

Rifles

WHAT'S NEW IN RIFLES AND RIFLE PRODUCTS

BY JON R. SUNDRA: Shooter's Bible Rifle Consultant

The big news in the world of rifles is not so much the introduction of new guns, but variations on existing models, especially among centerfire rifles. New permutations of barrel lengths, calibers, stock composition and even *color* are what help keep the rifle scene a dynamic one.

Of equal interest is the fact that three *shotgun* manufacturers—Ithaca, Mossberg and U.S. Repeating Arms—have recently introduced *rifled* 12 gauge slug barrels in their pump shotgun models, thus qualifying them as—well, *rifles*. The use of conventional Foster-type slugs in any of these rifled shotgun barrels may or may not produce better accuracy than conventional smoothbore barrels. These specialized pipes really come into their own when they are used in conjunction with sabot-clad .50 caliber slugs of BRI (which is now distributed by Mossberg). The BRI slug is far more aerodynamic than the cup-shaped chunks of lead used in Remington, Winchester and Federal ammo. As a result of its flatter trajectory and higher terminal energy/velocity values, the BRI slug is efficient enough to make a 100-yard plus gun. That's based not only on superior ballistics, but on the higher level of accuracy these rifled barrels can provide. Assuming a scope is mounted and shooting is done from benchrest, any of these three guns is capable of punching three-inch groups at 100 yards.

Of the three gunmakers, Ithaca and Mossberg offer the easiest scope mounting, because their rifled slug barrels come equipped with mount bases affixed to the barrels, thereby maintaining the instant barrel

BRI's .50 caliber wasp-waist projectile in rifled bores (above) makes rifle-like performance available to slug shooters.

interchangeability feature. As such, an IER-type (Intermediate Eye Relief) scope is required on the Ithaca and Mossberg, while a conventional scope and receiver-based mount is called for in the 1300 Winchester.

BROWNING

Not long ago, this famed Utah-based firm introduced an unusual rifle called the A-Bolt Stalker, which fea-

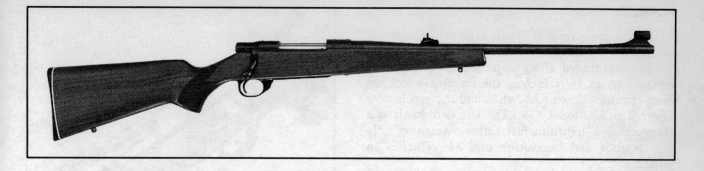

Interarm's new Howa line of centerfire rifles includes the Hunter grade, shown here, with its straight comb classic styling.

tured a black stock. With nearly every rifle manufacturer now offering black fiberglass handles, Browning's Stalker hardly raised an eyebrow—until folks learned that Browning's stock was fashioned from a chunk of hardwood painted black. The original Stalker had none of the advantages of a synthetic stock—strength, stability and light weight—only the color. The new A-Bolt Stalker is still black, but underneath the textured paint is a well made stock of graphite-reinforced fiberglass, complete with molded-in checkering panels. Actually, the Stalker offers three permutations: one is a silvery, matte-finished barreled action in stainless steel; another sports matte blue metalwork; and a third type features a laminated stock of black-green veneers. The last, called the A-Bolt Camo Stalker, appeals to the growing number of shooters who like the added strength and stability of the synthetic stock but not the hollow sound and toy-like feel of a "plastic" one.

Also new in Browning's growing A-Bolt line is the Micro Hunter grade with its shortened, slimmed-down stock and barrel, similar in concept to Remington's Mountain Rifle. A new Gold Medallion model goes a step farther than the regular Medallion grade with its top quality wood and embellishment. And the great .375 H&H Magnum has been added to the A-Bolt list of chamberings, which now total an impressive 13. Finally, the popular BAR semiauto is once again available in the potent .338 Winchester Magnum, which was dropped a few years ago.

INTERARMS

The news from this well-known importer is its exclusive U.S. distribution of the Howa line of centerfire rifles. Howa is the Japanese firm that makes Weatherby's guns, as well as the rifles once marketed in this country by Smith & Wesson, then Mossberg, and now Interarms.

Three Howa stocks are offered. The Trophy grade sports a Monte Carlo; the Hunter grade is a straight comb classic; and the third stock variety, called Lightning, features a black synthetic style by Bell & Carlson. There's also a heavy-barreled Varminter model offered in .223 and .22-250. For a while, at least, game caliber selection will be limited. In standard chamberings Interarms lists the .243, .270 .30-06 and .308, and in magnums there are the 7mm Remington and .300 Winchester. In the future, look for an expanded Howa line—it's a good, sound rifle.

As for the already diversified line of Mauser-type Mark X rifles, actions and barreled actions, Interarms has added the same Bell & Carlson fiberglass stock option.

KIMBER

Two major developments coming out of Clackamas, Oregon, are the long-awaited Kimber BGR (Big Game Rifle), which is now in the production stage, and Model 82 .22LR target rifle, the same gun Kimber produces for Uncle Sam. Kimber's current price list reveals a suggested retail for the BGR of $985.00 for the Classic grade in both standard and magnum calibers. The Custom Classic is priced at $1,230.00, and the Super America at $1,385.00. The highly accurate Model 82-A Government .22 is set for $645.00. All in all, it seems fair to predict that Kimber will be hard pressed to make these guns fast enough.

MARLIN

The latest innovation at Marlin is its transformation of the basic Model 336 lever action .30-30. The barrel has been shortened, along with the tubular magazine beneath it, to 16¼ inches, the forearm wood has been trimmed down somewhat, and the gun is now referred to as Model 336 LTS. The end result is a transportable, lightning-fast carbine weighing only 6½ pounds and measuring just 34⅜ inches in length.

Marlin has also taken Model 1894 and chambered it for two cartridges that first became popular back when Teddy Roosevelt and his Rough Riders were charging up San Juan Hill: the .25-20 Winchester and .35-20 Winchester. Both rounds may be obsolete, but that doesn't mean they can't be a lot of fun in a gun like Marlin's 1894-CL lever action. Moreover, they're just as effective at potting pests as they were 50 years ago. This model's straight buttstock, square finger lever and vintage open sights are sure to appeal to all those who share a nostalgic bent.

REMINGTON

The major development at Remington has to be its introduction of the long-time wildcat .35 Whelen, which it now offers with the Model 700 rifle (along with the factory ammo that goes with it). The Whelen makes its debut as a member of Remington's ongoing Limited Edition Classic series only, and will not be offered in the standard ADL, BDL or Mountain Rifle models.

As for the factory-loaded fodder, two loads are offered: a 200 grain pointed soft-point (PSP) at 2675 fps and 3177 foot pounds of muzzle energy, and a 250 grain round-nosed soft point at 2400 fps and 3197 foot pounds of muzzle energy.

Remington's Mountain Rifle has become so popular that it's now being offered in a short action version chambered in .243 Winchester, 7mm-08 Remington and .308 Winchester. Until now, only long action calibers were available in this lightweight version of the 700. Now that the Mountain Rifle is available in some of the same short action calibers as the Model 7, shooters will have a hard time deciding between the two.

Remington has also added a laminated stock version of its Model ADL 700 (in 30-06 only), thereby joining Mauser, Ruger, Savage, Sako, Browning and U.S. Repeating Arms in offering at least one version of its bolt action rifle with a laminated stock.

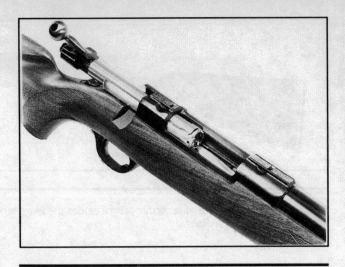

Ruger's Model 77 (above) has a Mauser-type extractor but with plunger ejection. The new Mark II version features mechanical ejection.

RUGER

We may be seeing the start of an eventual wholesale revision of Ruger's Model 77 bolt action rifle. A prototype recently unveiled features a new chambering—.223 Remington—and its familiar plunger ejector was replaced by a mechanical one similar to that found in the pre-1964 Model 70 Winchester. As for Ruger's plan to change Model 77 to the '98 Mauser system, the big outboard extractor is already there, of course, but the 77's action still does not include the controlled-round feeding of the '98. Cartridges feeding up from the magazine of the 77 are simply pushed ahead of the bolt, as on any other plunger-type design. By contrast, the Mauser extractor takes control of the cartridge rim the moment it clears the feed rails, which makes it far more "idiot-proof." In any event, Ruger now has the mechanical ejection on what they're calling the Model 77 Mark II in .223 caliber. Modification of the bolt face required to make the 77 a controlled-round action cannot be far behind.

SAKO

Over in Finland, Sako has pulled off a real coup by modifying its petite AI action to a solid-bottom single shot, adding a match-quality trigger and screwing on a target-grade bull barrel chambered for the world's two most accurate catridges—the .22 and

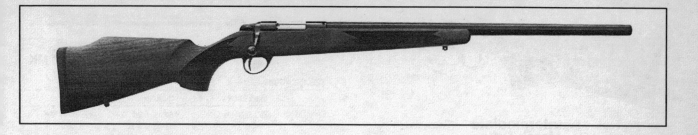

Sako's .22 and 6mm PPC rifles feature solid-bottom, single shot action, target grade bull barrel, and a 24-ounce match-quality trigger.

6mm PPC's. Together, these two calibers have dominated benchrest competition for more than a decade. Sako is offering its own factory-loaded ammunition to such high standards that in either caliber groups of well below half an inch at 100 yards are the norm.

As for velocity, neither of these benchrest cartridges is considered a barn burner, at least not in factory-loaded form. The .22 version is loaded with a 52 grain hollow point at a normal 3400 fps; and the 6mm 68 grain HP exits at 3140 fps. While that doesn't put them in the .22-250 or .240 Weatherby category, the exceptional accuracy of these PPC's makes them genuine 300-yard varmint rifles. The PPC's are being offered in the single shot version only with a Monte Carlo-type stock. A repeater version with Sako's regular straight-comb varmint stock will soon be available, along with a lightweight sporter version. Surely other companies will follow Sako's lead and eventually chamber their rifles for these extremely accurate PPC cartridges.

SAVAGE

With the introduction of its Model 100-F, Savage has joined the swelling ranks of centerfire rifle makers who are offering a fiberglass stock as a standard option. This newest Savage sports the black color and stippled texture that have become standard features of the synthetic stock.

Fortunately, Savage has produced a more attractive, better proportioned stock than the ones supplied with its Model 110-E, with its stained hardwood, and Model 110-B, with its all-brown laminate. Savage's synthetic stock is finished in a conservative, straight-comb classic pattern. There's nice detail around the pistol grip and flute areas where shortcuts are usually taken to reduce costs. The new 110-F is a good-looking rifle and an excellent value.

U.S. REPEATING ARMS

Stock variations are the name of the game at the Winchester shop. Just about every variety of Model 70 is now offered in a choice of McMillan-made fiberglass handles, which USRAC calls "Winlite," and two versions of a laminated stock—one in all-brown, called "Win-Tuff," and the other a tri-color combo called "Win-Cam." These same laminated options are available in Models 94 and 9422 lever actions, as well as in several variations of the Winchester Model 1300 pump shotgun.

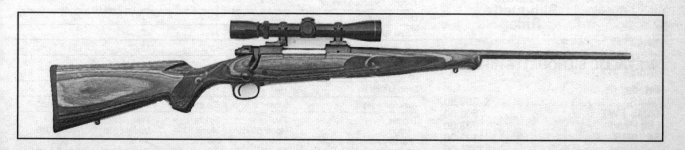

U.S. Repeating Arms' commitment to laminates is reflected in this new Model 70 Featherweight in Win-Tuf.

ANSCHUTZ MATCH RIFLES

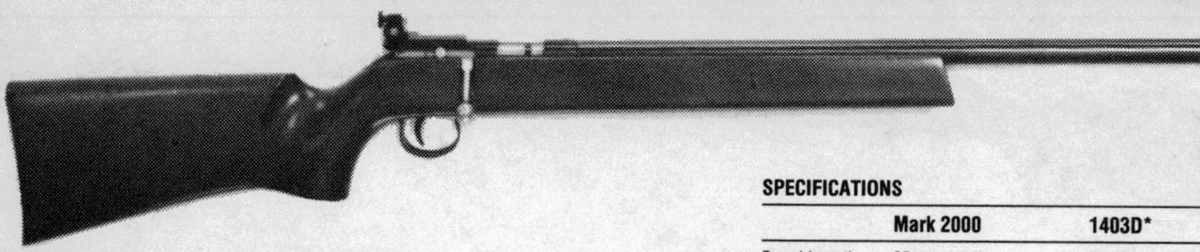

MODEL MARK 2000 MK

Intermediate Match Rifles

INTERMEDIATE MATCH RIFLES

Prices

Mark 2000	**$399.50**
1403D	667.50
Left Hand	724.50
1803D	739.00
Left Hand	842.50

SPECIFICATIONS

	Mark 2000	1403D*	1803D*
Barrel Length	25¼″ ¾″ dia.	Precision rifled .22 long rifle only 25″ medium heavy ¹¹/₁₆″ dia.	25½″ ¾″ dia.
Action	Match 2000	Match 64	Match 64
Trigger	Single stage. Factory set for crisp trigger pull 3 lbs.	1.1 lbs. Single stage, adjustable* for weight of pull, take-up over travel. #5093	#5091 2 stage adjustable* from 9.2 to 10.6 oz.
Safety	Slide safety locks trigger.	Slide safety locks sear and bolt.	Slide safety looks sear and bolt.
Stock	Walnut finished hard-woood. Swivel rail.	Walnut finished hard-wood. Cheek piece/ Swivel Rail. Stippling.	Blonde finish, adjustable cheek piece. stippled pistol grip and fore stock. Swivel rail.
Sights	Front: Insert type globe sight. Rear Micrometer with clock adjustments (available separately as S.S.#2, #3)	Takes Anschutz 6723 Sight Set (available separately.)	Takes Anschutz 6723 Sight Set (available separately.)
Overall Length	43¼″	43¼″	43¼″
Weight (avg.)	7½ lbs.	8.6 lbs. with sights	8.6 lbs.
Left Hand			1803D Left

MODEL 64MS

MODEL 54.18MS

Metallic Silhouette Rifles

METALLIC SILHOUETTE RIFLES

Prices

64MS	**$ 399.50**
64MS-FWT	596.00
Left Hand	733.00
54.18MS	1129.00
Left Hand	1228.00
54.18MS-ED	1215.00
Left Hand	1321.00

Specifications and Features

	* 64MS	64MS-FWT	* 54.18MS	* 54.18MS-ED
Grooved for scope	•	•	•	•
Tapped for scope mount	•	•		
Overall length	39.5″	38¼″	41″	49″
Barrel length	21¼″	21¼″	22″	30″
Length of pull	13½″	13½″	13¾″	13¾″
High cheek piece with Monte Carlo effect	•	•	•	•
Drop at Comb	1½″	1½″	1½″	1½″
Average weight	8 lbs.	6¼ lbs.	8 lbs. 6 oz.	8 lbs. 6 oz.
Trigger: Stage	Two	Single	Two	Two
Model	Model 5091	Model 5094	Model 5018	Model 5018
Factory adjusted weight	5.3 oz.	3.0 lbs.	3.9 oz.	3.9 oz.
Adjustable weight	4.9---7 oz.	2.2---4.4 lbs.	2.1---8.6 oz.	2.1---8.6 oz.
Safety	Slide	Slide	Slide	Slide

* Left-hand rifles are built to same specifications except with left-hand stock cast off.

ANSCHUTZ TARGET RIFLES

**MODEL 1913
SUPER MATCH**
$2067.00 ($2237.00 Left Hand)

**MODEL 1911
PRONE MATCH**
$1444.00 ($1570.00 Left Hand)

**MODEL 1907
ISU STANDARD**
$1232.00 ($1340.00 Left Hand)

**MODEL 1808ED
SUPER RUNNING**
$1235.00 ($1359.00 Left Hand)

INTERNATIONAL MATCH RIFLES

Specifications and Features

	1913	1911	1910	1907	1808ED
Barrel Length	27¹/₄"	27¹/₄"	27¹/₄"	26"	32¹/₂"
O/D	1"	1"	1"	⁷/₈"	⁷/₈"
Stock	Int'l.- Thumb Hole Adj. Palm Rest Adj. Hand Rest	Prone	Int'l.- Thumb Hole	Standard	Thumb Hole
Cheek Piece	Adj.	Adj.	Adj.	Removable	Adj.
Butt Plate	Adj. Hook 10 Way Hook	Adj. 4 Way	Adj. Hook 10 Way Hook	Adj. 4 Way	Adj. 4 Way
Overall Length	45"-46"	45"-46"	45"-46"	43³/₄"-44¹/₂"	50¹/₂"
Overall Length to Hook	49.6"-51.2"		49.6"-51.2"		
Weight without sights (approx)	15.4 lbs.	11.9 lbs.	13.9 lbs.	10 lbs.	9¹/₄ lbs.
True Left-Hand Version	1913Left	1911Left	1910Left	1907Left	1808Left

ANSCHUTZ RIFLES

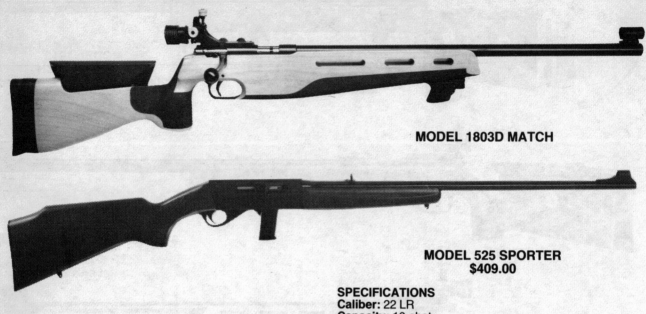

MODEL 1803D MATCH

MODEL 525 SPORTER
$409.00

SPECIFICATIONS
Caliber: 22 LR
Capacity: 10-shot
Barrel length: 24″
Overall length: 43″
Weight: 6$\frac{1}{2}$ lbs.
Sights: Hood ramp front; folding leaf rear
Stock/forend: Checkered Monte Carlo stock and beavertail forend of European hardwood
Length of pull: 14″
Drop at comb: 1$\frac{1}{4}$″
Drop at heel: 2$\frac{5}{8}$″
Features: Rotary-style safety; swivel studs; grooved for scope

THE ACHIEVER 22 LR
$319.50

SPECIFICATIONS
Capacity: 5 shot
Barrel length: 19$\frac{1}{2}$″
Overall length: 36$\frac{1}{4}$″
Weight: 5 lbs.
Action: Mark 2000 type repeating
Trigger: #5066-two stage 2.6 lbs.
Safety: Slide
Stock pull: 11$\frac{7}{8}$″-13″
Sights: Hooded ramp front; rear marble folding leaf; adj. for windage and elevation

ANSCHUTZ SPORTER RIFLES

MODEL 1422D CUSTOM
$939.99

BAVARIAN 1700
$967.00 (22 LR and 22 Mag.)
$1099.00 (22 Hornet and 222 Rem.)

Specifications	Classic 1422D 1522D	Bavarian .221LR .22 Mag.	Custom 1422D 1522D	Bavarian .22 Hor. .222 Rem.
Length—Overall	43″	43″	43″	43″
Barrel	24″	24″	24″	24″
Dia. at muzzle	11/16″	11/16″	11/16″	11/16″
Pull	14″	14″	14″	14″
Drop at—Comb	1¼″	1¼″	1″	1″
Monte Carlo	—	—	1″	—
Heel	1½″	1½″	1¾″	1½″
Average Weight	6½ lbs.	7¼ lbs.	7¼ lbs.	7¼ lbs.
Rate of Twist	Right Hand—one turn in 16.5″ for .22 LR; 1-16″ for .22 Mag & .22 Hornet; 1-14″ for .222 Rem.			
Take Down Bolt Action With Removable Firing Pin	•	•	•	•
Swivel Studs	•	•	•	•
Grooved for Scope	•	•	•	•
Tapped for Scope Blocks	•	•	•	•
Sights—Front—Hooded Ramp	•	•	•	•
Rear—Folding Leaf	•	•	•	•
Trigger Single Stage	5063	5096	5063	5096 .22 Hor 5095 .222 Rem.
*Adjustable for Creep & Pull	•	•	•	•
Factory Set for 2.6 lbs.	•	•	•	•
Adjustable for Overtravel		•		•
Clip Magazine	•	•	•	•
Safety—Wing	•	•	•	•
Stock—Monte Carlo			•	•
Cheek Piece		•	•	•
Roll Over Cheek Piece			•	•

BEEMAN RIFLES

BEEMAN/WEIHRAUCH HW 60 SMALLBORE RIFLE
$698.00 (Right) $739.95 (Left)

22 caliber LR, single shot. Improved bolt action. Adjustable match trigger with push button safety. Precision rifled barrel. Stippled forearm and pistol grip. Precision aperture sights, hooded front sight ramp. **Barrel length:** 26.8″. **Overall length:** 45.7″. **Weight:** 10.8 lbs.

BEEMAN/FWB 2000
From $1225.00

22 caliber LR. Micrometer match aperture sights. Foresight with interchangeable inserts. Meets ISU standard rifle specifications. Short lock time. Precision match trigger adjustable for weight, release point, finger length, lateral position, or advanced electronic trigger. **Barrel length:** 22″ and 26¼″. **Overall length:** 39″ and 43¾″. **Weight:** 9⅛ lbs. and 9¾ lbs. Left-hand and electronic trigger versions available.

BEEMAN/FWB 2000
SUPER MATCH
$2190.00 Mech. Trigger $2570.00 Elect. Trigger

22 caliber LR. Developed from the highly successful design of the FWB 2000. Available with same outstanding mechanical trigger of the 2000 or the new electronic trigger. Anatomically correct thumbhole stock, accessory rails for moveable weights; adj. palm rest, adj. cheekpiece, adj. hooked buttplate; superb match sights. Left-hand versions available.

BEEMAN/FWB 2600
$1375.00 (Right) $1550.00 (Left)

22 caliber LR. Designed as an identical small bore companion to the Beeman/FWB 600 Match air rifle. Super rigid stock made of laminated hardwood. Bull barrel free floats. Stock is cut low to permit complete ventilation around barrel. Match trigger has fingertip weight adjustment dial. Adjustable comb; match sights; single shot.

BEEMAN/KRICO RIFLES

Beeman/Krico rifles bring West German tradition to the world of varmint and big game hunting and target shooting in North America. Noted worldwide for their superb balance and handling, these rifles feature hammer forged, precision rifled barrels, exceptionally fine triggers, smoothly operating bolt actions, and interchangeable trigger modules. All models have cheekpieces and fine handcut checkering on the grips and forearms (except target models, which are stippled). All Beeman/Krico rifles are proofed at the factory for accuracy (at 100 meters, hunting rifles must group shots under 1.2 inches; target rifles are under .75 inches).

MODEL 400
$1225.00

Classic German-style 22 Hornet varmint rifle. Beautifully designed for natural balance and easy handling. Detachable 5-shot magazine. Exceptional accuracy. Grooved for scopes. Smooth sliding bolt and crisp trigger action. **Overall length:** 43″. **Weight:** 6.8 lbs.

MODEL 420
$1425.00 (scope not included)

22 Hornet varmint rifle with exceptionally sleek full stock. Has same features as Model 400, but with a double-set trigger for carefully aimed, precision shots. Detachable 5-shot magazine. The 22 Hornet caliber's light report and moderate power make it suitable for areas too populated for heavy cartridge use. **Overall length:** 38″. **Weight:** 6.5 lbs. Grooved for scopes.

MODEL 640 VARMINT
$1697.00
(shown with optional Beeman scope)

Heavy barrel varmint rifle 222 Rem., 223 Rem., 22-250. Walnut stock has high, Monte Carlo comb, full cheekpiece, checkered grip with Wundhammer palm swell and rosewood forend tip and grip cap. **Heavy barrel length:** 23³/₄″ long; 4-shot magazine. **Overall length:** 43¹/₂″. **Weight:** 9.6 lbs.

MODEL 340
METALLIC SILHOUETTE RIFLE
$1186.00

Heavy bull barrel adds extra control and steadiness. Tests produce 5-shot groups under ¹/₂″ ctc at 100 yards. Large, ³/₄″ diameter bolt knob for fast handling. 5-shot magazine. Double extractors. Match trigger adjusts from 14 to 28 oz. Franchi rubber buttplate. Stippled grip and forearm. Grooved for scopes. **Overall length:** 39¹/₂″. **Weight:** 7.5 lbs.

BEEMAN/KRICO RIFLES

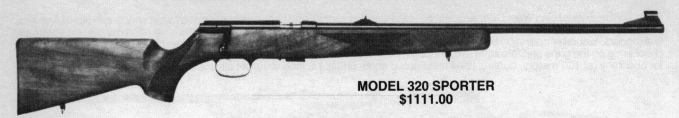

MODEL 320 SPORTER
$1111.00

SPECIFICATIONS
Caliber: 22 LR
Overall length: 43″

Capacity: 5-shot magazine
Weight: 6½ lbs.
Features: Straight stock and full forearm; receiver ground for scope mounts

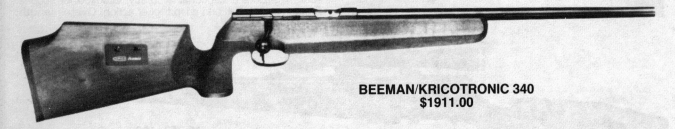

BEEMAN/KRICOTRONIC 340
$1911.00

22 caliber LR. The only rifle with an operational electronic ignition system designed for conventional ammunition. The system eliminates the need for a firing pin, as ammunition is ignited by an electronic current. Lock time is virtually instantaneous. On-Off switch activates electronic system. Operates like a normal bolt action rifle. Stock design by Texas Silhouette Champion Mike Massey. Bull barrel.

MODEL 600/700
$1898.00---$1953.00

SPECIFICATIONS
Calibers: 243 Rem., 308 Win., 270, 30-06
Overall length: 44″
Weight: 7 lbs.
Capacity: 3-shot magazine

Features: Drilled and tapped for scopes; double forward bolt lugs; silent safety; hammer swaged, chrome moly steel barrels
Model 620/720: Same specifications as 600/700 series except it features full stock style.

MODEL 640 SUPER SNIPER
$2363.00

SPECIFICATIONS
Caliber: 308 Win. and 223 Rem.
Overall length: 44¾″
Weight: 9.4 lbs.

Capacity: 3-shot magazine
Features: Adjustable buttplate and cheekpiece; oversize bolt knob; match grade trigger w/trigger shoe; heavy barrel w/ military-style muzzle brake; drilled and tapped for scopes

BLASER RIFLES

MODEL K 77A SINGLE SHOT

SPECIFICATIONS
Calibers: (interchangeable)
    Standard: 22-250, 243 Win., 6.5x55, 270 Win., 280 Rem., 7x57R, 7x65R, 30-06
    Magnum: 7mm Rem. Mag., 300 Win. Mag., 300 Weatherby Mag.
Barrel lengths: 23″ (Standard) and 24″ (Magnum)
Overall length: 39$^{1}/_{2}$″ (Standard); 40$^{1}/_{2}$″ (Magnum)
Weight: (w/scope mounts) 5$^{1}/_{2}$ lbs. (Standard) and 5$^{3}/_{4}$ lbs. (Magnum)
Safety: Tang-mounted safety slide provides cocking and de-cocking of hammer spring

Stock: Two-piece Turkish walnut stock and forend; solid black recoil pad; handcut checkering (18 lines/inch, borderless)
Length of pull: 14″
Scope mounts: Low-profile Blaser one-piece steel (for 1″ dia. scopes)
Prices:
Standard calibers w/scope mounts **$2280.00**
Magnum calibers w/scope mounts 2330.00
Interchangeable barrels—Standard 730.00
    Magnum 778.00

ULTIMATE BOLT ACTION

SPECIFICATIONS
Calibers: (interchangeable)
    Standard: 22-250, 243 Win., 25-06, 270 Win., 280 Rem., 308 Win., 30-06
    Magnum: 264 Win. Mag., 7mm Rem. Mag., 300 Win. Mag., 300 Weatherby Mag., 338 Win. Mag., 375 H&H
Barrel lengths: 23$^{1}/_{2}$″ (22″ in 25-06 and 243 Win.)
Weight: 6 to 6.75 lbs.
Safety: Cocks and uncocks the firing pin spring; spring is not under tension when safety lever is rearward, so gun can be loaded and unloaded with safety on; to cock gun, push safety forward
Prices:
All calibers, right or left hand **$1295.00**
"Ultimate Deluxe" Model 1595.00
Interchangeable barrels (all calibers) 401.00

Note: Special Order models are also available, from **Ultimate Carbine** w/19$^{1}/_{2}$″ barrel (**$1800.00**) to **Ultimate Royal** (**$11,500.00**) plus interchangeable barrels (**$700.00** to **$1200.00**).

MODEL R 84 BOLT ACTION

SPECIFICATIONS
Calibers: (interchangeable)
    Standard: 22-250, 243 Win., 6mm Rem., 25-06, 270 Win., 280 Rem., 30-06
    Magnum: 257 Weatherby Mag., 264 Win. Mag., 7mm Rem. Mag., 300 Win. Mag., 300 Weatherby Mag., 338 Win. Mag., 375 H&H
Barrel lengths: 23″ (Standard) and 24″ (Magnum)
Overall length: 41″ (Standard) and 42″ (Magnum)
Weight: (w/scope mounts) 7 lbs. (Standard) and 7$^{1}/_{4}$ lbs. (Magnum)
Safety: Locks firing pin and bolt handle
Stock: Two-piece Turkish walnut stock and forend; solid black recoil pad, handcut checkering (18 lines/inch, borderless)
Length of pull: 13$^{3}/_{4}$″
Prices:
Standard calibers w/scope mounts **$1495.00**
Magnum calibers w/scope mounts 1545.00
Left-Hand Standard w/scope mounts 1595.00
Left-Hand Magnum w/scope mounts 1656.00
Interchangeable barrels—Standard 495.00
    Magnum 545.00

BRNO RIFLES

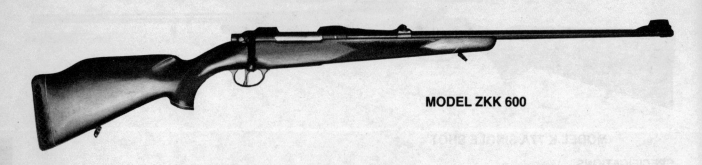

MODEL ZKK 600

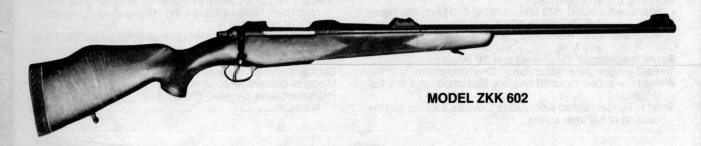

MODEL ZKK 602

MODEL ZKK
SPECIFICATIONS

Model	Action Type	Cal.	Barrel Specifications			Overall Length	Weight	Magazine Capacity	Sighted In
			Length	Rifling Twist	#Lands				
ZKK 600	bolt	270 Win	23.5 in	1 in 10"	4	44.0 in.	7 lbs. 2 oz.	5	110 yd.
		7×57		1 in 9"	4				
		7×64		1 in 9"	4				
		30.06 Spring			4				
ZKK 601	bolt	223 Rem	23.5 in.	1 in 12"	4	43.0 in.	6 lbs. 13 oz.	5	110 yd.
		243 Win		1 in 10"	4				
		308 Win		1 in 12"	4				
ZKK 602	bolt	300 Win mag	25.0 in.	1 in 10"	4	45.5 in.	9 lb. 4 oz.	5	110 yd.
		8×68		1 in 11"	4				
		375 H&H		1 in 12"	4				
		458 Win mag		1 in 14"	4				

Prices:
Model ZKK 600 Standard $599.00
Model ZKK 601 Monte Carlo Stock 599.00
Model ZKK 602 Standard 689.00
Monte Carlo Stock 749.00

BROWNING LEVER ACTION RIFLES

MODEL 1885

MODEL 1885
$639.95

Calibers: 22-250; 223, 30-06, 270, 7mm Rem. Mag., 45-70 Govt. **Bolt system:** Falling block. **Barrel length:** 28″ (recessed muzzle). **Overall length:** 43½″. **Weight:** 8 lbs. 8 oz. **Action:** High wall type, single shot, lever action. **Sights:** Drilled and tapped for scope mounts; two-piece scope base

available. **Hammer:** Exposed, serrated, three-position with inertia sear. **Stock and Forearm:** Select Walnut, straight grip stock and Schnabel forearm with cut checkering. Recoil pad standard.

MODEL 81 BLR RIFLE

MODEL 81 BLR SPECIFICATIONS

Calibers: 222 Rem., 223 Rem. 22-250 Rem., 243 Win., 257 Roberts, 7mm-08 Rem., 308 Win. and 358 Win. **Approximate Weight:** 6 lbs. 15 oz. **Overall length:** 39¾″. **Action:** Lever action with rotating head, multiple lug breech bolt with recessed bolt face. Side ejection. **Barrel length:** 20″. Individually machined from forged, heat treated chrome-moly steel; crowned muzzle. **Rifling:** 243 Win., one turn in 10″; 308 and 358 Win., one turn in 12″. **Magazine:** Detachable, 4-round capacity. **Trigger:** Wide, grooved finger piece. Short crisp pull of 4½ pounds. Travels with lever. **Receiver:** Non-glare top. Drilled and tapped to accept most top scope mounts. Forged and milled steel. All parts are machine-finished and hand-fit-

ted. Surface deeply polished. **Sights:** Low profile, square notch, screw adjustable rear sight. Gold bead on a hooded raised ramp front sight. Sight radius: 17¾″. **Safety:** Exposed, 3-position hammer. Trigger disconnect system. Inertia firing pin. **Stock and forearm:** Select walnut with tough oil finish and sure-grip checkering, contoured for use with either open sights or scope. Straight grip stock. Deluxe recoil pad installed.

Length of pull . . . . 13¾″
Drop at comb . . . . 1¾″
Drop at heel . . . . 2⅜″

Price (with sights) $449.95

BROWNING RIFLES

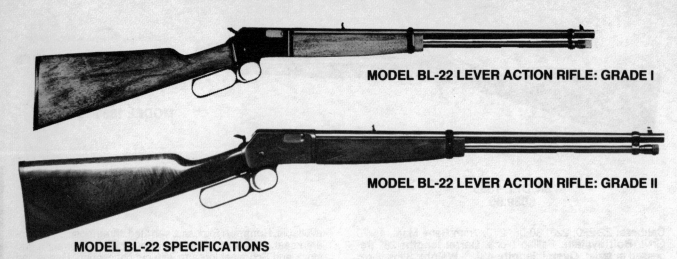

MODEL BL-22 LEVER ACTION RIFLE: GRADE I

MODEL BL-22 LEVER ACTION RIFLE: GRADE II

MODEL BL-22 SPECIFICATIONS

Action: Short throw lever action. Lever travels through an arc of only 33 degrees and carries the trigger with it, preventing finger pinch between lever and trigger on the upward swing. The lever cycle ejects the fired shell, cocks the hammer and feeds a fresh round into the chamber. **Magazine:** Rifle is designed to handle 22 caliber ammunition *in any combination* from tubular magazine. Magazine capacity is 15 Long Rifles, 17 Longs and 22 Shorts. The positive magazine latch opens and closes easily from any position. **Safety:** A unique disconnect system prevents firing until the lever and breech are fully closed and pressure is released from and reapplied to the trigger. An inertia firing pin and an exposed hammer with a half-cock position are other safety features. **Receiver:** Forged and milled steel. Grooved. All parts are machine-finished and hand-fitted. **Trigger:** Clean and crisp without creep. Average pull 5 pounds. Trigger gold-plated on Grade II model. **Stock and forearm:** Forearm and straight grip butt stock are shaped from select, polished walnut. Hand checkered on Grade II model. Stock dimensions:

Length of Pull . . . . 13¹/₂″
Drop at Comb . . . . 1⁵/₈″
Drop at Heel . . . . 2¹/₄″

Sights: Precision, adjustable folding leaf rear sight. Raised bead front sight. **Scopes:** Grooved receiver will accept the Browning 22 riflescope (Model 1217) and two-piece ring mount (Model 9417) as well as most other groove or tip-off type mounts or receiver sights. **Engraving:** Grade II receiver and trigger guard are engraved with tasteful scroll designs. **Barrel length:** 20″; recessed muzzle. **Overall length:** 36³/₄″. **Weight:** 5 pounds

Price: Grade I **$286.95**
 Grade II 326.95

MODEL A-BOLT 22 BOLT ACTION
$319.95 ($329.95 w/Sights)

Caliber: 22 LR. **Barrel length:** 22″. **Overall length:** 40¹/₄″. **Average weight:** 5 lbs. 9 oz. **Action:** Short throw bolt. Bolt cycles a round with 60° of bolt rotation. Firing pin acts as secondary extractor and ejector, snapping out fired rounds at prescribed speed. **Magazine:** Five and 15-shot magazine standard. Magazine/clip ejects with a push on magazine latch button. **Trigger:** Gold colored, screw adjustable. Pre-set at approx. 4 lbs. **Stock:** Laminated walnut, classic style with pistol grip. **Length of pull:** 13³/₄″. **Drop at comb:** ³/₄″. **Drop at heel:** 1¹/₂″. **Sights:** Available with or without sights (add **$10** for sights). Ramp front and adjustable folding leaf rear on open sight model. **Scopes:** Grooved receiver for 22 mount. Drilled and tapped for full-size scope mounts.

SPECIFICATIONS RIMFIRE RIFLES

Model	Caliber	Barrel Length	Sight Radius	Overall Length	Average Weight
A-Bolt 22	22 Long Rifle	22″	17⁵/₈″	40¹/₄″	5 lbs. 9 oz.
22 Semi-Auto	22 Long Rifle	19¹/₄″	16¹/₄″	37″	4 lbs. 4 oz.
BL-22	22 Long Rifle, Longs, Shorts	20″	15³/₈″	36³/₄″	5 lbs.

BROWNING RIFLES

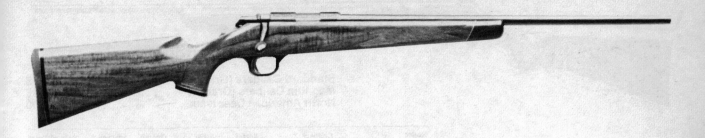

NEW: GOLD MEDALLION MODEL. Features classic-style stock of high-grade select walnut with high-gloss finish; detailed engraving; brass spacers; double-bordered checkering (22 lines per inch). **Price: $423.95.**

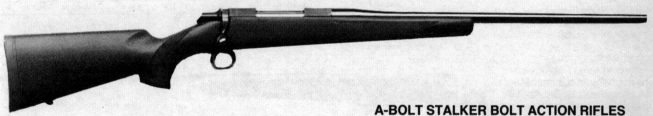

A-BOLT COMPOSITE STALKER

A-BOLT STALKER BOLT ACTION RIFLES

Browning's new graphite-fiberglass composite stock resists the nicks and scrapes of hard hunting and is resistant to weather and humidity. Its recoil-absorbing properties also make shooting a more pleasant experience. This series is available in three models: Stainless Stalker, Composite Stalker and Camo Stalker. The newest of these—the A-Bolt Composite Stalker—has the same features as Browning's A-Bolt Hunter plus the graphite-fiberglass composite stock, which helps ensure accuracy as well as durability. The stock is checkered for a good grip and has a nonglare textured finish. All exposed metal surfaces have a nonglare matte blued finish.

22 SEMIAUTOMATIC RIMFIRE RIFLES GRADES I AND VI

SPECIFICATIONS
Caliber: 22 LR. **Overall length:** 37". **Barrel length:** 19¼". **Weight:** 4 lbs. 4 oz. **Safety:** Cross-bolt type. **Capacity:** 11 cartridges in magazine, 1 in chamber. **Trigger:** Grade I is blued; Grade VI is gold colored. **Sights:** Gold bead front, adjustable folding leaf rear; drilled and tapped for Browning scope mounts. **Length of pull:** 13¾". **Drop at comb:** 1³/₁₆". **Drop at heel:** 2⅝". **Stock & Forearm:** Grade I, select walnut with checkering (18 lines/inch); Grade VI, high-grade walnut with checkering (22 lines/inch).

Grade I $328.50
Grade VI 674.95

GRADE VI

BROWNING RIFLES

BAR SEMIAUTOMATIC RIFLES

Standard Calibers (Grade I) $541.95
Magnum Calibers (Grade I) 587.95
North American Deer Issue 3550.00

BAR SEMIAUTOMATIC RIFLE

Model	Calibers	Barrel Length	Sight Radius*	Overall Length	Average Weight	Rate of Twist (Right Hand)
Magnum	338 Win. Mag.	24"	19 1/2"	45"	8 lbs. 6 oz.	1 in 12"
Magnum	300 Win Mag.	24"	19 1/2"	45"	8 lbs. 6 oz.	1 in 10"
Magnum	7mm Rem Mag.	24"	19 1/2"	45"	8 lbs. 6 oz.	1 in 9 1/2"
Standard	30-06 Sprg.	22"	17 1/2"	43"	7 lbs. 6 oz.	1 in 10"
Standard	280 Rem.	22"	17 1/2"	43"	7 lbs. 9 oz.	1 in 10"
Standard	270 Win.	22"	17 1/2"	43"	7 lbs. 9 oz.	1 in 10"
Standard	308 Win.	22"	17 1/2"	43"	7 lbs. 9 oz.	1 in 12"
Standard	243 Win.	22"	17 1/2"	43"	7 lbs. 10 oz.	1 in 10"
Big Game Series Ltd. Edition	30-06 Sprg.	22"	—	43"	7 lbs. 6 oz.	1 in 10"

*All models (except Big Game Series) are available with or without open sights. All models drilled and tapped for scope mounts.

Calibers: 25-06 Rem., 270 Win., 280 Rem., 30-06 Sprg., 7mm Rem. Mag., 300 Win. Mag., 338 Win. Mag. **Action:** Short throw bolt of 60 degrees. Plunger-type ejector. **Magazine:** Detachable. Depress the magazine latch and the hinged floorplate swings down. The magazine can be removed from the floorplate for reloading or safety reasons. **Trigger:** Adjustable within the average range of 3 to 6 pounds. Also grooved to provide sure finger control. **Stock and forearm:** Stock is select grade American walnut cut to the lines of a classic sporter with a full pistol grip. Stock dimensions:
Scopes: Closed. Clean tapered barrel. Receiver is drilled and tapped for a scope mount; or select **Hunter** model w/open sights. **Barrel length:** 24". Hammer forged rifling where a precision machined mandrel is inserted into the bore. The mandrel is a reproduction of the rifling in reverse. As hammer forces are applied to the exterior of the barrel, the barrel is actually molded around the mandrel to produce flawless rifling and to guarantee a straight bore. Free floated. **Overall length:** 44¼". **Weight:** 7 lbs. 8 oz. in Magnum; 6 lbs. 8 oz. in Short Action; 7 lbs. in Standard (Long Action).

Hunter $411.95
Hunter w/open sights 463.95
Medallion 478.95
Left-Hand Model 499.95
Medallion 375 H&H (open sights) 560.00
Micro Medallion (no sights) 478.95
Gold Medallion 624.95
Stainless Stalker (no sights) 524.95
Camo Stalker (no sights) 437.95

A-BOLT BOLT ACTION RIFLE

Short Action A-Bolt available in 223 Rem., 22-250 Rem., 243 Win., 257 Roberts, 7mm-08 Rem., 308 Win.

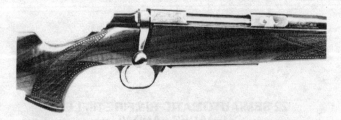

A-BOLT HIGH GRADE BOLT ACTION RIFLE
BIG HORN SHEEP LIMITED EDITION
$1365.00

Calibers: 270. Win. **Barrel length:** 22". **Overall length:** 42¾". **Approx. weight:** 6 lbs. 11 oz. **Stock:** High grade walnut profiled in classic style, embellished with cut skipline checkering with pearl border design. Rosewood forearm and grip caps. Brass spacers between stock and forearm and grip caps; also between recoil pad and stock. **Engraving:** Deep relief engraving on receiver, barrel, floorplate and trigger guard as setting for game species displayed in 24K gold. **Pronghorn Antelope Issue** (243 Win.): **$1240.00**

CHURCHILL RIFLES

REGENT BOLT ACTION RIFLE
$505.00 ($526.00 w/sights)

SPECIFICATIONS—REGENT, HIGHLANDER & HIGHLANDER COMBO

Calibers: 243 Win., 25-06, 270 Win., 308 Win., 30-06, 7mm Rem. Mag., 300 Win. Mag.
Capacity: 4 rounds; 3 rounds in 7mm Rem. Mag. and 300 Win. Mag.
Barrel length: 22"
Overall length: 42 1/2"
Weight: 7 1/2 lbs.; 8 lbs., Highlander Combo
Stock: Oil-finished standard grade European walnut (Highlander); extra select European walnut with 23-line hand-checkering, Monte Carlo comb and cheekpiece (Regent)
Prices: Highlander, $323.00; $345.00 w/sights.

Highlander Combo includes Highlander rifle with QD swivels, cobra-style sling, set of rings and bases, and 3-9 x 32mm Vistascope riflescope. **$375.00.**

Action: Bolt Action repeating
Receiver: Machined from solid block of forged high strength steel with hinged floorplate
Bolt: Machined forged steel with twin locking lugs and one large gas relief port
Barrel: Cold hammer forged steel
Safety: Positive non-slip thumb type on right side; locks trigger but allows bolt to be safely opened for unloading and inspection of the chamber
Stock: Select European Walnut with hand checkering and oil rubbed finish; swivel posts; recoil pad
Sights: Streamlined, contoured ramp; front gold bead; rear sight fully adjustable for windage and elevation

	ARTICLE NO.		CALIBER	BARREL LENGTH in/cm	OVERALL LENGTH in/cm	NOMINAL WEIGHT lb/kg	MAGAZINE CAPACITY rounds
	Without Sights	With Sights					
REGENT™	GA5433	GA6073	.243 Win.	22/56	42.5/108	7.5/3.4	4
	GA5441	GA6081	.25-06 Rem.	22/56	42.5/108	7.5/3.4	4
	GA5468	GA6103	.270 Win.	22/56	42.5/108	7.5/3.4	4
	GA5476	GA6111	.308 Win.	22/56	42.5/108	7.5/3.4	4
	GA5506	GA6146	.30-06 Sp.	22/56	42.5/108	7.5/3.4	4
	GA5565	GA6278	7mm Rem. Mag.	22/56	42.5/108	7.5/3.4	3
	GA5581	GA6286	.300 Win. Mag.	22/56	42.5/108	7.5/3.4	3
HIGHLANDER™	GA4089	GA5085	.25-06 Rem.	22/56	42.5/108	7.5/3.4	4
	GA4097	GA5093	.243 Win.	22/56	42.5/108	7.5/3.4	4
	GA4100	GA5107	.270 Win.	22/56	42.5/108	7.5/3.4	4
	GA4151	GA5131	.308 Win.	22/56	42.5/108	7.5/3.4	4
	GA4178	GA5158	.30-06 Sp.	22/56	42.5/108	7.5/3.4	4
	GA4267	GA5263	7mm Rem. Mag.	22/56	42.5/108	7.5/3.4	3
	GA4283	GA5271	.300 Win. Mag.	22/56	42.5/108	7.5/3.4	3
HIGHLANDER™ COMBO	GA7029		.25-06 Rem.	22/56	42.5/108	8/3.6	4
	GA7037		.243 Win.	22/56	42.5/108	8/3.6	4
	GA7045		.270 Win.	22/56	42.5/108	8/3.6	4
	GA7061		.308 Win.	22/56	42.5/108	8/3.6	4
	GA7088		.30-06 Sp.	22/56	42.5/108	8/3.6	4
	GA7126		7mm Rem. Mag.	22/56	42.5/108	8/3.6	3
	GA7207		.300 Win. Mag.	22/56	42.5/108	8/3.6	3

CLASSIC RIFLES

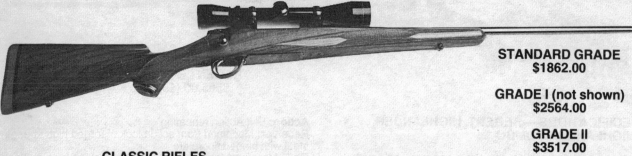

STANDARD GRADE
$1862.00

GRADE I (not shown)
$2564.00

GRADE II
$3517.00

CLASSIC RIFLES

Classic Rifles are presently offered in three grades: Standard, Grade I and Grade II. All stocks are made from French walnut and are fitted with forend tips (except Standard Grade), which are either ebony or striped ebony. Stocks are finished with a glass-type finish that is guaranteed for durability.

Standard Grade models feature A Grade French walnut stocks, Sako actions, Shilen Match Grade barrels, Pachmayr "Old English" recoil pads, Leonard Brownell steel grip caps, studs (for sling swivels), and checkering in a 3-point pattern with no wrap-around on the forend.

Grade I is the same as Standard except for the AAA Grade French walnut and checkering (a belted panel on the bottom of the forend).

Grade II features AAA Grade French walnut with fleurs-de-lis on each forend and checkering completely wrapped around. Two fleurs-de-lis appear on the pistol grip area and the floor plate is engraved with scrollwork (plus an animal of the owner's choice).

Specifications include the following: **Barrel lengths:** 22" (medium calibers) and 24" (long-action calibers and magnums). **Weight:** 6 lbs. (medium calibers) and 7¼ lbs. (long-action magnums). **Length of pull:** 13⅝". Recoil pads are standard. Stocks can be made to order.

DAKOTA ARMS

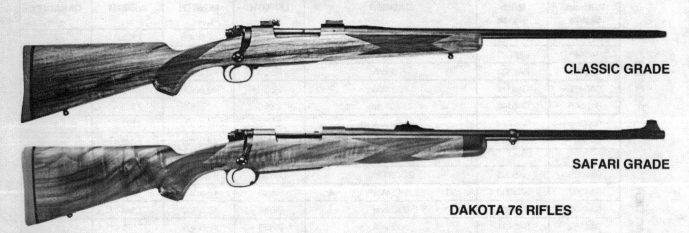

CLASSIC GRADE

SAFARI GRADE

DAKOTA 76 RIFLES

SPECIFICATIONS
Calibers:
    Safari Grade: 338 Win. Mag., 300 Win. Mag., 375 H&H Mag., 458 Win. Mag.
    Classic Grade: 257 Roberts, 270 Win., 280 Rem., 30-06, 7mm Rem. Mag., 338 Win. Mag., 300 Win. Mag., 375 H&H Mag., 458 Win. Mag.
Barrel length: 23"
Weight: 7½ lbs. (Classic); 8½ lbs. (Safari)
Safety: Three-position striker-blocking safety allows bolt operation with safety on
Sights: Ramp front sight; standing leaf rear sight
Stock: Medium fancy walnut stock fitted with recoil pad (Classic); fancy walnut with ebony forend tip and recoil pad (Safari)

Prices:

Safari Grade	$2750.00
Classic Grade	1750.00
Barreled actions: Safari Grade	1750.00
Classic Grade	1350.00
Actions: Safari Grade	1350.00
Classic Grade	1100.00

Note: Numerous options are available, including choice of wood (English, Black/Claro, Bastogne), quarter rib, ebony forend tip, wraparound checkering, etc.

HECKLER & KOCH RIFLES

Based on the design of its dependable military firearms, which have been a standard of the industry for more than 25 years, Heckler & Koch has introduced three hunting rifles—Models 940, 770 and 630. Each one features a polygonal cold hammer-forged barrel that increases bullet velocities, prolongs barrel life and maintains accuracy. All three models feature a delayed roller-locked bolt system, providing soft recoil for big game rifles. They also include one-piece European walnut stocks and come designed for scope mounting.

MODEL HK 940
$917.00

SPECIFICATIONS
Caliber: 30-06
Capacity: 3 rounds
Barrel length: 21.6″
Rifling: Polygonal
Twist: 10.0″, right hand

Overall length: 47.2″
Weight: 8.62 lbs.
Sights: V-notch rear (adjustable for windage); post front (adjustable for elevation)
Stock: European walnut
Finish: Polished blue

MODEL HK 770
$797.00

SPECIFICATIONS
Caliber: 308
Capacity: 3 rounds
Barrel length: 19.7″
Rifling: Polygonal
Twist: 11″, right hand

Overall length: 44.4″
Weight: 7.92 lbs.
Sights: V-notch rear (adjustable for windage); post front (adjustable for elevation)
Stock: European walnut
Finish: Polished blue

MODEL HK 630
$784.00

SPECIFICATIONS
Caliber: 223
Capacity: 4 rounds
Barrel length: 17.7″
Rifling: Polygonal
Twist: 10.6″, right hand

Overall length: 42.1″
Weight: 7.04 lbs.
Sights: V-notch rear (adjustable for windage); post front (adjustable for elevation)
Stock: European walnut
Finish: Polished blue

HECKLER & KOCH RIFLES

MODEL HK PSG-1 HIGH PRECISION MARKSMAN'S RIFLE
$8599.00

SPECIFICATIONS
Caliber: 308
Capacity: 5 rounds and 20 rounds
Barrel length: 25.6"
Rifling: 4 groove, polygonal
Twist: 12", right hand
Overall length: 47.5"
Weight: 17.8 lbs.
Sights: Hensoldt 6x42 telescopic
Stock: Matte black, high-impact plastic
Finish; Matte black, phosphated

SEMIAUTOMATIC VARMINT RIFLES
MODEL HK 300

The Model HK 300 features a European walnut checkered stock. All metal parts are finished in a high-luster custom blue. The receiver is fitted with special bases for HK 05 quick snap-on clamp mount with 1-inch rings that will fit all standard scopes. The positive locking action of the HK 05 provides for instant scope mounting with no change in zero, even after hundreds of repetitions. The rifle has a V-notch rear sight, adjustable for windage, and a front sight adjustable for elevation. Scope mounts are available as an additional accessory.

Caliber: 22 Winchester Magnum
Weight: 5.7 lbs.
Barrel length: 19.7" (all-steel hammer forged, polygonal profile)
Overall length: 39.4"
Magazine: Box type; 5- and 15-round capacity
Sights: V-notch rear, adjustable for windage; post front, adjustable for elevation
Trigger: Single stage, 3½ lb. pull
Action: Straight blow-back inertia bolt
Stock: Top-grade European walnut, checkered pistol grip and forearm
Price: $598.00

HEYM RIFLES

SAFETY MODEL 22S SHOTGUN/RIFLE
$2400.00

The Model 22S offers a special break-open action in which the cocking is accomplished by manually pushing forward a cocking slide located on the tang. For ultimate safety, the gun will automatically uncock by means of a built-in rocker weight if it is dropped or jostled about.

The Model 22S comes with single-set trigger, left-side barrel selector, arabesque engraving, walnut stock and an integral dovetail base for scope mounting.

SPECIFICATIONS
Shotgun barrels: 12 ga., 2³/₄″, 16 ga., 2³/₄″; 20 ga., 2³/₄″ and 3″. **Rifle barrels:** 22 Mag., 22 Hornet; 222 Rem.; 222 Rem. Mag.; 5.6 × 50 R Mag.; 6.5 × 57 R; 7 × 57 R; 243 Win. **Barrel length:** 24″. **Length of pull:** 14¹/₂″. **Overall length:** 40″.
MODEL 22SZ:
Same as above, take-down model . . . . **add'l $250.00**

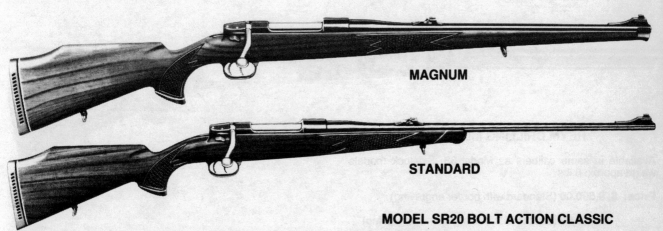

MAGNUM

STANDARD

Features two rugged Mauser-type locking lugs. A special guide rail allows the bolt to operate smoothly through the full length of travel. All parts are interchangeable. The magazine holds five regular or three Magnum cartridges. A hinged floorplate with convenient latch makes unloading easy. **A full selection of a left-hand version is available.**

SPECIFICATIONS
Calibers: (Standard) 243 Win., 270 Win., 308 Win., 30-06; (Magnum) 7mm Rem. Mag., 300 Win. Mag., 375 H&H Mag., plus metric calibers.

MODEL SR20 BOLT ACTION CLASSIC

Barrel length: 24″ (Standard) and 25″ (Magnum)
Length of pull: 14″
Weight: (Standard) 7 lb. 10 oz.; (Magnum) 8 lbs.
Stock: French walnut, hand checkering, Pachmayr Old English pad, oil finish, steel grip cap
Prices:
Model SR20 (Standard) $1125.00
   Left Hand version 1290.00
Model SR20 (Magnum) 1150.00
   Left Hand version 1340.00
Single set trigger for all models 75.00

Features a hand-checkered, oil-finished stock, all-steel bottom metal with straddled floorplate and inside release, plus steel grip cap. Other specifications same as Model SR20.

MODEL SR20 CLASSIC

Prices:
Model SR20 Classic Sporter $1350.00
Model SR20 Classic Magnum Sporter 1450.00
Model SR20 Classic Left-Hand Sporter 1600.00
Model SR20 Classic Left-Hand Magnum
   Sporter 1700.00
Custom open sights 450.00

HEYM RIFLES

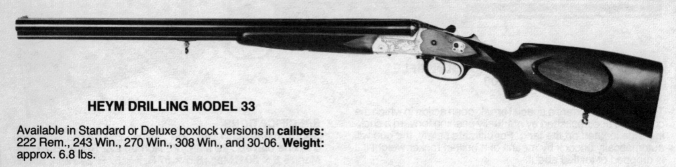

HEYM DRILLING MODEL 33

Available in Standard or Deluxe boxlock versions in **calibers:** 222 Rem., 243 Win., 270 Win., 308 Win., and 30-06. **Weight:** approx. 6.8 lbs.

Price: **$6500.00** (Standard with arabesque engraving)

7500.00 (Deluxe with hunting scene engraving)

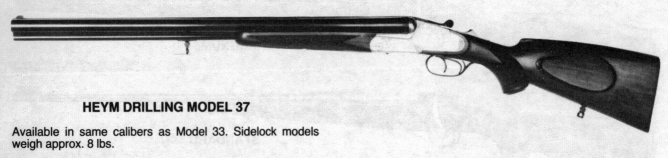

HEYM DRILLING MODEL 37

Available in same calibers as Model 33. Sidelock models weigh approx. 8 lbs.

Price: **$ 9,500.00** (Standard with border engraving)

12,000.00 (Deluxe with hunting scene engraving)

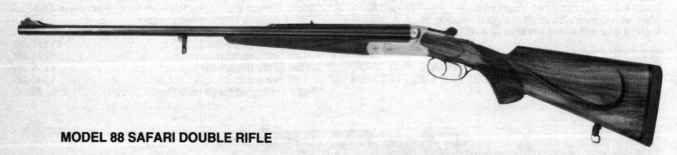

MODEL 88 SAFARI DOUBLE RIFLE

This German-built boxlock model has a modified Anson & Deeley action with standing sears, plus Purdey-type double underlocking lugs and Greener extension with crossbolt. Actions are furnished with sliding safeties and cocking indicators on the top tang, nonbreakable coil springs, front single set triggers and steel trigger guards.

Overall length: 42″
Weight: 10 lbs. (approx.)
Sights: Three-leaf express sight with standing, shallow V-sight; large gold bead front sight

SPECIFICATIONS
Calibers: 375 H&H, 458 Winchester, 470 Nitro Express
Barrel length: 25″

Prices:
Model 88 Safari in 375 H&H and 458 Win. $9800.00
Same model in 470 Nitro Express 9800.00

HOWA RIFLES

HUNTER SPORTING RIFLES
$440.00
($455.00 in 7mm Rem. Mag., 300 Win. Mag.)

SPECIFICATIONS
Calibers: 22-250, 223, 243 Win., 270 Win., 308 Win., 30-06
Capacity: 5 rounds
Barrel length: 22″
Overall length: 42¹/₂″
Weight: 7¹/₂ lbs.
Also available:
Model 1500 Trophy Grade **$465.00**
   In 7mm Rem. Mag and 300 Win. Mag. 480.00

HOWA LIGHTNING
$465.00
($480.00 in 7mm Rem. Mag.)

SPECIFICATIONS
Calibers: 270, 30-06, 7mm Rem. Mag.
Barrel length: 22″
Overall length: 42¹/₂″
Weight: 7 lbs.
Stock: Lightweight Carbolite

HOWA BARRELED ACTIONS
$255.00 (not shown)

SPECIFICATIONS
Calibers: 243 Win., 270 Win., 30-06, 308 Win. (standard); 223 Rem., 22-250 Rem. (heavy barreled varmint); 7mm Rem. Mag., 300 Win. Mag. (Magnum)
Capacity: 5 rounds (3 rounds in Magnum)
Barrel lengths: 22″ (standard); 24″ (heavy barreled varmint and Magnum)
Overall lengths: 27³/₄″ (standard); 29³/₄″ (heavy barreled and Magnum)
Weight: 5 lbs. 5 oz. (standard); 7 lbs. 1 oz. (heavy barreled varmint); 7 lbs. 9 oz. (Magnum)

HEAVY-BARRELED VARMINT RIFLES
$5l5.00 (not shown)

SPECIFICATIONS
Calibers: 223 and 22-250
Barrel length: 24″
Overall length: 44¹/₂″
Weight: 9¹/₄ lbs.

IVER JOHNSON RIFLES

WAGONMASTER LEVER ACTION
$166.50 (22 S, L, LR)
$187.50 (22 Win. Mag.)

SPECIFICATIONS
Caliber: 22 Short, Long, Long Rifle (also available in 22 Win. Mag.)
Barrel length: 18 1/2"
Weight: 5 3/4 lbs.
Overall length: 36 1/2"

Sights: Hooded ramp front; adjustable rear
Capacity: 21 Short, 17 Long, or 15 Long Rifle; can be mixed and loaded simultaneously; Magnum has 12-shot capacity
Finish: Blue
Stock: Hardwood

U.S. CARBINE MODEL .22
$166.50

SPECIFICATIONS
Caliber: 22 LR
Barrel length: 18 1/2"
Weight: 5.8 lbs.
Overall length: 38"
Sights: Military-style front and rear; rear sight is peep-type adjustable for windage and elevation

Capacity: 15 rounds
Finish: Blue
Stock: Hardwood

L'IL CHAMP SINGLE SHOT BOLT .22
$89.00

SPECIFICATIONS
Caliber: 22 S, L & LR
Barrel length: 16 1/4"
Overall length: 32 1/2"

Weight: 2 lbs. 11 oz.
Finish: Molded stock; nickel-plated bolt

K.D.F. RIFLES

MODEL K-15 IMPROVED
$1275.00 ($1325.00 in Magnum)

SPECIFICATIONS

Calibers: 243, 25-06, 270, 7x57, 30-06, 308 Win., 308 Norma, 300 Win. Mag., 7mm Rem. Mag., 375 H&H Mag., 270 Weatherby Mag., 300 Weatherby Mag., 257 Weatherby Mag. Other calibers available on special request.
Magazine capacity: Standard, 4 cartridges; Magnum, 3 cartridges
Barrel length: Standard, 24"; Magnum, 26"
Overall length: Standard, 44⁷/₈"; Magnum, 46⁷/₈"
Weight: Approx. 8 lbs.
Trigger pull: 13⁷/₈"
Shortest ignition time: Striker travels only 158-thousands of an inch. The extremely light striker is accelerated by a powerful striker spring . . . A patented two cocking cam design enables a very light and smooth cocking of the striker assembly . . . Two-piece firing pin.
Clip feature: Removable; can also be fed from top.
3 locking lugs: With large contact area . . . also Stellite locking insert.
60-Degree bolt lift only: For fast reloading.

Safety: Located on right-hand side . . . locking trigger and sear . . . Most convenient location.
Fine adjustable crisp trigger: 2¹/₂ lbs. to 7 lbs. . . . Two major moving parts only.
Stocks: American or European Walnut stocks with 1-inch recoil pad . . . Rosewood pistol grip cap . . . 20-line hand-checkering . . . Quick detachable swivels . . . Barrel is free floating . . . Oil finish . . . Available in right- or left-hand stocks . . . AAA grade stocks available. Monte Carlo style is standard. Classic, featherweight, thumbhole and competition-style stocks available.
Receiver: Drilled and tapped for scope mounts
Options: Iron sights . . . Set trigger . . . Recoil arrestor . . . KDF offers own bases to take 1" or 30mm rings.

Also available: **.411 KDF Magnum Dangerous Game Rifle.** Choice of iron sights or scope mounts and rings; also choice of finish. KDF recoil arrester included. Guaranteed to shoot 3 shots in ¹/₂" and 5 shots within 1" at 100 yards with proper loads. **Price: $1800.**

MODEL K-22 BOLT ACTION DELUXE
$495.00 (22 LR)
$545.00 (22 WMR)

SPECIFICATIONS

Caliber: 22 LR, 22 Mag.
Barrel length: 21.7"; chrome-moly steel, 4 grooves
Overall length: 40"
Weight: 6.6 lbs.

Action: Two locking lugs w/large contact area 60° bolt lift
Receiver: Two rails for scope mounting; scope mounts available from K.D.F.
Stock: European walnut, hand-checkered, rosewood forend, oil finish; sling swivels

KIMBER RIFLES

MODEL 82B CLASSIC

The Model 82 bolt-action sporter is available in calibers: 22 LR, 22 Hornet, .218 Bee & .25-20. The action is machined from solid steel and features a rear locking bolt with twin horizontally opposed locking lugs. The trigger is adjustable for pressure, overtravel and depth of sear engagement. The LR sporter is available with a 5- or 10-shot magazine; the Hornet a 3-shot flush fitting magazine; .218 & .25-20 are single shot. Special Kimber one-inch scope mount rings, machined from steel to fit the dovetailed receiver, are available in two heights. Also offered are open iron sights, hooded ramp front sight with bead and adjustable folding leaf rear sight.

Three stock styles are available: "Classic" style features a straight comb with no cheekpiece; "Cascade" style features a cheekpiece and Monte Carlo comb; and "Custom Classic" features fancy grade walnut, an ebony forend tip and Niedner-type butt plate.

Kimber's top of the line supergrade model is called the "Super America." It features high grade AAA fancy claro walnut, a classic style stock with a beaded cheekpiece, ebony forend tip, 22 line per inch full coverage checkering, skeleton grip cap.

Prices: (without sights)
Model 82 Classic, plain barrel . . . . $ 750.00
   In 22 Hornet and 22 WMR 795.00
Model 82 Continental, plain barrel 850.00
   In 22 Hornet and 22 WMR 895.00
Model 82 Custom Classic, plain barrel 995.00
   In 22 Hornet and 22 WMR 1040.00
Additional feature: Iron sights fitted 55.00
Model 82 Super America 1150.00
   In 22 WMR and 22 Hornet 1195.00
Model 82B Super Continental 1465.00
   In 22 WMR and 22 Hornet 1510.00
Model 82A Mini-Classic (18" barrel) 589.00
Model 82 Target 645.00

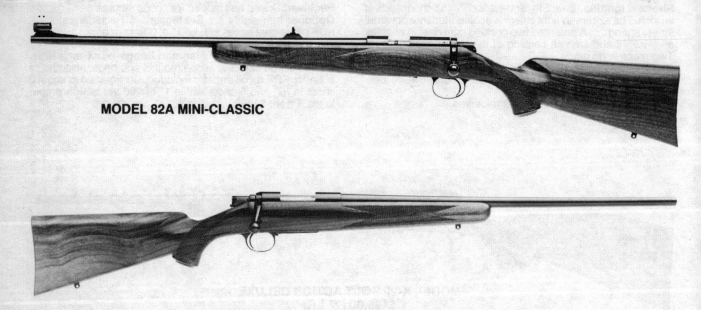

MODEL 82A MINI-CLASSIC

MODEL 84 SPORTER (MINI-MAUSER)

The Kimber Model 84 bolt-action sporter is a small Mauser-style front-locking action designed for the .222 family of cartridges (.222 Rem., .223 Rem., .222 Rem. Mag., .221 Fireball, .17 Rem., 17 Mach IV, 5.6×50mm, 6×47, 6×45). It features a traditionally Mauser-type extractor claw, twin front locking lugs, a fully adjustable trigger and a steel-hinged floorplate and trigger guard. Magazine capacity is 5 rounds. The receiver is grooved to accept Kimber's one-inch steel scope mount rings.

Prices:
Model 84 Classic, plain barrel . . . . $ 885.00
Model 84 Custom Classic, plain barrel 1130.00
Model 84 Super America 1285.00
Model 84 Continental
   222 Rem. and 223 Rem. only 985.00
Model 84 Super Continental
   222 Rem. and 223 Rem. only 1600.00

KIMBER RIFLES

BIG GAME RIFLE

The design of this big bore centerfire bolt action sporting rifle draws on the famous breeching concepts of Paul Mauser. Its key features include the following: a receiver machined from solid chrome moly steel; integral bolt handle and bolt head; Mauser extractor; Model 70 override trigger design,3-position safety, "inner collar" breeching concept for gas flow protection, ejector riding underneath left locking lug of bolt head; one-piece steel trigger guard and floor plate with positive locking of floorplate for heavy recoil protection; Model 84 style bolt stop.

Chambered for 270 Win., 280 Rem., 7mm Rem. Mag., 30-06, 338 Win. Mag., 300 Win. Mag. and 375 H&H Mag. Available in late summer of 1987 in Classic, Custom Classic and Super America models.

Prices:
Classic . . . . **$ 985.00**
In 375 H&H **1185.00**
Custom Classic **1230.00**
In 375 H&H **1430.00**
Super America **1385.00**
In 375 H&H **1585.00**

Kimber Rifles Technical Specifications

				STOCK STYLES								ACTION							BARREL		
Model	Caliber	Barrel Weight	Right Hand Left Hand	Classic	Custom Classic	SuperAmerica	Continental	Super Continental	Hunter Grade	Super Grade	Target	Front Locking	Rear Locking	Repeater	Single Shot	Magazine	Weight (pounds)	Overall Length	Length (inches)	Grooves	Twist (inches/turn)
82B	.22 LR	Light Sporter	R				•	•					•	•		5	6	37⅝	18	6	16
82B	.22 LR	Varmint	R	•	•								•	•		5	7½	42½	24	6	16
82A	.22 LR	Sporter	L	•	•								•	•		5	6½	40½	22	6	16
82B	.22 LR	Sporter	R	•	•	•							•	•		5	6½	40½	22	6	16
82A Gvt Mtch	.22 LR	Target	R								•		•		•		10¾	43	25	6	16
82B	.22 WMR	Light Sporter	R				•	•					•	•		5	6	37⅝	18	6	16
82B	.22 WMR	Sporter	R	•	•	•							•	•		5	6½	40½	22	6	16
82B	.22 Hornet	Light Sporter	R				•	•					•	•		3	6	37⅝	18	6	14
82B	.22 Hornet	Varmint	R	•	•								•	•		3	7½	42½	24	6	14
82A	.22 Hornet	Sporter	L	•	•								•	•		3	7½	40½	22	6	14
82B	.22 Hornet	Sporter	R	•	•	•							•	•		3	7½	40½	22	6	14
84B	.17 Rem	Sporter	R	•	•	•						•		•		5	6¼	40½	22	6	10
84B	.17 Rem	Varmint	R	•	•							•		•		5	7¼	42½	24	6	10
84A	.17 Rem	Sporter	L	•	•							•		•		5	6¼	40½	22	6	10
84B	.221 Fireball	Light Sporter	R				•	•				•		•		5	6	37⅝	18	6	12
84A	.221 Fireball	Sporter	L	•	•							•		•		5	6¼	40½	22	6	12
84B	.221 Fireball	Sporter	R	•	•							•		•		5	6½	40½	22	6	12
84B	.221 Fireball	Varmint	R	•	•							•		•		5	7¼	42½	24	6	14
84B	.222 Rem	Sporter	R	•	•	•						•		•		5	6¼	40½	22	6	14
84B	.222 Rem	Varmint	R	•	•							•		•		5	7¼	42½	24	6	14
84A	.222 Rem	Sporter	L	•	•							•		•		5	6¼	40½	22	6	14
84A	.222 Rem	Varmint	L	•	•							•		•		5	7¼	42½	24	6	14
84B	.223 Rem	Sporter	R	•	•	•						•		•		5	6¼	40½	22	6	12
84B	.223 Rem	Varmint	R	•	•							•		•		5	7¼	42½	24	6	12
84A	.223 Rem	Sporter	L	•	•							•		•		5	6¼	40½	22	6	12
84A	.223 Rem	Varmint	L	•	•							•		•		5	7¼	42½	24	6	12
BGR	.270 Win	Feather Weight	R	•	•	•						•		•		5	7¾	42	22	6	10
BGR	.280 Rem	Feather Weight	R	•	•	•						•		•		5	7¾	42	22	6	9
BGR	7mm Rem Mag	Medium Magnum	R	•	•	•						•		•		3	7¾	44	24	6	9
BGR	.30-06	Feather Weight	R	•	•	•						•		•		5	7¾	42	22	6	10
BGR	.300 Win Mag	Medium Magnum	R	•	•	•						•		•		3	8½	44	24	6	12
BGR	.338 Win Mag	Medium Magnum	R	•	•	•						•		•		3	8½	44	24	6	10
BGR	.375 H&H	Heavy Magnum	R	•	•	•						•		•		3	8½	44	24	6	12
PRED	.221 Fireball	Sporter	R						•	•		•			•		5¼	22⅝	14⅞	6	12
PRED	.223 Rem	Sporter	R						•	•		•			•		5¼	22⅝	14⅞	6	12
PRED	7mm TCU	Sporter	R						•	•		•			•		5¼	22⅝	14⅞	6	9

NOTE: All Model 84A rifles have a Kimber style rocker safety.
All Model 84B rifles have a Winchester Model 70 type 3 position lever safety.

RIFLES

KRIEGHOFF DOUBLE RIFLES

MODEL TECK OVER/UNDER

SPECIFICATIONS
Calibers: 308, 30-06, 300 Win. Mag., 375 H&H, 458 Win. Mag.
Barrel length: 25″
Action: Boxlock; double greener-type crossbolt and double barrel lug locking, steel receiver
Weight: 7¹/₂ lbs.
Triggers: Double triggers; single trigger optional
Safety: Located on top tang
Sights: Open sight with right angle front sight
Stock: German-styled with pistol grip and cheekpiece; oil-finished
Length of stock: 14³/₈″
Finish: Nickel-plated steel receiver with satin grey finish
Prices:
Model Teck (Boxlock) $6990.00
In 375 H&H and 458 Win. Mag. 7850.00
Teck-Handspanner (16 ga. receiver only; 7x65R, 30-06, 308 Win.) 7990.00
Also available:
TRUMPF SBS (Side-by-side boxlock) 8400.00

MODEL ULM OVER/UNDER

SPECIFICATIONS
Calibers: 308 Win., 30-06, 300 Win. Mag., 375 H&H, 458 Win. Mag.
Barrel length: 25″
Weight: 7.8 lbs.
Triggers: Double triggers (front trigger = bottom; rear trigger = upper
Safety: Located on top tang
Sights: Open sight w/right angle front sight
Stock: German-styled with pistol grip and cheekpiece; oil-finished
Length of stock: 14³/₈″
Forearm: Semi-beavertail
Prices:
Model ULM (Sidelock) $11,500.00
Primus (Deluxe Sidelock) 14,500.00
Dekor (Light scroll engraving) 10,500.00
Also available:
NEPTUN SBS (Side-by-side sidelock) 13,500.00

MARK X RIFLES
ACTIONS & BARRELED ACTIONS

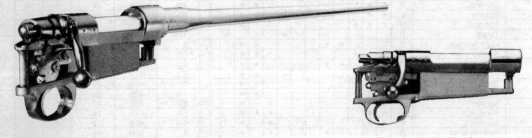

BARRELED ACTIONS
$255.00
$270.00 in 7mm Rem. Mag., 300 Win. Mag.

Hand-fitted with premium hammer-forged barrels created from corrosion resistant chrome vanadium steel. Each barreled action is carefully proofed and marked under close government control, ready to drop into the stock of your choice.

Calibers: 22-250, 243, 25-06, 270, 7×57, 7mm Rem. Mag., 300 Win. Mag., 308, 30-06. **Barrel length:** 24″. **Weight:** 5¹/₂ lbs. (5³/₄ lbs. in 22-250, 243, and 25-06). **Rifling twist:** 10 (14 in 22-250 and 9.5 in 7×57).

Also available in 375 H&H Mag. and 458 Win. Mag. Same barrel length but different weights: 6 lbs. (375 H&H Mag.) and 5.75 lbs. (458 Win. Mag.). **Rifling twist:** 12 (375 H&H Mag.) and 14 (458 Win. Mag.). **Price: $340.00**

MAUSER SYSTEM ACTIONS
$185.00 (Single Shot)

Type A: 7×57mm to 30-06. Standard magazine (3³/₈″) and bolt face (.470″) **$215.00**
Type B: 22-250 to 308. Short magazine (2⁷/₈″); standard bolt face. **$215.00**
Type C: 7mm Rem. Mag. to 458 Win. Mag. Standard magazine and Magnum bolt face (.532″) **$220.00**

Also available:
Type D: 300 Win. Mag. to 375 H&H. Magnum magazine (3¹¹/₁₆″) and Magnum bolt face **$245.00**
Mini-Mark X (.17 to .223) **$205.00**

MARK X RIFLES

MINI-MARK X
$460.00

The miniature Mark X Mauser-system rifle features the proven Mauser action scaled down to handle the high-velocity .223 caliber.

SPECIFICATIONS
Caliber: 223
Capacity: 5 rounds
Barrel length: 20″
Twist: l turn in 10″
Overall length: 39³/₄″
Weight: 6.35 lbs.
Trigger: Adjustable

MINIATURE ACTION MARK X
$265.00 (not shown)

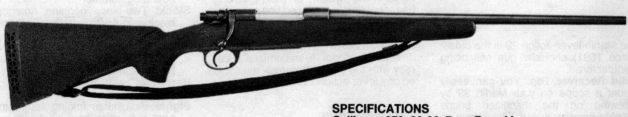

MARK X LTW SPORTER
$465.00
$480.00 in 7mm Rem. Mag.

SPECIFICATIONS
Calibers: 270, 30-06, 7mm Rem. Mag.
Capacity: 5 rounds; 3 in 7mm Rem. Mag.
Barrel length: 20″
Twist: 1 turn in 10″
Weight: 7 lbs.
Stock: Carbolite

AMERICAN FIELD SPORTING RIFLE SERIES
$499.00

Features forged and machined Mauser System actions . . . Hammer-forged, chrome, vanadium steel barrels . . . Drilled and tapped for scope mounts and receiver sights . . . Hooded ramp front and fully adjustable rear sight . . . All-steel button release magazine floor plate . . . Detachable sling swivels . . . Silent sliding thumb safety . . . Prime European walnut stocks . . . Sculpted, low-profile cheekpiece . . . Rubber recoil butt plate . . . Steel grip cap.

Calibers: 22-250, 243 Win., 25-06, 270 Win., 7 × 57, 308 Win., 30-06, 7mm Rem. Mag., 300 Win. Mag. **Barrell length:** 24″. **Overall length:** 44″. **Weight:** 7 lbs. **Capacity:** 5 rounds.

MARLIN LEVER ACTION CARBINES

MODEL 444SS
$385.95

Caliber: 444 Marlin
Capacity: 5-shot tubular magazine
Barrel: 22″ Micro-Groove®
Overall length: 40½″
Stock: American black walnut pistol grip stock with rubber rifle butt pad
Sights: Ramp front sight with brass bead and Wide-Scan® hood; receiver tipped for scope mount or receiver sight
Weight: 7½ lbs.

MARLIN GOLDEN 39AS
$318.95

The Marlin lever-action 22 is the oldest (since 1891) shoulder gun still being manufactured.

Solid Receiver Top. You can easily mount a scope on your Marlin 39 by screwing on the machined scope adapter base provided. The screw-on base is a neater, more versatile method of mounting a scope on a 22 sporting rifle. The solid top receiver and scope adapter base provide a maximum in eye relief adjustment. If you prefer iron sights, you'll find the 39 receiver clean, flat and sandblasted to prevent glare.

Exclusive brass magazine tube.
Micro-Groove® Barrel. Marlin's famous rifling system of multi-grooving has consistently produced fine accuracy because the system grips the bullet more securely, minimizes distortion, and provides a better gas seal.

And the Model 39 maximizes accuracy with the heaviest barrels available on any lever-action 22.

SPECIFICATIONS
Caliber: 22 Short, Long and Long Rifle
Capacity: Tubular magazine holds 26 Short, 21 Long and 19 Long Rifle Cartridges
Action: Lever action; solid top receiver; side ejection; one-step takedown; deeply blued metal surfaces; re-

ceiver top sandblasted to prevent glare; hammer block safety; rebounding hammer
Stock: Two-piece genuine American black walnut with fluted comb; full pistol grip and forend; blued-steel forend cap; swivel studs; grip cap; white butt plate and pistol-grip spacers; tough Mar-Shield® finish
Barrel: 24″ with Micro-Groove® rifling (16 grooves)
Sights: Adjustable folding semi-buckhorn rear, ramp front sight with new Wide-Scan™ hood; solid top receiver tapped for scope mount or receiver sight; scope adapter base; offset hammer spur for scope use—works right or left
Overall length: 40″
Weight: About 6½ lbs.

MODEL 39 TAKE-DOWN
$355.95

SPECIFICATIONS
Caliber: 22 Short, Long or Long Rifle
Capacity: Tubular magazine holds 16 Short, 12 Long, or 10 Long Rifle cartridges
Barrel length: 16½″ lightweight barrel (16 grooves)
Overall length: 32⅝″

Weight: 5¼ lbs.
Safety: Hammer block safety
Sights: Adjustable semi-buckhorn rear, ramp front with brass bead and Wide-Scan™ hood; top receiver tapped for scope mount and receiver sight; scope adapter base; offset hammer spur (right or left hand) for scope use

Stock: Two-piece straight-grip American black walnut with scaled-down forearm and blued steel forend cap; Mar-Shield® finish
Action: Lever action; solid top receiver; side ejection; rebounding hammer; one-step take-down; deep blued metal surfaces; gold-plated trigger

MARLIN LEVER ACTION CARBINES

MODEL 1894 CLASSIC
$383.95

SPECIFICATIONS
Calibers: 25/20 Win. and 32/20 Win.
Capacity: 6-shot tubular magazine
Barrel length: 22″ (6-groove rifling)
Overall length: 38³/₄″
Weight: 6¹/₄ lbs.

Action: Lever action with squared finger lever; side ejection; solid receiver top sandblasted to prevent glare; hammer block safety
Sights: Adjustable semi-buckhorn folding rear, brass bead front; solid top

receiver tapped for scope mount and receiver sight; offset hammer spur
Stock: Straight-grip American black walnut with Mar-Shield® finish; blued steel forearm cap

MARLIN 336CS
$325.95 (without scope)

SPECIFICATIONS
Caliber: 30/30 Win., 35 Rem., 375 Win.
Capacity: 6-shot tubular magazine
Action: Lever action w/hammer block safety; deeply blued metal surfaces; receiver top sandblasted to prevent glare

Stock: American black walnut pistol grip stock w/fluted comb and Mar-Shield® finish; deeply blued metal surfaces
Barrel: 20″ Micro-Groove® barrel
Sights: Adjustable folding semi-buckhorn rear; ramp front sight w/brass bead and removable Wide-Scan™

hood; tapped for receiver sight and scope mount; offset hammer spur for scope use (works right or left)
Overall length: 38¹/₂″
Weight: 7 lbs.

MODEL 336 LIGHTWEIGHT
$325.95

SPECIFICATIONS
Caliber: 30/30 Win.
Capacity: 5-shot tubular magazine
Barrel length: 16¹/₄″ with Micro-Groove® rifling (12 grooves)
Overall length: 34³/₈″

Weight: 6¹/₂ lbs.
Safety: Hammer block safety
Sights: Adjustable semi-buckhorn folding rear, brass bead front; offset hammer spur (right or left hand) for scope use

Stock: Straight-grip American black walnut with scaled-down forearm and rubber rifle butt pad
Action: Lever action; side ejection; solid top receiver; squared finger lever; deep blued metal surfaces

MARLIN LEVER ACTION CARBINES

MARLIN 1895SS
$385.95

SPECIFICATIONS
Caliber: 45/70 Government
Capacity: 4-shot tubular magazine
Action: Lever action w/square finger lever; hammer block safety; receiver top sandblasted to prevent glare

Stock: American black walnut pistol grip stock w/rubber rifle butt pad and Mar-Shield® finish; white pistol grip and butt spacers
Barrel: 22″ Micro-Groove® barrel
Sights: Ramp front sight w/brass bead and Wide-Scan™ hood; receiver tapped for scope mount or receiver sight
Overall length: 40½″
Weight: 7½ lbs.

MARLIN 1894S
$357.95

SPECIFICATIONS
Calibers: 41 Mag., 44 Rem. Mag., 44 Special, 45 Colt
Capacity: 10-shot tubular magazine
Action: Lever action w/square finger lever; hammer block safety

Stock: American black walnut stock w/ Mar-Shield™ finish; blued steel for-end cap
Barrel: 20″ Micro-Groove® barrel
Sights: Ramp front sight w/brass bead and Wide-Scan™ hood; solid top receiver tapped for scope mount or receiver sight
Overall length: 37½″
Weight: 6 lbs.

MARLIN 1894CS 357 MAGNUM
$357.95

SPECIFICATIONS
Caliber: 357 Magnum, 38 Special
Capacity: 9-shot tubular magazine
Action: Lever action w/square finger lever; hammer block safety; side ejection; solid top receiver; deeply blued metal surfaces; receiver top sandblasted to prevent glare

Stock: Straight-grip two-piece genuine American black walnut with white butt plate spacer; tough Mar-Shield® finish.
Barrel: 18½″ long with modified Micro-Groove® rifling (12 grooves)
Sights: Adjustable semi-buckhorn folding rear, bead front; solid top receiver tapped for scope mount or receiver sight; offset hammer spur for scope use—adjustable for right- or left-hand use
Overall length: 36″
Weight: 6 lbs.

MARLIN RIFLES

MODEL 30AS
$320.95

SPECIFICATIONS
Caliber : 30/30
Capacity: 6-shot tubular magazine
Action: Lever action w/hammer block safety; solid top receiver w/side ejection; hammer block safety

Stock: Walnut-finish hardwood stock w/ pistol grip; Mar-Shield® finish
Sights: Tapped for scope mount and receiver sight; also available in combination w/4x, 32mm, 1" scope

Barrel: 20" Micro-Groove® barrel
Overall length: 38¼"
Weight: Approx. 7 lbs.

MODEL 25M
$141.95 with scope

SPECIFICATIONS
Caliber: 22 Win. Mag Rimfire (not interchangeable with any other 22 cartridge)
Capacity: 7-shot clip magazine

Stock: One-piece walnut-finished hardwood Monte Carlo with full pistol grip
Barrel length: 22" with Micro-Groove® rifling
Overall length: 41"

Weight: 6 lbs.
Sights: Adjustable open rear, ramp front sight; receiver grooved for tip-off scope mount

MODEL 25 MB MIDGET MAGNUM
$172.95 with scope

SPECIFICATIONS
Same specifications as Model 25M except **barrel length** (16¼"), **overall length** (35¼") and **weight** (4¾ lbs.).

MARLIN BOLT ACTION RIFLES

MARLIN 780
$161.95

MARLIN 781
$168.95

SPECIFICATIONS (MODEL 780)
Caliber: 22 Short, Long or Long Rifle
Capacity: Clip magazine holds 7 Short, Long or Long Rifle cartridges
Action: Bolt action; serrated, anti-glare receiver top; positive thumb safety; red cocking indicator

Stock: Monte Carlo genuine American black walnut with full pistol grip; checkering on pistol grip and underside of forend; white butt plate spacer; tough Mar-Shield® finish
Barrel: 22″ with Micro-Groove® rifling (16 grooves)
Sights: Adjustable folding semi-buckhorn rear; ramp front with Wide-

Scan™ with hood; receiver grooved for tip-off scope mount
Overall length: 41″
Weight: About 5½ lbs.
MARLIN 781: Specifications same as Marlin 780, except with tubular magazine that holds 25 Short, 19 Long or 17 Long Rifle cartridges. **Weight:** About 6 lbs.

MARLIN 783 MAGNUM
$185.95

SPECIFICATIONS
Caliber: 22 Win. Magnum Rimfire (not interchangeable with any other 22 cartridge)
Capacity: 12-shot tubular magazine with patented closure system
Action: Bolt action; serrated, anti-glare receiver top; positive thumb safety; red cocking indicator

Stock: Monte Carlo genuine American black walnut with full pistol grip; checkering on pistol grip and underside of forend; white butt plate spacer; swivel studs; tough Mar-Shield® finish
Barrel: 22″ with Micro-Groove® rifling (20 grooves)
Sights: Adjustable folding semi-buck-

horn rear; ramp front with Wide-Scan™ hood; receiver grooved for tip-off scope mount
Overall length: 41″
Weight: About 6 lbs.

MARLIN 782 MAGNUM: Specifications same as 783 Magnum, except with 7-shot clip magazine **$168.95**

MARLIN 15Y "LITTLE BUCKAROO™"
Single Shot 22 Beginner's Rifle
$120.95 (without scope)

SPECIFICATIONS
Caliber: 22 Short, Long or Long Rifle
Capacity: Single shot
Action: Bolt action; easy-load feed throat; thumb safety; red cocking indicator
Stock: One-piece walnut finish hard-

wood Monte Carlo with full pistol grip; tough Mar-Shield® finish
Barrel length: 16¼″ (16 grooves)
Sights: Adjustable open rear; ramp front sight; free 4 × 15 scope included
Overall length: 33¼″
Weight: 4¼ lbs.

MARLIN RIFLES

MODEL 9 CAMP CARBINE
$294.95

SPECIFICATIONS
Caliber: 9mm
Capacity: 12-shot clip (20-shot magazine available)
Action: Semi-automatic. Manual bolt hold-open. Garand-type safety, magazine safety, loaded chamber indicator. Solid-top, machined steel receiver is sandblasted to prevent glare, and is drilled and tapped for scope mounting.
Stock: Walnut finished hardwood with pistol grip; tough Mar-Shield™ finish; rubber rifle butt pad.
Barrel length: 16½″ with Micro-Groove® rifling.
Sights: Adjustable rear, ramp front sight with brass bead; Wide-Scan™ hood. Receiver drilled and tapped for scope mount.
Overall length: 35½″
Weight: 6¾ lbs.

MODEL 45
$294.95

SPECIFICATIONS
Caliber: 45 Auto
Capacity: 7-shot clip
Barrel length: 16½″
Overall length: 35½″
Weight (approx.): 6.75 lbs.
Stock: Walnut finished hardwood with pistol grip; rubber rifle butt pad
Sights: Adjustable open rear; ramp front sight with brass bead; Wide-Scan hood

MARLIN 60
$124.95 (without scope)

SPECIFICATIONS
Caliber: 22 Long Rifle
Capacity: 17-shot tubular magazine with patented closure system
Barrel length: 22″
Weight: 5½ lbs.
Overall length: 40½″
Sights: Ramp front sight; adjustable open rear, receiver grooved for tip-off scope mount
Action: Semiautomatic; side ejection; manual and automatic "last-shot" hold-open devices; receiver top has serrated, non-glare finish; cross-bolt safety
Stock: One-piece walnut-finished hardwood Monte Carlo stock with full pistol grip; Mar-Shield® finish

MARLIN RIFLES

MODEL 70HC
$130.95

SPECIFICATIONS
Caliber: 22 LR
Capacity: 25-shot clip magazine
Barrel length: 18″ (with Micro-Groove® rifling)
Overall length: 36½″

Weight: 5 lbs.
Action: Semiautomatic; side ejection; manual bolt hold-open; receiver top has serrated, non-glare finish; cross-bolt safety
Sights: Adjustable open rear, ramp front; receiver grooved for tip-off scope mount
Stock: Monte Carlo walnut-finished hardwood with full pistol grip and Mar-Shield® finish

MODEL 70P "PAPOOSE"
$153.95 (with scope)

SPECIFICATIONS
Caliber: 22 LR
Barrel length: 16¼″
Overall length: 35¼″
Weight: 3.75 lbs.

Capacity: 7-shot clip
Sights: Adjustable open rear; ramp front
Stock: Walnut-finished hardwood with full pistol grip

Action: Semiautomatic; side ejection; manual bolt hold-open; cross-bolt safety

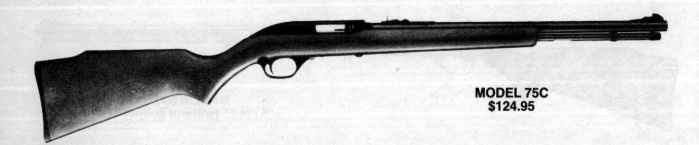

MODEL 75C
$124.95

SPECIFICATIONS
Caliber: 22 LR
Capacity: 13-shot tubular magazine
Barrel length: 18″
Overall length: 36½″

Weight: 5½ lbs.
Stock: Monte Carlo walnut finish hardwood
Action: Semiautomatic; side ejection; manual and "last-shot" automatic bolt hold-opens
Sights: Adjustable open rear; ramp front sight

MARLIN 22 RIFLES

MARLIN 995
$156.95

SPECIFICATIONS
Caliber: 22 Long Rifle
Action: Semiautomatic
Capacity: 7-shot clip magazine
Barrel: 18″ with Micro-Groove® rifling (16 grooves)

Stock: Monte Carlo genuine American black walnut with full pistol grip; checkering on pistol grip and forend
Sights: Adjustable folding semi-buckhorn rear; ramp front sight with brass bead, Wide-Scan™ hood

Overall length: 36³/₄″
Weight: About 5¹/₂ lbs.
Features: Receiver grooved for tip-off scope mount; bolt hold-open device; cross-bolt safety

MAUSER RIFLES

MODEL 66
$2500.00

This short-action repeater rifle is internationally known for its outstanding handling qualities. The interchangeable barrel system allows the shooter to own one rifle with several extra barrels in different calibers. Includes special detachable sights, adjustable for windage and elevation, selected walnut stock, oiled and polished, fitted with Pachmayr recoil pad. Double trigger.

SPECIFICATIONS
Calibers: 243 Win., 270 Win., 30-06, 308 Win.
Barrel length: 24″
Weight: 7¹/₄ lbs.
Also available:
Model 66 Ultra (21″ barrel)
Model 66 Magnum version in calibers 7mm Rem. Mag., 300 Win. Mag. **Barrel length:** 26″. **Weight:** 9¹/₄ lbs.
Model 66 Big Game Rifle (26″ barrel) in 375 H&H Mag. and 458 Win. Mag.

PARKER-HALE RIFLES

MODEL M81 CLASSIC
$799.95

SPECIFICATIONS
Calibers: 22/250, 243 Win., 6mm Rem., 270 Win., 308 Win., 30-06, 300 Win. Mag., 7mm Rem. Mag.
Barrel length: 24″
Overall length: 44$\frac{1}{2}$″
Capacity: 4 rounds
Weight: 7.75 lbs.
Length of pull: 13$\frac{1}{2}$″

MODEL M81 AFRICAN
$999.95

SPECIFICATIONS
Caliber: 375 H&H
Barrel length: 24″
Overall length: 44$\frac{1}{2}$″
Weight: 7.75 lbs.
Stock: Hand-checkered walnut
Features: All-steel trigger guard, adjustable trigger, barrel band front swivel, African express rear sight, hand-engraved receiver

MODEL 1100 LIGHTWEIGHT
$559.95

SPECIFICATIONS
Calibers: 22/250, 243 Win., 6mm Rem., 270 Win., 308 Win., 30-06
Barrel length: 22″
Overall length: 43″
Weight: 6$\frac{1}{2}$ lbs.
Capacity: 4 rounds
Length of pull: 13$\frac{1}{2}$″
Model 1100M African Magnum (404 and 458 Win. Mag. only). **Barrel length:** 24″. **Overall length:** 46″. **Weight:** 9$\frac{1}{2}$ lbs. **Price:** $899.95.

PARKER-HALE RIFLES

MODEL 1000 STANDARD
$499.95

SPECIFICATIONS
Calibers: 22/250, 243 Win., 6mm Rem., 270 Win., 308 Win.,
   30-06
Barrel length: 22″ (24″ in cal. 22/250)
Overall length: 43″
Weight: 7¼ lbs.
Capacity: 4 rounds
Length of pull: 13½″

MODEL 2100 MIDLAND
$369.95

SPECIFICATIONS
Calibers: 22/250, 243 Win., 6mm Rem., 270 Win., 308 Win.,
   30-06
Barrel length: 22″ (24″ in cal. 22/250)
Overall length: 43″
Weight: 7 lbs.
Capacity: 4 rounds
Length of pull: 13½″

MODEL 1200 SUPER
$659.95

SPECIFICATIONS
Calibers: 22/250, 243 Win., 6mm Rem., 270 Win., 308 Win.,
   30-06
Barrel length: 24″
Overall length: 44½″
Weight: 7½ lbs.
Capacity: 4 rounds
Length of pull: 13½″
Model 1200M Super Magnum (300 Win. Mag. and 7mm
   Rem. Mag. only): Same specifications as Model 1200
   Super but capacity is 3 rounds. **Price: $659.95.**
Model 1200C Super Clip (243 Win., 6mm Rem., 270 Win.,
   30-06 and 308 Win. only). Same specifications as Model
   1200 Super but weighs 7¾ lbs. **Price: $699.95.** Also avail-
   able in 300 Win. Mag. and 7mm Rem. Mag. (3 rounds only).
Model 1200V Super Varmint (22/250, 6mm Rem., 243 Win.,
   25/06 only). Same specifications as Model 1200 Super but
   weighs 9 lbs. **Price: $659.95.**

PARKER-HALE TARGET RIFLES

MODEL M87
$1175.95

This all-round high precision long range target rifle is available in several calibers suitable for silhouette or practical rifle competition and varmint shooting. The bolt is designed for smooth and rapid operation. The handle is tipped with a large diameter ball and allows ample clearance for aperture or telescopic sights. Integral dovetails on the action body provide positive scope mounting with Parker-Hale "Roll-Off" mounts.

SPECIFICATIONS
Calibers: 308 Win., 243 Win., 30-06 Springfield, 300 Win. Mag. (others on request) **Weight:** 10 lbs. (empty) **Barrel length:** 26" **Overall length:** 45" **Sights:** None fitted; action body dovetailed for Parker-Hale "Roll-Off" Scope mounts

MODEL M84 MK11 CANBERRA (not shown)
$1250.00 (7.62mm × 51 NATO)

Receiver is specifically designed for maximum rigidity with the framework of the rifle and a solid flat base with heavily reinforced flat top side. Action is securely fixed to the stock by two 1/4" socket head screws.

SPECIFICATIONS
Caliber: 7.62 × 51 NATO **Barrel length:** 27 1/2" **Overall length:** 48" **Weight:** 11 1/2 lbs. (w/sights & handstop) **Rifle twist:** 1 in 14" (1 in 10 and 1 in 12 made to order) **Capacity:** Single shot **Trigger pull weight:** 3 1/2 lbs.

Also available: **MODEL M84 MK11 BISLEY.**
Same as "Canberra" but is produced in an alternative stock style (one for right-handed shooters and one for left-handers).

REMINGTON BOLT ACTION RIFLES

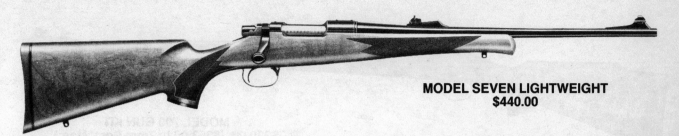

MODEL SEVEN LIGHTWEIGHT
$440.00

Every Model Seven is built to the accuracy standards of our famous Model 700 and is individually test fired to prove it. Its 18½" Remington special steel barrel is free-floating out to a single pressure point at the forend tip. And there is ordnance-quality steel in everything from its fully enclosed bolt and ex-

tractor system to its steel trigger guard and floor plate. Ramp front and fully adjustable rear sights, sling swivel studs are standard.

Also available with Kevlar Reinforced Fiberglass Stock in 243 Win., 7mm-08 Rem., and 308 Win. **Price:.....$600.00.**

	223 Rem.	243 Win.	7mm-08 Rem.	6mm Rem.	308 Win.
Clip mag. capacity	5	4	4	4	4
Barrel length	18½"	18½"	18½"	18½"	18½"
Overall length	37½"	37½"	37½"	37½"	37½"
Twist R-H (1 turn in)	12"	9⅛"	9¼"	9⅛"	10"
Average weight (lbs.)	6¼	6¼	6¼	6¼	6¼

Standard Stock Dimensions: 13½" length of pull, 1" drop at heel, ⅝" drop at comb (measured from centerline of bore).

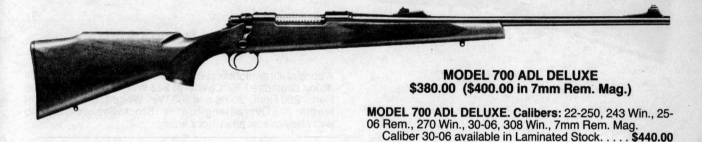

MODEL 700 ADL DELUXE
$380.00 ($400.00 in 7mm Rem. Mag.)

MODEL 700 ADL DELUXE. Calibers: 22-250, 243 Win., 25-06 Rem., 270 Win., 30-06, 308 Win., 7mm Rem. Mag. Caliber 30-06 available in Laminated Stock.....**$440.00**

MODEL 700 CLASSIC
(Chambered for 35 Whelen)

MODEL 700 CLASSIC LIMITED EDITION
$440.00

Caliber: 35 Whelen
Capacity: 5 shots (1 in chamber)
Barrel length: 22"
Overall length: 42½"
Weight: 7¼ lbs.
Bolt: Jeweled with shrouded firing pin

Receiver: Drilled and tapped for scope mounts; fixed magazine with or without hinged floor plate
Stock: Cut-checkered select American walnut with quick detachable sling swivels installed; recoil pad standard equipment on Magnum rifles; installed at extra charge on others

REMINGTON BOLT ACTION RIFLES

MODEL 700 GUN KIT
$330.00 ($353.00 in 7mm Rem. Mag.)

The Model 700 Gun Kit includes the Model 700 ADL barreled action (long and short), blind magazine (no floor plate), factory iron sights, and receiver drilled and tapped for scope mounts. The walnut stock with sling swivel studs and butt plate is furnished ready for final shaping, sanding and finishing. Stock inletting for the barreled action is completed to accurate dimensions requiring no additional internal inletting or cutting. The kit package also includes an owner's manual with complete instructions on how to finish the stock and three checkering pattern templates. Choice of cartridges for which the barreled actions are chambered include the 243 Win., 270 Win., 30-06, 308 Win. and 7mm Rem. Mag.

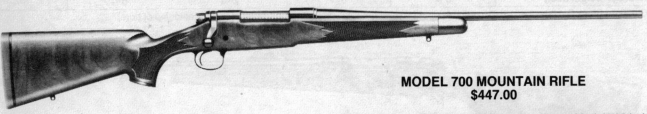

MODEL 700 MOUNTAIN RIFLE
$447.00

A special lightweight version of the Remington Model 700 bolt action centerfire rifle. **Calibers:** 243 Win., 270 Win., 7mm-08 Rem., 280 Rem., 30-06 and 308 Win. **Weight:** 6³/₄ lbs. **Barrel length:** 22″. **Overall length:** 41⁵/₈″. **Stock:** Straight-line comb with cheekpiece; satin stock finish.

MODEL 700 CUSTOM MOUNTAIN RIFLE
showing left side of synthetic stock reinforced with Kevlar

MODEL 700 CUSTOM GRADE RIFLES
(not shown)

GRADE I	$1200.00
GRADE II	2133.00
GRADE III	3333.00
GRADE IV	5200.00

REMINGTON BOLT ACTION RIFLES

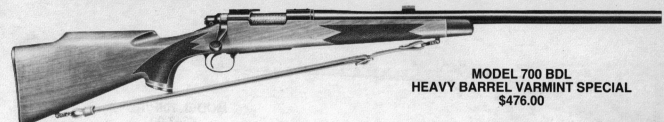

MODEL 700 BDL
HEAVY BARREL VARMINT SPECIAL
$476.00

The Model 700 BDL heavy barrel "Varmint Special" comes equipped with a 24-inch heavy target-type barrel. The "Varmint Special" is available in a wide range of popular high-velocity, varmint calibers, which include the 222 Rem., 223 Rem., 22-250 Rem., 308 Win., 6mm Rem., 243 Win., 25-06 Rem., and 7mm-08 Rem. The "Varmint Special" was designed for maximum-range precision shooting, suitable for chucks, foxes and other varmints.

Features include: hinged floor plate; quick release, swivels and strap; crisp trigger pull; American walnut stock, Monte Carlo style with cheekpiece; positive cut skip-line checkering on grip and all three sides of forend, grip cap with white line spacer and butt plate; DuPont developed RK-W wood finish. Stock dimensions are: 13 3/8-inch length of pull; 1 3/8 inch drop at heel; 1/2-inch drop at comb (from open sight line). The safety

is a thumb-lever type and is serrated. The bolt knob is oval shaped, serrated top and bottom. As in the Model 700 BDL, the cartridge head is completely encased by the bolt face and is supported by three rings of steel when the action is closed. The model is a very popular choice for metallic silhouette shooting.

SPECIFICATIONS

Calibers	Clip Mag. Cap.	Overall Length	Av. Wt. Lbs.	Twist R-H 1 turn in
22-250 Remington	4	43 1/2"	9	14
222 Remington	5	43 1/2"	9	14
223 Remington	5	43 1/2"	9	12
243 Winchester	4	43 1/2"	9	9 1/8
308 Winchester	4	43 1/2"	8 3/4	10
7mm-08 Remington	4	43 1/2"	8 3/4	9 1/4
6mm Remington	4	43 1/2"	9	9 1/8

Also available:
MODEL 700 BDL SHORT ACTION LEFT HAND in 243 Win., 270 Win., 30-06, 308 Win., and 7mm Rem. Mag. **Price: $487.00**; in 7mm Rem. Mag., **$507.00**.
CUSTOM DELUXE MODEL $447.00; in 7mm Rem. Mag. and 338 Win. Mag., **$467.00**.

MODEL 700 SAFARI GRADE in 375 H&H Mag., 458 Win. Mag., and 8mm Rem. Mag. (Classic and Monte Carlo style). **Price: $827.00**.

MODEL 700 SPECIFICATIONS

Calibers	Mag. Cap.	Barrel Length1	"Mountain Rifle"*	"Limited Classic"	Varmint Special	ADL, BDL & "Custom"	Twist R-H 1 turn in
17 Rem.	5	24"	—	—	—	43 1/2"/7 1/4	9"
222 Rem.	5	24"	—	—	43 1/2"/9	43 1/2"/7 1/4	14"
22-250 Rem.	4	24"	—	—	43 1/2"/9	43 1/2"/7 1/2	14"
223 Rem.	5	24"	—	—	43 1/2"/9	43 1/2"/7 1/4	12"
6mm Rem.*	4	22"	—	—	43 1/2"/9	41 1/2"/7 1/4	9 1/8"
243 Win.	4	22"	—	—	43 1/2"/9	41 1/2"/7 1/4	9 1/8"
25-06 Rem.	4	24"	—	—	—	41 1/2"/7 1/4	10"
270 Win.	4	22"	42 1/2"/6 3/4	—	—	41 1/2"/7 1/4	10"
280 Rem.	4	22"	42 1/2"/6 3/4	—	—	—	—
7mm-08 Rem.	4	22"	—	—	43 1/2"/9	41 1/2"/7 1/4	9 1/4"
30-06 & 30-06 "Accelerator"	4	22"	42 1/2"/6 3/4	—	—	41 1/2"/7 1/4	10"
308 Win. & 308 "Accelerator"	4	22"	—	—	43 1/2"/9	41 1/2"/7 1/4	10" 12"
7mm Rem. Mag.2	3	24"	—	—	—	44 1/2"/7 3/4	9 1/4"
300 Win. Mag.2	3	24"	—	—	—	44 1/2"/7 3/4	10"
338 Win. Mag.2	4	24"	—	44 1/2"/7 7/4	—	—	10"
Safari Grade*							
8mm Rem. Mag.	3	24"	—	—	—	44 1/2"/10	10"
375 H&H Mag.2	3	24"	—	—	—	44 1/2"/9	12"
458 Win. Mag.2	3	24"	—	—	—	44 1/2"/9	14"

1"Varmint Special" equipped only with a 24" barrel.   2Recoil pad included.

REMINGTON BOLT ACTION RIFLES

MODEL 700 "RS"
$547.00

MODEL 700 SYNTHETIC STOCKS

In answer to the demand for the lighter weight, strength and stability of synthetic stocks, Remington has introduced two new versions of its Model 700 centerfire rifle, as well as one version of its Model Seven. **Model 700 "RS"** introduces a new synthetic stock material called "Rynite", a DuPont thermoplastic resin with 35 percent glass reinforcement. This material provides more strength, stiffness and stability under a wide range of temperature and humidity conditions. This model includes the "Mountain Rifle" stock style featuring a straight comb and cheekpiece with Monte Carlo. A black, solid rubber recoil pad and pistol grip cap (with the "RA" logo) offer a smooth, uncluttered profile. Model 700 "RS" is available with a 22" barrel in right hand, long action with hinged floor plate in 270 Win., 280 Rem. and 30-06. **Price: $533.00**

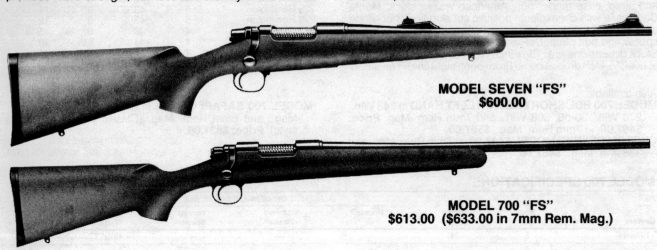

MODEL SEVEN "FS"
$600.00

MODEL 700 "FS"
$613.00 ($633.00 in 7mm Rem. Mag.)

Model 700 "FS" features a fiberglass stock reinforced with DuPont "Kevlar" aramid fiber for extra strength. The stock is shaped in the classic style with straight comb, no cheekpiece or Monte Carlo, and a black, Old English-style rubber recoil pad. The action has a blind magazine without floor plate. Model 700 "FS" is available in both long and short and right- and left-hand actions. Right-hand actions are chambered for 243 Win., 308 Win. and 7mm Rem. Mag. Left-hand actions are available in 270 Win., 30-06 and 7mm Rem. Mag.

   MODEL SEVEN "FS" is available in 243 Win., 7mm-08 Rem. and 308 Win.

SYNTHETIC STOCK RIFLES

Calibers	Mag. capacity	Barrel length	Overall length	Avg. Wt.	Twist R-H 1 turn in
Model 700 RS Rynite Stock BDL					
270 Win.	4	22"	42¹/₂	7¹/₄	10"
280 Rem.	4	22"	42¹/₂"	7¹/₄	9¹/₄"
30-06	4	22"	42¹/₂"	7¹/₄"	10"
Model 700 FS Fiberglass Stock ADL					
243 Win.	4	22"	41⁵/₈"	6¹/₄	9¹/₈"
270 Win.	4	22"	42¹/₂	6¹/₄	10"
30-06	4	22"	42¹/₂	6¹/₄	10"
308 Win.	4	22"	41⁵/₈	6¹/₄	10"
7mm Rem. Mag.	3	24"	44¹/₂	6³/₄	10"
Model Seven FS Fiberglass Stock					
243 Win.	4	18¹/₂"	37¹/₂	5¹/₄	9¹/₈"
7mm-08 Rem.	4	18¹/₂"	37¹/₂	5¹/₄	9¹/₄"
308 Win.	4	18¹/₂"	37¹/₂	5¹/₄	10"

REMINGTON RIFLES

BIG GAME REPEATING RIFLES
"SPORTSMAN" 78 BOLT ACTION
$313.00

The popularly priced "Sportsman" 78 bolt-action centerfire rifle is chambered for the 243 Win., 308 Win., 270 Win. and 30-06 Springfield. It features the same rugged Remington action, bolt and barrel long recognized for their strength and accuracy by hunters and bench rest shooters alike. The straight comb, walnut-finished hardwood stock has classic lines and a rounded forend. Sights are fully adjustable and the receiver is drilled and tapped for easy scope mounting.

Calibers: 223 Rem., 243 Win., 270 Win., 30-06 Springfield and 308 Win.
Capacity: 4-shot clip magazine
Barrel length: 22″
Overall length: 42 1/2″
Weight: 7 lbs.
Length of pull: 13 3/8″
Drop at heel: 1″ (from centerline of bore)
Drop at comb: 9/16″ (from centerline of bore)

RIFLES

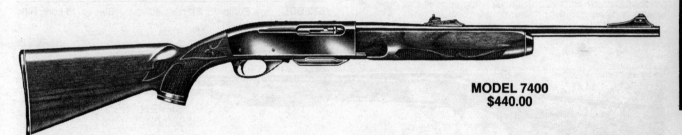

MODEL 7400
$440.00

Calibers: 243 Win., 270 Win., 280 Rem., 30-06, 308 Win., and 30-06 Carbine (see below)
Capacity: 5 centerfire cartridges (4 in the magazine, 1 in the chamber); extra 4-shot magazine available
Action: Gas-operated; receiver drilled and tapped for scope mounts
Barrel length: 22″
Weight: 7 1/2 lbs.
Overall length: 42″

Sights: Standard blade ramp front; sliding ramp rear
Stock: Checkered American walnut stock and forend; curved pistol grip
Length of pull: 13 3/8″
Drop at heel: 2 1/4″
Drop at comb: 1 13/16″

Also available:
MODEL 7400 CARBINE with 18 1/2″ barrel; chambered for 30-06 cartridge

MODEL 7600
$400.00

Calibers: 243 Win., 270 Win., 280 Rem., 30-06, 308 Win., 35 Whelen, and 30-06 Carbine (see below)
Capacity: 5-shot capacity in all six calibers (4 in the removable magazine, 1 in the chamber)
Action: Pump action
Barrel length: 22″ (18 1/2″ in 30-06 Carbine)
Weight: 8 lbs.
Overall length: 42″
Sights: Standard blade ramp front sight; sliding ramp rear,

both removable
Stock: Checkered American walnut
Length of pull: 13 3/8″
Drop at heel: 15/16″
Drop at comb: 9/16″

Also available:
MODEL 7600 CARBINE with 18 1/2″ barrel; chambered for 30-06 cartridge

REMINGTON RIMFIRE RIFLES

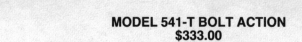

MODEL 541-T BOLT ACTION
$333.00

RIMFIRE RIFLE SPECIFICATIONS

Model	Action	Barrel Length	Overall Length	Average Wt. (lbs.)	Magazine Capacity
541-T	Bolt	24″	42½″	5⅞	5-Shot Clip
581-S	Bolt	24″	42½″	5⅞	5-Shot Clip
552 BDL Deluxe Speedmaster	Auto	21″	40″	5¾	15 Long Rifle
572 BDL Deluxe Fieldmaster	Pump	21″	40″	5½	15 Long Rifle

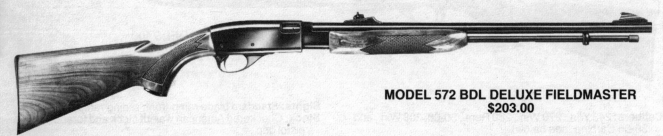

MODEL 572 BDL DELUXE FIELDMASTER
$203.00

MODEL 572 DELUXE

Features of this rifle with big-game feel and appearance are: DuPont's beautiful, tough RK-W finish; centerfire-rifle-type rear sight fully adjustable for both vertical and horizontal sight alignment; big-game style ramp front sight; handsome Remington impressed checkering on both stock and forend.

Action: Pump repeater
Caliber: 22 Short, Long and Long Rifle rimfire
Capacity: Tubular magazine holds 20 Short, 17 Long, 15 Long Rifle cartridges

Stock and forend: Model A, walnut finished hardwood; Model BDL, American walnut with tough DuPont RK-W lustrous finish and fine-line custom checkering
Sights: Model A, adjustable rear, bead front; Model BDL, fully adjustable rear, ramp front; screw removable
Safety: Positive cross bolt
Receiver: Grooved for "tip-off" scope mounts
Overall length: 40″
Barrel length: 21″
Average weight: 5½ lbs.

MODEL 552 BDL DELUXE SPEEDMASTER
$192.00

A deluxe model with all the tried and proven dependable mechanical features on the inside, plus special design and appearance extras on the outside. The 552 BDL sports tasteful Remington custom-impressed checkering on both stock and forend. Tough DuPont RK-W lifetime finish brings out the lustrous beauty of the walnut while protecting it. Sights are ramp-style in front and rugged big-game type fully adjustable in rear.

REMINGTON TARGET RIFLES

MODEL 40-XR
Rimfire Position Rifle
$933.00 ($1067.00 w/Kevlar Stock)

Stock designed with deep forend for more comfortable shooting in all positions. Butt plate vertically adjustable. Exclusive loading platform provides straight line feeding with no shaved bullets. Crisp, wide, adjustable match trigger. Meets all International Shooting Union standard rifle specifications.

Action: Bolt action, single shot
Caliber: 22 Long Rifle rimfire
Capacity: Single loading
Sights: Optional at extra cost. Williams Receiver No. FPTK and Redfield Globe front match sight
Safety: Positive serrated thumb safety
Receiver: Drilled and tapped for receiver sight
Barrel: 24″ medium weight target barrel countersunk at muz-

zle. Drilled and tapped for target scope blocks. Fitted with front sight base
Bolt: Artillery style with lock-up at rear. 6 locking lugs, double extractors
Trigger: Adjustable from 2 to 4 lbs.
Stock: Position style with Monte Carlo, cheekpiece and thumb groove; 5-way adjustable butt plate and full length guide rail
Overall length: 42$\frac{1}{2}$″
Average weight: 9$\frac{1}{4}$ lbs.

Also available: **MODEL 40-XR CUSTOM SPORTER** (22 cal.). Grade I **$1200.00**. Grade II **$2133.00** Grade III **$3333.00** Grade IV **$5200.00**

MODEL 40-XC
National Match Course Rifle
$1000.00 ($1133.00 w/Kevlar Stock)

Chambered solely for the 7.62mm NATO cartridge, this match rifle was designed to meet the needs of competitive shooters firing the national match courses. Position-style stock, five-shot repeater with top-loading magazine, anti-bind bolt and receiver and in the bright stainless steel barrel. Meets all International Shooting Union Army Rifle specifications. Weighs about 11 lbs.

Action: Bolt action, single shot
Caliber: 22 Long Rifle rimfire
Capacity: Single loading
Sights: Optional at extra cost. Williams Receiver No. FPTK

and Redfield Globe front match sight
Safety: Positive thumb safety
Length of pull: 13$\frac{1}{2}$″
Receiver: Drilled and tapped for receiver sight or target scope blocks
Barrel: 24″ heavy barrel
Bolt: Heavy, oversized locking lugs and double extractors
Trigger: Adjustable from 2 to 4 lbs.
Stock: Position style with front swivel block on forend guide rail
Overall length: 43$\frac{1}{2}$″
Average weight: 11 lbs.

REMINGTON TARGET RIFLES

MODEL 40-XB "RANGEMASTER"
Centerfire Rifle
$933.00

Barrels, in either standard or heavy weight, are unblued steel. Comb-grooved for easy bolt removal. Mershon White Line non-slip rubber butt plate supplied.

Action: Bolt—single shot in either standard or heavy barrel versions; repeater in heavy barrel only; receiver bedded to stock; barrel is free floating
Calibers: Single-shot, 222 Rem., 22-250 Rem., 6mm Rem., 243 Win., 7.62mm NATO (308 Win.), 30-06, 30-338 (30-7mm Mag.), 300 Win. Mag., 25-06 Rem., 7mm Rem. Mag.
Sights: No sights supplied; target scope blocks installed
Safety: Positive thumb operated
Receiver: Drilled and tapped for scope block and receiver sights

Barrel: Drilled and tapped for scope block and front target iron sight; muzzle diameter S2—approx. ³/₄″, H2—approx. ⁷/₈″; unblued stainless steel only, 27¹/₄″ long
Trigger: Adjustable from 2 to 4 lbs. pull; special 2-oz. trigger available at extra cost; single shot models only
Stock: American walnut; adjustable front swivel block on rail; rubber non-slip butt plate
Overall length: Approx. 45³/₄″
Average weight: S2—9¹/₄ lbs.; H2—11¹/₄ lbs.

·Also available: **MODEL 40-XB KEVLAR "Varmint Special."**
Barrel length: 27¹/₄″. **Overall length:** 45³/₄″. **Weight:** 9³/₄ lbs. **Price:** $1067.00.

MODEL 40XB-BR
Bench Rest Centerfire Rifle
$1000.00

Built with all the features of the extremely accurate Model 40-XB-CF but modified to give the competitive bench rest shooter a standardized rifle that provides the inherent accurracy advantages of a short, heavy, extremely stiff barrel. Wider, squared off forend gives a more stable rest on sandbags or other supports and meets weight limitations for the sporter and light-varmint classes of National Bench Rest Shooters Association competition.

Action: Bolt, single shot only
Calibers: 222 Rem., 22 Bench Rest Rem., 7.62 NATO (308 Win.), 6mm Bench Rest Rem., 223 Rem., 6x47
Sights: Supplied with target scope blocks
Safety: Positive thumb operated
Receiver: Drilled and tapped for target scope blocks
Barrel: Unblued stainless steel only; 20″ barrel for Light Varmint Class; 24″ barrel for Heavy Varmint Class.
Trigger: Adjustable from 1¹/₂ to 3¹/₂ lbs.; special 2-oz. trigger available at extra cost
Stock: Selected American walnut; length of pull—12″
Overall length: 38″ with 20″ barrel; 44″ with 24″ barrel
Average weight: Light Varmint Class (20″ barrel) 9¹/₄ lbs.; Heavy Varmint Class (24″ barrel) 11 lbs.

ROSSI RIFLES

MODEL M62 SAC
$192.00

SPECIFICATIONS
Caliber: 22 LR
Capacity: 12 rds.
Barrel length: 16¹/₂″
Overall length: 32³/₄″
Weight: 4¹/₄″
Finish: Blue
Model M62 SAC w/Nickel finish $207.00

PUMP-ACTION GALLERY GUNS
MODEL M62 SA
$192.00

SPECIFICATIONS
Caliber: 22 LR
Capacity: 13 rds.
Barrel length: 23″
Overall length: 39¹/₄″
Weight: 5¹/₂″ lbs.
Finish: Blue
Model M62 SA w/Octagonal barrel $217.00
Model 59 22 Magnum 237.00

PUMA LEVER ACTION CARBINES
MODEL M92 SRS
$282.00

SPECIFICATIONS
Caliber: 38 Special or 357 Magnum
Capacity: 7 rounds
Barrel length: 16″
Overall length: 33″
Weight: 5 lbs.
Finish: Blue

MODEL M92 SRC
$282.00 ($327.00 Engraved)

SPECIFICATIONS
Caliber: 38 Special or 357 Magnum
Capacity: 10 rounds
Barrel length: 20″
Overall length: 37″
Weight: 5³/₄″
Also available in 44 Magnum: $297.00

RUGER CARBINES

RUGER MINI-14

Materials: Heat-treated chrome molybdenum and other alloy steels as well as music wire coil springs are used throughout the mechanism to ensure reliability under field-operating conditions. **Safety:** The safety blocks both the hammer and sear. The slide can be cycled when the safety is on. The safety is mounted in the front of the trigger guard so that it may be set to Fire position without removing finger from trigger guard. **Firing pin:** The firing pin is retracted mechanically during the first part of the unlocking of the bolt. The rifle can only be fired when the bolt is safely locked. **Stock:** One-piece American hardwood reinforced with steel liner at stressed areas. Handguard and forearm separated by air space from barrel to promote cooling under rapid-fire conditions. **Field stripping:** The Carbine can be field stripped to its eight (8) basic sub-assemblies in a matter of seconds and without use of special tools.

MINI-14 SPECIFICATIONS
Caliber: 223 (5.56mm). **Length:** 37¼". **Weight:** 6 lbs. 4 oz. **Magazine:** 5-round, detachable box magazine. 20-shot and 30-shot magazines available. **Barrel length:** 18½".

Mini-14/5 Blued. $405.50
Mini-14/5F Blued (folding stock) 483.50
K-Mini-14/5 Stainless Steel 447.00
K-MINI-14/5F (Stainless steel, folding stock) 514.50
Scopes not included

MINI-14 RANCH RIFLE

Caliber: 223 (5.56mm) or 7.62×39. **Length:** 37¼". **Weight:** 6 lbs. 8 oz. **Magazine:** 10-shot and 20-shot magazines available. **Barrel length:** 18¼".

Mini-14/5R Blued $437.00
K-Mini-14/5R Stainless Steel 478.50
K-Mini-14/5RF Stainless Steel (folding stock) 541.00

RUGER CARBINES

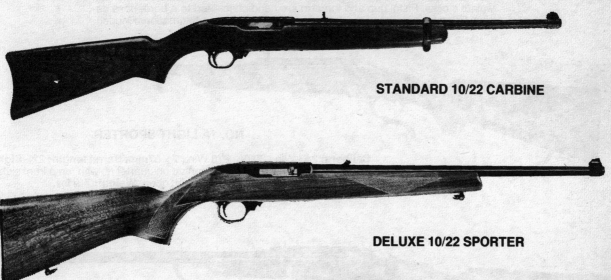

STANDARD 10/22 CARBINE

DELUXE 10/22 SPORTER

MODEL 10/22 CARBINE
22 LONG RIFLE CALIBER

Identical in size, balance and style to the Ruger 44 Magnum Carbine and nearly the same in weight, the 10/22 is a companion to its high-power counterpart. Construction of the 10/22 Carbine is rugged and follows the Ruger design practice of building a firearm from integrated sub-assemblies. For example, the trigger housing assembly contains the entire ignition system, which employs a high-speed, swinging hammer to ensure the shortest possible lock time. The barrel is assembled to the receiver by a unique dual-screw dovetail system that provides unusual rigidity and strength—and accounts, in part, for the exceptional accuracy of the 10/22.

SPECIFICATIONS
Caliber: 22 Long Rifle, high-speed or standard-velocity loads.
Barrel: 18$^{1}/_{2}$" long; barrel is assembled to the receiver by unique dual-screw dovetail mounting for added strength and rigidity. **Weight:** 5 lbs. **Overall length:** 37". **Sights:** $^{1}/_{16}$" gold bead front sight; single folding leaf rear sight, adjustable for elevation; receiver drilled and tapped for scope blocks or tip-off mount adapter. **Magazine:** 10-shot capacity, exclusive Ruger rotary design; fits flush into stock. **Trigger:** Curved finger surface, $^{3}/_{8}$" wide. **Safety:** Sliding cross-button type; safety locks both sear and hammer and cannot be put in safe position unless gun is cocked. **Stocks:** 10/22 R Standard Carbine is walnut; 10/22 RB is birch; 10/22 SP Deluxe Sporter is American walnut. **Finish:** Polished all over and blued or anodized.

Model 10/22-R Standard (walnut stock) $196.00
Model 10/22-RB Standard (birch stock) 176.00
Model 10/22-DSP Deluxe Sporter 222.00

MINI THIRTY

This modified version of the Ruger Ranch rifle is chambered for the 7.62 × 39mm Russian service cartridge (used in the SKS carbine and AKM rifle). Designed for use with telescopic sights, it features a low, compact scope mounting for greater accuracy and carrying ease. **Barrel length:** 18$^{1}/_{2}$". **Overall**

length: 37$^{1}/_{4}$". **Weight:** 7 lbs. 3 oz. (empty). **Magazine capacity:** 5 shots. **Rifling:** 6 grooves, right-hand twist, one turn in 10". **Finish:** polished and blued overall.
Price. $437.00

RUGER SINGLE-SHOT RIFLES

The following illustrations show the variations currently offered in the Ruger No. 1 Single-Shot Rifle Series. Ruger No. 1 rifles come fitted with selected American walnut stocks. Pistol grip and forearm are hand-checkered to a borderless design. **Price for any listed model is $575.00** (except No. 1 International Model).

NO. 1A LIGHT SPORTER

Calibers: 243 Win.; 30/06; 270 Win., 7×57mm. **Barrel length:** 22″. **Sight:** Adjustable folding-leaf rear sight mounted on quarter rib with ramp front sight base and dovetail-type gold bead front sight; open. **Weight:** 7¼ lbs.

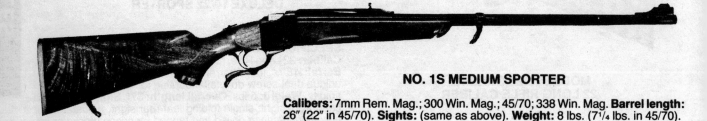

NO. 1S MEDIUM SPORTER

Calibers: 7mm Rem. Mag.; 300 Win. Mag.; 45/70; 338 Win. Mag. **Barrel length:** 26″ (22″ in 45/70). **Sights:** (same as above). **Weight:** 8 lbs. (7¼ lbs. in 45/70).

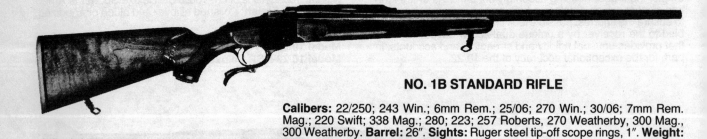

NO. 1B STANDARD RIFLE

Calibers: 22/250; 243 Win.; 6mm Rem.; 25/06; 270 Win.; 30/06; 7mm Rem. Mag.; 220 Swift; 338 Mag.; 280; 223; 257 Roberts, 270 Weatherby, 300 Mag., 300 Weatherby. **Barrel:** 26″. **Sights:** Ruger steel tip-off scope rings, 1″. **Weight:** 8 lbs.

NO. 1V SPECIAL VARMINTER

Calibers: 22/250; 25/06; 220 Swift; 223; 6mm. **Barrel length;** 24″. **Sights:** Ruger steel blocks and tip-off scope rings, 1″. **Weight:** 9 lbs.

RUGER RIFLES

NO. 1H TROPICAL RIFLE

Calibers: 375 H&H Mag.; 458 Win. Mag. **Barrel length:** 24″ (heavy). **Sights:** Adjustable folding-leaf rear sight mounted on quarter rib with ramp front sight base and dovetail-type gold bead front sight; open. **Weight:** 8¼ lbs. for 375; 9 lbs. for 458.
Price **$575.00**

NO. 1RSI INTERNATIONAL
With Mannlicher Style Forearm

SPECIFICATIONS
Caliber: 243 Win., 30-06, 270 Win., and 7×57mm. **Barrel length:** 20″ (lightweight). **Overall length:** 36½″. **Weight:** 7¼ lbs. **Sights:** Adjustable folding leaf rear sight mounted on quarter rib with ramp front sight base and dovetail-type gold bead front sight.
Price **$595.00**

BOLT ACTION RIFLES

MODEL 77/22 RS

SPECIFICATIONS
Caliber: 22LR. **Barrel length:** 20″. **Overall length:** 39¼″. **Weight:** 5¾ lbs. (w/o scope, magazine empty). **Feed:** Detachable 10-Shot Ruger Rotary Magazine.
Prices:
77/22R (plain barrel w/o sights; 1″ Ruger rings) **$364.50**
77/22S (gold bead front sight, folding leaf rear sight). **364.50**
77/22RS (sights included; 1″ Ruger rings) **384.50**

MODEL 77/22 BOLT ACTION RIMFIRE RIFLE

The Ruger 22-caliber rimfire 77/22 bolt-action rifle offers the sportsman quality and value. It represents a blend of characteristics long associated with the famous Ruger M-77 rifle and the internationally popular Ruger 10/22 semiautomatic rimfire rifle. It has been built especially to function with the patented Ruger 10-Shot Rotary Magazine concept. The magazine throat, retaining lips, and ramps that guide the cartridge into the chamber are solid alloy steel that resists bending or deforming.

The bolt assembly is built to military rifle standards of quality, but it has been modified to function with the 22 rimfire cartridge. Accordingly, the front part of the bolt is nonrotating and the locking lugs have been moved back to the middle of the action. The rear part of the bolt rotates and cams like that of the Ruger M-77 rifle, and it is connected to the nonrotating forward part of the bolt by a sturdy joint.

The new 77/22 weighs just under six pounds and provides the smallbore shooter with a compact, featherweight arm that delivers performance and reliability. The heavy-duty receiver incorporates the integral scope bases of the patented Ruger Scope Mounting System, with 1-inch Ruger scope rings. A new 3-position safety offers a new dimension in security. With safety in its "lock" position, a dead bolt is cammed forward, locking the bolt handle down. In this position the action is locked closed and the handle cannot be raised.

A simplified bolt stop fits flush with the left side of the receiver and permits the bolt to be withdrawn from receiver merely by pressing down tightly. The new bolt locking system ensures positive lock-up by two large locking lugs on rotating part of bolt. A nonadjustable trigger mechanism is set for medium weight trigger pull. This mechanism includes a single strong coil spring for both sear recovery and trigger return. Lock time is 2.7 milliseconds.

All metal surfaces are finished in a deep, lustrous blue with nonglare surfaces on top of receiver. Stock is selected straight-grain American walnut, hand checkered with an attractive and durable polyurethane finish.

RUGER BOLT ACTION RIFLES

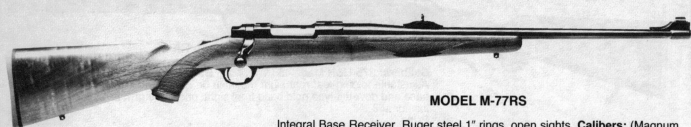

MODEL M-77RS

Integral Base Receiver, Ruger steel 1″ rings, open sights. **Calibers:** (Magnum action) 270, 7 × 57mm, 30-06 (with 22″ barrels), 25-06, 7mm Rem. Mag., 300 Win. Mag., 338 Win. Mag. (with 24″ barrels); and (Short Stroke action) 243, 308 (with 22″ barrels). **Weight:** Approx. 7 lbs.

Price **$518.00**

MODEL M-77RL ULTRA LIGHT

New 6-pound big game rifle in both long- and short-action versions, with Integral Base Receiver and 1″ Ruger scope rings. Luxury detailing throughout. **Calibers:** (Magnum action) 270, 30-06, 257 (all with 20″ barrels); and (Short Stroke action) 22-250, 243, .250-3000, 308 (with 22″ barrels). **Weight:** Approx. 6 lbs.

Price **$498.00**

MODEL M-77RLS ULTRA LIGHT

This big game bolt-action rifle encompasses the traditional features that have made the Ruger M-77 one of the most popular centerfire rifles in the world. It includes a sliding top tang safety, a one-piece bolt with Mauser-type extractor and diagonal front mounting system. American walnut stock is hand-checkered in a sharp diamond pattern. A rubber recoil pad, pistol grip cap and studs for mounting quick detachable sling swivels are standard. **Calibers:** 270, 30-06 (Magnum action); 243 and 308 (short stroke action). **Barrel length:** 18 1/2″. **Overall length:** 38 7/8″. **Weight:** 6 lbs. (empty). **Sights:** Open.

Price **$498.00**

RUGER BOLT ACTION RIFLES

MODEL M-77RSI INTERNATIONAL

Mannlicher-type stock, Integral Base Receiver, open sights, Ruger 1″ steel rings.
Calibers: (Short Stroke action) 22-250, 250-3000, 243, 270, 30-06, and 308 (all with 18$\frac{1}{2}$″ barrels). **Weight:** Approx. 7 lbs.

Price **$524.00**

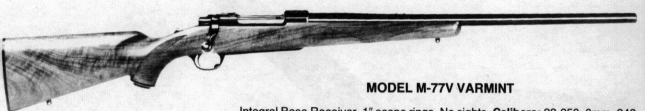

MODEL M-77V VARMINT

Integral Base Receiver, 1″ scope rings. No sights. **Calibers:** 22-250, 6mm, 243, 25-06, 308 (with heavy 24″ barrels); 220 Swift (with 26″ barrel). **Weight:** Approx. 9 lbs.

Price **$482.00**

MODEL M-77R (not shown)

Integral Base Receiver, 1″ scope rings. No sights. **Calibers:** (Magnum action) 270, 7×57mm, 257 Roberts, 280 Rem., 30-06 (all with 22″ barrels); 25-06, 7mm Rem. Mag., 300 Win. Mag., 338 Win. Mag. (all with 24″ barrels); and (Short Stroke action) 22-250, 6mm, 243, 308 (all with 22″ barrels); 220 Swift (with 24″ barrel). **Weight:** Approx. 7 lbs.

Price **$460.00**

MODEL M-77RS TROPICAL (not shown)

Integral Base Receiver (Magnum action only). Equipped with open sights and Ruger steel rings. **Caliber:** 458 Win. Mag. only. Steel trigger guard and floor plate. **Weight:** Approx. 8.75 lbs.

Price: **$600.00**

SAKO FIBERCLASS RIFLES

NEW ALL WEATHER FIBERGLASS-STOCKED CENTERFIRE RIFLE

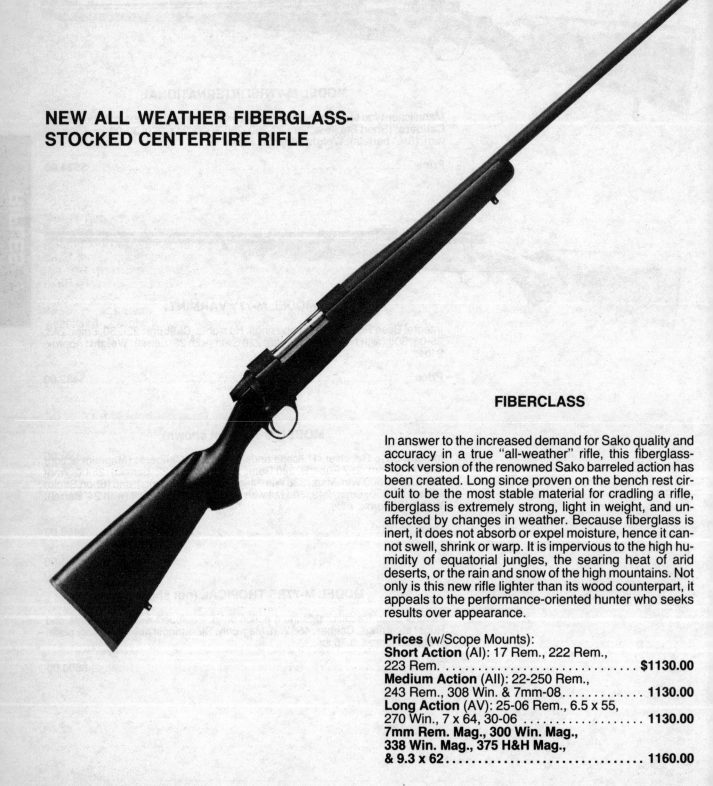

FIBERCLASS

In answer to the increased demand for Sako quality and accuracy in a true "all-weather" rifle, this fiberglass-stock version of the renowned Sako barreled action has been created. Long since proven on the bench rest circuit to be the most stable material for cradling a rifle, fiberglass is extremely strong, light in weight, and unaffected by changes in weather. Because fiberglass is inert, it does not absorb or expel moisture, hence it cannot swell, shrink or warp. It is impervious to the high humidity of equatorial jungles, the searing heat of arid deserts, or the rain and snow of the high mountains. Not only is this new rifle lighter than its wood counterpart, it appeals to the performance-oriented hunter who seeks results over appearance.

Prices (w/Scope Mounts):
Short Action (AI): 17 Rem., 222 Rem.,
223 Rem. **$1130.00**
Medium Action (AII): 22-250 Rem.,
243 Rem., 308 Win. & 7mm-08 . . . . 1130.00
Long Action (AV): 25-06 Rem., 6.5 x 55,
270 Win., 7 x 64, 30-06 . . . . 1130.00
**7mm Rem. Mag., 300 Win. Mag.,
338 Win. Mag., 375 H&H Mag.,
& 9.3 x 62** 1160.00

SAKO RIFLES

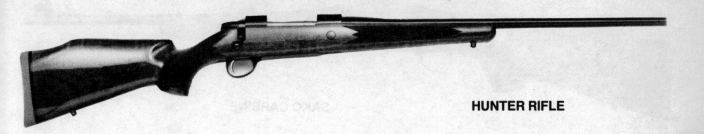

HUNTER RIFLE

HUNTER

Here's one case of less being more. Sako has taken its famed bolt-action, centerfire rifle, redesigned the stock and trimmed the barrel contour. In fact, in any of the short action (A1) calibers—.17 Rem., .222 or .223 Rem.—the Hunter weighs in at a mere 5¾ pounds, making it the lightest wood stock production rifle in the world.

The same cosmetic upgrading and weight reduction have been applied to the entire Hunter line in all calibers and action lengths, standard and magnum. All the precision, quality and accuracy for which this Finnish rifle has been so justly famous are still here. Now it just weighs less.

The Sako Trigger is a rifleman's delight—smooth, crisp and fully adjustable. If these were the only Sako features, it would still be the best rifle available. But the real quality that sets Sako apart from all others is its truly outstanding accuracy.

While many factors can affect a rifle's accuracy, 90 percent of any rifle's accuracy potential lies in its barrel. And the creation of superbly accurate barrels is where Sako excels.

The care that Sako takes in the cold-hammering processing of each barrel is unparalleled in the industry. As an example, after each barrel blank is drilled, it is diamond-lapped and then optically checked for microscopic flaws. This extra care affords the Sako owner lasting accuracy and a finish that will stay "new" season after season.

You can't buy an unfired Sako. Every gun is test fired using special overloaded proof cartridges. This ensures the Sako owner total safety and uncompromising accuracy. Every barrel must group within Sako specifications or it's scrapped. Not recycled. Not adjusted. Scrapped. Either a Sako barrel delivers Sako accuracy, or it never leaves the factory.

And hand-in-hand with Sako accuracy is Sako beauty. Genuine European walnut stocks, flawlessly finished and checkered by hand.

Prices (include lacquer finish without sights, or oil finish with sights)

Short Action (AI)

In 17 Rem.	$850.00
In 222 Rem, 223 Rem, & 6mm PPC	820.00

Medium Action (AII)

In 22-250 Rem., 7mm-08, 243 Win. & 308 Win.	820.00

Long Action (AV)

In 25-06 Rem., 270 Win., 30-06, 6.5x55, 7x64	840.00
In 7mm Rem. Mag., 300 Win. Mag., 9.3x62, & 338 Win. Mag.	850.00
In 375 H&H Mag.	860.00
In 300 Weatherby Mag.	870.00

SAKO CARBINES

Sako's Carbines combine the handiness and carrying qualities of the traditional, lever action "deer rifle" with the power of modern, high-performance cartridges. An abbreviated 18½ inch barrel trims the overall weight of the Carbine to just over 40 inches in the long (or AV) action calibers, and 39½" in the medium (or All) action calibers. Weight is a highly portable 7 and 6½ pounds, respectively (except in the .338 and .375 H&H calibers, which tip the scale at 7½ pounds).

As is appropriate for a rifle of this type, the Carbine is furnished with an excellent set of open sights; the rear is fully adjustable for windage and elevation, while the front is a nonglare serrated ramp with protective hood.

The Carbine is available in a choice of stocks: the traditional wood stock of European walnut done in a contemporary Monte Carlo style with a choice of hand-rubbed oil or gloss lacquer finish. Either way, hand-cut checkering is standard. The Mannlicher-style full stock Carbine wears Sako's exclusive two-piece forearm, which joins beneath the barrel band. This independent forward section of the forearm eliminates the bedding problems normally associated with the full forestock. A blued steel muzzle cap puts the finishing touches on this European-styled Carbine.

For the hunter whose primary concerns are ruggedness and practicality, there's the Fiberclass Carbine. Stocked in the same distinctive black fiberglass stock as Sako's famed Fiberclass Rifle model, the Carbine offers the same advantages but in a shorter, lighter configuration. The fiberglass Carbines in .338 and .375 H&H have become favorites withe Alaskan guides, bush pilots, and all those who work or travel regularly in big bear country.

SAKO CARBINE

Prices:

Sako Carbine w/Scope Mounts in 22-250 Rem.,
  243 Rem., 308 Win. & 7mm-08 (Medium Action) **$820.00**
In 25-06 Rem., 6.5×55, 270 Win., 7 × 64 & 30-06 (Long Action) **840.00**
In 7mm Rem. Mag., 300 Win. Mag., 338 Win. Mag., & 375 H&H Mag. (Long Action) **850.00**

Sako Fiberclass Carbine w/Scope Mounts
In 25-06, 270 Win., & 30-06 (Long Action) . . **$1130.00**
In 7mm Rem. Mag., 300 Win. Mag., 338 Win. Mag. & 375 H&H Mag. (Long Action) **1160.00**

Sako Mannlicher-Style Carbine w/Scope Mounts
In 222 Rem. (Short Action) **$885.00**
In 243 Win. & 308 Win. (Medium Action) **885.00**
In 25-06, 270 Win., & 30-06 (Long Action) **885.00**
In 7mm Rem. Mag., 300 Win. Mag. & 338 Win. Mag. (Long Action) **915.00**
In 375 H&H Mag. **935.00**

Also available:
Left-Handed Models (Long Action only)
In 25-06, 270 Win. Mag., 30-06. . . . . **$890.00**
In 7mm Rem. Mag., 300 Win. Mag, 338 Win. Mag. **950.00**
In 375 H&H Mag. **950.00**

SAKO MANNLICHER-STYLE CARBINE

SAKO RIFLES

LAMINATED STOCK MODELS

In response to the growing number of hunters and shooters who seek the strength and stability that a fiberglass stock provides, coupled with the warmth and feel of real wood, Sako introduces its Laminated Stock models.

Machined from blanks comprised of 36 individual layers of $1/16$-inch hardwood veneers that are resin-bonded under extreme pressure, these stocks are virtually inert. Each layer of hardwood has been vacuum-impregnated with a permanent brown dye. The bisecting of various layers of veneers in the shaping of the stock results in a contour-line appearance similar to a piece of slab-sawed walnut. Because all Sako Laminated Stocks are of real wood, each one is unique, with its own shading, color and grain.

These stocks satisfy those whose sensibilities demand a rifle of wood and steel, but who also want state-of-the-art performance and practicality. Sako's Laminated Stock provides both, further establishing it among the most progressive manufacturers of sporting rifles—and the *only* one to offer hunters and shooters their choice of walnut, fiberglass or laminated stocks in 18 calibers (10 in Left-Handed models), from .17 Remington to .375 H&H.

Prices:

Laminated with Scope Mounts

In 17 Rem., 222 Rem. & 223 Rem. (Short Action) and
   22-250, 243 Rem., 308 Win. and 7mm-08
   (Medium Action). **$925.00**
In 25-06 Rem., 6.5 × 55, 270 Win., 7 × 64 & 30-06
   (Long Action) 940.00
In 7mm Rem. Mag., 300 Win. Mag. & 338 Win. Mag.
   (Long Action) 945.00
In 375 H&H Mag. (Long Action) 955.00

Laminated Left-Handed with Scope Mounts

In 25-06, 6.5 × 55, 270 Win., 7 × 64, 30-06
   (Long Action) 960.00
In 7mm Rem. Mag., 300 Win. Mag., 338 Win. Mag.,
   & 9.3 × 62 (Long Action). 980.00
In 375 H&H Mag. (Long Action) 995.00

SAKO CUSTOM RIFLES

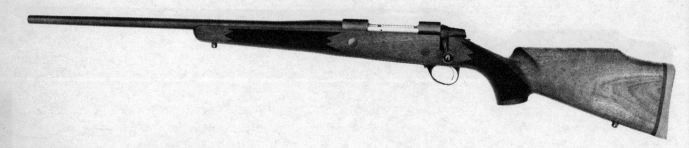

LEFT-HANDED MODELS

Sako's new Left-Handed models are based on mirror images of the right-handed models enjoyed by Sako owners for many years, with handle, extractor and ejection port all located on the port side. Naturally, the stock is also reversed, with the cheekpiece on the opposite side and the palm swell on the port side of the grip.

Otherwise these guns are identical to the right-hand models. That means hammer-forged barrels, one-piece bolts with integral locking lugs and handles, integral scope mount tails, three-way adjustable triggers, Mauser-type inertia ejections, and one-piece steel trigger guard/magazine frames.

Sako's Left-Handed rifles are available in all Long Action models. The Hunter Grade carries a durable, hand-rubbed oil finish with generous-size panels of hand-cut checkering, a presentation-style recoil pad, scope mounts, and sling swivel studs installed. The Deluxe model is distinguished by its rosewood forend tip and grip cap, its skip-line checkering and gloss lacquer finish atop a select-grade of highly figured European walnut. The metal work carries a deep, mirro-like blue that looks more like black chrome. Laminated and Fiberclass Long Action models are also available for lefthfanders.

Prices

Hunter Lightweight w/Scope Mounts
In 25-06, 6.5 × 55, 270 Win., 7 × 64 & 30-06..**$950.00**
In 7mm Rem. Mag., 300 Win. Mag., 338 Win. Mag., and 9.3 × 62..........................**960.00**
In 375 H&H Mag............................**970.00**

Deluxe (all Long Action) w/Scope Mounts
In 25-06, 6.5 × 55, 270 Win. Mag., 7 × 64 & 30-06................................**$1210.00**
In 7mm Rem. Mag, 300 Win. Mag., 338 Win. Mag. and 9.3 × 62......................**1240.00**
In 375 H&H Mag............................**1290.00**

Fiberclass (all Long Action) w/Scope Mounts
In 25-06, 6.5 × 55, 270 Win., 7 × 64 & 30-06..............................**$1300.00**
In 7mm Rem. Mag., 300 Win. Mag., 338 Win. Mag. & 9.3 × 62............................**1320.00**
In 375 H&H Mag............................**1310.00**

SAKO RIFLES

SAFARI GRADE
$2115.00

Crafted in the tradition of the classic British express rifles, Safari Grade is truly a professional's rifle. Every feature has been carefully thought out and executed with one goal in mind: functionality. The magazine is extended, allowing four belted magnums to be stored inside (instead of the usual three). The steel floorplate straddles the front of the trigger guard bow for added strength and security.

An express-style quarter rib provides a rigid, non-glare base for the rear sight, which consists of a fixed blade and one auxiliary fold-down. The front swivel is carried by a contoured barrel band to keep the stud away from the off-hand under the recoil of big calibers. The front sight assembly is also a barrel-band type for maximum strength. The blade sits on a non-glare ramp and is protected by a steel hood.

The Safari's barreled action carries a subtle semi-matte blue, which lends an understated elegance to this eminently practical rifle. The functional, classic-style stock is of European walnut selected especially for its strength with respect to grain orientation as well as for color and figure. A rosewood forend tip, a steel grip cap, an elegant, beaded cheekpiece and presentation—style recoil pad complete the stock embellishments.

Calibers: 300 Win. Mag., 338 Win. Mag & 375 H&H Mag. See also **Specifications Table**.

VARMINTER
$1035.00

The Sako Varminter is specifically designed with a prone-type stock for shooting from the ground or bench. The forend is extra wide to provide added steadiness when rested on sandbags or makeshift field rests.

Calibers: 222 Rem. & 223 Rem. (Short Action); 22-250, 243 Rem. & 308 Win. (Medium Action). Also available in 6mm PPC and 22 PPC (single shot only). **Price: $925.00.**

SAKO RIFLES

DELUXE SHORT ACTION

DELUXE

All the fine-touch features you expect of the deluxe grade Sako are here—beautifully grained French Walnut, superbly done high-gloss finish, hand-cut checkering, deep rich bluing and rosewood forend tip and grip cap. And of course the accuracy, reliability and superior field performance for which Sako is so justly famous are still here too. It's all here—it just weighs less than it used to. Think of it as more for less.

In addition, the scope mounting system on these Sakos is among the strongest in the world. A tapered dovetail is milled into the receiver, to which the scope rings and separate bases are mounted. A beautiful system that's been proven by over 20 years of use. Sako scope rings are available in *low* (2½ to 3-power scopes), *medium* (4-power scopes) and *high* (6-power scopes). Available in one-inch only.

Prices (w/Scope Mounts)
Short Action (AI) in 17 Rem., 222 Rem.
& 223 Rem. **$1065.00**
Medium Action (AII) in 22-250
Rem., 243 Rem., 7mm-08 & 308 Win. **1065.00**
Long Action (AV) in 25-06 Rem.,
270 Win., 30-06 . . . . **1065.00**
In 7 mm Rem. Mag., 300 Win. Mag.,
338 Win. Mag., 9.3 × 62, 375 H&H Mag. **1090.00**
In 300 Weatherby Mag. **1100.00**

SAKO SUPER DELUXE $2115.00

Sako offers the Super Deluxe to the most discriminating gun buyer. This one-of-a-kind beauty is available on special order.

SAKO RIFLES

SAKO Rifle Specifications
The Closest To "Custom" in a Production Rifle

	CUSTOM			CARBINES			RIFLES				
	VARMINT	TARGET	SAFARI	FIBERCLASS	CARBINE	CARBINE MANNLICHER STYLE	LAMINATED	FIBERCLASS	SUPERDELUXE	DELUXE	HUNTER
Action*	AI / AI / AII	AI / AII	AV	AV	AV / AV / AV	AV / AV / AV	AI / AII / AV / AV	AI / AII / AV / AV	AI / AII / AV / AV	AI / AV / AV / AV	AI / AV / AV / AV
Left-handed							• • •	• • •	• • •	• • •	• • •
Total length (in)	43¾ / 42¾ / 43¼	42¾ / 45	43	40½ / 40½ / 40½	39½ / 40½ / 40½ / 40½	39½ / 40½ / 44 / 46	41½ / 42½ / 44 / 46	41½ / 42½ / 43½ / 45½	41½ / 42½ / 43½ / 45½	41½ / 42½ / 44 / 46	41½ / 42½ / 44 / 46
Barrel length (in)	23¾ / 25¼ / 22¾	23¾ / 25¼	22	18½ / 18½ / 18½	18½ / 18½ / 18½	18½	21¼ / 21¾ / 22 / 24	21¼ / 21¾ / 22 / 24	21¼ / 21¾ / 22 / 24	21¼ / 21¾ / 22 / 24	21¼ / 21¾ / 22 / 24
Weight (lbs)	8¾ / 8½ / 8½	10 / 10	8¾	7½ / 7¼ / 7¼	6½ / 7 / 7¼ / 7¾	7½	5¾ / 6¾ / 7¼ / 7¾	5¾ / 6¾ / 7¼ / 7¾	6¼ / 7 / 7½ / 8	5¾ / 6¾ / 7¼ / 7¾	5¾ / 6¾ / 7¼ / 7¾

Caliber / Rate of Twist

Caliber / Twist	VARMINT	TARGET	SAFARI	FIBERCLASS (carb)	CARBINE	CARBINE MANN.	LAMINATED	FIBERCLASS (rifle)	SUPERDELUXE	DELUXE	HUNTER
17 Rem / 10"	•									•	•
222 Rem / 14"	•								•	•	•
223 Rem / 12"	•								•	•	•
22 PPC / 14"	•										•
6mm PPC / 14"	•										•
22-250 Rem / 14"	•				•	•	•	•			•
243 Win / 10"	•				•	•	•	•	•	•	•
7mm-08 / 9½"	•				•	•	•	•			•
308 Win / 12"	•				•	•	•	•	•	•	•
25-06 Rem / 10"				•	•	•	•	•	•	•	•
6.5 x 5.5 / 10"					•	•			•	•	•
270 Win / 10"				•	•	•	•	•	•	•	•
7 x 64 / 10"									•	•	•
30-06 / 10"				•	•	•	•	•	•	•	•
7mm / Rem Mag / 9½"				•	•	•	•	•	•	•	•
300 Win Mag / 10"				•		•			•	•	•
300 Wby Mag / 10"										•	•
338 Win Mag / 10"	•	•	•	•	•	•	•	•	•	•	•
9.3 x 62 / 14"	•	•	•	•	•	•	•	•	•	•	•
375 H&H Mag / 12"	•	•	•	•	•	•	•	•	•	•	•

Stock Finish / Sights / Mag. / Buttplate

	VARMINT	TARGET	SAFARI	FIBERCLASS (carb)	CARBINE	CARBINE MANN.	LAMINATED	FIBERCLASS (rifle)	SUPERDELUXE	DELUXE	HUNTER
Stock Finish — Lacquered							• • • • •				• • • •
Stock Finish — Oiled	• • •	• •		• • •	• • •	• • •					• • • •
Sights — Without sights	• • •	• •					• • • •	• • • •	• • • •	• • • •	• • • •
Sights — Open sights				•		•					• • • •
Sights — Base for telescopic sight mounts	• • •	• •	•	• • •	• • •	• • •	• • •	• • •	• • •	• • •	• • •
Magazine capacity	5	6	4	5 / 3	5 / 3	3	5 / 3	5 / 3	5 / 3	6 / 5 / 3	6 / 5 / 3
Buttplate — Rubber		• •	•	• • •	• • •	• • •	• • •	• • •	• • •	• • •	• • •
Buttplate — Hard	• • •	• •	•								

* HUNTER MODELS ONLY: OIL FINISHED HAVE OPEN SIGHTS

SAKO ACTIONS

Only by building a rifle around a Sako action do shooters enjoy the choice of three different lengths, each scaled to a specific family of cartridges. The A1 (Short) action is miniaturized in every respect to match the .222 family, which includes everything from .17 Remington to .222 Remington Magnum. The A11 (Medium) action is scaled down to the medium-length cartridges of standard (30-06) bolt face—.22-250, .243, .308 or similar length cartridges. The AV (Long) action is offered in either standard or Magnum bolt face and accommodates cartridges of up to 3.65 inches in overall length, including rounds like the .300 Weatherby and .375 H&H Magnum. **For lefthanders, only the Long Action is offered in either standard or Magnum bolt face.** All actions are furnished in-thewhite only.

AI-1 (SHORT ACTION)
CALIBERS:
17 Rem.
222 Rem.
222 Rem. Mag.
223 Rem.
$370.00

AII-1 (MEDIUM ACTION)
CALIBERS:
22-250 Rem. (AII-3)
243 Win.
308 Win.
$370.00

AV-4 (LONG ACTION)
CALIBERS:
25-06 Rem. (AV-1)
270 Win. (AV-1)
7 × 64
30-06 (AV-1)
7mm Rem. Mag.
300 Win. Mag.
338 Win. Mag.
375 H&H Mag.
$370.00

Also available:
LEFT-HANDED ACTIONS
Long Action only: $385.00

SAUER RIFLES

Maker of fine rifles and shotguns since 1751, the J.P. Sauer & Sohn Company of West Germany announces its Sauer 90 Bolt Action Rifle series in four configurations—Supreme, Lux, Stutzen and Safari. Each features a hammer-forged barrel and machined steel receiver; cam-activated lugs ensure positive lockup, while the 65° bolt facilitates rapid reloading.

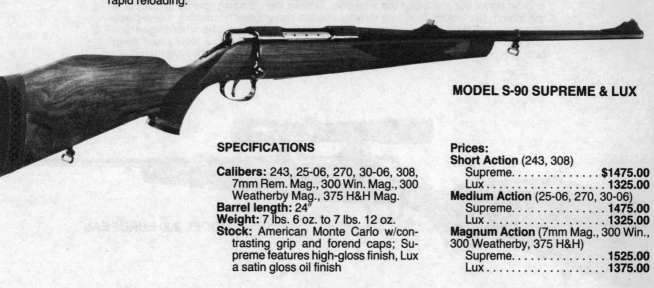

MODEL S-90 SUPREME & LUX

SPECIFICATIONS

Calibers: 243, 25-06, 270, 30-06, 308, 7mm Rem. Mag., 300 Win. Mag., 300 Weatherby Mag., 375 H&H Mag.
Barrel length: 24″
Weight: 7 lbs. 6 oz. to 7 lbs. 12 oz.
Stock: American Monte Carlo w/contrasting grip and forend caps; Supreme features high-gloss finish, Lux a satin gloss oil finish

Prices:
Short Action (243, 308)
Supreme $1475.00
Lux 1325.00
Medium Action (25-06, 270, 30-06)
Supreme 1475.00
Lux 1325.00
Magnum Action (7mm Mag., 300 Win., 300 Weatherby, 375 H&H)
Supreme 1525.00
Lux 1375.00

MODEL S-90 STUTZEN

SPECIFICATIONS
Calibers: 30-06, 270
Barrel length: 20″
Weight: 7½ lbs.
Stock: European Monte Carlo w/satin gloss oil finish
Price:
W/sights, no swivels $1675.00

MODEL S-90 SAFARI

SPECIFICATIONS
Caliber: 458 Win.
Barrel length: 24″
Weight: 10 lbs. 12 oz.
Stock: American Monte Carlo with matte oil finish
Price:
Incl. sights, swivels $1675.00

SAUER RIFLES

MODEL 200

The Sauer 200 is a take-down rifle featuring an interchangeable barrel system. Take-down is made simply by removing the buttstock bolt and pulling the buttstock off the receiver. To change barrels, remove the forend and clamping screws, then pull the original barrel out and insert the new one. Tighten the clamping screws and replace the forend. Six locking lugs lock directly into the barrel breech, creating a one-piece barrel and bolt for maximum strength and accuracy. Also features hammer-forged barrels and machined steel receivers, hand-checkered select walnut stocks and deep bluing. A push-button safety is located in front of the trigger for use by either hand.

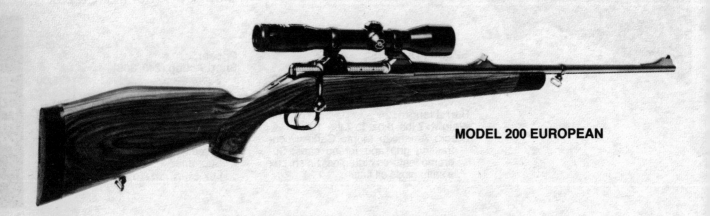

MODEL 200 EUROPEAN

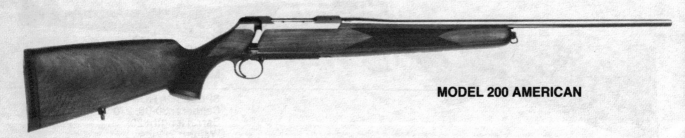

MODEL 200 AMERICAN

MODEL 200 AMERICAN & EUROPEAN

SPECIFICATIONS
Calibers: 243, 25-06, 270, 30-06, 308
Barrel length: 24″ (American); 26″ (European)
Weight: 7 lbs. 12 oz.
Stock: American Monte Carlo w/high-gloss finish, contrasting forend and pistol grip caps (American); Classic style w/cheekpiece and schnabel forend, satin gloss oil finish, contrasting forend and grip caps (European)
Features: Both models drilled and tapped for scope bases and shipped without swivels; sights provided on European model only
Prices:
MODEL 200 . . . . $1175.00
Left Hand 1270.00

SAVAGE CENTERFIRE RIFLES

MODEL 110 BOLT-ACTION
CENTERFIRE RIFLES
STANDARD AND MAGNUM CALIBERS

The Savage 100 Series features solid lockup, positive gas protection, precise head space, precision-rifled barrels, and select walnut Monte Carlo stocks.

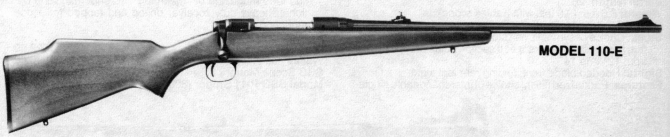

MODEL 110-E

MODEL 110-E
Calibers: 223, 22-250, 243 Win., 30-06, 270 Win., 7mm Rem. Mag.

A specially designed version of the 110 bolt action rifle featuring a free floating barrel, satin blue receiver (to reduce light reflections), and Wundhammer swell pistol grip. Internal box holds 4 rounds plus one in the chamber. Stock is select walnut with high Monte Carlo.

SPECIFICATIONS
Barrel length: 22″ (24″ Magnum). **Overall length:** 43″ (45″ Magnum). **Pull:** 13¹/₂″. **Drop at comb:** 1⁵/₈″. **Drop at heel:** 2¹/₄″. **Weight:** 7 lbs. **Capacity:** 5. **Rate of twist:** 1 turn in 9¹/₂· (7mm Rem. Mag.); 1 turn in 10″ (243, 30-06, 270); 1 turn in 12″ (308); 1 turn in 14″ (223, 22-250)

MODEL 99-C LEVER ACTION

Clip magazine allows for the chambering of pointed, high velocity big bore cartridges. **Action:** Hammerless, lever action, cocking indicator, top tang safety. **Magazine:** Detachable clip; holds 4 rounds plus one in the chamber. **Stock:** Select walnut with high Monte Carlo and deep fluted comb. Cut checkered stock and fore-end with swivel studs. Recoil pad and pistol grip cap. **Sights:** Detachable hooded ramp front sight, bead front sight on removable ramp adjustable rear sight. Tapped for top mount scopes. **Barrel length:** 22″ **Overall length:** 42³/₄″. **Weight:** 7 lbs. **Calibers:** 243 Win., 308 Win.

RIFLES

STEYR-MANNLICHER RIFLES

MODEL SSG MARKSMAN
(Shown with synthetic stock and optional Kahles ZF69 scope)

SPECIFICATIONS

Calibers: 243 Win., 308 Win. (7.62mm NATO)
Barrel length: 26"
Weight: 8.6 lbs. (9.9 lbs. with Kahles scope)
Overall length: 44.5"
Stock: Choice of synthetic half stock of ABS "Cycolac" or walnut; removable spacers in butt section adjusts length of pull from 12³/₄" to 14"
Sights: Hooded blade front; folding rear leaf sight
Features: Parkerized finish; choice of interchangeable single-or double-set triggers; detachable 5-shot rotary straight-line feed magazine of "Makrolon"; 10-shot magazine optional; heavy-duty receiver drilled and tapped for scope mounting.

Prices:
Cycolac half stock. **$1598.00**
Walnut half stock 1995.00
SSG Scope Mount 155.00
Model SSG P-11 Sniper (308 Win.) 1682.00

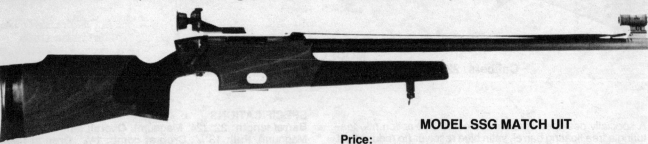

Features 26" heavy barrel, 10-shot box magazine, match bolt, Walther target peep sights, mirage cover, and adjustable rail in forend to adjust sling travel. **Weight:** 11 lbs. **Caliber:** 308 Win.

MODEL SSG MATCH UIT

Price:
With walnut half stock. **$2350.00**
Also available:
SSG Match Rifle w/26" heavy barrel; 308 caliber; synthetic stock. **Price:**. . . . .**$1875.00.**

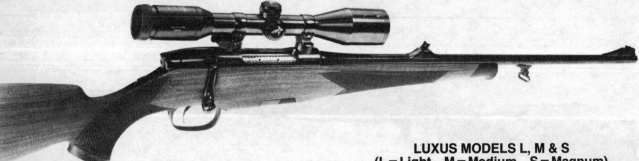

LUXUS MODELS L, M & S
(L=Light   M=Medium   S=Magnum)

SPECIFICATIONS

Calibers:
Model L (standard calibers) 22-250 Rem., 6mm Rem., 243 Win., 308 Win.
Model L (optional metric calibers) 5.6×57
Model M (standard calibers) 25-06 Rem., 270 Win., 7×57, 7×64, 30-06
Model M (optional metric calibers) 6.5×55, 6.5×57, 7.5 Swiss, 9.3×62
Model S 300 Win. Mag., 7mm Rem. Mag., 6.5×68, 8×68S
Barrel lengths: 20" (full stock); 23.6" (half stock); 26" (Model S)
Weight: 6.8 lbs. (full stock); 6.9 lbs. (half stock)
Overall length: 39" (full stock); 43" (half stock)

Stock: Hand-checkered walnut with Monte Carlo cheekpiece; either full Mannlicher or half stock; European hand-rubbed oil finish or high-gloss lacquer finish
Sights: Ramp front adjustable for elevation; open U-notch rear adjustable for windage
Features: Single combination trigger (becomes hair trigger when moved forward before firing); detachable 3-shot steel straight-line feed magazine (6-shot optional). 6 rear locking lugs; drilled and tapped for scope mounts

Prices:
Full stock (in **Model L & M** calibers) $2495.00
Half stock (in **Model L & M** calibers) 2364.00
Half stock (in **Model S** calibers) 2567.00

STEYR-MANNLICHER RIFLES

MODEL L (LIGHT)
shown with full stock
and double triggers

MODEL M (MEDIUM)
shown with half stock
and single trigger

MODEL M PROFESSIONAL
with synthetic stock
& parkerized finish

SPECIFICATIONS
Calibers:

Model SL (Super Light, standard calibers only) 222 Rem., 222 Rem. Mag., 223 Rem.

Model L (standard calibers) 22-250 Rem., 6mm Rem., 243 Win., 308 Win.

Model L (optional metric caliber) 5.6×57

Model M (standard calibers) 25-06 Rem., 270 Win., 7×57, 7×64, 30-06 Spr.

Model M (optional metric calibers) 6.5×57, 7.5 Swiss, 8×57JS, 9.3×62

Barrel length: 20″ (full stock); 23.6″ (half stock)
Weight: 6.8 lbs. (full stock); 6.9 lbs. (half stock); 7.5 lbs. (Professional)
Overall length: 39″ (full stock); 43″ (half stock)
Stock: Full Mannlicher or standard half stock with Monte Carlo cheekpiece and rubber recoil pad; hand-checkered walnut in skip-line pattern; Model M with half stock is available in a "Professional" version with a parkerized finish and synthetic stock made of ABS "Cycolac" (made with right-handed action only); left-handed action available in full stock and half stock.

Features: Choice of fine-crafted single- or double-set triggers. Detachable 5-shot rotary magazine of "Makrolon"; 6 rear locking lugs; drilled and tapped for scope mounting.

Prices:

Models SL, L, M Full stock	**$1939.00**
Models SL, L, M Half stock	**1812.00**
Full stock, with left-handed action	2112.00
Half stock, with left-handed action	2083.00
Professional, with iron sights	1532.00
Model SL, L Varmint (270 Win., 30-06)	1939.00

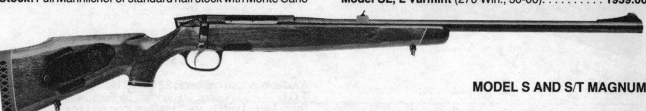

MODEL S AND S/T MAGNUM

SPECIFICATIONS
Calibers:

Model S 257 Weatherby Mag., 264 Win. Mag., 300 Win. Mag., 7mm Rem. Mag., 300 H&H Mag., 375 H&H Mag.

Model S (Optional calibers) 6.5×68

Model S/T (Heavy barrel) 375 H&H Mag., 458 Win. Mag.

Model S/T (Optional caliber) 9.3×64

Barrel length: 26″ Model S/T (with 26″ heavy barrel)
Weight: 8.4 lbs. (Model S); 9.02 lbs. (Model S/T); add .66 lbs. for butt mag. opt.

Overall length: 45″
Stock: Half stock with Monte Carlo cheekpiece and rubber recoil pad; hand-checkered walnut in skip-line pattern; available with optional spare magazine inletted in butt stock.
Features: Choice of fine-crafted single- or double-set triggers; detachable 4-shot rotary magazine of "Makrolon"; 6 rear locking lugs; drilled and tapped for scope mounting.

Prices:

Model S	**$1952.00**
Model S/T with opt. butt magazine	2176.00

THOMPSON/CENTER RIFLES

TCR '87 HUNTER (Single Shot Rifle)
$395.00
Calibers: 22 Hornet, 222 Rem., 223 Rem., 22/250 Rem., 243 Win., 270 Win., 7mm-08, 308 Win., or 30-06

Barrels quickly interchange from one caliber to the next

Chambered for nine popular hunting cartridges, this superbly accurate sports rifle offers the simplicity and strength of a break-open design coupled with the unique feature of interchangeable barrels. Triggers function double set or single stage. A positive lock cross-bolt safety offers maximum security. Wood is hand-selected American black walnut from the Thompson/Center mill. All barrels are equipped with iron sights, removable for scope mounting.

SPECIFICATIONS
Barrel lengths: 23″ (Light Sporter) and 25⅞″ (Medium Sporter)
Overall length: 39½″ (Light Sporter) and 43⅜″ (Medium Sporter)
Weight: 6 lbs. 14 oz. (Light Sporter) and 7 lbs. 8 oz. (Medium Sporter)

THE CONTENDER CARBINE
$370.00

Available in nine **calibers:** 22 LR, 22 Hornet, 223 Rem., 7mm T.C.U., 7 × 30 Waters, 30/30 Win., 35 Rem., 44 Mag. and 357 Rem. Max. Barrels are 21 inches long and are interchangeable, with adjustable iron sights and tapped and drilled for scope mounts.
Also available:
Accessory rifle barrels $160.00
.410 gauge shotgun barrel (3″ shotshell) . . . . 180.00.

TIKKA RIFLES

Tikka Bolt Action Rifles combine aesthetic beauty, good balance and hard, rugged construction for bolt-action shooting. The barrels are rifled by the cold forging method. The double lugged chrome-moly bolt rides smoother and easier on double rails for efficient ejection and locking. The select grain walnut stock and palm-swelled grip are enhanced by the hand-cut checkering on both grip and forestock. Trigger adjustment can be done without action removal. Extra magazine clips are available. Sling swivels and front sight hood are packed with each gun.

M55 DELUXE

M55 STANDARD

MODEL M55

SPECIFICATIONS
Calibers: 222 Rem., 223 Rem., 22-250 Rem., 243 Win., 308 Win. (17 Rem. available in Standard and Deluxe models only)
Barrel length: 23.2″ (24.8″ in Sporter and Heavy Barrel models)
Overall length: 42.8″ (44″ in Sporter and Heavy Barrel models)
Weight: 7.25 lbs. (8.8 lbs. in Heavy Barrel; 9 lbs. in Sporter)

Prices:
Standard $630.00
Deluxe 680.00
Trapper 650.00
Continental 680.00
Super Sporter 803.00
    With sights 820.00

TIKKA RIFLES

M65 WILD BOAR

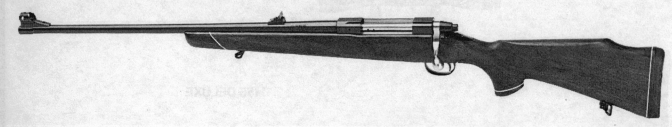

M65 DELUXE LEFT HAND

M65 SUPER SPORTER

MODEL M65

SPECIFICATIONS

Calibers: 270 Win., 308 Win., 338 Win. Mag., 30-06, 7mm Rem. Mag., 9, 3 × 62, 300 Win. Mag. (Sporter and Heavy Barrel models in 270 Win., 308 Win., and 30-06 only)
Barrel length: 22.4″ (24.8″ in Sporter and Heavy Barrel models)
Overall length: 43.2″ (44″ in Sporter; 44.8″ in Heavy Barrel)
Weight: 7.5 lbs. (9.9 lbs. in Sporter and Heavy Barrel models)

Prices:
Standard	$671.00
Deluxe	715.00
Deluxe Left Hand	770.00
Super Sporter	870.00
With sights	880.00
Trapper (w/o sights)	650.00
Continental	730.00
Wild Boar	725.00

A. UBERTI RIFLES & CARBINES

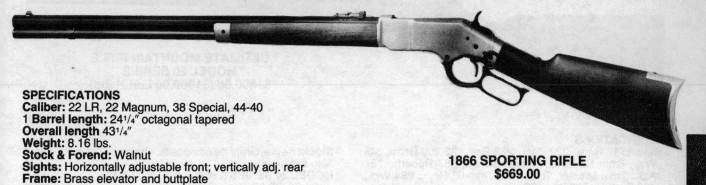

SPECIFICATIONS
Caliber: 22 LR, 22 Magnum, 38 Special, 44-40
1 **Barrel length:** 24¼" octagonal tapered
Overall length 43¼"
Weight: 8.16 lbs.
Stock & Forend: Walnut
Sights: Horizontally adjustable front; vertically adj. rear
Frame: Brass elevator and buttplate

1866 SPORTING RIFLE
$669.00

SPECIFICATIONS
Calibers: 22 LR, 22 Magnum, 38 Special, 44-40, 45 LC
Barrel length: 19" round, tapered
Overall length: 38¼"
Weight: 7.38 lbs.
Sights: Fixed front; vertically adjustable rear
Also available:
1873 Rifle w/24¼" barrel (43¼" overall). **$830.00.**

1873 CARBINE
$769.00

SPECIFICATIONS
Caliber: 44 Magnum (44-40 convert.)
Barrel length: 18" round
Overall length: 34"
Weight: 4.41 lbs.
Stock: Walnut with brass buttplate
Also available:
Buckhorn S.A. Buntline w/23" overall length. **$419.00.**
Cattleman w/slightly smaller frame. **Calibers:** 22 LR, 22 Magnum, 32-20, 38 Special, 38-40, 357 Magnum, 44 Special, 44-40, 45 LC. **$459.00**

BUCKHORN REVOLVING CARBINE
$469.00

ULTRA LIGHT ARMS

ULTIMATE MOUNTAIN RIFLE
MODEL 20 SERIES
$1800.00 ($1900.00 Left Hand)

SPECIFICATIONS
Calibers: 17 Rem., 222 Rem., 223 Rem., 22-250 Rem., 243 Win., 6mm Rem., 250-3000 Savage, 257 Roberts, 257 Ack., 7mm Mauser, 7mm Ack., 7mm-08 Rem., 284 Win., 300 Savage, 308 Win., 358 Win.
Barrel length: 22″
Weight: 4.75 lbs.
Safety: Two-position safety allows bolt to open or lock with sear blocked

Stock: Kevlar/Graphite composite; choice of 7 or more colors
Also available:
MODEL 24 SERIES (Long Action) in 270 Win., 30-06, 25-06, 7mm Express. **$1875.00**
Same as above in Left-Hand Model. **1975.00**
MODEL 28 SERIES (Magnum Action) in 264 Win., 7mm Rem., 300 Win., 338 . . . . **2350.00**
Same as above in Left-Hand Model. **2450.00**

VALMET RIFLES

VALMET HUNTER RIFLE
$795.00

The most reliable semiautomatic sporting rifle available, the Hunter incorporates the durability and reliability of Valmet's military weapons manufactured for the Finnish Defense Forces. Its main features are as follows:
Durability: Precision-machined steel receiver.
Reliability: Simple but rugged design with few moving parts. Dependable gas piston mechanism. Proven to function in arctic sub-zero extremes as well as hot, muggy conditions.
Minimal recoil: Barrel is positioned centerline from barrel tip through the stock, minimizing barrel lift. Gas piston mechanism reduces recoil.
Accuracy: Heavy barrel with precision rifling. Less recoil and reduced barrel lift add to accuracy of following shots. Gas-operated rotating bolt ensures a secure lockup. Locked-down dust cover provides secure surface accommodating quick detachable scope mount with 1″ rings.
Caliber versatility: Available in 223, 243, 308 and 30-06.
Fast sighting: Flush-folding rear sight with luminous dots. Luminous vertical bar front sight assures fast, accurate sight picture.

Speed: Fast sighting, minimal recoil and barrel lift, plus large magazine capacity, enable shooter to stay "on target" with fast, accurate firepower.
American walnut stock: Deep-cut checkering and palm swell for added control. Length and angle (pitch) adjustable with factory spacers. Quick, detachable sling swivel.
Ejection buffer: Optional buffer protects brass for reloading.

SPECIFICATIONS
Type: Gas-operated semiautomatic
Calibers: 223, 243, 308, 30-06
Capacity:
 223 cal., 15 rounds (30 rds. optional)
 243 cal., 9 rounds (5 rds. optional)
 308 cal., 5 rounds (9 and 20 rds. optional)
 30-06 cal., 5 rounds (9 rds. optional)
Barrel length: 20¹/₂″
Overall length: 42″
Weight: 8 lbs.

VALMET RIFLES

VALMET 412S DOUBLE RIFLE
$1205.00 ($1315.00 in 9.3 × 74R)

Valmet's double rifle offers features and qualities no other action can match: rapid handling and pointing qualities and the silent, immediate availability of a second shot. As such, this model overcomes the two major drawbacks usually associated with this type of firearm: price and accuracy. Other features include:

Barrel regulation: Regulate windage through adjustment at the muzzle. Elevation is regulated by the sliding wedge between the barrels. Shooters can use their favorite loads and are not limited to the specific load used by the factory. Point-of-impact can be changed for any desired distance.

Accuracy: Compares favorably with most lever actions, pumps and autoloaders.

Speed: Faster initial shot due to excellent handling qualities inherent to a double rifle. Second shot is as fast as you can pull the trigger. No noise or distraction from a lever, moving bolt or pumping action.

Excellent handling qualities: Bulk of the weight is between the hands, enabling the gun to come up fast and swing smoothly.

American walnut stock: Available either cast-on or cast-off for right- or left-handed shooters. Deep-cut checkering for secure grip with palm swell for greater control and comfort.

Length and angle adjustable with factory spacer. Quick, detachable sling swivel. Semi-Monte Carlo design.

Interchangeability: Receiver will accept Valmet over/under shotgun barrels in both 12 and 20 gauge, plus shotgun/rifle barrels, with minor initial fitting.

Optional triggers: Equipped with single selective trigger. Double triggers also available.

Mechanical triggers: Operate mechanically and do not depend on inertia from recoil to activate trigger for second shot.

Automatic safety: Automatically goes to safe position when gun is opened. Optional safety locks safety out and in fire position.

Other features: Strong steel receiver, superior sliding locking mechanism, cocking indicators, and two-piece firing pin.

SPECIFICATIONS
Calibers: 30-06, 9.3 × 74R
Barrel length: 24″
Overall length: 40″
Weight: 8 1/2 lbs.
Stock: American walnut
Other: Extractors, automatic ejectors

VARNER SPORTING ARMS

FAVORITE MODEL (SINGLE SHOT)
$249.00

SPECIFICATIONS (FIELD GRADE)
Caliber: 22SS
Barrel length: 21 1/2″; 12-groove, match grade; half-round, half-octagonal
Weight: 5 lbs.
Sights: Peep and open rear sights adjustable for windage and elevation

Stock: Straight-grain American walnut
Finish: Blued steel
Also available:
SPORTER GRADE $369.00
PRESENTATION GRADE (w/AAA Fancy American walnut stock; hand-checkered grip and forearm) . . 495.00

WALTHER TARGET RIFLES

U.I.T. MATCH
$1500.00

Caliber: 22 LR
Action: Bolt action, single shot
Barrel length: 25½"
Overall length: 44¾"
Weight: 13 lbs.
Also available:
U.I.T. BV Universal. $1625.00

MODEL GX-1
$2100.00

Caliber: 22 LR
Action: Bolt action, single shot
Barrel length: 25½"
Overall length: 46"
Weight: 16½"

KK/MS SILHOUETTE
$1050.00

Caliber: 22 LR
Action: Bolt action, single shot
Barrel length: 25½"
Overall length: 44¾"
Weight: 8¾ lbs

RUNNING BOAR (not shown)
$1200.00

Caliber: 22 LR
Action: Bolt action, single shot
Barrel length: 23½"
Overall length: 42"
Weight: 10¼ lbs.

WEATHERBY RIFLES

MARK V FIBERMARK

The Fibermark's hand-molded fiberglass stock is impervious to climatic changes. It shoots with constant accuracy no matter what the weather—from desert heat to mountain snow. The stock is finished with a non-glare black wrinkle finish for a positive grip, even in wet, humid weather. Available in right-hand only, 24″ or 26″ barrels. **Weight:** 7¼ lbs. (24″) and 8 lbs. (26″).

Additional specifications listed on the previous page.

Calibers	Prices
240, 257, 270, 7mm & 300 W.M. and 30-06	$1123.00
(24″ barrel; add $20 for 26″ barrel)	
340 Win. Mag. (26″ barrel)	1143.00

MARK V EUROMARK

Calibers	Prices
240, 257, 270, 7mm, 300 W.M., 30-06	$1040.00
340 Win. Mag.	1060.00
378 Win. Mag. (right/left hand)	1214.00
460 Win. Mag. (right/left hand; includes custom stock, customized action, integral muzzle brake)	1354.00

The principal features of this Mark V model include a hand-rubbed, satin oil finish Claro walnut stock and non-glare special process blue matte barreled action. Left-hand models are available. Specifications are listed on previous table.

WEATHERBY RIFLES

MARK V DELUXE RIFLE

Calibers	Prices
224 Weatherby Mag., 22/250 Varmintmaster	$ 971.00
240, 257, 270, 7mm, 300 W.M., 30-06	
24" barrel	991.00
26" barrel	987.00
340 Weatherby Mag. only	1011.00
378 Weatherby Mag. only	1165.00
460 Weatherby Mag. only	1305.00

CALIBER	.224	.22/250	.240	.257	.270	7mm	.30-06	.300	.340	.378	.460
Model	Right hand 24" or 26" bbl. Left hand model not available		Right or left hand 24" bbl. Right hand 26" bbl. Left hand 26" bbl. **available in .300 cal. only**						Right or left hand 26" bbl. only.	Right or left hand 26" bbl. only.	Right or left hand 26" bbl. only.
**Weight w/o sights	6½ lbs.		7¼ lbs.						8½ lbs.		10½ lbs.
Overall length	43¼" or 45¼" dependent on barrel length		44½" or 46½" dependent on barrel length						46½"		
Magazine Capacity	4, +1 in chamber	3, +1 in chamber	4, +1 in chamber	3, +1 in chamber			4, +1 in chamber	3, +1 in chamber	2, +1 in chamber		
Barrel	24" standard or 26" semi-target		24" standard or 26" #2 contour						26" #2 contour	26" #3 contour	26" #4* contour
Rifling	1-14" twist		1-10" twist						1-12" twist		1-16" twist
Sights	Scope or iron sights extra										
Stocks:	Drop dimensions from bore centerline: Mark V— Comb: ¾" Monte Carlo: ½" Heel: 1½" Varmintmaster— Comb: ⁹⁄₁₆" Monte Carlo: ¼" Heel: 1⅛"										
Deluxe	American walnut, individually hand-bedded to assure precision accuracy. High lustre, durable stock finish. Quick detachable sling swivels. Basket weave checkering. Monte Carlo style with cheek piece, especially designed for both scope and iron sighted rifles. Length of pull 13½."										European Walnut Pull: 13⅞"
Euromark	American walnut, individually hand-bedded to assure precision accuracy. Satin finish. Ebony pistol grip cap and fore end tip. Custom fine line hand checkering with extension on pistol grip. Solid black recoil pad. Quick detachable sling swivels. Monte Carlo style with cheek piece, especially designed for both scope and iron sighted rifles. Length of pull 13½."										European Walnut Pull: 13⅞"
Lazermark	American walnut, individually hand-bedded to assure precision accuracy. High lustre, durable stock finish. Quick detachable sling swivels. Laser carving on forearm, pistol grip and under cheek piece. Monte Carlo style with cheek piece, especially designed for both scope and iron sighted rifles. Length of pull 13½."										European Walnut Pull: 13⅞"
Fibermark	Not available		Molded fiberglass, individually hand-bedded to assure precision accuracy. Non-glare, black, wrinkle finish. Quick detachable sling swivels. Monte Carlo style with cheek piece, especially designed for both scope and iron sighted rifles. Length of pull 13½."						Not available		
Action	A scaled-down version of the popular Mark V action, with 6 precision locking lugs in place of 9.		Featuring the Mark V, world's strongest and safest action. The nine locking lugs have almost double the shear area of the lugs found on conventional bolt rifles. The cartridge case head is completely enclosed in the bolt and barrel. .460: action includes hand honing, bolt knob fully checkered, bolt and follower damascened, custom engraved floor plate.								
Safety	Forward moving release, accessible and positive										

WEATHERBY RIFLES

MARK V LAZERMARK

With its intricately carved stock pattern, this Mark V model captures the beauty of Old World craftsmanship using today's most modern technology—laser. (Prices do not include scope.)

Calibers   **Prices**
224 and 22-250 Varmintmaster (24″ barrel) $1085.00

240, 257, 270, 7mm & 300 W.M. and 30-06
  (24″ barrel) **1105.00**
378 W.M. **1281.00**
340 W.M. **1127.00**
460 W.M. (includes customized action, custom
  stock, integral muzzle brake) **1421.00**

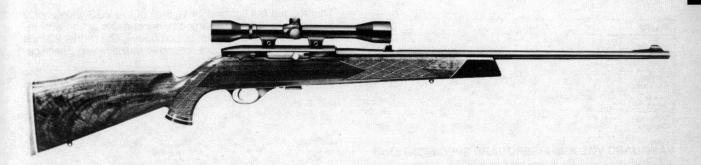

MARK XXII DELUXE 22 SEMIAUTOMATIC

Although lighter and handier than Weatherby's big game rifle, this .22 semiautomatic boasts the same pointing characteristics and basic stock design. It is also the only .22 which allows hunters to choose single shot or semiautomatic fire. The Mark XXII is available in both clip and tubular models. The tubular model has a 15 shot capacity; the clip model comes with a 10 shot magazine. Folding leaf rear iron sights adjustable for windage and elevation and ramp front sights are standard. The receiver is precision-grooved for dovetailed scope mounts. Other features include non-skid rubber butt pad, Monte Carlo stock, and rosewood forend tip.

Price (clip or tube) $454.00

MARK XXII .22 AUTOMATIC SPECIFICATIONS

Action	Semi-automatic with single shot selector
Caliber	.22 long rifle cartridges only
Barrel	24″, special steel, contoured barrel
Overall length	42¼″
Magazine	Clip model—comes with 10-shot magazine. Extra 5 or 10-shot magazines available. Tubular model—15-shot capacity.
Stock	Select walnut, hand-checkered, Monte Carlo stock with cheek piece, Rosewood fore-end tip and pistol grip cap with diamond inlay. Non-skid rubber butt pad. Length of pull 13½″.
Sights	Adjustable folding rear sight; ramp front sight.
Safety	Shotgun type tang safety.
Weight	Approx. 6 lbs. without scope.
Trigger	Crip, clean precision trigger pull.
Mounts	Receiver is precision-grooved for dovetail scope mounts.

WEATHERBY RIFLES

VANGUARD FIBERGUARD
$560.00

The Fiberguard rifle weighs less than 6½ lbs. and features a 20″ barrel. Its fiberglass stock eliminates warping and swelling. See Specifications table below.

VANGUARD VGL (not shown)

This rugged but lightweight version of the VGS weighs only 6½ pounds. It features smooth, dependable action with recessed bolt face and enclosed bolt sleeve. The shorter 20-inch barrel is streamlined from breech to muzzle. See Specifications table below.

Price: (without sights) $467.00

VANGUARD VGL AND FIBERGUARD SPECIFICATIONS
Vanguard rifles available in right hand models only

Calibers	223 Rem.	243 Win.	270 Win.	7mm Rem. Mag.	30-06	308 Win.
Barrel Length	20″	20″	20″	20″	20″	20″
Barrel Contour	No.1	No.1	No.1	No.1	No.1	No.1
Approx. Weight	6lb. 8oz.	6lb. 8oz.	6lb. 10oz.	6lb. 10oz.	6lb. 10oz.	6lb. 8oz.
Overall Length	*40 in.	*40 in.	40½ in.	40½ in.	40½ in.	*40 in.
Magazine Cap	6 rnds.	5 rnds.	5 rnds.	3 rnds.	5 rnds.	5 rnds.
Rifling	1-12″	1-10″	1-10″	1-10″	1-10″	1-10″
Sights	Scope or iron sights available at extra cost.					
Stock	Fiberglass hand molded stock with non-glare, forest green wrinkle finish, 13½″ pull, black butt pad. (Recoil pad on 7mm Rem. Mag.)					
Action	Vanguard action of the improved Mauser type. *Short action is ½″ shorter than the standard action.					
Safety	Side operated, forward moving release, accessible and positive.					
Mounts	Vanguard action accepts same bases as Mark V action.					

WEATHERBY RIFLES

VANGUARD VGX
Shown with Weatherby Supreme 3-9/XX44S
Variable Scope on Buehler mount
$600.00 (without sights)

VANGUARD VGX SPECIFICATIONS (available in right-hand models only)

Calibers	.22-250 Rem.	.22-250 Rem.	.243 Win.	.25-06 Rem.	270 Win.	7mm Rem. Mag.	.30-06	.300 Win. Mag.
Barrel Length	24"	24"	24"	24"	24"	24"	24"	24"
Barrel Contour	No. 3	No. 2	No. 2	No. 2	No. 2	No. 2	No.2	No.2
Approx. Weight	8lb.8oz.	7lb.12oz.	7lb.14oz.	7lb.14oz.	7lb.14oz.	7lb.14oz.	7lb.14oz.	7x
Overall Length	44"*	44"*	44"*	44½"	44½"	44½"	44½"	44½"
Magazine Cap.	5 rnds.	5 rnds.	5 rnds.	5 rnds.	5 rnds.	3 rnds.	5 rnds.	3 rnds.
Rifling	1–14"	1–14"	1–10"	1–10"	1–10"	1–10"	1–10"	1–10"
Sights	Scope or iron sights available at extra cost							
Stock	American walnut, 13½" pull, custom checkering, recoil pad, high lustre finish; rosewood tip and cap.							
Action	Vanguard action of the improved Mauser type.							
Safety	Side operated, forward moving release, accessible and positive.							
Mounts	Van guard action accepts same bases as Mark V action.							

*.22–250 and .243 action is ½" shorter than the standard action.

VANGUARD VGS

The VGS offers the same performance and workmanship as the VGX. The hand-bedded, hammer-forged barrel guarantees accuracy of a 1½" or less 3-shot group at 100 yards.

Price (without sights) **$467.00**

VANGUARD VGS SPECIFICATIONS
(available in right-hand models only)

Calibers	.22-250 Rem.	.22-250 Rem.	.243 Win.	.25-06 Rem.	270 Win.	7mm Rem. Mag.	.30-06	.300 Win. Mag.
Barrel length	24″	24″	24″	24″	24″	24″	24″	24″
Barrel Contour	No. 3	No. 2	No. 2	No. 2	No. 2	No. 2	No. 2	No. 2
Approx. Weight	8lb. 8oz.	7lb. 12oz.	7lb. 12oz.	7lb. 14oz.	7lb. 14oz.	7lb. 14oz.	7lb. 14oz.	7lb. 14oz.
Overall Length	44″*	44″*	44″*	44½"	44½"	44½"	44½"	44½"
Magazine Cap.	5 rnds.	5 rnds.	5 rnds.	5 rnds.	5 rnds.	3 rnds.	5 rnds.	3 rnds.
Rifling	1-14″	1-14'in	1-10″	1-10″	1-10″	1-10″	1-10″	1-10″
Sights	Scope or iorn sights available at extra cost							
Stock	American walnut, 13½″ pull, hand checkered, satin finish, butt pad. (Recoil pad on magnum models.)							
Action	Vanguard action of the improved Mauser type.							
Safety	Side operated, forward moving release, accessible and positive.							
Mounts	Vanguard action accepts samebases as Mark V action.							

*.22–250 and .243 action is 1/2" shorter than the standard action.

WHITWORTH SPORTING RIFLES

SAFARI GRADE EXPRESS RIFLE
$690.00

Features three safety-lug bolt design for added strength and security . . . Hand-rubbed European walnut stocks with sculpted continental-style cheekpiece . . . Custom three-leaf Express sight . . . Ramp mounted front sight with detachable hood . . . Three-point adjustable trigger . . . Premium hammer-forged chrome-vanadium steel barrels . . . Premium milled-steel Mauser System Action.

SPECIFICATIONS
Calibers: 375 H&H Magnum and 458 Win. Mag. **Barrel length:** 24". **Overall length:** 44.75". **Weight:** 7½ lbs. **Capacity:** 3 rounds.

WINCHESTER BOLT ACTION RIFLES

MODEL 70 LIGHTWEIGHT RIFLE
$399.00

Available in **calibers:** 22-250 Rem., 223 Rem., 243 Win., 270 Win., 280 Rem., 308 Win. and 30-06 Springfield. **Barrel length:** 22" (hammer forged barrel). **Weight:** 6 to 6¼ lbs. **Stock:** Classic straight stock with satin finish and point pattern cut-checkering. Furnished with sling swivel studs.

MODEL 70 WIN-TUFF

RIFLES/WINC/253C

SPECIFICATIONS

Model	Caliber	Mag. Capacity	Barrel Length	Overall Length	Nominal Length of Pull	Nominal Drop at Comb	Nominal Drop at Heel	Nom. Wt.	Rate of Twist 1 Turn in	Prices
70 WIN-TUFF LTWT	22-250 Rem.	5	22"	42"	13½"	9/16"	7/8"	6¼	14"	$409.00
FWT	243 Win.	5	22	42	13½	9/16	7/8	6½	10	476.00
LTWT	243 Win.	5	22	42	13½	9/16	7/8	6¼	10	409.00
FWT	270 Win.	5	22	42½	13½	9/16	7/8	6¾	10	476.00
LTWT	270 Win.	5	22	42½	13½	9/16	7/8	6½	10	409.00
FWT	30-06 Spgfld.	5	22	42½	13½	9/16	7/8	6¾	10	476.00
LTWT	30-06 Spgfld.	5	22	42½	13½	9/16	7/8	6½	10	409.00

WINCHESTER BOLT ACTION RIFLES

MODEL 70XTR FEATHERWEIGHT
$465.00

Model 70 XTR Featherweight hunting rifles minimize weight for easy handling and carrying. A new Model 70 European Featherweight in 6.5×55mm Swedish Mauser is being offered for the first time in the U.S. Barrel and receiver have integral recoil lug machined from chrome molybdenum steel. Bolt body and locking lugs are machined from a single steel bar. Thermoplastic bedding mates the receiver recoil lug and the stock for maximum strength and accuracy. Bolt features a

jeweled finish and knurled bolt handle. Three-position safety. Receivers drilled and tapped for scope mounting. One-piece walnut stocks are hand-worked and finished with genuine cut checkering.

Also available: **MODEL 70 XTR WIN-CAM FEATHER-WEIGHT** in 270 Win. and 30-06. **Weight:** 6¾ lbs. Camouflage stock. **Price: $476.00.**

MODEL 70XTR FEATHERWEIGHT SPECIFICATIONS

Model	Caliber	Magazine Capacity(a)	Barrel Length	Overall Length	Nominal Length of Pull	Nominal Drop at Comb	Nominal Drop at Heel	Nominal Weight (lbs.)	Rate of Twist (R.H.) 1 Turn in
70 XTR Featherweight	270 Win.	5	22″	42½″	13½″	9/16″	7/8″	6¾″	10″
Long Action	30-06	5	22″	42½″	13½″	9/16″	7/8″	6¾″	10″
70 XTR Featherweight	243 Win.	5	22″	42″	13½″	9/16″	7/8″	6½	10″
Short Action	308 Win.	5	22″	42″	13½″	9/16″	7/8″	6½	12″

(a) For additional capacity, add one round in chamber when ready to fire.
Also available: Calibers 22-250 Rem., 223 Rem. and 280 Rem.

MODEL 70 WINLITE
$636.00
($654.00 in 300 Weatherby Mag.)

The fiberglass stock on this new model sets high standards for lightness, strength, and accuracy. Receiver bedding stability is assured with the use of thermoplastic and by fitting the barreled action individually to the stock. Critical inletted areas are molded into the stock, and the action bed and forend are reinforced Kevlar/Graphite for strength and rigidity. Special

bedding pads are easily removed for "free-floating" the barrel if desired. Despite a dramatic weight reduction, there is no increase in the recoil sensation since the fiberglass material compresses during recoil, becoming a total recoil absorption device.

SPECIFICATIONS

Caliber:	270 Win.	30-06 Spfd.	7mm Rem. Mag.	338 Win. Mag.	280 Rem.	300 Win. Mag.	300 Weath. Mag.
Mag. Cap.:	4*	4*	3*	3*	4	3	3
Barrel Length:	22″	22″	24″	24″	22″	24″	24″
Overall Length:	42½″	42½″	44½″	44½″	42½″	44½″	44½″
Length of Pull:	13½″	13½″	13½″	13½″	13½″	13½″	13½″
**Drop at Comb:	9/16″	9/16″	9/16″	9/16″	9/16″	9/16″	9/16″
**Drop at Heel:	1/2″	1/2″	1/2″	1/2″	1/2″	1/2″	1/2″
Weight (lbs.)	6½″	6½″	7½″	7½″	6¼-6½	6¼-7	6¼-7
Rate of Twist:	10″	10″	9½″	10″	10″	10″	10″

*For additional capacity, add one round in chamber when ready to fire.
**Drops are measured from centerline of bore.

WINCHESTER BOLT ACTION RIFLES

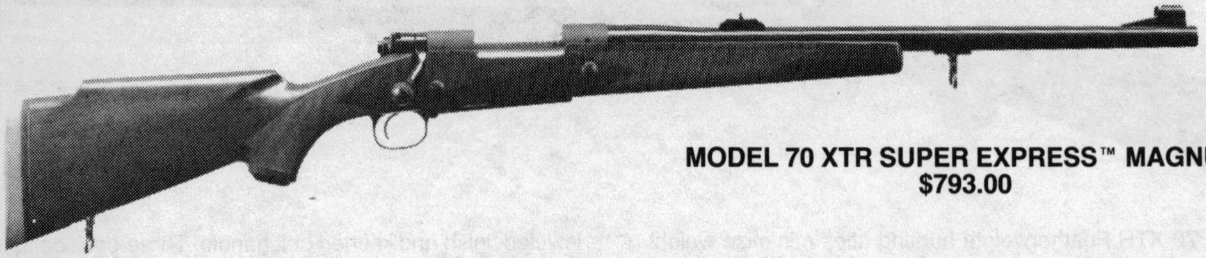

MODEL 70 XTR SUPER EXPRESS™ MAGNUM
$793.00

Go after the biggest game in true Sporter style with these new Model 70 XTR Super Express Magnum rifles. Their high performance and dependability stem from the proven Model 70 African™ . . . now improved and upgraded with XTR styling and convenience features. This big game pair of rifles boasts all the Sporter Magnum features in 375 H&H and 458 Winchester Magnum calibers. The crisply styled Sporter stock design has the same innovative cheekpiece for shooter comfort, but is reinforced with two steel crossbolts for added strength.

The forward sling swivel is mounted directly on the rifle barrel for improved carrying balance and strength. Magazine capacity is three Magnum cartridges.

The new Monte Carlo stock with sculpted cheekpiece on Model 70 XTR Sporter Magnum and Super Express Magnum rifles is shown in the photo above.

XTR elegance checkering is custom-patterned at 18 lines per inch; wraps around forend for improved handling, gripping and appearance.

SPECIFICATIONS FOR MODEL 70XTR SPORTER

Caliber	Magazine Capacity (A)	Barrel Length	Overall Length	Nominal Length Of Pull	Nominal Drop At Comb	Nominal Drop At Heel	Nominal Drop At MC	Nominal Weight (Lbs.)	Rate of Twist 1 Turn In	Sights	
22-250 Rem.	5	24″	44″	13 1/2″	9/16″	1 5/16″	3/4″	7 3/4	14″	—	**Prices:**
223 Rem.	6	24	44	13 1/2	9/16	1 5/16	3/4	7 3/4	12	—	**$451.00**
243 Rem.	5	24	44	13 1/2	9/16	1 5/16	3/4	7 3/4	10	—	**to**
264 Win. Mag.	3	24	44 1/2	13 1/2	9/16	1 5/16	3/4	7 3/4	9	—	**$468.00**
270 Win.	5	24	44 1/2	13 1/2	9/16	1 5/16	3/4	7 3/4	10	Rifle	
270 Win.	5	24	44 1/2	13 1/2	9/16	1 5/16	3/4	7 3/4	10	—	
270 Weath. Mag.	3	24	44 1/2	13 1/2	9/16	1 5/16	3/4	7 3/4	10	—	
7mm Rem. Mag.	3	24	44 1/2	13 1/2	9/16	1 5/16	3/4	7 3/4	9 1/2	Rifle	
7mm Rem. Mag.	3	24	44 1/2	13 1/2	9/16	1 5/16	3/4	7 3/4	9 1/2	—	
30-06 Spgfld.	5	24	44 1/2	13 1/2	9/16	1 5/16	3/4	7 3/4	10	Rifle	
30-06 Spgfld.	5	24	44 1/2	13 1/2	9/16	1 5/16	3/4	7 3/4	10	—	
300 Win. Mag.	3	24	44 1/2	13 1/2	9/16	1 5/16	3/4	7 3/4	10	Rifle	
300 Win. Mag.	3	24	44 1/2	13 1/2	9/16	1 5/16	3/4	7 3/4	10	—	
300 Weath. Mag.	3	24	44 1/2	13 1/2	9/16	1 5/16	3/4	7 3/4	10	—	
338 Win. Mag.	3	24	44 1/2	13 1/2	9/16	1 5/16	3/4	7 3/4	10	Rifle	
338 Win. Mag.	3	24	44 1/2	13 1/2	9/16	1 5/16	3/4	7 3/4	10	—	

WINCHESTER BOLT ACTION RIFLES

WINCHESTER RANGER®
BOLT ACTION CENTERFIRE RIFLE
$336.00

The Ranger Bolt Action Rifle comes with an American hardwood stock, a wear-resistant satin walnut finish, ramp bead-post front sight, steel barrel, three-position safety and engine-turned, anti-bind bolt. The receiver is drilled and tapped for scope mounting; accuracy is enhanced by thermoplastic bedding of the receiver. Barrel and receiver are brushed and blued.

SPECIFICATIONS

Model	Caliber	Magazine Capacity(a)	Barrel Length	Overall Length	Nominal Length of Pull	Nominal Drop at Comb	Nominal Drop at Heel	Nominal Weight (lbs.)	Rate of Twist (R.H.) 1 Turn in
Ranger	270 Win.	4	22″	42 1/2″	13 1/2″	1 5/8″	2 1/8″	7 1/8	10″
Bolt Action Rifle	30-06 Springfield	4	22″	42 1/2″	13 1/2″	1 5/8″	2 1/8″	7 1/8	10″

(a) For additional capacity, add one round in chamber when ready to fire.

WINCHESTER RANGER®
YOUTH BOLT ACTION CARBINE
$345.00

This carbine offers dependable bolt action performance combined with a scaled-down design to fit the younger, smaller shooter. It features anti-bind bolt design, jeweled bolt, three-position safety, contoured recoil pad, ramped bead front sight, semi-buckhorn folding leaf rear sight, and sling swivels. Receiver is drilled and tapped for scope mounting. Stock is of American hardwood with protective satin walnut finish. Pistol grip, length of pull, overall length, and comb are all tailored to youth dimensions (see table).

SPECIFICATIONS

Model	Caliber	Magazine Capacity(a)	Barrel Length	Overall Length	Nominal Length of Pull	Nominal Drop at Comb	Nominal Drop at Heel	Nominal Weight (lbs.)	Rate of Twist (R.H.) 1 Turn in
Ranger Youth Short Action Rifle	243 Win.	4	20″	39″	12 1/2″	3/4″	1″	5 3/4	10″

(a) For additional capacity, add one round in chamber when ready to fire.

Manufacturer does not furnish suggested retail prices; above figures are estimated average prices.

WINCHESTER LEVER ACTION CARBINES & RIFLES

Model 94™ Side Eject™ Lever Action Centerfire carbines have been developed and refined through almost a century of sporting use and technological advancement. The new angled ejection system throws the spent cartridge away from the shooter's line of vision and does not interfere with top-mounted scopes. It features an improved, stabilized trigger mechanism with controlled pre-travel and short, crisp let-off.

Receivers are of forged steel. Chromium molybdenum barrels assure long-lasting strength. Chamber and rifling are cold-forged in a single operation for precise alignment and accuracy. The receiver is ported for angled ejection and scopes can be top-mounted.

Model 94 XTR is top choice for lever-action styling and craftsmanship. Metal surfaces are highly polished and blued. American walnut stock and forearm have a protective stain finish with precise-cut XTR wrap-around checkering. It has a 20-inch barrel with hooded blade front sight and semi-buckhorn rear sight. Available in 30-30 Winchester caliber.

Model 94 Trapper is a 16-inch short-barrel lever action with straight forward styling. Compact and fast-handling in dense cover, it has a magazine capacity of five shots. Available in 30-30 Winchester caliber, 45 Colt, and 44 Rem. Mag./44 S&W Special.

MODEL 94 SIDE EJECT SPECIFICATIONS

Model	Caliber	Magazine Capacity (A)	Barrel Length	Overall Length	Nominal Length Of Pull	Nominal Drop At Comb	Nominal Drop At Heel	Nominal Weight (Lbs.)	Rate of Twist 1 Turn In	Sights	Prices
94 Deluxe	30-30 Win.	6	20″	37³/₄″	13″	1¹/₈″	1⁷/₈″	6¹/₂	12″	Rifle *	$426.00
94 WIN-TUFF	30-30 Win.	6	20″	37³/₄″	13″	1¹/₈″	1⁷/₈″	6¹/₂	12″	Rifle	299.00
94XTR	30-30 Win.	6	20″	37³/₄″	13″	1¹/₈″	1⁷/₈″	6¹/₂	12″	Rifle	299.00
XTR/Scope	30-30 Win.	6	20	37³/₄	13	1¹/₈	1⁷/₈	6¹/₂	12	R/S	342.00
	Low-mount scope 1.5-4.5 variable										
Standard	30-30 Win.	6	20	37³/₄	13	1¹/₈	1⁷/₈	6¹/₂	12	Rifle	274.00
Long Rifle	30-30 Win.	7	24	41³/₄	13	1¹/₈	1⁷/₈	7	12	Rifle	286.00
7-30 Waters	7-30 Waters	7	24	41³/₄	13	1¹/₈	1⁷/₈	7	12	Rifle	312.00
Big Bore	307 Win.	6	20	37³/₄	13	1¹/₈	1⁷/₈	6¹/₂	12	Rifle	299.00
Big Bore	356 Win.	6	20	37³/₄	13	1¹/₈	1⁷/₈	6¹/₂	12	Rifle	299.00
94 Trapper	30-30 Win.	5	16″	33³/₄″	13″	1¹/₈″	1⁷/₈″	6¹/₈	12″	Rifle	274.00
	44 Rem. Mag./ 44 S&W Spec.	9	16	33³/₄	13	1¹/₈	1⁷/₈	6	38	Rifle	296.00
	45 Colt	9	16	33³/₄	13	1¹/₈	1⁷/₈	6	38	Rifle	296.00
Ranger	30-30 Win.	6	20″	37³/₄″	13″	1¹/₈″	1⁷/₈″	6¹/₂	12″	Rifle	244.00
Lever Action	30-30 Win.	6	20	37³/₄	13	1¹/₈	1⁷/₈	6¹/₂	12	R/S	278.00
	Scope 4 × 32 see-through mounts										

(A) For additional capacity, add one round in chamber when ready to fire. Drops are measured from center line of bore. R/S-Rifle sights and optional Bushnell® Sportview® scope with mounts.

* Indicates NEW. Rate of twist is right-hand.

WINCHESTER LEVER ACTION RIFLES

MODEL 9422 XTR
LEVER-ACTION RIMFIRE RIFLES

These Model 9422 XTR rimfire rifles combine classic 94 styling and handling in ultra-modern lever action 22s of superb craftsmanship. Handling and shooting characteristics are superior because of their carbine-like size.

Positive lever action and bolt design ensure feeding and chambering from any shooting position. The bolt face is T-slotted to guide the cartridge with complete control from magazine to chamber. A color-coded magazine follower shows when the brass magazine tube is empty. Receivers are grooved for scope mounting. Other functional features include exposed hammer with half-cock safety, hooded bead front sight, semi-buckhorn rear sight and side ejection of spent cartridges.

Stock and forearm are American walnut with XTR checkering, high-luster finish, and straight-grip design. Internal parts are carefully finished for smoothness of action.

Model 9422 XTR Classic combines original styling and advanced lever action technology. The walnut stock has a fluted comb and ends in a crescent steel buttplate. Additional features include an extended forearm with barrel band and a 22½" barrel for longer range accuracy.

Model 9422 XTR Standard is considered one of the world's finest production sporting arms. It holds 21 Short, 17 Long or 15 Long Rifle cartridges.

Also available: **Win-Cam Magnum** featuring laminated non-glare, green-shaded stock and forearm. American hardwood stock is bonded to withstand all weather and climates.

Model 9422 XTR Magnum gives exceptional accuracy at longer ranges than conventional 22 rifles. It is designed specifically for the 22 Winchester Magnum Rimfire cartridge and holds 11 cartridges.

SPECIFICATIONS

Model	Caliber	Magazine Capacity	Barrel Length	Overall Length	Nominal Length Of Pull	Nominal Drop At Comb	Nominal Drop At Heel	Nominal Weight (Lbs.)	Rate of Twist 1 Turn In	Sights	Prices
9422XTR	22	21S,17L,15LR	20½"	37⅛"	13½"	1⅛"	1⅞"	6¼	16"	Rifle	$324.00
	22WMR	11	20½	37⅛	13½	1⅛	1⅞	6¼	16	Rifle	
9422XTR with Pistol Grip Stock	22	21S,17L,15LR	22½"	39⅛"	13"	1⅛"	1⅞"	6½	16"	Rifle	324.00
	22WMR	11	22½	39⅛	13	1⅛	1⅞	6½	16	Rifle	
9422 WIN-TUFF	22	21S,17L,15LR	20½"	37⅛"	13½"	1⅛"	1⅞"	6¼	16"	Rifle	331.00
	22WMR	11	20½	37⅛	13½	1⅛	1⅞	6¼	16	Rifle	
9422 WIN-CAM	22WMR	11	20½"	37⅛"	13½"	1⅛"	1⅞"	6¼	16"	Rifle	331.00

WMR-Winchester Magnum Rimfire. S-Short, L-Long, LR-Long Rifle. Drops are measured from center line of bore. * Indicates NEW.

Manufacturer does not furnish suggested retail prices; above figures are estimated average prices.

WINCHESTER LEVER ACTION RIFLES

MODEL 94 STANDARD
$274.00

Model 94 Standard is an economical version of the 94 XTR. Lever action is smooth and reliable. In 30-30 Winchester, the rapid-firing six-shot magazine capacity provides two more shots than most centerfire hunting rifles.

Also available: **Model 94 Long Rifle** (24") in 30-30 Win. (7-shot) with extra long forearm.

MODEL 94 SIDE EJECT™
STANDARD BIG BORE CARBINE
$299.00

Winchester's powerful .307 and .356 hunting calibers combined with maximum lever-action power and angled ejection provide hunters with improved performance and economy.

MODEL 94 WIN-TUFF RIFLE
$299.00 (20" Barrel)

Includes all features and specifications of standard Model 94 plus tough laminated hardwood styled for the brush-gunning hunter who wants good concealment and a carbine that can stand up to all kinds of weather.

WINSLOW RIFLES

SPECIFICATIONS

Stock: Choice of two stock models. **The Plainsmaster** offers pinpoint accuracy in open country with full curl pistol grip and flat forearm. **The Bushmaster** offers lighter weight for bush country; slender pistol with palm swell; beavertail forend for light hand comfort. Both styles are of hand-rubbed black walnut. Length of pull—13½ inches; plainsmaster ⅜ inch castoff; Bushmaster 3/16 inch castoff; all rifles are drilled and tapped to incorporate the use of telescopic sights; rifles with receiver or open sights are available on special order; all rifles are equipped with quick detachable sling swivel studs and white-line recoil pad. All Winslow stocks incorporate a slight castoff to deflect recoil, minimizing flinch and muzzle jump. **Magazine:** Staggered box type, four shot. (Blind in the stock has no floor plate). **Action:** Mauser Mark x Action. **Overall length:** 43″ (Standard Model); 45″ (Magnum); all Winslow rifles have company name and serial number and grade engraved on the action and caliber engraved on barrel. **Barrel:** Douglas barrel

premium grade, chrome moly-type steel; all barrels, 20 caliber through 35 caliber, have six lands and grooves; barrels larger than 35 caliber have eight lands and grooves. All barrels are finished to (.2 to .4) micro inches inside the lands and grooves.
Total weight (without scope): 7 to 7½ lbs. with 24″ barrel in standard calibers 243, 308, 270, etc; 8 to 9 lbs. with 26″ barrel in Magnum calibers 264 Win., 300 Wby., 458 Win., etc. Winslow rifles are made in the following calibers:
Standard cartridges: 22-250, 243 Win., 244 Rem., 257 Roberts, 308 Win., 30-06, 280 Rem., 270 Win., 25-06, 284 Win., 358 Win., and 7mm (7×57).
Magnum cartridges: 300 Weatherby, 300 Win., 338 Win., 358 Norma, 375 H.H., 458 Win., 257 Weatherby, 264 Win., 270 Weatherby, 7mm Weatherby, 7mm Rem., 300 H.H., 308 Norma.
Left-handed models available in most calibers.

WINSLOW BASIC RIFLE

The Basic Rifle, available in the Bushmaster stock, features one ivory diamond inlay in a rosewood grip cap and ivory trademark in bottom of forearm. Grace 'A' walnut jeweled bolt and follower **$1375.00**. Plainsmaster stock **$100.00** extra. **Left-hand** model **$1475.00**

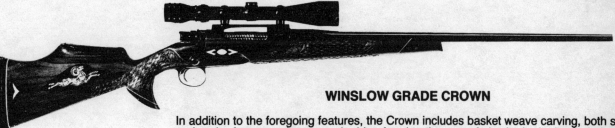

WINSLOW GRADE CROWN

In addition to the foregoing features, the Crown includes basket weave carving, both sides and under forearm, also on each side of and to the rear of pistol grip. It also includes two eight-point ivory and ebony inlays, one on each side of the magazine box, two large triangle ivory and ebony inlays, one on each side of the buttstock. **Price upon request.**

WINSLOW VARMINT

This 17 caliber is available in the Bushmaster stock and the Plainsmaster stock, which is a miniature of the original high roll-over cheekpiece and a round leading edge on the forearm, modified spoon billed pistol grip. Available in 17/222, 17/222 Mag. 17/233, 222 Rem. and 223. Regent grade shown. **Price upon request.**

Shotguns

FOR ADDRESSES AND PHONE
NUMBERS OF MANUFACTURERS AND
DISTRIBUTORS INCLUDED IN THIS
SECTION, SEE *DIRECTORY OF
MANUFACTURERS AND SUPPLIERS*

WHAT'S NEW IN SHOTGUNS AND SHOTGUN PRODUCTS

BY NICK SISLEY: Shooter's Bible Shotgun Consultant

The biggest news in shotgunning this season centers around the thickness of your wallet. If it's on the thin side these days, you'll herald the arrival of the 3¹/₂-inch 12 gauge Magnum, along with the shotguns being made to handle it. If your wallet is reasonably well padded, you'll be excited about the news from Parker Reproductions (about which more later on). So let's take a closer look at these and other new products in the shotgun world, starting with the new 3¹/₂-inch Magnum shell.

Federal continues its leadership in the steel shot field with the industry's first 12 gauge 3¹/₂" shotgun shell optimized for steel shot.

FEDERAL/MOSSBERG

The future success of Federal's 3¹/₂-inch Magnum depends naturally on how well it performs in the field. This new shell ups the payload in steel from 1¹/₄ ounces in the 3-inch steel load to 1⁹/₁₆ ounces, or a 23 percent increase. Since there are only five more steel pellets in the 3¹/₂-inch 10 gauge Magnum, it follows that the 3¹/₂-inch 12 gauge steel load might literally steal the thunder from the 10 bore, perhaps putting it permanently on the back burner.

The shotgun Federal picked to help them develop this load was Mossberg's Model 835 pump. The receiver on this beefed-up Model 500 (Mossberg) was lengthened to accept and handle the larger shell. It comes with a 28-inch barrel and Accu-Mag chokes, which were designed especially for patterning steel shot effectively. The barrel was also back-bored to reduce the heavy recoil of this 7³/₄-pound gun. Shooters are well advised to add a recoil reducer to the stock, and perhaps another in the forend.

This new Federal load has a muzzle velocity of 1300 fps and is offered in steel #2, BB, T and F sizes. Federal is also introducing its Top Gun line, which is a target-type load with a very attractive price. Available only in 12 gauge, it uses extra hard shot, Federal's own 209 primer and 12S3 wad. It's offered in 2³/₄ dram 7¹/₂ and 8. The company's Premium line now offers a 28 gauge with ³/₄-ounce of coppered 6, 7¹/₂, or 8 shot. And in its Premium Buckshot lineup, Federal has introduced coppered 00 and #4 buck in 10 gauge, plus #4 buck in 2³/₄-inch 12 gauge.

Federal's new 10 gauge 3½" Premium buckshot load contains 54 pellets of hard, copper-plated #4 buckshot with granulated plastic filler.

PARKER REPRODUCTIONS

Back in 1981, Bill Jaqua, who runs one of the best equipped gun shops in the world in Findlay, Ohio, paid $95,000 for one of eight existing 28 gauge A-1 Special Parkers. It's probably safe to say that these original American Parker A-1 Specials are the most valuable guns ever produced in this country.

The "new" Parker story begins with Jack Skeuse, who has been a Parker collector for years. He saw the intense interest many Americans had in this side-by-side, so he explored the possibility of having it manufactured. He ended up traveling to Japan, having selected the factory there which produced the Winchester Model 101 and 23 doubles. Skeuse introduced his first Parkers—all 20 gauge in DHE grade—at the 1984 S.H.O.T. Show. After carefully expanding the Parker line for a few years, Skeuse decided early in 1988 to "open the dikes." The options now are quite varied, but heading the list is the Parker Reproduction A-1 Special.

When it comes to fine doubles, whether original Parkers or reproductions, the bottom line will always be guided by craftsmanship. These new Par-

kers, especially the A-1 Specials, are truly magnificent, and they're available in all four gauges: 12, 20, 28 and even the .410. If your pocketbook isn't quite fat enough to spring for the A-1 Special, which goes for less than $9,000, there's a new BHE grade line, which features bank-note engraving in all four gauges and sells for less than $4,000. Twelve-gauge Parker Reproductions are also available now in the Sporting Clay Classic Model. Featuring screw-in chokes, it's even suitable for shooting steel shells and retails for around $3,120.

BROWNING

Browning is bringing back a famous old smoothbore, too—the Model 12, previously of Winchester fame. This pump shotgun once made doubles guns take a back seat with the American shooting public. It was so well balanced and reliable, in fact, that pump repeaters replaced side-by-sides as the darlings of water-fowlers, upland purists, and clay target champions.

Browning's Model 12 is available in 20 gauge only, although a 28 gauge will probably be out soon, perhaps followed by a .410. There's only one barrel length (26 inches) and only two choke choices (full or improved cylinder), all with 2¾-inch chambers. Two grades—I and V—are offered in limited editions (8,500 in Grade I and 4,000 in Grade V). Grade V sports fancy engraving and gold scenes on both sides of its richly blued receiver. On the right, four mallards skim some cattails, while on the left a ruffed grouse flushes ahead of a pointing dog. Pricing is set at $700 for Grade I and $1,100 for Grade V. Upon first inspection of these guns, you may think you're looking at one of the original Model 12's. The stock dimensions are the same, with the fluted comb, semi-pistol grip and metal grip cap, and the action is smooth and slick.

Browning has brought back Model 12 in 20 gauge. The model shown here is part of the company's Grade I line.

Remington has expanded its steel line with, among others, this Special Purpose Duplex shell.

Also new from Browning is their BPS pump in 10 gauge Magnum with Invector Chokes (modified, improved modified and full), which is designed especially for steel shot. A 30-inch barrel is standard, but 28- and 32-inchers are available.

REMINGTON

Remington Arms purchased Parker Brothers shortly before World War II. And while they never produced many of the Parker side-by-sides, the company continues to own the production rights. Remington's first modern version was unveiled at the 1988 S.H.O.T. Show in Las Vegas. A superb AHE grade, it was auctioned off in behalf of the National Shooting Sports Foundation for $20,500. But you can now get an original, modern-day Parker direct from Remington's Custom Shop, which plans to produce about 50 guns a year.

Remington's shotgun line also includes a re-designed Model 970 TC Trap gun, the 870 Express, which is now available in a combo set (regular Rem-Choke barrel and 20-inch I.C. choked barrel with rifle sights). Several new Remington shot loads are on the market as well. In Duplex lead, there's a 2×4 and a 4×6, both $2^{3}/_{4}$ and 3-inch Magnums. The steel line has been expanded with 10 gauge $3^{1}/_{2}$-inch, $1^{3}/_{4}$-ounce 1, 2 and 3 sizes in 12 and 20 gauge, plus Duplex steel $BB \times 1$ and 1×3, $2^{3}/_{4}$- and 3-inch Magnum.

WEATHERBY

Weatherby's Japanese-made Athena and Orion over/under lines have been expanded. Previously available only in 12 and 20 gauges, 28 and .410 choices are now being offered in a variety of standard choke options. The 28's have $2^{3}/_{4}$-inch chambers, while the .410's bear 3-inch chambers. For skeet buffs, Weatherby's 12-gauge Athena skeet gun has been fitted with Briley skeet tubes in .410, 28 and 20. The package comes in a fitted aluminum case. These 12 gauge over-unders are fitted with high-tensile strength aluminum and full-length small gauge tubes, which are all the rage in competition skeet these days. No matter what gauge is used, these tubes all weigh the same (14 ounces), so they feel and swing the same.

KASSNAR

New for this year at Kassnar is the Royal Grade Churchill side-by-side. Its price is attractive, and yet it's replete with worthwhile features, including a case-hardened frame, minimal weight, chromed barrels, concave ribs, and hand checkering. The Royal offers seven options as well: 12 gauge 28-inch M/F; 12 gauge 26-inch IC/M; 16 gauge 28-inch M/F; 20

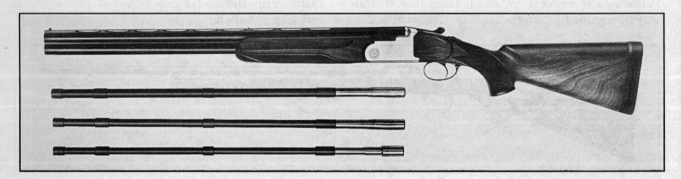

Weatherby's 12-gauge Athena skeet gun is fitted with high-tensile strength aluminum, full-length tubes.

gauge 28-inch M/F; 20 gauge 26-inch IC/M; 28 gauge 25-inch M/F; and .410 26-inch F/F.

U.S. REPEATING ARMS

Winchester's Model 1300 pump has a new version: a Turkey gun. It was selected by the National Wild Turkey Federation as their "Gun of the Year." A turkey and the Federation's name are engraved on one side of the receiver, with another turkey scene and the Federation's initials appearing on the other side. The finish of both barrel and receiver is non-reflective matte. And the stock, with its laminated hardwood, is naturally camouflaged in varying shades of green and brown. The price of walnut continues to rise, which means that laminated stocks will become increasingly important over the long term for both shotguns and rifles.

The 22-inch barrel on this Model 1300 Turkey gun features vent rib and Winchoke tubes—extra full, full and modified. The 1300 also features a Cordura camo sling that's quickly detachable, a rubber recoil pad, and one-pin receiver disassembly. Weatherby offers a new 1300 Featherweight model as well; it comes in 12 or 20 gauge with Winchokes and 22-inch barrel.

ACTIV INDUSTRIES

Activ continues to make inroads into the shotshell market. Their Ultra line of shells now includes the following: 3-inch, 4 dram, $1^5/8$-ounce in 2, 4, 6 and $7^1/2$; and a 3-inch 20 bore $3^1/4$ dram load with either 4, 6, or $7^1/2$. These Ultra shells contain hard, nickel-plated shot.

Activ's new Super Shot line is also nickel-plated. The offerings are as follows:

12 gauge $2^3/4$-inch 4 dram $1^3/8$-ounce 4, 6 & $7^1/2$
12 gauge $2^3/4$-inch $3^3/4$ dram $1^1/4$-ounce BB, 2, 4, 5, 6, $7^1/2$ & 9
16 gauge $2^3/4$-inch $3^1/4$ $1^1/8$ ounce 4, 6 & $7^1/2$
20 gauge $2^3/4$-inch $2^3/4$ dram 1 ounce 4, 5, 6, $7^1/2$ & 9

ITHACA

Ithaca nearly fell by the financial wayside a while back, but they've been resurrected. They've dropped their Model 51 gas-operated autoloader and sold their Mag-10 10 gauge operation to Remington. Ithaca's major new effort, however, is their all-time best

seller: the Model 37 pump, the lightweight bottom ejector that was first introduced in 1937. Now this pump from yesteryear is called the Model 87. It offers four basic possibilities. First is the Supreme, in 12 or 20 gauge, with vent rib and a choice (in 12 gauge) of 30-inch full, 28-inch modified, or 26-inch improved cylinder. In 20 gauge, barrel lengths are all 26 inches, but there's still a choice of three choke options.

The Deluxe grade comes with vent rib, screw chokes, and barrel lengths of 30, 28 or 26 inches in 12 gauge (25 inches only in 20 bore). A third choice is the Ultralight model, made from a milled bar of aircraft aluminum instead of steel. In 12 or 20 gauge, it sports a 25-inch barrel with screw-in chokes and weighs 6 and 5 pounds, respectively. The fourth choice in Ithaca's Model 87 is Camo Vent. It has a 28-inch screw-choke barrel and its stock and metal parts are all finished in camo matte.

BERETTA

What's especially newsworthy at Beretta is a new finish, part of their Onyx Series. Three models are offered—Model 686 and 687, both over-and-unders, and Model 626 side-by-side. The new finish is a lustrous, black semi-matte, and it appears on the barrels as well as the receivers. The result is less glare and maintenance, since the material is corrosion-resistant and provides improved heat dissipation.

SKB

Two side-by-sides are new from SKB. They are Models 200 and 400. The former is a box lock with scroll engraving; the latter has false side plates with more elaborate engraving. You can choose from either 12 or 20 gauge, with Interchokes in each. There's only one barrel length—26 inches—and they weigh in at six pounds three ounces for the 20 gauge Model 200, and six pounds 10 ounces in 12 gauge. Model 400 weighs six pounds five ounces in 20 gauge and six pounds 12 ounces for the 12 gauge.

CLASSIC DOUBLES INTERNATIONAL

No longer will the Winchester name appear on Models 101 or 23. They've been taken over by Classic Doubles. There are reportedly nine new 101 and 23 variations on the company's drawing boards, but for now these Classic Doubles shotguns will be much the same as their Winchester forebears.

AMERICAN ARMS

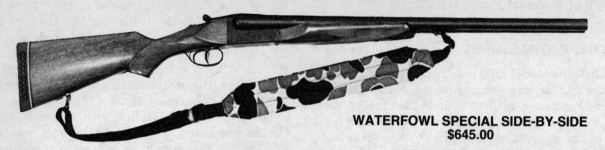

WATERFOWL SPECIAL SIDE-BY-SIDE
$645.00

WATERFOWL SPECIAL O/U 10 GAUGE

SPECIFICATIONS
Gauge: 10
Chambers: 3¹/₂″
Barrel length: 32″ with F/F (steel full)
Weight: 10 lbs. 13 oz.
Triggers: Double
Stock: Dull finish walnut, pistol-grip stock and beavertail forend with hand-checkering
Length of pull: 14⁵/₁₆″
Drop at comb: 1³/₈″
Drop at heel: 2³/₈″
Features: Flat rib; fitted rubber recoil pad; precision-made boxlocks; one-piece, steel-forged receiver; manual thumb safety; sling swivels and camouflaged sling

Also available:

WATERFOWL SPECIAL OVER/UNDER 10 GAUGE. Same specifications as side-by-side model, except for the following. **Weight:** 9 lbs. 15 oz. **Length of pull:** 14¹/₂″. Also includes ¹/₄″ vent rib. **Price: $875.00**

WATERFOWL SPECIAL OVER/UNDER 12 GAUGE. Same specifications as 10 gauge model, except for the following. **Chambers:** 3″. **Barrel length:** 28″. **Trigger:** Single selective. **Weight:** 6 lbs. 15 oz. Also has automatic selective ejectors. **Price: $650.00**

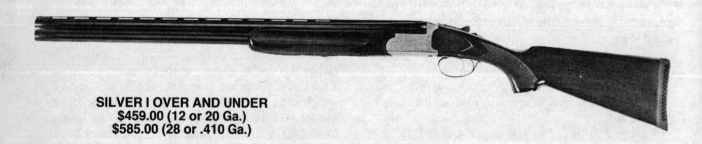

SILVER I OVER AND UNDER
$459.00 (12 or 20 Ga.)
$585.00 (28 or .410 Ga.)

SPECIFICATIONS
Gauges: 12, 20, 28 or .410
Chambers: 3″ (2³/₄″ in 28 ga.)
Barrel lengths: 26″, choked IC/M (all gauges); 28″, choked M/F (12 and 20 ga.)
Trigger: Single selective
Weight: 6 lbs. 15 oz. (12 ga.); 6 lbs. 10 oz. (20 ga.); 5 lbs. 14 oz. (28 ga.); 6 lbs. 6 oz. (.410 ga.)
Stock: Hand-checkered, walnut, pistol-grip stock and forend
Length of pull: 14¹/₈″
Drop at comb: 1³/₈″

Drop at heel: 2³/₈″
Features: Fitted recoil pad; ¹/₄″ vent rib; manual thumb safety; scroll-engraved, precision-made boxlocks; one-piece, steel-forged receiver; locking cross bolt; monobloc chrome-lined barrels; extractors

Also available:
SILVER II OVER/UNDER. Same specifications as above, but available in only 12 or 20 gauge. Includes choke tubes and automatic selective ejectors. **Price: $620.00**

AMERICAN ARMS

BRISTOL OVER AND UNDER
$850.00

SPECIFICATIONS
Gauge: 12 or 20
Chambers: 3″
Barrel length: 26″ (28″ barrel avail. with 12 ga.)
Trigger: Single selective with gold color
Weight: 7 lbs. 1 oz. (12 ga.); 6 lbs. 12 oz. (20 ga.)
Frame: Old silver finish
Stock: Oil-finished walnut stock and forend with hand-checkering; pistol grip

Length of pull: 14$\frac{1}{8}$″
Drop at comb: 1$\frac{3}{8}$″
Drop at heel: 2$\frac{3}{8}$″
Features: Precision-made boxlocks with hand-engraved scrollwork on false side plates; one-piece, steel-forged receiver; monbloc chrome-lined barrels; locking cross bolt; manual thumb safety; fitted recoil pad; automatic selective ejector; $\frac{1}{4}$″ vent rib with matte finish; choke tubes

SINGLE BARREL SHOTGUN
$108.00

SPECIFICATIONS
Gauges: 12, 20 and .410
Chamber: 3″
Barrel length: 28″, choked M/F (12 and 20 ga.); 26″, choked F (.410 ga. only)

Features: Manual thumb safety; chrome-lined barrels; checkered stock and forearm with walnut-style finish; non-folding

SINGLE BARREL WATERFOWL SPECIAL
$160.00

SPECIFICATIONS
Gauge: 10
Chamber: 3$\frac{1}{2}$″
Barrel length: 30″ choked Full
Finish: Same as above with non-reflective finish

Also available:
SINGLE BARREL TURKEY SPECIAL. Same specifications as above, except for the following. **Barrel length:** 26″ with choke tube. **Price: $189.00**

CAMPER SPECIAL

CAMPER SPECIAL. Same specifications as the single barrel model, except for the following. **Barrel length:** 21″, choked Modified only. **Overall length:** 27″. **Price: $108.00**

SHOTGUNS

AMERICAN ARMS

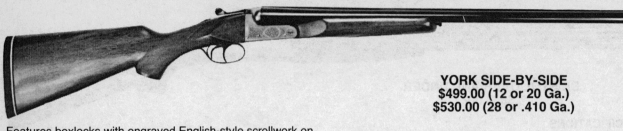

YORK SIDE-BY-SIDE
$499.00 (12 or 20 Ga.)
$530.00 (28 or .410 Ga.)

Features boxlocks with engraved English-style scrollwork on side plates; one-piece, steel-forged receiver; chrome barrels; manual thumb safety; independent floating firing pin.

SPECIFICATIONS
Gauges: 12, 20, 28, .410
Chambers: 3″ (except 28 gauge, 2³/₄″)
Barrel lengths: 26″, choked IC/M (all gauges); 28″, choked M/F (12 and 20 gauges)

Weight: 6 lbs. 14 oz. (12 and .410 ga.); 6 lbs. 4 oz. (20 and 28 ga.)
Drop at comb: 1³/₈″
Drop at heel: 2³/₈″
Other features: Fitted recoil pad; flat matted rib; walnut pistol-grip stock and beavertail forend with hand-checkering; gold front sight bead

DERBY SIDE-BY-SIDE
Single or Double Trigger

Features functioning side locks with English-style hand-engraving on side plates; one-piece, steel-forged receiver; chrome barrels; automatic safety

SPECIFICATIONS
Gauges: 12, 20, 28, .410 (20/28 gauge in two-barrel set)
Chambers: 3″
Barrel lengths: 26″, choked IC/M (all gauges); 28″, choked M/F (12 and 20 gauges)
Weight: 7 lbs. 1 oz. (12 ga.); 6¹/₄ lbs. (20, 28 and .410 ga.)
Sights: Gold bead front sight
Stock: Walnut and splinter forend with hand-checkering

Length of pull: 14¹/₈″
Drop at comb: 1³/₈″
Drop at heel: 2³/₈″
Finish: Hand-rubbed oil finish wood

Prices:
12 or 20 ga. double trigger	$ 830.00
12 or 20 ga. single trigger	875.00
28 or .410 ga. double trigger	875.00
28 or .410 ga. single trigger	900.00
20/28 ga. double trigger set	1095.00
20/28 ga. single trigger set	1125.00

TURKEY SPECIAL SIDE-BY-SIDE
$695.00

SPECIFICATIONS
Gauge: 10
Chambers: 3¹/₂″
Barrel length: 26″ with choke tubes
Weight: 9 lbs. 15 oz.
Stock: Dull finish walnut stock and beavertail forend with hand-checkering; pistol grip
Length of pull: 14⁵/₁₆″
Drop at comb: 1³/₈″
Drop at heel: 2³/₈″
Features: Fitted recoil pad; flat rib; precision-made boxlocks with one-piece, steel-forged receiver; non-reflective,

chrome-lined barrels; manual thumb safety; sling swivels and camouflaged sling
Also available:
TURKEY SPECIAL SIDE-BY-SIDE 12 GAUGE. Same specifications as 10 gauge model, except for the following. **Chambers:** 3″. **Weight:** 6 lbs. 14 oz. **Length of pull:** 14¹/₈″. **Price: $550.00**
TURKEY SPECIAL OVER/UNDER. Same specifications as side-by-side model, except for the following. **Length of pull:** 14¹/₂″. Also includes ¹/₄″ vent rib, choke tubes and extractors. **Price: $940.00**

ARMSPORT SHOTGUNS

MODEL 2717 O/U SINGLE SELECTIVE TRIGGER WITH EXTRACTORS
$550.00

MODEL 2733 (12 GAUGE) DELUXE BOSS ACTION SINGLE SEL. TRIGGER
$590.00

This is a superbly designed, handsomely engraved over-and-under shotgun with ventilated rib. The single selective trigger allows you to fire either barrel at will. It has exceptionally fine hand-picked walnut stock and forend, hand-crafted and fitted for generations of fine shooting. Gloss or oil finish. 12 gauge. 28-inch barrels choked Mod. and Full (Extractors). 3-inch Mag. shells.

Also available:
Model 2719 20 Ga. 26" O/U 3" Mag. Imp. & Mod. . . **$550.00**
Model 2720 .410 Ga. 26" O/U 3" Mag. Imp. & Mod.
Non-selective trigger **650.00**
Model 2735 20 Ga. 26" O/U 3" Mag. Imp. & Mod. ·
Deluxe Boss Action **590.00**

MODEL 2741 (12 GAUGE) DELUXE BOSS ACTION O/U SINGLE SEL. TRIGGER w/AUTO EJECTORS
$650.00

Also available:
Model 2727 12 Ga. 28" Barrel O/U 3" Mag. Mod. &
Full **$615.00**
Model 2729 20 Ga. 26" Barrel 3" Mag.
Imp. & Mod. **615.00**
Model 2743 20 Ga. 26" Barrel 3" Mag. Imp. & Mod.
Deluxe Boss Action **650.00**

Beautifully designed boss action over/under shotguns with both top and lateral vent ribs. Swell pistol grip and flare forend. Gloss or oil-finished stock. Chambered for 3-inch Magnum shells with chemically engraved silver finished receiver. 12 gauge with 28-inch barrels. Mod. and full chokes.

ARMSPORT SHOTGUNS

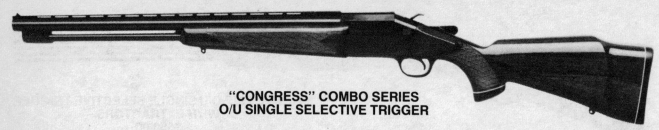

"CONGRESS" COMBO SERIES
O/U SINGLE SELECTIVE TRIGGER

Both shotgun and rifle barrels of these "Turkey" guns are mated to shoot groups as close to perfect as possible. The fine-grained palm swell full pistol grip rollover cheekpiece, walnut stock and forend are all hand-checkered. Both 12 and 20 gauge top shotgun barrels are chambered to accept 3" magnum shells. The Deluxe Single Selective Trigger models are available in both 12 and 20 gauge over either .222, .243 or .270.

Model 2783 Deluxe 12 gauge/222 w/lateral rib . . **$1600.00**
Model 2784 Deluxe 12 gauge/243 w/lateral rib 1600.00
Model 2785 Deluxe 12 gauge/270 w/lateral rib 1600.00
Model 2786 Deluxe 20 gauge/222 w/lateral rib 1600.00
Model 2787 Deluxe 20 gauge/243 w/lateral rib 1600.00
Model 2788 Deluxe 20 gauge/270 w/lateral rib 1600.00

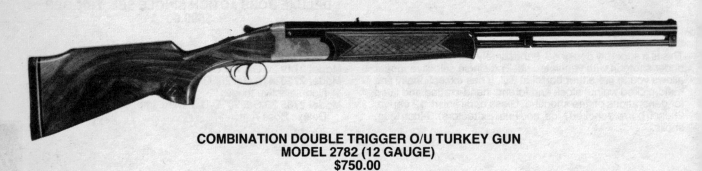

COMBINATION DOUBLE TRIGGER O/U TURKEY GUN
MODEL 2782 (12 GAUGE)
$750.00

Armsport's over/under shotgun/rifle combination turkey gun is manufactured by one of Italy's finest gun factories. This 12 gauge, 3" mag. shotgun with .222 caliber rifle features chrome-lined barrels with an extra wide upper vent rib. The frame is built from a special solid steel block and has tempered antique silver finish or basic blue, both beautifully engraved. Its high luster walnut palm swell pistol grip and stock are gracefully made with schnabel forend, both checkered for sure grip. Fitted with rubber recoil pad.

MODEL 2704 OVER/UNDER

"SENATOR" SERIES
O/U DOUBLE TRIGGER WITH EXTRACTORS
From $490.00—$595.00

The Armsport over/unders with double triggers are lightweight, well balanced and are chambered for 3" Mag. shells. The special grade steel barrels are chrome lined, with both an upper vent rib and lateral vent rib. The fine grain walnut stock has a palm swell pistol grip and both the stock and schnabel-type forend have a deep, sure-grip checkering. The beautifully engraved antique silver receiver is engineered from the finest gun steel. The double trigger instantly allows the shooter his barrel choice.

Available in:
Model 2702 12 Ga. 28" O/U 3" Mag. 2 Trig. Ext. Mod. & Full
Model 2704 20 Ga. 26" O/U 3" Mag. 2 Trig. Ext. Imp. & Mod.
Model 2705 .410 Ga. 26" O/U 3" Mag. 2 Trig. Ext. Imp. & Mod.

ARMSPORT SHOTGUNS

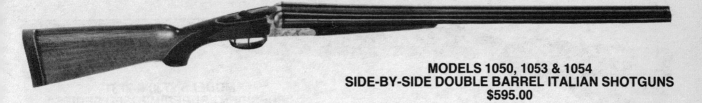

MODELS 1050, 1053 & 1054
SIDE-BY-SIDE DOUBLE BARREL ITALIAN SHOTGUNS
$595.00

Chambered for 3″ magnum with hard chrome-lined barrels, these shotguns feature center ribs, fluorescent front sights, Italian box lock actions and gloss finish stocks and forends. Also antique silver finish receivers engraved with bird scenes.

Model 1050 is 12 gauge with 28″ barrel with Modified & Full choke. Model 1053 is 20 gauge with 26″ barrel with Imp. & Modified choke. Model 1054 is .410 gauge with 26″ barrel with Imp. & Modified choke.

MODEL 2700
10 GAUGE OVER & UNDER GOOSE GUN
$950.00

This 10 gauge 3¹/₂″ "Fowler" Magnum Boss-type action O/U Goose gun has two bottom locking lugs on its OM8 steel barrels attached to an antiqued silver finished action. Three Canada geese scenes are engraved on the two sides and bottom of the receiver. The hard chrome-lined barrels have an extra wide 12mm top vent rib with a fluorescent front sight and a brass mid-bead sight. Both the 32″ barrels choked full and the 28″ barrels choked Imp. and Mod. will shoot steel BB's effectively. The walnut stock with rubber recoil pad and matching forend are hand-checkered.

MODEL 2900
ITALIAN TRI-BARREL SHOTGUN
$1450.00

The only three-barrel shotgun being manufactured, Model 2900 features 28″ barrels (12 gauge) lined and chambered for 3″ magnum shells choked improved, modified and full. The front trigger fires the top two barrels and the rear trigger fires the bottom barrel. Made on a boss type action from special steel, the shotgun frame has two bottom locking lugs. The select grain walnut palm swell pistol grip stock and forend has a rubber recoil pad, high gloss finish and checkering.

ARMSPORT SHOTGUNS

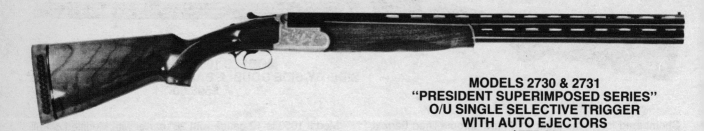

MODELS 2730 & 2731
"PRESIDENT SUPERIMPOSED SERIES"
O/U SINGLE SELECTIVE TRIGGER
WITH AUTO EJECTORS
$775.00

Milled from special high-strength steel, these shotguns feature engraved antique silver finished boss-type receiver fitted to special steel barrels with jeweled engine turned barrel lugs and hand-checkered walnut stock with rubber recoil pad, palm swell full pistol grip and matching checkered semi-schnabel forend. Also, extra wide 12mm top vent rib with front fluorescent sight and brass mid-bead sight, plus lateral vent rib. All President models have single selective triggers and are chambered 3" magnum. Barrel lengths are 26" in 20 gauge and 27" in 12 gauge. Chokes are Skeet and Skeet 6 Interchangeable.

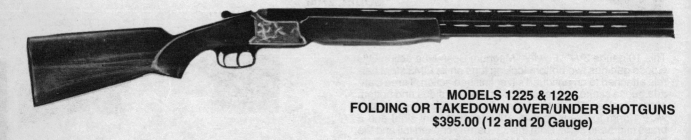

MODELS 1225 & 1226
FOLDING OR TAKEDOWN OVER/UNDER SHOTGUNS
$395.00 (12 and 20 Gauge)

Chambered for 3" magnum shells. Can shoot steel shot. Top vent rib with front and mid-bead sights. Lateral vent rib. Engraved antique finish receiver. Walnut palm swell pistol grip stock. Schnabel-type forend. Cut checkering on stock and forend. Two triggers. Model 1225 is 12 gauge with 28" barrel with Modified and Full choke. Model 1226 is 20 gauge with 26" barrel and Imp. and Modified choke.

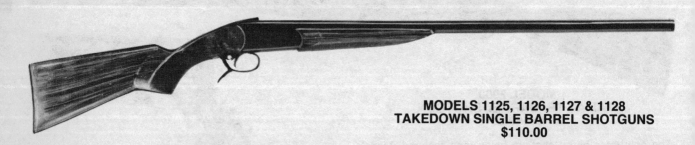

MODELS 1125, 1126, 1127 & 1128
TAKEDOWN SINGLE BARREL SHOTGUNS
$110.00

Machined from solid block of gun steel drop forging. Features a bottom lever takedown opening action and a complete iron cross removable forend. Barrels are chambered for 3" magnum shells with hard chrome-lined barrels and bores for steel shot use. High-gloss walnut finish stock and forend are checkered. **Models 1125 and 1126** are 12 gauge with 28" barrels (Model 1125 has Modified choke; Model 1126 has Full). **Model 1127** is 20 gauge with 26" barrel, Modified choke. **Model 1128** is .410 gauge with full choke.

BENELLI SHOTGUN

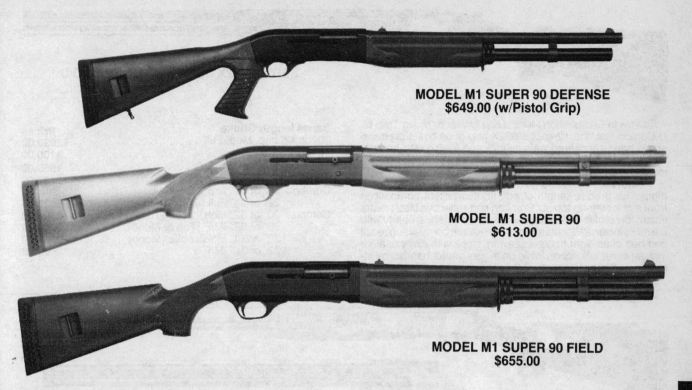

MODEL M1 SUPER 90 DEFENSE
$649.00 (w/Pistol Grip)

MODEL M1 SUPER 90
$613.00

MODEL M1 SUPER 90 FIELD
$655.00

This 12 gauge autoloader functions on a rotating bolt system that minimizes recoil and maximizes accuracy. It features an adjustable rear sight as standard equipment, a one-piece alloy receiver for lighter weight and quick maneuverability, and a stock and forend made of a rugged fiberglass reinforced polymer. The Super 90 has a free carrier and an external shell release for lightning-like ammo changes or speedy reloads. A pistol grip stock is available as an accessory and the grip is enclosed in molded rubber to insulate the hand from recoil.

Also available with 28″ vent rib (screw-in choke tubes: Full, Improved and Modified). **Price: $655.00**

SPECIFICATIONS
Gauge: 12
Chamber: 3″
Mag. capacity: 7
Barrel length: 19³/₄″
Choke: Cylinder
Overall length: 39³/₄″
Weight: 7 lbs. 4 oz.
Finish: Matte black
Stock: High impact polymer
Sights: Post front; fixed buckhorn rear drift adjustable

MONTEFELTRO SUPER 90
$664.00 ($724.00 Left Hand)

The Montefeltro Super 90 combines the fast firing characteristics of the M1 Super 90 with the look of a classic sporting shotgun. The heart of this Benelli remains the Montefeltro rotating bolt system, a rugged and simple inertia recoil design that functions with all types of 3″ and 2³/₄″ loads. A drop adjustment kit allows the stock to be custom-fitted to any shooter.

SPECIFICATIONS
Gauge: 12
Capacity: 5 rounds
Chamber: 3″
Chokes: Screw-in, Full, Improved & Modified
Barrel length: 28″
Overall length: 47″
Weight: 6 lbs. 14 oz.
Stock: High-gloss walnut
Finish: Matte black

SHOTGUNS

BERETTA SHOTGUNS

SERIES 682X COMPETITION TRAP O/U

Available in Competition Mono, Over/Under or Mono Trap-O/U Combo Set, the 12-gauge 682X trap guns boast premium grade hand-checkered walnut stock and forend with International or Monte Carlo left- or right-hand stock and choice of 3 stock dimensions.

Features: Adjustable gold-plated, single selective sliding trigger for precise length of pull fit; fluorescent competition front sight; step-up top rib; Bruniton non-reflective black matte finish; low profile improved boxlock action; manual safety with barrel selector; 2³/₄″ chambers; auto ejector; competition recoil pad butt plate; light hand-engraving; stock with silver oval for initials; silver inscription inlaid on trigger guard; handsome fitted case. **Weight:** Approx. 8 lbs.

Barrel length/Choke	Prices
30″ or 32″ Imp. Mod./Full	$2030.00
30″ or 32″ Mobilchoke	2100.00
Top Single 32″ or 34″ Full	1960.00
Top Single 32″ or 34″ Mobilchoke	2030.00
Combo.: 30″ or 32″ Imp. Mod./Full 32″ or 34″ Full (Mono)	2520.00
Combo.: 30″ or 32″ Mobilchoke (Top)	2800.00
30″ or 32″ IM/F (Top or Mono)	2660.00
32″ or 34″ Mobilchoke (Mono)	2660.00
32″ or 34″ IM/F	2660.00

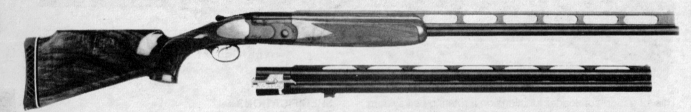

682X COMPETITION W/MONO AND COMBO O/U BARRELS

682 COMPETITION SKEET O/U
26″ or 28″ SK/SK $2030.00
4-Barrel Set (28″) $4830.00
12, 20, 28, .410 Gauge

This skeet gun sports hand-checkered premium walnut stock, forged and hardened receiver, manual safety with trigger selector, auto ejector, stock with silver oval for initials, silver inlaid on trigger guard. Price includes fitted case.

Action: Low profile hard chrome-plated boxlock
Trigger: Single adjustable sliding trigger
Barrels: 26″ or 28″ rust blued barrels with 2³/₄″ chambers
Stock dimensions: Length of pull 14³/₈″; drop at comb 1¹/₂″; drop at heel 2¹/₃″
Sights: Fluorescent front and metal middle bead
Weight: Approx. 8 lbs.

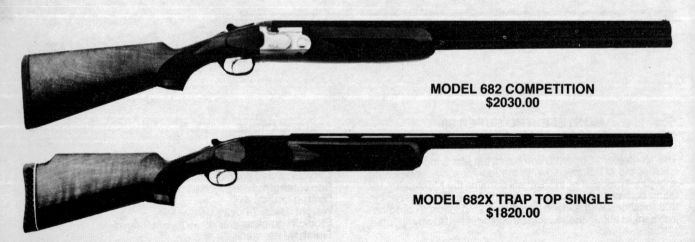

MODEL 682 COMPETITION
$2030.00

MODEL 682X TRAP TOP SINGLE
$1820.00

BERETTA SHOTGUNS

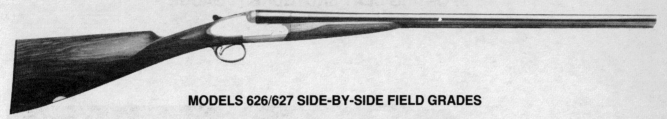

MODELS 626/627 SIDE-BY-SIDE FIELD GRADES

These good-looking field models feature low profile solid box-lock design, hand-fitted stocks and forends of handsome European walnut with deep diamond hand-checkering, tang-mounted safety/barrel selectors, single-selective trigger, metal bead sight and knurled rib. 12 gauge barrels are chambered 2³/₄"; 20 gauge barrels, 3" Mag. **Model 626** has bright chrome finish, full hand-engraving. **Model 627** boasts hand-engraved side plates.

MODEL 626 ONYX SERIES

The **Model 626 Onyx** has a full-figured American walnut stock, lustrous black semi-matte finish on the barrels and receiver, and front and center sighting beads on a vent rib.

Model 626 Field $995.00
12 ga., 26" Imp. Cyl./Mod.
12 ga., 28" Mod./Full

Model 626 Onyx $1265.00
12 ga., 26" Mobilchoke
20 ga., 26" Mobilchoke

Model 627EL $1995.00
12 ga., 28" Mod./Full
12 ga., 26" Imp. Cyl./Mod.

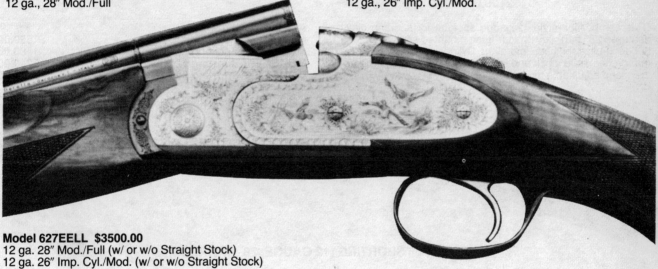

Model 627EELL $3500.00
12 ga. 28" Mod./Full (w/ or w/o Straight Stock)
12 ga. 26" Imp. Cyl./Mod. (w/ or w/o Straight Stock)

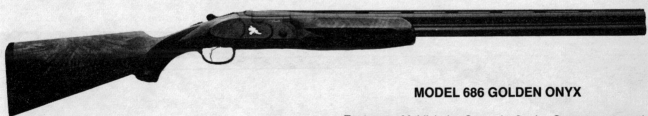

SPECIFICATIONS
Gauges: 12, 20
Chamber: 3"
Barrel lengths: 26" and 28"
Chokes: Full, Modified and Improved Cylinder
Stock: American walnut with recoil pad

MODEL 686 GOLDEN ONYX

Features: Mobilchoke Screw-in Choke System; automatic ejectors; vent ribs; Golden Onyx features game birds on both sides of the receiver

Prices:
MODEL 686 Onyx Over/Under $1035.00
MODEL 686 Golden Onyx Over/Under 1665.00
MODEL 686 Onyx Side/Side. 1035.00

BERETTA SHOTGUNS
SPORTING CLAY SHOTGUNS 12 GAUGE

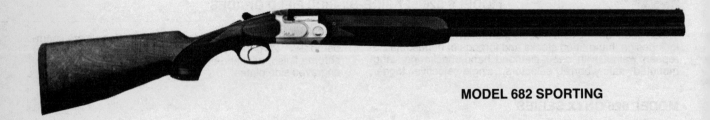

MODEL 682 SPORTING

MODEL 682 SPORTING
$2100.00

This competition-style 12 gauge shotgun for sporting clays features 28″ barrels with four flush-mounted screw-in choke tubes (Full, Modified, Improved Cylinder and Skeet), plus hand-checkered stock and forend of fine walnut, 2³/₄″ chambers and adjustable trigger.

Also available:
MODEL A303 Sporting . . . . $ 660.00
MODEL 686 Sporting 1680.00
MODEL 687 Sporting 12 Ga. 2240.00
MODEL 687 Sporting 20 Ga. 2240.00

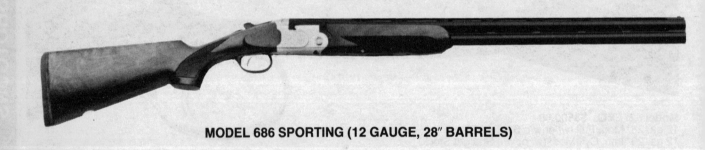

MODEL 686 SPORTING (12 GAUGE, 28″ BARRELS)

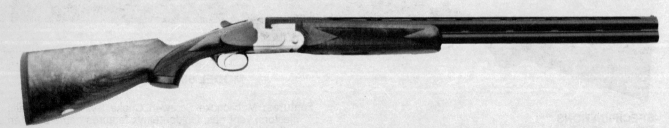

MODEL 687 SPORTING (12-GAUGE, 28″ BARRELS)

BERETTA SHOTGUNS

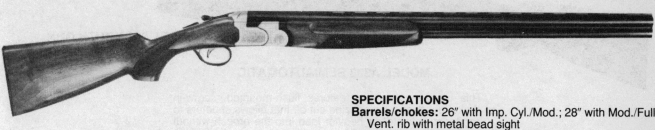

**MODEL 686 OVER/UNDER
28 Gauge**

SPECIFICATIONS
Barrels/chokes: 26″ with Imp. Cyl./Mod.; 28″ with Mod./Full. Vent. rib with metal bead sight
Action: Low profile, improved boxlock
Trigger: Selective single trigger, auto safety
Extractors: Auto ejectors
Stock: Choice walnut, hand-checkered and hand-finished with a tough gloss finish
Weight: Less than 7 lbs.

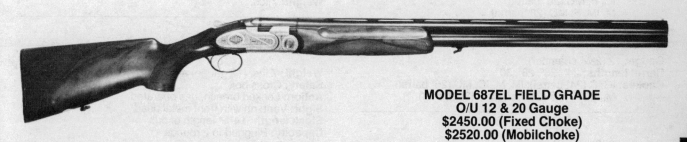

**MODEL 687EL FIELD GRADE
O/U 12 & 20 Gauge
$2450.00 (Fixed Choke)
$2520.00 (Mobilchoke)**

The **687EL** features new variations with Mobilchoke, Full, Modified and Improved Cylinder in 12 and 20 gauge; strong boxlock action handsomely tooled with floral hand-engraved decorative side plates, finest quality walnut stock accented with silver monogram plate, selective auto ejectors and fitted case.

Also available: **Model 687EELL,** featuring a special premium walnut, custom-fitted stock and exquisitely engraved side-plate, game-scene motifs. With fixed choke: **$3500.00;** with Mobilchoke: **$3640.00**

SPECIFICATIONS
Barrels/chokes: 26″ with Imp. Cyl./Mod.; 28″ with Mod./Full.
Action: Low-profile improved boxlock
Trigger: Single selective with manual safety
Extractors: Auto ejectors
Weight: 7 lbs. 2 oz.

**MODEL 1200F
$440.00**

This All-Weather 12 gauge semiautomatic shotgun features space-age technopolymer stock and forend. Lightweight (only 7+ pounds), it has a 28″ barrel chamber for 2³/₄″ shells and sports a unique weather-resistant matte black finish to reduce glare, resist corrosion and aid in heat dispersion.

SPECIFICATIONS
Gauge: 12
Chamber: 2³/₄″

Barrel length: 28″
Choke: Modified
Weight: 7.3 lbs.
Length of pull: 14³/₈″
Mag. Capacity: 6

Also available: **MODEL 1200 FP** (Law Enforcement) with 20″ barrel and Improved Cylinder choke (7-round capacity).
Price: $440.00

BERETTA SHOTGUNS

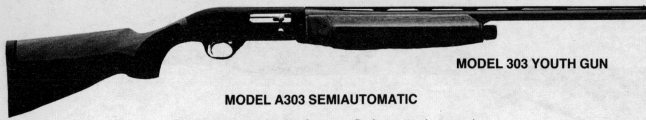

MODEL 303 YOUTH GUN

MODEL A303 SEMIAUTOMATIC

This unique autoloader features flush-mounted, screw-in choke tubes, and a magazine cut off that allows shooters to hand-feed a lighter or heavier load into the breech without emptying the magazine. Disassembly takes one minute.

SPECIFICATIONS
Gauge: 12 (3″ Magnum chamber)
Barrel lengths: 26″, 28″, 30″
Chokes: F, MC (24″, 30″ and 32″ barrels)
     IC, F, MC (26″ barrel)
     M, IM, F, MC (28″ barrel)

Gauge: 12 (2³/₄″ chamber)
Barrel lengths: 24″, 26″, 28″, 30″
Chokes: IC, C (24″ barrel); IM, M, IC, MC (26″ barrel)
     M, IM, F, MC (28″ barrel); F (30″ barrel)

Gauge: 20 (2³/₄″ or 3″ Magnum)
Barrel lengths: 26″ and 28″
Chokes: IC, M, MC (26″ barrel)
     M, IM, F, MC (28″ barrels)

A303 YOUTH
Gauge: 20 (3″ chamber)
Barrel length: 24″
Chokes: F, M, IC
Length of pull: 13¹/₂″

A303 SLUG
Gauges: 12, 20 (2³/₄″ and 3″ chambers)
Barrel lengths: 22″
Choke: Slug (C)
Weight: 7 lbs.

GENERAL A303 SPECIFICATIONS

Weight: 7 lbs. (12 gauge) and 6 lbs. (20 gauge)
Safety: Cross bolt
Action: Locked breech, gas operated
Sight: Vent. rib with front metal bead
Stock length: 14⁷/₈″ length of pull
Capacity: Plugged to 2 rounds

Prices:
A303 w/fixed choke, 3″ Magnum $506.00
A303 w/mobilchoke, 2³/₄″ or 3″ Magnums 574.00
A303 Slug 554.00
A303 Youth 574.00
A303 Skeet 12 & 20 ga., 2³/₄″, 26″ Skeet 606.00
A303 Trap 12 ga., 2³/₄″, 30″ and 32″ Full 606.00
A303 Trap w/Monte Carlo 12 ga., 2³/₄″, 30″ and 32″
    mobilchoke. 660.00

MODEL A303 COMPETITION TRAP
(not shown)

The Beretta A303 Trap is the competition version of the proven A303 semiautomatic. Its gas-operated system lessens recoil; other features include wide floating vent rib with flourescent front and mid-rib bead sights, plus Monte Carlo stock fitted with American trap pad. The A303 also comes with hand-checkered stock and forend of select European walnut, plus gold-plated trigger.

SPECIFICATIONS
Gauge: 12
Barrel lengths: 30″ and 32″ (M,IM,F,MC)

Sight: Ventilated rib with flourescent front bead, metal middle bead
Action: Semiautomatic, locked breech, gas operated
Safety: Cross bolt
Ejector: Auto
Trigger: Gold plated
Stock: Select walnut
Weight: 8 lbs.
Butt plate: Special trap recoil pad
Chamber: 2³/₄″

BERNARDELLI SHOTGUNS

Bernardelli shotguns are the creation of the Italian firm of Vincenzo Bernardelli, known for its fine quality firearms and commitment to excellence for more than a century. Most of the long arms featured below can be built with a variety of options, customized for the discriminating sportsman. With the exceptions indicated for each gun respectively, options include choice of barrel lengths and chokes; pistol or straight English grip stock; single selective or non-selective trigger; long tang trigger guard; checkered butt; beavertail forend; hand-cut rib; automatic safety; custom stock dimensions; standard or English recoil pad; extra set of barrels; choice of luggage gun case.

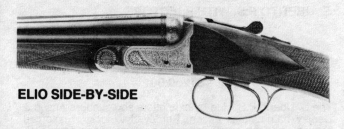

ELIO SIDE-BY-SIDE

ELIO SIDE-BY-SIDE
$1350.00
With Ejectors $1300.00

For gunners who prefer a lightweight 12 gauge double, the Elio weighs about 6¼ pounds and is designed around the Anson-Deeley action with Purdey locks. Intricate English rosette and scroll engraving and a coin finished receiver, fine hand-checkered European walnut stock, hinged front trigger on double trigger models.

BRESCIA SIDE-BY-SIDE

BRESCIA SIDE-BY-SIDE
$1550.00

Available in 12, 16, or 20 gauge, the Brescia side-by-side features Greener or Purdey locks, small engravings, hardened marbled mounting, chrome-lined barrels, finely grained stock.

SLUG LUSSO DELUXE

SLUG SIDE-BY-SIDE
$1080.00 ($1130.00 w/Single Trigger)
SLUG LUSSO DELUXE
$1680.00 ($1730.00 w/Single Trigger)

Especially designed to pattern well with slugs and buckshot, this 12 gauge side-by-side has Anson & Deeley action, Purdey-type locks, reinforced breech, richly engraved hunting scene on white-finish receiver, automatic ejectors, rear adjustable sight with overturning leafs, cheekpiece, double triggers. Deluxe model has fully engraved sideplates.

HEMINGWAY SIDE-BY-SIDE
$1680.00 (not shown)
W/Single Non-selective Trigger $1760.00

An elegant and light 12 gauge side-by-side suitable for upland bird hunting, the Hemingway features 23½-inch barrels without monobloc, right bore open and left one slightly Improved Cylinder, automatic ejectors, special rib with white bead front sight, hinged front trigger, woodcock hunting scenes engraved, long-type trigger guard and forend, hand-checkered walnut woods, metal shield for intials. Special steel frame and barrels. **Weight:** 6¼ lbs.

BERNARDELLI SHOTGUNS

HOLLAND LUSSO

HOLLAND V.B.

HOLLAND LUSSO
HOLLAND V.B.
HOLLAND LISCIO (not shown)

These 12 gauge Holland & Holland style sidelock side-by-sides feature sidelocks with double safety levers, reinforced breech, three round Purdey locks, automatic ejectors, right trigger folding, striker retaining plates, best-quality walnut stock and finely chiselled high-grade engravings. The three shotguns differ only in the amount and intricacy of engravings.

S. UBERTO F.S. WITH EJECTORS

S. UBERTO F.S.
$1140.00
S. UBERTO F.S. WITH EJECTORS
$1250.00

The S. Uberto F.S. side-by-side offers shotgunners Anson & Deeley hammerless action, Purdey-style locks, reinforced breech, fine relief engravings with hunting scenes, finest walnut checkered stock and forend, right trigger folding. Available in 12 and 20 gauge.

S. **Uberto 1** with modest engraving, marbled
   mounting . . . . $ 910.00
S. **Uberto 1E** w/ejectors 1025.00
S. **Uberto 1E** w/ejectors and single trigger 965.00
S. **Uberto 2 E** w/ejectors 1080.00

ROMA 6

ROMA 6
$1655.00
ROMA 6E WITH EJECTORS
$1775.00

Available in 12, or 20 gauge, the Roma 6 is Bernardelli's premier boxlock and a most popular model. This side-by-side shotgun features Anson & Deeley action with Purdey-style locks, sideplated and coin-finished receiver with elaborate scroll engraving covering 100% of the action, precision-bored barrels made of superior chromium steel, double triggers with front hinged trigger, hand-selected European walnut stock and forend with fine, hand-cut checkering.

BROWNING AUTOMATIC SHOTGUNS

"SWEET SIXTEEN"
AUTO-5

AUTO-5

The Browning Auto-5 Shotgun is offered in an unusually wide variety of models and specifications. The Browning 12-gauge 3-inch Magnum accepts up to and including the 3-inch, 1⁷/₈ ounce, 12-gauge Magnum load, which contains only ¹/₈ ounce of shot less than the maximum 3¹/₂-inch 10-gauge load. The 2³/₄-inch Magnums and 2³/₄-inch high velocity shells may be used with equal pattern efficiency. Standard features include a special shock absorber and a hunting-style recoil pad. The Auto-5 is also available with the Invector screw-in choke system.

Browning also offers the 20 gauge in a 3-inch Magnum model. This powerful, light heavyweight offers maximum versatility to 20-gauge advocates. It handles the 20-gauge, 2³/₄-inch high velocity and Magnums, but it literally thrives on the 3-inch, 1¹/₄-ounce load which delivers real 12-gauge performance in a 20-gauge package.

The 12-gauge Auto-5, chambered for regular 2³/₄-inch shells, handles all 12-gauge, 2³/₄-inch shells, from the very lightest 1 ounce field load to the heavy 1¹/₂-ounce Magnums. The Browning 20-gauge Auto-5 is lightweight and a top performer for the upland hunter. Yet, with 2³/₄-inch high velocity or 2³/₄-inch Magnums, it does a fine job in the duck blind.

24-inch barrels are available as an accessory.

Hunting Models:
Light 12, Sweet 16 and Light 20 gauge, Invector . . . **$632.95**
3" Magnum 12 and Magnum 20 gauge, Invector. 652.95
Gold Classic edition, 500 issued 6500.00

BT-99
SINGLE SHOT TRAP SPECIAL

SPECIFICATIONS
Receiver: Machined steel, tastefully hand-engraved and richly blued
Barrel: Choice of 32" or 34" lengths; choke choice of Full, Improved Modified or Modified; chambered for 12 gauge, 2³/₄" shells only
Trigger: Gold-plated, crisp, positive, pull approximately 3¹/₂ lbs.
Stock and forearm: Select French walnut, hand-rubbed finish, sharp 20-line hand-checkering; Monte Carlo or conventional stock available; full pistol grip; length of pull 14³/₈";

drop at comb 1³/₈"; drop at heel 2"; full beavertail forearm
Safety: No manual safety, a feature preferred by trap shooters
Sights: Ivory front and center sight beads
Rib: High post, ventilated, full floating, matted, ¹¹/₃₂" wide
Recoil pad: Deluxe, contoured trap style
Weight: 8 lbs. with 32" barrel; 8 lbs. 3 oz. with 34" barrel
Automatic ejection: Fired shell ejected automatically on opening action, unfired shell elevated from chamber for convenient removal
Grade I Competition, Invector (32" or 34" barrel) . . . **$957.50**
Grade I Competition, Non-Invector **$934.50**

BROWNING AUTOMATIC SHOTGUNS

12 GAUGE B-80 HUNTING MODEL

B-80 PLUS GAS-OPERATED SEMI-AUTOMATIC SHOTGUN

The B-80 now shoots all popular loads, from 2³/₄″ field loads to 3″ magnum steel shot loads, without changing barrels or any adjustments. All barrels are chambered for 3″ shells and fitted with invector choke tubes. Other features include flawless gas operation, softer recoil, square receiver (for longer sighting plane), interchangeable barrels, choice of steel or alloy receivers.

SPECIFICATIONS
Trigger: Crisp and positive
Chamber: All models have 3″ chambers and are designed to shoot all popular loads from 2³/₄″ field to 3″ magnums, including steel shot.
Safety: Cross bolt; red warning band visible when in fire position
Receiver: High strength alloy in light and Magnum models will accept either field or Magnum barrel

Stock and forearm: Walnut skillfully cut-checkered; full pistol grip; length of pull 14¹/₄″; drop at comb 1⁵/₈″; drop at heel 2¹/₂″; a field recoil pad is fitted
Gauge: 12 and 20 gauge
Barrels: 12 and 20 gauge interchangeable spare barrels available with either 2³/₄″ or 3″ chambers; barrels are equipped with ventilated ribs except Buck Special barrels which have adjustable rifle sights; barrels of the same gauge are interchangeable; all models except Buck Special barrels are fitted with Invector Choke Tube System
Magazine capacity (including one in chamber): 4 (2³/₄″ or 3″ loads); reduced to 3 (2³/₄″ or 3″ magnum)

Prices
Invector, Alloy & Steel (12 and 20 Ga.) $561.95
Extra barrels $125.00–198.00

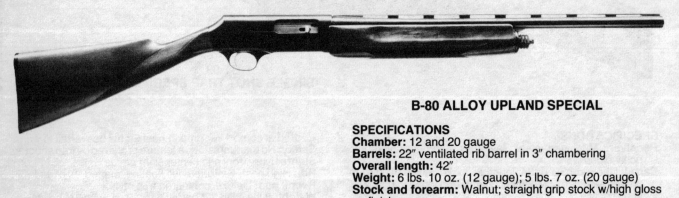

B-80 ALLOY UPLAND SPECIAL

SPECIFICATIONS
Chamber: 12 and 20 gauge
Barrels: 22″ ventilated rib barrel in 3″ chambering
Overall length: 42″
Weight: 6 lbs. 10 oz. (12 gauge); 5 lbs. 7 oz. (20 gauge)
Stock and forearm: Walnut; straight grip stock w/high gloss finish
Length of pull: 14″
Drop at comb: 1¹/₂″
Drop at heel: 2¹/₂″

B-80 Upland Special $561.95

BROWNING SHOTGUNS

CITORI STANDARD

CITORI TRAP & SKEET MODELS

FIELD GRADE
Gauge: 12, 16, 20, 28 and .410 gauge
Barrels: 24", 26", 28", or 30" in 12 gauge; 28" in 16 gauge; 24", 26", or 28" in 20 gauge; ventilated rib with matted sighting plane; medium raised German nickel-silver sight bead; 26" or 28" in 28 gauge; 26" or 28" in .410 gauge
Overall length: All gauges 41" with 24" barrels; 43" with 26" barrels; 45" with 28" barrels; 47" with 30" barrels
Chokes: Mod.-Full, Invector in 30" barrels; choice of Invector, Mod.-Full or Imp. Cyl.-Mod. in 28" and 26" barrels
Trigger: Single selective; gold-plated, fast and crisp
Chamber: All 20-gauge Field models and all 12-gauge Field models accept all 3" Magnum loads as well as 2³/₄" loads; 16 and 28-gauge accepts 2³/₄" loads; .410-gauge accepts 2¹/₂", 3", or 3" Mag. loads

Safety: Manual thumb safety; combined with barrel selector mechanism
Automatic ejectors: Fired shells thrown out of gun; unfired shells are elevated for easy removal
Approximate Weight:

	12 gauge	16 gauge	20 gauge
24" barrels	6 lbs. 9 oz.		5 lbs. 12 oz.
26" barrels	7 lbs. 9 oz.		6 lbs. 11 oz.
28" barrels	7 lbs. 11 oz.	7 lbs	6 lbs. 13 oz.
30" barrels	7 lbs. 13 oz		

Stock and forearm: Dense walnut; skillfully checkered; full pistol grip; hunting Beavertail forearm; field-type recoil pad installed on 12 gauge models.

	12 gauge	20 gauge
Length of pull	14¹/₄"	14¹/₄"
Drop at comb	1⁵/₈"	1¹/₂"
Drop at heel	2¹/₂"	2³/₈"

HUNTING, SUPERLIGHT, UPLAND SPECIAL & SPORTER MODELS*

HUNTING & LIGHTNING 28 GAUGE & .410 BOREPRICES

Grade I Hunting	$ 892.00
Grade I Lightning	902.00
Grade III Hunting	1342.00
Grade III Lightning	1352.00
Grade VI Hunting	1895.00
Grade VI Lightning	1905.00

SUPERLIGHT 12 & 20 GAUGE

Grade I Invector	928.00
Grade III Invector	1220.00
Grade VI Invector	1790.00

UPLAND SPECIAL 12 & 20 GAUGE

Grade I	902.00
Grade I Lightning	912.00
Grade III	1220.00
Grade III Lightning	1230.00
Grade VI	1790.00
Grade VI Lightning	1800.00

*NOTE : All Invector model Citori's are available in the High Grades.

SUPERLIGHT 28 GAUGE & .410 BORE

Grade I	$ 892.00
Grade III	1342.00
Grade VI	1895.00

TRAP MODELS (High Post Target Rib)
Standard 12 Gauge

Grade I Invector	$1010.00
Grade III	1342.00
Grade VI Invector	1895.00

SKEET MODELS (High Post Target Rib)
Standard 12 and 20 Gauge

Grade I Invector	998.00
Grade I	966.00
Grade III	1342.00
Grade VI	1895.00

Standard 28 Gauge and .410 Bore

Grade I	1010.00
Grade III	1342.00
Grade VI	1895.00

4-BARREL SKEET SET
12 Gauge with one removable forearm and four sets of barrels, 12, 20, 28 and .410 gauges, high post target rib.
(Furnished with fitted luggage case for gun and extra barrels)

Grade 1	$3235.00
Grade III	3550.00
Grade VI	4035.00

BROWNING SHOTGUNS

BPS PUMP

BPS PUMP SHOTGUN

Gauge: 10, 12 and 20
Barrels: Choice of 22″, 26″, 28″, 30″ or 32″ lengths with high-post ventilated rib; Hunting model has German nickel sight bead
Action: Pump action with double-action bars; bottom loading and ejection; serrated slide release located at rear of trigger guard
Choke: Invector only
Trigger: Crisp and positive; let-off at 4¹/₂ lbs.
Chamber: 3″ chamber in Hunting models accepts all 2³/₄″, 2³/₄″ Magnum and 3″ Magnum shells; target models 2³/₄″ shells only
Safety: Convenient knurled-thumb, top-receiver safety; slide forward to shoot

Approximate weight: 7 lbs. 12 oz. with 28″ barrel
Overall length: 42³/₄″ with 22″ barrel; 46³/₄″ with 26″ barrel; 48³/₄″ with 28″ barrel; 50³/₄″ with 30″ barrel
Stock and forearm: Select walnut, weather-resistant finish, sharp 18-line checkering; full pistol grip; semi-beavertail forearm with finger grooves; length of pull 14¹/₄″; drop at comb 1¹/₂″; drop at heel 2¹/₂″

Invector Hunting, 12 and 20 ga., V.R. **$412.50**
Invector Hunting, 10 ga.. . . . . **471.95**
Upland Special, 22 ″ barrel with Invector,
    12 and 20 ga., V.R. **412.50**
Invector Stalker, 12 ga. only **412.50**
Buck Special, 12 ga. only **418.50**

BPS YOUTH & LADIES MODEL

SPECIFICATIONS
Chamber: 20 gauge only
Barrels: 22″ invector w/ventilated rib; interchangeable within gauge
Overall length: 41³/₄″
Weight (approx.): 6 lbs. 11 oz.
Stock and forearm: Straight grip stock of select walnut in durable gloss finish
Length of pull: 13¹/₄″
Drop at comb: 1¹/₂″
Drop at heel: 2¹/₂″

BPS Youth & Ladies Model **$412.50**

BROWNING SHOTGUNS

MODEL 12 PUMP SHOTGUN

After more than 75 years, the ageless Winchester Model 12, one of the most popular shotguns ever produced (over 2 million), is offered as part of Browning's Limited Edition Model 12 Program. The first Model 12 is available in 20 gauge, with 28 gauge and .410 bore (Model 42) to follow. A total of 12,500 20 gauge Model 12's will be produced, including 8,500 Grade I models and 4,000 Grade V's.

SPECIFICATIONS
Gauge: 20
Barrel length: 26″
Overall length: 45″
Chamber: 2³/₄″
Choke: Modified
Weight: 7 lbs. 1 oz.
Length of pull: 14″
Drop at heel: 2¹/₂″
Drop at comb: 1¹/₂″
Trigger: Approx. 4¹/₂ lbs. trigger pull

Capacity: 5 loads in magazine (w/plug removed), one in chamber; 2 loads in magazine (w/plug installed), one in chamber
Receiver: Grade I: deeply blued. Grade V: engraved with gold game scenes
Stock and forearm: Grade I: select walnut w/semi-gloss finish and cut checkering. Grade V: select high grade walnut with high gloss finish (both grades include steel grip cap)

GRADE I . . . . $ 699.95
GRADE V 1100.00

MODEL A-500 12 GAUGE SEMIAUTOMATIC

Designed and built in Belgium, the A-500 employs a short recoil system with a strong four-lug bolt design. There is no gas system to collect powder residues or grime, and no pistons, ports or cylinders to clean. Only one extractor is needed to pull the shell from the chamber. The stock has no drilled holes to accommodate action springs, making it that much stronger (especially where it bolts against the receiver).

SPECIFICATIONS
Barrel lengths: 26″, 28″ and 30″
Overall lengths: 45¹/₂″, 47¹/₂″ and 49¹/₂″

Weight: 7 lbs. 3 oz. (26″ barrel); 7 lbs. 5 oz. (28″ barrel) and 7 lbs. 7 oz. (30″ barrel)
Chamber: 3″
Choke: Invector
Stock dimensions: length of pull 14¹/₄″; drop at comb 1¹/₂″; drop at heel 2¹/₂″
Safety: cross bolt, right or left hand
Action: short recoil operated with four lug rotary bolt
Barrel/receiver finish: deep high polish blued finish; receiver lightly engraved with scroll pattern
Model A-500 . . . . $552.00
Extra barrels 199.95

CHURCHILL SHOTGUNS

REGENT VII
$889.00 (with full side plates)

The Regent Grade over/under shotguns feature an 11 mm-wide ventilated rib, single selective trigger, automatic top tang safety, selective automatic ejectors and 2³/₄-inch (70 mm) chambers.

Barrels: 27″ long; chrome molybdenum steel with silver braised monobloc; insides of barrels are fully chromed; wide ventilated rib

Gauge/chokes: 12 and 20 gauge with ICT (interchangeable choke tubes) in Imp. Cyl./Mod./Full

Action: Forged nickel-chrome steel heat-treated for hardness before and after machining; engraved hunting scene in antique silver finish

Locks: Double bottom lock, made up of two smooth-fitting lugs, formed by an ingenious sliding bolt that inserts into special slots in the lugs

Trigger: Single-selective trigger working off an inertia block; selection of the barrel is done by moving the safety button; the recoil of the first shot moves the block from one sear to the other to set up the second shot

Ejectors: Selective automatic

Stock: Fashioned from extra select fancy walnut in a genuine oil-rubbed finish with pistol grip; precise 22 line hand-checkering

REGENT GRADE COMPETITION SHOTGUNS

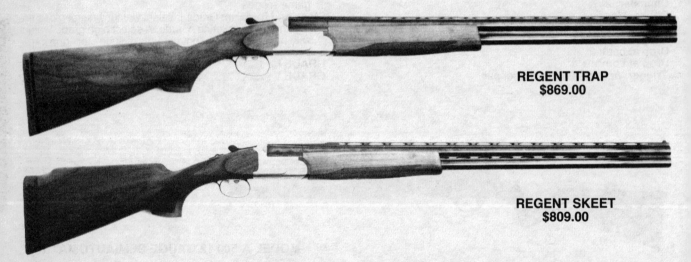

REGENT TRAP
$869.00

REGENT SKEET
$809.00

These competition shotguns feature selective automatic ejectors, chrome bores, single-selective triggers, safety and wide ventilated ribs. The Regent Trap model, in 12 gauge, has ventilated side ribs and is furnished with Monte Carlo stock and Supercushion recoil pad. The Regent Skeet is available in both 12 and 20 gauge.

MODEL	Gauge	Chamber	Barrel Length	Chokes	Overall Length	Length of Pull	Drop at Comb	Drop at Heel	Nominal Weight
GP7802 TRAP	12	2.75″	30″	IM & F	47.25″	14.5″	1.36″	1.5″	8 lbs.
GP7829 SKEET	12	2.75″	26″	SK & SK	43.94″	14.5″	1.5″	2.36″	7 lbs.
GP7853 SKEET	20	2.75″	26″	SK & SK	43.94″	14.5″	1.5″	2.36″	7 lbs.

CHURCHILL SHOTGUNS

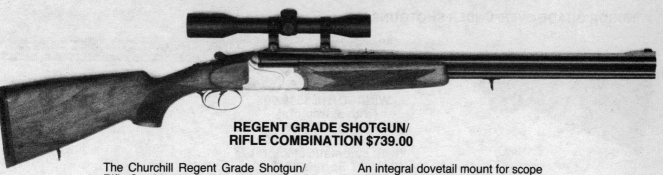

REGENT GRADE SHOTGUN/ RIFLE COMBINATION $739.00

The Churchill Regent Grade Shotgun/ Rifle Combination is the ultimate in performance and classic design for the over/under enthusiast. The multi-purpose gun is available in 12 gauge (Modified choke with 3″ chamber) over the following caliber rifle barrels: .222 Rem., .223 Rem., .243 Win., .270 Win., .308 Win. and 30-06 Spfd.

An integral dovetail mount for scope mounting, integral iron sights and a finely engraved antique silver finish reinforced receiver are all standard features. The extra-select European walnut stock has been meticulously hand-checkered in a natural oil finish. Incorporated in the buttstock is a Monte-Carlo cheekpiece.

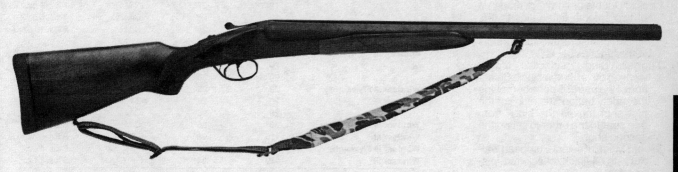

WINDSOR I GRADE SIDE-BY-SIDE SHOTGUNS

WINDSOR I $559.00
WINDSOR I 10 GA. $679.00
WINDSOR I w/ICT $629.00
WINDSOR I 10GA. w/ICT $759.00
WINDSOR I 28GA. & .410 GA.
$569.00

Perfect balance, elegance of line, richness of beautiful woods and careful fitting of metal to wood are the essence of Churchill shotguns.

Windsor I side-by-side shotguns are available in all gauges from 10 to .410 and in a wide range of barrels and chokes.

Windsor I Specifications (Side by Side)

Model	Gauge	Barrel Length	Chokes	Weight
Windsor I	10	32″	F/F	11 lbs. 6 oz.
	10	32″	IC/M/M	11 lbs. 8 oz.
	10	26″	IC/M/F	10 lbs. 15 oz.
	12	32″	F/F	8 lbs. 4 oz.
	12	30″	F/F	8 lbs.
	12	30″	M/F	8 lbs.
	12	28″	M/F	7 lbs. 9 oz.
	12	27″	IC/M/F	7 lbs. 9 oz.
	12	26″	IC/M	7 lbs. 4 oz.
Windsor I Flyweight	12	25″	IC/M	7 lbs.
Windsor I	16	28″	M/F	6 lbs. 8 oz.
Windsor I Flyweight	16	25″	IC/M	6 lbs. 6 oz.
Windsor I	20	28″	M/F	6 lbs. 6 oz.
	20	27″	IC/M/F	6 lbs. 8 oz.
	20	26″	IC/M	6 lbs. 4 oz.
	20	24″	M/F	6 lbs.
Windsor I Flyweight	20	23″	IC/M	6 lbs.
Windsor I	28	25″	SK/SK	6 lbs. 6 oz.
	28	25″	M/F	6 lbs. 6 oz.
Windsor I Flyweight	28	23″	IC/M	6 lbs. 3 oz.
Windsor I	.410	26″	M/F	6 lbs. 7 oz.
	.410	24″	M/F	6 lbs.
Windsor I Flyweight	.410	23″	F/F	5 lbs. 12 oz.

CHURCHILL SHOTGUNS

WINDSOR GRADE OVER/UNDER SHOTGUNS

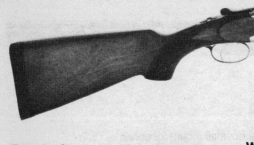

WINDSOR III OVER/UNDER

WINDSOR III $549.00
(with extractors)
With ICT Barrels $649.00
WINDSOR IV $619.00
(with automatic ejectors)
With ICT Barrels $719.00
WINDSOR III .410GA. $599.00

Barrels: Chrome molybdenum steel with silver braised monobloc; insides of barrels are fully chromed; ventilated rib

Action: Forged nickel-chrome steel heat-treated for hardness before and after machining; richly engraved game scenes on antique silver finish

Locks: Double bottom lock made up of two smooth fitting lugs that is formed by an ingenious sliding bolt which inserts into special slots in the lugs

Trigger: Single selective trigger working off an inertia block. Selection of the barrel is done by moving the safety button; the recoil of the first shot moves the block from one sear to the other to set up the second shot

Stock: Made of select European walnut with oil finish; checkered; pistol grip

WINDSOR III SPECIFICATIONS (OVER/UNDER)

Model	Gauge	Barrel Length	Chokes	Weight
Windsor III	12	30″	M/F,F/F	7 lbs. 8 oz.
	12	30″	M/F/XF	7 lbs. 10 oz.
	12	28″	M/F	7 lbs. 7 oz.
	12	27″	IC/M/F	7 lbs. 8 oz.
	12	26″	IC/M	7 lbs. 6 oz.
Windsor III Flyweight	12	25″	IC/M	6 lbs. 10 oz.
Windsor III	20	28″	M/F	6 lbs. 8 oz.
	20	27″	IC/M/F	6 lbs. 8 oz.
	20	26″	IC/M	6 lbs. 6 oz.
Windsor III Flyweight	20	25″	IC/M	5 lbs. 12 oz.
Windsor III	28	28″	M/F	6 lbs. 8 oz.
	28	26″	IC/M	6 lbs. 4 oz.
Windsor III Flyweight	28	25″	IC/M	6 lbs. 2 oz.
Windsor III	.410	26″	F/F	6 lbs. 6 oz.
Windsor III Flyweight	.410	25″	F/F	6 lbs. 4 oz.
Windsor III	.410	24″	F/F	6 lbs. 3 oz.

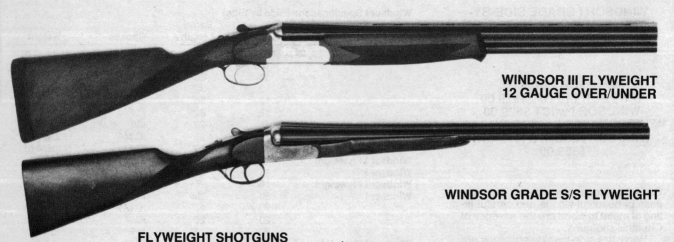

WINDSOR III FLYWEIGHT 12 GAUGE OVER/UNDER

WINDSOR GRADE S/S FLYWEIGHT

FLYWEIGHT SHOTGUNS

Churchill Flyweight shotguns are right for ultra-responsive, fast-handling upland game hunting. The English-style straight grip buttstock and 23-inch or 25-inch barrels contribute to the line's fast and sure handling characteristics.

Churchill Flyweights are available with either Interchangeable Choke Tubes (ICT) or traditional chokes, in a wide range of side by sides, over/unders. They incorporate all the standard features found in the traditional line of Churchill shotguns.

CHURCHILL SHOTGUNS

Windsor IV Specifications (Over/Under)

Model	Gauge	Barrel Length	Chokes	Weight
Windsor IV	12	30″	F/F	7 lbs. 8 oz.
	12	30″	M/F	7 lbs. 8 oz.
	12	30″	M/F/XF	7 lbs. 10 oz.
	12	28″	M/F	7 lbs. 7 oz.
	12	27″	IC/M/F	7 lbs. 8 oz.
	12	26″	IC/M	7 lbs. 6 oz.
	12	26″	SK/SK	7 lbs. 6 oz.
Windsor IV Flyweight	12	25″	IC/M	6 lbs. 13 oz.
Windsor IV	20	28″	M/F	6 lbs. 8 oz.
	20	27″	IC/M/F	6 lbs. 8 oz.
	20	26″	IC/M	6 lbs. 6 oz.
	20	26″	SK/Sk	6 lbs. 6 oz.
Windsor IV Flyweight	20	25″	IC/M	6 lbs. 3 oz.
Windsor IV	28	28″	M/F	6 lbs. 8 oz.
	28	26″	IC/M	6 lbs. 5 oz.
Windsor IV Flyweight	28	25″	IC/M	6 lbs. 4 oz.
Windsor IV	.410	26″	F/F	6 lbs. 4 oz.
Windsor IV Flyweight	.410	25″	F/F	6 lbs. 3 oz.
Windsor IV	.410	24″	F/F	6 lbs. 3 oz.

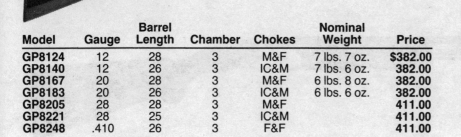

Model	Gauge	Barrel Length	Chamber	Chokes	Nominal Weight	Price
GP8124	12	28	3	M&F	7 lbs. 7 oz.	$382.00
GP8140	12	26	3	IC&M	7 lbs. 6 oz.	382.00
GP8167	20	28	3	M&F	6 lbs. 8 oz.	382.00
GP8183	20	26	3	IC&M	6 lbs. 6 oz.	382.00
GP8205	28	28	3	M&F		411.00
GP8221	28	25	3	IC&M		411.00
GP8248	.410	26	3	F&F		411.00

MONARCH OVER/UNDER

The Churchill Monarch over/under shotguns feature a high-lustre blued receiver, gold plated single selective trigger, ventilated rib, and European walnut stock with checkering and a protective polyurethane finish. Double bottom lock, made up of two smooth fitting lugs, is formed by an ingenious sliding bolt which inserts into special slots in the lugs. Available in 12, 20, and new flyweight 28 and .410 gauge models.

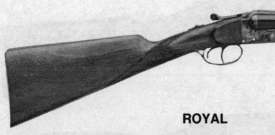

ROYAL

The new Royal side-by-side features chromed barrels with concave rib, double-hinged triggers, extractors, case-hardened receivers and English-style checkered European walnut stock.

SPECIFICATIONS

Gauges: 12, 16, 20. 28 and .410
Barrel lengths: 25″ (28 ga.), 26″ (12, 16 and .410 ga.), and 28″ (12, 16, 20 ga.)
Chamber: 2¾″ (16 ga.) and 3″ (12, 20, 28, .410 ga.)
Chokes: M/F (12, 16, 20, 28 ga.); IC/M (12, 20 ga.) and F/F (.410 ga.)
Weight: 5 lbs. 13 oz. (28 and .410 ga.); 6 lbs. (20 ga. IC/M); 6 lbs. 2 oz. (16 and 20 ga.M/F); 6 lbs. 6 oz. 12 ga. IC/M); 6 lbs. 8 oz.(12 ga. M/F)
Prices:
12, 16 and 20 Gauge $559.00
28 Gauge 579.00
.410 Gauge 58.00

CLASSIC DOUBLES

MODEL 101 OVER/UNDER

Formerly distributed by Olin/Winchester, Model 101 has been acquired by Classic Doubles International. These guns will continue to be produced in Japan by OK Firearms. All models feature chrome molybdenum steel barrels with chrome-lined chambers and bores suitable for steel shot, plus forged steel frames and trigger guards, single selective triggers, and top-grade semi-fancy American walnut.

Included in the new Classic Doubles line is Olin/Winchester's former Model 23 side-by-side, which is now Model 201. Prices and specifications for all models are listed below.

Prices:

MODEL 101 FIELD GRADE I	$2335.00
Waterfowler	1865.00
MODEL 101 FIELD GRADE II	2685.00
Field Set	4190.00
MODEL 101 SPORTERS	2425.00
Combo (28" and 30" Barrels)	3610.00
MODEL 101 TRAP SINGLE BARREL	2535.00
Over/Under	2335.00
Combo (Over/Under Single)	3460.00
MODEL 101 SKEET	2335.00
Four-Barrel Set (12, 20, 28, .410)	5840.00
MODEL 201 SIDE/SIDE GRADE I (12 Ga.)	2335.00
20 Ga. Skeet/Skeet Choke	2830.00
Set (28 & .410 Ga.)	4500.00

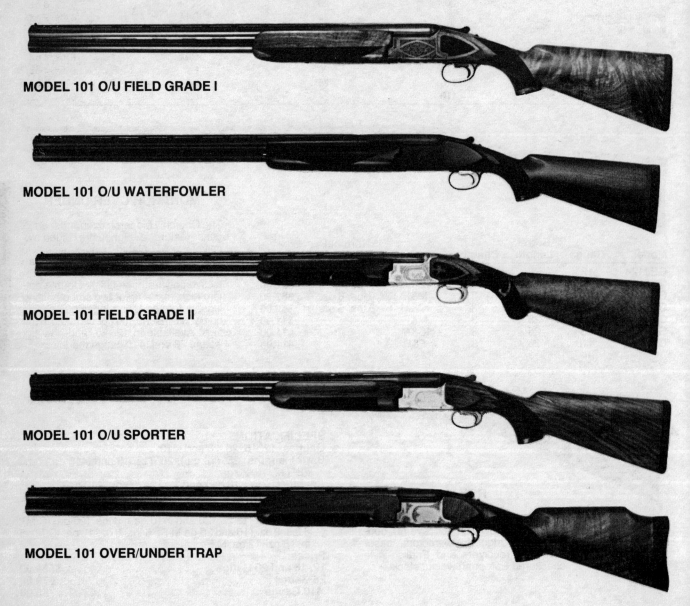

MODEL 101 O/U FIELD GRADE I

MODEL 101 O/U WATERFOWLER

MODEL 101 FIELD GRADE II

MODEL 101 O/U SPORTER

MODEL 101 OVER/UNDER TRAP

CLASSIC DOUBLES

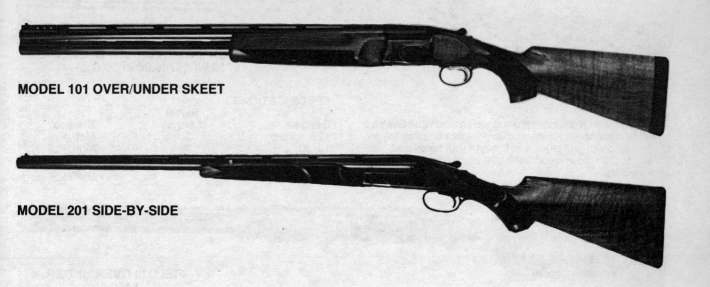

MODEL 101 OVER/UNDER SKEET

MODEL 201 SIDE-BY-SIDE

Model	Symbol	Gauge	BBL Lgth.	O/A Lgth.	Lgth. of Pull	Drop at Comb	Drop at Heel	Nominal Weight	Choke	Stock
M101 Field-Grade I	B1012W	12	28"	44⁷/₈"	14½"	1½"	2¼"	7	In Choke 6	Standard
	B1012EW	12	25½"	42¼"	14½"	1½"	2½"	6¾	In Choke 6	Straight English
	B1015W	20	28"	44⁷/₈"	14½"	1½"	2¼"	6½	In Choke 4	Standard
	B1015EW	20	25½"	42¼"	14½"	1½"	2½"	6¼	In Choke 4	Straight English
M101 Field-Grade II	A1012W	12	28"	44⁷/₈"	14½"	1½"	2¼"	7	In Choke 6	Standard
	A1015W	20	28"	44⁷/₈"	14½"	1½"	2¼"	6½	In Choke 4	Standard
	A1017W	28	28"	44⁷/₈"	14½"	1½"	2¼"	6½	In Choke 4	Standard
	A1019	410	28"	44⁷/₈"	14½"	1½"	2¼"	6¼	M/F	Standard
SET	A10128W2	12/20	28"/26"	44⁷/₈"/42⁷/₈"	14½"	1½"	2¼"	7/6½	In Choke 6/4	Standard
M101 Waterfowler	101CWF	12	30"	46⁷/₈"	14½"	1½"	2¼"	7½	In Choke 4	Standard
M101 Sporter *New Model*	101SP28W	12	28"	44⁷/₈"	14½"	1½"	2⅛"	7	In Choke 6	Standard
	101SP20W	12	30"	46⁷/₈"	14½"	1½"	2⅛"	7¼	In Choke 6	Standard
COMBO	101SP28W2	12	28"/30"	44⁷/₈"/46⁷/₈"	14½"	1½"	2⅛"	7/7¼	In Choke 6	Standard
M101 Trap Single	101T014M	12	34"	51¼"	14½"	1⁷/₁₆"	2³/₁₆"	8½	In Choke 4	Monte Carlo
Single	101T014S	12	34"	51¼"	14½"	1⁷/₁₆"	1⁷/₁₆"	8½	In Choke 4	Standard
Single	101T0112M	12	32"	49¼"	14½"	1⁷/₁₆"	2³/₁₆"	8½	In Choke 4	Monte Carlo
Single	101T012S	12	32"	49¼"	14½"	1⁷/₁₆"	1⁷/₁₆"	8½	In Choke 4	Standard
O/U	101T20M	12	30"	47¼"	14½"	1⅜"	2⅛"	8¾	In Choke 4	Monte Carlo
O/U	101T20S	12	30"	47¼"	14½"	1⅜"	1⅜"	8¾	In Choke 4	Standard
O/U	101T22M	12	32"	49¼"	14½"	1⅜"	2⅛"	9	In Choke 4	Monte Carlo
O/U	101T22S	12	32"	49¼"	14½"	1⅜"	1⅜"	9	In Choke 4	Standard
COMBO; O/U-Single	101T30M	12	30"–34"	47¼"–51¼"	14½"	1⅜"	2⅛"	9–8¾	In Choke 4	Monte Carlo
O/U-Single	101T30S	12	30"–34"	47¼"–51¼"	14½"	1⅜"	1⅜"	9–8¾	In Choke 4	Standard
O/U-Single	101T302M	12	30"–32"	47¼"–49¼"	14½"	1⅜"	2⅛"	9–8¾	In Choke 4	Monte Carlo
O/U-Single	101T302S	12	30"–32"	47¼"–49¼"	14½"	1⅜"	1⅜"	9–8¾	In Choke 4	Standard
O/U-Single	101T32M	12	32"–34"	49¼"–51¼"	14½"	1⅜"	2⅛"	9–8¾	In Choke 4	Monte Carlo
O/U-Single	101T32S	12	32"–34"	49¼"–51¼"	14½"	1⅜"	1⅜"	9–8¾	In Choke 4	Standard
M101 Skeet	101527W	12	27½"	44⅝"	14¼"	1⅜"	2⅛"	7¼	In Choke 4	Standard
	101557	20	27½"	44⅝"	14¼"	1⅜"	2⅛"	6½	SK/SK	Standard
	10154	12,20,28,410	27½"	44⅝"	14¼"	1½"	2⅛"	7½	SK/SK	Standard
M201 Side-by-Side *New Model*	201C2	12	26"	43¼"	14½"	1½"	2¼"	7	IC/M	Standard
	201C2W	12	26"	43¼"	14½"	1½"	2¼"	7	In Choke 6	Standard
	201C5	20	26"	43¼"	14½"	1½"	2¼"	7	IC/M	Standard
	201C5E	20	26"	43¼"	14½"	1½"	2¼"	7	IC/M	Straight English
SET	201C79	28/410	28"	45¼"	14½"	1½"	2¼"	6½/5⁷/₈	IC/M,M/F	Standard

CHARLES DALY SHOTGUNS

SUPERIOR II OVER/UNDER 12 GAUGE
$710.00   ($749.00 in 20 Ga.)

The Superior II Over/Under is a rugged shotgun that boasts a beautifully engraved silver receiver, single selective trigger, checkered pistol grip stock and forearm with recoil pad, ventilated rib, high-gloss wood finish with blued barrels. Selective auto ejectors.

SPECIFICATIONS

Gauge	Barrel Length	Chokes
12 Magnum	30"	Mod./Full
12, 20	28"	Mod./Full
12, 20	26"	Imp. Cyl./Mod.
12, 20	26"	Skeet

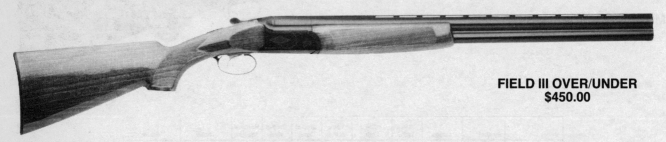

FIELD III OVER/UNDER
$450.00

This field grade over/under offers the same fine features as the other Charles Daly shotguns: excellent construction with a sound marriage of metal to wood. Checkered pistol grip and forearm, straight stock with high-gloss finish, 26- or 28-inch barrels with ventilated rib and single selective trigger. Non-selective extractors.

SPECIFICATIONS

Gauge	Barrel Length	Chokes
12 or 20	28"	Mod./Full
12 or 20	26"	Imp. Cyl./Mod.

GAS AUTOMATIC
From $365.00

The Charles Daly gas automatic features Invector Choke System with wrench; 12 gauge model available with 27-inch barrels; 12 gauge Magnum comes with 30-inch barrels. Ventilated rib.

Also available is a 12 gauge slug gun model with a 20" barrel and a "Super Field" model with a 23" barrel and Invector Choke System. The "Multi-XII" model (12 gauge only) features vent. rib w/Invector choke and fires 2³/₄"or 3" magnum shells interchangeably.

OVER/UNDER DIAMOND TRAP AND SKEET (not shown)
TRAP: $1050.00   SKEET: $1000.00

The 12 gauge Trap gun features a 30-inch ventilated rib barrel choked Improved Modified/Full, Monte Carlo stock with non-slip recoil pad, extra strong reinforced receiver, selective trigger and shell ejector.

The 12 gauge Skeet version is available with 26-inch barrels choked Skeet/Skeet, competition ventilated rib, oil-finished stock with non-slip recoil pad, selective trigger, separate shell ejectors.

FERLIB SHOTGUNS

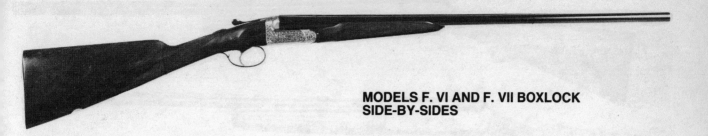

MODELS F. VI AND F. VII BOXLOCK SIDE-BY-SIDES

Hand-crafted by the small European artisan firm of the same name, Ferlib shotguns are high-quality, hand-fitted side-by-sides. With Anson & Deeley boxlock design, all Ferlib doubles are available in 12, 16, 20 and 28 gauge and .410 bore, with automatic ejectors, double triggers with front trigger hinged (non-selective single trigger is optional), hand-rubbed oil-finished straight grip stock with classic forearm (beavertail optional). Dovetail lump barrels have soft-luster blued finish; top rib is concave with file-cut matting. **Barrel length:** 25"-28". **Stock dimensions:** Length of pull, 14$\frac{1}{2}$"; drop at comb, 1$\frac{1}{2}$"; drop at heel, 2$\frac{1}{4}$. **Weight:** 12 ga., 6 lbs. 8 oz.–6 lbs. 14 oz.; 16 ga., 6 lbs. 4 oz.–6 lbs. 10 oz.; 20 ga., 5 lbs. 14 oz.–6 lbs. 4 oz.; 28 ga. and .410, 5 lbs. 6 oz.–5 lbs. 11 oz.

Model F. VI w/scalloped frame, border-line engraving, case-hardened colors, select walnut stock **$3750.00**
Model F. VII w/scalloped frame, full-coverage English scroll engraving, coin finish, select walnut stock **$4750.00**
Model F. VII/SC w/scalloped frame, game scene with either bulino engraved or gold inlayed birds and scroll accents with coin finish, special walnut stock with extra figure and color **$6100.00**
Model F. VII/SC sideplated game scene engraving with gold inlayed birds and coin finish, special walnut stock, extra figure and color **$7100.00**

F.I.E. SHOTGUNS

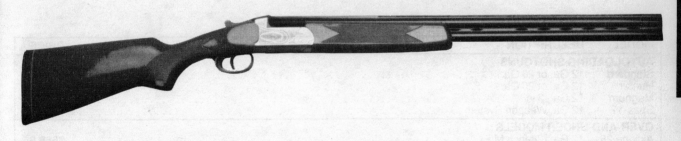

OVER/UNDER 12 & 20 GAUGE

Built in Brescia, Italy, for the shooting enthusiast who wants an over-under shotgun at an affordable price, F.I.E.'s over/under models accommodate all shells, including 3" Magnums. Other features include chrome-lined 26" and 28" barrels, modified and full chokes, ventilated rib, brass bead front sight, automatic safety, checkered European walnut stock and forend, and crossbolt locking system. The receiver is finished in brushed chrome engraved with game scenes.

In addition, the Deluxe model features a single selective trigger, screw-in choke tubes (full, modified, I.C., I.M., and cyl-

inder), epoxy wood finish, auto ejectors, and scroll engraving. The "Priti" Model has all the same features as the standard model, but with epoxy wood finish, scroll engraving, and rubber recoil pad.

Prices:
Standard O/U **$349.95**
Deluxe O/U 519.95
Priti Deluxe O/U 379.95

FRANCHI AUTOLOADING SHOTGUNS

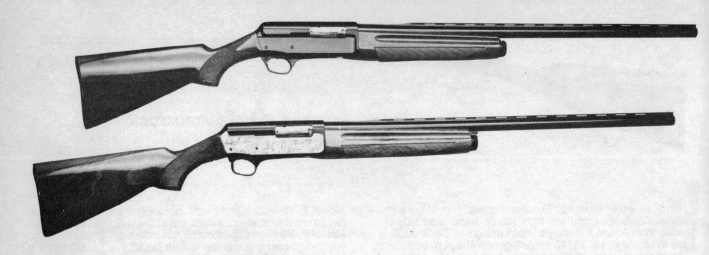

MODEL 48/AL ULTRA LIGHT
12 or 20 GAUGE WITH VENT RIB

Model 48/AL Ultra Lights feature specially selected European stock, forend; fully engraved light weight receiver covered by a lifetime guarantee; the automatic safety, which securely locks the hammer, is silent and positive; hand safety can be reversed for left-handed shooters; chrome-lined barrel for light weight and maximum strength; checkered pistol grip; reliable recoil action requiring no maintenance and no cleaning. Chambered for 2¾ shells.

SPECIFICATIONS
Gauge: 12, 20, 12 ga. Magnum

Barrel lengths (and chokes): 24″ (slug w/rifled sights; cylinder bore; improved cylinder); 26″ (cylinder bore; improved cylinder; modified); 28″ (full & modified); 30″ (full); 32″ (full)
Mechanism: Recoil
Chamber: 2¾″ (3″ in 12 ga. Magnum)
Overall length: 47⅞″ (w/28″ barrel)
Weight: 6 lbs. 4 oz. (12 ga.); 5 lbs. 2 oz. (20 ga)
Capacity: 5 shots
Safety: Lateral push button safety
Stock: Stock and forearm have machine cut diamond checkering (Magnum models equipped with recoil pads)

MODEL 48 ULTRA-LIGHT AUTOLOADERS

MODEL	DESCRIPTION	PRICE
AUTOLOADING SHOTGUNS		
Standard	12 Ga. or 20 Ga..................................	**$439.95**
Hunter	12 Ga. or 20 Ga..................................	474.95
Magnum	12 Ga., 3 in.	474.95
Spas-12	12 Ga. Weapon System	559.95
OVER-AND-UNDER MODELS		
Alcione 28	12 Ga. (28-inch M/F)	**$669.95**
Alcione 26	12 Ga. (26-inch I.C./M).........................	669.95

BARREL LENGTH AND CHOKE SELECTION		24″ Slug. R/S	24″ Cyl. V/R	24″ IC V/R	26″ Cyl. V/R	26″ Skeet V/R	24″ IC V/R	26″ Mod. V/R	28″ Mod. V/R	28″ Full V/R	30″ Full V/R	32″ Full V/R
	12 Gauge	X	X	X	X	X	X	X	X	X	X	X
	20 Gauge	X	X	X	X	X	X	X	X	X	X	

R/S = Rifle sights   V/R = Vent. rib

FRANCHI AUTOLOADING SHOTGUNS

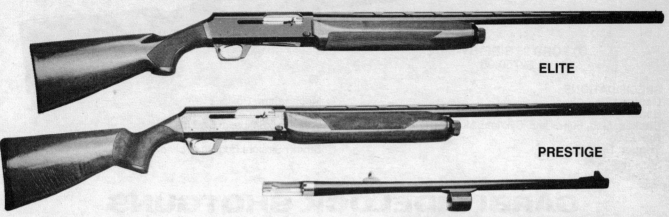

ELITE

PRESTIGE

GAS-OPERATED SEMIAUTOMATICS
PRESTIGE & ELITE MODELS

SPECIFICATIONS
Gauge: 12 (2¾" chamber)
Mechanism: Gas operated semiautomatic
Magazine capacity: 5
Barrel lengths (and chokes): 24" (slug barrel w/rifles sights); 26" (Modified, Improved cylinder); 28" (Full/Modified); 30" (Full)
Overall length: 50"
Weight: 7 lbs. 6 oz.
Features: Double cocking slide (dual rails); chrome plated sleeve; stainless steel piston; patented magazine disconnect system; gold plated trigger
Finish: Hand rubbed satin finish; grip holding checkering
Note: Elite Model features hand filed ventilated rib (7mm wide to reduce glare); red phosphorescent front sight; European walnut stock and forend; oil finish w/hand patterned checkering on forend and pistol grip stock; engraved receiver illustrates shooting scenes
Prices: $474.95 (Prestige)
　　　　524.95 (Elite)

GAMBA SHOTGUNS

PRINCIPESSA SIDE-BY-SIDE
$2000.00

SPECIFICATIONS
Gauges: 12 and 20
Barrel length: 28" or 26¾" (20 ga.)
Chokes: Modified full or Imp. Cycl./Imp. Modified (4/2)
Rib: Plain
Trigger: Double or single trigger by request
Ejectors: Automatic

Mechanism: Boxlock
Stock: Straight English
Forend: Standard
Weight: 6.62 lbs. (12 ga.) or 6.18 lbs. (20 ga.)
Action: Made from special heat-treated chrome-nickel-molybdenum steel; case hardened finish (or color casehardened by request)

GAMBA SHOTGUNS

OXFORD 90 SIDE-BY-SIDE
$2750.00

SPECIFICATIONS
Gauge: 12
Barrel lengths: 27½″ or 26¾″
Chokes: Mod. Full or Imp. Cyl./Imp. Modified (4/2)
Rib: Plain
Trigger: Double or single

Mechanism: Boxlock
Locking: Purdey system
Weight: 6.84 lbs. or 5.96 lbs.
Forend: Standard
Stock: Straight English or pistol grip

GARBI SIDELOCK SHOTGUNS

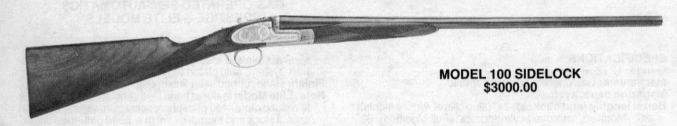

MODEL 100 SIDELOCK
$3000.00

Like this Model 100 shotgun, all Spanish-made Garbi models featured here are Holland & Holland pattern sidelock ejector guns with chopper lump (demibloc) barrels. They are built to English gun standards with regard to design, weight, balance and proportions, and all have the characteristic "feel" associated with the best London guns. All of the models offer fine 24-line hand-checkering, with outstanding quality wood-to-metal and metal-to-metal fit. The Model 100 is available in 12, 16, 20 and 28 gauge and sports Purdey-style fine scroll and rosette engraving, partly done by machine.

MODEL 200

MODELS 101, 102 AND 103A (not shown)
$4500.00

Available in 12, 16, 20, and 28 gauge, the sidelocks are hand-crafted with hand-engraved receiver and select walnut straight grip stock.

SPECIFICATIONS
Barrels: 25″ to 30″ in 12 ga.; 25″ to 28″ in 16, 20 and 28 ga.; high-luster blued finish; smooth concave rib (optional Churchill or level, file-cut rib)
Action: Holland & Holland pattern sidelock; automatic ejectors; double triggers with front trigger hinged; case-hardened

Stock/forend: Straight grip stock with checkered butt (optional pistol grip); hand-rubbed oil finish; classic (splinter) forend (optional beavertail)
Weight: 12 ga. game, 6 lbs. 8 oz. to 6 lbs. 12 oz.; 12 ga. pigeon or wildfowl, 7 lbs.—7 lbs. 8 oz.; 16 ga., 6 lbs. 4 oz. to 6 lbs. 10 oz.; 20 ga., 5 lbs. 15 oz.—6 lbs. 4 oz.; 28 ga., 5 lbs. 6 oz.—5 lbs. 10 oz.
Also available:
MODEL 200 in 12, 16, 20 or 28 gauge; features Holland pattern stock ejector double, heavy-duty locks, Continental-style floral and scroll engraving, walnut stock. **Price: $6250.00**

ITHACA SHOTGUNS

MODEL 87 FIELD GRADES

Made in much the same manner as 50 years ago, Ithaca's Model 37 pump (now designated as Model 87) features Rotoforged barrels hammered from 11″ round billets of steel, then triple-reamed, lapped and polished. The receivers are milled from a solid block of ordnance grade steel, and all internal parts—hammer, extractors, slides and carriers—are milled and individually fitted to each gun.

Models	Prices
MODEL 87 w/Supreme Vent Rib	$831.00
MODEL 87 w/Deluxe Vent Rib and choke tubes	395.00
MODEL 87 ULTRALIGHT w/Choke Tubes	430.00
MODEL 87 Deluxe Combo	472.00

MODEL 87 FIELD GRADE

SPECIFICATIONS

Model	Grade	Gauge	Chamber	Barrel Length	Choke	Weight (Lbs.)
87	Supreme Vent Rib	12	3″	30″	Full	7
		12	3″	28″	Mod	7
		12	3″	26″	I.C.	7
		20	3″	26″	Full	6³/₄
		20	3″	26″	Mod	6³/₄
		20	3″	26″	I.C.	6³/₄
87	Deluxe Vent, Choke Tubes	12	3″	30″	CT Full*	7
		12	3″	28″	CT Mod*	7
		12	3″	26″	CT Mod*	7
		20	3″	25″	CT Mod*	6³/₄
87	Ultralight, Choke Tubes	12	2³/₄″	25″	CT Mod*	6
		20	2³/₄″	25″	CT Mod*	5
87	Camo Vent, Choke Tubes	12	3″	28″	CT Full*	7

*Furnished with one tube indicated. Other interchangeable tubes available.

MODEL 87 DEERSLAYER

The first shotgun developed to handle rifled slugs successfully, Ithaca's Deerslayer shotgun remains first choice for many big game hunters around the world. The Deerlayer's design results in an "undersized" cylinder bore—from the forcing cone all the way to the muzzle. This enables the slug to travel smoothly down the barrel with no gas leakage or slug rattle. The new Deerslayer II features the world's first production rifled barrel for shotguns; moreover, the Deerslayer's barrel is permanently screwed into the receiver for solid frame construction, which insures better accuracy to about 85 yards.

Models	Prices
MODEL 87 DEERSLAYER	$377.00
MODEL 87 DEERSLAYER ULTRALIGHT	412.00
MODEL 87 DEERSLAYER w/Rifled Barrel	472.00

MODEL 87 DEERSLAYER

SPECIFICATIONS

Model	Grade	Gauge	Chamber	Barrel Length	Choke	Weight (Lbs.)
87	Deluxe Combo	12	3″	28″	CT Mod.*	7
				20″	Special Bore	
		20	3″	28″	CT Mod.*	6³/₄
				20″	Special Bore	
87	Deerslayer	12	3″	20″	Special Bore	6³/₄
		12	3″	25″	Special Bore*	6³/₄
		20	3″	20″	Special Bore	6
		20	3″	25″	Special Bore	6
	Ultralight	20	2³/₄″	20″	Special Bore	5
87	Deerslayer II	12	3″	25″	Special Rifled Barrel Bore	7

ITHACA SHOTGUNS

CUSTOM TRAP

SINGLE BARREL CUSTOM TRAP

Model	Gauge	Chamber	Barrel Length	Choke	Weight (Lbs.)
Custom	12	2³/₄″	32″	Full	8¹/₂
	12	2³/₄″	34″	Full	8¹/₂
Trap	12	2³/₄″	32″	Full	8¹/₂
	12	2³/₄″	34″	Full	8¹/₂

Standard dimensions are: Length of pull is 14³/₈″ with 1³/₄″ drop at both comb and heel. Custom stock fitting at no extra charge.

Models	Prices
CUSTOM TRAP 32″ and 34″ Barrel	$ 7,176.00
DOLLAR TRAP w/Grade AA Fancy American walnut stock & forend	$10,000.00

KRIEGHOFF SHOTGUNS

MODEL ULM-P
O/U SIDELOCK LIVE PIGEON GUN
Standard $12,500.00
Bavaria $14,350.00

SPECIFICATIONS

Gauge: 12

Chamber: 2³/₄″

Barrel: 28″ or 30″ long; tapered, ventilated rib

Choke: Top, Full; bottom, Imp. Mod.

Trigger action: Single trigger, non-selective bottom-top; hand-detachable sidelocks with coil springs; optional release trigger

Stock: Selected fancy English walnut, oil finish; length, 14³/₈′, drop at comb, 1³/₈″; optional custom-made stock

Forearm: Semi-beavertail

Engraving: Light scrollwork; optional engravings available

Weight: Approx. 8 lbs.

Also available in Skeet (28″) and Trap (30″) models (same prices as above)

KRIEGHOFF SHOTGUNS

K-80 LIVE PIGEON

MODEL K-80 TRAP, SKEET, SPORTING CLAY AND LIVE PIGEON

Barrels: Made of Boehler steel; free-floating bottom barrel with adjustable point of impact; standard rib is ventilated tapered step; Trap, Skeet, Live Pigeon, Sporting Clay and International barrels all interchangeable; tapered step ribs standard on all models
Receivers: Hard satin-nickel finish; case hardened; blue finish available as special order
Triggers: Wide profile, single selective, position adjustable

Weight: 8¹/₂ lbs. (Trap); 8 lbs. (Skeet)
Ejectors: Selective automatic
Sights: White pearl front bead and metal center bead
Stocks: Hand-checkered and epoxy-finished Select European walnut stock and forearm; silver soldered metal-to-metal assemblies; quick-detachable palm swell stocks available in five different styles and dimensions
Safety: Push button safety located on top tang.

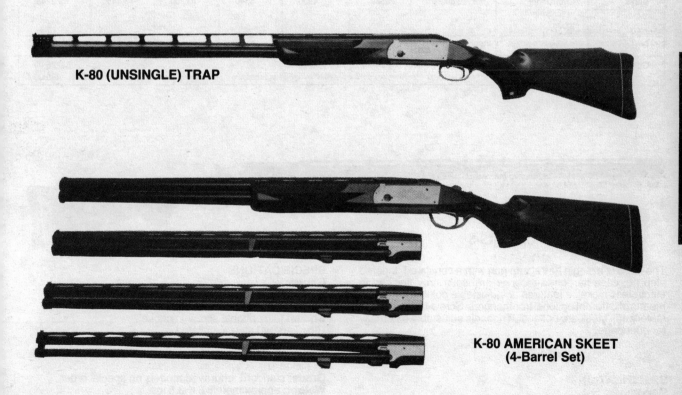

K-80 (UNSINGLE) TRAP

K-80 AMERICAN SKEET
(4-Barrel Set)

KRIEGHOFF SHOTGUNS

Specifications And Prices

Model	Description	Bbl Length	Choke	Standard	Bavaria	Danube	Gold Target	Extra Barrels
Trap	Over & Under	30"/32"	IM/F	$4480.	$ 7890.	$ 9800.	$12,955.	$1795
	Unsingle	32"/34"	Full	5350.	8650.	10,650.	13,750.	2400.
	Top Single	34" only	Full	4745.	8045.	10,045.	13,145.	1795.
		30" + 32"						
	Combo	30" + 34"	IM/F	6880.	10,350.	12,300.	15,450	
		32" + 34"	+F					
Optional Features:								
Screw-in chokes (O/U, Top or Unsingle)		$300.						
Single factory release		270.						
Double factory release		440.						
Skeet		28"/12 ga.	Tula					1950.
		28"/20 ga.	Skeet					1895.
	4-Barrel Set	28"/28 ga.	Skeet	8980.	12,800.	14,700.	18,950.	1895.
		28"/.410 ga.	Skeet					1895.
	2-Barrel Set	28"/12 ga.	Tula	6200.	9640.	11,600.	N/A	N/A
	Lightweight	28"/12 ga.	Skeet	4250.	7780.	9600.	N/A	1795.
	Standardweight	28"/12 ga.	Tula	4550.	7990.	9950.	13,200.	1950.
		28"/12 ga.	Skeet	4390.	7890.	9800.	12,995.	1795.
	International	28"/12 ga.	Tula	4725.	7990.	9950.	13,200.	1950.
Sporting Clays	Over/Under w/screw-in tubes (5)	28"/12 ga.	Tubes	4930.	8340.	10,250.	13,445.	2245.
Pigeon	Pigeon	28"/29"/30"	IM/SF	4480.	7890.	9800.	12,995.	1795.
Optional engravings: Super Standard								$$225.00
Super Scroll								495.00

MODEL KS-5

The KS-5 is a single barrel trap gun with a ventilated, tapered step rib, case-hardened receiver and satin grey finished in electroless nickel. It features an adjustable point of impact by means of different optional fronthangers. Screw-in chokes and factory adj. stock are optional. Trigger is adjustable externally for poundage.

SPECIFICATIONS
Gauge: 12
Chamber: 2³/₄"
Barrel length: 32" or 34"
Choke: full; optional screw-in chokes
Rib: Tapered step; ventilated
Trigger: weight of pull adjustable; optional release
Receiver: case-hardened; satin grey finished in electroless nickel
Grade: standard; engraved models on special order
Weight: approximately 8.6-8.8 lbs.
Case: aluminum
Price: $2395.00 (with full choke and case)
　　　　2695.00 (with screw-in choke and case)
Screw-in choke barrels: $1550.00
Regular barrels: $1250.00
Engraved models: $5450.00 and up

LEBEAU-COURALLY SHOTGUNS

For generations, Lebeau-Courally has enjoyed the distinction of supplying guns to the royal houses of Europe. Rated among the world's best for more than a century, these hand-crafted shotguns are available with an extensive selection of intricate engraving patterns, and can be tailored to the custom specifications of the most demanding shooter.

BOXLOCK SIDE-BY-SIDE (not shown)
$11,000.00 and up

Available in 12, 16, 20, and 28 gauge, this Anson & Deeley boxlock side-by-side shotgun features automatic ejectors, Purdey-type third fastener, and double triggers with front trigger hinged. It is offered with choice of classic or rounded action, with or without sideplates, concave or level rib, file-cut or smooth, and choice of numerous engraving patterns. **Barrels:** Dovetail lump barrels 26"–30" long with high-luster rust blued finish. **Stock/forend:** Hand-rubbed, oil-finished straight grip select French walnut stock with checkered butt and classic (splinter) forend (optional pistol grip and beavertail forend). **Weight:** 12 ga., 6 lbs. 6 oz.–8 lbs. 4 oz.; 16 ga., 6–6½ lbs.; 20 ga., 5½ lbs.–6 lbs. 4 oz.; 28 ga., 5 lbs. 4 oz.-6 lbs.

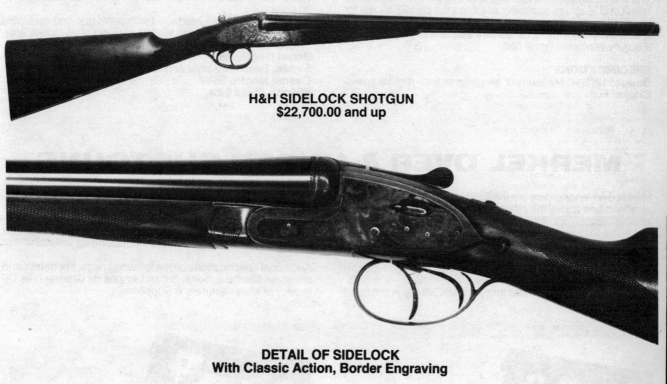

H&H SIDELOCK SHOTGUN
$22,700.00 and up

DETAIL OF SIDELOCK
With Classic Action, Border Engraving

This Holland & Holland pattern sidelock double is a gunner's dream—with automatic ejectors, chopper lump barrels of Walhreyne compressed steel, choice of classic or rounded action, concave or level rib, file-cut or smooth, double triggers with front trigger hinged (non-selective single trigger optional), coin finish or casehardened in colors, optional hand-detachable lock and H&H type self-opening mechanism, choice of a wide variety of engravings. **Barrel length:** 26"-30". **Gauges:** 12, 16, 20, and 28. **Stock/forend:** Best-quality French walnut stock with straight grip (pistol grip optional) and checkered butt; classic (splinter) forend (beavertail available). **Weight:** Same as Boxlock Side-by-Side.

MARLIN SHOTGUNS

MARLIN MODEL 55
GOOSE GUN
$213.95

High-flying ducks and geese are the Goose Gun's specialty. The Marlin Goose Gun has an extra-long 36-inch full-choked barrel and Magnum capability, making it the perfect choice for tough shots at wary waterfowl. It also features a quick-loading 2-shot clip magazine, a convenient leather carrying strap and a quality ventilated recoil pad.

SPECIFICATIONS
Gauge: 12; 2³/₄″ Magnum, 3″ Magnum or 2³/₄″ regular shells
Choke: Full

Capacity: 2-shot clip magazine
Action: Bolt action; positive thumb safety; red cocking indicator
Stock: Walnut-finish hardwood with pistol grip and ventilated recoil pad; swivels and leather carrying strap; tough Mar-Shield® finish
Barrel length: 36″
Sights: Bead front sight and U-groove rear sight
Overall length: 56³/₄″
Weight: About 8 lbs.

MERKEL OVER & UNDER SHOTGUNS

Merkel over-and-unders are the first hunting guns with barrels arranged one above the other, and they have since proved to be able competitors of the side-by-side gun. Merkel superiority lies in the following details:
- Available in 12, 16, 20 and .410 gauges
- Lightweight (5³/₄ to 6³/₄ lbs.)
- The high, narrow forend protects the shooter's hand from the barrel in hot or cold climates.
- The forend is narrow and therefore lies snugly in the hand

to permit easy and positive swinging.
- The slim barrel line provides an unobstructed field of view and thus permits rapid aiming and shooting.
- The over-and-under barrel arrangement reduces recoil error; the recoil merely pushes the muzzle up vertically.

Additional specifications on the following page. For details and prices on Merkel options, contact Armes de Chasse (see Directory of Manufacturers & Suppliers).

MODEL 200E
$3009.00

MODEL 201E
$4003.00

MERKEL OVER/UNDER SHOTGUNS

MERKEL OVER/UNDER SHOTGUN SPECIFICATIONS

Gauges: 12, 16, 20, 28, .410
Barrel lengths: 26″, 26³/₄″, 28″
Weight: 6 to 7 lbs.
Stock: English or pistol grip in European walnut
Features: Models 200E and 201E are boxlocks; Models 203E and 303E are sidelocks. All models include three-piece

forearm, automatic ejectors, articulated front triggers. Automatic safety, selective and nonselective triggers are optional, as are upgraded wood, recoil pad and special engraving. All Merkel shotguns are made by VEB Fahrzeug and Jagdwaffenwerk Ernst Thalman, West Germany, and are distributed in the U.S. by Armes de Chasse.

MODEL 203E
$10,000.00

MODEL 303E
$16,000.00

MERKEL SIDE-BY-SIDE SHOTGUNS

MERKEL SIDE-BY-SIDE SHOTGUN SPECIFICATIONS

Gauges: 12, 16, 20
Barrel lengths: 26″, 26³/₄″, 28″
Weight: 6 to 7 lbs.
Stock: English or pistol grip in European walnut
Features: Models 47E, 147E and 122 are boxlocks; Models 47S and 447S are sidelocks. All guns have cold hammer-

forged barrels, double triggers, double lugs and Greener crossbolt locking systems and automatic ejectors. Choking and patterning for steel shot (using U.S. Steel shotshells), upgraded wood, automatic safety, recoil pad and special engraving are available as options.

347S

147E

MERKEL SIDE-BY-SIDE SHOTGUNS

MODEL 47S SIDE-BY-SIDE
$4370.00

MODEL 147S & 247S
$5436.00

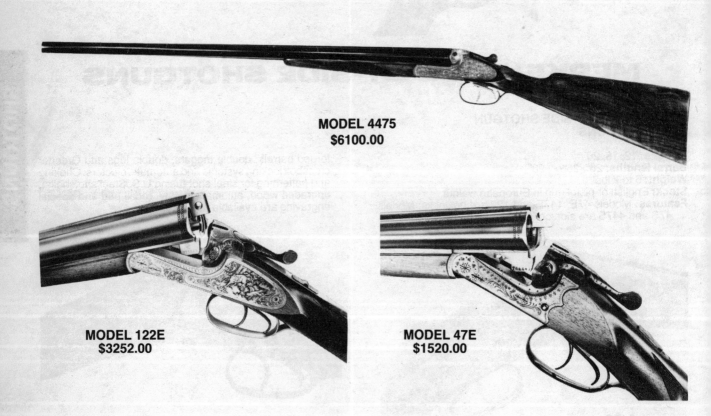

MODEL 4475
$6100.00

MODEL 122E
$3252.00

MODEL 47E
$1520.00

MOSSBERG PUMP SHOTGUNS

These slide-action Model 500's offer lightweight action and high tensile-strength alloys. They also feature the famous Mossberg "Safety on Top" and a full range of interchangeable barrels. Stocks are walnut-finished birch with rubber recoil pads with combs checkered pistol grip and forend.

MODEL 500 SPECIFICATIONS

Action: Positive slide-action

Barrel: 12 or 20 gauge and .410 bore with free-floating vent. rib; ACCU-CHOKE II interchangeable choke tubes; chambered for $2\frac{3}{4}$" standard and Magnum and 3" Magnum shells

Receiver: Aluminum alloy, deep blue/black finish; ordnance steel bolt locks in barrel extension for solid "steel-to-steel" lockup

Capacity: 6-shot (one less when using 3" Magnum shells); plug for 3-shot capacity included

Safety: Top tang, thumb-operated; disconnecting trigger

Stock/forend: Walnut-finished American hardwood with checkering; rubber recoil pad

Standard stock dimensions: 14" length of pull; $2\frac{1}{2}$" drop at heel; $1\frac{1}{2}$" drop at comb

Sights: Metal bead front

Overall length: 48" with 28" barrel

Weight: 12 ga. $7\frac{1}{2}$ lbs.; 20 ga. $6\frac{3}{4}$ lbs.; .410 bore $6\frac{1}{2}$ lbs.; Slugster $6\frac{3}{4}$ lbs.; Magnums $8\frac{1}{2}$ lbs. (weight varies slightly due to wood density)

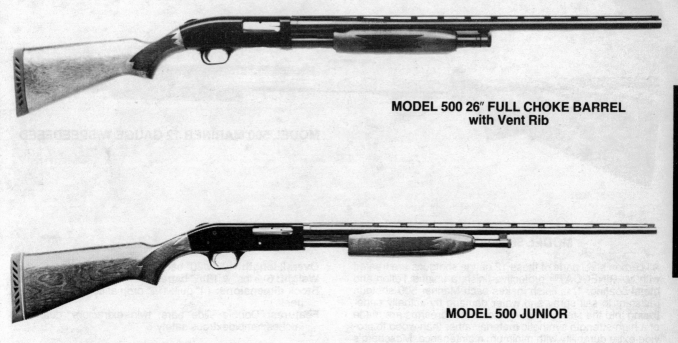

MODEL 500 26" FULL CHOKE BARREL
with Vent Rib

MODEL 500 JUNIOR

MOSSBERG SHOTGUNS

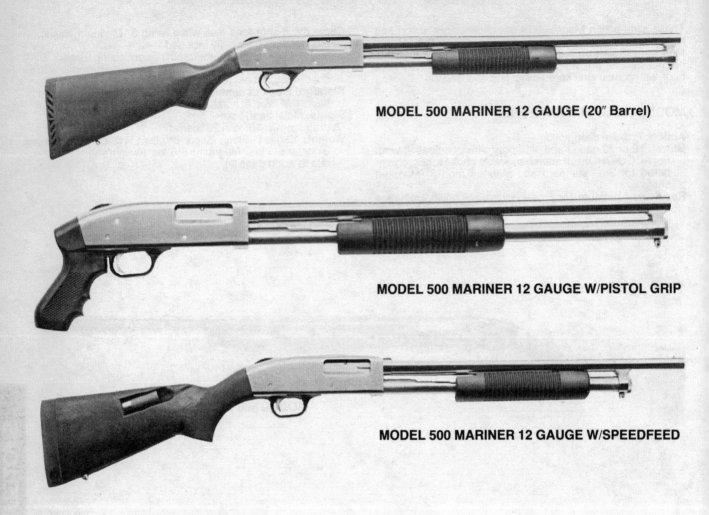

MODEL 500 MARINER 12 GAUGE (20″ Barrel)

MODEL 500 MARINER 12 GAUGE W/PISTOL GRIP

MODEL 500 MARINER 12 GAUGE W/SPEEDFEED

MODEL 500 MARINER

All carbon steel parts of these 12 gauge shotguns are treated with MARINECOAT™ protective finish, a unique Teflon and metal coating. This finish makes each Mariner 500 shotgun resistant to salt spray and water damage by actually penetrating into the steel pores. All stock and forearms are made of a high-strength synthetic material rather than wood to provide extra durability with minimum maintenance. Mossberg's Speedfeed stock allows shooters to carry up to four extra 2³/₄″ rounds in the buttstock—two on each side. Mariners are available in a variety of 6- or 8-shot versions. The Mini-Combo offers a full-length buttstock and extra pistol grip.

SPECIFICATIONS
Gauge: 12
Chambers: 2³/₄″ and 3″
Capacity: 6-shot model—5-shot (3″ chamber) and 6-shot (2³/₄″ chamber)
8-shot model—7-shot (3″ chamber) and 8-shot (2³/₄″ chamber)
Barrel lengths: 18¹/₂″ and 20″

Overall length: 40″ w/20″ barrel; 38¹/₂″ w/18¹/₂″ barrel
Weight: 6¹/₂ lbs. w/18¹/₂″ barrel
Stock dimensions: 14″ pull; 1¹/₂″ drop at comb; 2¹/₂″ drop at heel
Features: Double slide bars; twin extractors; dual shell latches; ambidextrous safety

Prices:
MARINER 6-SHOT
Cruiser & Synthetic Field Models **$349.95**
Speedfeed Model 382.95
MARINER 8-SHOT
Cruiser & Synthetic Field Models 366.95
Speedfeed Mode 399.95
MARINER 6-SHOT MINI-COMBO
Synthetic Field 357.95
Speedfeed Model 389.95
MARINER 8-SHOT MINI-COMBO
Synthetic Field Model 373.95
Speedfeed Model 406.95

MOSSBERG SHOTGUNS

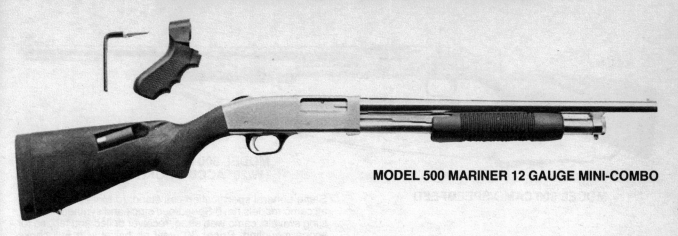

MODEL 500 MARINER 12 GAUGE MINI-COMBO

MODEL 500 CAMO SLUGSTER

MODEL 500 TROPHY SLUGSTER

SPECIFICATIONS
Gauge: 12
Barrel length: 24″
Finish: Blued; gloss-finished high-comb wood buttstock and forearm
Features: Scope mounting is permanently affixed to barrel (not to the receiver) for constant scope/bore alignment; barrel is rifled for better accuracy downrange; buttstock is cut straighter with a high comb for quick, precise sighting; designed to use BRI flat-shooting Sabot loads for 5-shot groups under 3″ at 100 yards.
Prices: **$310.00** Rifled barrel
       290.00 Plain barrel

MOSSBERG PUMP SHOTGUNS

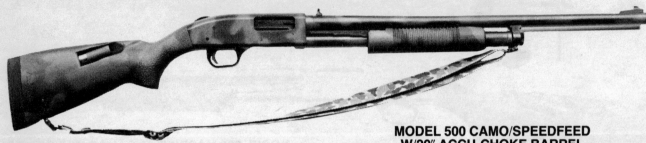

MODEL 500 CAMO/SPEEDFEED

MODEL 500 CAMO/SPEEDFEED W/20″ ACCU-CHOKE BARREL

Same general specifications as standard Model 500, except all camo models have Speedfeed stock and synthetic forend, sling swivels, camo web strap, receiver drilled and tapped for scope mounting. **Price:** 30″ vent rib barrel with Full choke **$316.95;** 24″ vent rib ACCU II Turkey **$336.95;** 24″ Slugster **$313.95.**

MODEL 500 WATERFOWL/DEER CAMO COMBO

SPECIFICATIONS
Gauge: 12
Barrel length: 28″ (Accu-Choke w/one Accu-Steel choke tube and 24″ Slugster barrel
Features: Synthetic forearm and Speedback buttstock; receiver drilled and tapped for scope mounting; quick disconnect posts and swivels, plus camo web sling, are supplied
Price: $372.95
     369.00 w/Accu-II choke and 20″ barrel

MODEL 500 CAMPER

SPECIFICATIONS
Gauges: 12, 20 & .410
Chambers: 2¹/₂″ and 3″ Magnum
Barrel length: 18¹/₂″
Weight: 4¹/₂ lbs. (.410 ga.); 5 lbs. (20 ga.); 5¹/₂ lbs. (12 ga.)
Features: Synthetic pistol grip; camo carrying case
Price: $282.95

MOSSBERG PUMP SHOTGUNS

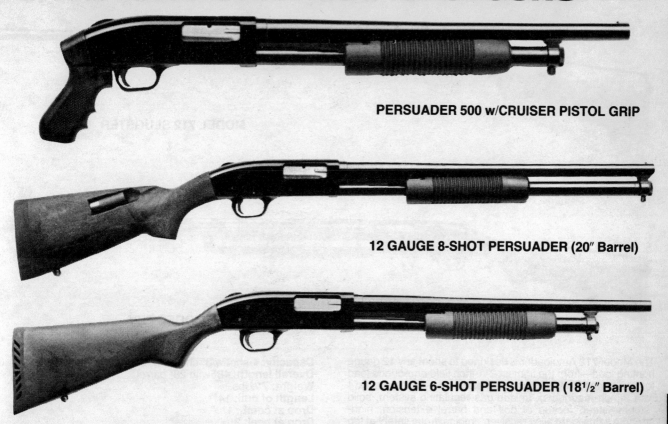

PERSUADER 500 w/CRUISER PISTOL GRIP

12 GAUGE 8-SHOT PERSUADER (20" Barrel)

12 GAUGE 6-SHOT PERSUADER (18½" Barrel)

MODEL 500 SLIDE-ACTION LAW ENFORCEMENT "PERSUADER"

These slide-action shotguns are available in 6- or 8-shot versions, chambered for both 2¾-inch and 3-inch shells.

Six-shot models have 18½-inch barrel, overall length of 37¾ inches and a weight of 6¼ pounds with full buttstock. (Also available in 20 gauge and .410 bore.)

Eight-shot models have 20-inch barrels, overall length of 39¾ inches and weigh 6¾ pounds with full buttstock.

Both 6- and 8-shot models are available in choice of blued, parkerized or nickel metal finish; satin or oiled walnut wood finish. Lightweight aluminum alloy receiver with steel locking bolt into barrel extension affords solid "steel-to-steel" lockup. Heavy-duty rubber recoil pads come on all full stock models; sling swivels on all models. Optional pistol grip and other accessories.

PRICES 8-SHOT MODELS:
PERSUADER 8-SHOT Blued **$267.95**
  Synthetic Field Model 267.95
  With rifle sight 287.95
  Speedfeed Model 299.95
PERSUADER 8-SHOT w/Parkerized Finish
  With wood stock 308.95
  With rifle sight 328.95
PERSUADER 8-SHOT MINI-COMBO Blued 274.95
PERSUADER 8-SHOT MAXI-COMBO Blued 298.95
  With vent rib 308.95
  Synthetic Field Model 298.95

PRICES 6-SHOT MODELS:
PERSUADER 6-SHOT Blued
  With wood stock, bead sights **$251.95**
  Synthetic Field stock, blued, bead sight 251.95
  Both models w/rifle sights 269.95
  Cruiser Model, blued 251.95
  Speedfeed stock, blued (12, 20 ga.) 283.95
  Speedfeed stock w/rifle sight 302.95
PERSUADER 6-SHOT w/Parkerized Finish (12 ga.) 291.95
  Same as above w/rifle sights 311.95
PERSUADER 6-SHOT w/Camo Finish 309.95
  Synthetic Field Model 274.95
PERSUADER 6-SHOT MINI-COMBO
Blued, 12 and 20 gauge 258.95
  Speedfeed Model (Blued) 291.95
  With Camo Finish 316.95
  Synthetic Field Model (Camo) 284.95
PERSUADER 6-SHOT MAXI-COMBO Blued 279.95
  Wood stock model 289.95
  With ACCU-II Choke 299.95
  Wood stock Model 20 gauge 279.95
PERSUADER 6-SHOT MAXI-COMBO w/Camo
Finish 362.95
  Synthetic Field Model w/ACCU-II Choke 329.95

MOSSBERG AUTOLOADING SHOTGUNS

MODEL 712 SLUGSTER

MODEL 712A

The Model 712 Autoloader is designed to shoot any 12 gauge hunting load—from the lightest 2³/₄-inch field one-ounce load to the heaviest 3-inch magnums. **Features:** 5-shot capacity (4 with 3-inch magnums), unique gas regulating system, solid "steel-to-steel" lockup of bolt and barrel extension, high-strength lightweight alloy receiver, ambidextrous safety at top rear of receiver, dual shell latches, self-adjusting action bars, walnut-finished stock with checkering and recoil pad, internal ACCU-CHOKE II choke tubes that sit flush with the muzzle.

SPECIFICATIONS
Gauge: 12
Chambers: 2³/₄" and 3"

Capacity: 4-shot w/3" chamber; 5-shot w/2³/₄" chamber
Overall length: 48" with 28" barrel
Weight: 7¹/₂ lbs.
Length of pull: 14"
Drop at comb: 1¹/₂"
Drop at heel: 2¹/₂"
Features: Double slide bars; twin extractors; dual shell latches; ambidextrous safety; checkered walnut-stained hardwood; recoil pad; ACCU-CHOKE tube system; Bradley-style white front sights plus mid-point bead
Prices:
MODEL 712 w/vent rib and Accu-II Choke $344.95
MODEL 712 w/Accu-Steel Choke 348.95

MODEL 835 ULTI-MAG

The world's first shotgun chambered specifically for Federal Cartridge's new 3¹/₂" 12 gauge Magnum shotshell, the **Ulti-Mag** fires all standard 12 gauge 2³/₄" and 3" field and target loads as well. Designed for waterfowlers who need a shotshell capable of delivering larger payloads of steel shot, the high-velocity (1300+ fps) load provides a 23 percent or more increase in steel shot capacity compared to conventional 12 gauge 3" Magnums.

The **Ulti-Mag** also features a "backbored" barrel, thus in-creasing diameter bore, reducing recoil, and improving patterns. There is also a new **ACCU-MAG** choke tube system, in which stainless steel tubes fit flush with the muzzle to handle high-velocity steel shot loads with efficiency. Capacity is five shots with 3" or 3¹/₂" shells, and six shots with 2³/₄" shells. Other features include an ambidextrous safety, solid "steel-to-steel" lockup, and high-strength aluminum alloy receivers with anodized finish. For further information, contact O.F. Mossberg & Sons, 7 Grasso Avenue, North Haven, CT 06473.

NAVY ARMS SHOTGUNS

MODEL 96
$715.00

Five fully interchangeable chokes make the Model 96 Over/ Under a versatile shotgun, useful for all types of upland and waterfowl hunting as well as target shooting. Italian made, this 12-gauge gun features 28-inch chrome-lined barrels with 3-inch chambers, ejectors, double ventilated rib construction, an engraved hard chrome reciver, European walnut stock with checkered wrist and forend and gold-plated single trigger. Chokes: Full; Imp. Cyl./ Mod.; Mod.; Imp. Cyl./Skeet; Cyl.

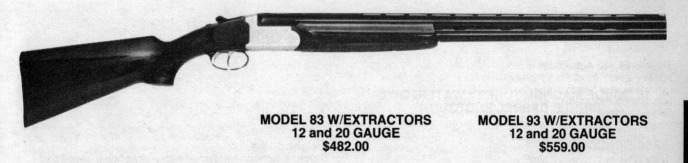

MODEL 83 W/EXTRACTORS
12 and 20 GAUGE
$482.00

MODEL 93 W/EXTRACTORS
12 and 20 GAUGE
$559.00

The Model 83/93 Bird Hunter is a quality field grade over/under available in 12 or 20 gauge. Manufactured in Italy, it features 28-inch chrome-lined barrels with 3-inch chambers; double vent rib construction, European walnut stock, hand-checkered wrist and forend, chrome engraved receiver and gold-plated triggers. Both gauges available in Mod./Full or Imp. Cyl./ Mod. chokes.

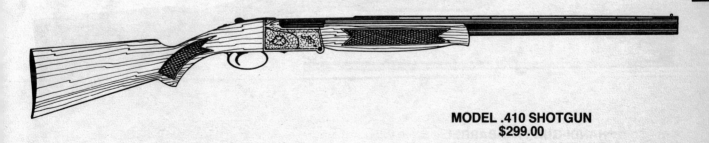

MODEL .410 SHOTGUN
$299.00

The Model 410 Italian-made over/under shotgun features European walnut stock checkered at the wrist and forend, 26-inch chrome-lined barrels with 3-inch chambers, ventilated rib barrel and an engraved, hard chrome receiver. **Chokes:** Full/Full or Skeet/Skeet. **Weight:** 6¹/₄ lbs.

NEW ENGLAND FIREARMS

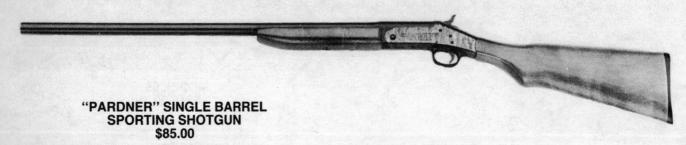

"PARDNER" SINGLE BARREL SPORTING SHOTGUN
$85.00

SPECIFICATIONS
Gauges: 12, 20 and .410
Chamber: 3″
Action: Break open, side lever release, positive ejection
Barrel lengths: 26″ and 28″
Overall length: 43″ w/28″ barrel; 39″ w/26″ Youth barrel

Weight: 5 to 6 lbs.
Stock: Straight, walnut finish American hardwood
Length of pull: 13³/₄″ (12¹/₂″ Youth model)
Drop at comb: 1¹/₂″
Drop at heel: 2¹/₂″ (2³/₈″ Youth model)

10 GAUGE MAGNUM TURKEY/WATERFOWL SINGLE BARREL SHOTGUN
$169.00

SPECIFICATIONS
Gauge: 10
Chamber: 3¹/₂″ Magnum
Action: Break open, side lever release, positive ejection
Barrel length: 32″
Overall length: 47″

Weight: 10 lbs.
Stock: American hardwood with walnut finish, recoil pad
Forend: Extended; walnut finish American hardwood
Length of pull: 13¹/₂″
Drop at comb: 1¹/₂″
Drop at heel: 2¹/₂″

HANDI-GUN TWO-BARREL RIFLE/SHOTGUN SYSTEM

SPECIFICATIONS
Gauge/Caliber: 20/22 Hornet or 20/30-30
Chamber: 3″
Action: Break open, side lever release, positive ejection
Barrel length: 22″ (rifle or shotgun)

Weight: 6¹/₂ lbs. (9¹/₂ lbs. combined)
Sights: Shotgun, front brass bead; rifle, ramp front and adjustable folding rear; tapped for scope mounts
Stock: American hardwood
Forend: Semi-beavertail, walnut finish American hardwood

OMEGA SHOTGUNS

Omega side-by-side shotguns are available in two models, both with double triggers and non-automatic safety. The Standard model has a checkered beechwood stock and semi-pistol grip. The Deluxe model has a checkered European walnut stock and low barrel rib. Both models come in .410 gauge with 26-inch barrels and Full/Full chokes. **Overall length:** 40½". **Weight:** 5½ lbs.

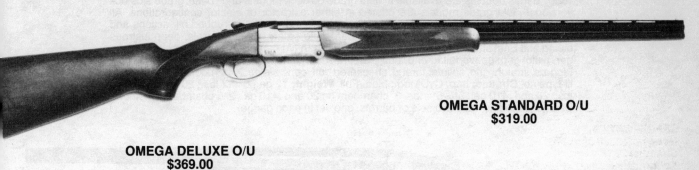

OMEGA STANDARD O/U
$319.00

OMEGA DELUXE O/U
$369.00

The Omega over/under is truly a premium shotgun featuring single trigger, automatic safety, ventilated rib and checkered European walnut stock.

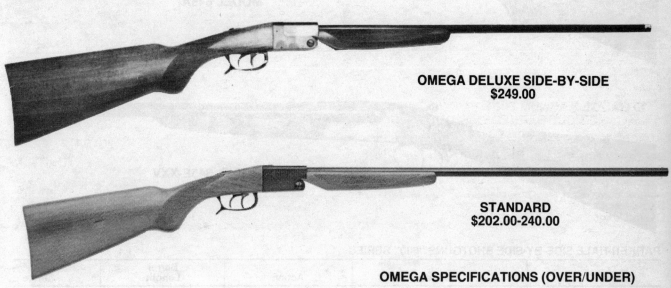

OMEGA DELUXE SIDE-BY-SIDE
$249.00

STANDARD
$202.00-240.00

OMEGA SPECIFICATIONS (OVER/UNDER)

Movel	Gauge	Barrel Length	Chokes	Weight
Deluxe	12	28"	M/F	7 lbs. 6 oz.
Deluxe	12	26"	IC/M	7 lbs. 2 oz.
Standard	12	28"	M/F	7 lbs. 6 oz.
Standard	12	26"	IC/M	7 lbs. 2 oz.
Standard	20	28"	M/F	6 lbs. 2 oz.
Standard	20	26"	IC/M	6 lbs.
Standard	28	26"	IC/M	6 lbs. 1 oz.
Standard	28	26"	M/F	6 lbs. 1 oz.
Standard	.410	26"	F/F	6 lbs.

OMEGA SPECIFICATIONS (SIDE-BY-SIDE)

Deluxe	.410	26"	F/F	5 lbs. 7 oz.
Standard	20	26"	IC/M	5 lbs. 7 oz.
Standard	28	26"	M/F	5 lbs. 7 oz.
Standard	.410	26"	F/F	5 lbs. 7 oz.

PARKER-HALE SHOTGUNS

Now available in the U.S., Parker-Hale side-by-side shotguns have long been favorites in Great Britain. Superbly crafted by the Spanish gunmaking firm of Ignacio Ugartechea, the "600" Series doubles are available in field grade boxlock models and "best" grade sidelock versions. Field grade models are offered in either extractor or ejector configurations. All models boast stocks of hand-checkered walnut finished with hand-rubbed oil, actions and parts machined from ordnance steel, standard auto safety, forged barrels, deep lustrous bluing and English scroll design engraving. **American** (A) models: Single non-selective trigger, pistol grip, beavertail forend, butt plate, raised matted rib. **English** (E) models: Double triggers, straight grip, splinter forend, checkered butt, concave rib; XXV models have Churchill-type rib. **Chokes:** Imp. Cyl./Mod.; Mod./Full. **Weight:** 12 ga., 6¾-7 lbs.; 20 ga. 5¾ lbs.-6 lbs.; 28 and .410 ga., 5¼-5½ lbs. 3" chambers on 20 and .410 ga.; 2¾ chambers on others. Bi-Gauge models have two sets of barrels, one set in each gauge.

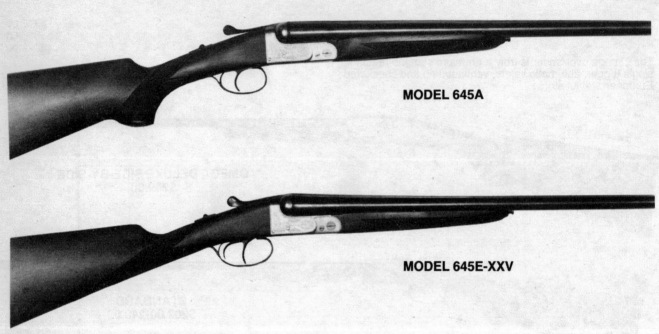

MODEL 645A

MODEL 645E-XXV

PARKER-HALE SIDE-BY-SIDE SHOTGUNS "600" SERIES

Model	Gauges	Action	Barrel Length	Price
640E (English)	12, 16, 20	Boxlock	26", 28"	$ 529.95
640E (English)	28, .410	Boxlock	27"	599.95
640A (American)	12, 16, 20, 28, .410	Boxlock	26", 28"	629.95
640A	28, .410	Boxlock	27"	699.95
645E (Bi-Gauge)	20/28 or 28/410	Boxlock	26"	1199.95
645E (English)	12, 16, 20	Boxlock	26", 28"	679.95
645E (English)	28, .410	Boxlock	27"	749.95
645A (American)	12, 16, 20	Boxlock	26", 28"	779.95
645A	28, .410	Boxlock	27"	849.95
645A (Bi-Gauge)	20/28 or 28/410	Boxlock	27"	1299.95
645E-XXV (English)	12, 16, 20	Boxlock	25"	699.95
645E-XXV (English)	28, .410	Boxlock	25"	779.95
670E (English)	12, 16, 20	Sidelock	26", 28"	2900.00
670E (English)	28, .410	Sidelock	27"	3100.00
680E-XXV (English)	12, 16, 20	Sidelock	25"	2700.00
680E-XXV (English)	28, .410	Sidelock	25"	2900.00

PARKER REPRODUCTIONS

PARKER A-1 SPECIAL

Recognized by the shooting fraternity as the finest American shotgun ever produced, the Parker A-1 Special is again available. Exquisite engraving and rare presentation grade French walnut distinguish the A-1 Special from any other shotguns in the world. Currently offered in 12, 20 and 28 gauge (.410 is pending), all gauges are available with ventilated rib. Each gun is custom-fitted in its own oak and leather trunk case. Two models are offered: Hand Engraved and Custom Engraved. For specifications, see the table below.

Prices:

A-1 SPECIAL
One barrel set . . . . $ 8740.00
Two barrel set 9740.00

A-1 SPECIAL CUSTOM ENGRAVED
With two sets of barrels 10500.00

B-GRADE BANK NOTE LTD. EDITION
One barrel set 3970.00
Two sets of barrels. 4970.00

D-GRADE
One barrel set 2970.00
Two sets of barrels. 3600.00
12 ga. w/internal screw chokes 3120.00

SPECIFICATIONS

Gauge	Barrel Length	Chokes	Chambers	Drop At Comb	Drop At Heel	Length Of Pull	Nominal Weight	Overall Length
12	26	Skeet I & II or IC/M	2¾	1⅜	2³⁄₁₆	14⅛	6¾	42⅝
12	28	IC/M or M/F	2¾	1⅜	2³⁄₁₆	14⅛	6¾	44⅝
12*	28	Internal Screw Choke	3	1⅜	2³⁄₁₆	14⅛	7+	44⅝
12+	28	IC/M	3	1⅜	2³⁄₁₆	14⅛	7+	44⅝
20	26	Skeet I & II or IC/M	2¾	1⅜	2³⁄₁₆	14⅜	6½	42⅝
20	28	M/F	3	1⅜	2³⁄₁₆	14⅜	6½	44⅝
28	26	Skeet I & II or IC/M	2¾	1⅜	2³⁄₁₆	14⅜	5⅓	42⅝
28	28	M/F	2¾	1⅜	2³⁄₁₆	14⅜	5⅓	44⅝
†28/.410	26	IC/M	3	1⅜	2³⁄₁₆	14⅜	5½	42⅝
†28/.410	26	Skeet I & II	3	1⅜	2³⁄₁₆	14⅜	5½	42⅝
★.410	26	IC/M	3	1⅜	2³⁄₁₆	14⅜	under 5	42⅝
★.410	26	Skeet I & II	3	1⅜	2³⁄₁₆	14⅜	under 5	42⅝

Note: *Dimensions may vary slightly as each stock is hand-carved.*
+ Steel Shot Special, 3-inch chambers, IC/M chokes—note weight
★ Sporting Clays Classic, six choke tubes: Skeet I, Skeet II, IC, M, IM, F

† .410 Bore barrels on 28 gauge, 00 frame
★ .410 Bore on 0000 frame, projected weight

SHOTGUNS

PERAZZI SHOTGUNS

For the past 20 years or so, Perazzi has concentrated solely on manufacturing competition shotguns for the world market. Today the name has become synonymous with excellence in competitive shooting. The heart of the Perazzi line is the classic over/under, whose barrels are soldered into a monobloc that holds the shell extractors. At the sides are the two locking lugs that link the barrels to the action, which is machined from a solid block of forged steel. Barrels come with flat, step or raised ventilated rib. The walnut forend, finely checkered, is available with schnabel, beavertail or English styling, and the walnut stock can be of standard, Monte Carlo, Skeet or English design. Double or single non-selective or selective triggers. Sideplates and receiver are masterfully engraved and transform these guns into veritable works of art.

MODEL MX3C GAME

GAME SHOTGUNS OVER/UNDER 12 GAUGE

MODEL		GAUGE	BARREL LENGTHS	PRICE
MX5		12	26³/₈"-27⁵/₈"	$3150.00
MX5C	equipped with 5 choke tubes	12	27⁵/₈"	3450.00
MX3		12	27⁵/₈"	3750.00
MX3C	equipped with 5 choke tubes	12	27⁵/₈"	4050.00
MX3 special		12	27⁵/₈"	4400.00
MX3C special	equipped with 5 choke tubes	12	27⁵/₈"	4700.00
MX12		12	26³/₈"-27⁵/₈"	4550.00
MX12C	equipped with 5 choke tubes	12	27⁵/₈"	4850.00

GAME SHOTGUNS OVER/UNDER 12 GAUGE

MODEL			GAUGE	BARREL LENGTHS	PRICE
MX20	SC3		20-28-410	26"	$ 8,000.00
MX20C	SC3		20	26"	8,300.00
MX20	SCO		20-28-410	26"	13,450.00
MX20C	SCO		20	26"	13,750.00
SCO			20-28-410	26"-27⁵/₈"	15,350.00
MX20	gold		20-28-410	26"	14,950.00
MX20C	gold		20	26"	15,250.00
SCO	gold		20-28-410	26"-27⁵/₈"	17,100.00
SCO		SIDEPLATES	20-28-410	26"-27⁵/₈"	19,950.00
SCO	gold	SIDEPLATES	20-28-410	26-27⁵/₈"	23,150.00
EXTRA			20-28-410	26"-27⁵/₈"	37,150.00

PERAZZI SHOTGUNS

MODEL MX3 SKEET

AMERICAN SKEET SHOTGUNS OVER AND UNDER 4 GAUGE SETS

MODEL		GAUGE	BARREL LENGTHS	PRICE
MX3		12-20-28-410	27⁵/₈"	$ 8,500.00
MX3	special	12-20-28-410	27⁵/₈"	10,200.00
MX3L		12-20-28-410	27⁵/₈"	10,200.00
MIRAGEspecial		12-20-28-410	27⁵/₈"	11,400.00
MX3S	SC3	12-20-28-410	27⁵/₈"	14,900.00
MX3	SCO	12-20-28-410	27⁵/₈"	18,250.00
MX3S	SCO	12-20-28-410	27⁵/₈"	20,250.00
MX3	gold	12-20-28-410	27⁵/₈"	19,900.00
MX3S	gold	12-20-28-410	27⁵/₈"	22,300.00

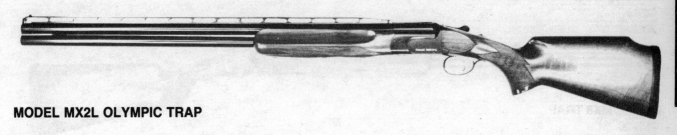

MODEL MX2L OLYMPIC TRAP

AMERICAN TRAP SHOTGUNS COMBO SETS

MODEL		GAUGE	BARREL LENGTHS	PRICE
MX3	COMBO*	12		$5000.00
MX3L	COMBO*	12		6200.00
MX3 special	COMBO*	12		5800.00
MX8 special	COMBO* adjustable selective trigger	12	single barrel 32"-34"	6700.00
GRAND AMERICA 88	special COMBO* adjustable selective trigger	12	O/U BBL 29¹/₂"-31¹/₂"	6700.00
DB81 special	COMBO*	12		7100.00

PERAZZI SHOTGUNS

MODEL DB81 TRAP

OLYMPIC & AMERICAN TRAP, SKEET & SPORTING OVER AND UNDERS

MODEL	GAUGE	BARREL LENGTHS	PRICE
MX3	12	27⁵⁄₈″-29¹⁄₂″-31¹⁄₂″	$3750.00
MX3B	12	27⁵⁄₈″-29¹⁄₂″-31¹⁄₂″	3750.00
MX3C equipped with 5 choke tubes	12	27⁵⁄₈″	4050.00
MX3 special adjustable selective trigger	12	27⁵⁄₈″-29¹⁄₂″-31¹⁄₂″	4400.00
MX3C special with 5 chokes-adjustable, selective trigger	12	27⁵⁄₈″	4700.00
MIRAGE*	12	27⁵⁄₈″-29¹⁄₂″-31¹⁄₂″	4700.00
MX8	12	27⁵⁄₈″-29¹⁄₂″-31¹⁄₂″	4700.00
MX8 special	12	27⁵⁄₈″-29¹⁄₂″-31¹⁄₂″	4900.00
DB81	12	29¹⁄₂″-31¹⁄₂″	4900.00
MX1	12	27⁵⁄₈″	4800.00
MX1B	12	27⁵⁄₈″	4800.00
MX2	12	29¹⁄₂″	4800.00
MX2L	12	29¹⁄₂″	4800.00
MX3L	12	27⁵⁄₈″-29¹⁄₂″-31¹⁄₂″	4550.00
MX3BL	12	27⁵⁄₈″-29¹⁄₂″-31¹⁄₂″	4550.00
MX3CL equipped with 5 choke tubes	12	27⁵⁄₈″	4850.00

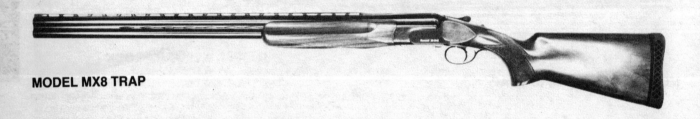

MODEL MX8 TRAP

AMERICAN TRAP SINGLE BARREL SHOTGUNS

MODEL	GAUGE	BARREL LENGTHS	PRICE
MX3 *	12	32″-34″	$3550.00
MX3 special* adjustable selective trigger	12	32″-34″	4150.00
TM1 special* adjustable trigger	12	32″-34″	3700.00
TMX special* adjustable trigger	12	32″-34″	3700.00
MX3L *	12	32″-34″	4300.00
MX8 special* adjustable selective trigger	12	32″-34″	4650.00
GRANDAMERICA special* adjustable selective trigger	12	32″-34″	4650.00

PIOTTI SHOTGUNS

One of Italy's top gunmakers, Piotti limits its production to a small number of hand-crafted, best-quality double-barreled shotguns whose shaping, checkering, stock, action and barrel work meets or allegedly exceeds the standards achieved in London prior to WWII. The Italian engravings are the finest ever and are becoming recognized as an art form in themselves.

All of the sidelock models exhibit the same overall design, materials and standards of workmanship; they differ only in the quality of the wood, shaping and sculpturing of the action, type of engraving and gold inlay work and other details. The Model Piuma differs from the other shotguns only in its Anson & Deeley boxlock design.

SPECIFICATIONS
Gauges: 10, 12, 16, 20, 28, .410
Chokes: As ordered
Barrels: 12 ga., 25″ to 30″; other gauges, 25″ to 28″; chopper lump (demi-bloc) barrels with soft-luster blued finish; level, file-cut rib or optional concave or ventilated rib
Action: Boxlock, Anson & Deeley; Sidelock, Holland & Holland pattern; both have automatic ejectors, double triggers with front trigger hinged (non-selective single trigger optional), coin finish or optional color case-hardening
Stock: Hand-rubbed oil finish (or optional satin luster) on straight grip stock with checkered butt (pistol grip optional)
Forend: Classic (splinter); optional beavertail
Weight: Ranges from 4 lbs. 15 oz. (.410 ga.) to 8 lbs. (12 ga.)

MODEL MONTE CARLO SIDELOCK
$10,200.00

Best-quality Holland & Holland pattern sidelock ejector double with chopper lump barrels. Choice of Purdey-style scroll and rosette or Holland & Holland-style large scroll engraving.

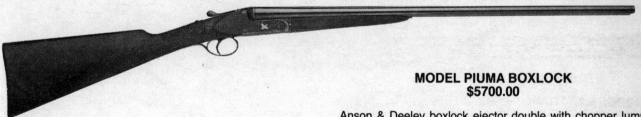

MODEL PIUMA BOXLOCK
$5700.00

Anson & Deeley boxlock ejector double with chopper lump (demi-bloc) barrels, and scalloped frame. Very attractive scroll and rosette engraving is standard. A number of optional engraving patterns including game scene and gold inlays are available at additional cost.

PIOTTI SHOTGUNS

MODEL KING NO. 1 SIDELOCK
$12,500.00

Best-quality Holland & Holland pattern sidelock ejector double with chopper lump barrels, level file-cut rib, very fine, full coverage scroll engraving with small floral bouquets, gold crown in top lever, name in gold, and gold crest in forearm, finely figured wood.

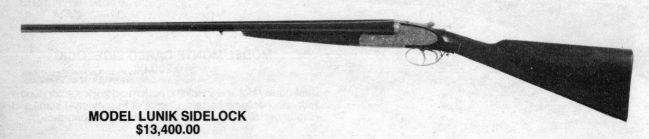

MODEL LUNIK SIDELOCK
$13,400.00

Best-quality Holland & Holland pattern sidelock ejector double with chopper lump (demi-bloc) barrels, level, filecut rib, Renaissance-style, large scroll engraving in relief, gold crown in top lever, gold name, and gold crest in forearm, finely figured wood.

MODEL KING EXTRA (With Gold)
$18,600.00

Best-quality Holland & Holland pattern sidelock ejector double with chopper lump barrels, level filecut rib, choice of either bulino game scene engraving or game scene engraving with gold inlays, engraved and signed by a master engraver, exhibition grade wood.

REMINGTON SHOTGUNS

PARKER AHE SHOTGUN
$12,500

Produced by the Parker Gun Works (a division of Remington Arms Company at Ilion, N.Y.), this new version of a time-honored American firearms tradition is available in 20 gauge AHE Grade. It will be handcrafted in limited quantities on special order from the Remington Custom Shop. The Parker model features a new single selective trigger mechanism, the first new side-by-side trigger design in over 60 years. Automatic ejectors have a more simplified and reliable design, as do the updated automatic safeties. Stocks are produced from highly select Circassian or American walnut, and custom checkering

(28 lines/inch) adorns both forend and butt stock, with AHE-grade side panels on each side of the tang. Fine-scroll engraving and game scenes decorate the casehardened receivers.

Additional specifications include **Barrel length:** 28". **Chambers:** 2³/₄". **Weight:** 6¹/₂ lbs. Raised ventilated ribs are standard, with front and mid-barrel ivory beads. Customers may specify stock dimensions and any combination of chokes, including Skeet, Improved Cylinder, Modified and Full.

MODEL 870 EXPRESS MAGNUM

MODEL 870 EXPRESS (12 GAUGE)
$223.00

Model 870 Express features the same action as the Wingmaster and is available with 3" chamber and 28" vent-rib barrel only. It has a hardwood stock with low-luster finish and solid butt pad. Choke is Modified REM Choke tube and wrench. **Overall length:** 48¹/₂". **Weight:** 7¹/₄ lbs.

MODEL 870 EXPRESS COMBO (not shown)
$320.00

Model 870 Express offers all the features of the standard Model 870, including twin-action bars, quick-changing barrels, REM Choke plus low-luster, checkered hardwood stock and no-shine finish on barrel and receiver. The Model 870 Combo is packaged with an extra 20" deer barrel, fitted with rifle sights and fixed, Improved Cylinder choke (additional REM chokes can be added for special applications). The 3-inch chamber handles all 12 gauge ammo without adjustment.

REMINGTON PUMP SHOTGUNS

MODEL 870 "TC" TRAP (12 GAUGE ONLY)
$547.00 ($560.00 w/Monte Carlo Stock)

The **870 "TC"** is a single-shot trap gun that features a unique gas-assisted recoil-reducing system, REM, Choke and a high step-up ventilated rib. REM chokes include regular full, extra full and super full. **Stock:** Redesigned stock and forend of select American walnut with cut-checkering and satin finish; length of pull 14³/₈"; drop at heel 1⁷/₈"; drop at comb 1³/₈". **Weight:** 8¹/₂ lbs. **Barrel length:** 30".

Also available in **Fixed Full Choke: $533.00**; with Monte Carlo stock: **$547.00.**

MODEL 870 · 20 GAUGE LIGHTWEIGHT
$427.00

This is the pump action designed for the upland game hunter who wants enough power to stop fast flying game birds but light enough to be comfortable for all-day hunting. The 20-gauge Lightweight handles all 20-gauge 2³/₄-inch shells. **Stock:** American walnut stock and forend. **Barrel length:** 26" and 28". **Average weight:** 6 lbs.

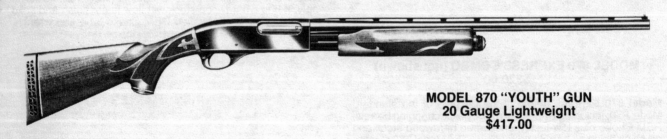

MODEL 870 "YOUTH" GUN
20 Gauge Lightweight
$417.00

The Model 870 "Youth" Gun brings Remington's pump action perfection to a whole new range of shooters. The Model 870 shotgun has been specially designed for youths and smaller-sized adults. It's a 20-gauge lightweight with a 1-inch shorter stock and 5-inch shorter barrel. Yet it is still all 870, complete with REM Choke and ventilated rib barrel. **Barrel length:** 21". **Stock Dimensions:** Length of pull 12¹/₂" (including recoil pad); drop at heel; 2¹/₂" drop at comb 1⁵/₈". **Overall length:** 40". **Average Weight:** 6 lbs. **Choke:** Mod. and Imp. Cyl.

REMINGTON PUMP SHOTGUNS

MODEL 870 WINGMASTER 12 GAUGE
$429.00 ($472.00 Left Hand)

This new restyled 870 "Wingmaster" pump has cut checkering on its satin finished American walnut stock and forend for confident handling, even in wet weather. An ivory bead "Bradley" type front sight is included. Rifle is available with 26", 28" and 30" barrel with REM Choke and handles 3" and 2¾" shells interchangeably. **Overall length:** 46½ (26" barrel), 48½" (28" barrel), 50½ (30" barrel). **Weight:** 7¼ lbs.

Also available: **WINGMASTER DEER GUN** with Imp. Cyl. and rifle sights, 12 gauge only. **Barrel length:** 20". **Price: $367.00.** Left-hand model: **$423.00**

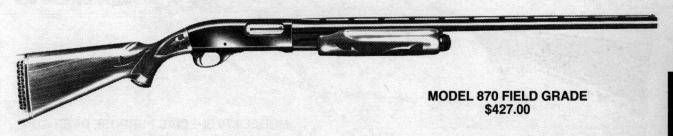

MODEL 870 FIELD GRADE
$427.00

Receiver made from ordnance-quality steel. Barrel extension locks in the breech block to assure constant headspace. Cross-bolt safety switch. Vibra-horned metal finish, chrome-plate bolt. Metal bead front sight. **Gauges:** 20, 28 and .410. **Chamber:** 3". **Stock:** American walnut stock and forend have deep, sure checkering; fluted comb; wood protected by Du Pont's RK-W finish; distinctive white spacers at recoil pad and grip cap; length of pull 14"; drop at heel 2½"; drop at comb 1⅝"; 3-shot plug furnished. 28 gauge and .410 guns have butt plates, not recoil pads. **Weight** (approx): 20 gauge, 6½ lbs.; 28 gauge and .410, 6¼ lbs. **Barrel lengths:** 25" (28 ga. and .410); 26" and 28" (20 ga.)

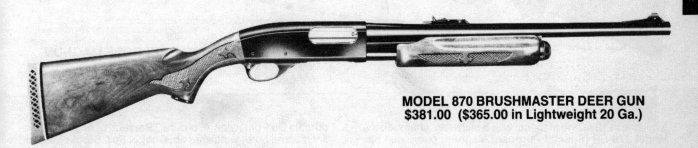

MODEL 870 BRUSHMASTER DEER GUN
$381.00 ($365.00 in Lightweight 20 Ga.)

The **Model 870 Brushmaster** is made to handle rifled slugs and buck shot. It features a 20-inch barrel with 3-inch chamber and fully adjustable rifle-type sights. Stock fitted with rubber recoil pad and white-line spacer. Also available in standard model, but with lacquer finish, no checkering, recoil pad, grip cap; special handy short forend. **Choke:** Imp. Cyl. **Weight:** 6¼ lbs.

REMINGTON PUMP SHOTGUNS

MODEL 870 SPECIAL FIELD
$429.00

The **Model 870 "Special Field"** shotgun combines the traditional, straight-stock styling of years past with features never before available on a Remington pump. Its 21-inch vent rib barrel, slimmed and shortened forend, straight, cut-checkered stock offers upland hunters a quick, fast-pointing shotgun. The

"Special Field" is chambered for 3-inch shells and will also handle all 2³/₄-inch shells interchangeably. Barrels will not interchange with standard 870 barrels. **Overall length:** 41¹/₂". **Weight:** 7 lbs. (12 ga.); 6 lbs. (20 ga.).

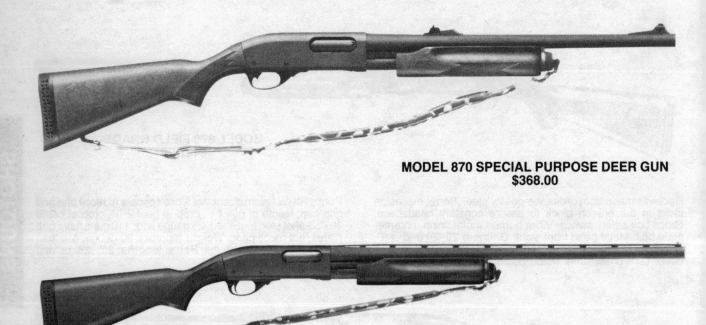

MODEL 870 SPECIAL PURPOSE DEER GUN
$368.00

MODEL 870 SPECIAL PURPOSE MAGNUM
$420.00

Available in 12 gauge Magnum with 3-inch Mag. chamber, the **Model 870 SP (Special Purpose) Magnum** pump gun has been designed with waterfowlers and turkey hunters in mind. For concealment, all metal surfaces have been finished in non-glare, non-reflective Parkerized black. And all wood surfaces have been given a dull, non-reflective oil finish with a slightly rough feel for firmer grip. For ease of carrying, the SP Mag. Pump comes factory-equipped with a camo-patterned padded sling, attached at both ends by quick-detachable sling swivels. More than 2 inches wide at the shoulder, the sling is made of

durable Du Pont nylon "Cordura." **Barrel:** 26" or 30" chrome-lined barrel bore; ventilated rib. **Choke:** Full. **Stock:** Supplied with dark-colored recoil pad and black line spacers. **Overall length:** 46¹/₂" with 26" barrel; 50¹/₂" with 30" barrel. **Weight:** Approx. 7¹/₄ lbs.

Also available: **SPECIAL PURPOSE DEER GUN** (12 gauge) with rifle sights, recoil pad, Imp. Cyl. **Barrel length:** 20". **Overall length:** 40¹/₂." **Average weight:** 7 lbs.

REMINGTON SHOTGUNS
MODEL 11-87 PREMIER

MODEL 11-87 PREMIER
$527.00 ($573.00 Left Hand)

The new Remington **Model 11-87 "Premier"** with REM Choke offers the dependability of a pump along with the easy shootability of an autoloader, the magnum power of a waterfowl gun, and the light handling of an upland gun. This new shotgun's standout attraction to the practical shooter is its ability to handle a broad variety of 12-gauge ammunition interchangeably. Switching from light, 2¾" field loads to heavy 3" magnums is simply a matter of inserting different shotgun shells. A new, patented pressure compensating gas system accomplishes this without the need for adjustments. An additional bonus to shooters is a 50 percent increase in overall performance endurance, revealed by extensive testing. Among the factors contributing to this high level of dependability and durability are:

• Extractor 30 percent thicker
• A redesigned, more durable firing pin retractor spring
• Heat treated pistol and piston seal
• Corrosion and rust resistant stainless steel magazine tube

The standard version of the 11-87 "Premier" shotgun is available in three ventilated rib barrel lengths: 26", 28" and 30"—all with REM Choke. A left-hand mirror image version is available in 28" only. The stock is satin finished with new cut-checkering (20 lines per inch), featuring a "floating diamond" motif. Also, there's a solid brown presentation-type butt pad and a grip cap with Remington's new "RA" logo. Forend has the same satin finish and checkering pattern. Barrel and receiver have Bradley-type white-faced front sight and metal bead on barrel.

MODEL 11-87 PREMIER TRAP 12 GAUGE
$580.00
$593.00 (w/Monte Carlo Stock)

A 30" trap barrel offers trap shooters a REM Choke system with three interchangeable choke constrictions: trap full, trap extra full, and trap super full.

Also available in **Fixed Full Trap Choke: $567.00**; with Monte Carlo stock: **$580.00**

MODEL 11-87 PREMIER SHOTGUNS

Gauge	Barrel Length & Choke	Overall length	Avg. Wt. (lbs.)
	30" REM Choke	50½	8⅜
12	28" REM Choke	48¼	8¼
	28" REM Choke	48¼	8¼
	26" REM Choke	46	8⅛

EXTRA BARRELS. 11-87 barrels are not interchangeable with the Remington Model 1100. Also, target barrels are designed for optimal performance with target loads and therefore are not pressure compensated. These guns will, however, be pressure compensating and shoot all 12-gauge loads when equipped with an 11-87 Premier field barrel.

REMINGTON SHOTGUNS

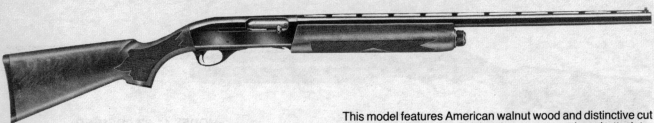

MODEL 11-87 PREMIER SKEET 12 GAUGE
$573.00

This model features American walnut wood and distinctive cut checkering with satin finish, plus new two-piece butt plate. REM Choke system includes option of two skeet chokes— skeet and improved skeet. Trap and skeet guns are designed for 12-gauge target loads and are set to handle 2³/₄" shells only.

Also available in **Fixed Skeet Choke: $560.00.**

MODEL 11-87 SPECIAL PURPOSE MAGNUM
$525.00

Features nonreflective wood and metal finish for all types of hunting where concealment is critical. Exposed metal surfaces of both barrel and receiver are Parkerized; bolt and carrier have non-glare blackened coloring. Barrel lengths: 26" and 30". Chamber: 3". Choke: REM Choke.

MODEL 11-87 SPECIAL PURPOSE DEER GUN
3" MAGNUM
$499.00

Features same finish as other SP models plus a padded, ca-mostyle carrying sling of Cordura nylon with Q.D. sling swivels. Barrel is 21" with rifle sights and slug choke (handles all 2³/₄" and 3" rifled slug and buckshot loads as well as high velocity field and magnum loads; does not function with light 2³/₄" field loads).

REMINGTON AUTOLOADING SHOTGUNS

MODEL 1100 SPECIAL FIELD
AUTOLOADING SHOTGUNS
12 and 20 Gauge

The Remington Model 1100 is a 5-shot gas-operated auto-loading shotgun with a gas metering system designed to reduce recoil effect. This design enables the shooter to use all 2¾-inch standard velocity "Express" and 2¾-inch Magnum loads without any gun adjustments. Barrels, within gauge and versions, are interchangeable. The 1100 is made in gauges of 12, 20, 28 and .410. All 12 and 20 gauge versions include REM Choke; interchangeable choke tubes in 26", 28" and 30" (12 gauge only) barrels. The solid-steel receiver features decorative scroll work. Stocks come with fine-line checkering in a

fleur-de-lis design combined with American walnut and a scratch-resistant finish. Features include white-diamond inlay in pistol-grip cap, white-line spacers, full beavertail forend, fluted-comb cuts, chrome-plated bolt and metal bead front sight. Made in U.S.A.

HIGH GRADE:
Model 1100 D Tournament with vent. rib barrel . . $2290.00
Model 1100 F Premier vent. rib barrel 4720.00
Model 1100 F Premier with gold inlay 7080.00

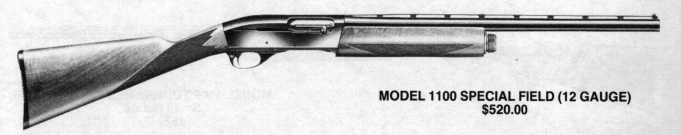

MODEL 1100 SPECIAL FIELD (12 GAUGE)
$520.00

The **Model 1100 "Special Field"** shotgun combines traditional, straight-stock styling with its 21-inch vent-rib barrel and slimmed and shortened forend, which offer upland hunters a quick, fast-pointing shotgun. Non-engraved receiver; non-Magnum extra barrels are interchangeable with standard

Model 1100 barrels. **Overall length: 41". Stock dimensions:** Length of pull 14⅛"; drop at comb 1½"; drop at heel 2½". **Choke:** REM Choke system. **Weight:** 7¼ lbs. (12 ga.); 6½ lbs. (20 ga.).

MODEL 1100 3" MAGNUM
20 & Lightweight 20 Gauges
$533.00

Designed for 3-inch and 2¾-inch Magnum shells; accepts and functions with any 1100 standard 2¾-inch chambered barrel. Available in 12 gauge 30-inch or 28-inch plain or ventilated rib, and 28-inch in 20 gauge, plain or ventilated rib barrels. **Stock**

dimensions: 14" long including pad; 1½" drop at comb; furnished with recoil pad. **Weight:** About 8 lbs., 12 ga.; 6¾ lbs., 20 ga.

MODEL 1100 DEER GUN
Lightweight 20 Gauges
$480.00

Features 2-inch (12 gauge) and 20-inch (LT-20 gauge) barrels, Improved Cylinder choke. Rifle sights adjustable for windage and elevation. Recoil pad. Choked for both rifled slugs and

buck shot. **Weight:** 12 gauge, 7¼ lbs.; 20 gauge, 6½ lbs. **Overall length:** 41" (12 gauge), 40" (LT-20 gauge).

REMINGTON AUTOLOADING SHOTGUNS

MODEL 1100 TOURNAMENT SKEET
$589.00

The world's winningest skeet gun, with high-grade positive cut-checkering on selected American walnut stock and forend. The LT-20 and 28 gauge Model 1100 Tournament Skeet guns have a higher vent rib to match the sight picture of the 12-gauge model. A true "matched set," with all the reliability, superb balance, and low recoil sensation that make it the choice of over 50% of the entrants in the world skeet shooting championships. Available in LT-20 and 28 gauges. **Barrel length:** 26". **Choke:** REM Choke. **Weight:** 6³/₄ lbs. (20 ga.), 6¹/₂ lbs. (28 ga.).

MODEL 1100 TOURNAMENT SKEET
Small Gauge
$589.00

Quality and economy, American walnut stock and forend, and receiver engraving identical to that of the higher grade models distinguish this SA Grade Model 1100 auto Skeet gun. Available in 28 ga., and .410 bore. **Stock dimensions:** Length of pull 14"; drop at heel 2¹/₂"; drop at comb 1¹/₂". **Barrel length:** 25" **Choke:** Skeet.

MODEL 1100 LT-20 YOUTH GUN • LIGHTWEIGHT
20 Gauge Only
$525.00

The Model 1100 LT-20 Youth Gun autoloading shotgun features a shorter barrel (21") and stock. **Overall length:** 39¹/₂". **Weight:** 6¹/₂ lbs.

MODEL 1100 • 28 & .410 GAUGES
$533.00

The Remington Model 1100 Autoloading shotguns in 28 and .410 gauges are scaled-down models of the 12-gauge version. Built on their own receivers and frames, these small gauge shotguns are available in full (.410 only) and modified chokes with either plain or ventilated rib barrels.

SPECIFICATIONS. Type: Gas-operated. **Capacity:** 5-shot with 28 ga. shells; 4-shot with 3" .410 ga. shells; 3-shot plug furnished. **Barrel:** 25" of special Remington ordnance steel; extra barrels interchangeable within gauge. **Chamber:** 3" in .410, 2³/₄" in 28 ga. **Overall length:** 45". **Safety:** Convenient cross-bolt type. **Receiver:** Made from solid steel, top matted, scroll work on bolt and both sides of receiver. **Stock dimensions:** Walnut; 14" long; 2¹/₂" drop at heel; 1¹/₂" drop at comb. **Average weight:** 6¹/₂ lbs. (28 ga.); 7 lbs. (.410).

ROSSI SHOTGUNS

THE OVERLAND

OVERLAND DOUBLE. Available in a .410 bore and 12 or 20 gauge for both standard 2¾-inch shells or 3-inch Magnum. The 12 and 20 gauges are offered in the Coach Gun version with abbreviated 20-inch barrels with Improved and Modified chokes. All models feature a raised rib with matted sight surface, hardwood stocks, rounded semi-pistol grips, blued hammers, triggers and locking lever.

Gauge	Barrel Length	Choke	Price
12	20″	IC&M	$332.00
12	28″	M&F	332.00
20	20″, 26″	IC&M	332.00
.410 bore	26″	F&F	337.00

THE SQUIRE

SQUIRE DOUBLE. Available in .410 bore or 12 or 20 gauge, the Squire has 3-inch chambers to handle the full range of shotgun loads. Features double triggers, raised matted rib, beavertail forend and pistol grip. Twin underlugs mesh with synchronized sliding bolts for double-safe solid lockup.

Gauge	Barrel Length	Choke	Price
12	20″	IC&M	$352.00
12	28″	M&F	352.00
20	26″	IC&M	352.00
.410 bore	26″	F&F	357.00

ROTTWEIL SHOTGUNS

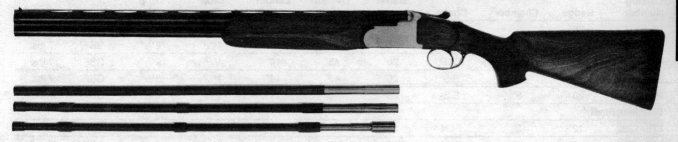

ROTTWEIL AMERICAN SKEET
$2395.00

SPECIFICATIONS
Gauge: 12 ga.
Action: Boxlock
Barrel: 27″ Skeet and Skeet choke, vent rib
Weight: 7½ lbs.
Overall length: 44½″

Stock: Selected European walnut, hand-checkered, modified forend
Sights: Plastic front housed in metallic sleeve with additional center bead
Features: Interchangeable inertia-type trigger group; receiver milled from solid block of special gun steel; retracting firing pins are spring mounted; all coil springs; first shotgun specially designed for tube sets

RUGER SHOTGUNS

No Slots

3 Slots

2 Slots

1 Slot

RUGER RED LABEL OVER/UNDER 20 GAUGE
$798.00

WITH STAINLESS STEEL RECEIVER 12 GAUGE
$798.00

Hardened chrome molybdenum, other alloy steels and music wire coil springs are used throughout. Features single-selective trigger, automatic top safety, standard gold bead front sight. Stock and semi-beavertail forearm are shaped from American walnut with hand-cut checkering (20 lines per inch). Pistol grip cap and rubber recoil pad are standard, and all wood surfaces are polished and beautifully finished. Stainless steel receiver available on 12 gauge version; 20 gauge is satin polished and blued.

RUGER SCREW-IN CHOKE INSERTS

Designed especially for the popular 12 gauge "Red Label" over/under shotgun. Easily installed with a key wrench packaged with each shotgun. Choke fits flush with the muzzle. Every shotgun is equipped with a Full, Modified, Improved Cylinder and two Skeet screw-in chokes. The muzzle edge of the chokes has been slotted for quick identification in or out of the barrels. Full choke has 3 slots; Modified has 2 slots, and Improved Cylinder has 1 slot (Skeet has no slots).

Models with Screw-In Chokes $987.50

SPECIFICATIONS

RUGER OVER & UNDER SHOTGUN SPECIFICATIONS

Catalog Number	Gauge	Chamber	Choke	Barrel Length	Overall Length	Length of Pull	Drop at Comb	Drop at Heel	Sights	Weight
RL 2008	20	3"	F&M	28"	45"	14"	1½"	2½"	GBF	7 lbs.
RL-2016	20	3"	IC&M	26"	43"	14"	1½"	2½"	GBF	7 lbs.
RL-2018	20	3"	IC&M	28"	45"	14"	1½"	2½"	GBF	7 lbs.
RL-2026	20	3"	S/S	26"	43"	14"	1½"	2½"	GBF	7 lbs.
RL-2028	20	3"	S/S	28"	45"	14"	1½"	2½"	GBF	7 lbs.
Stainless Steel										
KRL-1232	12	3"	F&M	26"	42⅞"	14"	1½"	2½"	GBF	7½ lbs.
KRL-1235	12	3"	F&M	28"	44⅞"	14"	1½"	2½"	GBF	7½ lbs.
KRL-1230	12	3"	IC&M	26"	42⅞"	14"	1½"	2½"	GBF	7½ lbs.
KRL-1233	12	3"	IC&M	28"	44⅞"	14"	1½"	2½"	GBF	7½ lbs.
KRL-1231	12	3"	S/S	26"	42⅞"	14"	1½"	2½"	GBF	7½ lbs.
KRL-1234	12	3"	S/S	28"	44⅞"	14"	1½"	2½"	GBF	7½ lbs.
Screw-in Chokes										
KRL-1226	12	3"	F,M,IC,S	26"	42⅞"	14"	1½"	2½"	GBF	7½ lbs.
KRL-1227	12	3"	F,M,IC,S	28"	42⅞"	14"	1½"	2½"	GBF	7½ lbs.

F-Full, M-Modified, IC-Improved Cylinder, S-Skeet, GBF-Gold Bead Front Sight

SAVAGE RIFLE/SHOTGUNS

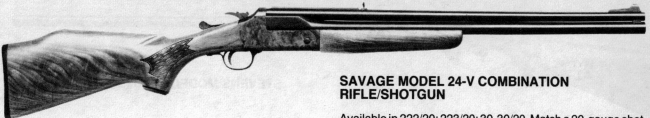

SAVAGE MODEL 24-V COMBINATION RIFLE/SHOTGUN

Available in 222/20; 223/20; 30-30/20. Match a 20-gauge shotgun with any of five popular centerfire calibers. Frame is color case hardened and barrel is a deep, lustrous blue and tapped, ready for scope mounting. Two-way top opening lever.

SAVAGE MODEL 24-C "CAMPER'S COMPANION"

SAVAGE MODEL 24 FIELD GRADE

24-C Campers Companion Combination: 22 long rifle/20 gauge. At 5³/₄ pounds, it's a pound lighter and five inches shorter than other 24's. When stored in special case, it measures just 5 inches × 22 in. The case has handles for carrying, thongs for tying to pack or saddle. Recess in stock holds extra shells.

24 Field Grade Combinations: 22 long rifle/20 or .410 gauge; 22 Magnum/20. A combination gun at a field grade price makes this model an ideal first gun. It combines the ever popular 22 cartridge with either of two popular shotgun gauges. Walnut-finished hardwood stock and forend are coated with sturdy electro-cote. Barrel alignment band.

Model	389	24	24V	24C
Caliber	.308/.222	22LR/22 Mag.	.222/.223/.30-30	22LR
Gauge/Choke	12/IC,MF	20/Full	20/Full	20/C
Barrel Length	25³/₄	24"	24"	20"
Chambered for	2³/₄" & 3"	2³/₄" & 3"	2³/₄" & 3"	2³/₄" & 3"
Length Overall	43"	40"	40"	36¹/₂"
Length Taken Down	25³/₄"	24"	24"	20"
Approx. Weight	7 lbs.	6¹/₂ lbs.	6³/₄-7¹/₂ lbs.	5³/₄ lbs.

C - Cylinder IC - Improved Cylinder MF - Modified Full
LR - Long Rifle Mag. - Magnum

SAVAGE & STEVENS PUMP SHOTGUNS

STEVENS MODEL 67 PUMP SHOTGUN

A trim-looking, smooth-functioning pump shotgun economically priced. **Action:** Hammerless, pump action, with side ejection solid steel receiver; top tang safety. **Stock:** Walnut finish hardwood, "corn cob" style forend; rubber recoil pad. **Barrel:** All chambered for 2³/₄" or 3" shells in 12, 20 gauges and .410 bore. **Magazine:** Tubular, 4 shots plus one in the chamber. **Barrel lengths and chokes:** 12 gauge, 28" Mod.; 12 gauge 30" Full; 20 gauge 28" Mod.; .410 bore, 26" Full. **Overall length:** 45" (.410); 47" (20); 47⁵/₈" (12). **Approx. weight:** 6¹/₄–6³/₄ lbs.

STEVENS MODEL 67-VR PUMP ACTION SHOTGUN

Same as Model 67, except all barrels have ventilated ribs.

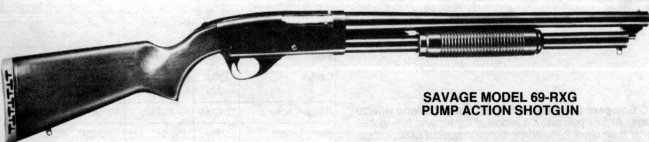

SAVAGE MODEL 69-RXG PUMP ACTION SHOTGUN

Compact, smooth-functioning law enforcement version of the Model 67 pump shotgun. **Stock:** Tung oil-finished hardwood stock and forend; ventilated rubber recoil pad; studs for QD sling loops attached. **Magazine:** Tubular, 7 shots, plus one in the chamber. **Barrel length:** 18¹/₄" Cylinder bore. **Overall length:** 39". **Gauge:** 12. **Chamber:** 2³/₄" and 3" shells. **Approx. weight:** 6³/₄ lbs.

SKB SHOTGUNS
GAS-OPERATED AUTOMATICS FOR FIELD & TRAP

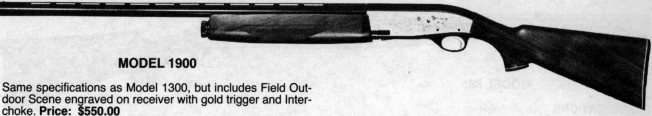

MODEL 1900

Same specifications as Model 1300, but includes Field Outdoor Scene engraved on receiver with gold trigger and Interchoke. **Price: $550.00**
Also available: **Deluxe Auto Trap** (12 ga. only with 2³/₄" chamber). **Price: $575.00**

MODEL 3000

Same specifications as Models 1300 and 1900, but with Field Presentation features. **Price: $585.00**
Also available: **Presentation Auto Trap** (12 ga. only with 2³/₄" chamber). **Price: $595.00**

MODEL 1300

SPECIFICATIONS
Gauges: 12 and 20
Chambers: 3"
Choke: Interchoke
Barrel lengths: 26" and 28" (Field); 30" (Trap)
Overall length: 48¹/₄" (Field); 50¹¹/₁₆" (Trap)
Weight: 6 lbs. 6 oz. (20 ga.); 7 lbs. 4 oz. (12 ga.)
Price: $495.00
Also available: **Slug Gun** with sights (22" barrel), 12 ga. only: **$499.00**

SIDE BY SIDES

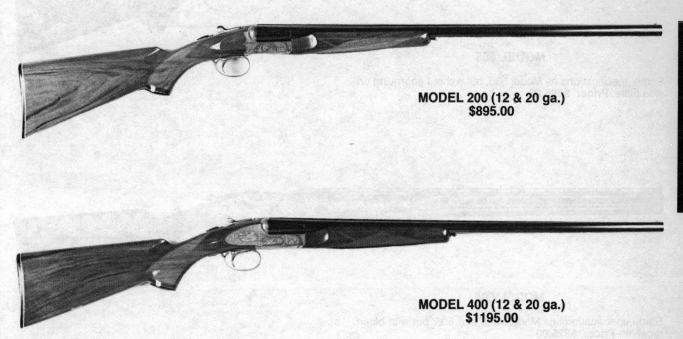

MODEL 200 (12 & 20 ga.)
$895.00

MODEL 400 (12 & 20 ga.)
$1195.00

SKB SHOTGUNS

OVER & UNDER TRAP GUNS

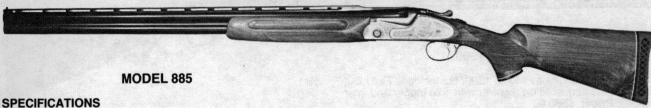

MODEL 885

SPECIFICATIONS
Gauge: 12
Chambers: 2³/₄″
Choke: Interchoke
Barrel lengths: 30″, 32″, 34″
Overall length: 47³/₈″
Weight: 8 lbs. 2 oz.
Stock: Standard or Monte Carol
Finish: Silver engraved receiver
Price: $1495.00

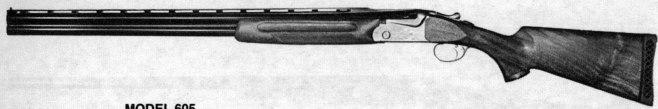

MODEL 605

Same specifications as Model 885, but without engraving on side plate. **Price:** $995.00

MODEL 505

Same specifications as Models 885 and 605, but with blued receiver. **Price:** $825.00

SOVEREIGN SHOTGUNS

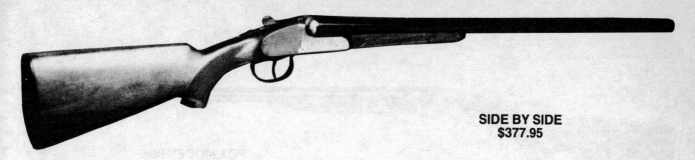

SIDE BY SIDE
$377.95

SPECIFICATIONS

Gauge: 12 (3″ chamber)
Barrel length: 28″
Choke: Mod./full
Weight: 6 lbs.
Stock: Walnut w/checkered pistol grip and forearm

Length of pull: $14\frac{1}{2}$″
Drop at comb: $1\frac{1}{2}$″
Drop at heel: 2″
Safety: Automatic
Receiver: Chrome engraved; monobloc construction

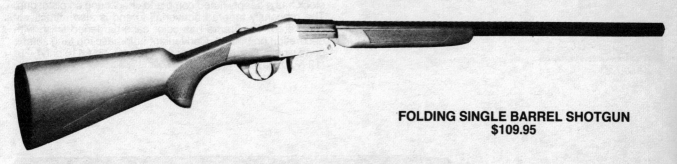

FOLDING SINGLE BARREL SHOTGUN
$109.95

SPECIFICATIONS

Gauge: 12, 16, 20 and .410 (3″ chamber)
Barrel length: 28″ (12, 16 and 20 ga.); 26″ (.410 ga.)
Weight: 6 lbs.
Choke: 12 and 20 ga. full/modified; 16 and .410 ga. full only

Stock: Walnut finished hardwood; chrome plated chamber and bore
Receiver: chrome engraved
Safety: Tang operated; automatic reset

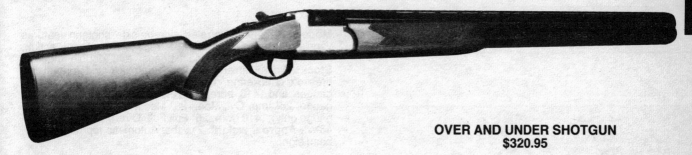

OVER AND UNDER SHOTGUN
$320.95

SPECIFICATIONS

Gauge: 12 or 20 ($2\frac{3}{4}$″ chamber)
Barrel length: 28″
Choke: Modified/full
Weight: 7 lbs. (12 ga.); $6\frac{3}{4}$ lbs. (20 ga.)
Stock: Walnut stock w/checkered pistol grip and forearm

Safety: Automatic
Receiver: Chrome engraved; monobloc construction
Length of pull: $14\frac{5}{8}$″
Drop at comb: $1\frac{3}{8}$″
Drop at heel: $2\frac{1}{4}$″

STEVENS & FOX SHOTGUNS

FOX MODEL BSE
$525.00

Fox B-SE. Gauges: 12, 20 and .410. Automatic ejectors are standard equipment on the Fox B-SE. Other fine gun features are the single trigger and ventilated rib. The B-SE has the lines found only in a double gun, enriched with materials and finishes typical of expensive custom guns. Its selected walnut stock has a deeply fluted comb and checkering on pistol grip. The gracefully tapered beavertail forend is also attractively checkered. The frame has color case-hardened finish with decoration on bottom. Convenient automatic top tang safety; bead sights. **Barrel lengths:** 24″ (12 ga.) 26″ (.410 only), 28″ (12 & 20 .ga), 30″ (12 ga. only).

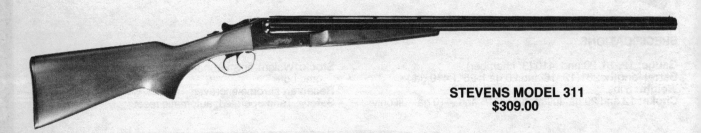

STEVENS MODEL 311
$309.00

Model 311 double-barreled side-by-side shotgun features ventilated rib and lightweight barrels. **Action:** Break action, hammerless, with coil mainsprings, and double triggers. **Stock:** Walnut finish hardwood buttstock and forend; impressed checkering. **Gauges:** 3″ chambering for 12, 20 gauges and .410 bore. **Barrels and chokes:** 12 and 20 gauge, 26″ Imp. Cyl./Mod.; 28″ Mod./Full; 30″ Mod./Full (12 gauge only); .410 bore, 26″ Full/Full. **Overall length:** 41³/₄″–45³/₄″. **Approx. weight:** 7¹/₂ lbs. Automatic top tang safety, bead sight.

Also available: **Model 311R** designed for law enforcement use. **Barrel length:** 18¹/₄″. **Weight:** 6³/₄ lbs.

STOEGER SHOTGUNS

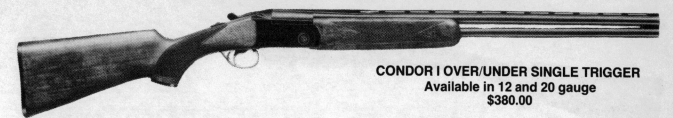

CONDOR I OVER/UNDER SINGLE TRIGGER
Available in 12 and 20 gauge
$380.00

The **STOEGER OVER/UNDER SINGLE TRIGGER** is a workhorse of a shotgun, designed for maximum dependability in heavy field use. The super-safe lock-up system makes use of a sliding underlug, the best system for over/under shotguns. A massive monobloc joins the barrel in a solid one-piece assembly at the breech end. Reliability is assured, thanks to the mechanical extraction system. Upon opening the breech, the spent shells are partially lifted from the chamber, allowing easy removal by hand. Stoeger barrels are of chrome-moly steel with micro-polished bores to give tight, consistent patterns.

They are specifically formulated for use with steel shot where Federal migratory bird regulations require. Atop the barrel is a sighting rib with an anti-glare surface. The buttstock and forend are of durable hardwood, hand-checkered and finished with an oil-based formula that takes dents and scratches in stride.

The Stoeger over/under shotgun is available in 12 or 20 gauge with 26-inch barrels choked Imp. Cyl./Mod. with 3-inch chambers; 12 or 20 gauge with 28-inch barrels choked Mod./Full, 3-inch chambers.

COACH GUN
Available in 12 and 20 gauge
$260.00

The **STOEGER CLASSIC SIDE-BY-SIDE COACH GUN** sports a 20-inch barrel. Lightning fast, it is the perfect shotgun for hunting upland game in dense brush or close quarters. This endurance-tested workhorse of a gun is designed from the ground up to give you years of trouble-free service. Two massive underlugs provide a super-safe, vise-tight locking system for lasting strength and durability. The mechanical extraction of spent shells and double-trigger mechanism assure reliability. The automatic safety is actuated whenever the action is

opened, whether or not the gun has been fired. The polish and blue is deep and rich, and the solid sighting rib is matte-finished for glare-free sighting. Chrome-moly steel barrels with micro-polished bores give dense, consistent patterns. The classic stock and forend are of durable hardwood . . . oil finished, hand-rubbed and hand-checkered.

Improved Cylinder/Modified choking and its short barrel make the Stoeger coach gun the ideal choice for hunting in close quarters, security and police work. 3-inch chambers.

UPLANDER SIDE-BY-SIDE
Available in 12, 20, 28 and .410 gauge
$265.00

The **STOEGER SIDE-BY-SIDE** is a rugged shotgun, endurance-tested and designed to give years of trouble-free service. A vise-tight, super-safe locking system is provided by two massive underlugs for lasting strength and durability. Two design features which make the Stoeger a standout for reliability are its positive mechanical extraction of spent shells and its traditional double-trigger mechanism. The safety is automatic

in that every time the action is opened, whether the gun has been fired or not, the safety is actuated. The polish and blue is deep and rich. The solid sighting rib carries a machined-in matte finish for glare-free sighting. Barrels are of chrome-moly steel with micro-polished bores to give dense, consistent patterns. The stock and forend are of classic design in durable hardwood . . . oil finished, hand-rubbed and hand-checkered.

STOEGER SHOTGUNS

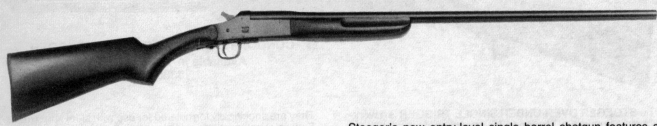

SINGLE BARREL
$95.00

Stoeger's new entry-level single barrel shotgun features a unique locking system. By pulling rearward on the trigger guard, the underlug engagement is released, thus opening the action. Single mechanical extraction makes for convenient removal of spent shells. For ease of operation and maximum safety, this single barrel shotgun is equipped with an exposed hammer, which must be cocked manually. A half-cocked setting on the hammer provides the safety mode.

The buttstock and semi-beavertail forearm are of durable Brazilian hardwood. Stoeger's new single barrel shotgun is available in 12, 20 gauge, and .410 bore.

STOEGER SHOTGUN SPECIFICATIONS

Model	Gauge	Chokes	Chamber	Barrel Length	Length of Pull	Drop at Comb	Drop at Heel	Approx. Average Weight	Safety	Extractors
Single Barrel	12	M, F, IC	2³/₄"	28"/26"	14¹/₂"	1¹/₂"	2¹/₂"	5¹/₈ lbs.	Manual	Yes
	20	M, F, IC	3"	28"/26"	14¹/₂"	1¹/₂"	2¹/₂"	5¹/₈ lbs.	Manual	Yes
	.410	M, F, IC	3"	28"	14¹/₂"	1¹/₂"	2¹/₂"	5¹/₈ lbs.	Manual	Yes
Side-by-Side	12	M/F IC&M	3"	28"/26"	14¹/₂"	1¹/₂"	2¹/₂"	7 lbs.	Automatic	Yes
	20	M/F IC&M	3"	28"/26"	14¹/₂"	1¹/₂"	2¹/₂"	6³/₄ lbs.	Automatic	Yes
	28	IC/M	2³/₄"	26"	14¹/₂"	1¹/₂"	2¹/₂"	7 lbs.	Automatic	Yes
	.410	F/F, IC/M	3"	26"	14¹/₂"	1¹/₂"	2¹/₂"	7 lbs.	Automatic	Yes
Over/Under	12	M/F IC&M	3"	28"/26"	14¹/₂"	1¹/₂"	2¹/₂"	7 lbs.	Manual	Yes
	20	M/F IC/M	3"	28"/26"	14¹/₂"	1¹/₂"	2¹/₂"	7 lbs.	Automatic	Yes
Coach Gun	12	M/F IC/M	3"	20"	14¹/₂"	1¹/₂"	2¹/₂"	6³/₄ lbs.	Automatic	Yes
Coach Gun	12	IC&M	3"	20"	14¹/₂"	1¹/₂"	2¹/₂"	6¹/₂ lbs.	Automatic	Yes
	20	IC&M	3"	20"	14¹/₂"	1¹/₂"	2¹/₂"	6¹/₂ lbs.	Automatic	Yes
	20	M/F IC/M	3"	20"	14¹/₂"	1¹/₂"	2¹/₂"	6³/₄ lbs.	Automatic	Yes

VALMET SHOTGUNS

VALMET 412 ST TRAP & SKEET
$1149.00 STANDARD
$1449.00 PREMIUM

To the sophisticated shooter, Valmet's clay target series is one of the best values in trap and skeet guns available. The 412 ST boasts an impressive array of features usually found on only more expensive guns. Both Trap and Skeet models are available in Standard or Premium Grade.

The **Trap models** have—

High stepped, tapered vent rib: Gets the shooter "on target" quickly. Cross-file pattern reduces glare and improves heat dissipation. Fluorescent front and metal middle beads are standard.

Perfectly balanced: Lines up easily, swings smoothly and provides a superior sighting plane.

Reliable and durable 412 action: Designed to withstand large centerfire rifle calibers. Incorporates precision honing to ensure satisfaction from demanding competitive shooters.

Mechanical triggers: Not dependent upon the inertia from recoil to reset the trigger. Provides a faster and more reliable second shot.

Elongated forcing cones: Greatly reduce recoil.

Stainless steel screw-in choke tubes: Add versatility; corrosion-resistant stainless steel gives added strength over common carbon or alloy steel.

American walnut stock: Double palm swells for both right- and left-handed shooters with Monte Carlo and full comb stock in trap models. Quick-change stock bolt and key permit fast and easy removal. Pachmayr competition recoil pad is standard.

Single selective trigger: Selector button is located on wide target-style trigger for quick, easy selection.

Target safety: Locked in "fire" position. Removal of set screw permits conversion to automatic safety.

Sliding lock bolt: Provides secure barrel lockup. Wears in, not loose.

Steel receiver: Forged and machined for durability.

Automatic ejectors: Eject fired rounds.

Two-piece firing pin: For better durability.

Trap combo sets: Lets the shooter add barrels; precision tolerances require only minor initial fitting.

Skeet 12 and 20 gauge: Start with the gauge of your choice and add the other barrel/gauge at your convenience.

Premium Grade Models: Offer additional features such as Select, semi-fancy American walnut stock and forearm.

Matte nickel receiver: More resistant to wear and corrosion.

Matte blued locking bolt and lever: With non-reflective finish.

Pre-drilled stock: 1-inch diameter hole is provided for insertion of recoil reducer.

Gold trigger: For a subtle touch of class.

Stock wrist checkering: For improved grip.

MODEL 412 ST PREMIUM GRADE SKEET

SPECIFICATIONS MODEL 412 ST PREMIUM & STANDARD GRADE SKEET

Gauges: 12 and 20
Chambers: 2³/₄"
Barrel length: 28"
Chokes: Stainless steel, screw-in Skeet/Skeet
Weight: 8 lbs.
Stock: Premium Grade, Select semi-fancy American walnut; Standard Garde, American walnut

Length of pull: 14¹/₈"
Drop at comb: 1¹/₂"
Drop at heel: 2¹/₈"
Trigger: Single selective mechanical

VALMET SHOTGUNS

MODEL 412 ST Standard Mono Trap

SPECIFICATIONS MODEL 412 ST PREMIUM GRADE TRAP

Gauge: 12
Chambers: 2³/₄"
Barrel lengths: 30" and 32"
Chokes: Stainless steel, screw-in M, IM, F
Weight: 9 lbs.
Stock: Select semi-fancy American walnut
Length of pull: 14⁵/₈"

Drop at comb: 1¹/₂"
Drop at heel: 1¹/₂"
Trigger: Single selective mechanical
Combo sets: 30" o/u bbl. w/32" or 34" single bbl.
32" o/u bbl. w/32" or 34" single bbl.
Optional hard case available

SPECIFICATIONS MODEL 412 ST STANDARD GRADE TRAP

Gauge: 12
Chambers: 2³/₄"
Barrel lengths: 30" and 32"
Chokes: Stainless steel, screw-in M, IM, F
Weight: 9 lbs.
Stock: American walnut
Length of pull: 14⁵/₈"

Drop at comb: 1¹/₂"
Drop at heel: 1¹/₂"
Trigger: Single selective mechanical
Combo sets: 30" o/u bbl. w/32" or 34" single bbl.
32" o/u bbl. w/32" or 34" single bbl.
Optional hard case available

VALMET 412S SHOTGUN/RIFLE
$1099.00

Valmet's unique 412S Shotgun/Rifle combination continues to be the most popular gun of its type in the U.S. Its features are identical to the 412S Field Grade over/under shotguns, including strong steel receiver, superior sliding locking mechanism with automatic safety, cocking indicators, mechanical triggers and two-piece firing pin. In addition, note the other features of this model—

Barrel regulation: Adjusts for windage simply by turning the screw on the muzzle. Elevation is adjustable by regulating the sliding wedge located between the barrels.

Compact: 24-inch barrels mounted on the low-profile receiver limit the overall length to 40 inches (about 5" less than most bolt-action rifles with similar 24-inch barrels).

Single selective trigger: A barrel selector is located on the trigger for quick, easy selection. Double triggers are also available.

Wide choice of calibers: Choose from 222, 30-06, 308

or the new 9.3 × 74R. All are under the 12 gauge, 3" chamber with Improved Modified choke.

Sighting options: The vent rib is cross-filed to reduce glare. The rear sight is flush-folding and permits rapid alignment with the large blade front sight. The rib is milled to accommodate Valmet's one-piece scope mount with 1" rings. Scope mount is of "quick release" design and can be removed without altering zero.

American walnut stock: Stocks are available either cast-on or cast-off for either right- or left-handed shooters, with palm swell for greater control and comfort. Quick detachable sling swivel. Length or pitch adjustable with factory spacers. Semi-Monte Carlo design.

Interchangeability: Receiver will accommodate Valmet's 12 and 20 gauge over/under shotgun barrels and double-rifle barrels with minor initial fitting.

SPECIFICATIONS MODEL 412S SHOTGUN/RIFLE

Gauge/Caliber: 12/.222, 12/30-06, 12/308 or 12/9.3 × 74R
Chamber: 3" with Improved Modified choke
Barrel length: 24"

Overall length: 40"
Weight: 8 lbs.
Stock: American walnut with semi-Monte Carlo design

VALMET SHOTGUNS

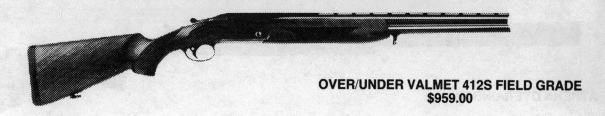

OVER/UNDER VALMET 412S FIELD GRADE
$959.00

Designed for the experienced hunter, Valmet's 412S represents the pride and skill of "Old World" European craftsmanship. The barrels are polished to a mirror finish and deeply blued. Select American walnut stock and forearm highlight fine, deep-cut checkering. Other features include:

Time-proven action: Designed to handle large centerfire calibers for more durability and reliability.

Mechanical trigger: Fires two shots as fast as you can pull the trigger. Does not rely on the inertia from the recoil of the first shot to set the trigger for the second. In the event of a faulty primer or light hit, inertia trigger shotguns cannot function on the second round.

Single selective trigger: Selector button is located on the trigger for fast, easy selection.

Large trigger guard opening: Designed for cold weather shooting; permits easy finger movement when wearing gloves.

American walnut stock and forearm: Add greatly to overall appearance.

Superior stock design: A straight stock that is not cast or "bent." Double palm swell for added comfort for both right- and left-handed shooters. Length and angle (pitch) can be altered for a perfect fit with addition of factory spacers. Fine, deep-cut checkering.

Palm-filling forearm: Rounded and tapered for comfort and smooth, true swing, plus fine, deep-cut checkering.

Automatic ejectors: Select and eject fired rounds. Raise unfired shells for safe removal.

Chrome-lined barrels: For more consistent patterns. Eliminates pitting and corrosion, extends barrel life even with steel shot.

Stainless steel choke tubes: Added strength over regular carbon and alloy materials. Easily handles steel shot. Recessed so as not to detract from appearance. Tight tolerances enable truer patterns and enhance choke versatility.

Sliding locking bolt: Secure lockup between receiver and barrels. Wears in, not loose.

Matte nickel receiver: Non-glare and more resistant to wear and corrosion.

Wide vent rib: Cross-file pattern reduces glare. Fluorescent front and middle beads.

Automatic safety: Goes to safe position automatically when gun is opened.

Cocking indicators: Allow shooter to determine (through sight or feel) which barrel has been fired.

Steel receiver: Forged and machined for durability.

Chamber: 3-inch on all models

Two-piece firing pin: For more durability

Versatility: Change from 12 to 20 gauge simply by adding a barrel. Change from over/under shotgun to shotgun/rifle, trap, skeet or double rifle. Precision tolerances require only minor initial fitting.

SPECIFICATIONS MODEL 412S FIELD GRADE OVER/UNDER

Gauge: 12
Chambers: 3"
Weight: 7 1/4 lbs. w/26" barrels; 7 1/2 lbs. w/28" or 30" barrels

Barrel lengths/chokes:
26", IC, M, IM
28", M, IM, F
30" M, IM, F

WEATHERBY SHOTGUNS

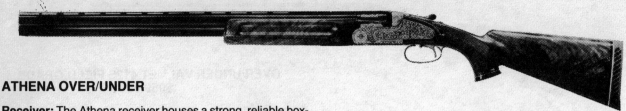

ATHENA OVER/UNDER

Receiver: The Athena receiver houses a strong, reliable box-lock action, yet it features side lock-type plates to carry through the fine floral engraving. The hinge pivots are made of a special high strength steel alloy. The locking system employs the time-tested Greener cross-bolt design. **Single selective trigger:** It is mechanically rather than recoil operated. This provides a fully automatic switchover, allowing the second barrel to be fired on a subsequent trigger pull, even in the event of a misfire. A flick of the trigger finger and the selector lever, located just in front of the trigger, is all the way to the left enabling you to fire the lower barrel first, or to the right for the upper barrel. The Athena trigger is selective as well. **Barrels:** The breech block is hand-fitted to the receiver, providing closest possible tolerances. Every Athena is equipped with a matted, ventilated rib and bead front sight. **Selective automatic ejectors:** The Athena contains ejectors that are fully automatic both in selection and action. **Slide safety:** The safety is the traditional slide type located conveniently on the upper tang

on top of the pistol grip. **Stock:** Each stock is carved from specially selected Claro walnut, with fine line hand-checkering and high luster finish. Trap model has Monte Carlo stock only. **Weight:** 12 ga. Field, 8 lbs.; 20 ga. Field, 7 lbs.; Trap, 8½ lbs.

Prices:
Fixed Choke:
Field (28 or .410 Ga.)	$1590.00
Skeet (12 or 20 Ga.)	1601.00

IMC Multi Choke:
Field (12 or 20 Ga.)	1590.00
Trap (12 Ga.)	1611.00
Trap, single barrel (12 Ga.)	1611.00
Trap Combo (12 Ga.)	2100.00
Athena Master Skeet (tube set w/case)	3200.00

MODEL 82 AUTOMATIC IMC (12 Ga.)
$555.00
BUCKMASTER AUTO SLUG $555.00

EIGHTY-TWO AUTOMATIC

Gas-operated means no friction rings and collars to adjust for different loads. The barrel holds stationary instead of plunging backward with every shot. To these natural advantages, Weatherby has added revolutionary "Floating Piston" action.

In the Weatherby Eighty-two, the piston "floats" freely on the magazine tube completely independent of every other part of the action. Nothing to get out of alignment. Nothing to cause drag or friction. **Weight:** 7½ lbs.

Model Eighty-Two Auto Shotgun Specifications

All guns are 12 gauge and have ventilated rib barrels.
Magazine capacity is three shells (2¾") with a removable plug limiting capacity to two shells in the magazine.

Model	Chamber	Bbl Length	Chokes	Overall Length	Length of Pull	Drop at: Comb	Drop at: Heel	Bead Sights	Approx. Weight
Choked Barrels									
Buckmaster	2¾"	22"	Skeet	46¼"	14¼"	1⅜"	2½"	Rifle	7½ lb.
IMC Barrels									
Field	2¾"	26"	M/IC/Sk	46½"	14¼"	1⅜"	2½"	Front bead	7½ lb.
Field	2¾"	28"	F/M/IC	48½"	14¼"	1⅜"	2½"	Front bead	7½ lb.
Field	2¾"	30"	F/M/IC	50½"	14¼"	1⅜"	2½"	Front bead	7½ lb.
Field	3"	28"	F/M/IC	48½"	14¼"	1⅜"	2½"	Front bead	7½ lb.
Field	3"	30"	F/M/IC	50½"	14¼"	1⅜"	2½"	Front bead	7½ lb.

WEATHERBY SHOTGUNS

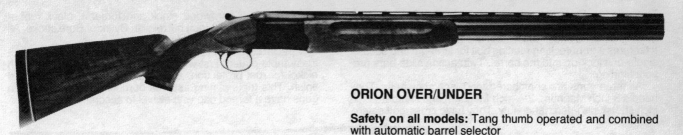

ORION OVER/UNDER

Safety on all models: Tang thumb operated and combined with automatic barrel selector
Stocks on all models: American walnut

ORION OVER/UNDER

For greater versatility, the Orion incorporates the integral multi-choke (IMC) system. Available in Extra-full, Full, Modified, Improved Modified, Improved Cylinder and Skeet, the choke tubes fit flush with the muzzle without detracting from the beauty of the gun. Three tubes are furnished with each gun. The precision hand-fitted monobloc and receiver are machined from high-strength steel with a highly polished finish. The box-lock design uses the Greener cross-bolt locking system and special sears maintain hammer engagement. Pistol grip stock and forearm are carved of Claro walnut with hand-checkered diamond inlay pattern and high-gloss finish. Chrome moly steel barrels, and the receiver, are deeply blued. The Orion also features selective automatic ejectors, single

selective trigger, front bead sight and ventilated rib. The Trap model boasts a curved trap-style recoil pad and is available with Monte Carlo stock only. **Weight:** 12 ga. Field, 7¹/₂ lbs.; 20 ga. Field, 7¹/₂ lbs.; Trap, 8 lbs.

Prices:
Fixed Choke:
    Field (28 or .410 Ga.) **$1000.00**
    Skeet (12 or 20 Ga.) 1011.00
IMC Multi Choke:
    Field (12 or 20 Ga.). 1000.00
    Trap (12 Ga.) 1051.00

Athena & Orion Over/Under Shotgun Specifications

Fixed Choke Models (12 Ga. and 20 Ga.)

Model	Chamber	Bbl Length	Chokes	Overall Length	Length of Pull	Comb	Drop at: Heel	**MC	Bead Sights	*Approx. Weight
Skeet/Skeet	3"	26"	S/S	43¹/₄"	14¹/₄"	1¹/₂"	2¹/₂"		White Fr, Mid Br	6¹/₂-7¹/₂ lb.
†Skeet/Skeet	2³/₄"	28"	S/S	45¹/₄"	14¹/₄"	1¹/₂"	2¹/₂"		White Fr, Mid Br	6¹/₂-7¹/₂ lb.
IMC Multi-Choke Field Models (12 Ga. and .410 Ga.)										
Field	3"	26"	M/IC/Sk	43¹/₄"	14¹/₄"	1¹/₂"	2¹/₂"		Brilliant Front	6¹/₂-7¹/₂ lb.
Field	3"	28"	F/M/IC	45¹/₄"	14¹/₄"	1¹/₂"	2¹/₂"		Brilliant Front	6¹/₂-7¹/₂ lb.
Field (12 Ga. only)	3"	30"	F/M/F	47¹/₄"	14¹/₄"	1¹/₂"	2¹/₂"		Brilliant Front	7¹/₂-8 lbs.
IMC Multi-Choke Field Models (28 Ga. only)										
Field	2³/₄"	26"	M/IC/Sk	43¹/₄"	14¹/₄"	1¹/₂"	2¹/₂"		Brilliant Front	6¹/₂-7¹/₂ lb.
Field	2³/₄"	28"	F/M/IC	45¹/₄"	14¹/₄"	1¹/₂"	2¹/₂"		Brilliant Front	6¹/₂-7¹/₂ lb.
IMC Multi-Choke Trap Models (12 Ga. only)**										
Trap	2³/₄"	30"	F/M/IM	47¹/₂"	14³/₈"	1³/₈"	2¹/₈"	1³/₄"	White Fr, Mid Br	8-8¹/₂ lb.
Trap	2³/₄"	32"	F/M/IM	49¹/₂"	14³/₈"	1³/₈"	2¹/₈"	1³/₄"	White Fr, Mid Br	8-8¹/₂ lb.
†Sgl Bbl Trap	2³/₄"	32"	F/M/IM	49¹/₂"	14³/₈"	1³/₈"	2¹/₈"	1³/₄"	White Fr, Mid Br	8-8¹/₂ lb.
†Sgl Bbl Trap	2³/₄"	34"	F/M/IM	51¹/₂"	14³/₈"	1³/₈"	2¹/₈"	1³/₄"	White Fr, Mid Br	8¹/₂-9 lb.

**TRAP STOCKS AVAILABLE ONLY WITH MONTE CARLO.

Three tubes shown are furnished with IMC models. An Extra Full tube is also available as a separate item.

*Weight varies due to wood density.

†Available in Athena Model only.

WINCHESTER SECURITY SHOTGUNS

This trio of tough 12-gauge shotguns provides backup strength for security and police work as well as all-around utility. The action is one of the fastest second-shot pumps made. It features a front-locking rotating bolt for strength and secure, single-unit lock-up into the barrel. Twin-action slide bars prevent binding.

All three guns are chambered for 3-inch shotshells. They handle 3-inch Magnum, 2³/₄-inch Magnum and standard 2³/₄-inch shotshells interchangeably. They have cross-bolt safety, walnut-finished hardwood stock and forearm, black rubber butt pad and plain 18-inch barrel with Cylinder Bore choke. All are ultra-reliable and easy to handle.

Special chrome finishes on Police and Marine guns are actually triple-plated: first with copper for adherence, then with nickel for rust protection, and finally with chrome for a hard finish. This triple-plating assures durability and quality. Both guns have a forend cap with swivel to accommodate sling.

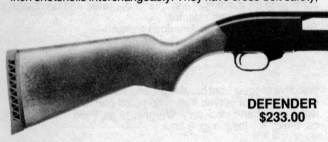

DEFENDER
$233.00

Also available: **DEFENDER COMBO** with pistol grip and extra hunting barrel. **$261.00 ($280.00 with vent. rib)**

Security Defender™ is ideal for home security use. The compact 35⁵/₈-inch overall length handles and stores easily. The Defender has a deep blued finish on metal surfaces and features a traditional ribbed forearm for sure pumping grip. It has a metal bead front sight. The magazine holds eight 12-gauge 2³/₄-inch shells. New version offers shotshell capacity of five 2³/₄" shells with optional metal bead front sight or rifle type (front and rear). **$224.00** (metal bead) and **$240.00** (rifle).

STAINLESS MARINE
$387.00

Security Police™ is designed for police and security force work. It features an 18-inch ordnance stainless steel barrel and a satin chrome finish on all external metal parts. The distinctive satin chrome finish diffuses light and resists corrosion. The magazine has a capacity of six 2³/₄-inch shotshells, plus one shell in the chamber. Optional metal bead front sight or rifle-type front and rear sights. **Price: $387.00.**

Also available: **Stainless Marine** model. Same specifications as Stainless Police model w/o satin finish.

Model	Current Symbol Number	New Symbol Number	Gauge	Chamber	Shotshell Capacity (A)	Choke	Barrel Length & Type	Overall Length	Nominal Length of Pull	Nominal Drop At Comb	Nominal Drop At Heel	Nominal Weight (Lbs.)	Sights
Stainless Marine	G120321SR	7467	12	3" Mag.	7†	Cyl.	18"	38⁵/₈"	14"	1³/₈"	2³/₄"	7	RT
Stainless Police	G120319PR	7517	12	3" Mag.	7†	Cyl.	18"	38⁵/₈"	14"	1³/₈"	2³/₄"	7	RT
Defender	G1203DM1	7566	12	3" Mag.	8†	Cyl.	18"	38⁵/₈"	14"	1³/₈"	2³/₄"	6³/₄	MBF
Pistol Grip	G1203DM1PG	7616	12	3" Mag.	8†	Cyl.	18	25⁵/₈	—	—	—	5¹/₂	MBF
	G1203DM2B	7665	12	3" Mag.	5	Cyl.	18	38⁵/₈	14	1³/₈	2³/₄	6¹/₄	MBF
Rifle Sights	G1203DM2R	7715	12	3" Mag.	5	Cyl.	18	38⁵/₈	14	1³/₈	2³/₄	6¹/₄	RT
Defender COMBO	G1203S CP	7764	12	3" Mag.	5	Cyl.	18"	38⁵/₈"	14"	1³/₈"	2³/₄"	6¹/₄	MBF
Extra Barrel: Plain			12	3" Mag.	5	W1M	28	48⁵/₈	14	1³/₈	2³/₄	6¹/₄	MBF
Defender COMBO	G1203S CV	7814	12	3" Mag.	5	Cyl.	18	38⁵/₈	14	1³/₈	2³/₄	6¹/₄	MBF
Extra Barrel: Vent Rib			12	3" Mag.	5	W1M	28 VR	48⁵/₈	14	1³/₈	2³/₄	6¹/₂	MBF

(A) Includes one round in chamber when ready to fire. †-One less for 3" shells. Cyl.-Cylinder Bore. VR-Ventilated rib. MBF-Metal bead front. RT-Rifle type front and rear sights.

WINCHESTER SHOTGUNS

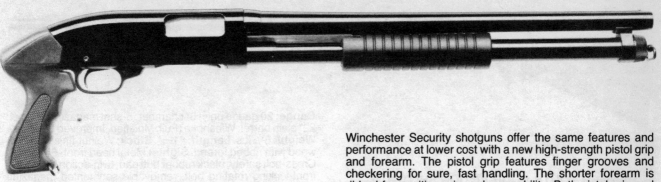

PISTOL GRIP SLIDE-ACTION DEFENDER
$233.00

Winchester Security shotguns offer the same features and performance at lower cost with a new high-strength pistol grip and forearm. The pistol grip features finger grooves and checkering for sure, fast handling. The shorter forearm is ribbed for positive grip and pumpability. Both pistol grip and forearm are high-impact-resistant ABS plastic with non-glare matte black finish. The Pistol Grip series is lighter in weight, compact, easily stored and fast handling.

RANGER SEMIAUTOMATIC SHOTGUN
$291.00 ($288.00 w/22″ Barrel Deer)

Gauge: 12 and 20; 2³/₄″ chamber; 3-shot magazine. **Barrel:** 28″ vent rib with Full, Modified and Improved Cylinder Winchoke tubes or 28″ plain barrel Modified. **Weight:** 7 to 7¹/₄ pounds. **Overall length:** 48⁵/₈″. **Stock:** Walnut-finished hardwood with cut-checkering. **Sights:** Metal bead front. **Features:** Cross-bolt safety; front-locking rotating bolt; black serrated butt plate, gas-operated action. Also available in deer barrel.

Ranger Pump Action Shotguns

Ranger Field Winchoke	G120385R	6519	12	3″ Mag.	5	W3	28″VR	48⁵/₈″	14″	1¹/₂″	2¹/₂″	7¹/₄	MBF
	G120387R	6568	20	3″ Mag.	5	W3	28 VR	48⁵/₈	14	1¹/₂	2¹/₂	7¹/₄	MBF
Ranger Deer COMBO	G1203RC	6618	12	3″ Mag.	5	Cyl.	22	42³/₄″	14″	1¹/₂″	2¹/₂″	6¹/₂	RT
12 ga. Extra Barrel			12	3″ Mag.	5	W3	28	48⁵/₈	14	1¹/₂	2¹/₂	7¹/₄	MBF
Ranger Deer COMBO	G120320RC	6667	20	3″ Mag.	5	Cyl.	22	42³/₄″	14″	1¹/₂″	2¹/₂″	6¹/₂	RT
20 ga. Extra Barrel			20	3″ Mag.	5	W3	28	48⁵/₈	14	1¹/₂	2¹/₂	7¹/₄	MBF
Ranger Deer Gun	G120310R	6717	12	3″ Mag.	5	Cyl.	22″	42³/₄″	14″	1¹/₂″	2¹/₂″	6¹/₂	RT
	G120320R	6766	20	3″ Mag.	5	Cyl.	22	42³/₄	14	1¹/₂		6¹/₂	RT
Ranger Utility Winchoke	G120353R1	6816	12	3″ Mag.	5	W1M	28″VR	48⁵/₈″	14″	1¹/₂″	2¹/₂″	7¹/₄	MBF
	G120373R1	6865	20	3″ Mag.	5	W1M	28 VR	48⁵/₈	14	1¹/₂	2¹/₂	7¹/₄	MBF
	G120351R1	6923	12	3″ Mag.	5	W1F	30 VR	50⁵/₈	14	1¹/₂	2¹/₂	7¹/₂	MBF
Ranger Youth	G120330R	7111	20	3″ Mag.	5	W3	22″VR	41⁵/₈″	13″	1¹/₂″	2¹/₂″	6¹/₄	MBF
Pump Action Winchoke	G120333R1	7178	20	3″ Mag.	5	W1M	22	41⁵/₈	13	1¹/₂	2¹/₂	6	MBF

(A) Includes one shotshell in chamber when ready to fire. VR-Ventilated rib. Cyl.-Cylinder Bore. R-Rifled barrel. MBF-Metal bead front. RT-Rifle type front and rear sights. Model 1300 and Ranger pump action shotguns have factory-installed plug which limits capacity to three shells. Ranger Youth shotgun has factory-installed plug which limits capacity to one, two or three shells as desired. Extra barrels for Model 1300 and Ranger shotguns are available in 12 or 20 gauge, plain or ventilated rib, in a variety of barrel lengths and chokes; interchangeable within gauge. Winchoke sets with wrench come with gun as follows: W3W-Extra Full, Full, Modified tubes. W3-Full, Modified, Improved Cylinder tubes. W1M-Modified tube. W1F-Full Tube.
*Indicates NEW. Cyl./R-Cylinder Bore with rifling

WINCHESTER SHOTGUNS

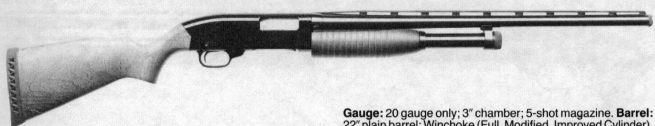

Gauge: 20 gauge only; 3″ chamber; 5-shot magazine. **Barrel:** 22″ plain barrel; Winchoke (Full, Modified, Improved Cylinder). **Weight:** 6½ lbs. **Length:** 41⅝″. **Stock:** Walnut-finished hardwood with ribbed forend. **Sights:** Metal bead front. **Features:** Cross-bolt safety; black rubber butt pad; twin-action slide bars; front-locking rotating bolt; removable segmented magazine plug to limit shotshell capacity for training purposes; discount certificate for full-size adult stock. Also available in plain barrel w/Mod. choke.

RANGER YOUTH SLIDE-ACTION SHOTGUN
$230.00 ($268.00 w/vent. rib)

MODEL 1300 FEATHERWEIGHT™ SLIDE-ACTION
$324.00 (12 & 20 GAUGE)

The Model 1300 Featherweight 12- and 20-gauge pump guns are designed with shorter 22-inch barrels for upland shooting and small, quick game. At 6⅜ pounds, both are light-carrying, easy-swinging and lightning fast.

Their perfected slide action is one of the fastest, surest ever made. Twin-action slide bars prevent binding. The action permits ultra-fast follow-up shots. The front-locking rotating bolt locks the bolt into barrel with maximum strength and security. The ventilated rib barrel is chromium molybdenum steel, hot-formed for high strength.

Both 12- and 20-gauge versions handle 3-inch Magnum, 2¾-inch Magnum, and 2¾-inch standard shotshells interchangeably. Their 22-inch barrel is specially adapted for the Winchoke system, and each comes equipped with Full, Modified and Improved Cylinder Winchoke tubes and wrench. The Winchoke system and 3″ Magnum capability give these new shotguns the versatility for most upland game—and great potential as utility guns.

Model 1300 Featherweight styling is clean-cut and handsome. Stock and forearm are American walnut with high-luster finish. Deep cut-checkering on pistol grip and traditional ribbing on the short, contoured forearm. Receivers are roll-engraved. Metal surfaces are highly polished and blued. Other features include cross-bolt safety with red indicator and metal front bead sight.

The 20-gauge Model 1300 Featherweight makes short work of upland birds. Equipped with serrated butt plate. The 12-gauge version delivers maximum versatility and performance for rabbits and small, fast game. The short barrel makes shotgun hunting for small game quick and responsive while the Winchoke system maximizes utility value. Equipped with rubber recoil pad. **Chamber:** 3″. **Barrel length:** 22″. **Overall length:** 42⅝″. **Weight:** 6⅜ lbs.

Also available: **Model 1300 XTR** with 28″ barrel. **Weight:** 7¼ lbs. **Price:** $324.00.

WINCHESTER SHOTGUNS

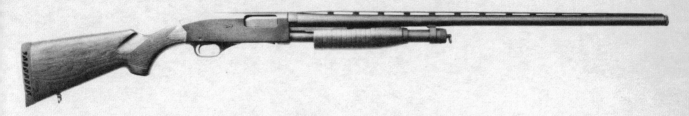

MODEL 1300 MAGNUM WATERFOWL
$338.00 (12 GAUGE)

The Model 1300 Magnum Waterfowl pump is designed specifically for hunting ducks and geese. It features a 30-inch ventilated rib barrel with the Winchoke System of interchangeable choke tubes (Extra Full, Full and Modified). Stock and forearm are of American walnut with a low-luster protective finish. All exterior metal surfaces have a special non-glare matte finish to aid in hunter concealment. Other features include metal front bead sight, cross-bolt safety, rubber recoil pad and sling swivels. **Chamber:** 3″ Mag. **Barrel length:** 30″. **Overall length:** 50⅝″. **Stock dimensions:** Length of pull, 14″; drop at comb, 1½″; drop at heel, 2½″; **Weight:** 7 lbs.
Also available with WIN-TUFF Laminated stock and forearm: **$349.00.**

MODEL 1300 TURKEY SHOTGUN
WITH WINCHOKE®, V.R. (not shown)
$338.00

Available in 12 gauge only, the Model 1300 Turkey gun comes equipped with a 22-inch ventilated rib barrel, which includes the Winchester Winchoke system with Extra Full, Full and Modified choke tubes and wrench. Its walnut stock and forearm have a special low-luster protective finish; the receiver, barrel and all exterior metal surfaces feature a non-glare matte finish. The receiver is roll engraved. The pistol grip has deep-cut checkering; the contoured forearm is ribbed for sure gripping and has been modified for positioning and comfort. Other features include cross-bolt safety with red indicator blocks and metal bead sights. The 1300 Turkey Gun handles 3″ magnum, 2¾″ Magnum and 2¾″ standard shotshells interchangeably.

Chamber: 3″ Mag., 5-shot capacity. **Overall length:** 42⅝″. **Stock dimensions:** Length of pull, 14″; drop at comb, 1½″; drop at heel, 2½″. **Weight:** 6⅜″.

Also available:
Turkey Win-Cam Camouflage model w/vent ribs: **$349.00.**
Special Turkey NWTF (National Wild Turkey Federation) Model with Win-Cam Camouflage: **$368.00.**
Combo Pac Win-Cam Camouflage with extra barrel (12 ga. 30″ waterfowl w/12 ga. 22″ upland game); stock laminated w/ Win-Cam camouflage green and all metal parts with low reflecting matte finish. **Price: $425.00**

Model	Current Symbol Number	New Symbol Number	Gauge	Chamber	Shotshell Capacity (A)	Choke	Barrel Length & Type	Overall Length	Nominal Length Of Pull	Nominal Drop At Comb	Nominal Drop At Heel	Nominal Weight (Lbs.)	Sights
1300 XTR	G130385XTR	6014	12	3″ Mag.	5	W3	28″VR	48⅝″	14″	1½″	2½″	7¼	MBF
Featherweight	G1303RP	6063	12	3″ Mag.	5	W3	22 VR	42⅝″	14	1½	2½	6⅜	MBF
Featherweight	G1303QD	6113	20	3″ Mag.	5	W3	22 VR	42⅝″	14	1½	2½	6⅜	MBF
1300 Waterfowl	G1303WF	6162	12	3″ Mag.	5	W3W	30″VR	50⅝″	14″	1½″	2½″	7	MBF
WIN-TUFF	*G1303WFLAM	6196	12	3″ Mag.	5	W3W	30 VR	50⅝	14	1½	2½	7	MBF
1300 Deer Gun	*G1303D	6212	12	3″ Mag.	5	Cyl/R	22″	42¾″	14″	1½″	2½″	6½	RT
WIN-TUFF	*G1303DLAM	6238	12	3″ Mag.	5	Cyl/R	22	42¾	14	1½	2½	6½	RT
1300 Turkey Gun	G1303TK	6261	12	3″ Mag.	5	W3W	22″VR	42⅝″	14″	1½″	2½″	6⅜	MBF
WIN-CAM	G1303TCAM	6295	12	3″ Mag.	5	W3W	22 VR	42⅝	14	1½	2½	6⅜	MBF
Spec. NWTF	*G1303NWTF	6303	12	3″ Mag.	5	W3W	22 VR	42⅝	14	1½	2½	6⅜	MBF
1300 CamoPack WIN-CAM	G1303TWC	6469	12	3″ Mag.	5	W3W	22″VR	42⅝″	14″	1½″	2½″	6⅜	MBF
Extra Barrel			12	3″ Mag.	5	W1M	30 VR	50⅝	14	1½	2½	7	MBF

Paramilitary

FOR ADDRESSES AND PHONE
NUMBERS OF MANUFACTURERS AND
DISTRIBUTORS INCLUDED IN THIS
SECTION, SEE *DIRECTORY OF
MANUFACTURERS AND SUPPLIERS*

AMERICAN CARBINE

CALICO M·100 CARBINE
$299.95

Caliber: 22 LR
Barrel length: 16.1″
Overall length: 29.8″ (stock folded); 35.8″ (stock extended)
Weight: 5.7 lbs. (loaded); magazine w/100 rds 24 oz.
Height: 7.3″ (max.)
Magazine capacity: 100 rds.
Safety: ambidextrous, trigger and hammer block

Sights: post, adj. for elevation (front); notch, adj. for windage (rear)
Sight radius: 12.2″
Also available:
Calico M·100P Pistol (22 LR): **$249.95**
Calico M·100S Sporter (16″ barrel, 22 LR only, 100-round capacity): **$318.95**

AUTO-ORDNANCE

MODEL 1927A5 THOMPSON
SEMIAUTOMATIC (45 Caliber)
$559.95

Featuring lightweight alloys for maximum shooting balance, this .45 semiautomatic pistol has an overall length of 26″ and is supplied with a 30-round magazine. Modeled after the famous Model 1928 but without the detachable buttstock, it is precision rifled; its 13″ barrel complements the gun's overall fine detail. It accepts all accessories common to the 1927A-1.

AUTO-ORDNANCE

1927A1 THOMPSON DELUXE SEMIAUTOMATIC
CARBINE (45 Caliber)
$614.95

The frame and receiver of this classic are durably manufactured from solid milled steel. It features finger-grooved vertical foregrip, a 16" finned barrel, and an adjustable rear sight and compensator.

Model 1927A-1C Lightweight. $567.00

THOMPSON M1 SEMIAUTOMATIC
CARBINE (45 Caliber)
$574.95

1911 A1 THOMPSON GOVERNMENT MODEL
45 Caliber: $344.95

Considered by many to be the best and most popular .45 caliber automatic pistol in the world, this Model 1911 is now available in three other calibers as well—9mm, 38 Super and 41 Action Express. All parts are interchangeable with all other Government 1911 pistols. Constructed of durable 4140 steel, the frame and slide are finished in deep blue; each radius features a non-glare finish and both grips are enhanced by a special medallion.

1911A1 Government Model
In 9mm, 38 Super or 41 Action Express $381.95

BARRETT SEMIAUTOMATIC RIFLES

BARRETT MODEL 82A1
$7400.00

Barrett's Model 82A1 (military configuration) features 4140 steel Match Grade barrel; high efficiency, low signature muzzle brake, two magazines; airtight and watertight fitted hard case.

SPECIFICATIONS
Caliber: 50 BMG (12.7mm)
Operation: Recoil, semiautomatic
Barrel length: 33"
Overall length: 61"
Capacity: 11 round detachable box magazine
Weight: 32.5 lbs.
Muzzle velocity: 2,848 fps
Sights: Leupold MI Ultra 10X telescope and rings w/iron sight backup

BERETTA SEMIAUTOMATIC RIFLES

BERETTA AR-70 SPORTER
SEMIAUTOMATIC RIFLE
$800.00

Optimum firepower and rugged dependability characterize this Beretta semiautomatic 223-caliber centerfire rifle. Special features include simple, fast take-down with no special tools needed. Far fewer component parts than similar centerfires. Every inch is crafted from the toughest materials in modern arsenal technology for all-weather, year-round use in any terrain. Comes with 8- and 30-round magazines, three-piece cleaning kit and military-style carrying strap.

SPECIFICATIONS
Action: Medium length. **Barrel length:** 17.72". **Magazine:** 8 or 30 rounds. **Sights:** Diopter sighting device adjustable for windage and elevation. **Finish:** Military-like exterior of antiabrasive, corrosion-free epoxy resins. **Weight:** 8.31 lbs.

COLT SEMIAUTOMATIC RIFLES

AR-15A2 GOVERNMENT MODEL
Rifle $815.95
Carbine 835.95

AR-15A2 GOVERNMENT CARBINE (223 Cal.)
$835.95

Designed from the famous Colt M-16 military rifle, the Colt AR-15 A2 is lightweight, with simple maintenance, easy handling and extreme accuracy. Semiautomatic 223 (5.56 mm) with 5-round magazine capacity. Features forward bolt assist, stiffer barrel with 1 turn in 7" rifling twist, strong nylon ribbed round handguard, buttstock and pistol grip, improved heat deflector and muzzle compensator. Front sight post adjustable for elevation. Quick flip rear sight assembly with short-range and long-range tangs, adjustable for windage. **Weight:** 5.8 lbs. **Barrel length:** 16". **Overall length:** 35" with buttstock extended; 32" closed.

AR-15A2 H-BAR (223 Rem.)
$869.95

The new Colt AR-15A2 H-BAR features the new target-style rear sight adopted by the U.S. Military on their M16A2, which is fully adjustable for windage and elevation out to 800 meters and is capable of fine adjustment at the longer ranges. This model also has a cartridge case deflector for left-handed shooters. **Weight:** Approximately 8 lbs. **Barrel length:** 20".

COLT SEMIAUTOMATIC RIFLE

DELTA H-BAR AR-15A2 RIFLE
$1359.95

This rifle has been selectively chosen and equipped with a 3×9 variable rubber armored scope, leather sling, shoulder stock cheekpiece, cleaning kit and carrying case.
Caliber: 223 Rem. **Barrel length:** 20″. **Weight:** 10 lbs.

EMF SEMIAUTOMATIC CARBINES

AP-74 MILITARY
$295.00 ($320.00 in .32 ACP)

An outstanding copy of the U.S. Army Colt M-16 rifle, the AP-74 is extremely durable and dependable. Available with original military-type stock or in the sporter model with finely finished wood stock. In 22 Long Rifle or 32 ACP caliber. Military model available in 22 LR only; "dressed" with Cyclops scope, military mounts, Colt bayonet, sling and bipod.

SPECIFICATIONS
Magazine capacity: 15 rounds. **Barrel length:** 20″ w/flash reducer. **Overall length:** 38″. **Weight:** 6¾ lbs. **Front sight:** Protected pin. **Rear sight:** Selective protected peep, with apertures for long and close ranges. **Stock:** Strong, lightweight plastic; ventilated snap-out forend; fixed buttstock.

FABRIQUE NATIONALE RIFLES

LIGHT AUTOMATIC LAR
7.62 NATO (308 MATCH)
$3179.00

This 308 Win. Match gas-operated semiautomatic has a rifled bore with 4 lands and grooves, plus right-hand twist, one turn in 12 inches. The rear sight is adjustable from 200 to 600 yards in 100 yard increments. Sight radius is 21³/₄ inches. Synthetic stock with ventilated forend. **Weight** (without magazine): 9 lbs. 7 oz. **Overall length:** 44¹/₂″. **Barrel length:** 21″ (24¹/₂″ with flash hider).

LAR PARA (308 MATCH)
MODEL 50.63 w/18″ Bbl., Short Flash Hider
$3239.00

HEAVY BARREL MODEL 50.42 W/Wood Stock & Metal Bipod (not shown): $4175.00
MODEL 50.41 With Synthetic Stock: $3776.00

FNC SEMIAUTOMATIC 223 REM. (5.56mm)
PARATROOPER $2322.00
STANDARD (not shown) $2204.00

The FNC is a short, relatively light weapon with a fully locked mechanism functioning by an adjustable gas flow, plus smooth recoil and high accuracy. It is remarkably rugged, impervious to any adverse weather conditions and field strips effortlessly.

SPECIFICATIONS
Caliber: 223 Rem. (5.56mm). **Capacity:** 30-round magazine. **Action:** Gas-operated, semiautomatic. **Barrel length:** 18″. **Weight:** 9.6 lbs. with magazine. **Rifling:** 6 lands and grooves with right-hand twist, 1 turn in 12″. **Overall length:** 40″; 30″ with butt folded.

F.I.E./FRANCHI

PARA RIMFIRE RIFLE
$234.95

This takedown semiautomatic rifle comes in its own contour-fitted carrying case, which features steel reinforced corners, latches and hinges. Rifle has an artillery-type rear sight, hooded front sight, interior and exterior threaded muzzle, skeleton buttstock. Other features include oil finished walnut forend, matte black receiver finish. O.D. web sling and disassembly tool.

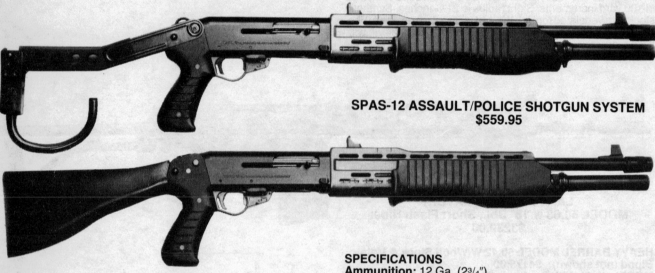

SPAS-12 ASSAULT/POLICE SHOTGUN SYSTEM
$559.95

A slide-action or gas-operated semiautomatic shotgun featuring dual firing system, using all types of 2³/₄″ shotshells. Offers maintenance-free parkerized finish, lightweight alloy receiver, anti-corrosive chrome-lined steel barrel and folding stock, plus nylon-resin pistol grip and forearm.

SPECIFICATIONS
Ammunition: 12 Ga. (2³/₄″)
Choke: Cylinder bore
Capacity: 9 (8 plus 1 in chamber)
Barrel length: 21¹/₂″
Length w/stock folded: 31³/₄″
Length w/stock extended: 41″
Weight: 9.6 lbs.
Finish: Matte black

MODEL LAW-12 SEMIAUTOMATIC SHOTGUN
$559.95

SPECIFICATIONS
Gauge: 12 (2³/₄″ chamber)
Choke: Cylinder bore
Action: Gas-operated semiautomatic
Barrel length: 21¹/₂″
Overall length: 41″

Weight: 6.7 lbs.
Sights: Front bead
Safety: Dual quick deployment; positive 180° swivel type
Stock type: Fixed
Finish: Military spec. matte black

F.I.E./FRANCHI

MODEL SAS-12 PUMP ACTION SHOTGUN
$359.95

SPECIFICATIONS: Same as LAW-12, except it operates with pump action. Length folded is 31³/₄″ (same as SPAS-12). Chambered for 3″ Magnum as well as 2³/₄″ shells.

GALIL SEMIAUTOMATIC RIFLES

MODEL 308 ARM 7.62 mm (.308 WIN.) SEMIAUTOMATIC RIFLE

Based on the battle-proven 5.56 mm (223) semiautomatic, the 7.62 mm (308) version is built for hard use and rough handling. Features ease of handling by right- or left-handed marksmen and functions under adverse weather conditions, humidity and dust. Post-type front sight; L flip-type rear sight set for 300 and 500 meters (330 and 550 yards); folding night sights are fitted with tritium lights. Telescopic, infrared or starlight sights can be fixed using special sight mounts.

SPECIFICATIONS (MODELS AR and ARM)
Ammunition: 223 REM. (5.56 mm) and 308 Win. (7.62 mm)
Finish: Black
Barrel length: 16.1″ (223) and 18¹/₂″ (308)
Weight (empty): 8.6 lbs (AR) and 9.6 lbs. (ARM)
Length, stock folded: 27.2″ (223) and 29.7″ (308)
Overall length: 36¹/₂″ (223) and 39″ (308)

GALIL MODEL 223 AR SEMIAUTO RIFLE

GALIL RIFLE SYSTEM SEMIAUTOMATIC	PRICE
223 AR	$795.00
223 ARM	875.00
308 AR	849.00
308 ARM	940.00

AR —Folding stock only
ARM—Folding stock, bipod, carrying handle and wood forearm

HECKLER & KOCH
SEMIAUTOMATIC RIFLES

HK91 SEMIAUTOMATIC RIFLES
308 Caliber (7.62mm)

All HK91, 93 and 94 series semiautos feature delayed roller-locked bolt system to reduce recoil, cold hammer-forged barrels that provide maximum durability, matte black finish, choice of fixed stock of high-impact plastic or retractable metal stock, diopter sights adjustable for windage and elevation, plus ring front sight with post.

SPECIFICATIONS	A2	A3
Overall length:	40.35"	33.07"
Length of barrel:	17.71"	17.71"
Sight radius:	22.44"	22.44"
Weight w/o magazine:	9.7 lbs.	10.5 lbs.
Weight of 20-round magazine, empty:	9.88 oz.	

Price
HK91 A2 (w/20-round mag., fixed stock, muzzle cap & sling) . . . . $ 932.00
HK91 A3 (w/retractable metal stock) 1098.00

HK93 SEMIAUTOMATIC RIFLES (not shown)
223 Caliber

HK94 SEMIAUTOMATIC CARBINE
9mm

HK93 SEMIAUTOMATIC RIFLES (not shown)
223 Caliber

SPECIFICATIONS	A2	A3
Overall length:	37.0"	29.92"
Length of barrel:	16.14"	16.14"
Sight radius:	19.09"	19.09"
Weight without magazine:	7.94 lbs.	8.6 lbs.

Price
HK93 A2 (w/25-round mag., fixed stock, muzzle cap & sling) . . . . $ 932.00
HK93 A3 (w/retractable metal stock) 1098.00

HK94 SEMIAUTOMATIC CARBINE
9mm

SPECIFICATIONS	A2	A3
Overall length:	34.59"	27.58"
Barrel length:	16.54"	16.54"
Weight w/o magazine:	6.43 lbs.	7.18 lbs.
Rifling:	6 groove	6 groove
Twist:	10" R.H.	10" R.H.

Price
HK94 A2 (w/fixed stock) . . . . $ 932.00
HK94 A3 (w/retractable stock) 1098.00
Prices include 15-round magazine, barrel shroud and assault grip.

INTRATEC SEMIAUTOMATIC PISTOLS

TEC-9
$247.95

Caliber: 9mm Luger/Parabellum
Operation: Closed bolt blowback system
Barrel length: 5"
Weight: 50 oz. unloaded
Magazine capacity: 36 rounds

Weight of magazine: 22 oz. loaded
Sights: Open; fixed front, adjustable rear
Sight radius: 10"
Muzzle velocity: 1200-1400 fps
Finish: Military non-glare blue

TEC-9S (not shown)
$306.00

Caliber: 9mm Luger/Parabellum
Barrel length: 5" threaded
Weight: 51 oz.
Capacity: 36 rounds
Operation: Closed bolt blowback system
Safety: Firing pin block safety

Sights: Open; fixed front, adjustable rear
Finish: Stainless steel non-glare

Also available: **TEC-9M** with 3" barrel, blued finish, 20-round magazine. **Weight:** 44 oz. **Price: $226.95.** In stainless steel: **$286.95.**

IVER JOHNSON/AMAC

M1 30 CAL. CARBINE $291.50
W/Hardwood Stock $265.00

SPECIFICATIONS
Caliber: 30
Capacity: 5, 15 and 30 rounds
Barrel length: 18"
Overall length: 35 1/2"
Weight: 5 1/2 lbs.
Sights: Military front and peep rear
Finish: Blue

MODEL DELTA 786
$665.00

SPECIFICATIONS
Caliber: 9mm
Barrel length: 4 3/4"
Overall length: 15.2"
Weight: 6 lbs. (7 1/2 lbs. w/loaded magazine)
Muzzle velocity: 1246 to 1375 ft./sec.
Effective fire: Max. to 235 yards
Type of fire: Semiautomatic/full auto
Features: Open-bolt firing system; easy barrel attachment; heavy-duty sight; fold-down trigger guard; triple positive safety; rotary selective fire switch; 20, 25, 32 round magazines; snap-on shoulder stock; hand grip; easy field stripping

ENFORCER
$333.20

SPECIFICATIONS
Caliber: 30
Mag. Capacity: 5, 15 and 30 rounds
Barrel length: 9 1/2"
Action: Semiautomatic
Weight: 5 1/2 lbs.
Sights: Adjustable
Stock: Walnut
Also available:
Super Enforcer. 30 caliber full auto with 9 1/2" barrel. **Price: $496.91.**

M.A.C. SEMIAUTOMATIC PISTOL

MODEL M10A1S
9mm or 45 ACP
$399.00

This semiautomatic pistol offers compact firepower coupled with the same integrity as the original Military Armament Corporation's Ingram Model 10 submachine guns. Redesigned Garand-type safety combined with closed bolt operation provide a safe and dependable defensive side arm. Incredibly rugged and functional under adverse weather conditions.

SPECIFICATIONS
Operation: Closed bolt blowback system
Barrel length: 5³/₄"
Overall length: 10¹/₂"
Width: 2"
Height w/magazine: 10¹/₂" (9mm); 12¹/₂" (.45 ACP)
Weight: 6¹/₄ lbs. unloaded
Magazine weight: 1.37 lbs. (32-round mag., 9mm loaded); 2.15 lbs. (30-round mag., .45 ACP loaded)
Magazine capacity: 32 rounds (9mm); 30 rounds (.45 ACP)
Sights: Front, protected post; rear, fixed aperture 100 meters
Safety: Manually operated Garand type located in trigger guard

MITCHELL SEMIAUTOMATIC RIFLES

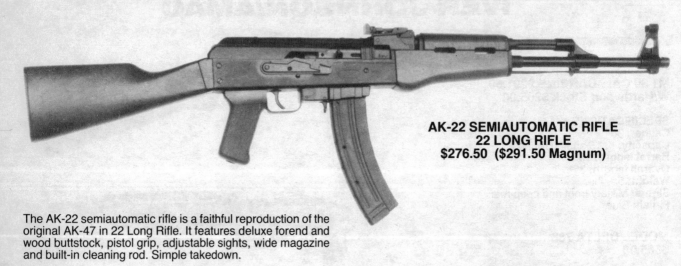

AK-22 SEMIAUTOMATIC RIFLE
22 LONG RIFLE
$276.50 ($291.50 Magnum)

The AK-22 semiautomatic rifle is a faithful reproduction of the original AK-47 in 22 Long Rifle. It features deluxe forend and wood buttstock, pistol grip, adjustable sights, wide magazine and built-in cleaning rod. Simple takedown.

MODEL M70
AK-47 WOODSTOCK
$675.00

Features flip up, fully adjustable night sights, scope rail, hammer forged barrel, all-weather teak stock, pistol grip and forend. 30-round magazine holds bolt open after last round. Also, fitted rubber butt plates, factory scopes and scope mounts. All in 7.62 × 39 caliber. Full line of accessories available. Made in Yugoslavia.
Also available:
AK-47 with Folding Stock . . . . $ 698.00
AK-47 with Heavy Barrel 995.00
COUNTER SNIPER Rifle with Match Grade
Scope 1995.00
SKS M59 Rifle with Folding Bayonet 666.00

SPECTRE PISTOL 9mm CALIBER
$670.00

Features double action (fires from a closed bolt) on the first round and single action semiauto after that; 50-round magazine; Sinusoidal rifling allows rapid fire without heat build-up; heat dissipating frame-bolt-barrel combination.
Also available:
SPECTRE CARBINE with Folding Stock $680.00

MOSSBERG RIFLES

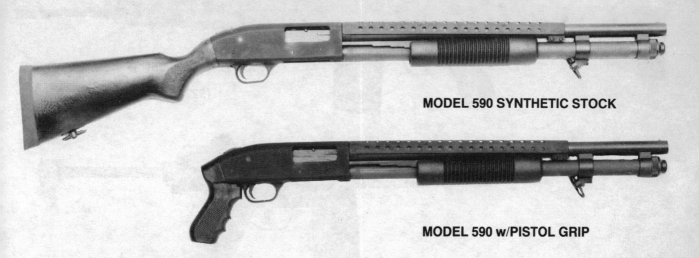

MODEL 590 SYNTHETIC STOCK

MODEL 590 w/PISTOL GRIP

MODEL 590 MILITARY 9-SHOT
$328.95

SPECIFICATIONS
Gauge: 12
Barrel length: 20″
Chamber: 2³/₄″
Finish: Blue
Sight: Bead
Choke: Cylinder Bore
Capacity: 9 shot

Features: Barrel heat shield; bayonet lug; meets MILSPEC
  344E
Also available:
Model 590 w/Speedfeed $361.95
Model 590 w/Wood or Synthetic Stock 328.95
Model 590 Parkerized 369.95
  With Speedfeed 402.95

MODEL 500 BULLPUP 6-SHOT
$394.95

SPECIFICATIONS
Gauge: 12
Barrel length: 18¹/₂″
Choke: Cylinder Bore
Sight: Rifle
Weight: 9¹/₂ lbs.
Overall length: 26¹/₂″

Features: action and trigger group enclosed and protected
  from exposure to elements; all models equipped w/venti-
  lated barrel shield; rifle type sights protected within molded
  carrying handle; dual pistol grips; full rubber recoil pad
  (ready for instant shoulder firing.

Also available:
Model 500 8-Shot w/20″ barrel (28¹/₂″ overall) $409.95

SIGARMS

MODEL SG 550/551 SP ASSAULT RIFLE
$1950.00
($2200.00 w/16″ Barrel)

SPECIFICATIONS
Caliber: 223
Barrel length: 20.8″; Model 551, 16″
Rifling twist: 7″
No. grooves: 6
Overall length: 39.3″; Model 551, 32½″
Length w/butt folded: 30.4″; Model 551, 32½″
Weight: 9 lbs.; Model 551, 7.7 lbs.
Trigger pull weight: 6.6 lbs.

Sights: Diopter
Features: On-the-weapon folding bipod fitted into recessed hand guard; high-graded synthetics used for butt, hand guard, pistol grip and magazine; magazine "multipack" system and bolt hold-open device; ambidextrous design for left- and right-handed shooters; gas operation with rotating bolt

SPRINGFIELD ARMORY

MODEL G3 SEMIAUTOMATIC RIFLE
$650.00—$700.00

This HK-91-type rifle in .308 caliber is an exact duplicate of the original German-manufactured G3 military rifle. It will be offered in late 1988 in both standard and retractable stock models.

SPECIFICATIONS
Caliber: 7.62 × 51mm NATO. **Magazine:** Six 20-round magazines. **Rifling:** 1-in-10 twist standard. **Stock:** Glass bedded heavy walnut w/adj. cheekpiece & rubber recoil pad. **Features and Accessories:** Folding and removable bipod; knurled shoulder (accepts figure-8 style op rod guide; test target supplied; adj. leather military sling; cleaning kit. **Options:** 3.5 x 10 variable power Leupold-Stevens scope and Springfield Armory Third Generation Scope Mount w/two mounting screws.

SPRINGFIELD ARMORY

**BERETTA BM-59 STANDARD GRADE
WITH INTEGRAL FOLDING BIPOD
Italian model $1248.00
Nigerian Model $1365.00
Alpine Paratrooper Model $1624.00**

SPECIFICATIONS

Type: Gas-operated, semiautomatic, clip-loaded, detachable box magazine. **Grade:** Standard grade with European walnut stock. **Caliber:** 7.62mm NATO (308 Win.). **Weight:** 9.5 lbs. **Barrel length:** 19.3″. **Overall length:** 43.11″. **Magazine capacity:** 20-round box type. **Rifling:** Right-hand twist, 1 turn in 11.96″. **Sights:** Military; rear aperature; front square post; also direct and indirect grenade launcher sights. **Sight radius:** 21.37″. **Accessories:** Cleaning kits; bayonets; extra magazines; scope mounts; scopes; slings. Also comes with winter trigger, grenade launcher and sights, muzzle tricompensator bipod and 20-round Beretta magazine.
Also available:
BM-59 Alpine (w/folding stock) **$1435.00**

**MODEL M-21 MIA SEMIAUTOMATIC
SNIPER RIFLE
$1881.00 (w/o Accessories)**

SPRINGFIELD ARMORY

MODEL SAR-48
$899.00 (Standard)

SPECIFICATIONS

Caliber: 308 **Barrel length:** 21″ (Standard, Model 22, Heavy Barrel & Para standard barrel); 18″ (Bush & Para short barrel). **Overall length:** 43.3″ (Standard & Model 22); 40.3″ (Bush); 45.3″ (Heavy Barrel); 40.2″ (Para short barrel); 43.2″ (Para standard barrel). **Weight:** 9.5 lbs. (Standard & Model 22); 8.6 lbs. (Bush); 13.23 lbs. (Heavy Barrel); 8.3 lbs. (Para short barrel); 9.2 lbs. (Para standard barrel). **Magazine:** 20 rounds (10 round box in Model 22). **Sights:** Front and rear adjustable. **Rifling:** Four groove, right hand twist, 1 turn in 12″. **Operation:** Gas, adjustable (blowback in Model 22).

Also available:
SAR-48 Model 22 (22 LR) $760.00
Heavy Barrel SAR-48 w/att. bipod, forward
   assist cocking handle, chrome-lined barrel
   (and more) 899.00
SAR-48 Bush Rifle w/18″ barrel 899.00
SAR-48 Para Model 969.00

M1 GARAND STANDARD MODEL
$761.00

SPECIFICATIONS

Type: Gas-operated, semiautomatic, clip-fed. **Grade:** Standard "Issue-Grade" w/walnut stock. **Caliber:** 30M2 (30-06) and 308 (7.62mm) **Weight:** 9 lbs. 8 ozs. **Barrel length:** 24″. **Overall length:** 43½″. **Magazine capacity:** 8 rounds. **Stock dimensions:** Length of pull 13″; drop at comb 2″; drop at heel 2½″. **Sights:** Front, military square blade; rear, full click-adjustable aperture.

Also available:
National Match Model. . . . . $ 897.00
Ultra-Match Model 1033.00
M1 "Tanker" Rifle 797.00

M1A STANDARD MODEL
$782.00

SPECIFICATIONS

Type: Gas-operated, semiautomatic, clip-loaded, detachable box magazine. **Caliber:** 7.62mm NATO (308 Winchester). **Weight:** 8 lbs. 15 oz. w/empty magazine. **Barrel length:** 22″ w/o flash suppressor. **Overall length:** 44½″. **Magazine capacity:** 5, 10, 20, 25 rounds. **Sights:** Military; square post; full-click adjustable aperture rear. **Sight radius:** 21¹/₁₆″. **Rifling:** 6-groove, right-hand twist; 1 turn in 11″. **Accessories:** Combination muzzle brakeflash suppressor-grenade launcher; bipod; grenade launcher-winter trigger; grenade launcher sight; bayonet; field oiling & cleaning equipment.

Also available
National Match Model. . . . . $ 998.00
Super Match Model. 1231.00
M1A-A1 Bush Assault Model 806.00

STEYR-MANNLICHER

SSG-PII SNIPER RIFLE
$1682.00

The SSG-PII Sniper Rifle features a 26-inch heavy match barrel without sights and functional synthetic ABS Cycolac stock. **Caliber:** 308 Winchester.

STEYR AUG-SA
SEMIAUTOMATIC RIFLE
$1362.00

SPECIFICATIONS
Caliber: 223 Rem.
Barrel length: 20″
Overall length: 31″
Weight: 8½ lbs.
Stock: Synthetic, green
Sights: 1.5X scope, scope and mount form the carrying handle.
Features: Semiautomatic, gas-operated action; can be converted to suit right- or left-hand shooters (including ejection port). Folding vertical front grip.
Extra barrels: 16″ or 20″ $295.00
24″ heavy barrel w/folding, adjustable bipod 485.00

UZI
SEMIAUTOMATIC CARBINE

Action Arms' UZI Semiautomatic Carbine incorporates modifications of the submachine gun so that it meets the requirements of U.S. Federal regulations.

In appearance, the UZI Semiautomatic is virtually identical to the submachine gun, except for a longer barrel. The semiautomatic works from a closed breech with floating firing pin, while the submachine gun has an open breech with fixed firing pin. The semiautomatic's 16.1-inch barrel length delivers a muzzle velocity of 1,250 to 1,500 feet per second, depending on the type of ammunition used.

Price includes molded case, 25-round magazine, carrying sling, 16.1-inch barrel, short display barrel, detailed owner's manual, sight adjustment key. A conversion kit is also available to convert the carbine to accept 22 LR rimfire cartridges. Kit includes Precision Breech-Block/Bolt assembly, 20-round magazine and safety-keyed barrel.

SPECIFICATIONS
Caliber: 9mm Parabellum, 41 A.E., or .45 ACP
Operation principle: Blowback, closed breech with floating firing pin
Magazine: Staggered box-type holding 25 or 32 rounds
Safety systems: (1.) Fire selector in position "S" (2.) Pistol grip safety
Sights: Front, "post" type; rear, L flip-type adjustable for 100m (330 ft.) and 200m (660 ft.)
Stock: Folding metal stock
Weight: Empty magazine, 25 round, 200g (7.0 oz.); 32 round, 220g (7.8 oz.)
Length: (Metal stock folded) 620mm (24.4"); (Metal stock extended) 800mm (31.5")

UZI 9mm SEMIAUTOMATIC CARBINE
$698.00

Barrel length: 410mm (16.1")
No. lands & grooves: 4; right-hand twist; 1 turn in 10"
*Approx. muzzle velocity: 380—460 m/sec (1250—1500 ft/sec)
*Maximum range: Up to 2000m (2200 yds.) at 30° elevation

Also available:
MINI-CARBINE. Barrel length: 19.75". **Weight:** 7.2 lbs. **Overall length:** 35.75". **Price:** $698.00.

*Depending upon type of ammunition used. Specifications subject to change without notice

UZI SEMIAUTOMATIC PISTOL

UZI 9mm SEMIAUTOMATIC PISTOL
$579.00

Like the 9mm carbine, the UZI 9mm semiautomatic pistol features the same simplicity of design, rugged reliability, perfect balance and numerous safety features. Price includes 20-round magazine, sight adjustment key, molded carrying case and detailed instruction manual. Imported by Action Arms Ltd.

SPECIFICATIONS
Operation principle: Blowback; closed breech with floating firing pin
Type of fire: Semiautomatic only
Ammo: 9mm Parabellum or 45 ACP
Safety systems: Fire selector in position "S"; grip safety
Sights: Front post-type; rear open-type, both adjustable for windage and elevation; twin white dots
Barrel length: 4.5" (115 mm)
Overall length: 9.45" (240 mm)
Rifling: 4 grooves; right-hand twist, 1 turn in 10" (254 mm)
Muzzle velocity: 1100 fps (335 m/sec)
Weight: Unloaded, 3.8 lbs. (1.73 kg)
Magazine weights: loaded, 20-round, 14.4 oz. (410 g); 25-round, 17.3 oz. (490 g); 32-round, 21.2 oz. (600 g)

VALMET SEMIAUTOMATIC RIFLES

M76 MILITARY RIFLE (Wood Stock)

M78 SEMIAUTOMATIC RIFLE

VALMET
M76 & M78 MILITARY RIFLES

Developed for the Finnish Defense Forces to withstand the climatic extremes and rugged environment of that country, the M76 provides the highest level of reliability, durability and accuracy. Its major features include:

Gas-operated mechanism: Reliable gas-operated action. Reduces recoil.

Rotating bolt: Provides secure lockup. Increases accuracy.

Barrel on centerline: Minimizes barrel lift. Enables shooter to get "on target" quickly for subsequent shots.

Combat sights: Adjustable front sight is located in a tunnel-guard for protection from accidental misalignment when bumped or dropped. The rear sight, with range adjustments of from 100 to 600 meters, is a folding leaf with peep sight blade. Equipped with night sight, flipped forward, they reveal luminous spots.

Accuracy: Precision rifling, minimal recoil and minimal barrel lift, rotating bolt with solid lockup, fast sight picture, all help to get "on target" with speed and accuracy.

Positive selector lever, cocking handle: Located on the right side, but convenient for left-handed shooters to operate. Functions as a dust cover in the upper position.

Simplicity of design: Easily field-stripped into the following components: cover with rear sights, gas tube, return spring assembly, slide with gas piston and bolt assembly. No tools required.

Caliber versatility: Available in 308 and 223 (M78 in 308 only).

Stock design Available in folding, wood or synthetic stock (M78 in full wood stock only).

Firepower: Magazines hold 20 rounds (M76/308); 15 and 30 rounds (M76/223); and 20 rounds (M78/308).

Optional accessories: Include bipod, cleaning kit, bayonet with scabbard, military sling, ejection buffer, dust cover with scope mount attachment, one-piece scope mount with rings.

SPECIFICATIONS M76

Caliber: 223, 308

Mag. Capacity: 15 rounds standard; 20 and 30 rounds optional

Barrel length: $16^3/_4$" (223); $20^1/_2$" (308)

Overall length: 37" (223); $40^1/_2$" (308)

Weight: 8 to $8^1/_4$ lbs.

Stock: Wood, synthetic or folding

Prices:

Wood Stock	$699.00
Synthetic Stock	795.00
Folding Stock	825.00
LMG $24^1/_2$" Barrel	999.00

Black Powder Guns

FOR ADDRESSES AND PHONE
NUMBERS OF MANUFACTURERS AND
DISTRIBUTORS INCLUDED IN THIS
SECTION, *SEE DIRECTORY OF
MANUFACTURERS AND SUPPLIERS*

ARMSPORT

TRYON TRAILBLAZER

The only mass-produced muzzleloading back-action lock hunting and target rifle. The all-steel working parts are heat treated to proper hardness; all others decorative steel furniture is polished and bright blued to complement the select-grained European walnut stock. The chrome-lined barrel is available in 28- or 32-inch lengths, with both a folding leaf sight (windage and elevation adjustable) and a regular sight for primitive shooting.

Price (finished): $445.00 (Models 5128, 5129 & 5130)
495.00 (Engraved Model)

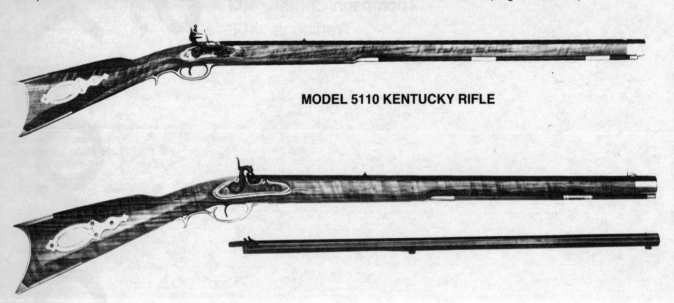

MODEL 5110 KENTUCKY RIFLE

MODEL 5115
KENTUCKY RIFLE-SHOTGUN COMBINATION

Armsport's Kentucky rifle-shotgun combination has been designed with a 28-inch grooved rifle barrel and a 28-inch 20-gauge smoothbore shotgun barrel. This model also boasts a "one-piece" select grain walnut stock, with long barrels rifled for accuracy and proof-tested for safety. All brass fittings—patch box, ferrules, butt plate—are polished to a bright finish. Kentucky rifle kits are completely inletted and pre-assembled to assure perfect wood-to-metal fitting and no missing parts.

KENTUCKY RIFLE SPECIFICATIONS

Model No. Finished	Model No. Kit	Cal.	Description	Ignition	Price (finished)
5108	5208	45	Kentucky Rifle Chr. Lined	P	$285.00
5108V		36	Kentucky Rifle	P	285.00
5109	5209	50	Kentucky Rifle Chr. Lined	P	285.00
5110	5210	45	Kentucky Rifle Chr. Lined	F	299.00
5110A	5210A	50	Kentucky Rifle Chr. Lined	F	299.00
5115		50/20	Kentucky Rifle & Shotgun Com. 2 Barrel Set	P	355.00
5115C		45/20	Kentucky Rifle & Shotgun Com. 2 Barrel Set	P	355.00

ARMSPORT

HAWKEN MODEL 5104 (50 Cal.)

HAWKEN MODELS 5101/5102/5103

HAWKEN RIFLE KITS WITH CHROME-LINED BARRELS

Each of these rifle-shotgun combinations is available with a 50-caliber rifle barrel and a 20-gauge shotgun barrel—two guns in one, a game shooting rifle that converts in less than 10 seconds to a shotgun in three simple steps. The smooth-bore Hawken shotgun barrels have been manufactured with the same care as the Italian trap and skeet barrels. The walnut stocks have been sanded, hand-rubbed and given a high-luster finish. All brass parts have been fitted exactly and highly polished. Rear sights are adjustable for windage and elevation. All Hawken rifles and kits are available in 45, 50, 54 and 58 calibers.

Hawken Rifles	Hawken Kits	Cal.	Description	Ignition	Price (finished)
5101	5201	45	Hawken Rifle	P	$280.00
5102	5202	50	Hawken Rifle	P	280.00
5103	5203	54	Hawken Rifle	P	280.00
5103C	5203C	58	Hawken Rifle	P	280.00
5104	5204	50	Hawken Rifle	F	315.00
5104B	5204B	54	Hawken Rifle	F	315.00

DOUBLE BARREL SHOTGUNS (MODEL 5124 & 5125)

These hook breech 12-gauge double-barrel muzzleloading shotguns combine English tradition with modern finished wood and metal. Checkered select-grain walnut stocks with bright blued chrome-lined barrels combine with the finely en-graved lock plate to make these rugged, well-balanced shotguns. Available also in 10 gauge.
Price (finished): $450.00 (Model 5124)
500.00 (Model 5125/10 gauge)

ARMSPORT
REPLICA REVOLVERS

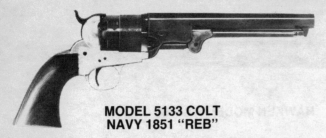

MODEL 5133 COLT NAVY 1851 "REB"

A modern replica of a Confederate Percussion Revolver. It has a polished brass frame, a rifled blued barrel and polished walnut grips. **Price: $110.00**

MODEL 5136 COLT NAVY 1851 STEEL

This authentic reproduction of the Colt Navy Revolver, which helped shape the history of America, features a rifled barrel, blued steel frame, engraved cylinder, polished brass trigger guard and walnut grips. **Price: $150.00**

MODEL 5120 REMINGTON ARMY 44 CALIBER STEEL REVOLVER

One of the most accurate cap and ball revolvers of the 1880's. Its rugged steel frame and top strap made this the favorite of all percussion cap revolvers. **Price: $180**; w/brass frame **$165.00**

MODEL 5138 STAINLESS STEEL REMINGTON ARMY 44 CALIBER

This stainless steel version of the 44-caliber New Remington Army Revolver is made for the shooter who seeks the best. Its stainless steel frame assures lasting good looks. **Price: $295.00**

MODEL 5139 1860 COLT ARMY

This authentic reproduction offers the same balance and ease of handling for fast shooting as the original 1860 model. **Price: $160.00**

Replica Revolvers Description	Model No. Finished	Barrel Length	Caliber	Recommended Ball Dia.
New Remington Army Stainless Steel	5138	8"	44	.451
New Remington Army	5120	8"	44	.451
1851 Navy Reb Brass	5133	7"	36	.376
1851 Navy Reb Brass	5134	7"	44	.451
1851 Navy Steel	5135	7"	36	.376
1851 Navy Steel	5136	7"	44	.451
1860 Colt Army*	5139	8"	44	.451

ARMSPORT

COLLECTOR'S PREMIUM REVOLVERS
.44 CALIBER REMINGTON, COLT ARMY & COLT NAVY

**MODEL 5152 ENGRAVED REMINGTON
OR COLT ARMY .44 CALIBER
$250.00 ($275.00 COLT ARMY)**

**MODEL 5153 ENGRAVED COLT ARMY
$225.00**

**MODEL 5154 ENGRAVED COLT NAVY
$210.00**

Also available:
Model 5138 Remington Army SS. . . . **$295.00** (Kit **$140.00**)
Model 5150 1860 Colt Army SS. . . . . **$295.00** (Kit **$140.00**)
Model 5133/5134 1851 Colt Navy Brass
(36 & 44 Cal.). . . . . **$110.00** (Kit **$99.00**)
Model 5135/5136 1851 Colt Navy Steel
(36 & 44 Cal.). . . . . **$150.00** (Kit **$137.00**)

CVA

1858 REMINGTON ARMY STEEL FRAME REVOLVER
$164.95 ($182.95 w/Target Sights)

Caliber: 44
Cylinder: 6-shot
Barrel length: 8″ octagonal
Overall length: 13″
Weight: 38 oz.
Sights: Blade front; groove in frame (rear)
Grip: Two-piece walnut
Also available:
1858 REMINGTON ARMY Brass Frame Revolver: $134.95. Kit: $112.95.

COLT WALKER REVOLVER
$189.95

Caliber: 44
Barrel: 9″ rounded with hinged-style loading lever
Cylinder: 6-shot engraved
Grip: One-piece walnut
Front sight: Blade
Finish: Solid brass trigger guard
Overall length: 15½″
Weight: 71 oz.

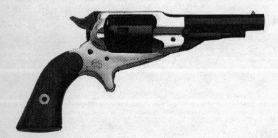

NEW MODEL POCKET REMINGTON
Finished $91.95
Kit $76.95

This single-action 31-caliber percussion revolver is a reproduction of a valued collector's item. Manufactured originally in the mid-1800s, the five-shot revolver was most effective at close ranges. Its brass frame and 4-inch blued barrel provide beauty as well as ruggedness.

Caliber: 31 percussion
Barrel length: 4″ octagonal
Cylinder: 5 shots
Overall length: 7½″
Sights: Post in front; groove in frame in rear
Weight: 15½ oz.
Finish: Solid brass frame

CVA

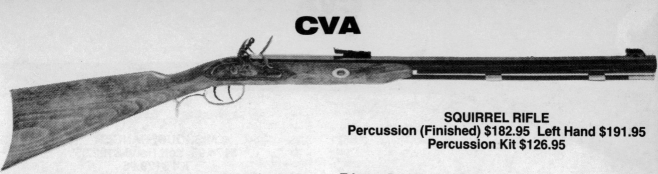

SQUIRREL RIFLE
Percussion (Finished) $182.95   Left Hand $191.95
Percussion Kit $126.95

Ignition: Color case-hardened and engraved lockplate; bridle, fly, screw-adjustable sear engagement; authentic V-type mainspring
Caliber: 32 percussion
Stock: Select hardwood
Barrel: 25″ octagonal; $^{11}/_{16}$″ across flats; hooked breech for easy take down and cleaning; rifling, one turn in 48″; 8 lands, deep grooves; blued steel
Overall length: 40$^3/_4$″
Weight: 5 lbs. 12 oz.

Trigger: Double set (will fire set or unset)
Front sight: Dovetail, beaded blade
Rear sight: Fully adjustable, open hunting-style dovetail
Finish: Solid brass butt plate, trigger guard, wedge plates and thimbles
Accessories: Stainless steel nipple or flash hole liner; aluminum ramrod with brass tips, cleaning jag
Also available:
SQUIRREL RIFLE HUNTING COMBO KIT (32 and 45 caliber percussion): **$142.95**

BLAZER RIFLE
Finished $114.95
Kit $97.95

Caliber: 50 percussion
Barrel length: 28″ octagonal ($^{15}/_{16}$″ across flats); in-line breech and nipple
Rifling: 1 turn in 66″ (8 lands and deep grooves)
Overall length: 43$^1/_2$″

Weight: 7 lbs.
Sights: Brass blade front; fixed open rear
Stock: Select hardwood
Lock: Straight-through ignition (removable for cleaning and adjustment)

BLAZER II RIFLE (50 Caliber Perc.)
Finished $99.95

Barrel: 24$^1/_2$″ octagonal, $^{11}/_{16}$″ across flats; in-line breech and nipple; deeply grooved custom rifling, one turn in 66″
Overall length: 43$^1/_2$″
Weight: 5 lbs. 12 oz.

Sights: Brass blade (front); fixed semi-buckhorn (rear)
Stock: Select hardwood with pistol grip
Lock: Straight-through ignition, removable; screw-adjustable sear engagement

ST. LOUIS HAWKEN RIFLE (50 Cal. Perc.)
Finished $199.95
Kit $151.95

Barrel: 28″ octagonal $^{15}/_{16}$″ across flats; hooked breech; rifling one turn in 66″, 8 lands and deep grooves
Overall length: 44″
Weight: 7 lbs. 13 oz.
Sights: Dovetail, beaded blade (front); adjustable open hunting-style dovetail (rear)

Stock: Select hardwood with beavertail cheekpiece
Triggers: Double set; fully adjustable trigger pull
Finish: Solid brass wedge plates, nose cap, ramrod thimbles, trigger guard and patch box
Also available:
PERCUSSION COMBO (50 and 54 calibers): **$167.95**

CVA

MISSOURI RANGER
$174.95 Left Hand $182.95
Kit $129.95

Caliber: 50 percussion
Barrel length: 28″ octagonal
Rifling: 1 turn in 66″; 8 lands, deep grooves; $^{15}/_{16}$″ across flats; hooked breech for easy takedown
Overall length: 44″
Weight: 7 lbs. 8oz.
Stock: Select hardwood

Triggers: Double set (will fire set and unset)
Sights: Brass blade in front; fixed semi-buckhorn in rear
Finish: Blackened nose cap, trigger guard, black rubber butt plate, thimbles and wedge plates
Lock: Color case hardened and engraved
Features: bridle, fly, screw-adj. sear engagement; v-type mainspring

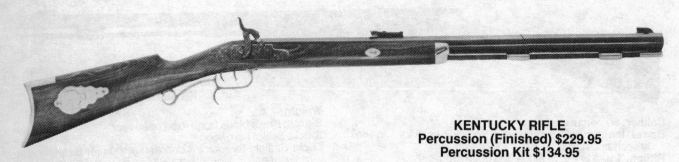

KENTUCKY RIFLE
Percussion (Finished) $229.95
Percussion Kit $134.95

Caliber: 50 and 54 percussion
Ignition: Color case-hardened; bridle, fly, screw adjustable sear engagement and authentic V-type mainspring; two lock screws
Barrel: 28″ octagon; rifled one turn in 66″; 1″ across the flats, barrel tenon, hooked breech
Overall length: 44″
Weight: 7 lbs. 15 oz.
Finish: Solid-brass patchbox, wedge plates, nose cap, ramrod thimbles, trigger guard and butt plate; blued steel finish

Triggers: Double set; will fire set and unset; fully adjustable for trigger pull
Sights: Beaded blade front sight; fully adjustable dovetail open hunting rear sight
Stock: Select walnut with fully formed beavertail cheekpiece
Accessories: Stainless steel nipple or flash hole liner; hardwood ramrod with brass tips and cleaning jag; kits available

HAWKEN RIFLE
Percussion (Finished) $322.95

Ignition: Engraved color case-hardened; screw adjustable sear engagement; V-type mainspring
Caliber: 45 percussion or flintlock
Barrel: 33¹/₂″, rifled, octagon
Overall length: 48″
Weight: 7 lbs. 4 oz.

Finish: Deep-luster blue, polished brass hardware
Sights: Kentucky-style front and rear
Stock: Dark, walnut tone
Accessories: Brass-tipped, hardwood ramrod, stainless steel nipple or flash hole liner

CVA

DOUBLE BARREL CARBINE
$441.95

Caliber: 50 Over/Under
Barrel length: 26″
Overall length: 41¼″
Twist: 1 in 66″; 8 lands & grooves

Features: Checkered English-style straight grip and beaver-tail forestock
Weight: 8 lbs. 8 oz.

TRAPPER SHOTGUN
Finished $227.95
Kit $189.95

Gauge: 12
Barrell length: 28″ round
Stock: Select hardwood; English-style straight grip
Trigger: Early-style steel
Sights: Brass bead in front

Finish: Solid brass wedge plates; color-hardened lock plates, hammer, black trigger guard and tang
Features: Stainless steel nipple, wooden ramrod w/brass tip
Chokes: Interchangeable Improved, Modified and Full

MOUNTAIN RIFLE
$307.95

Calibers: 50 and 54 percussion
Barrel length: 32″ octagonal (¹⁵⁄₁₆″ across flats); with hooked breech for easy takedown and cleaning
Rifling: 1 turn in 66″ (8 lands and deep grooves)
Overall length: 48″
Weight: 9 lbs.
Sights: German silver blade front; screw adjustable ramp rear
Triggers: Double set, fully adjustable trigger pull

Stock: Select European walnut with fully formed cheekpiece
Finish: Pewter nose cap, trigger guard and butt plate
Lock: Plate is color casehardened and engraved; internal features include bridle, fly, screw-adjustable sear engagement, V-type mainspring
Accessories: Stainless steel nipple, hardwood ramrod with aluminum tips

CVA

PENNSYLVANIA LONG RIFLE
Percussion (Finished) $322.95
Flintlock $331.95

Ignition: Color case-hardened and engraved lockplate; bridle, fly, screw-adjustable sear engagement; authentic V-type mainspring
Caliber: 50 percussion or flintlock
Stock: Select walnut
Barrel: 40″ octagonal, ⅞″ across flats; rifling 8 lands, deep grooves
Length: 55¾″ overall

Weight: 8 lbs. 3 oz.
Trigger: Double set (will fire set or unset)
Rear sight: Fixed semi-buckhorn, dovetail
Finish: Brass butt plate, patchbox, trigger guard, thimbles and nose cap
Accessories: Stainless steel nipple or flash hole liner; hardwood ramrod and brass tips

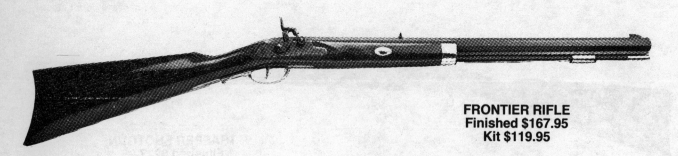

FRONTIER RIFLE
Finished $167.95
Kit $119.95

Caliber: 50 percussion
Barrel length: 24″ octagonal (¹⁵/₁₆″ across flats)
Rifling: 1 turn in 48″ (8 lands and deep grooves)
Overall length: 40″
Weight: 6½ lbs.
Sights: Brass blade front; fixed open rear

Trigger: Early-style brass with tension spring
Stock: Select hardwood
Finish: Solid brass butt plate, trigger guard wedge plate, nose cap and thimble
Accessories: Stainless steel nipple, hardwood ramrod with brass tips and cleaning jag

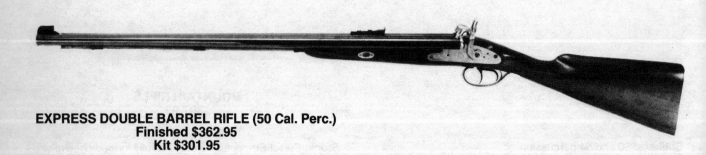

EXPRESS DOUBLE BARREL RIFLE (50 Cal. Perc.)
Finished $362.95
Kit $301.95

Barrels: Two laser aligned tapered 28″ round; hooked breech; rifling, 1 turn in 48″
Overall length: 44¼″
Weight: 9 lbs. 3 oz.
Locks: Plate is color hardened and engraved; includes bridle, fly, screw-adjustable sear engagement
Triggers: Double, color case hardened

Sights: Fully adjustable for windage and elevation, hunting style (rear); dovetail, beaded blade (front)
Stock: Select hardwood
Finish: Polished steel wedge plates; color case hardened locks, hammers, triggers and trigger guard; engraved locks, hammers and tang

CVA

1861 COLT NAVY BRASS FRAMED REVOLVER
Finished $112.95
Kit $92.95

Caliber: 44
Barrel length: 7¹/₂″ rounded; creeping style
Weight: 44 oz.
Cylinder: 6-shot, engraved
Sights: Blade front; hammer notch rear
Finish: Solid brass frame, trigger guard and backstrap; blued
 barrel and cylinder
Grip: One-piece walnut

Also available in 36 caliber with steel frame: **$137.95.**

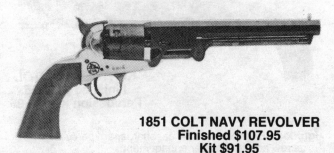

1851 COLT NAVY REVOLVER
Finished $107.95
Kit $91.95

Caliber: 36
Barrel length: 7¹/₂″ octagonal; hinged-style loading lever
Overall length: 13″
Weight: 44 oz.
Cylinder: 6-shot, engraved
Sights: Post front; hammer notch rear
Grip: One-piece walnut
Finish: Solid brass frame, trigger guard and backtrap; blued
 barrel and cylinder; color case-hardened loading lever and
 hammer

Also available with steel frame: **$132.95**

COLT SHERIFF'S MODEL REVOLVER
$91.95

Caliber: 36
Barrel length: 5¹/₂″ (rounded w/creeping style loading lever)
Overall length: 11¹/₂″
Weight: 40¹/₂ oz.
Cylinder: 6-shot semi-fluted
Grip: One-piece walnut
Sight: Hammer notch in rear
Finish: Solid brass frame, trigger guard and backstrap

Also available **Engraved Nickel Plated Model: $179.95** (w/
matching flask). With steel frame: **$126.95.**

1860 COLT ARMY REVOLVER
$132.95

Caliber: 44
Barrel length: 8″ rounded; creeping-style loading lever
Overall length: 13″
Weight: 44 oz.
Cylinder: 6-shot, engraved and rebated
Sights: Blade front; hammer notch rear
Grip: One-piece walnut
Finish: Solid brass trigger guard; blued barrel and cylinder
 with color casehardened loading lever, hammer and frame

CVA

THIRD MODEL COLT DRAGOON
$182.95

Caliber: 44
Cylinder: 6-shot engraved
Barrel length: 7¹/₂″ rounded with hinged-style loading lever
Overall length: 14″
Weight: 75 oz.
Sights: Blade front; hammer notch rear
Grip: One-piece walnut

KENTUCKY PISTOL
Finished $112.95
Percussion Kit $74.95

REMINGTON BISON
$199.95

Caliber: 44
Cylinder: 6-shot
Barrel length: 10¹/₄″ octagonal
Overall length: 18″
Weight: 48 oz.
Sights: Fixed blade front; screw adjustable target rear
Grip: Two-piece walnut
Finish: Solid brass frame

Ignition: Engraved, color casehardened percussion lock, screw adjustable sear engagement
Caliber: 45 percussion or flintlock
Barrel: 10¹/₄″, rifled, octagon
Overall length: 15¹/₄″
Weight: 40 oz.
Finish: Blued barrel, brass hardware
Sights: Dovetailed Kentucky front and rear
Stock: Select hardwood
Accessories: Brass-tipped, hardwood ramrod; stainless steel nipple or flash hole liner

COLONIAL PISTOL
Finished $86.95
Percussion Kit $57.95

Ignition: Engraved, color case-hardened lock
Caliber: 45 (451 bore) percussion
Barrel: 6³/₄″, rifled, octagon
Overall length: 12³/₄″
Weight: 31 oz.
Finish: Casehardened lock; blued barrel; brass hardware
Sights: Dovetail rear; brass blade front
Stock: Select hardwood
Accessories: Steel ramrod, stainless steel nipple; kits available for percussion and flintlock

PHILADELPHIA DERRINGER
Finished $74.95
Kit $41.95

Ignition: Color casehardened and engraved, coil-spring back-action lock
Caliber: 45 percussion
Barrel: 3¹/₄″ rifled
Overall length: 7¹/₈″
Weight: 16 oz.
Finish: Brass hardware; blued barrel
Stock: Select hardwood
Accessories: Stainless steel nipple

DIXIE

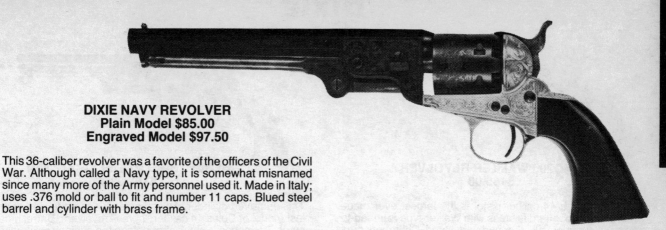

DIXIE NAVY REVOLVER
Plain Model $85.00
Engraved Model $97.50

This 36-caliber revolver was a favorite of the officers of the Civil War. Although called a Navy type, it is somewhat misnamed since many more of the Army personnel used it. Made in Italy; uses .376 mold or ball to fit and number 11 caps. Blued steel barrel and cylinder with brass frame.

SPILLER & BURR 36 CALIBER BRASS FRAME REVOLVER
$85.00

The 36-caliber octagon barrel on this revolver is 7 inches long. The cylinder chambers mike .378. The cylinder is a six-shot and the hammer engages a slot between the nipples on the cylinder as an added safety device. It has a solid brass trigger guard and frame with backstrap cast integral with the frame, two-piece walnut grips and Whitney-type case-hardened loading lever.

"WYATT EARP" REVOLVER
$115.00

This 44-caliber revolver has a 12-inch octagon rifled barrel; cylinder is rebated. Highly polished brass frame, backstrap and trigger guard. The barrel and cylinder have a deep blue luster finish. Hammer, trigger, and loading lever are case-hardened. Walnut grips. Recommended ball size is .451.

DIXIE 1860 ARMY REVOLVER
$135.00

The Dixie 1860 Army has a half-fluted cylinder and its chamber diameter is .447. Use .451 round ball mold to fit this 8-inch barrel revolver. Cut for shoulder stock.

DIXIE

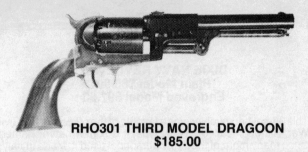

RHO200 WALKER REVOLVER
$185.00

This 4¹/₂-pound, 44-caliber pistol is the largest ever made. Steel backstrap; guard is brass with Walker-type rounded-to-frame walnut grips; all other parts are blued. Chambers measure .445 and take a .450 ball slightly smaller than the originals.

RHO301 THIRD MODEL DRAGOON
$185.00

This engraved-cylinder, 4¹/₂-pounder is a reproduction of the last model of Colt's 44 caliber "horse" revolvers. Barrel measures 7³/₈ inches, ¹/₈ inch shorter than the original; color case-hardened steel frame, one-piece walnut grips. Recommended ball size: .454.

DSB-58 SCREW BARREL DERRINGER
$84.00

Overall length: 6¹/₂″. Unique loading system; sheath trigger, color case-hardened frame, trigger and center-mounted hammer; European walnut, one-piece, "bag"-type grip. Uses #11 percussion caps.

FHO201 FRENCH CHARLEVILLE FLINT PISTOL
$140.00

Reproduction of the Model 1777 Cavalry, Revolutionary War-era pistol. Has reversed frizzen spring; forend and lock housing are all in one; case-hardened, round-faced, double-throated hammer; walnut stock; case-hardened frizzen and trigger; shoots .680 round ball loaded with about 40 grains FFg black powder.

DIXIE BRASS FRAMED "HIDEOUT" DERRINGER
Plain $49.95
Engraved $59.95

Made with brass frame and walnut grips and fires a .395 round ball.

DIXIE PENNSYLVANIA PISTOL
Percussion $105.00 (Kit $72.50)
Flintlock $119.95 (Kit $88.75)

Available in 44-caliber percussion or flintlock. Bright luster blued barrel measures 10 inches long; rifled, ⁷/₈-inch octagon, takes .430 ball; barrel held in place with a steel wedge and tang screw; brass front and rear sights. The brass trigger guard, thimbles, nose cap, wedge plates and side plates are highly polished. Locks are fine quality with early styling. Plates measure 4³/₄ inches × ⁷/₈ inch. Percussion hammer is engraved and both plates are left in the white. Flint is an excellent style lock with the gooseneck hammer having an early wide thumb piece. Stock is walnut stained and has a wide bird-head-type grip.

LINCOLN DERRINGER
$285.00

This 41-caliber, 2-inch browned barrel gun has 8 lands and 8 grooves and will shoot a .400 patch ball.

ABILENE DERRINGER
$69.95

An all-steel version of Dixie's brass-framed derringers. The 2¹/₂-inch, 41-caliber barrel is finished in a deep blue black; frame and hammer are case-hardened. Bore is rifled with 6 lands and grooves. Uses a tightly patched .395 round ball and 15 or 20 grains of FFFg powder. Walnut grips. Comes with wood presentation case.

DIXIE

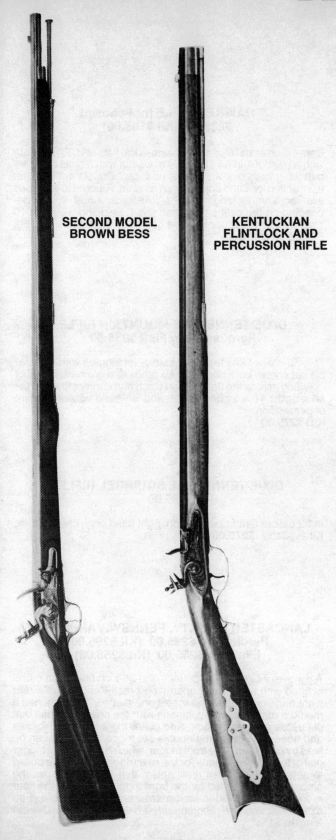

**SECOND MODEL
BROWN BESS**

**KENTUCKIAN
FLINTLOCK AND
PERCUSSION RIFLE**

SECOND MODEL BROWN BESS MUSKET
$399.95

This 75-caliber Brown Bess has a 41³/₄-inch smoothbore barrel that takes a .730 round ball. In keeping with the traditional musket, it has brass furniture on a walnut-stained stock. The lock is marked "Tower" and has the crown with the "GR" underneath. Barrel, lock and ramrod are left bright.
Kit: $275.00

THE KENTUCKIAN FLINTLOCK AND
PERCUSSION RIFLE
Flintlock $209.00
Percussion $195.00

This 45-caliber rifle has a 33¹/₂-inch blued octagon barrel that is ¹³/₁₆ inch across the flats. The bore is rifled with 6 lands and grooves of equal width and about .006 inch deep. Land-to-land diameter is .453 with groove-to-groove diameter at. 465. Ball size ranges from .445 to .448. The rifle has a brass blade front sight and a steel open rear sight. The Kentuckian is furnished with brass butt plate, trigger guard, patch box, side plate, thimbles and nose cap plus case-hardened and engraved lock plate. Highly polished and finely finished stock in European walnut. **Overall length:** 48″. **Weight:** Approx. 6¹/₄ lbs.

DIXIE DOUBLE BARREL MAGNUM
MUZZLE LOADING SHOTGUN (not shown)
$299.00

A full 12-gauge, high-quality, double-barreled percussion shotgun with 30-inch browned barrels. Will take the plastic shot cups for better patterns. Bores are choked modified and full. Lock, barrel tang and trigger are case-hardened in a light gray color and are nicely engraved. Also available: **10 gauge Magnum,** double-barrel-choke cylinder bored, otherwise same specs as above: **$365.00.** In **12 gauge: $325.00.**

DIXIE

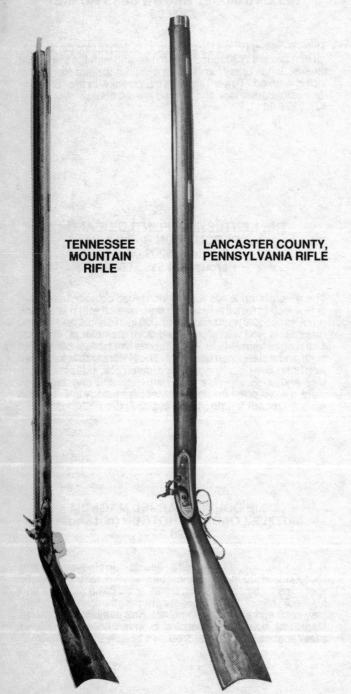

TENNESSEE MOUNTAIN RIFLE

LANCASTER COUNTY, PENNSYLVANIA RIFLE

HAWKEN RIFLE (not shown)
$225.00 (Kit $185.00)

Barrel is charcoal blued, $^{15}/_{16}$" across the flats and 30" in length with a twist of 1 in 64". Stock is of walnut with a steel crescent buttplate, halfstock with brass nosecap. Double set triggers, front action lock and adjustable rear sight. Ramrod is equipped with jag. Overall length is 46½". Average actual weight, depending on the caliber, is about 8 lbs. Shipping weight is 10 lbs. Available in either finished gun or kit. Available in 45, 50, 54 and 58 calibers.

DIXIE TENNESSEE MOUNTAIN RIFLE
Percussion or Flint $335.00

This 50-caliber rifle features double-set triggers with adjustable set screw, bore rifled with six lands and grooves, barrel of $^{15}/_{16}$ inch across the flats, brown finish and cherry stock. **Overall length:** 41½ inches. Right- and left-hand versions in flint or percussion.
Kit: $275.00

DIXIE TENNESSEE SQUIRREL RIFLE
$335.00

In 32 caliber flint or percussion, right hand only, cherry stock. Kit available: **$275.00**

LANCASTER COUNTY, PENNSYLVANIA RIFLE
Percussion $295.00 (Kit $255.00)
Flintlock $255.00 (Kit $255.00)

A lightweight at just 7½ pounds, the 36-inch blued rifle barrel is fitted with a standard open-type brass Kentucky rifle rear sight and front blade. The maple one-piece stock is stained a medium darkness that contrasts with the polished brass butt plate, toe plate, patchbox, side plate, trigger guard, thimbles and nose cap. Featuring double-set triggers, the rifle can be fired by pulling only the front trigger, which has a normal trigger pull of four to five pounds; or the rear trigger can first be pulled to set a spring-loaded mechanism that greatly reduces the amount of pull needed for the front trigger to kick off the sear in the lock. The land-to-land measurement of the bore is an exact .450 and the recommended ball size is .445. **Overall length:** 51½".

DIXIE

PRO401 MISSISSIPPI RIFLE
$430.00

Commonly called the U.S. Rifle Model 1841, this Italian-made replica is rifled in a 58 caliber to use a round ball or a Minie ball; 3 grooves and regulation sights; solid brass furniture; case-hardened lock.

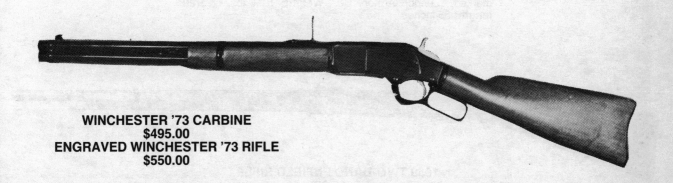

WINCHESTER '73 CARBINE
$495.00
ENGRAVED WINCHESTER '73 RIFLE
$550.00

This 44-40 caliber gun can use modern or black powder cartridges. **Overall length:** 39". **Barrel:** 20" round. Its full tubular magazine will hold 11 shots. The walnut forearm and buttstock complement the high-luster bluing of the all steel parts such as the frame, barrel, magazine, loading lever and butt plate.

Comes with the trap door in the butt for the cleaning rod; leaf rear sight and blade front sight. This carbine is marked "Model 1873" on the tang and caliber "44-40" on the brass carrier block.

WESSON RIFLE
$395.00

The lock work for this rifle is housed in a steel frame or receiver. Barrel is a heavy 1$\frac{1}{8}$" × .50 caliber measuring 28" and fitted with a false muzzle. Two-piece European walnut stock is hand checkered at wrist and forearm. Barrel and underrib are finished in bright blue; receiver is case colored. Double set triggers and adjustable rear sight. **Overall length:** 43$\frac{1}{2}$". **Weight:** 10$\frac{1}{4}$ lbs.

DIXIE

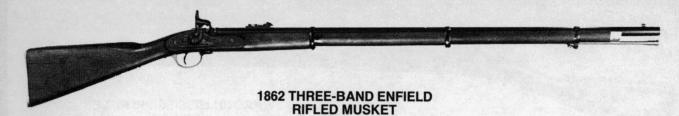

1862 THREE-BAND ENFIELD RIFLED MUSKET
$385.00

One of the finest reproduction percussion guns available, the 1862 Enfield was widely used during the Civil War in its original version. This rifle follows the lines of the original almost exactly. The .58 caliber musket features a 39-inch barrel and walnut stock. Three steel barrel bands and the barrel itself are blued; the lock plate and hammer are case colored and the remainder of the furniture is highly polished brass. The lock is marked, "London Armory Co." **Weight:** 10½ lbs. **Overall length:** 55 inches.

1858 TWO-BAND ENFIELD RIFLE
$315.00

This 33-inch barrel version of the British Enfield is an exact copy of similar rifles used during the Civil War. The .58 caliber rifle sports a European walnut stock, deep blue-black finish on the barrel, bands, breech-plug tang and bayonet mount. The percussion lock is color casehardened and the rest of the furniture is brightly polished brass.

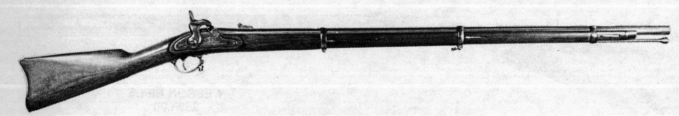

1863 SPRINGFIELD CIVIL WAR MUSKET
$385.00 (Kit $330.00)

An exact copy of the Model 1863 Springfield, which was the last of the regulation muzzleloading rifles. The barrel on this .58 caliber gun measures 40 inches. The action and all metal furniture is finished bright. The oil-finished walnut stock is 53 inches long. **Overall length:** 56 inches. **Weight:** 9½ lbs.

EMF

SHERIFF'S MODEL 1851 REVOLVER
$114.00

SPECIFICATIONS
Caliber: 36 Percussion
Ball diameter: .376 round or conical, pure lead
Barrel length: 5″
Overall length: 10 1/2″
Weight: 39 oz.
Sights: V-notch groove in hammer (rear); truncated cone in front
Percussion cap size: #11
Also available in complete **cased set** (36 caliber steel frame): **$160.00**

MODEL 1860 ARMY REVOLVER
$180.00

SPECIFICATIONS
Caliber: 44 Percussion
Barrel length: 8″
Overall length: 13 5/8″
Weight: 41 oz.
Frame: Casehardened
Finish: High-luster blue with walnut grips
Also available as a **cased set** with wood case, flask and mold: **$300.00**

MODEL 1862 POLICE REVOLVER
$225.00

SPECIFICATIONS
Caliber: 36 Percussion
Capacity: 5-shot
Barrel length: 6 1/2″
Also available as a **cased set: $325.00**

MODEL 1851 STEEL NAVY REVOLVER
36 Caliber $170.00

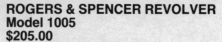

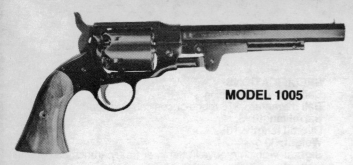

MODEL 1005

ROGERS & SPENCER REVOLVER
Model 1005
$205.00

Caliber: 44 Percussion; #11 percussion cap
Barrel length: 7¹/₂″
Sights: Integral rear sight notch groove in frame; brass truncated cone front sight
Overall length: 13³/₄″
Weight: 47 oz.
Finish: High-gloss blue; flared walnut grip; solid-frame design; precision-rifled barrel
Recommended ball diameter: .451 round or conical, pure lead

ROGERS & SPENCER ARMY REVOLVER
Model 1006 (Target)
$221.00

Caliber: 44; takes .451 round or conical lead balls; #11 percussion cap
Weight: 47 oz.
Barrel length: 7¹/₂″
Overall length: 13³/₄″
Finish: High-gloss blue; flared walnut grip; solid-frame design; precision-rifled barrel
Sights: Rear fully adjustable for windage and elevation; ramp front sight

MODEL 1006

ROGERS & SPENCER REVOLVER
Model 1007, London Gray
$233.00

Revolver is the same as Model 1005, except for London Gray finish, which is heat treated and buffed for rust resistance; same recommended ball size and percussion caps.

MODEL 1020

REMINGTON 1858
NEW MODEL ARMY REVOLVER
Model 1020: $177.00

This model is equipped with blued steel frame, brass trigger guard in 44 caliber.

Weight: 40 oz.
Barrel length: 8″
Overall length: 14³/₄″
Finish: Deep luster blue rifled barrel; polished walnut stock; brass trigger guard.
Model 1010: Same as Model 1020 except with 6¹/₂″ barrel and in 36 caliber: **$177.00**

REMINGTON 1858
NEW MODEL ARMY ENGRAVED
Model 1040: $254.00

Classical 19th-century style scroll engraving on this 1858 Remington New Model revolver.

Caliber: 44 Percussion; #11 cap
Barrel length: 8″
Overall length: 14³/₄″
Weight: 41 oz.
Sights: Integral rear sight notch groove in frame; blade front sight
Recommended ball diameter: .451 round or conical, pure lead

EUROARMS OF AMERICA

1851 NAVY SHERIFF

SCHNEIDER & GLASSICK
1851 NAVY SHERIFF
Model 1080: $124.00

Caliber: 36 Percussion; #11 cap
Barrel length: 5″
Overall length: 11 1/2″
Weight: 38 oz.
Sights: Rear sight is traditional V-notch groove in hammer; truncated cone front sight of brass
Finish: High-gloss blue on barrel and cylinder; backstrap frame and trigger guard polished yellow brass; walnut grips; hammer and loading lever color casehardened
Recommended ball diameter: .375 round or conical, pure lead

SCHNEIDER & GLASSICK
1851 NAVY SHERIFF (not shown)
Model 1090: $124.00

Same as Model 1080 except in 44 caliber, with .451 round or conical ball.

SCHNEIDER & GLASSICK
1851 NAVY (not shown)
Model 1120: $158.00

Caliber: .36 percussion, #11 cap
Barrel length: 7 1/2″, octagonal barrel, precision rifled
Overall length: 13″
Weight: 42 oz.
Finish: Blued barrel and frame; backstrap and trigger guard are polished brass; walnut grips.

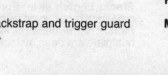

REMINGTON 1858
NEW MODEL ARMY TARGET
Model 1045: $250.00

Caliber: 44 Percussion; #11 cap
Barrel length: 8″, precision rifled
Overall length: 14 3/4″
Weight: 41 oz.
Sights: Integral rear sight notch groove in frame; dovetailed stainless steel front sight adjustable for windage
Finish: Stainless steel; polished yellow brass trigger guard; walnut grips
Recommended ball diameter: .451 round or conical, pure lead
Model 1048: 44 caliber, 8″ barrel. **$237.00**

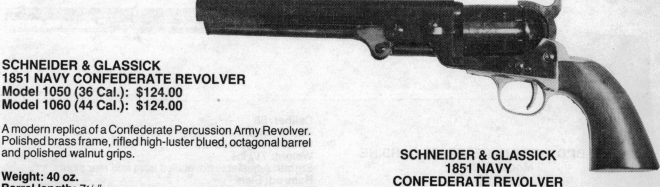

SCHNEIDER & GLASSICK
1851 NAVY CONFEDERATE REVOLVER
Model 1050 (36 Cal.): $124.00
Model 1060 (44 Cal.): $124.00

A modern replica of a Confederate Percussion Army Revolver. Polished brass frame, rifled high-luster blued, octagonal barrel and polished walnut grips.

Weight: 40 oz.
Barrel length: 7 1/2″
Overall length: 13″
Finish: Brass frame, backstrap and trigger guard; blued rifled barrel; casehardened hammer and loading lever; engraved cylinder with naval battle scene

SCHNEIDER & GLASSICK
1851 NAVY
CONFEDERATE REVOLVER

EUROARMS OF AMERICA

HAWKEN RIFLE
Model 2210A: $293.00

Caliber: 50 percussion
Barrel: 28″ long; blued precision rifled, octagonal
Weight: 9½ — 9¾ lbs., depending on density of wood
Stock: Solid one-piece walnut
Ramrod: Wooden, with brass tips threaded for cleaning jag, worm or ball puller
Sights: Target rear sight adjustable for windage and elevation; front sight dovetail cut
Triggers: Double-set triggers adjustable for hair trigger, if desired
Furniture: Polished brass mountings, barrel key

SINGLE-BARRELED MAGNUM CAPE GUN
Model 2295: $400.00

Euroarms of America offers a beautiful reproduction of a classic English-styled single-barreled shotgun. The lock is left in the white and displays a scroll engraving, as does the bow of the trigger guard. Uses #11 percussion caps and recommended wads are felt overpowder and cardboard overshot.

Gauge: 12
Barrel: 32″, open choke
Overall length: 47½″
Weight: 7½ lbs.
Stock: English style; European walnut with satin oil finish; moderate recoil, even with relatively heavy powder charges
Finish: Barrel, underrib, thimbles, nose cap, trigger guard and butt plate are deep, rich blue

COOK & BROTHER CONFEDERATE CARBINE
Model 2300
$367.00

Classic re-creation of the rare 1861, New Orleans-made Artillery Carbine. Lock plate is marked "Cook & Brother N.O. 1861" and is stamped with a Confederate flag at rear of hammer.

Caliber: 58
Barrel length: 24″
Overall length: 40⅓″
Weight: 7½ lbs.
Sights: Adjustable dovetailed front and rear sights
Ramrod: Steel
Finish: Barrel is antique brown; butt plate, trigger guard, barrel bands, sling swivels and nose cap are polished brass; stock is walnut
Recommended ball sizes: .575 r.b., .577 Minie and .580 maxi; uses musket caps

EUROARMS OF AMERICA

LONDON ARMORY COMPANY
2-BAND RIFLE MUSKET
Model 2270
$393.00

Caliber: 58
Barrel length: 33″, blued and rifled
Overall length: 49″
Weight: 8¹/₂–8³/₄ lbs., depending on wood density
Stock: One-piece walnut; polished "bright" brass butt plate, trigger guard and nose cap; blued barrel bands
Sights: Inverted 'V' front sight; Enfield folding ladder rear
Ramrod: Steel

LONDON ARMORY COMPANY
ENFIELD MUSKETOON
Model 2280
$367.00

Caliber: 58; Minie ball
Barrel length: 24″; round high-luster blued barrel
Overall length: 40¹/₂″
Weight: 7 to 7¹/₂ lbs., depending on density of wood
Stock: Seasoned walnut stock with sling swivels
Ramrod: Steel
Ignition: Heavy-duty percussion lock
Sights: Graduated military-leaf sight
Furniture: Brass trigger guard, nose cap and butt plate; blued barrel bands, lock plate, and swivels

LONDON ARMORY COMPANY
3-BAND ENFIELD RIFLED MUSKET
Model 2260: $427.00

Caliber: 58
Barrel length: 39″, blued and rifled
Overall length: 54″
Weight: 9¹/₂ — 9³/₄ lbs., depending on wood density
Stock: One-piece walnut; polished "bright" brass butt plate, trigger guard and nose cap; blued barrel bands
Ramrod: Steel; threaded end for accessories
Sights: Traditional Enfield folding ladder rear sight; inverted 'V' front sight

HOPKINS & ALLEN ARMS

KENTUCKY PISTOL MODEL 10
Flint $124.25
Percussion $102.25
Kit $64.25

The Kentucky Pistol features a convertible ignition system, heavy-duty ramrod and special Hopkins & Allen breech and tang.

Caliber: 45
Barrel: Rifled, 10" long; $^{15}/_{16}$" wide
Overall length: 15$^1/_2$"
Weight: 3 lbs.

BOOT PISTOL MODEL 13
$86.55
Kit $66.85

The Boot Pistol comes with a sculptured walnut pistol grip and is fitted with open sights—post type front sight and open rear sight with step elevator. The H&A Boot Pistol features a rich blue-black finish and is equipped with a match trigger.

Caliber: 45
Barrel: $^{15}/_{16}$" × 6" octagonal
Overall length: 13"

BRUSH RIFLE MODEL 345
$228.69
Kit $120.39

Caliber: 45 and 36
Barrel: 25" octagon, $^{15}/_{16}$" across flats
Weight: 7 lbs.
Stock: Selected hardwood
Sights: Notched rear; silver blade front
Features: Compact, light, quick pointing rifle; convertible ignition

HOPKINS & ALLEN ARMS

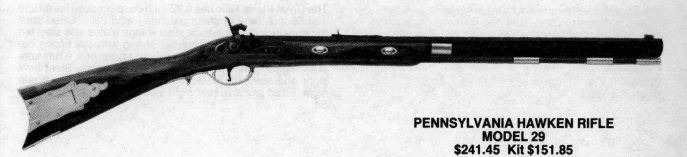

UNDERHAMMER RIFLE
MODEL 32

Calibers: 31, 36, 45, 50 and 58
Stock: American walnut and walnut forend
Barrel: Octagonal; avail. in lengths of 20″, 25″, or 32″; $^{15}/_{16}$″ across the flats; cut rifled with uniform round ball twist
Special features: Only three moving parts in the action give the shooter years of trouble-free performance; uninterrupted sighting plane; target trigger; positive ignition

Four Underhammer Rifles available:
Buggy (31, 36, and 45 cal.); 20″ or 25″ barrel; weighs 6-7 lbs.
  Price: $247.75
Heritage (31, 36, 45, 50 cal.); 32″ barrel; weighs 7$^1/_2$-8 lbs.
  Price: $261.65
Deerstalker (58 cal.); 32″ barrel; weighs 9$^1/_2$ lbs. **Price: $270.25**
Target (45 cal.); 42″ barrel; weighs 11 lbs. **Price: $284.10**
Kits available: **$152.85 to $192.70**

PENNSYLVANIA HAWKEN RIFLE
MODEL 29
$241.45 Kit $151.85

Caliber: 50
Lock mechanism: Flintlock or percussion
Barrel: 29″ long; octagonal; $^{15}/_{16}$″ across the flats; cut rifled with round ball twist
Overall length: 44″
Weight: 7$^1/_2$ lbs.
Stock: Walnut with cheekpiece and dual barrel wedges for added strength
Furniture: Brass fixtures, incl. patch box
Special feature: Convertible ignition system

LYMAN

LYMAN PLAINS PISTOL
$159.95
Percussion Kit $129.95

This replica of the pistol carried by the Western pioneers of the 1830s features a pistol-sized Hawken lock with dependable coil spring and authentic rib and thimble styling. It has a richly stained walnut stock, blackened iron furniture and polished brass trigger guard and ramrod tips. Equipped with a spring-loaded trigger and a fast twist (1 in 30 inches both calibers) barrel for target accuracy. **Caliber:** 50 or 54 percussion.

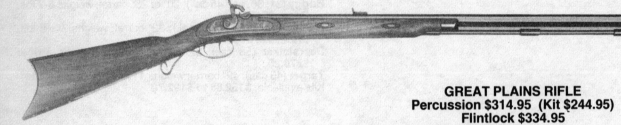

GREAT PLAINS RIFLE
Percussion $314.95 (Kit $244.95)
Flintlock $334.95

The Great Plains Rifle has a 32-inch deep-grooved barrel and 1 in 66-inch twist to shoot patched round balls. Blued steel furniture including the thick steel wedge plates and steel toe plate; correct lock and hammer styling with coil spring dependability; and a walnut stock without a patch box. A Hawken-style trigger guard protects double-set triggers. Steel front sight and authentic buckhorn styling in an adjustable rear sight. Fixed primitive rear sight also included. **Caliber:** 50 or 54.

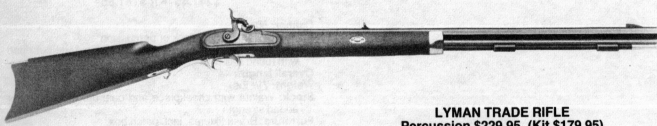

LYMAN TRADE RIFLE
Percussion $229.95 (Kit $179.95)
Flintlock $254.95 (Kit $209.95)

The Lyman Trade Rifle features a 28-inch octagonal barrel, rifled one turn at 48 inches, designed to fire both patched round balls and the popular maxistyle conical bullets. Polished brass furniture with blued finish on steel parts; walnut stock; hook breech; single spring-loaded trigger; coil-spring percussion lock; fixed steel sights; adjustable rear sight for elevation also included. Steel barrel rib and ramrod ferrule. **Caliber:** 50 or 54 percussion and flint. **Overall length:** 45".

MICHIGAN ARMS

THE WOLVERINE

This new black powder rifle features an in-line ignition system using a standard 209 non-corrosive shotgun primer to fire the charge. One screw disassembles the barrel, breech plug and receiver for easy cleaning. The barrel is made of aircraft quality steel, and there's a choice of Michigan walnut, cherry or curly maple stock. Other features include a modern rifle trigger, positive safety, soft recoil pad, O-ring barrel seal, solid aluminum ramrod drilled and tapped for shotgun and standard black powder.

SPECIFICATIONS
Caliber: 45, 50 or 54. **Barrel length:** 26″ octagonal (1″ diameter, 1 turn in 66″). **Overall length:** 44″. **Weight:** 7³/₄″ (54 cal.). **Length of pull:** 13⁵/₈″. **Sights:** Adjustable folding leaf rear and brass-bead tipped front sights, both dovetailed; receiver drilled and tapped for optional Williams peep sight. **Price: $398.00.**

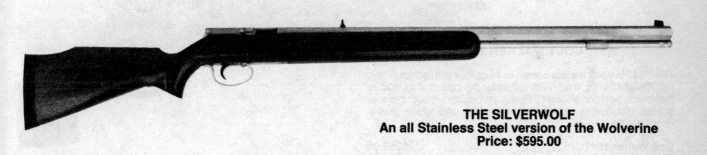

THE SILVERWOLF
An all Stainless Steel version of the Wolverine
Price: $595.00

THE FRIENDSHIP SPECIAL MATCH

While the design of this match rifle is the same as **Wolverine,** it features several extra components, including specially selected barrel, fully adjustable Lyman Globe front sight with inserts, Morgan adjustable recoil pad, fully adjustable trigger, special barrel lengths up to 30 inches, custom stock configuration with deep "C" pistol grip, and custom stock finish. **Price: $599.00**

NAVY ARMS REVOLVERS

LE MAT REVOLVERS

Once the official sidearm of many Confederate cavalry officers, this 9 shot .44 caliber revolver with a central single shot barrel of approx. 65 caliber gave the cavalry man 10 shots to use against the enemy. **Barrel length:** 7⅝″. **Overall length:** 14″. **Weight:** 3 lbs. 7 oz.

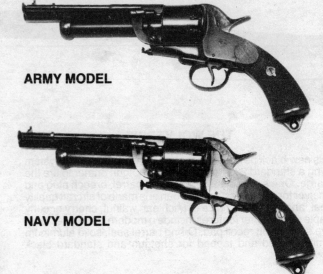

ARMY MODEL

Cavalry Model	$550.00
Navy Model	550.00
Army Model	550.00

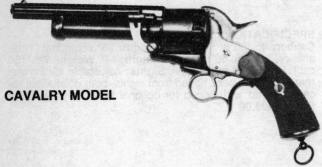

CAVALRY MODEL

NAVY MODEL

COLT WALKER 1847

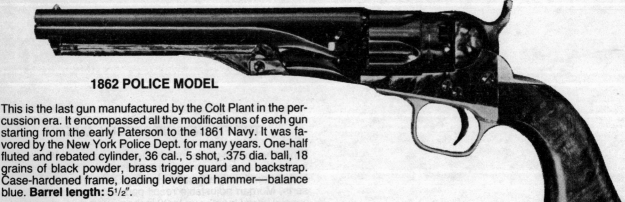

The 1847 Walker replica comes in 44 caliber with a 9-inch barrel. **Weight:** 4 lbs. 8 oz. Well suited for the collector as well as the black powder shooter. Features include: rolled cylinder scene; blued and case-hardened finish; and brass guard. Proof tested.

Colt Walter 1847	$250.00
Single Cased Set	350.00

1862 POLICE MODEL

This is the last gun manufactured by the Colt Plant in the percussion era. It encompassed all the modifications of each gun starting from the early Paterson to the 1861 Navy. It was favored by the New York Police Dept. for many years. One-half fluted and rebated cylinder, 36 cal., 5 shot, .375 dia. ball, 18 grains of black powder, brass trigger guard and backstrap. Case-hardened frame, loading lever and hammer—balance blue. **Barrel length:** 5½″.

1862 Police	$225.00
Law and Order set	300.00

NAVY ARMS REVOLVERS

REB MODEL 1860

A modern replica of the confederate Griswold & Gunnison percussion Army revolver. Rendered with a polished brass frame and a rifled steel barrel finished in a high-luster blue with genuine walnut grips. All Army Model 60's are completely proof-tested by the Italian government to the most exacting standards. **Calibers:** 36 and 44. **Barrel length:** 7¼". **Overall length:** 13". **Weight:** 2 lbs. 10 oz.-11 oz. **Finish:** Brass frame, backstrap and trigger guard, round barrel hinged rammer on the 44 cal. rebated cylinder.

Reb Model 1860 . . . . $119.50
Single Cased Set 230.00
Double Cased Set 370.00
Kit 88.00

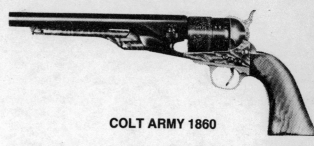

COLT ARMY 1860

These guns from the Colt line are 44 caliber and all six-shot. The cylinder was authentically roll engraved with a polished brass trigger guard and steel strap cut for shoulder stock. The frame, loading lever and hammer are finished in high-luster color case-hardening. Walnut grips. **Weight:** 2 lbs. 9 oz. **Barrel length:** 8". **Overall length:** 13⅝". **Caliber:** 44. **Finish:** Brass trigger guard, steel back strap, round barrel creeping cylinder, rebated cylinder engraved. Navy scene. Frame cut for s/stock (4 screws). Also available with full fluted cylinder and in 5½" barrel (Sheriff's model).

Army 1860 . . . . $164.00
Single Cased Set 274.00
Double Cased Set 460.00
Kit 123.00

1851 NAVY "YANK"

Originally manufactured by Colt from 1850 through 1876, this model was the most popular of the Union revolvers, mostly because it was lighter and easier to handle than the Dragoon. **Barrel length:** 7½". **Overall length:** 14". **Weight:** 2 lbs. **Rec. ball diam.:** .375 R.B. (.451 in 44 cal) **Calibers:** 36 and 44. **Capacity:** 6 shot. **Features:** Steel frame, octagonal barrel, cylinder roll-engraved with Naval battle scene, backstrap and trigger guard are polished brass.

1851 Navy "Yank" $140.00
Kit 100.00
Single Cased Set 250.00
Double Cased Set 414.00

ROGERS & SPENCER NAVY REVOLVER

This revolver features a six-shot cylinder, octagonal barrel, hinged-type loading lever assembly, two-piece walnut grips, blued finish and case-hardened hammer and lever. **Caliber:** 44. **Barrel length:** 7½". **Overall length:** 13¾". **Weight:** 3 lbs.

Rogers & Spencer $240.00
With satin finish 259.00

NAVY ARMS REVOLVERS

STAINLESS STEEL 1858 REMINGTON

Exactly like the standard 1858 Remington except that every part with the exception of the grips and trigger guard is manufactured from corrosion-resistant stainless steel. This gun has all the style and feel of its ancestor with all of the conveniences of stainless steel. **Caliber:** 44.

1858 Remington $279.00

TARGET MODEL REMINGTON REVOLVER

With its top strap and frame, the Remington Percussion Revolver is considered the magnum of Civil War revolvers and is ideally suited to the heavy 44-caliber charges. Based on the Army Model, the target gun has target sights for controlled accuracy. Ruggedly built from modern steel and proof tested.

Remington Percussion Revolver $190.00

DELUXE 1858 REMINGTON-STYLE .44 CALIBER

Built to the exact dimensions and weight of the original Remington .44, this model features an 8″ barrel with progressive rifling, adjustable front sight for windage, all-steel construction with walnut stocks and silver-plated trigger guard. Steel is highly polished and finished in rich charcoal blue. **Barrel length:** 8″. **Overall length:** 14¼″. **Weight:** 2 lbs. 14 oz.

Deluxe 1858 Remington-Style .44 Cal. $315.00

REMINGTON NEW MODEL ARMY REVOLVER
(not shown)

This rugged, dependable, battle-proven Civil War veteran with its top strap and rugged frame was considered the magnum of C.W. revolvers, ideally suited for the heavy 44 charges. Nickel finish in 44 cal. only. **Calibers:** 36 and 44. **Barrel length:** 8″. **Overall length:** 13½″. **Weight:** 2 lbs. 9 oz.

Remington Army Revolver, blue	**$167.00**
Single cased set, blue	277.00
Double cased set, blue	467.00

ARMY 60 SHERIFF'S MODEL
(not shown)

A shortened version of the Army Model 60 Revolver. The Sheriff's model version became popular because the shortened barrel was fast out of the leather. This is actually the original snub nose, the predecessor of the detective specials or belly guns designed for quick-draw use. A piece of traditional Americana, the Sheriff's model was adopted by many local police departments. **Calibers:** 36 and 44.

Army 60 Sheriff's Model	**$119.50**
Kit	88.00

NAVY ARMS PISTOLS

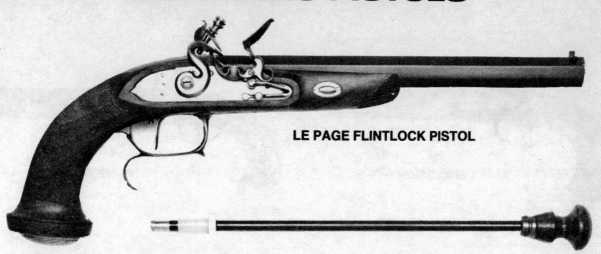

LE PAGE FLINTLOCK PISTOL

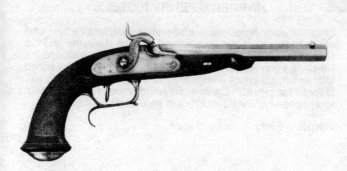

LE PAGE FLINTLOCK PISTOL
(45 Caliber)

Beautifully hand-crafted reproduction featuring hand-check-ered walnut stock with hinged buttcap and carved motif of a shell at the forward portion of the stock. Single-set trigger and highly polished steel lock and furniture together with a brown finished rifled barrel make this a highly desirable target pistol. **Barrel length:** 10½″. **Overall length:** 17″. **Weight:** 2 lbs. 2 oz.

Le Page Flintlock (rifled or smoothbore) $340.00
Single Cased Set 659.00

CASED LE PAGE PISTOL SETS
(45 Caliber)

The case is French-fitted and the accessories are the finest quality to match.

Double Cased Flintlock Set $1100.00

LE PAGE PERCUSSION PISTOL
(45 Caliber)

The tapered octagonal rifled barrel is in the traditional style with 7 lands and grooves. Fully adjustable single-set trigger. Engraved overall with traditional scrollwork. The European walnut stock is in the Boutet style. Spur-style trigger guard. Fully adjustable elevating rear sight. Dovetailed front sight ad-justable for windage. **Barrel length:** 9″. **Overall length:** 15″. **Weight:** 2 lbs. 2 oz. **Rec. ball diameter:** 440 R.B.

Le Page Percussion $312.00

Double Cased Set
French- fitted double-cased set comprising two Le Page Pis-tols, turn screw, nipple key, oil bottle, cleaning brushes, leather covered flask and loading rod.

Double Cased Percussion Set. $900.00

Single Cased Set
French-fitted single-cased set comprising one Le Page pistol, turn screw, nipple key, oil bottle, cleaning brushes, leather covered flask and loading rod.

Single Cased Percussion Set $560.00

NAVY ARMS PISTOLS

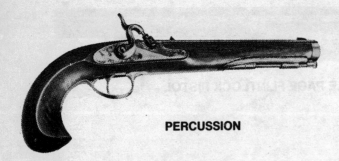

PERCUSSION

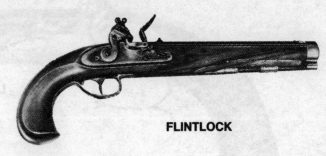

FLINTLOCK

KENTUCKY PISTOLS

The Kentucky Pistol is truly a historical American gun. It was carried during the Revolution by the Minutemen and was the sidearm of "Andy" Jackson in the Battle of New Orleans. Navy Arms Company has conducted extensive research to manufacture a pistol truly representative of its kind, with the balance and handle of the original for which it became famous.

Flintlock.	$134.00
Single Cased Flintlock Set.	235.00
Double Cased Flintlock Set.	389.00
Percussion	115.00
Single Cased Percussion Set	230.00
Double Cased Percussion Set.	360.00

HARPER'S FERRY PISTOLS

Of all the early American martial pistols, Harper's Ferry is one of the best known and was carried by both the Army and the Navy. Navy Arms Company has authentically reproduced the Harper's Ferry to the finest detail, providing a well-balanced and well-made pistol. **Weight:** 2 lbs. 9 oz. **Barrel length:** 10". **Overall length:** 16". **Caliber:** 58 smoothbore. **Finish:** Walnut stock; case-hardened lock; brass mounted browned barrel.

Harper's Ferry.	$199.00

ELGIN CUTLASS PISTOL

Part of Navy Arm's Classic Collection, this pistol represents the only combination gun (knife and pistol) ever issued by any U.S. military service. It was also the first percussion handgun officially used by the U.S. **Overall length:** 9" (12" blade). **Rec. ball diam.:** .440 R.B. **Weight:** 2 lbs.

Elgin Cutlass Pistol	$104.95
Kit.	78.50

NAVY ARMS RIFLES

PARKER-HALE WHITWORTH MILITARY TARGET RIFLE

Recreation of Sir Joseph Whitworth's deadly and successful sniper and target weapon of the mid-1800s. Devised with a hexagonal bore with a pitch of 1 turn in 20 inches. Barrel is cold-forged from ordnance steel, reducing the build-up of black powder fouling. Globe front sight; open military target rifle rear sight has interchangeable blades of different heights. Walnut stock is hand-checkered. **Caliber:** 451. **Barrel length:** 36". **Weight:** 9½ lbs.

Parker-Hale Whitworth Military Target Rifle (incl. accessory kit) **$750.00**

PARKER-HALE 451 VOLUNTEER RIFLE

Originally designed by Irish gunmaker, William John Rigby, this relatively small-caliber rifle was issued to volunteer regiments during the 1860s. Today it is rifled by the cold-forged method, making one turn in 20 inches. Sights are adjustable: globe front and ladder-type rear with interchangeable leaves; hand-checkered walnut stock. **Weight:** 9½ lbs.

Parker-Hale 451 Volunteer Rifle (incl. accessory kit) **$725.00**

Other Parker-Hale muskets available:
2-BAND MUSKET MODEL 1858
    Barrel length: 33". **Overall length:** 48½". **Weight:** 8½ lbs. **500.00**
MUSKETOON MODEL 1861
    Barrel length: 24". **Overall length:** 40¼". **Weight:** 7½ lbs. **400.00**
3-BAND MUSKET MODEL 1853
    Barrel length: 39". **Overall length:** 55". **Weight:** 9 lbs. **550.00**

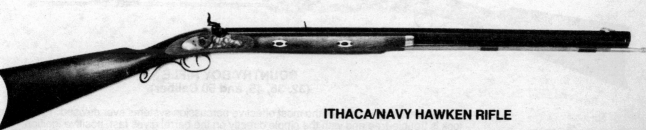

ITHACA/NAVY HAWKEN RIFLE

Features a 31½" octagonal blued barrel crowned at the muzzle with buckhorn-style rear sight, blade front sight. Color case hardened percussion lock is fitted on walnut stock. Furniture is all steel and blued (except for nose cap and escutcheons). Available in 50 and 54 cal.

Ithaca/Navy Hawken Rifle **$480.00**
Kit **374.00**

NAVY ARMS RIFLES

#2 CREEDMOOR TARGET RIFLE

Features a color casehardened rolling block receiver, checkered walnut stock and forend, 30″ tapered barrel in 45/70 caliber with blued finish, hooded front sight and Creedmoor tang sight. **Barrel length:** 30″. **Overall length:** 46″. **Weight:** 9 lbs.

#2 Creedmoor Target Rifle	$640.00
Rolling Block Action	125.00

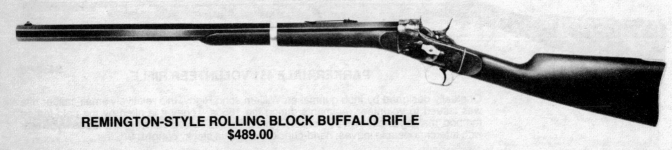

REMINGTON-STYLE ROLLING BLOCK BUFFALO RIFLE
$489.00

Features 26″ or 30″ octagonal/half-round barrel; color casehardened receiver; solid brass trigger guard, walnut stock and forend. Available in 45/70 caliber only. Tang is drilled and tapped for Creedmoor sight.

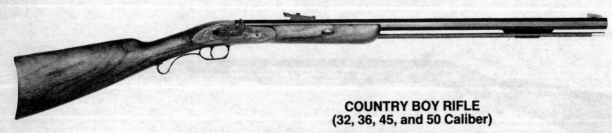

COUNTRY BOY RIFLE
(32, 36, 45, and 50 Caliber)

An authentic copy of one of the most effective percussion systems ever devised. The simple lock is trouble-free and with the nipple directly on the barrel gives fast, positive ignition. The quickest handling, fastest shooting rifle on the market today; ideal for the young beginner shooter. Features hooked breech and fully adjustable hunting sights. Simple, efficient and trustworthy. **Barrel length:** 26″. **Weight:** 5½ lbs.

Rifle	$250.00
Rifle Kit	192.00

NAVY ARMS RIFLES

1853 ENFIELD RIFLE MUSKET

The Enfield Rifle Musket marked the zenith in design and manufacture of the military percussion rifle and this perfection has been reproduced by Navy Arms Company. This and other Enfield muzzleloaders were the most coveted rifles of the Civil War, treasured by Union and Confederate troops alike for their fine quality and deadly accuracy. **Caliber:** 557. **Barrel length:** 39″. **Weight:** 9 lbs. **Overall length:** 55″. **Sights:** Fixed front; graduated rear. **Rifling:** 3 groove, cold forged. **Stock:** Seasoned walnut with solid brass furniture.

1853 Enfield Rifle Musket. **$475.00**

1858 ENFIELD RIFLE

In the late 1850s the British Admiralty, after extensive experiments, settled on a pattern rifle with a 5-groove barrel of heavy construction, sighted to 1100 yards, designated the Naval rifle, Pattern 1858. In the recreation of this famous rifle Navy Arms has referred to the original 1858 Enfield Rifle in the Tower of London and has closely followed the specifications even to the progressive depth rifling. **Caliber:** 557. **Barrel length:** 33″. **Weight:** 8 lbs. 8 oz. **Overall length:** 48.5″. **Sights:** Fixed front; graduated rear. **Rifling:** 5-groove; cold forged. **Stock:** Seasoned walnut with solid brass furniture.

1853 Enfield Rifle. **$450.00**

1861 ENFIELD MUSKETOON

The 1861 Enfield Musketoon is a Limited Collector's edition, individually serial numbered with certificate of authenticity. **Caliber:** 557. **Barrel length:** 24″. **Weight:** 7 lbs. 8 oz. **Overall length:** 40.25″. **Sights:** Fixed front; graduated rear. **Rifling:** 5-groove; cold forged. **Stock:** Seasoned walnut with solid brass furniture.

1861 Enfield Musketoon. **$325.00**
Kit. 270.00

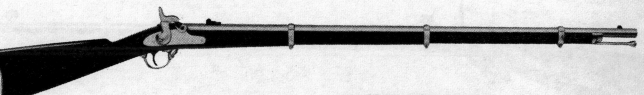

1863 SPRINGFIELD RIFLE

An authentically reproduced replica of one of America's most historical firearms, the 1863 Springfield rifle features a full-size, three-band musket and precision-rifled barrel. **Caliber:** 58. **Barrel length:** 40″. **Overall length:** 56″. **Weight:** 9½ lbs. **Finish:** Walnut stock with polished metal lock and stock fittings.

1863 Springfield Rifle. **$500.00**
Springfield Kit. 400.00

NAVY ARMS

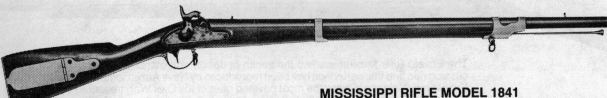

MISSISSIPPI RIFLE MODEL 1841

The historic percussion lock weapon that gained its name as a result of its performance in the hands of Jefferson Davis' Mississippi Regiment during the heroic stand at the Battle of Buena Vista. Also known as the "Yager" (a misspelling of the German Jaeger), this was the first rifle adopted by Army Ordnance to fire the traditional round ball. In 58 caliber, the Mississippi is handsomely furnished in brass, including patch box for tools and spare parts. **Weight:** 9¹/₂ lbs. **Barrel length:** 32¹/₂″. **Overall length:** 48¹/₂″. **Caliber:** 58. **Finish:** Walnut finish stock, brass mounted.

Model 1841 . . . . **$400.00**

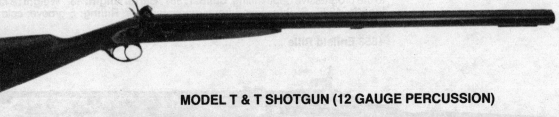

MODEL T & T SHOTGUN (12 GAUGE PERCUSSION)

This Turkey and Trap side-by-side percussion shotgun is choked full/full. It features a genuine walnut stock with checkered wrist and oil finish, color casehardened locks, and 28-inch blued barrels. It will pattern a load of #6 shot size in excess of 85% in a 30-inch circle at 30 yards and in excess of 65% at 40 yards, using 96 grains of FFg, 1¹/₄ oz. #6 shot and 13 gauge overshot, over powder and cushion wads.

Model T & T **$432.00**

RIGBY-STYLE TARGET RIFLE

This affordable reproduction of the famed Rigby Target Rifle of the 1880s features a 32-inch blued barrel, target front sight with micrometer adjustment, fully adjustable vernier rear sight (adjustable up to 1000 yards), hand-checkered walnut stock color casehardened breech plug, hammer lock plate, and escutcheons. This .451 caliber gun is cased with loading accessories, including bullet starter and sizer and special ramrod.

Rigby-Style Target Rifle **$550.00**

NAVY ARMS

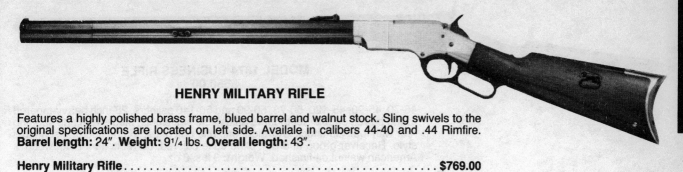

HENRY MILITARY RIFLE

Features a highly polished brass frame, blued barrel and walnut stock. Sling swivels to the original specifications are located on left side. Availale in calibers 44-40 and .44 Rimfire. **Barrel length:** ?4". **Weight:** 9¼ lbs. **Overall length:** 43".

Henry Military Rifle **$769.00**

IRON FRAME HENRY

Same specifications as the Henry Military Rifle, except with iron frame.

Iron Frame Henry **$933.00**

HENRY TRAPPER MODEL

This short, lightweight .44/40 is ideal for the hunter. **Barrel length:** 16½". **Overall length:** 34½". **Weight:** 7¼ lbs.

Henry Trapper Model **$769.00**

HENRY CARBINE

The arm first utilized by the Kentucky Cavalry. Available in either original 44 rimfire caliber or in 44/40 caliber. Oil-stained American walnut stock, blued finish with brass frame. **Barrel length:** 23⅝". **Overall length:** 45".

Henry Carbine **$769.00**

HENRY CARBINE ENGRAVED

This carbine version of the orginal Henry Rifle (produced between 1850 and 1866) served as a revolutionary weapon in the Civil War. Only 50 engraved units are available in .44/40 or .44 rimfire. **Barrel length:** 24". **Overall length:** 39". **Weight:** 8¼ lbs.

Henry Carbine Engraved **$1750.00**

SHILOH SHARPS

MODEL 1874 BUSINESS RIFLE
$650.00

45-70, 45-90, 45-120, 50-70, 50-90 and 50-140 calibers. 28-inch heavy-tapered round barrel, double-set triggers adjustable set, sights, blade front and sporting rear with leaf. Buttstock is straight grip rifle butt plate, forend sporting schnabel style. Receiver group and butt plate case-colored, barrel is dark blue; wood is American walnut oil-finished. **Weight:** 9 lbs. 8 oz.

MODEL 1874 MILITARY RIFLE
$800.00

45-70 and 50-70 calibers. 30-inch round barrel. Blade front and Lawrence-style sights. Military-style forend with 3 barrel bands and 1¼-inch swivels. Receiver group, butt plate and barrel bands case-colored. Barrel is dark blue, wood with oil finish. **Weight:** 8 lbs. 2 oz.

MODEL 1874 CARBINE
$650.00

45-70 and 45-90 calibers. 24-inch round barrel, single trigger, blade front and sporting rear sight, buttstock straight grip, steel rifle butt plate, forend sporting schnabel style. Case-colored receiver group and butt plate; barrel is dark blue; wood has oil finish. **Weight:** 8 lbs. 4 oz.

Sharps Model 1874 Rifle and Cartridge Availability Table

MODEL	CALIBER										
	40-50 1 11/16"BN	40-70 2 1/4"BN	40-90 2 5/8"BN	45-70 2 1/10"ST	45-90 2 4/10"ST	45-100 2 6/10"ST	45-110 2 7/8"ST	45-120 3 1/4"ST	50-70 1 3/4"ST	50-100 2 1/2"ST	50-140 3 1/4"ST
LONG RANGE EXPRESS	●	●	●	●	●	●	●	●		●	●
NO. 1 SPORTING RIFLE	●	●	●	●	●	●	●	●		●	●
NO. 3 SPORTING RIFLE	●	●	●	●	●				●	●	●
SADDLE RIFLE	●	●		●	●						
BUSINESS RIFLE	★	★●	★●	●	●			●	●	●	●
CARBINE	★	★●	★●	●	●	●	●		●	●	●
1874 MILITARY ●RIFLE	★	★●	★●	●					●		

● Standard
★ Available on special order. Add $75.00 to the suggested retail price for special order fee
BN = Bottleneck, ST = Straight

SHILOH SHARPS

MODEL 1874 SPORTING RIFLE NO. 1
$775.00

Calibers: 45-70, 45-90, 45-120, 50-70, 50-90 and 50-140. Features 28-inch or 30-inch tapered octagon barrel. Double-set triggers with adjustable set, blade front sight, sporting rear with elevation leaf and sporting tang sight adjustable for elevation and windage. Buttstock is pistol grip, shotgun butt, sporting forend style. Receiver group and butt plate case colored. Barrel is high finish blue-black; wood is American walnut oil finish. **Weight:** 9 lbs. 8 oz.

MODEL 1874 SPORTING RIFLE NO. 3
$675.00

45-70, 45-90, 45-120, 50-70, 50-90 and 50-140 calibers. 30-inch tapered octagon barrel, double-set triggers with adjustable set, blade front sight, sporting rear with elevation leaf and sporting tang sight adjustable for elevation and windage. Buttstock is straight grip with rifle butt plate; trigger plate is curved and checkered to match pistol grip. Forend is sporting schnabel style. Receiver group and butt plate is case colored. Barrel is high finish blue-black; wood is American walnut oil-finished. **Weight:** 9 lbs. 12 oz.

MODEL 1863 SPORTING RIFLE
$695.00

Caliber: 54; 30" tapered octagon barrel, blade front sight, sporting rear with elevation leaf, double-set triggers with adjustable set; curved trigger plate, pistol grip buttstock with steel butt plate, forend schnable style; optional Tang sight. **Weight:** 9 lbs.
Also available: **MODEL 1863 PERCUSSION MILITARY RIFLE** $800.00
MODEL 1863 PERCUSSION CARBINE 650.00

THOMPSON/CENTER

THE PATRIOT

Features a hooked breech, double-set triggers, first-grade American walnut stock, adjustable (Patridge-type) target sights, solid brass trim, beautifully decorated and color case-hardened lock with a small dolphin-shaped hammer. **Weight:** Approximately 36 oz. Inspired by traditional gallery and dueling-type pistols, its carefully selected features retain the full flavor of antiquity, yet modern metals and manufacturing methods have been used to ensure its shooting qualities.

Patriot Pistol 36 and 45 caliber $235.00
Kit 180.00

THOMPSON/CENTER

PENNSYLVANIA HUNTER (not shown)

For the hunter who prefers (or is required to use) a round ball, the Pennsylvania Hunter offers a firearm designed especially for that purpose. Its 31″ barrel is cut rifled (.010″ deep) with 1 turn in 66″ twist. The outer contour of the barrel is distinctively stepped from octagon to round. Sights are fully adjustable for both windage and elevation. The single hunting style trigger with large trigger guard bow allows the rifle to be fired with gloves on. Stocked with select American black walnut; metal hardware is all blued steel. Features a hooked breech system and coil spring lock. **Caliber:** Caplock and flintlock models are available in .50 caliber only. **Overall length:** 48″. **Weight:** Approx. 7.6 lbs.

Pennsylvania Hunter Caplock .50 caliber $265.00
Pennsylvania Hunter Flintlock .50 caliber 280.00

THE HAWKEN
45, 50 and 54 caliber

Similar to the famous Rocky Mountain rifles made during the early 1800's, the Hawken is intended for serious shooting. Button-rifled for ultimate precision, the Hawken is available in 45, 50 or 54 caliber, flint or percussion. Featuring a hooked breech, double-set triggers, first-grade American walnut, adjustable hunting sights, solid brass trim, beautifully decorated and color casehardened lock.

Hawken Caplock 45, 50 or 54 caliber $325.00
Hawken Flintlock 50 caliber. 340.00
Kit: Percussion. 230.00
Flintlock 245.00

THE NEW ENGLANDER SHOTGUN

This new 12-gauge muzzleloading percussion shotgun weighs only 5 lbs. 2 oz. It features a 28-inch (improved cylinder) round barrel and is stocked with selected American black walnut.

New Englander Shotgun. $210.00

THE NEW ENGLANDER RIFLE

Features 26″ round, .50 or .54 caliber rifle barrel (1 in 48″ twist); weighs 7 lbs. 15 oz.

New Englander Rifle (Right or Left Hand) $210.00

THOMPSON/CENTER

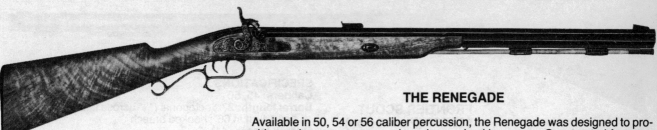

THE RENEGADE

Available in 50, 54 or 56 caliber percussion, the Renegade was designed to provide maximum accuracy and maximum shocking power. Constructed from superior modern steel with investment cast parts fitted to an American walnut stock, the rifle features a precision-rifled (26-inch carbine-type) octagon barrel, hooked-breech system, coil spring lock, double-set triggers, adjustable hunting sights and steel trim. **Weight:** Approx. 8 lbs.

Renegade Caplock 50 and 54 caliber and 56 caliber smoothbore (left
    or right hand) **$275.00**
Renegade Flintlock 50 caliber. 290.00
Kit: Caplock (left or right hand) 200.00
Flintlock 215.00

RENEGADE HUNTER
50 Caliber

This single trigger hunter model, fashioned after the double triggered Renegade introduced in 1974 with great success, features a large bow in the shotgun style trigger guard. This allows shooters to fire the rifle in cold weather without removing their gloves. The octagon barrel measures 26″ and the stock is made of select American walnut. **Weight:** About 8 pounds.

Renegade Hunter 50 caliber **$255.00**

THE CHEROKEE

A light percussion sporting rifle with interchangeable barrels. **Caliber:** 32 or 45. **Barrel length:** 24″. **Weight:** About 6 lbs. Sights are open hunting style fully adjustable for windage and elevation. Stock is American walnut with contoured cheekpiece on left-hand side.

Cherokee Caplock **$265.00**
Kit 200.00
Interchangeable barrels (w/ramrod) in 32 and 45 caliber 115.00
Kit barrels 80.00

TRADITIONS

FRONTIER SCOUT
$156.00 (Percussion)

SPECIFICATIONS
Calibers: 45, 50
Barrel length: 27"; octagonal ($7/8$" across flats) with tenon; rifled 1 turn in 66"; hooked breech
Overall length: $41^{1}/_{4}$"
Weight: 4.75 lbs.
Length of pull: $12^{1}/_{4}$"
Sights: Fully adjustable rear, brass blade front
Stock: Beech
Lock: Adjustable sear engagement with fly and bridle
Furniture: Solid brass, blued steel

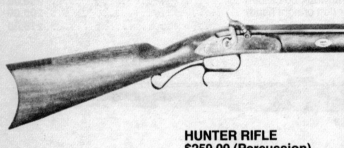

HUNTER RIFLE
$259.00 (Percussion)

SPECIFICATIONS
Calibers: 50, 54
Barrel length: 29"; octagonal (1" across flats) with 2 tenons; hooked breech, rifled 1 turn in 66"
Overall length: 46"
Weight: $7^{1}/_{2}$ lbs.
Lock: Adjustable sear engagement with fly and bridle
Stock: Walnut with contoured beavertail cheekpiece
Sights: Fully screw adjustable for windage and elevation; beaded blade front with Patridge-style open rear; both dovetailed
Furniture: Black-chromed brass with German silver wedge plates and stock ornaments

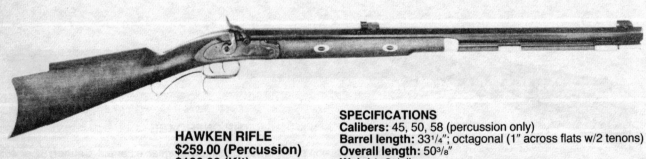

HAWKEN RIFLE
$259.00 (Percussion)
$198.00 (Kit)

SPECIFICATIONS
Calibers: 45, 50, 58 (percussion only)
Barrel length: $33^{1}/_{4}$"; octagonal (1" across flats w/2 tenons)
Overall length: $50^{3}/_{8}$"
Weight: $8^{1}/_{2}$ lbs.
Lock: Adjustable sear engagement with fly and bridle
Stock: Walnut, beavertail cheekpiece
Triggers: Double set; will fire set and unset
Sights: Fully screw adjustable for windage and elevation; beaded front sight with Patridge-style open rear; both are dovetailed
Furniture: Solid brass, blued steel

TRADITIONS

HAWKEN WOODSMAN
$200.00 (Percussion)
$153.00 (Kit)

SPECIFICATIONS
Caliber: 50
Barrel length: 29″ (octagonal); hooked breech; rifled 1 turn in 66″
Overall length: 46″
Weight: $7\frac{1}{2}$ lbs.
Triggers: Double set; will fire set or unset
Lock: Adjustable sear engagement with fly and bridle
Stock: Beech
Sights: Fully screw adjustable for windage and elevation; beaded blade front with Patridge-style open rear
Furniture: Solid brass, blued steel

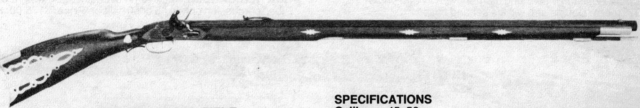

PENNSYLVANIA RIFLE
$300.00 (Flintlock)
$290.00 (Percussion)

SPECIFICATIONS
Calibers: 45, 50
Barrel length: $41\frac{3}{8}$″; octagonal ($\frac{7}{8}$″ across flats) with 3 tenons; rifled 1 turn in 66″
Overall length: $56\frac{5}{8}$″
Weight: 9 lbs.
Lock: Adjustable sear engagement with fly and bridle
Stock: Select hardwood, beavertail style
Triggers: Double set; will fire set and unset
Sights: Fully adjustable rear; brass blade front
Furniture: Solid brass, blued steel

SHENANDOAH RIFLE
$196.00 (Flintlock)
$186.00 (Percussion)

SPECIFICATIONS
Caliber: 50
Lock: Color casehardened with V-type mainspring
Barrel: $34\frac{1}{2}$″; octagonal ($\frac{7}{8}$″ across flats) with two tenons
Overall length: 49″
Weight: 6 lbs.
Triggers: Double set; will fire set and unset
Stock: Beech
Sights: Fixed rear, blade-type front
Furniture: Brass buttplate, nose cap and trigger guard

TRADITIONS

FRONTIER RIFLE
$185.00 (Flintlock)
$175.00 (Percussion)

SPECIFICATIONS
Calibers: 45 (percussion only) and 50
Barrel: Octagonal ($^{15}/_{16}''$ across flats) with tenon; hooked breech, rifled 1 turn in 66''
Overall length: $44^1/_4''$
Weight: 8 lbs.
Lock: Adjustable sear engagement with fly and bridle
Triggers: Double set; will fire set and unset
Stock: Beech

Sights: Fully screw adjustable for windage and elevation; beaded blade front with Patridge-style open rear (dovetailed)
Furniture: Solid brass, blued steel
Also available:
FRONTIER CARBINE with $40^1/_2''$ overall length; weight $6^1/_2$ lbs.; percussion only in 45 or 50 caliber. **Price: $175.00;** Kit $127.00.

TRAPPER RIFLE
$178.00 (Percussion)

SPECIFICATIONS
Calibers: 36, 45, and 50
Barrel length: 25''; 45 and 50 calibers rifled 1 turn in 66''; 36 caliber rifled 1 turn in 48''; hooked breech; octagonal ($^7/_8$ across flats)
Overall length: $40^1/_2''$
Weight: 5 lbs.

Stock: Beech
Lock: Adjustable sear engagement with fly and bridle
Triggers: Double set, will fire set and unset
Sights: Fully screw adjustable for windage and elevation; beaded blade front with Patridge-style open rear
Furniture: Solid brass, blued steel

TRAPPER PISTOL
$108.00 (Percussion)
$85.00 (Kit)

SPECIFICATIONS
Calibers: 36, 45, 50
Barrel length: $10^3/_4''$; octagonal ($^7/_8''$ across flats) with tenon
Overall length: $16^5/_8''$
Weight: $1^3/_4$ lbs.
Stock: Beech
Lock: Adjustable sear engagement with fly and bridle
Triggers: Double set, will fire set and unset
Sights: Fully adjustable rear; brass blade front
Furniture: Solid brass; blued steel on assembled pistol

A. UBERTI

1st MODEL DRAGOON REVOLVER

SPECIFICATIONS
Caliber: 44
Capacity: 6 shots
Barrel length: 7¹/₂" round forward of lug
Overall length: 13¹/₂"
Weight: 4 lbs.
Frame: Color casehardened steel
Grip: One-piece walnut
Features: Brass backstrap and trigger guard; engraved cylinder
Also available:
2nd Model Dragoon w/square cylinder bolt shot . . . **$240.00**
3rd Model Dragoon w/loading lever latch, steel
   backstrap, cut for shoulder stock 269.00
Texas Dragoon w/squareback trigger guard 240.00

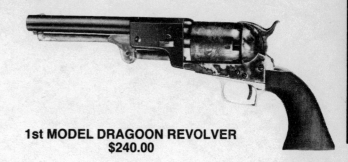

1st MODEL DRAGOON REVOLVER
$240.00

1861 NAVY REVOLVER

SPECIFICATIONS
Caliber: 36
Capacity: 6 shots
Barrel length: 7¹/₂"
Overall length: 13"
Weight: 2.75 lbs.
Grip: One-piece walnut
Frame: Color casehardened steel
Also available:
Civil Type w/brass backstrap and trigger guard **$229.00**
Western Type w/silver plated backstrap and trigger
   guard 249.00
Fluted Cylinder Type w/steel backstrap and trigger
   guard 249.00

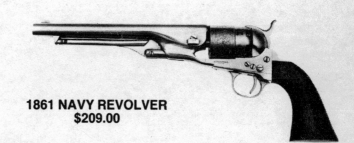

1861 NAVY REVOLVER
$209.00

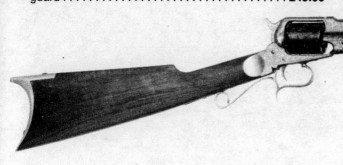

1858 NEW ARMY TARGET REVOLVING CARBINE
$385.00

SPECIFICATIONS
Caliber: 44
Barrel length: 18" octagonal, tapered
Overall length: 37"
Weight: 4.63 lbs.
Sights: Vertically adjustable rear; ramp front
Frame: Blued steel
Stock: Walnut
Features: Brass trigger guard and butt plate
Also available:
1858 New Army .44 Revolver $209.00
   With Stainless Steel. 299.00
   Target Model, blued steel 239.00

SANTA FE HAWKEN RIFLE
$385.00

SPECIFICATIONS
Caliber: 50 of 54
Barrel length: 32" octagonal
Overall length: 50"
Weight: 9¹/₂ lbs.
Stock: Walnut with beavertail cheekpiece
Features: Brown finish; double trigger set; color casehardened lockplate; German silver wedge plates and stock turrule

Sights, Scopes & Mounts

FOR ADDRESSES AND PHONE
NUMBERS OF MANUFACTURERS AND
DISTRIBUTORS INCLUDED IN THIS
SECTION, SEE *DIRECTORY OF
MANUFACTURERS AND SUPPLIERS*

AIMPOINT SIGHTS

SERIES 2000 ELECTRONIC SIGHTS

Two versions of Aimpoint's new Series 2000 Sights. Two versions are available, Short and Long, and are offered in two finishes—black or stainless. The Short 2000 is a smaller version weighing only 5.35 ounces, with a length of 5 inches. Primarily designed for handgun users, its versatility allows for multi-use. Shooters can easily remove the sight from one firearm to another. Mounting requires standard one-inch rings and mounts. The Long 2000 is slightly larger—7¹/₄ inches overall—and weighs just over 6 ounces. The Long version can be mounted on all firearms and will work well for hunters and marksmen who use rifles and require magnification.

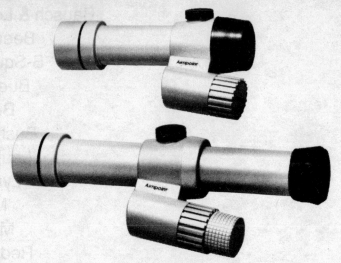

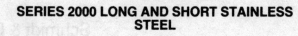

SERIES 2000 LONG AND SHORT STAINLESS STEEL

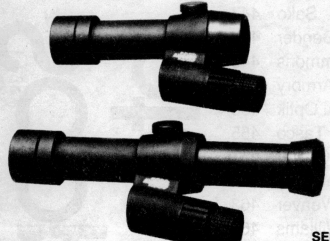

SERIES 2000 LONG AND SHORT BLACK FINISH

Series 2000 Specifications	Short	Long
Length	5″	7¹/₄″
Weight	5.35 oz.	6 oz.
Diameter	1″	1″
Magnification	None	None
Scope Attachments	None	3X
Material	Anodized Aluminum	Anodized Aluminum
Finish	Black or Stainless finish	Black or Stainless finish
Mounting	Standard 1″ rings	Standard 1″ rings
Positive sight adjustment	¹/₂″ at 100 yards	¹/₂″ at 100 yards
Lens coating	Standard	Standard
Battery types	Long cap—one piece lithium (DL ²/₃A) or two piece mercury (PX1/RM1N) Short cap—one piece lithium CR-¹/₃N, 2L76BP or DL¹/₃N	Same Same
Price: 2000 Black or Stainless	**$209.95**	**$229.95**

ARMSPORT SCOPES

JAPANESE MULTICOATED WATERPROOF EXTRA WIDE ANGLE RIFLESCOPES

4x32mm Wide Angle Duplex Reticle $146.00
4x40mm Wide Angle Duplex Reticle 167.00
2x5x32mm Wide Angle Duplex Reticle. 207.00
3x9x32mm Wide Angle Duplex Reticle. 202.00
3x9x40mm Wide Angle Duplex Reticle. 215.00

432XT

W3940AX

W3932AX

JAPANESE MULTICOATED WATERPROOF RIFLESCOPES

4x32mm Duplex Reticle $122.00
4x40mm Duplex Reticle 144.00
2x5x32mm Duplex Reticle 180.00
3x9x32mm Duplex Reticle 176.00
3x9x40mm Duplex Reticle 186.00

3940XTW

ARMSPORT STAR WATERPROOF RIFLESCOPES

4x32mm Duplex Reticle . . . . $ 80.00
4x40mm Duplex Reticle 98.00
3x9x32mm Duplex Reticle 96.50
3x9x40mm Duplex Reticle 117.00

ARMSPORT STAR WATERPROOF EXTRA WIDE ANGLE RIFLESCOPES

Same as above. Add **$6.00** per scope.

RINGS, BASES and RING SETS

1″ Detachable Rings (101 Low, 102 Medium, 103 High,
    104—22 Cal.). $10.50
Deluxe 1″ See-Thru Detachable Rings. 13.50
Complete Scope Mounting Set. 15.50
Bases for Detachable Mounts. 5.00
1″ Detachable Extension Ring Set 17.50

22 CALIBER RIFLESCOPES with MOUNTS

4x15mm Crosshair Reticle w/20mm Objective Bell . . **$26.50**
3x7 20mm Crosshair Reticle. 66.00

BAUSCH & LOMB

Since 1853 the name Bausch & Lomb has stood for superior optical performance. The repeatability—a critical factor—of Bausch & Lomb's variable and fixed power rifle-scopes enables sportsmen to enjoy optimum tracking accuracy with positive return to zero each time. The advanced design of these scopes eliminates point-of-impact shifts at high and low powers. To insure brightness, internal lens surfaces are multi-coated so light loss from reflection is minimized. Strong, durable one-piece body maintains optical alignment. All scopes are waterproof and fogproof.

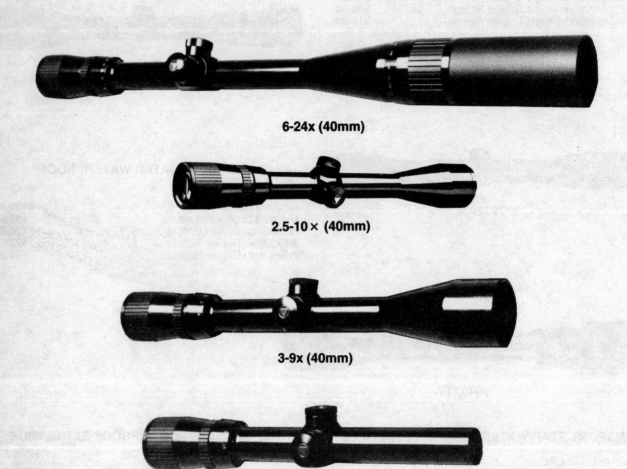

6-24x (40mm)

2.5-10 × (40mm)

3-9x (40mm)

1.5x-6 (20mm)

BALVAR RIFLESCOPES

Bausch & Lomb's variable 6-24x40, 3-9x40, and 1.5-6x21 riflescopes have been redesigned, reducing their weight by 15 percent each. When set at its lowest power, the variable 1.5-6x provides a full 60-foot field at 100 yards, making it an ideal optical sight for stalking in tall timber and dense brushy areas. For maximum visibility, this scope can also zoom up to a full 6x for long range shots at big game. It weighs only 13.9 ounces and measures 11 inches in length. For benchrest competitors, long-range varmint hunters and silhouette shooters, the 6x-24x scope is sufficiently short and light. Its 40mm focusing objective lens eliminates problems with parallax regardless of distance to target. Features positive click steel windage and elevation adjustments, plus precision internal adjustments for repeatability and return to zero.

Model 64 Balvar Riflescope

6-24x40mm.	$509.95
3-9x40mm.	409.95
1.5-6x20mm	399.95
2.5-10x40mm	495.95

BAUSCH & LOMB

TARGET SCOPES

Feature crisp, repeatable ⅛″ MOA click adjustments in two styles, plus hard surface, multi-coated optics, sunshades (3″ and 5″). Fogproof and waterproof.

36x(40mm) Dot Reticle $599.95
36x(40mm) Fine Crosshair Reticle 589.95
24x(40mm) Dot Reticle 599.95
24x(40mm) Fine Crosshair Reticle 589.95
6x-24x(40mm) Fine Crosshair Reticle 599.95

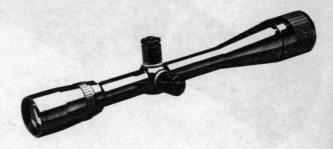

TARGET SCOPES

COMPACTS

Offer same features and performance as full-size Bausch & Lomb riflescopes in lightweight design. Include four times zoom ratio, resettable ¼″ MOA click adjustments, hard surface multi-coated optics, one-piece body tube. Fogproof and waterproof.

2x-8x(32mm) Balvar Compact $419.95
4x(32mm) Balfor Compact 319.95

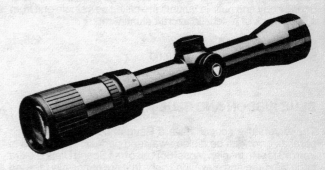

COMPACTS

HANDGUN SCOPES

Feature one-piece body tube, resettable ¼″ MOA click adjustments, wide margin of eye relief, hard surface, multi-coated optics. Fogproof and waterproof.

4x(28mm) $289.95
2x(20mm) 269.95

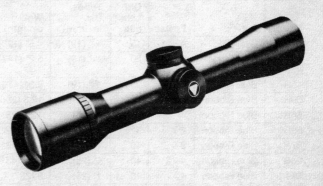

HANDGUN SCOPES

BEEMAN SCOPES

SS-3 SERIES

Offers 1.5-4x zoom power for greater flexibility. Glare-free black matte finish is anodized into metal for deep sheen and extra toughness. Instant action dial around front of scope dials away parallax error and dials in perfect focus from 10 feet to infinity. Scope measures only 5³/₄ inches in length and weighs only 8.5 ounces. **SS-3 Series: $250.00**

SS-1 AND SS-2 SERIES

Beeman SS-1 and SS-2 short scopes are extra compact and rugged, due largely to breakthroughs in optical engineering and computer programming of lens formulas. Less than 7 inches long, both scopes pack 11 lenses that actually gather light for bigger, brighter targets than "projected spot" targets. Scope body and built-in mounts are milled as a single unit from a solid block of hi-tensile aircraft aluminum.

SS-1 Series: $179.50
SS-2 Series: $225.00—$250.00

BLUE RIBBON AND BLUE RING SCOPES

These versatile scopes have a Range Focus Ring by which parallax error can be dialed away and perfect focus dialed in from 13 feet to infinity. Model 66R also has Speed Dials—extra large windage and elevation knobs that are especially fast and easy to use. Beeman economy scopes (Models 30A, 35R and 45R) are notable for their high lens counts.

BEEMAN SS-2L "SKYLITE" RIFLESCOPE

Features a brightly illuminated reticle powered by daylight and even moonlight (no batteries necessary). In addition to standard black reticle, supplementary color filters are available for different lighting and shooting situations. Filter options include: white (for silhouette or target); red (for twilight and general purpose); yellow (for haze, fog and low light); green (for bright light and snow). A small electrical illuminator is also available for use in total darkness.

Beeman SS-2L w/color reticle, 3x **$275.00**
Beeman SS-2L w/color reticle, 4x 295.00
Lamp 29.95
Filter Kit (green or yellow) 18.95

SCOPE SPECIFICATIONS:

Model	Series	Power	Obj. Lens mm	Tube Dia. in. (mm)	Wgt. oz. (gm)	Length in. (mm)	Field of View 100 yds. (100m)	Eye Relief in. (mm)	Reticle
30A	Blue Ring	4	15	³/₄" (19)	4.5* (128)	10.2 (259)	21 (7m)	2 (50)	5 pt. TL
35R	Blue Ring	3	20	³/₄" (19)	5.2* (147)	11 (280)	25 (8.3m)	2.5 (64)	5 pt. TL
45R	Blue Ring	3-7	20	³/₄" (19)	6.3* (179)	10.8 (275)	26-12 (8.7-4m)	2.5 (64)	5 pt. TL
50R	Blue Ribbon	2.5	32	1" (25)	12.3 (350)	12 (305)	33 (11m)	3.5 (90)	5 pt. TL
54R	Blue Ribbon	4	32	1" (25)	12.3 (35)	12 (305)	29' (8.8m)	3.5 (90)	5 pt. TL
66R	Blue Ribbon	2.7	32	1" (25)	14.9 (422)	11.4 (290)	62-16 (18.9-5.3m)	3 (76)	5 pt. TL
67R	Blue Ribbon	3-9	40	1" (25)	15.2 (431)	14.4 (366)	43.5-15' (13.3-4.6m)	3 (76)	5 pt. TL
68R	Blue Ribbon	4-12	40	1" (25)	15.2 (431)	14.4 (366)	30.5'-11' (9.3-3.4m)	3 (76)	5 pt. TL
MS-1	Blue Ribbon	4	18	1" (25)	8 (227)	7.5 (191)	23' (7m)	3.5	5 pt. TL
SS-1	Blue Ribbon	2.5	16	⁷/₈" (22)	6.9* (195)	5.5 (137)	32.5 (10.8m)	3 (76)	5 pt. TL
SS-2	Blue Ribbon	3	21	1.38" (35)	13.6* (385)	6.8 (172)	34.5 (11.5m)	3.5 (90)	5 pt. TL
SS-2	Blue Ribbon	4	21	1.38" (35)	13.7 (388)	7 (182)	24.6 (8.2m)	3.5 (90)	5 pt. TL
SS-3	Blue Ribbon	1.5-4	16	⁷/₈" (22)	8.6 (241)*	5.75 (146)	44.6'-24.6' (13.6-7.5m)	3 (76)	5 pt. TL

*Includes scope mount in price and weight.   TL = Thin Line reticle.

BEEMAN MOUNTS

DOUBLE ADJUSTABLE SCOPE MOUNTS

Beeman Professional Pivot Mounts. The finest scope mounts in existence for big bore. These allow scopes to be quickly and easily detached for transporting, protecting from bad weather or repairing. No tools required. Just lift mount latch, pivot scope 90° and lift out. Scope returns to zero when reattached. Built-in windage adjustment allows full use of scope's windage adjustment. Also, bases sit so low mechanical sights may be used when scope is off. **$269.50**
Beeman Professional Dovetail Mounts. These are the finest scope mounts in existence for 22 caliber rifles. Same superb construction and built-in windage adjustment as the Pivot Mounts (above). A locking screw arrangement absolutely locks the mount into position with 11mm dovetails. **No. 5085 w/25-26mm (1″) rings: $98.95**
Double Adjustable Scope Mounts. The first mounts to have both clamp size and windage adjustment features. Using spacer bars provided, clamp size adjusts to fit grooved receivers and scope bases on all known 22 rifles (¼ to ⅝″, 6mm to 15mm). Windage adjustment built into the mount center

scope so that scope retains its full range of windage adjustments. These high-quality mounts are for 22 rimrife and airgun shooters who wish to mount high-performance 1″ diameter scopes on their guns. **No. 5084: $29.98**
Beeman Deluxe Ring Mounts. Simpler version of 5084 without the double adjustable feature. Very sturdy and extremely solid. High tensile aviation aluminum with non-glare, honed blue-black finish. Blued steel clamping screws. **No. 5081: $28.98**
Beeman/Buehler Mounts and Bases. These bases were designed specifically for Beeman/Krico rifles. They will take any Buehler rings, however. Built-in windage adjustment. Only the medium and high rings recommended. Finest chrome moly steel, beautifully blued. Scope may be pivoted off, but this requires loosening two screws with a screwdriver. Two bases and ring heights available. **No. 5094** (base-smallbore) and **No. 5095** (base-large-bore): **$59.98**. **No. 5096** (medium rings) and **No. 5097** (high rings): **$59.98.**

MODEL 68R
$298.95

MODELS 68R & 67R

These two high power scopes—with 4-12 zoom power and 3-9 zoom power, respectively—are suitable for airguns, rimfire and centerfire rifles alike. Field shooters who must make precise head shots on small game will find the higher magnifications helpful. Both models incorporate the lens bracing required to protect them from the damaging two-way snap of spring piston airguns. Other features include a speed dial (for elevation) and range focus, plus a large 40mm objective lens that provides super-bright images. **Model 67R: $349.00**

MODEL M66R
$239.95

This scope, which was designed for centerfire, 22 caliber rimfire, and adult air rifles, can zoom instantly from 2 to 7x for long-range shots requiring pinpoint accuracy. It features speed dials with full saddle and range focus. There's also a special running target version—a delicate dot is set on each side of the horizontal member of a special, thin-line crosshair to provide proper leads for targets running right or left at 10 meters.

Also available: **Model 66RL** with color reticle (2x-7x): **$289.96.**

B-SQUARE SCOPE MOUNTS

44 MAGNUM RUGER BLACKHAWK MOUNTS
$49.95 (Stainless)
$39.95 (Blue)

M-94 ANGLE EJECT SCOPE MOUNT
For Winchester 94 Angle Eject
$49.95

1903 SPRINGFIELD SCOPE MOUNT
$59.95

ONE-PIECE BASES
$9.95

This new one-piece base fits both long and short actions. It provides better alignment than two-piece blocks for the straightest, strongest and best looking base available. It can be attached with socket screws and wrench provided. The Mauser 98 Large Ring and Small Ring bases have a notch that locates itself in the clip-lip, so there's no need to file for clip-lips or bolt handle clearance. Bases are available for Winchester 70, Savage 110, Browing A-Bolt, Remington 700, T/C Hawken, and many others.

MAUSER 98

OTHER POPULAR RIFLES

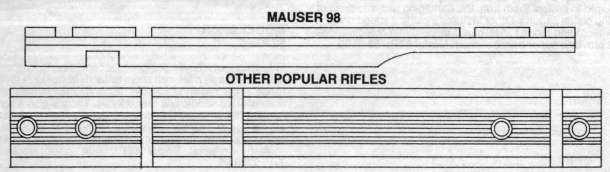

B-SQUARE SCOPE MOUNTS

PISTOL MOUNTS

RUGER MK I/II 22 AUTO (MONO-MOUNT)
$39.95 ($49.95 Stainless)

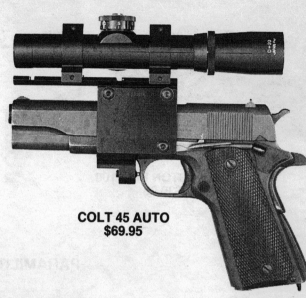

COLT 45 AUTO
$69.95

DAN WESSON/COLT PYTHON
$49.95 ($59.95 Stainless)

RIFLE MOUNTS

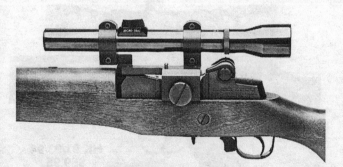

RUGER MINI-14
$49.95 ($59.95 Stainless)

RUGER MINI-14 RANCH/MINI-THIRTY
$49.95

B-SQUARE SCOPE MOUNTS

SHOTGUN MOUNTS

REMINGTON 870/1100
$39.95

MOSSBERG 500
$39.95

PARAMILITARY MOUNTS

1917/P14 ENFIELD
$39.95

BERETTA AR 70
$49.95

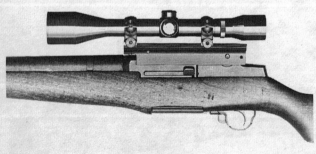

M1 GARAND
$59.95

HK 91/93/94
$69.95

BUEHLER SCOPE MOUNTS

BUEHLER TELESCOPIC SIGHT MOUNTS. By using one of the five basic styles of mount bases, you may position the scope of your choice in the best possible location—the one that positions the scope so that the shooter has a full field of view when his face is nestled in a comfortable, natural position against the stock. Scopes vary in eye relief from 3 to 5 inches. Sight adjustment turrets are in different locations. The amount of space available on the scope for the mount varies. Most important of all is the difference in shooters and in the way each one holds a rifle. One of the five styles of mounts will locate your scope in the best position for you. All Buehler mount rings fit and are interchangeable with all Buehler bases.

MICRO-DIAL UNIVERSAL MOUNT

Both windage and elevation features are built in. A twist of the fingers fixes the elevation desired on a dial clearly marked in minutes (one inch at 100 yards). Another twist on the lock wheel directly below the dial securely locks the setting. The windage screws are also calibrated in minutes on both sides. The Micro Dial is designed primarily for all scopes with internal adjustments, such as the Balvar 2½ to 8 (use Code 7 Rings for Balvar), but can be used to advantage with many other scopes. Dial also makes it possible to switch scopes between rifles. The ring spacing is 4 inches.

Prices:

Micro-Dial Base	$51.00
Mount Base, One or Two-piece	31.00
Mount Base, Sako, Mini-14	47.50
Mount Base, Pistol—Blue	31.00
Mount Base, Pistol—Stainless	39.00
Mount Base, Pistol M83, (Blue or Silver)	41.00

SHORT ONE-PIECE BASES

The short one-piece base locates the front ring over the top of the receiver ring about 1 inch aft of the long one-piece base. The rear ring is in about the same location. Thus, ring spacing averages 4 inches. The short base is recommended for shorter scopes, scopes with large and long objective bells, and scopes with turrets near the center of the tube. Each **$31.00**

TWO-PIECE BASE

Two-piece bases locate the front ring over the receiver ring in the same place as the short one-piece base. The rear ring, however, is over the bridge on bolt-action rifles, not ahead of it as is the case with the one-piece bases. The ring spacing averages 4½ inches. Will accommodate scopes described under the *short* one-piece bases. The eye relief is shorter than either one-piece base but adequate for the average installation.

Two-Piece Scope Mount Base **$31.00**

LOW SAFETY (not shown)
$21.25

For scoping bolt-action rifles. In the "ON" position, pressure of the striker spring holds both bolt and striker in closed position. Safety operates on right side of action, rotating through 70-degree arc with definite stops in "OFF" and "ON" positions. Can be used equally well with or without scope. Fits following models: Mauser M98 & F.N., Krag, Springfield, Winchester M54, 1891 Argentine Mauser, M93.

SAFETY ON

SAFETY OFF

BUEHLER SCOPE MOUNTS

M83 BUEHLER PISTOL MOUNT
(shown on Ruger Blackhawk)

M83 PISTOL MOUNT

Installs without drilling or tapping (wrench included). Base is made of high tensile Aircraft Aluminum Alloy, anodized and dyed in black or silver to match blue or stainless steel pistols. Designed for calibers up through 357 Magnum. Use code 7 rings.

M83 (Base only) $41.00

BUEHLER RINGS FOR BOTH ONE AND TWO-PIECE MOUNTS

A double split-type ring with the added beauty of a smoothly rounded "ball turret top." The steel spacer at the top of each ring is made of 16 laminations .002" thick which may be peeled off one or more at a time, thus accurately fitting all scopes up to .01" smaller in size than the normal dimension of the ring.

MOUNT RINGS

Double split rings, codes 6, 7 & 8 . . . . $41.50
Double split rings, codes 10, 11, 14, 15 . . . . 52.00
Spec. 30mm, code 30 . . . . 62.50
Engraved split rings, codes 6, 8 . . . . 98.75

BURRIS SCOPES

3X-9X FULLFIELD (illustrated)

A versatile scope for big game and varmint hunting. The most popular variable power scope because it fulfills a variety of purposes from long-range varmint shooting to shorter ranges of heavy brush shooting. A rugged, factory-sealed hunting scope with a big 14-foot field of view at 9X and a 38-foot field at 3X.

3x-9x FULLFIELD

Plex. $278.95
Plex w/satin finish 289.95
Post crosshair 289.95
3"–1" dot 290.95

2x-7x FULLFIELD (not illus.)
Field of view: at 7x, 18 ft.; at 2x, 47 ft.

Plex. $263.95
Plex w/satin finish 275.95
Post crosshair 275.95
3"–1" dot 276.95

1³/₄x-5x FULLFIELD (not illus.)
Field of view: at 5x, 25ft.; at 1³/₄x, 66 ft.

Plex. $238.95
Post crosshair 248.95
3"–1" dot 249.95

BURRIS SCOPES

MIKRO REVOLVER SCOPE

A scaled-down version of the big scopes, this ⅝-inch diameter tube weighs only four ounces. Designed to take the recoil of any magnum handgun. Packed with two ⅝-inch steel rings that fit standard handgun bases. Eye relief is nine inches minimum and 24 inches maximum.

Mikro Scope 2x and 3× Crosshair............ $142.95

GUNSITE SCOUT SCOPE

Made for hunters who need a seven to 14-inch eye relief to mount just in front of the ejection port opening, allowing hunters to shoot with both eyes open. The 15-foot field of view and 2¾x magnification are ideal for brush guns and handgunners who use the "two-handed hold."

Gunsite Scout Scope 2¾x Plex XER........... $162.95
  With satin finish............................ 172.95
Gunsite Scout Scope 1½x Plex XER........... 157.95
  With satin finish............................ 166.95

3x-9x FULLFIELD RAC SCOPE
with AUTOMATIC RANGEFINDER RETICLE

Once the crosshair has been zeroed in at 200 yards, it remains there regardless of the power setting. The range reticle automatically moves to a zero at ranges up to 500 yards as power is increased to fit the game between the stadia range wires. No need to adjust elevation knob. Bullet drop adjustment is automatic.

3x-9x Fullfield RAC Crosshair (Dot or Plex)...... $297.95
3x-9x RAC CHP Safari Finish.................. 306.95

BURRIS SCOPES

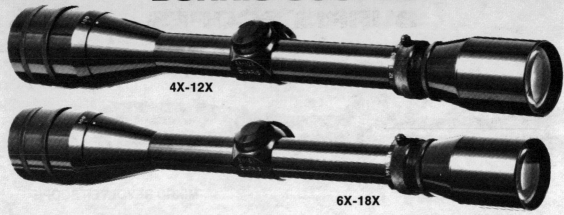

4X-12X

6X-18X

4X-12X FULLFIELD

The ideal scope for long-range varmint hunting and testing hand loads. Can also be used for big game hunting. Features crisp resolution, accurate parallax settings and a big field of view. Friction-type parallax settings from 50 yards to infinity with positive stop to prevent overturning. Fully sealed to withstand the worst field conditions and designed to deliver years of excellent service.

4x-12x FULLFIELD

Plex.	$326.95
Fine Plex.	326.95
2"–.7" Dot	339.95
ARC Crosshair Fine Plex	342.95

6X-18X FULLFIELD

This versatile, high magnification, variable scope can be used for hunting, testing hand loads or shooting bench rest. It features excellent optics, a precise parallax adjustment from 50 yards to infinity, accurate internal adjustments and a rugged, reliable mechanical design that will give years of dependable service. Fully sealed against moisture and dust.

6x-18x FULLFIELD

Plex.	$338.95
Fine Plex.	338.95
2"–.7" Dot	349.95
2"–.7" Dot Silhouette.	369.95
Fine Plex Silhouette	356.95

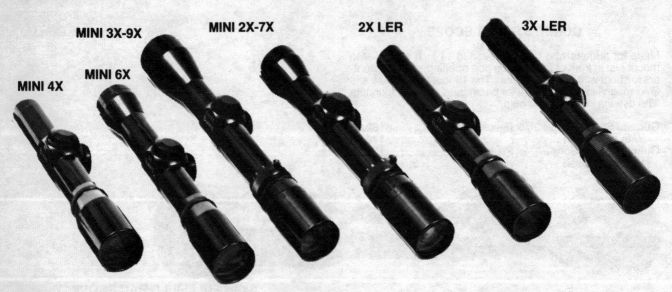

MINI 3X-9X   **MINI 2X-7X**   **2X LER**   **3X LER**

MINI 6X

MINI 4X

MINI SCOPES with PLEX RETICLE:

Mini 4x.	$156.95
Mini 6x.	171.95
Mini 6x 2" Dot P.A.	202.95
Mini 3x-9x.	218.95
Mini 3x-9x Silver Safari	238.95
Mini 2x-7x.	212.95
Mini 4x-12x	289.95

LONG EYE RELIEF SCOPE with PLEX RETICLE:

1x LER	$149.95
1½x-4x LER	253.95
2x LER	155.95
3x LER	168.95
4x LER	175.95
5x LER	189.95

INTERMEDIATE EYE RELIEF SCOPE with PLEX RETICLE:

7X IER.	$203.95
10x IER	252.95

BURRIS SCOPES

1¹/₂X SHOTGUN

2¹/₂X SHOTGUN

10X, 12X & 6X–18X FULLFIELD SILHOUETTE SCOPES

These three scopes, with their precision click target type knobs and Burris Hi-Lume lenses give silhouette shooters a real edge. All new design allows fast, precise reticle adjustments, free of backlash, on both windage and elevation. Graduated knobs are easy to read and can be reset to zero once initial sighting is made. Threaded dust covers included.

10x Fullfield Fine Plex Silhouette	$284.95
¹/₂" Dot Silhouette	293.95
12x Fullfield Fine Plex Silhouette	291.95
¹/₂" Dot Silhouette	302.95
6x-18x Fullfield Fine Plex Silhouette	356.95
6x-18x Fullfield 2"–.7" Dot Silhouette	369.95

1¹/₂X & 2¹/₂X FULLFIELD SHOTGUN SCOPES

The huge field-of-view and recoil proof construction allows shotgun slug hunters to improve their accuracy. Running shots during low-light conditions are made possible with either scope.

1¹/₂x Fullfield Plex	$178.95
2¹/₂x Fullfield Plex	188.95

10X SILHOUETTE SCOPE

12X SILHOUETTE SCOPE

6X–18X SILHOUETTE SCOPE

MOUNT BASE (For Ruger Mark I & II)

Installs in seconds without drilling or tapping. Accepts one-inch .22 rings and Burris long eye relief handgun scopes.

Price:	$34.95
With Silver Safari Finish	39.95

BUSHNELL RIFLESCOPES

BANNER RIFLESCOPES

All Banner riflescopes feature precise resettable click adjustments and fully coated optics. They are also waterproof and fogproof. Prismatic Range Finder and Bullet Drop Compensator are optional.

4x-12x (40mm) BDC	**209.95**
3x-9x (40mm)	**135.95**
6x (40mm)	**143.95**
4x (32mm), BDC.	**115.95**
2.5x (20mm)	**79.95**

BANNER 6X (40mm) Open Country

BANNER 4X-12X (40mm) Medium to Long Range

BANNER 4X (32mm) General-purpose w/BDC

BANNER 2.5X (20mm) Short Range

BUSHNELL RIFLESCOPES

ARMORLITE RIFLESCOPES

Bushnell's Armorlite riflescope offers a proven optical system in Graphlon-VI, a graphite composite material that is stronger than steel, lighter than aluminum, and impervious to any field hazard the hunter might encounter. The scope is available in 3 to 9 power variable and features multicoated optics. It is nitrogen-purged for waterproof and fogproof integrity. One-quarter-minute adjustments provide precise targeting, and the one-piece body tube ensures positive optical alignment.

MODEL 65-3940 . . . . **$349.95**

BANNER COMPACT RIFLESCOPES

Light in weight (11 ounces for the 2-8x and 8 ounces for the 4x), these scopes complement the popular lightweight rifles. They feature large 28mm objective lens for bright, sharp images, precise internal click adjustments, and a Multi-X reticle for a clearly visible aiming point.

2-8x (28mm) Banner Compact Riflescope **$179.95**
4x (28mm) Banner Compact Riflescope **119.95**

(A) 2-8X (28mm) BANNER COMPACT RIFLESCOPE

(B) 4x (28mm) BANNER COMPACT RIFLESCOPE

BUSHNELL RIFLESCOPES

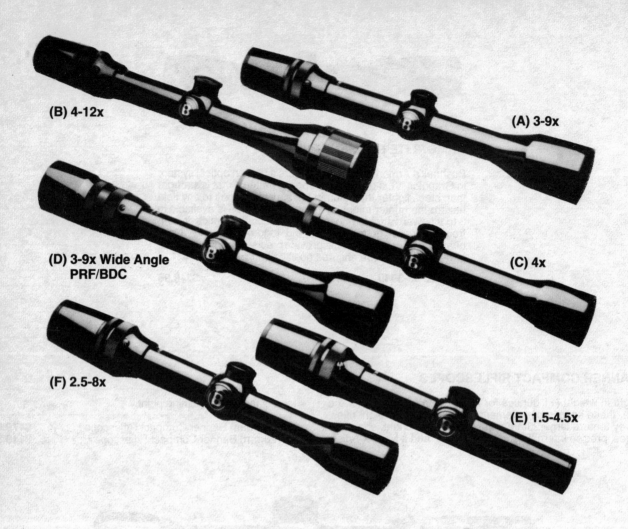

(B) 4-12x

(A) 3-9x

(D) 3-9x Wide Angle PRF/BDC

(C) 4x

(F) 2.5-8x

(E) 1.5-4.5x

SCOPECHIEF RIFLESCOPES

To maximize light transmission and image brightness, the precision ground polished lenses in the Scope Chief riflescope line are now multi-coated on all air-to-glass surfaces. Precision 1/4 M.O.A. click adjustments are standard, as is durable one-piece body tube. Scopes are hermetically sealed for full waterproof and fogproof integrity. Bullet Drop Compensator and Prismatic Range Finder included on 4-12x and 3-9x models.

3-9x40mm $241.95
4-12x40mm PRF/BDC 297.95
3-9x40mm Wide Angle PRF/BDC 301.95
1.5-4.5x20mm 211.95
2.5-8x32mm 215.95
4x32mm 153.95

SCOPECHIEF SPECIFICATION CHART

	Variable Powers			Fixed Power
Magnification	3x-9x	2.5x-8x	1.5x-4.5x	4x
Objective Lens Aperture (mm)	40	32	20	32
Field of View at 100 yards (ft)	3x-34 9x-13	2.5x-45 8x-14	1.5x-73.7 4.5x-24.5	28
Weight (oz)	13.6	11.6	9.5	9.3
Length (in)	12.1	11.2	9.6	12
Eye Relief (in)	3x-3.5 9x-3.3	2.5x-3.7 8x-3.3	1.5x-3.5 4.5x-3.5	3.5
Exit Pupil (mm)	3x-13.3 9x-4.4	2.5x-12.8 8x-4	15x-13.3 4.5x-4.4	8
Relative Light Efficiency	3x-267 9x-30	2.5x-247 8x-96	1.5x-267 4.5x-30	96
MX Center CH Width at 100 yards	3x-.67 9x-.22	2.5x-.8 8x-.25	1.5x-1.3 4.5x-44	.5
Mix Distance Post Tip to Post Tip (in) at 100 yards	3x-24 9x-8	2.5x-28.8 8x-9	1.5x-48 4.5x-16	18
100 yards (in)	.5			

BUSHNELL RIFLESCOPES

BANNER RIFLESCOPE SPECIFICATION CHART

VARIABLE POWER

Magnification	Bullet Drop Compensator	Field of view at 100 yds. (ft.)	Weight (oz.)	Length (inches)	Eye distance (inches)	Entrance pupil (mm)	Exit pupil (mm)	Relative Light Efficiency	MX center CH width at 100 yds. (inches)	MX distance post tip to post tip (inches)	Graduation at 100 yds. (inches)
4x-12x 40mm	BDC	29 at 4x / 10 at 12x	15.5	13.5	3.2	40	10 at 4x / 3.3 at 12x	150 / 17	0.5 / .17	18 / 6	.75
3x-9x 40mm		35 at 3x / 12.6 at 9x	13	13	3.5	40	13.3 at 3x / 4.4 at 9x	267 / 30	.66 / .22	24 / 8	.75
3x-9x 38mm	BDC	43 at 3x WIDE ANGLE / 14.6 at 9x	14	12.1	3	38	12.7 at 3x / 4.2 at 9x	241 / 26.5	.66 / .22	24 / 8	1.0
3x-9x 32mm	BDC	39 at 3x / 13 at 9x	11	11.5	3.5	32	10.7 at 3x / 3.6 at 9x	171 / 19	.66 / .22	24 / 8	1.0
1.75x-4.5x 21mm	BDC	71 at 1.75x WIDE ANGLE / 27 at 4.5x	11.5	10.2	2.9	21	12 at 1.75x / 4.7 at 4.5x	216 / 33	1.18 / .44	45.7 / 17.8	1.5
1.5x-4x 21mm		63 at 1.5x / 28 at 4x	10.3	10.5	3.5	21	14 at 1.5x / 5 at 4x	294 / 41	1.3 / 0.5	48 / 18	1.5

FIXED POWER

Magnification	Bullet Drop Compensator	Field of view at 100 yds. (ft.)	Weight (oz.)	Length (inches)	Eye distance (inches)	Entrance pupil (mm)	Exit pupil (mm)	Relative Light Efficiency	MX center CH width at 100 yds. (inches)	MX distance post tip to post tip (inches)	Graduation at 100 yds. (inches)
10x 40mm	BDC	12	14.0	14.5	3	40	4	24	0.2	7.2	.66
6x 40mm		19.5	11.5	13.5	3	40	6.7	67	0.3	12	.75
4x 40mm	BDC	37.3 WIDE ANGLE	12	12.3	3	40	10	150	0.6	21	1.0
4x 32mm	BDC	29	10	12.0	3.5	32	8	96	0.5	18	1.0
2.5x 20mm		45	8	10.9	3.5	20	8	96	0.8	28.8	1.5

SPORTSVIEW TRUSCOPE

Lets the hunter confirm that the rifle is shooting where he is aiming in the field (where firing a shot would spook the game).

Truscope w/22 & 30 caliber arbor **$47.95**

LEUPOLD RIFLE SCOPES

VARIABLE POWER SCOPES

VARI-X II LINE
Reticles are the same apparent size throughout power range, stay centered during elevation and windage adjustments. Eyepieces are adjustable and fog-free.
VARI-X II 1x4 . . . . **$250.80**

Vari-X II 2x7

VARI-X II 2x7
A compact scope, no larger than the Leupold M8-4X, offering a wide range of power. It can be set at 2X for close ranges in heavy cover or zoomed to maximum power for shooting or identifying game at longer ranges. **$301.90.** With Dot or CPC reticle: **$322.90**

Vari-X II 3x9

VARI-X II 3x9
A wide selection of powers lets you choose the right combination of field of view and magnification to fit the particular conditions you are hunting at the time. Many hunters use the 3X or 4X setting most of the time, cranking up to 9X for positive identification of game or for extremely long shots. The adjustable objective eliminates parallax and permits precise focusing on any object from less than 50 yards to infinity for extra-sharp definition. **$324.30.** With Dot or CPC reticle: **$345.30.** Also available with adjustable objective: **$361.80**

Vari-X II 4x12 A.O.

VARI-X II 4x12 (Adj. Objective)
The ideal answer for big game and varmint hunters alike. At 12.25 inches, the 4x12 is virtually the same length as Vari-X II 3x9. **$390.80**

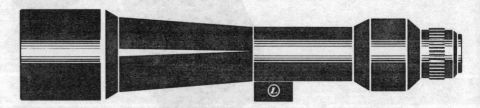

SPOTTING SCOPES
Leupold's Golden Ring 20x60mm Spotting Scope features extraordinary eye relief and crisp, bright roof prism optics housed in a lightweight, sealed, waterproof body. The 12.9-inch, 19.5-ounce Spotting Scope comes complete with a self-storing screw-on sunshade, lens caps, and a leather-trimmed green canvas case. **$476.80.** 30x60mm: **$503.55**

Now available: Leupold's new 20x50mm and 25x50mm compact Waterproof Spotting Scopes with nearly 1″ of eye relief for comfortable viewing with or without glasses.

20x50mm Compact **$450.00**
20x50mm Compact Armored 476.80
25x50mm Compact 476.80
25x50mm Compact Armored 503.55
   With reticle 530.65

LEUPOLD RIFLE SCOPES
VARIABLE POWER SCOPES
VARI-X III LINE

The Vari-X III scopes feature a power-changing system that is similar to the sophisticated lens systems in today's finest cameras. Some of the improvements include an extremely accurate internal control system and a sharp, superb-contrast sight picture. Reticles are the same apparent size throughout power range, stay centered during elevation/windage adjustments. Eyepieces are adjustable and fog-free.

VARI-X III 1.5x5
Here's a fine selection of hunting powers for ranges varying from very short to those at which big game is normally taken. The exceptional field at 1.5X lets you get on a fast-moving animal quickly. With the generous magnification at 5X, you can hunt medium and big game around the world at all but the longest ranges. **$344.20.** Also available in black matte finish: **$362.00**

Vari-X III 1.5 × 5

VARI-X III 2.5x8
This is an excellent range of powers for almost any kind of game, inlcuding varmints. In fact, it possibly is the best all-around variable going today. The top magnification provides plenty of resolution for practically any situation. **$388.20.** In matte finish: **$406.05**

Vari-X III 2.5 × 8

Vari-X III 3.5 × 10

VARI-X III 3.5x10
The extra power range makes these scopes the optimum choice for year-around big game and varmint hunting. The adjustable objective model, with its precise focusing at any range beyond 50 yards, also is an excellent choice for some forms of target shooting. **$406.10.** With adjustable objective: **$443.60**

Vari-X III 6.5 × 20
(with adjustable objective)

VARI-X III 6.5x20
This scope has the widest range of power settings in our variable line, with magnifications that are especially useful to hunters of all types of varmints. In addition, it can be used for any kind of big game hunting where higher magnifications are an aid. **$481.00**

LEUPOLD SCOPES
THE COMPACT SCOPE LINE

The introduction of the Leupold Compacts has coincided with the increasing popularity of the new featherweight rifles. Leupold Compact scopes give a more balanced appearance atop these new scaled-down rifles and offer generous eye relief, magnification and field of view, yet are smaller inside and out. Fog-free.

2.5X COMPACT
The 2.5X Compact is only 8½ inches long and weighs just 7.4 ounces. **$203.50**

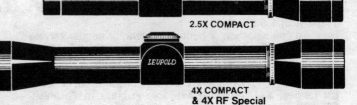

2.5X COMPACT

4X COMPACT
& 4X RF Special

4X COMPACT
The 4X Compact is over an inch shorter than the standard 4X. The 4X RF Special is focused to 75 yards and has a Duplex reticle with finer crosshairs. **$232.40**

6X COMPACT

6X COMPACT
To make the 6X Compact, Leupold's shaved an ounce and a half and .7 inch off the standard scope of the same magnification. **$237.15**

6X COMPACT
(with adjustable objective)

6X COMPACT (Adj. Objective)
The popularity of this magnification seems to be growing at the same rate as the availability of lighter or so-called "mountain" rifles. Now available with adjustable objective lens. **$279.95**

2X7 COMPACT

2X7 COMPACT
Two ounces lighter and a whole inch shorter than its full-size counterpart, this 2x7 is one of the world's most compact variable power scopes. It's the perfect hunting scope for today's trend toward smaller and lighter rifles. **$301.90**

3x9 COMPACT

3X9 COMPACT
The 3x9 Compact is a full-blown variable that's 3½ ounces lighter and 1.3 inches shorter than a standard 3x9. Also available in new flat black, matte finish. **$316.05**

3x9 COMPACT
(with adjustable objective)

3X9 COMPACT (Adj. Objective)
Big scope performance in a package compatible with the growing list of scaled down and featherweight rifles. Now available with adjustable objective lens. **$355.90**

LEUPOLD SCOPES
THE TARGET SCOPE LINE

Shooters using Leupold target scopes are dominating both local and national bench rest and silhouette matches. Fog-free. Adjustable objective.

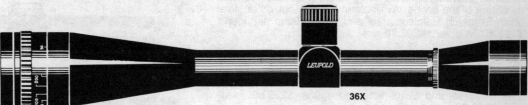

36X

36X TARGET SCOPE
A full 36 power magnification with clear, sharp resolution is possible with Leupold's 36X target scope, all in a package that is only 13.9 inches long and weighs just 15½ ounces. Adjustable objective. **$542.95.** With Target Dot: **$563.95**

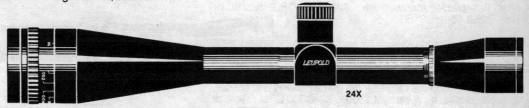

24X

24X TARGET SCOPE
The 24X is just 13.6 inches long and weighs only 14½ ounces. It is compact enough to be receiver mounted and light enough to permit transfer of significant weight from scope to rifle. Adjustable objective. **$542.95.** With ⅛ min. or ½ min. Target Dot: **$563.95**

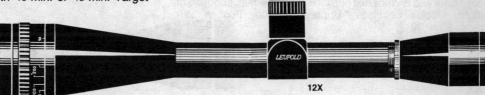

12X

12X TARGET SCOPE
The 12X target scope has the magnification and clear, sharp-contrast sight picture that target shooters need. Two types of redesigned windage/elevation adjustment knobs are included. Adjustable objective. **$408.85.** With CPC reticle or Dot: **$429.85**

VARI-X III 6.5x20

VARI-X III 6.5x20 TARGET SCOPE
The 6.5x20 target allows a shooter to not only change magnifications quickly to match target range, but also rapidly select the windage and elevation needed for each shot, knowing he can unerringly return to a previous setting with ease. Adjustable objective. **$542.95.** With CPC reticle or Dot: **$429.85**

LEUPOLD SCOPES

EXTENDED EYE RELIEF HANDGUN SCOPE LINE

2X EER

With an optimum eye relief of 12-24 inches, the 2X EER is an excellent choice for most handguns. It is equally favorable for carbines and other rifles with top ejection that calls for forward mounting of the scope. Available in black anodized or silver finish to match stainless steel and nickel-plated handguns. **$184.80.** In silver: **$202.70**

2X EER

4X EER

Only 8.4 inches long and 7.6 ounces. Optimum eye relief 12-24 inches. Available in black anodized or silver finish to match stainless steel and nickel-plated handguns. **$225.65.** In silver: **$243.50**

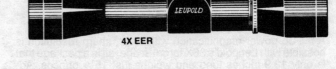

4X EER

FIXED-POWER SCOPE LINE

4X

The all-time favorite is the 4X, which delivers a widely used magnification and a generous field of view. Also available in new flat black, matte finish. **$232.40.** CPC reticle or Dot: **$253.40**

4X

6X

Gaining popularity fast among fixed power scopes is the 6X, which can extend the range for big game hunting and double, in some cases, as a varmint scope. **$248.15.** CPC reticle or Dot: **$269.15**

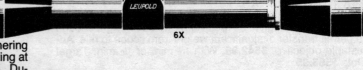

6X

6X42mm

Large 42mm objective lens features increased light gathering capability and a 7mm exit pupil. Great for varmint shooting at night. Duplex or Heavy Duplex: **$279.00.** Post & Duplex: **$300.00**

8X

A true varmint scope, the 8X has the sharp resolution, contrast and accuracy that also make it effective for some types of target shooting. Adjustable objective permits precise, parallax-free focusing. **$330.90.** CPC reticle or Dot: **$351.90**

  Also available: **8x36mm.** Features a target-style dot and thinner Duplex reticle for long-range use (focused at 300 yds. instead of 150). **$330.90.** With target-style dot: **$351.90.** With adj. objective: **$368.40**

8X

12X

Superlative optical qualities, outstanding resolution and magnification make the 12X a natural for the varmint shooter. Adjustable objective is standard for parallax-free focusing. **$335.30.** CPC reticle or Dot: **$356.30**

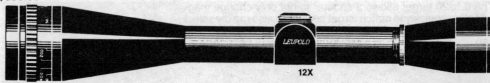

12X

LYMAN RECEIVER SIGHTS

LYMAN 57 and 66 UNIVERSAL RECEIVER SIGHTS

An unobtrusive micrometer receiver sight for hunting or target shooting with sporter, target or military rifle. This sight is equipped with a push-button quick release slide that makes it ideal for alternating use on a scope-equipped rifle.

Fully adjustable with audible ¼-minute clicks for windage and elevation. Coin-slotted stayset knobs for hunting.

Slide adjustments are equipped with precision scales to aid in pre-setting sights for specific ranges or wind conditions. Slide furnished with elevation stop screw that facilitates return to "zero" if removed and reattached. Slide operates in dovetail channel.

No. 57 and 66 Receiver Sights, complete **$54.95**

NO. 57 RECEIVER SIGHT

NO. 66 RECEIVER SIGHT

SERIES 17A TARGET FRONT SIGHTS

Teamed with a Lyman receiver sight, these low silhouette front sights provide precise, X-ring accuracy on the range. Designed for use with dovetail slot mounting, they are supplied with seven interchangeable inserts (see descriptions below) that are locked into place with a threaded cap.

Series 17A Target Front Sight w/inserts **$22.95**

LYMAN HUNTING FRONT SIGHTS

Despite the exceptionally sharp definition provided by a fine aperture receiver sight, an equally fine front sight is necessary for consistently accurate shooting, particularly in extreme glare and overcast in the field. Lyman ivory bead front sights are the ideal field front sights. They present a flat optical surface that's equally illuminated by bright or dull light, and they keep their "color" under all light conditions. The Lyman ivory bead front sight is the perfect teammate for your favorite Lyman receiver sight, and will give you a reliable, sharply defined, glareless aiming surface, even under the worst conditions. You can fit a ready adaptable Lyman bead front sight to your rifle in minutes.

NO. 18 SCREW-ON TYPE RAMP

The screw-on ramp is designed to be secured with a heavy 8-40 screw (it may be brazed on if desired). Screw-on ramps are ruggedly built and extremely versatile. They use A width front sights, and are available in the following heights:

18A—Low Ramp: .100-inch from top of barrel to bottom of dovetail.

18C—Medium Ramp: .250-inch from top of barrel to bottom of dovetail.

18E—High Ramp: .350-inch from top of barrel to bottom of dovetail.

No. 18 Screw-On Ramp less sight. **$13.50**

NO. 31 FRONT SIGHT
¹/₁₆-inch BEAD

This sight is designed to be used on ramps. Standard ³/₈-inch dovetail. Ivory bead. See Sight Selection Chart.

Price: No. 31 Front Sight **$7.50**

NO. 3 FRONT SIGHT
¹/₁₆-inch BEAD

This sight is mounted directly in the barrel dovetail. ³/₈-inch dovetail is standard. Ivory bead. See Sight Selection Chart.

Price: No. 3 Front Sight **$7.50**

MERIT SHOOTING AIDS

IRIS SHUTTER DELUX MASTER TARGET DISC WITH FLEXIBLE NEOPRENE LIGHT SHIELD

May be cut to size. Particularly adapted for use with extension, telescope height and tang sights. The 1½-inch diameter flexible neoprene light shield is permanently attached to the eye cup, which is replaceable by removing three screws. The shield is concentrically ribbed on its concave face for cutting to suitable size. It is more advantageous than a large metal disc since it protects the sighting equipment in case the disc is accidentally bumped.

The Master Target Disc may be used on all sights having clearance for a disc 7/16-inch thick and ¾-inch or larger in diameter.

Merit Delux Master Disc $60.00
Replacement Shield 8.95
Delux Replacement Shield and Steel Cup 10.00

MERIT DELUX NO. 3 SERIES DISC

Side View   **Front Views**
(minimum and maximum opening)

Other size apertures are obtained by simply turning the knurled eyepiece right or left respectively to decrease or increase the opening.

Merit Delux No. 3LS $50.00
   Outside diameter of disc 11/16″. Shank 11/32″ long.
Merit Delux No. 3A 50.00
   Outside diameter of disc 11/16″. Shank 15/32″ long. Disc thickness 7/32″.

Merit No. 4SS—Outside diameter of disc ½″. Shank 5/16″ long. Disc thickness ¼″. $40.00
Merit No. 4LS—Outside diameter of disc ½″. Shank 11/32″ long. Disc thickness ¼″. 40.00
Merit No. 4ELS—Outside diameter of disc ½″. Shank ½″ long. Disc thickness ¼″. 40.00

The merit optical attachment with aperture is the answer to a shooter's problem when eyesight is impaired. It (1) concentrates and sharpens the vision by increasing the focal depth of the eye, making pistol or rifle sights stand out sharp and clear; (2) cuts out objectionable side lights; (3) helps the shooter to take the same position for each shot; (4) gives instant and easy choice of the right aperture to suit your own eye and particular conditions at time of shooting. The Delux model has swinging arm feature so that the shooter can swing the aperture from the line of vision when not shooting.

Delux Optical Attachment $60.00

Replacement suction cup 8.00

SIGHT CHART

Popular Peep Sights and the proper Merit Discs to fit them. The Merit Master Target Disc may be had with any of the No. 3 series shanks. All of the sights marked ★ will take the Master Disc depending on the front sight used. See chart below:

LYMAN

Sight Model No.	Merit Discs Target	Hunting
48WH, 48WJ, 48WJS, 48W, 45, 35, *30½, *2, *2A, *103	Deluxe 3LS	4SS
All Other 48 Sights	Deluxe 3LS	
*All 52, 54, *524, *525, *Tube Sight		4LS
All 57, 34, All 38, All 41		
45, All 42, All 55, All 56, All 66		4SS
*58E	3A	4ELS
40		

WITTEK-VAVER

Sight Model No.	Merit Discs Target	Hunting
*All Wittek-Vaver Sights. Most of these sights will take the Master Disc with 3A shank	Deluxe 3A	4ELS
*Savage 3S, 4S, 5S, 6S, 7S	15 — 3LS / 3S	4LS
*Remington Model 37 Std. Peep Sight	3SL or Master Disc 3SL	
Remington 41P, 341P, 510P, 511P, 512P Springfield 084, 085, 086, 087	Deluxe 3S	

REDFIELD

Sight Model No.	Merit Discs Target	Hunting
All of Series 70-*75-80-90 and 100		4SS
*Olympic (See Adaptor Page)	3SS or 3LS	Deluxe 4LS
*International (See Adaptor Page)		
All of Series 102		

PACIFIC

Sight Model No.	Merit Discs Target	Hunting
All Williams FP		4SS
K1, S1, W1, SA1, S1R, L1, LB1, EN1, EN3, EN5		4SS
K2, S2, W2, SA2, S2R, LB2, EN2, EN4	Deluxe 3LS	4LS

WINCHESTER

Rifle Model	Sight Model	
74	88A	474
71, 64, 65	Win Special	4SS
*75	84A	3A — 4ELS
72, 69A	80A, 80A	3S72 — 4SP72
*All of Marble-Goss Receiver, Tang and Extension Sights	3LS	4LS
Ranger and Stevens Standard Peep Sights	3LS	4LS

Marlin Standard Peep Sights   4-S
Marble Flexible Rear Sights   4-S
King 210 Rear Sights   4-K

MILLET SIGHTS™
SCOPE MOUNTS

Adjustable Rear

Fixed Rear

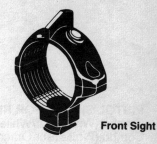

Front Sight

Scope-Site Ring Set Adjustable	**$69.95**
Scope-Site Ring Set Fixed	39.95
Convertible Top Cap Set Adjustable	56.95
Scope-Site Ruger M77-Fixed	39.95
Scope-Site Ruger M77-Adj.	69.95
Scope-Site Remington 870 & 1100 Shotguns, fixed	39.95
Same as above w/Adj.	69.95

SCOPE-SITE™ FOR RIFLES & SHOTGUNS

Scope-Site solves two major problems that arise in effective use of telescopic sights. First, scopes are not useable for low-light, close-in shots in densely wooded areas. Second, scopes on high magnification take too much time to align on distant shots for fast, elusive game.

Scope-Site provides open patridge-style high visibility sights above the telescopic sight. The rear sights are either click-adjustable or fixed. Both types come with white outline apertures. Front post sights are blaze orange.

Scope-Site is far superior to see-through type mounts, because the telescopic sight remains close to the bore for proper cheeking on the stock comb. Scope-Site requires the rifleman to move his head only one inch to see through his open sights.

ANGLE-LOC™ SCOPE RINGS (not shown)
(for Weaver-Type Bases and Ruger Rings)

Millett's 1″ Angle-Loc™ scope rings (for use with Weaver-type bases) feature positive clamping mounts for solid alignment of the base to the ring, and windage adjustment integral to the rings enabling shooters to fine-tune the scope rings to their firearms. Available in three heights. Choice of smooth, engraved or Scope-Site.

Angle-Loc Scope-Site Fixed (low, medium, high)	**$39.95**
Angle-Loc Scope-Site Adjustable (low, medium, high)	69.95
Angle-Loc Engraved Rings (low, medium, high)	39.95
Angle-Loc Smooth Rings (low, medium, high)	26.95
Ruger M77 or Super Redhawk Engraved Rings (front & rear, set), medium only	39.95
Same as above w/smooth rings, medium only	26.95

UNIVERSAL CUSTOM SCULPTURED BASES
(not shown)

Millett's 2-piece scope bases have outstanding features. Custom crafted style on the outside with all of the excess mass remove from the underside, makes these bases the lightest, heat treated, nickel steel bases on the market, 40% lighter.

700 Series (Two piece set)	SB70001	**$20.95**
FN Series (Two piece set)	FN00002	20.95
70 Series (Two Piece Set)	WB70003	20.95
Browning Bar, Blr (2 piece set)	BB00004	20.95
Browning A-Bolt (2 piece set)	BB00005	20.95
Rem 7400/7600/4/6 (2 piece set)	RB00006	20.95
Marlin 336 & Similar (2 piece set)	MB00007	20.95
Winchester 94, Angle Eject (2-pc set)	WB00008	20.95
Savage 110, All Models (2-pc set)	SB00009	20.95

MILLET SIGHTS™

PISTOL SIGHTS FOR RUGER P85
Combo (White rear/White front) **$59.79**
Combo (White rear/Orange front) 59.79
Rear only (White outline) .47.29
Front only (White ramp) .13.59
Front only (Orange ramp) 13.59
Front only (Serrated ramp) 13.59

SCOPE-SITE FOR HANDGUNS
Colt Python/Trooper/Diamondback/Peacekeeper (fully
adjustable) **$72.95**
Dan Wesson (calibers thru .357; fully adjustable; 2
rings) 72.95
Ruger Redhawk (also Ranch Rifle, #1, #3; adj. for
windage, medium) 39.95
   Fully adjustable, medium 69.95
Ruger Super Redhawk (also M77; adj. for
windage) 39.95
   Fully adjustable 69.95

MILLETT SCOPE MOUNTS FOR HANDGUNS
Colt Python/Trooper/Diamondback/Peacekeeper
(smooth rings) **$29.95**
   Engraved rings (front and rear, set) 42.95
Dan Wesson (calibers up thru .357; smooth rings, 2-
ring set) 26.95
   Same calibers, engraved rings (2-ring set) 39.95
   41/44 Magnum, smooth rings only (3-ring
set) 44.85
Ruger Redhawk (also Ranch Rifle, #1, #3; smooth
rings) 26.95
   Engraved rings (front and rear, set) 39.95
Ruger Super Redhawk (also M77; engraved rings
front & rear) 39.95
   Smooth rings (front & rear, set) 26.95

MILLETT SIGHTS™
Revolver Sights

COLT REVOLVER

The Series 100 Adjustable Sight System offers today's discriminating Colt owner the finest quality replacement sight available. 12 crisp click stops for each turn of adjustment, delivers $5/8''$ of adjustment per click at 100 yards with a 6" barrel. Easy to install, using factory front sight. Guaranteed to give your Colt that custom look.

For Colt Python, Trooper, Diamond Back, and new Frontier single action army.

Rear Only (White Outline)	CR00001	$41.95
Rear Only (Target Blade)	CR00002	41.95
Rear Only (Silhouette)	CR00003	41.95

Colt owners will really appreciate the high visibility feature of Colt front sights. Easy to install—just drill 2 holes in the new sight and pin on. All steel. Your choice of blaze orange or white bar. Fits 4", 6" & 8" barrels only.

Colt Python (White or Orange Bar)	FB00007–8	$11.59
Trooper, Diamond Back, King Cobra, Peacemaker	FB00015–16	11.59

SMITH & WESSON

The Series 100 Adjustable Sight System for Smith & Wesson revolvers provides the sight picture and crisp click adjustments desired by the discriminating shooter. $1/2''$ of adjustment per click, at 100 yards on elevation, and $5/8''$ on windage, with a 6" barrel. Can be installed in a few minutes, using factory front sight.

K&N frames manufactured prior to 1974 did not standardize on front screw hole location, so the front hole must be drilled and counterbored on these sights.

Smith & Wesson N Frame

N.312—Model 25-5, all bbl., 27-$3^1/2''$ & 5", 28-4" & 6"
N.360—Model 25, 27, 29, 57, & 629-4, 6 & $6^1/2''$ bbl.
N.410—Model 27, 29, 57, 629 with $8^3/8''$ bbl.

Smith & Wesson K&L Frame

K.312—Models 14, 15, 18, 48-4", & 53
K&L360—Models 16, 17, 19, 48-6", $8^3/8''$, 66, 686, 586

Smith & Wesson K&L-Frame		
Rear Only .312 (White Outline)	SK00001	$41.95
Rear Only .312 (Target Blade)	SK00002	41.95
Rear Only .360 (White Outline)	SK00003	41.95
Rear Only .360 (Target Blade)	SK00004	41.95
Rear Only .410 (White Outline)	SK00005	41.95
Rear Only .410 (Target Blade)	SK00006	41.95

Smith & Wesson K&N Old Style		
Rear Only .312 (White Outline)	KN00001	$41.95
Rear Only .312 (Target Blade)	KN00002	41.95
Rear Only .360 (White Outline)	KN00003	41.95
Rear Only .360 (Target Blade)	KN00004	41.95
Rear Only .410 (White Outline)	KN00005	41.95
Rear Only .410 (Target Blade)	KN00006	41.95

Smith & Wesson N-Frame		
Rear Only .312 (White Outline)	SN00001	$41.95
Rear Only .312 (Target Blade)	SN00002	41.95
Rear Only .360 (White Outline)	SN00003	41.95
Rear Only .360 (Target Blade)	SN00004	41.95
Rear Only .410 (White Outline)	SN00005	41.95
Rear Only .410 (Target Blade)	KN00006	41.95

RUGER

The high visibility white outline sight picture and precision click adjustments of the Series 100 Adjustable Sight System will greatly improve the accuracy and fast sighting capability of your Ruger. $3/4''$ per click at 100 yard for elevation, $5/8''$ per click for windage, with 6" barrel. Can be easily installed, using factory front sight or all-steel replacement front sight which is a major improvement over the factory front. Visibility is greatly increased for fast sighting. Easy to install by drilling one hole in the new front sight.

The Red Hawk all-steel replacement front sight is highly visible and easy to pickup under all lighting conditions. Very easy to install. Fits the factory replacement system.

SERIES 100 RUGER DOUBLE ACTION REVOLVER SIGHTS	
Rear Sight (fits all adjustable models)	$41.95
Front Sight (Security Six, Police Six, Speed Six)	11.59
Front Sight (Redhawk and GP-100)	13.59

SERIES 100 RUGER SINGLE ACTION REVOLVER SIGHTS	
Rear Sight (Black Hawk Standard & Super; Bisley Large Frame, Single-Six)	41.95
Front Sight (Millet Replacement sights not available for Ruger single action revolvers).	

DAN WESSON

This sight is exactly what every Dan Wesson owner has been looking for. The Series 100 Adjustable Sight System provides 12 crisp click stops for each turn of adjustment, with $5/8''$ per click for windage, with a 6" barrel. Can be easily installed, using the factory front or new Millett high visibility front sights.

Choice of white outline or target blade.

Rear Only (White Outline)	DW00001	$41.95
Rear Only (Target Blade)	DW00002	41.95
Rear Only (White Outline) 44 Mag.	DW00003	41.95
Rear Only (Target Blade) 44 Mag.	DW00004	41.95

If you want super-fast sighting capability for your Dan Wesson, the new Millett blaze orange or white bar front is the answer. Easy to install. Fits factory quick-change system. All steel, no plastic. Available in both heights.

Dan Wesson .44 Mag & 15-2 (White Bar) (high)	FB00009	$11.59
Dan Wesson .44 Mag & 15-2 (Orange Bar) (high)	FB00010	11.59
Dan Wesson 22 Caliber (White Bar) (low)	FB00011	11.59
Dan Wesson 22 Caliber (Orange Bar) (low)	FB00012	11.59

MILLET SIGHTS™

FLUSH-MOUNT SLING SWIVELS

Millett's flush-mount redesigned Pachmayr sling swivels are quick detachable and beautifully styled in heat treated nickel steel. The sling swivel loop has been redesigned to guide the sling into the loop, eliminating twisitng and fraying on edges of sling. Millett flush-mount bases are much easier to install than the old Pachmayr design, with no threading and an easy to use step drill.

Flush-Mount Swivels (pair)	SS00001	**$13.95**
Loops Only	SS00002	**6.95**
Piloted Counterbore	SS00003	**14.95**

FLUSH-MOUNT HARRIS BIPOD ADAPTER

Millett's flush-mount sling swivels have a simple-to-use adapter for the Harris bipod, that detaches quickly so the loop can then be installed in the bipod loop receptacle. Will also fit Pachmayr flush-mount bases.

Harris Bipod Adapter	SS00004	**$6.95**

DUAL-CRIMP INSTALLATION TOOL KIT

The Dual-Crimp System is a new revolutionary way of installing front sights on autos. Now it is not necessary to heliarc or silver solder to get a good secure job. Dual-Crimp has a two-post, hollow rivet design that works very much like an aircraft rivet and withstands the heavy abuse of hardball ammo. Your choice of four styles and nine heights. Dual-Crimp is the quick and easy system for professionals. Requires a drill press.

Dual-Crimp Tool Set, Complete	DC0002	**$129.95**
Application Tool		**69.95**
Reverse counterbore (solid carbide)		**33.50**
³/₁₆" Drill (solid carbide)		**15.50**
Drill Jig		**19.95**
		69.95
Service Kit (for Series 100 System)		**99.95**

SHURSHOT RIBBED SHOTGUN SIGHTS

The greatest deterrent to shotgun accuracy is raising your head from the stock when shooting. With the Millett ShurShot, accuracy is improved by giving the shooter a reference point to align his head position on the stock. The blaze orange inserts are highly visible in low light and aids the eye in picking up the target. Late in the day deer hunters or early morning duck hunters can get on the game quickly and accurately. ShurShot works great with slugs or shot. Shooting is quick and natural. Eye instinct will automatically align and center the rib and sight bar.

ShurShot Shotgun Sight Combo (Orange) Fits Rem. 1100 & 870	SG00001	**$15.95**
ShurShot Shotgun Sight (Rear Only Orange) Fits Rem. 1100 & 870	SG00002	**9.95**
ShurShot Shotgun Sight (Front Only Orange)	SG00003	**6.95**
ShurShot Shotgun Combo (Orange)	SG00004	**15.95**
Other Models ShurShot Shotgun Sight (Rear Only Orange)	SG00005	**9.95**
Other Models ShurShot Adj. Shotgun Sight Combo (Orange)	SG00006	**21.95**
ShurShot Adj. Shotgun Sight (Rear Only Orange)	SG00007	**15.95**

GLOCK 17 REPLACEMENT SIGHT

The Innovative Glock 17 pistol, the first production pistol to use plastic for the major part of its construction, leaves many shooters looking for better, fully adjustable sights. The Millet sight, in either white outline or target black blade) retrofits the factory dovetail. The plastic factory front sight must be replaced with a Millett Dual-Crimp front (.340 height) and is available in white, orange or black serrated ramp. Rear sight is fully adjustable with positive clicks for windage and elevation. All-steel construction.

GLOCK 17 Sight	
Rear Sight (white outline)	**47.29**
Rear Sight (target)	**47.29**

MILLETT SIGHTS™

SMITH & WESSON 39/59

This sight system provides fast and accurate sighting capability even under low light conditions. The unique white outline rear blade teamed up with the blaze orange or white bar front sight creates a highly visible sight picture, ideal for match or duty use.

Combo (White rear/Dual-Crimp White Front)	SW39591	$62.95
Combo (White rear/Dual-Crimp Orange Front	SW39592	62..95
Rear Only (White outline)	SW39595	50.39
Rear Only (Target Blade)	SW39596	50.39
Requires .340 Dual-Crimp Front		

SMITH & WESSON 469, 669, 659, 459, 645 AUTOPISTOL SIGHTS

Rear Sight (white outline)	**$47.29**
Front Sight DC 312 white or orange	13.59
Rear/Front Combination	59.79

SMITH & WESSON 400/500/600 SERIES AUTOPISTOL SIGHTS

Rear Sight (white outline)	**$48.29**
Front Sight DC 312 white or orange	13.59
Rear/Front Combination	60.95

BROWNING HI-POWER

The Series 100 Adjustable Sight System for Browning Hi-Power will provide accurate high visibility sighting for both fixed and adjustable slides with no machine modifications required to the dovetail. Most adjustable slide model Hi-Powers can use the factory front sight as shown in the photo. The fixed slide model requires a new front sight installation. We highly recommend the Dual-Crimp front sight installation on this gun.

Browning Hi-Power (Adjustable Slide Model)

Combo (White rear/Stake-On White Front)	BA00001	$59.79
Combo (White rear/Stake-On Orange Front)	BA00002	59.79
Combo (White rear/Dual-Crimp White Front)	BA00003	59.79
Combo (White rear/Dual-Crimp Orange Front)	BA00004	59.79
Rear Only (White Outline)	BA00009	47.29
Rear Only (Target Blade)	BA00010	47.29
Hi-Power Requires .340 High Front Sight.		

Browning Hi-Power (Fixed Slide Model)

Combo (White rear/Stake-On White Front)	BF00001	$59.79
Combo (White rear/Stake-On Orange Front)	BF00002	59.79
Combo (White rear/Dual-Crimp White Front)	BF00003	59.79
Combo (White rear/Dual-Crimp Orange Front)	BF00004	59.79
Rear Only (White Outline)	BF00009	47.29
Rear Only (Target Blade)	BF00010	47.29
Hi-Power Requires .340 High Front Sight		

MODELS CZ75/TZ75/TA90 AUTOPISTOL SIGHTS

Rear Sight (white and Target) only	**$47.29**

COLT 45

This Series 100 High Profile Adjustable Sight is rugged, all steel, precision sight which fits the standard factory dovetail with no machine modifications required. This sight provides a highly visible sight picture even under low light conditions. Blaze orange or white bar front sight, precision click adjustments for windage and elevation makes the Colt .45 Auto Combo the handgunner's choice.

Combo (White rear/Stake-On White Front)	CA00001	$59.79
Combo (White rear/Stake-On Orange Front)	CA00002	59.79
Combo (White rear/Dual-Crimp White Front)	CA00003	59.79
Combo (White rear/Dual-Crimp Orange Front)	CA00004	59.79
Rear Only (White Outline)	CA00009	47.29
Rear Only (Target Blade)	CA00010	47.29
Colt Gov. and Com. Require .312 High Front Sight.		

BERETTA ACCURIZER COMBO

This amazing new sight system not only provides a highly visible sight picture but also tunes the barrel lockup to improve your accuracy and reduce your group size by as much as 50%. The Beretta Accurizer sight system fits the 92S, 92SB, 84 and 85 models. Easy to install. Requires the drilling of one hole for installation. Your choice of rear blade styles. Front sight comes in white bar, serrated ramp or blaze orange.

Combo (White Rear/White Bar Front)	BE00001	$67.29
Combo (White Rear/Orange Bar Front)	BE00002	67.29
Rear Only (White Outline)	BE00005	47.95
Rear Only (Target Blade)	BE00006	47.95
Front Only (White Bar)	BE00007	20.95
Front Only (Orange Bar)	BE00008	20.95
Front Only (Serrated Ramp)	BE00009	20.95
Fits Models 92S, 92SB, 85, 84		

MILLETT SIGHTS™

RUGER STANDARD AUTO

The Ruger Standard Auto Combo provides a highly visible sight picture even under low light conditions. The blaze orange or white bar front sight allows the shooter to get on target fast. Great for target use or plinking. Uses Factory Front Sight on adjustable model guns when using Millett target rear only. All other installations use Millett Front Sight. Easy to install.

Combo (White rear/White front)	**$59.79**
Combo (White rear/Orange front)	59.79
Rear Only (White Outline)	47.29
Rear Only (Silhouette Target Blade)	47.29
Front Only (White)	13.59
Front Only (Orange)	13.59
Front Only (Serrated Ramp)	13.59
Front Only (Target-Adjustable Model/White Bar)	13.59
Front Only (Target-Adjustable Model/Orange Bar)	13.59
Front Only Bull Barrel (White or Orange Ramp)	14.95

INTERCHANGEABLE SIGHT BLADES

The Millett Series 100 Adjustable Sight System is the first group of completely interchangeable component gun sights. All of the sight blades will interchange so now you can have your choice and have extra blades for the differing shooting conditions.

Rear Blades Only

.312 (White Outline)	BL31201	**$16.79**
.312 (Target Blade)	BL31202	16.79
.312 (Target Silhouette Blade)	BL31206	16.79
.360 (White Outline)	BL36003	16.79
.360 (Target Blade)	BL36004	16.79
.360 (Target Silhouette Blade)	BL36007	16.79
.360 Narrow Notch (White Outline)	BL36008	16.79
.360 Rifle Peep Sight Blade .050 Dia. Aperture	BL00010	16.95
.360 Rifle Peep Sight Blade .080 Dia. Aperture	BL00011	16.95
.410 (White Outline)	BL41005	16.79
.410 (Target Blade)	BL41009	16.79

POCKET SIGHT ADJUSTMENT TOOL

This handy little tool prevents the bluing from being scratched and makes sight adjustment quick and easy.

Sight Adjusting Tool (Series 100 System)	SA00008	**$3.10**

MARKSMAN SPEED-COMBO

The Marksman Speed-Combo is State-of-the-art in sight technology. Designed specifically to meet the demands of the I.P.S.C. competition shooting. The large target rear blade is uniquely engineered to provide sharp crisp sighting under all daylight conditions. The extra deep angled rear notch provides the competitive edge for fast sight acquisition.

Colt Gold Cup Marksman Speed Rear Only (Target .410 Blade)	GC00018	**$41.95**
Custom Combat Low Profile Marksman Speed Rear Only (Target .410 Blade)	CC00015	47.29
Colt Government & Commander (High Profile) Marksman Speed Rear Only (Target .410 Blade)	CA00018	47.29
Gold Cup & Low Profile Front .275		13.59
Colt High Profile Front .410		13.59

SIG/SAUER P-220, P-225, P-226

Now Sig Pistol owners can obtain a Series-100 adjustable sight system for their guns. Precision click adjustment for windage and elevation makes it easy to zero when using different loads. The high visibility features assures fast sight acquisition when under the poorest light conditions. Made of high quality heat treated nickel steel and built to last. Extremely easy to install on P-225 and P-226. The P-220 and Browning BDA 45 require the Dual-Crimp front sight installation.

Sig P220 Combo (White Rear/Dual-Crimp White Front)	SP22001	**$59.79**
Sig P220 Combo (White Rear/Dual-Crimp Orange Front)	SP22002	59.79
Sig P220-25-26 Rear Only (White)	SP22003	47.29
Sig P220-25-26 Rear Only (Target)	SP22004	47.29
Sig P225-6 Combo (White Rear/Dovetail White Front)	SP22561	59.79
Sig P225-6 Combo (White Rear/Dovetail Orange Front)	SP22562	59.79
Sig P225-6 (White) Dovetail Front	SP22565	13.59
Sig P225-6 (Orange) Dovetail Front	SP22566	13.59

The Sig P220 Uses .360 Dual-Crimp Front Sight. The Sig P225-6 Uses a Dovetail Mount Front Sight

MILLETT SIGHTS™
Rifle Sights

COLT AR-15 (And similar models)

Riflemen will appreciate this new peep sight system for AR-15's. Fully adjustable for windage and elevation at the rear sight. No more difficult front sight adjustment. The Millett front sight is a serrated post design that provides a sharp, crisp sight picture under all lighting conditions. A real improvement over the round factory front sight. The rear peep sight blade has a large eye piece that blocks out the surrounding light and allows a sharp, crisp image to show through the cone-shaped aperture. Easy to install requiring no special tools.

Combo Peep Sight (Peep Sight Rear/Serrated Ramp Front)	AR15001	**$55.95**
Rear Only Peep Sight (.080 Dia. Aperture)	AR15002	**45.95**
Front Only Serrated Ramp	AR15003	**10.95**

RUGER MINI-14

Mini-14 owners will be elated with this new Series 100 adjustable sight system. Precision click adjustments for windage and elevation with easy return to zero. The large eye piece on the peep sight blade blocks out surrounding light to provide a sharp sight picture which greatly improves shooting accuracy. The cone-shaped aperture totally eliminates sighting error caused by reflected light. Easy to install with no special tools or gunsmithing required.

Mini-14 Rear Peep Sight (.080 Dia. Aperture)	**$45.95**
Mini-14 Front Sight	**15.95**
Mini-14 Combo (Rear peep/post front)	**60.95**
Rear Peep Blade only; .050 diam. aperture	**16.95**

H&K 91, 93 (And similar models)

Now H&K owners can have a traditional peep sight system, fully adjustable for windage and elevation, with precision click adjustments and an easy return to zero. The single aperture rear blade has a large eye piece that blocks out surrounding light to provide a sharp, crisp sight picture, greatly improving shooting accuracy. The cone-shaped aperture totally eliminates sighting error caused by reflected light. Easy to install with no special tools or gunsmithing required.

Rear Only Peep Sight (.080 Dia. Aperture)	HK91001	**$45.95**

RUGER 10/22 INTERCHANGEABLE COMBO

10/22 owners will love this new sight system. Highly visible and super accurate because the blaze orange and the white bar front sights contrast so well against the background. The rear sight blade provides a sharp horizontal sighting plane with a deep notch for fast sighting. The Ruger 10/22 Interchangeable Combo is sold with or without the quickchange front sight feature. Your choice of white outline or target rear blades. Interchangeable Combo includes 2 front sights white bar and blaze orange.

Ruger 10/22 Interchangeable Front Combo (White Rear/White & Orange Front)	RF00001	**$77.69**
Ruger 10/22 Interchangeable Front Combo (Target Rear/White & Orange Front)	RF00002	**77.69**
Ruger 10/22 Combo (White Rear/White Front)	RF00003	**56.69**
Ruger 10/22 Combo (White Rear/Orange Front)	RF00004	**56.69**
Ruger 10/22 Combo (Target Rear/White Front)	RF00005	**56.69**
Ruger 10/22 Combo (Target Rear/Orange Front)	RF00006	**56.69**
Interchangeable Front Sight Base Only (.157)	RF00009	**11.49**

Also fits Win. 77, 94 Carbine, & Rem. 740-760, 700 old model dovetail rear

OPEN RIFLE SIGHTS
Dovetail Rear Mount

The Series 100 Adjustable Sight System for Dovetail rear mount rifles provide a highly visible sight picture and fast, accurate sightings every time. Precision click adjustments for windage and elevation insure fine sighting. Made of heat treated steel and easy to install. Especially recommended for Marlin 336 owners. Front sights feature blaze orange and white bar enhance contrast, especially in dim light. Rear sight blade provides a sharp horizontal sighting plane with deep notch for fast sighting (choice of white outline or target rear blades). **Price: Rear Sight $47.29; Front Sight $10.49.**

FRONT SIGHT CHART	
HEIGHT	**MAKE & MODEL**
.540	Ruger 44 Carbine, #3, 375
.540	Marlin 336, 375
.540	Winchester 94 Trapper
.540	Browning, BLR 22
.500	Winchester 77, 94 Carbine
.500	Remington 740-760, 700 Old Model with Dovetail
.500	Ruger 10/22
.460	Marlin 44, 88-89, 39 A-M
.460	Remington 121, 241, 510-513T
.460	Savage 110, 170, 99T-E-C
.430	Savage 340 Old Model, 99 Old Model
.400	Winchester 88, 70 pre 1964, 94 pre 1964, 71 pre 1964
.400	Marlin 780 22 LR, 1894-1895
.400	Browning Bar 22
.400	Savage 340
.343	Winchester 9422
.343	Use with Interchangeable Base to make .500 height

REDFIELD SCOPES

THE ULTIMATE ILLUMINATOR

The first American-made scope with a 30mm one-piece outer tube and a 56mm adjustable objective. Engineered with quarter-minute positive click adjustments, the Ultimate Illuminator features a European #4 reticle. Comes complete with a set a 30mm steel rings with exclusive Rotary Dovetail System, lens covers and hardwood presentation box.

3x-12x Ultimate Illuminator 30mm Variable **$714.95**

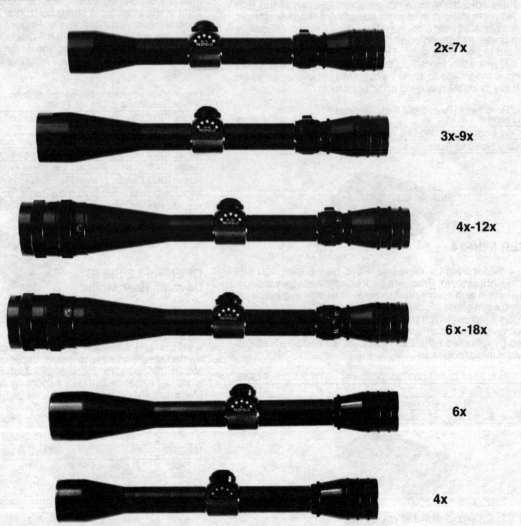

2x-7x

3x-9x

4x-12x

6x-18x

6x

4x

GOLDEN FIVE STAR SCOPES

This series of seven scopes incorporates the latest variable and fixed power scope features, including multi-coated and magnum recoil-resistant optical system, plus maximum light-gathering ability. Positive quarter-minute click adjustments for ease of sighting and optimum accuracy. Anodized finish provides scratch-resistant surface.

Golden Five Star Scopes:

1x-4x Variable Power	$234.95
2x-7x Variable Power	244.95
3x-9x Variable Power	262.95
4x-12x Variable Power (adj. objective)	337.95
6x-18x Variable Power (adj. objective)	357.95
4x Fixed Power	187.95
6x Fixed Power	206.95

REDFIELD SCOPES

LOW PROFILE WIDEFIELD 2X-7X VARIABLE

LOW PROFILE WIDEFIELD 3X-9X VARIABLE

3X-9X ACCU-TRAC VARIABLE POWER

LOW PROFILE WIDEFIELD

In heavy cover, game may jump out of the brush 10 feet away or appear in a clearing several hundred yards off, either standing or on the move.

The Widefield®, with 25% more field of view than conventional scopes, lets you spot game quicker, stay with it and see other animals that might be missed.

The patented Low Profile design means a low mounting on the receiver, allowing you to keep your cheek tight on the stock for a more natural and accurate shooting stance, especially when swinging on running game.

The one-piece, fog-proof tube is machined with high tensile strength aluminum alloy and is anodized to a lustrous finish that's rust-free and virtually scratch-proof. Available in 7 models.

WIDEFIELD LOW PROFILE SCOPES

1³/₄x-5x Low Profile Variable Power
113806 1³/₄x-5x 4 Plex **$294.95**
2x-7x Low Profile Variable Power
111806 2x-7x 4 Plex **304.95**
2x-7x Low Profile Accu-Trac Variable Power
111810 2x-7x 4 Plex AT **357.95**
3x-9x Low Profile Variable Power
112806 3x-9x 4 Plex **335.95**
3x-9x Low Profile Accu-Trac Variable Power
112810 3x-9x 4 Plex AT **388.95**
2³/₄x Low Profile Fixed Power
141807 2³/₄x 4 Plex **214.95**
4x Low Profile Fixed Power
143806 4x 4 Plex **239.95**
6x Low Profile Fixed Power
146806 6x 4 Plex **261.95**

REDFIELD SCOPES

THE TRACKER

The Tracker series brings you a superior combination of price and value. It provides the same superb quality, precision and strength of construction found in all Redfield scopes, but at an easily affordable price. Features include the tough, one-piece tube, machined and hand-fitted internal parts, excellent optical quality and traditional Redfield styling.

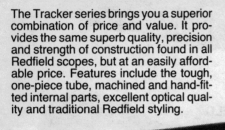

TRACKER

TRACKER SCOPES

2x-7x Tracker Variable Power
122300 2x-7x 4 Plex $172.95

3x-9x Tracker Variable Power
123300 3x-9x 4 Plex $192.95

4x Tracker Fixed Power
135300 4x 4 Plex $134.95

Matte Finish
122308 2x-7x 4 Plex $181.95
122308 3x-9x 4 Plex   200.95
122308 4x 4 Plex   140.95

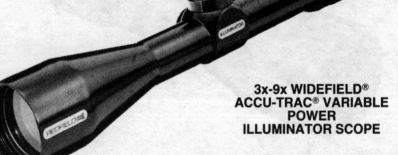

**3x-9x WIDEFIELD®
ACCU-TRAC® VARIABLE
POWER
ILLUMINATOR SCOPE**

THE ILLUMINATOR

Every sportsman knows that dawn and dusk are the most productive times to hunt. Game use the cover of darkness for security while feeding, blending in easily with the greens, grays and browns of the outdoors during dim light conditions.

With this new Illuminator series, you can add precious minutes to morning and evening hunting. These scopes actually compensate for the low light, letting you "see" contrasts between field and game.

Optimum resolution, contrast, color correction, flatness of field, edge-to-edge sharpness and absolute fidelity are improved by the unique air-spaced, tri-plet objective, and the advanced 5-element erector lens system.

The Illuminators also feature a zero tolerance nylon cam follower and thrust washers to provide absolute point of impact hold through all power ranges. The one-piece tube construction is virtually indestructible, tested at 1200g acceleration forces, and fog-free through the elimination of potential leak paths.

Offered in both the Traditional and Widefield® variable power configurations, the Illuminator is also available with the Accu-Trac® feature.

Also offered in a 30mm 3x-12x with a 56mm adjustable objective.

ILLUMINATOR SCOPES

3x-9x Traditional Variable Power
123886 3x-9x 4 Plex $414.95

3x-9x Widefield Variable Power
112886 3x-9x 4 Plex $468.95

3x-9x Widefield Accu-Trac Variable Power
112880 3x-9x 4 Plex $507.95

3x9 Widefield Matte Finish
112888 $450.95

3x12 Ultimate Illuminator Variable Power
112900 3x12 30mm $714.95

SAKO SCOPE MOUNTS

Weighing less than 3 ounces, these new Sako scope mounts are lighter, yet stronger than ever. Tempered steel allows the paring of every last gram of unnecessary weight without sacrificing strength. Like the original mount, these rings clamp directly to the tapered dovetails on Sako rifles, thus eliminating the need for separate bases and screws. Annular grooves inside the rings preclude scope slippage even under the recoil of the heaviest calibers. Nicely streamlined and finished in a rich blue-black to complement any Sako rifle.

Price: Low, medium, or high $40.00
Engraved (low, medium, high) 42.00

SCHMIDT & BENDER RIFLE SCOPES

These fine Schmidt & Bender rifle scopes offer brightness and resolution, color fidelity, and excellent field-of-view. Each model comes with a 30-year guarantee and incorporates the essential ingredients every hunter looks for in rough hunting conditions: recoil-proof, centered reticles; dust and moisture-proof assembly (nitrogen-filled), and precise click adjustments. To guarantee that its scopes will stand up to the most severe hunting conditions, Schmidt & Bender subjects them to vibration tests exceeding the demands of the most powerful cartridges, environmental tests from −40° F to + 122° F, and heavy rain testing. All variable scopes have 30mm center tubes; all fixed power scopes have 1″ tubes. **Prices on request.**

VARIABLE POWER SCOPE 1¼-4x20

VARIABLE POWER SCOPE 1½-6x42

VARIABLE POWER SCOPE 2½-10x56

SCHMIDT & BENDER

FIXED POWER SCOPE 1¹/₂x15
(steel tube w/o mounting rail)
$525.00

FIXED POWER SCOPE 4x36
(steel tube w/o mounting rail)
$550.00

FIXED POWER SCOPE 6x42
(steel tube w/o mounting rail)
$675.00

FIXED POWER SCOPE 12x42
(steel tube w/o mounting rail)
$800.00

FIXED POWER SCOPE 8x56
(steel tube w/o mounting rail)
$850.00

SIMMONS SCOPES

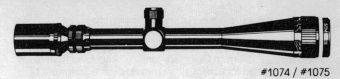

#1074 / #1075

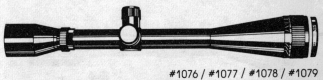

#1074 / #1075
with sun shade and lens covers on

#1076 / #1077 / #1078 / #1079

**GOLD MEDAL SERIES
MODEL 1044**

SILHOUETTE AND TARGET RIFLESCOPES

MODEL 1074
6.5-20x40mm

Field of view: 17.8'-6.2'
Eye relief: 3.5-3.3 Truplex
Weight: 16.2 oz.
Length: 15"
Price: $247.50

DOT RETICLE

MODEL 1075
6.5-20x40mm

Field of view: 17.8'-6.2'
Eye relief: 3.5-3.3 Dot
Weight: 16.2 oz.
Length: 15"
Price: $247.50

TRUPLEX RETICLE

MODEL 1076
15x40mm

Field of view: 11.5'
Eye relief: 3.4 Truplex
Weight: 15.6 oz.
Length: 15"
Price: $195.00

MODEL 1077
15x40mm

Field of view: 11.5'
Eye relief: 3.4 Dot
Weight: 15.6 oz.
Length: 15"
Price: $195.00

MODEL 1078
24x40mm

Field of view: 6.2'
Eye relief: 3.3 Truplex
Weight: 15.6 oz.
Length: 15"
Price: $202.50

MODEL 1079
24x40mm

Field of view: 6.2'
Eye relief: 3.3 Dot
Weight: 15.6 oz.
Length: 15"
Price: $202.50

GOLD MEDAL RIFLESCOPE SERIES

MODEL 1042 "44 MAG" WIDE ANGLE
6x44mm

Field of view: 22.5'
Eye relief: 3.0"
Weight: 14.5 oz.
Price: $180.00

MODEL 1043 "44 MAG" WIDE ANGLE
8x44mm

Field of view: 22.5'
Eye relief: 3.0"
Weight: 14.5 oz.
Price: $180.00

MODEL 1044 "44 MAG" WIDE ANGLE
3-10x44mm

Field of view: 36.2-10.5'
Eye relief: 3.4" -3.3"
Weight: 16.3 oz.
Price: $198.75

RANGER MODEL 1045
3-9x44mm

Field of view: 42-14
Eye relief: 4.0-3.3
Weight: 16.2 oz.
Length: 13"
Price: $348.75

MODEL 1046
4-12x44mm

Field of view: 31-11
Eye relief: 3.9-3.2
Weight: 19.1 oz.
Length: 14.2"
Price: $371.25

MODEL 1047
6.5-20x44mm

Field of view: 17.8-6.1
Eye relief: 3.4-3.2
Weight: 19.4 oz.
Length: 15.4"
Price: $390.00

MODEL 1050
4-x32 Compact

Field of view: 22" at 100 yds.
Eye relief: 4.8"
Weight: 9 oz.
Price: $150.00

MODEL 1054
3-9x32 Compact

Field of view: 40"-14"
Eye relief: 3.5"
Weight: 10.4 oz.
Price: $195.00

SIMMONS SCOPES

GOLD MEDAL PRESIDENTIAL SERIES

Features "SIMCOAT" multi-coating on all lenses . . . 360°
Wide-angle . . . 44mm Objective lens . . . Anodized high gloss
finish . . . Speed focusing . . . 1/4 minute click adjustments

Model 1065 (4x44mm) $262.50
Model 1066 (2-7x44mm) 300.00
Model 1067 (3-9x44mm) 330.00
Model 1068 (4-12x44mm) 337.50
Model 1069 (6.5-20x44mm) 360.00

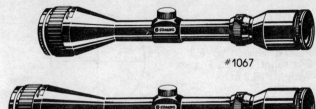

#1067

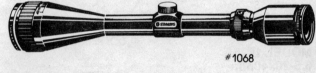

#1068

#1069

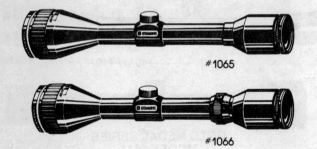

#1065

#1066

SIMMONS MODEL	X	Field of View (Feet)	Eye Relief (Inches)	Length (Inches)	Weight (Ounces)	Exit Pupil mm	Relative Brightness	Twilight Factor at High Power
#1065 4x44mm		35	3.5	13	15.5	11	121	13.3
#1066 2-7x44mm	2	55.1	3.3	12.6	16.6	22	484	
#1066 2-7x44mm	7	18.3	2.9			6.3	40	17.6
#1067 3-9x44mm	3	42	4.0	13	16.2	14.7	216	
#1067 3-9x44mm	9	14	3.3			4.9	54	19.9
#1068 4-12x44mm	4	31	3.9	14.2	19.1	11	121	
#1068 4-12x44mm	12	11	3.2			3.7	14	23
#1069 6.5-20x44mm	6.5	17.8	3.4	15.4	19.4	6.8	46	
#1069 6.5-20x44mm	20	6.1	3.2			2.2	5	30

RIFLESCOPE RINGS

Low 1" Set **Model 1401** . . . . $ 8.50
High 1" Set **Model 1403** 8.50
1" See-Thru Set **Model 1405** 9.75
1" Rings for 22 Grooved Receiver **Model 1406** 8.50
1" Rings extention for Compact Scopes
   Model 1409 . . . . 15.00

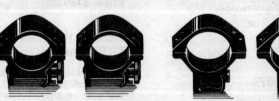

#1401   #1406

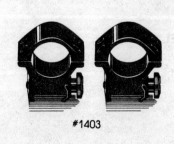

#1403

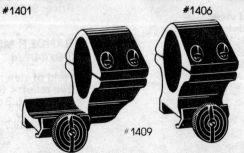

#1409

SIMMONS SCOPES

#1080

#1086

#1084

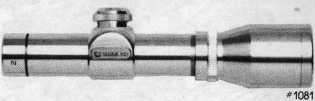

#1081

SILVER MEDAL PISTOLSCOPE SERIES

Fixed power, variable power and silhouette models are all available in this series in traditional blue or silver finish with multi-coated lenses and one-1/2 piece tubes (to withstand shock of magnum calibers).

Model 1080 2x20 . . . . $105.00
Model 1081 10x20 Polished Alum. 105.00

Model 1082 1x20 . . . . **116.25**
Model 1083 1x20 Polished Alum. **116.25**
Model 1084 4x32 . . . . **150.00**
Model 1085 4x32 w/Target Turret **165.00**
Model 1086 1-3x32 . . . . **240.00**
Model 1087 2-6x32 . . . . **281.25**
Model 1088 4x32 Polished Alum. **150.00**
Model 1089 7x32 w/Adj. Obj. & Tar. Tur. **202.50**
Model 1090 Long Eye Relief Scope 1.5x20 . . . . **117.00**

#1013

#1015

#1017

#1018

SILVER MEDAL RIFLESCOPE SERIES
QUAD VARIABLES

Model 1007 4x32 Compact w/Rings . . . . $ 84.75
Model 1013 1-4x20 Quad. 119.25
Model 1015 3-12x40 Quad. 110.25
Model 1017 4-16x40 Quad. 126.75
Model 1018 6-24x40 Quad. 148.50

Model 1023 4x40 Wide Angle 105.75
Model 1025 6x40 Wide Angle 111.75
Model 1026 1.5-4.5x32 . . . . 123.75
Model 1027 2-7x32 . . . . 123.75
Model 1029 3-9x40 Wide Angle 129.00
Model 1030 3-9x32 Polished Alum. 127.50
Model 1090 1.5x20 L.E.R. Matte 117.00
Model 1099 4x32 w/Adj. Objective 107.25

SPRINGFIELD ARMORY RIFLE SCOPES

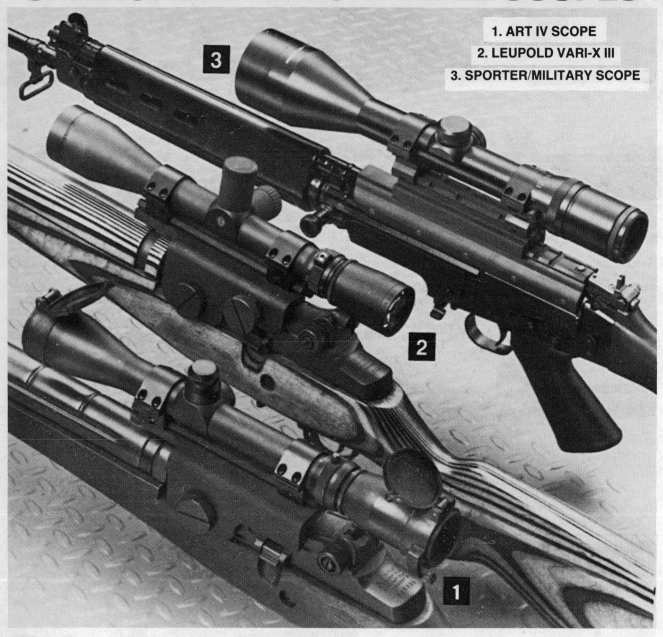

1. ART IV SCOPE
2. LEUPOLD VARI-X III
3. SPORTER/MILITARY SCOPE

SPORTER SCOPES
$257.40

Available in 3x9x56 Rangefinder and 4x14x56 Rangefinder, these scopes provide range-finding capabilities out to 1,000 yards. They also enable shooters to use any power setting without changing the ranging effect, while leaving their hands in position. An internal level maintains vertical and horizontal alignment for maximum accuracy at extended ranges. The Sporter model comes with a one-inch tube.

Also available:
MILITARY MODEL (30mm tube) **$384.40**
ART IV 3x9 Variable Powerf 335.00

LEUPOLD VARI-X III (3.5x10)
$378.50

This scope features infinitely variable power selector detents at regular intervals and a 15-minute dial with quarter-minute click adjustments for windage and elevation. It comes standard with a one-inch tube with matte black finish.

SWAROVSKI OPTIK

SPECIFICATIONS

Telescopic Sights	1.5x20	4x32	6x42	8x56	1.5-6x42	2.2-9x42	3-12x56
Magnification	1.5x	4x	6x	8x	1.5-6x	2.2-9x	3-12x
Max. effective objective dia.	20mm	32mm	42mm	56mm	42mm	42mm	56mm
Exit pupil dia.	12.7mm	8mm	7mm	7mm	14.3-7mm	14.3-4.7mm	14.3-4.7mm
Field of view at 100m	18.5m	10m	7m	5.2m	18.5-6.5m	12-4.5m	9-3.3m
Twilight effective factor (DIN 58388)	4.2	11.3	15.9	21.1	4.2-15.9	6.2-19.4	8.5-25.9
Intermediary tube dia. Steel-Standard	26mm	26mm	26mm	26mm	30mm	30mm	30mm
Objective tube dia.	26mm	38mm	48mm	62mm	48mm	48mm	62mm
Ocular tube dia.	40mm	40mm	40mm	40mm	40mm	40mm	40mm
Scope length	247mm	290mm	322mm	370mm	322mm	342mm	391mm
Weight Steel	360g	430g	500g	660g	570g	580g	710g
(approx.) Light metal with rail		370g	400g	490g	480g	470g	540g
A change of the impact point per click in mm/100m	12	7	6	4	9	6	4

AMERICAN LIGHTWEIGHT SCOPE

This new model features precision ground, coated and aligned optics sealed in a special aluminum alloy tube to withstand heavy recoil. Eye relief is 85mm and the recoiling eyepiece protects the eye. Positive click adjustments for elevation and windage change the impact point (approx. 1/4") per click at 100 yards, with parallax also set at 100 yards. Weight is only 13 ounces.

ZFM 6x42 MILITARY STYLE SNIPER SCOPE
Mounted on H&K G-3 Rifle w/ARMS G-3 Scope Base

Provides a detailed, color-true contrast image, even in adverse light conditions. Scope is corrosion resistant and durable.

SWAROVSKI OPTIK

HABICHT NOVA TELESCOPIC SIGHTS

These fine Austrian-made sights feature brilliant optics with high-quality lens coating and optimal sighting under poor light and weather conditions. The Nova ocular system with telescope recoil damping reduces the danger of injury, especially with shots aimed in an upward direction. The main tube is selectable in steel or light metal construction with a mounting rail. Because of Nova's centered reticle, the aiming mark remains in the center of the field of view regardless of corrections of the impact point.

VARIABLE POWER

1.5-6x42

2.2-9x42

3-12x56

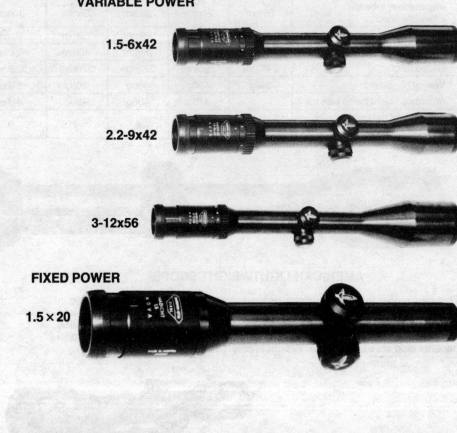

FIXED POWER

1.5 × 20

6 × 42

8 × 56

TASCO SCOPES

PRO-POINT MULTI-PURPOSE SCOPES

Pro-Point is an electronic aiming device for pistols, shotguns, rifles and bows, featuring the brightest red dot reticle available. Shooters merely focus on the illuminated dot and the target simultaneously to produce precise shots. Pro-Point also features a large 30mm tube which increases field of view and is stronger and more rigid than other comparable scopes. In addition, an on-off rheostat lets the shooter control the dot intensity under varying light conditions. A heavy gauge extension tube attaches to the front of the scope, converting it into a rifle or shotgun scope while also acting as a mirage hood. Pro-Point scopes come equipped with matching 30mm ring set with Allen wrench, adjustable polarizing filter, lens caps, two mercury batteries and lens cloth. Choice of aluminum or matte black finish. **Weight:** 5½ oz. **Length:** 5". **Price: $249.95**

RUBBER ARMORED SCOPES

Extra padding helps these rugged scopes stand up to rough handling. Custom-fitting rings are included. Scopes feature:
• Fully coated optics
• Windage and elevation controls

• Waterproofing, fogproofing, shockproofing
• ¼-minute positive click stops
• Opti-centered 30/30 rangefinding reticle
• Haze filter caps

Model	Power	Objective Diameter	Finish	Reticle	Field of View @ 100 Yards	Eye Relief	Tube Diam.	Scope Length	Scope Weight	Price
RC4X32A,B	4	32mm	Green Rubber	30/30	27'	3"	1"	11¾"	11.5 oz.	**$109.95**
RC39X32A,B	3-9	32mm	Green Rubber	30/30	35'-13'	3¼"	1"	12¾"	13oz.	129.95
RC4X40A,B	4	40mm	Green Rubber	30/30	27'	3¼"	1"	12½"	14.2 oz.	129.95
RC39X40A,B	3-9	40mm	Green Rubber	30/30	35'-14'	3¼"	1"	12⅝"	14.3 oz.	149.95

"A" fits standard dove tail base.
"B" fits ⅜" grooved receivers—most 22 cal. and airguns.

TASCO PISTOL SCOPES

PRO-CLASS PISTOL SCOPES

OBJECTIVE DIAMETER: 22mm
POWER: 1

Model	Finish	Reticle	Field of View @ 100 yds	Eye Relief	Scope Length	Scope Weight	Price
P1X22	Dull Satin	Dot	65'-24'	8-28"	7³/₄"	8 oz.	$199.95
P1X22PA	Pol. Alum.	Dot	65'-24'	8-28"	7³/₄"	8 oz.	199.95
IR1X22	Dull Satin	Illumin.	65'-24'	8-28"	7³/₄"	8.3 oz.	389.95
IR1X22PA	Pol. Alum.	Illumin.	65'-24'	8-28"	7³/₄"	8.3 oz.	389.95
POWER: 2							
P2X22	Dull Satin	Dot	26'-18'	10-24"	7³/₄"	7.6 oz.	199.95
P2X22PA	Pol. Alum.	Dot	26'-18'	10-24"	7³/₄"	7.6 oz.	199.95
IR2X22	Dull Satin	Illumin.	26'-18'	10-24"	8"	8.4 oz.	379.95
IR2X22PA	Pol. Alum.	Illumin.	26'-18'	10-24"	8"	8.4 oz.	379.95
POWER: 3							
P3X22	Dull Satin	Dot	13'-6'	12-24"	8¹/₄"	8.5 oz.	219.95
P3X22PA	Pol. Alumin.	Dot	13'-6'	12-24"	8¹/₄"	8.5 oz.	219.95
OBJECTIVE DIAMETER: 30mm							
POWER: 4							
P4X30	Dull Satin	Dot	7'-6'	12-24"	9³/₄"	12.1 oz.	259.95
P4X30PA	Pol. Alum.	Dot	7'-6'	12-24"	9³/₄"	12.1 oz.	259.95
IR4X30	Dull Satin	Illumin.	7'-6'	12-24"	10"	12.9 oz.	429.95
IR4X30PA	Pol. Alum.	Illumin.	7'-6'	12-24"	10"	12.9 oz.	429.95
OBJECTIVE DIAMETER: 40mm							
POWER: 6							
P6X40	Dull Satin	Dot	5'2"-5'5"	12-23"	11"	14.2 oz.	349.95
P6X40PA	Pol. Alum.	Dot	5'2"-5'5"	12-23"	11"	14.2 oz.	349.95
OBJECTIVE DIAMETER: 22mm							
POWER: 1							
P1X22S	Dull Satin	Dot	43'-22'	8-28"	6¹/₂"	7.7 oz.	239.95
POWER: 2							
P2X22S	Pol. Alum.	Dot	23'-18'	10-24"	6¹/₂"	7.7 oz.	219.95

TASCO TS® SCOPES

For silhouette and target shooting, Tasco's TS® scopes adjust for varying long-range targets, with 1/8-minute Positrac® micrometer windage and elevation adjustments. All TS® scopes are waterproof, fog-proof, shockproof, fully Supercon-coated, and include screw-in metal lens protectors. All include two metal mirage deflection and sunshade hoods, five and eight inches in length, which can be used separately or together to eliminate image distortion resulting from excessive barrel temperatures or to shade the objective lens from direct sunlight. All include a focusing objective for precise parallax correction and extra-large 44mm objective lenses for extra brightness at high magnifications. Each scope is available in a choice of three reticle patterns: 1/2-minute dot, fine crosshair, and opti-centered 30/30 range finding.

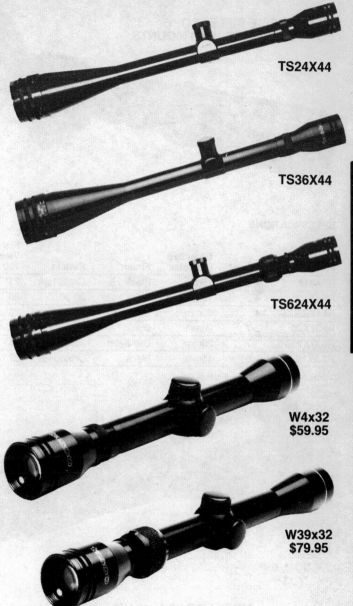

TS24X44

TS36X44

TS624X44

MODEL NO.	DESCRIPTION	PRICE
TS24X44B	24X (44mm)	$359.95
TS36X44B	36X (44mm)	389.95
TS624X44B	6X-24X Zoom (44mm)	449.95
TS832X44A	8X-32X (44 mm)	449.95
TS832X44B	8X-32X (44mm)	449.95

TS Scopes available in choice of three reticle patterns: Opti-centered 15/15/ Range Finding, Fine Crosshair & 1/4-minute dot.

Standard features: Two mirage deflection and sunshine hoods (3″ and 5″)

W4x32
$59.95

WATERPROOF RIFLESCOPES

Tasco's waterproof riflescopes can endure rain, snow, heat, dust, sand and altitude changes. They feature fully coated optics, non-removable eye bell, 1/4 minute positive click stops, Opti-Centered 30/30 rangefinding reticle, haze filter caps.

W39x32
$79.95

Model	Power	Objective Diameter	Finish	Reticle	Field of View @ 100 yards	Eye Relief	Tube Diam.	Scope Length	Scope Weight	Prices
W4X32	4	32mm	Black	30/30	28′	3″	1″	11³/₄″	9.5 oz.	**$59.95**
W4X40	4	40mm	Black	30/30	28′	3¹/₄″	1″	12¹/₂″	12.2 oz.	89.95
W39X32DS	3-9	32mm	Dull Satin	30/30	35′-14′	3¹/₄″	1″	12³/₄″	11.2 oz.	79.95
W39X32	3-9	32mm	Black	30/30	35′-14′	3¹/₄″	1″	12³/₄″	11.2 oz.	**79.95**
W39X40	3-9	40mm	Black	30/30	35′-14′	3¹/₄″	1″	12⁵/₈″	12.3 oz.	109.95
W4X32DS	4	32mm	Dull Stain	30/30	28′	3¹/₄″	1″	11³/₄″	9.5 oz.	39.95
SW39X32	3-9	32mm	Black	30/30	35′-13′	3¹/₄″	1″	11¹/₈	11 oz.	159.95
SW2.510X32	2.5-10	32mm	Black	30/30	41′-10¹/₂′	3¹/₄″	1″	11¹/₄″	8.5 oz.	169.95
W2.5X32	2.5	32mm	Black	30/30	42′	3¹/₄	1″	12¹/₄″	12.5 oz.	84.95

TASCO SCOPES

RIMFIRE RIFLESCOPE
FOR 22's WITH 22 RING MOUNTS

MODEL RF4 × 15
$14.95

SPECIFICATIONS

Model	Power	Objective Diameter	Finish	Reticle	Field of View @ 100 yards	Eye Relief	Tube Diam.	Scope Length	Scope Weight	Price
RF4X15	4	15mm	Black	Cross Hair	21'	2½"	¾"	11"	4 oz.	**$14.95**
RF4X18	4	18mm	Black	30/30	20'	2½"	¾"	10½"	3.8 oz.	29.95
RF4X20DS	4	20mm	Dull Satin	Cross Hair	20'	2½"	¾"	10½"	3.8 oz.	23.95
RF37X20	3-7	20mm	Black	30/30	24'-11'	2½"	¾"	11½"	5.7 oz.	44.95
RF37X20DS	3-7	20mm	Dull Satin	30/30	24'-11'	2½"	¾"	11½"	5.7 oz.	44.95
P1.5X15	1.5	15mm	Black	Cross Hair	22½'	9½"-20¾"	¾"	8¾"	3.25 oz.	29.95

MODEL TR 39 × 40 WA

TRAJECTORY-RANGE FINDING WORLD-CLASS
WIDE ANGLE® RIFLESCOPE
with Lifetime Warranty

All Tasco TR Scopes have fully coated optics, Opti-Centered® stadia reticle, ¼-minute positive click stops and haze filter caps. All are fog-proof, shockproof, waterproof and anodized.

MODEL NO.	DESCRIPTION	RETICLE	PRICE
TR312X32	3X-12X Zoom (32mm)	30/30 RF	$179.95
TR39X40WA	3X-9X Zoom (40mm) Wide Angle	30/30 RF	219.95
TR416X40	4X-16X Zoom (40mm)	30/30 RF	249.95
TR624X40	6X-24X Zoom (40mm)	30/30 RF	269.95

TASCO SCOPES

EURO-CLASS RIFLESCOPES

This new Tasco line of riflescopes features a 30mm tube providing great rigidity without undue point-of-impact change. It offers a large objective lens, fast focusing, hard anodized dull satin finsih, fully coated optics (plus Supercon-coated lenses for maximum light transmission), haze filter caps, and positive low-profile windage and elevation adjustments.

SPECIFICATIONS

**Model	Power	Objective Diameter	Finish	Reticle	Field of View @ 100 yards	Eye Relief	Tube Diam.	Scope Length	Scope Weight	Price
EU4X44	4	44mm	Dull Satin	30/30	29'	3"	30mm	12³/₈"	16 oz.	299.95
EU6X44	6	44mm	Dull Satin	30/30	20'	3"	30mm	12³/₈"	16 oz.	299.95
EU39X44	3-9	44mm	Dull Satin	30/30	37¹/₂'-14'	3"	30mm	12¹/₈"	18.5 oz.	319.95
EU312X52	3-12	52mm	Dull Satin	30/30	33"-8¹/₂'	3"	30mm	12¹/₄"	18.5 oz.	349.95
EU1.56X44	1.5-6	44mm	Dull Satin	30/30	52¹/₂'-16'	3³/₄"	30mm	12"	19.6 oz.	329.95
EUIR39X44	3-9	44mm	Dull Satin	SBD	37¹/₂'-13'	3¹/₄"	30mm	12⁵/₈"	18.5 oz.	599.95
EUR520X44	5-20	44mm	Dull Satin	30/30	21'-6'	3³/₄"	30mm	15¹/₂"	21.5 oz.	329.95

ILLUMINATED RETICLE RIFLE & PISTOL SCOPES

Specially designed for low-light conditions. Light intensity can be adjusted. Scope may also be used for normal viewing conditions. Includes illuminated cross hair reticle, fully coated optics, ¹/₄-minute positive click stops, fast focus eyepiece, nonremovable eye bell, haze filter caps.

SPECIFICATIONS

Model No.	Power	Objective Diameter (mm)	Finish	Reticle	Field of view @ 100 yards	Eye Relief	Tube Diam. (in.)	Scope Length (in.)	Scope Weight (oz.)	Price
IR1X22	1	22mm	Dull Satin	Illuminated	65'-24'	8-28"	1.2"	7³/₄"	8.3 oz.	$389.95
IR1X22PA	1	22mm	Polished Alum.	Illuminated	65'-24'	8-28"	1.2"	7³/₄"	8.3 oz.	$389.95
IR2X22	2	22mm	Dull Satin	Illuminated	26'-18'	10-24"	1.2"	8"	8.4 oz.	$379.95
IR2X22PA	2	22mm	Polished Alum.	Illuminated	26'-18'	10-24"	1.2"	8"	8.4 oz.	$379.95
IR39X40WA	3-9	40mm	Black	Illuminated	14'-38'	3"	1"	12³/₄"	14.8 oz.	399.95
IR4X30	4	30mm	Dull Satin	Illuminated	7'-6'	12-24"	1.2"	10"	12.9 oz.	429.95
IR4X30PA	4	30mm	Polished Alum.	Illuminated	7'-6'	12-24"	1.2"	10"	12.9 oz.	429.95
IR27X32WA	2-7	32mm	Black	Illuminated	15'-57'	3"	1"	11³/₄"	14.3 oz.	379.95

SCOPES

TASCO SCOPES

WORLD CLASS WIDE ANGLE® RIFLESCOPE

Features:
- 25% larger field of view
- Exceptional optics
- Fully coated for maximum light transmission
- Waterproof, shockproof, fog-proof
- Non-removable eye bell
- Free haze filter lens caps
- TASCO's unique World Class Lifetime Warranty

MODEL WA13.5 × 20

This member of Tasco's World Class Wide Angle line offers a wide field of view—115 feet at 1X and 31 feet at 3.5X—and quick sighting without depending on a critical view. The scope is ideal for hunting deer and dangerous game, especially in close quarters or in heavily wooded and poorly lit areas. Other features include 1/2-minute positive click stops, fully coated lenses (including Supercon process), nonremovable eyebell and windage/elevation screws. Length is 9³/₄″, with 1″ diameter tube. Weight is 10.5 ounces.

MODEL WA39 × 40

WIDE ANGLE VARIABLE ZOOM RIFLESCOPES (ALL WATERPROOF)

MODEL NO.	DESCRIPTION	RETICLE		PRICE
WA1 × 20	1X (20mm)	Wide Angle	30/30	$199.95
WA13.5 × 20	1X-3.5X Zoom (20mm)	Wide Angle	30/30	219.95
WA39X40TV	3X-9X (40mm)	Wide Angle	30/30	159.95
DS39X40WA	3X-9X (40mm)	Wide Angle	30/30	159.95
PA39X40WA	3X-9X (40mm)	Wide Angle	30/30	159.95
WA4 × 40	4X (40mm)	Wide Angle	30/30	129.95
DS4X40WA	4X (40mm)	Wide Angle	30/30	129.95
WA6 × 40	6X (40mm)	Wide Angle	30/30	129.95
DS6X40WA	6X (40mm)	Wide Angle	30/30	129.95
WA1.755 × 20	1.75X-5X Zoom (20mm)	Wide Angle	30/30	199.95
WA27 × 32	2X-7X Zoom (32mm)	Wide Angle	30/30	159.95
WA39 × 32	3X-9X Zoom (32mm)	Wide Angle	30/30	149.95
WA39 × 40	3X-9X Zoom (40mm)	Wide Angle	30/30	159.95
WA39 × 40D	3X-9X Zoom (40mm) Dot Ret.	Wide Angle	Dot	159.95

THOMPSON/CENTER SCOPES

RECOIL PROOF ELECTRA DOT RIFLE SCOPES

Designed and built to take the pounding of the heaviest Magnum loads, these scopes are subjected to a test force of 1,400 G's. All lenses and reticle house attachments are seated in neoprene and locked in place with finely threaded, double lock retaining rings. Waterproof construction, undetachable eye piece, anodized scope body and scratch-resistant finish. Electra Dot affords a clear, magnified view of the target under adverse light conditions. As the light fades, you simply switch on the battery-powered reticle. The center dot and a portion of both horizontal and vertical crosswires are instantly illuminated.

**TC 3/9V
#8620**

Model TC4 (No. 8610) $200.00
Model TC3/9V (No. 8620) 275.00

SPECIFICATIONS

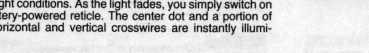

No. 8610 & No. 8620	TC 4 4 POWER with 1" tube Standard Turrets Electra Dot Reticle	TC 3/9V 3 to 9 VARIABLE with 1" tube Standard Turrets Electra Dot Reticle
Power	4X	3X to 9X
Field of View	29 ft. at 100 yds.	35.3 ft. on 3X 13.2 ft. on 9X
Eye Relief	3.3"	3.3"
Relative Brightness	64	177 on 3X 19 on 9X
Main Tube Diameter	1"	1"
Overall Length	12$^{15}/_{16}$"	12$^{7}/_{8}$"
Weight	12.3 ounces	15.5 ounces
Maximum Windage and Elevation Adjustment (at 100 yds.)	40" in either direction	40" in either direction
Click Value (at 100 yds.)	$^{1}/_{3}$"	$^{1}/_{4}$"
Dot with Crosshairs Reticle (Dot coverage at 100 yds.)	2"	4" (3X) 1$^{1}/_{3}$" (9X)

4X SHORT TUBE RIFLE SCOPE
#8640 (Rail Mount)
$195.00

LOBO SCOPES (not shown)

Designed for light to medium recoil calibers, these long eye relief scopes for pistols and black powder rifles feature adjustable eye pieces, are nitrogen filled and shock proof, and include self-centering crosswire reticles. Internal adjustments are protected by removable weather caps.

Lobo 1$^{1}/_{2}$X (No. 7550) $115.00
Lobo 3X (No. 7553) 120.00

Thompson/Center Scope Mounts are available for Contender, Smith & Wesson, Ruger, Hawken/Renegade and Seneca/Cherokee $13.50

SPECIFICATIONS LOBO SCOPES

	1$^{1}/_{2}$X	3X
Power	1$^{1}/_{2}$X	3X
Reticle	Crosshair	Crosshair
Field of View	16 ft. at 100 yds.	9 ft. at 100 yds.
Eye Relief	11 to 20 inches	11 to 20 inches
Relative Brightness	127	49
Main Tube Diameter	$^{7}/_{8}$"	$^{7}/_{8}$"
Overall Length	7$^{1}/_{4}$"	9"
Weight	5 ounces	6.3 ounces
Max. Windage & Elevation Adjustment (at 100 yds.)	5.25 ft. at 100 yards	5.25 ft. at 100 yards
Click Value (at 100 yds.)	$^{1}/_{3}$"	$^{1}/_{3}$"
Center of Crosshairs (Coverage at 100 yds.)	1.574"	1.181"

SCOPES

WEATHERBY SUPREME SCOPES

WEATHERBY SUPREME SCOPES

As every hunter knows, one of the most difficult problems is keeping running game in the field of view of the scope. Once lost, precious seconds fade away trying to find the animal in the scope again. Too much time wasted means the ultimate frustration. No second shot. Or no shot at all. The Weatherby Wide Field helps you surmount the problem by increasing your field of view.

FEATURES:

Optical excellence—now protected with multicoated anti-glare coating. • Fog-free and waterproof construction. • Constantly self-centered reticles. • Non-magnifying reticle. • 1/4" adjustments. • Quick variable power change. • Unique luminous reticle. • Neoprene eyepiece. • Binocular-type speed focusing. • Rugged score tube construction. Autocom point-blank system.

4 POWER

These are fixed-power scopes for big game and varmint hunting. Bright, clear image. Multicoated lenses for maximum luminosity under adverse conditions. 32-foot field of view at 100 yards.

3 TO 9 POWER

The most desirable variable for every kind of shooting from target to long-range big game. Outstanding light-gathering power. Fast, convenient focusing adjustment.

1³/₄ TO 5 POWER

A popular model for close-range hunting with large-bore rifles. Includes the Autocom system, which automatically compensates for trajectory and eliminates the need for range-finding without making elevation adjustments. Just aim and shoot!

Fixed Power:	PRICES
4 × 44	270.00
Variable Power:	
1.75-5 × 20	260.00
2-7 × 34	270.00
3-9 × 44	320.00

SUPREME RIFLESCOPES SPECIFICATIONS

Item	1.75-5X20	4X34	2-7X34	4X44	3-9X44
Actual Magnification	1.7-5	4	2.1-6.83	3.9	3.15-8.98
Field of View @ 100 yards	66.6-21.4 ft.	32 ft.	59-16 ft.	32 ft.	36-13 ft.
Eye Relief (inches)	3.4	3.1	3.4	3.0	3.5
Exit Pupil dia. in mm	11.9-4	8	10-4.9	10	10-4.9
Clear Aperture of Objective	20mm	34mm	34mm	44mm	44mm
Twilight Factor	5.9-10	11.7	8.2-15.4	13.3	11.5-19.9
Tube Diameter	1"	1"	1"	1"	1"
O.D. of Objective	1"	1.610"	1.610"	2"	2"
O.D. of Ocular	1.635"	1.635"	1.635"	1.635"	1.635"
Overall Length	10.7"	11.125"	11.125"	12.5"	12.7"
Weight	11 oz.	9.6 oz.	10.4 oz.	11.6 oz.	11.6 oz.
Adjustment Graduations					
Major Divisions:	1 MOA	1 MOA	1 MOA	1 MOA	1 MOA
Minor Divisions:	1/4 MOA	1/4 MOA	1/4 MOA	1/4 MOA	1/4 MOA
Maximum Adjustment (W&E)	60"	60"	60"	60"	60"
Reticles Available	LUMIPLEX	LUMIPLEX	LUMIPLEX	LUMIPLEX	LUMIPLEX

WEAVER RINGS AND BASES

1. **DETACHABLE TOP MOUNT RINGS.** Made with split rings in 7/8" and 1" diameters. The 1" blued rings are available in standard, medium, high and extension styles. New stainless steel rings in 1" medium also available. High Top Mount Rings and Medium Top Mount Rings (in 1" diameter only) provide adequate barrel and iron sight clearance for scopes with adjective diameters greater than 1 3/4". **$22.88** (**$34.98** for High Top Mount Rings and 1" Medium Stainless Steel)

2. **EXTENSION DETACHABLE MOUNT RINGS.** In 1" diameter only. Position scope 3/4" further forward, or backward, for improved eye relief. **$26.73**

3. **DETACHABLE SIDE MOUNTS.** Designed for Winchester 94 (except Angle Eject models) without drilling or tapping. Made with 1" diameter split-rings and brackets. Also offered in High style for greater clearance. **$23.32** (**27.28** for 1" Long)

4. **PIVOT MOUNT RINGS.** Change from scope to iron sights with a gentle push. Spring latch locks rings in place when scope is in sighting position. No drilling or tapping required. **$31.02**

5. **SEE-THRU MOUNT RINGS.** Attach to any bases which have square-cut cross bolt slots. Detach easily and offer built-in remounting precision. **$22.88** (**$26.73** for 1" Extension; **$16.28** for 7/8")

6. **INTEGRAL 1" SEE-THROUGH RINGS.** No drilling or tapping, and no base needed. Large aperature offers wide field of view with iron sights. **$16.28**

7. **1" TIP-OFF MOUNTS, SPLIT RINGS.** For mounting 1" scopes on rimfire rifles with 3/8" dovetailed factory-grooved receiver. No bases required. **$22.44**

8. **7/8" TIP-OFF MOUNTS, SOLID RINGS.** Designed to mount 7/8" scopes. Also available in 3/4" rings to fit 3/4" scopes. **$19.80**

9. **BLUED MOUNT BASE SYSTEMS.** **$59.50**

10. **STAINLESS STEEL MOUNT BASE SYSTEMS.** Require no drilling or tapping. Simply remove rear sight and slip on barrel yoke. Base attaches easily with two screws. Includes two Detachable Mount Rings, Mount Base, barrel yoke, screws and Allen wrench. **$83.27**

11. **SCOPE MOUNT SYSTEMS.** For fast mounting on Remington 870 or 1100 shotguns with no drilling or tapping. System meshes with existing trigger plate pins. Remove pins, replace with bolts. **$59.51**

12. **MODEL 94 ANGLE EJECT BASES.** For scoping Angle Eject Winchester 94's. **$9.63**

13. **BASES. $2.31-$11.99** top mount); **$5.06-$8.47** (pivot mount); **$8.80** (side mount)

WEAVER SCOPES

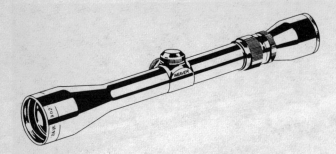

1. MODEL V9
   3x-9x Variable Hunting Scope

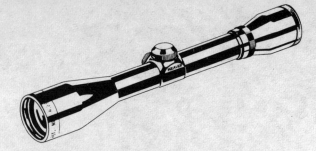

2. MODEL K4
   4x Fixed Power Hunting Scope

3. MODEL V3
   1x-3 Variable Hunting Scope

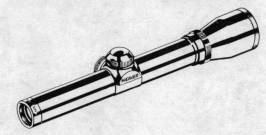

4. MODEL K2.5
   2$\frac{1}{2}$x Fixed Power Hunting Scope

5. MODEL V10
   2x-10x Variable All-Purpose Scope

6. KT15
   15x Target/Varmint Scope

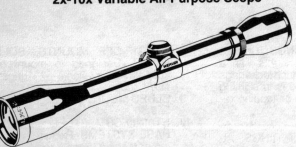

7. MODEL K6
   6x Fixed Power Hunting Scope

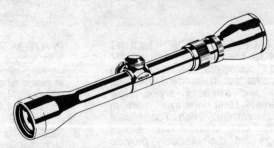

8. MODEL RV7
   2x-7x Rimfire Variable Scope

9. MODEL RK4
   4x Rimfire Fixed Power Scope

WILLIAMS SCOPE MOUNTS

MODEL SW-N-44-S (on S&W Model 629)

MODEL BH-S-357 (on Ruger Blackhawk)

GUIDELINE HANDGUN SCOPE MOUNTS
FOR REVOLVERS
$59.95

- Lightweight
- Hard anodized finish
- Precision-machined
- No drilling and tapping required
- High strength, heat-treated aluminum alloy
- Fits Ruger Blackhawk, Redhawk, Super Blackhawk and Bisley revolvers

- Fits Smith & Wesson "N" frames (.44 Magnum, 6″ and 8³/₈″ barrels)

Also available:
GUIDELINE HANDGUN SCOPE MOUNTS for Ruger Bull Barrel Auto Pistols: $49.95

TWO-PIECE DOVETAIL SCOPE MOUNT
(on Winchester 9422)

STREAMLINE DOVETAIL SCOPE MOUNTS
(ONE- and TWO-PIECE)
$29.95

Williams' unique double dovetail clamp-on system allows for simple installation and superior strength. These mounts are made to fit most dovetails found on rimfire rifles and air guns. Mounts are made for 1″ scopes and are constructed of precision-machined aluminum alloy.

ONE-PIECE DOVETAIL SCOPE MOUNT
(on Weatherby MKXXII)

WILLIAMS SCOPE MOUNTS

Shown on Model 70A Winchester

MODELS	Front	Rear
Remington Models 760, 740, 742, and Savage Model 170	1	2
Winchester Models 70 Standard, 670 and 770	4	3
*1917 Enfield	4	4
Remington Models 700, 721, 722, 725, Remington 700 L.H. and Remington 40X; BSA; Weatherby MK-V & Vanguard; Ruger 77ST; and S&W 1500	4	5
Savage Models 110, 111 and 112V	4	16
Winchester Models 88 and 100.	6	6
Browning BAR Auto and BLR Lever.	7	7
Marlin Models 336, 1894 & 1894C.	8	8
Remington Model 788	9	9
Thompson/Center 45 & 50 Cal. Hawken and 54 Cal. Renegade	10**	10**
Remington 541-S. Also, Remington Models 580, 581, 582 (require drilling & tapping)	11	11
Ruger Model 44	11	12
Ruger Model 10/22	13	12
Browning Safari Bolt and Mark X.	14	15
Ithaca LSA-55 and LSA-65 Bolt.	16	16
Rem. Models Four, Six, 7400 and 7600	17	18
Savage Model 99	19	20**
Winchester Model 94 Angle Eject	21	22

*With the rear receiver radiused the same diameter as the front receiver ring.

**Requires Sub-block

STREAMLINE TOP MOUNT

The Williams "Streamline" top mount is a revolutionary concept in two-piece mount design. Its solid ring-base construction allows the strongest possible installation of scope to rifle.

Because the bases are the rings, there can be no movement between the rings and bases as on other two-piece mounts. By design, the "Streamline" mount eliminates the need for extension rings as the mounts can be reversed allowing for installation of virtually all 1-inch scopes.

Features:
- Available for wide assortment of factory drilled rifles
- Precision-machined and lightweight
- Solid construction
- Eliminates need for extension rings—allows use of virtually all 1" scopes
- The bases are the rings
- Hard black anodized finish

Williams "Streamline" Two-Piece Top Mount
Complete **$21.00**
Williams "Steamline" Front or Rear Base Only **10.50**
Williams "Streamline" Two-Piece Top Mount with
Sub-Blocks for Hawken M/L **28.65**

Shown on Thompson/Center Renegade w/Sub-blocks

WILLIAMS SIGHT CHART

AMOUNT OF ADJUSTMENT NECESSARY TO CORRECT FRONT SIGHT ERROR

DISTANCE BETWEEN FRONT AND REAR SIGHTS	14"	15"	16"	17"	18"	19"	20"	21"	22"	23"	24"	25"	26"	27"	28"	29"	30"	31"	32"	33"	34"
Amount of 1	.0038	.0041	.0044	.0047	.0050	.0053	.0055	.0058	.0061	.0064	.0066	.0069	.0072	.0074	.0077	.0080	.0082	.0085	.0088	.0091	.0093
Error 2	.0078	.0083	.0089	.0094	.0100	.0105	.0111	.0116	.0122	.0127	.0133	.0138	.0144	.0149	.0155	.0160	.0156	.0171	.0177	.0182	.0188
at 3	.0117	.0125	.0133	.0142	.0150	.0159	.0167	.0175	.0184	.0192	.0201	.0209	.0217	.0226	.0234	.0243	.0251	.0259	.0268	.0276	.0285
100 Yards 4	.0155	.0167	.0178	.0189	.0200	.0211	.0222	.0234	.0244	.0255	.0266	.0278	.0289	.0300	.0311	.0322	.0333	.0344	.0355	.0366	.0377
Given in 5	.0194	.0208	.0222	.0236	.0250	.0264	.0278	.0292	.0306	.0319	.0333	.0347	.0361	.0375	.0389	.0403	.0417	.0431	.0445	.0458	.0472
Inches 6	.0233	.0250	.0267	.0283	.0300	.0317	.0333	.0350	.0367	.0384	.0400	.0417	.0434	.0450	.0467	.0484	.0500	.0517	.0534	.0551	.0567

When you replace an open rear sight with a receiver sight, it is usually necessary to install a higher front sight, to compensate for the higher plane of the new receiver sight. The table above shows the increase in front sight height that's required to compensate for a given error at 100 yards. Suppose your rifle has a 19 inch sight radius, and shoots 6 inches high at 100 yards, with the receiver sight adjusted as low as possible. The 19 inch column shows that the correction for a 6 inch error is .0317 inch. This correction is added to the over-all height of the front sight (including dovetail). Use a micrometer or similar accurate device to measure sight height. Thus, if your original sight measured .250 inch, it should be replaced with a sight .290 inch high.

WILLIAMS SIGHT-OVER-SCOPE

S-O-S
(SIGHT-OVER-SCOPE)
MOUNTING SYSTEMS
Shown on a Marlin Model 336

MODELS	S-O-S FRONT	S-O-S REAR
Remington Models 760-740-742, and Savage Model 170.	1	2
Winchester Models 70 Standard, 670 & 770	4	3
*1917 Enfield	4	4
Remington Models 700-721-722-725, L.H. and 40X; BSA; Weatherby MK-V and Vanguard; Ruger 77ST; and S&W 1500	4	5
Savage Models 110, 111 and 112V	4	16
Winchester Models 88 and 100	6	6
Browning BAR Auto and BLR Lever	7	7
Marlin Models 336, 1894 & 1894C	8	8
Remington Model 788	9	9
Thompson/Center 45 & 50 Cal. Hawken and 54 Cal. Renegade	10**	10**
Remington 541-S. Also, Remington Models 580-581-582 (require drilling & tapping)	11	11
Ruger Model 44.	11	12
Ruger Model 10/22	13	12
Browning Safari Bolt and Mark X	14	15
Ithaca LSA-55 and LSA-65 Bolt	16	16
Rem. Models Four, Six, 7400 and 7600	17	18
Savage Model 99.	19	20**
Winchester Model 94 Angle Eject	21	22**

*With the rear receiver radiused the same
diameter as the front receiver ring.
**Requires sub-block

The S-O-S System (on a Ruger 10/22)
S-O-S Kit Complete for Williams Rings **$47.00**
S-O-S Streamline Set (except w/sub-block) **54.15**
S-O-S Streamline Set 10 & 10 . . . . **61.75**
S-O-S Streamline Set 19 & 20, 21 & 22 . . . . **56.55**

This concept in sighting known as the S-O-S (Sight-Over-Scope) allows the scope to be mounted low and permits instant use of open sight for quick, fast action shots at close range. The compact S-O-S has both elevation and windage in the rear sight, and the front sight has additional windage.

The "Guide-Line" S-O-S ring top kit will work with all Williams mounts having the two-piece 1-inch rings. The sights are made from an aluminum alloy. They are rustproof and attractively anodized.

The S-O-S front sight is furnished with a fluorescent orange $3/32$-inch bead (white or gold is optional.) The S-O-S rear sight is furnished with the WGRS-M/L Guide Receiver Sight with the regular $3/8 \times .125$ Buckbuster long shank aperture. (Twilight or Regular apertures in the $3/8 \times .093$ and $3/8 \times .050$ are optional.) Specify the long shank aperture to fit the WGRS receiver sight.

WILLIAMS TWILIGHT SCOPES

1.5x-5x: $186.50

2¹/₂x: $132.00

4x: $138.00

3x-9X: $196.00

The "Twilight" series of scopes was introduced to accommodate those shooters who want a high-quality scope in the medium-priced field. The "Twilight" scopes are waterproof and shockproof, have coated lenses and are nitrogen-filled. Resolution is sharp and clear. All "Twilight" scopes have a highly polished, rich, black, hard anodized finish.

There are five models available: the 2¹/₂x, the 4x, the 1.5x-5x, the 2x-6x, and the 3x-9x. They are available in T-N-T reticle only (which stands for "thick and thin").

TWILIGHT SPECIFICATIONS

OPTICAL SPECIFICATIONS	2.5X	4X	1.5X – 5X At 1.5X	At 5X	2X – 6X At 2X	At 6X	3X – 9X At 3X	At 9X
Clear aperture of objective lens	20mm	32mm	20mm	Same	32mm	Same	40mm	Same
Clear aperture of ocular lens	32mm	32mm	32mm	Same	32mm	Same	32mm	Same
Exit Pupil	8mm	8mm	13.3mm	4mm	16mm	5.3mm	13.3mm	44.4mm
Relative Brightness	64	64	177	16	256	28	161.2	17.6
Field of view (degree of angle)	6°10'	5°30'	11°	4°	8°30'	3°10'	7°	2°20'
Field of view at 100 yards	32'	29'	57¾'	21'	45½'	16¾'	36½'	12¾'
Eye Relief	3.7"	3.6"	3.5"	3.5"	3"	3"	3.1"	2.9"
Parallax Correction (at)	50 yds.	100 yds.	100 yds.	Same	100 yds.	Same	100 yds.	Same
Lens Construction	9	9	10	Same	11	Same	11	Same
MECHANICAL SPECIFICATIONS								
Outside diameter of objective end	1.00"	1.525"	1.00"	Same	1.525"	Same	1.850"	1.850"
Outside diameter of ocular end	1.455"	1.455"	1.455"	Same	1.455"	Same	1.455"	Same
Outside diameter of tube	1"	1"	1"	Same	1"	Same	1"	Same
Internal adjustment graduation	¼ min.	¼ min.	¼ min.	Same	¼ min.	Same	¼ min.	Same
Minimum internal adjustment	75 min.	75 min.	75 min.	Same	75 min.	Same	60 min.	Same
Finish	Glossy		Hard	Black		Anodized		
Length	10"	11¾"	10¾"	Same	11½"	11½"	12¾"	12¾"
Weight	8½ oz.	9½ oz.	10 oz.	Same	11½ oz.	Same	13½ oz.	Same

WILLIAMS SIGHT-THRU MOUNTS

SHOWN ON REMINGTON MODEL 742

SHOWN ON WINCHESTER MODEL 70

Features:
- One-piece construction
- Large field of view for Iron Sights right under the scope
- Available for a wide assortment of factory-drilled rifles
- All parts are precision-machined
- Lightweight
- Hard black anodized finish
- Fast, accurate sighting under all field conditions

The Williams Sight-Thru Mount provides instant use of scope above, or iron sights below. Easily installed. Uses existing holes on top of receiver. No drilling or tapping necessary. The Sight-Thru is compact and lightweight—will not alter balance of the rifle. The high tensile strength alloy will never rust. All parts are precision-machined. Completely rigid. Shockproof. The attractive streamlined appearance is further enhanced by a beautiful, hard black anodized finish. Rings are 1″ in size; ⁷/₈″ sleeves available.

Williams "Sight-Thru" Mount Complete........ $21.00

MODELS	FRONT	REAR
Winchester Models 88 and 100; Sako Finnwolf; Ithaca 37†.	A	A
Remington Models 760, 740, 742 and Savage Model 170	A	B
Winchester Models 70 Standard, 670 and 770; Browning BBR	D	C
Remington Models 700 R.H. and L.H., 721, 722, 725; Weatherby MK-V and Vanguard; BSA round top receivers; Ruger 77ST; Smith & Wesson Model 1500.	D	E
Savage Models 110, 111 and 112V	D	F
Browning BLR Lever Action	O	O
Browning BAR High Power Auto; Mossberg 800; Remington 541S †. Will also fit Ward's Western Field Model 72 and Mossberg Model 472 lever action.*.	G	G
Late models Marlin 336, 1894 and 1894C	H	H
FN Mauser; Browning Bolt Action; J. C. Higgins 50-51; Interarms Mark X Mauser	D	I
Savage 99 (New Style)	J	K**
Schultz & Larsen.	A	G
1917 Enfield	J	J
Ruger 10/22	L	M
Ruger 44	O	M
Ruger 77R and RS Series †	H	P
Remington Models 4, 7400, 6, and 7600 . .	R	S

*When ordering 'G' bases for Western Field Model 72 and Mossberg Model 472, please specify that 360 screws must be furnished.
**Requires Sub-block   †Drilling and Tapping Required

WILLIAMS FRONT SIGHT RISER BLOCK

This riser block adds .250 inch to the height of the dovetail. It is especially handy on such guns as the Ruger 10/22 and any other models that require a higher than normal front sight (when installing a receiver sight). This model is available in two widths—the .250 for Williams Streamlined ramps and other ramps having a ¼-inch top width—and the .340 to work on all standard factory ramps (Winchester, Remington, Savage, etc.) having this base width. It incorporates the standard ³/₈-inch dovetail.

Price. $4.35

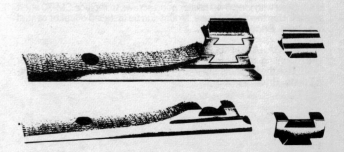

WILLIAMS

1.5X PISTOL & BOW SCOPE
$136.50

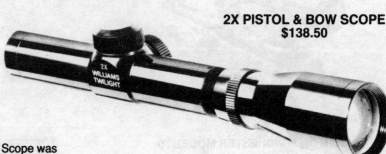

2X PISTOL & BOW SCOPE
$138.50

TWILIGHT SCOPES
FOR PISTOLS AND BOWS
WITH LONG EYE RELIEF

Built tough, compact and lightweight, the Twilight Scope was designed specifically for handgun hunters and precision target shooters. And for archers, these scopes offer the first practical scope-aiming device, including the new Wiliams bow scope mount, which opens up target and hunting possibilities never before available to the archer.

MECHANICAL SPECIFICATIONS	1.5X20	2.20
Outside Diameter of Objective End	1"	1"
Outside Diameter of Ocular End	36.5mm	36.5mm
Outside Diameter of Tube	1"	1"
Internal Adjustment Graduation	1/4"	1/4"
Minimum Internal Adjustment	170"	162"
Finish	Glossy Hard Black Anodized	
Length	209mm	216mm
Weight	6.4 oz.	6.6 oz.

OPTICAL SPECIFICATIONS	1.5X20	2X20
Clear Aperture of Objective Lens	20mm	20mm
Clear Aperture of Ocular Lens	30mm	30mm
Exit Pupil	13.3mm	10mm
Relative Brightness	177	100
Field of View (Degree of Angle)	3°4'	3°20'
Field of View at 100 Yards	19 ft.	17 1/2 ft.
Eye Relief	18"-25"	18"-25"
Parallax Correciton (at)	50 yds.	50 yds.
Lens Construction	6	6

NEW SM94/36 SIDE MOUNT ON THE
94 WINCHESTER $48.85

MOUNTING PLATES:
FOR 30-M1 CARBINE
(Attach with 8-40 fillister screws.) Use the Williams SM-740 side mount base with this mounting plate. Scope can be offset or high over bore. **Price: $11.50**

FOR SMLE NO. 1
(Attach with 8-40 fillister head mounting screws.) This mounting plate is supplied with long 8-40 fillister head screws to replace SM-70 short screws. Use the SM-70 base. Mount can be installed offset or central over bore. **Price: $7.40**

FOR M1 GARAND RIFLE
The mounting screws for this mounting plate are 8-40 × .475 fillister head. Use the Williams SM-740 (4 holes) side mount with this mounting plate. **Price: $11.50**

ZEISS RIFLESCOPES

EUROPEAN ZA SERIES

These five new scopes include the following features: large objective diameter and good twilight performance; metric graduation of reticle adjustment (1 click = 1cm/100m); traditional reticle types; and constant relationship between reticle and target when changing power (enabling use of reticle also for range estimation).

SCOPES

DIATAL-ZA 4x32T*
$525.00

DIATAL-ZA 6x42T*
$620.00

DIATAL-ZA 8x56T*
$710.00

DIAVARI-ZA 1.5-6x42T*
$870.00

DIAVARI-ZA 2.5-10x52T*
$1030.00

ZEISS RIFLESCOPES

THE C-SERIES

The C-Series was designed by Zeiss specifically for the American hunter. It is based on space-age alloy tubes with integral objective and ocular bells, and an integral adjustment turret. This strong, rigid one-piece construction allows perfect lens alignment, micro-precise adjustments and structural integrity. Other features include quick focusing, a generous 3 1/2″ of eye relief, rubber armoring, T-Star multi-layer coating, and parallax setting (free at 100 yards).

DIATAL-C 10x36T*
$675.00

DIAVARI-C 3-9x36T*
$915.00

DIATAL-C 6x32T*
$565.00

DIATAL-C 4x32T*
$525.00

DIAVARI-C 1.5-4.5x18T*
$790.00

PRODUCT SPECIFICATIONS	4×32	6×32	10×36	3-9×36		C1.5-4.5×18	
Magnification	4X	6X	10X	3X	9X	1.5X	4.5X
Objective Diameter (mm)/(inch)	1.26″	1.26″	1.42″	1.42″		15.0/0.6	18.0/0.7
Exit Pupil	0.32″	0.21″	0.14″	0.39″	0.16″	10.0	4.0
Twilight Performance	11.3	13.9	19.0	8.5	18.0	4.2	9.0
Field of View at 100 yds.	30′	20′	12′	36′	13′	72′	27′
Eye Relief	3.5″	3.5″	3.5″	3.5″	3.5″	3.5″	
Maximum Interval Adjustment (elevation and windage (MOA)	80	80	50	50		10.5′ @ 100 yds.	
Click-Stop Adjustment 1 click = 1 interval (MOA)	1/4	1/4	1/4	1/4		.36″ @ 100 yds.	
Length	10.6″	10.6″	12.7″	11.2″		11.8″	
Weight approx. (ounces)	11.3	11.3	14.1	15.2		13.4	
Tube Diameter	1″	1″	1″	1″		1″	
Objective Tube Diameter	1.65″	1.65″	1.89″	1.73″		1″	
Eyepiece O.D.	1.67″	1.67″	1.67″	1.67″		1.8″	

Ammunition

FOR ADDRESSES AND PHONE NUMBERS OF MANUFACTURERS AND DISTRIBUTORS INCLUDED IN THIS SECTION, SEE *DIRECTORY OF MANUFACTURERS AND SUPPLIERS*

ACTIV AMMUNITION

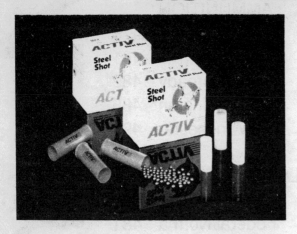

Buckshot Specifications

Model	Ga.	Length (in.)	# Of Pellets	Shot Size	Rnds. Per Box	Rnds. Per Case
*BK12Y	12	2¾	12	00	5	250
	12	2¾	20	1	5	250
	12	2¾	34	4	5	250
*BK12Z	12	2¾	9	00	5	250
	12	2¾	16	1	5	250
	12	2¾	27	4	5	250
BK12XL	12	2¾	15	00	5	250
	12	2¾	24	1	5	250
	12	2¾	41	4	5	250
BK12YL	12	2¾	12	00	5	250
	12	2¾	30	1	5	250
	12	2¾	34	4	5	250
BK12ZL	12	2¾	9	00	5	250
	12	2¾	16	1	5	250
	12	2¾	27	4	5	250

Steel Shot Specifications

Model	Ga.	Length (in.)	Dram Equiv.	Ounces Shot	Standard Shot Sizes	Rnds. Per Box	Rnds. Per Case
ST12E	12	3	Max	1⅜	BB, 1, 2, 4, 6	20	200
ST123F	12	3	Max	1¼	BB, 1, 2, 4	20	200
ST12F	12	2¾	Max	1¼	BB, 1, 2, 4, 6	20	200
ST12G	12	2¾	Max	1⅛	BB, 1, 2, 4	20	200
ST20H	20	3	Max	1	2, 4, 6	20	480
ST20J	20	2¾	Max	¾	4, 6	20	480

Steel Shot Information

Shot Sizes	Pellet Count Per Ounce	Average Pellet Count 1⅛	Average Pellet Count 1¼	Average Pellet Count 1⅜
BB	72	81	90	99
#1	103	116	129	142
#2	125	140	156	172
#4	192	216	240	264
#6	312	351	390	429

Target Load Specifications

Model	Ga.	Length (in.)	Dram Equiv.	Ounces Shot	Standard Shot Sizes	Rnds. Per Box	Rnds. Per Case
Tournament Grade: High Quality Target Loads. Trap and Skeet							
TG12G	12	2¾	3	1⅛	7½, 8, 8½, 9	25	500
TG12GL	12	2¾	2¾	1⅛	7½, 8, 8½, 9	25	500
TG12UL	12	Ultra Light		1⅛	7½, 8, 8½, 9	25	500
TG12H	12	2¾	2¾	1	7½, 8, 8½, 9	25	500
A20I	20	2¾	2½	⅞	7½, 8, 8½, 9	25	500
International Trap Loads. Nickel Plated Shot							
A12GH	12	2¾	3¼	1⅛	7½, 8, 9	25	500
Nickel Plated Pigeon Loads							
A12FH	12	2¾	3¼	1¼	6, 7½, 8, 9	25	500

Steel Shot Ballistics

ACTIV Loads	Average Pressure	Average Velocity	SAAMI Spec. Max. Dram
12 gauge – 1⅜ oz.	11.000	1280	1210
12 gauge – 1¼ oz.	10.800	1390	1375
12 gauge – 1⅛ oz.	11.000	1420	1365

Red Hornet Series Specifications

Model	Ga.	Length (in.)	Dram Equiv.	Ounces Shot	Standard Shot Sizes	Rnds. Per Box	Rnds. Per Case
Duck & Pheasant Promotional Loads							
H12F	12	2¾	3¾	1¼	4, 5, 6, 7½	25	500
H16G	16	2¾	3¼	1⅛	4, 5, 6, 7½	25	500
H20HH	20	2¾	2¾	1	4, 6, 7½	25	500
Small Game & Bird Promotional Loads							
H12FL	12	2¾	3¼	1¼	4, 6, 7½, 8	25	500
H12GL	12	2¾	3¼	1⅛	4, 6, 7½, 8	25	500
H16GL	16	2¾	2¾	1⅛	4, 6, 7½, 8	25	500
H20H	20	2¾	2½	1	4, 6, 7½, 8	25	500
Dove & Quail Promotional Loads							
H12HH	12	2¾	3¼	1	6, 7½, 8	25	500
H16H	16	2¾	2½	1	6, 7½, 8	25	500
H20I	20	2¾	2½	⅞	6, 7½, 8	25	500

Slugs Specifications

Model	Ga.	Length (in.)	Dram Equiv.	Weight	Rnds. Per Box	Rnds. Per Case
SL123F	12	3	Max	1¼ oz.	5	250
SL12F	12	2¾	Max	1¼ oz.	5	250
SL12H	12	2¾	Max	1 oz.	5	250
SL16H	16	2¾	Max	1 oz.	5	250
SL20I	20	2¾	Max	⅞ oz.	5	250

ACTIV AMMUNITION

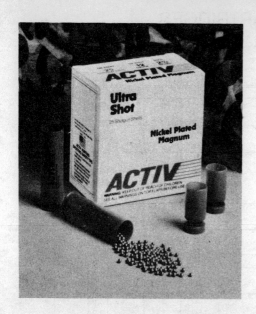

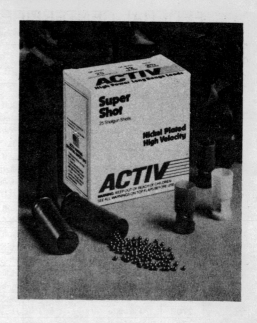

Ultrashot Nickel Magnum Loads Specifications

Model	Ga.	Length (in.)	Dram Equiv.	Ounces Shot	Standard Shot Sizes	Rnds. Per Box	Rnds. Per Case
N12B	12	3	4	1⅞	BB, 2, 4, 6	25	250
N12C	12	3	4	1⅝	2, 4, 6	25	250
N12D	12	2¾	4½	1½	BB, 2, 4, 6	25	250
N20F	20	3	3	1¼	2, 4, 6, 7½	25	500
N20G	20	3	3¼	1⅛	4, 6, 7½	25	500
N20GL	20	2¾	2¾	1⅛	4, 6, 7½	25	500

Super Shot Nickel High Velocity Loads Specifications

Model	Ga.	Length (in.)	Dram Equiv.	Ounces Shot	Standard Shot Sizes	Rnds. Per Box	Rnds. Per Case
N12E	12	2¾	4	1⅜	4, 6, 7½	25	250
N12F	12	2¾	3¾	1¼	BB, 2, 4, 5, 6, 7½, 9	25	250
N16GL	16	2¾	3¼	1⅛	4, 6, 7½	25	250
N20H	20	2¾	2¾	1	4, 5, 6, 7½, 9	25	500

Penetrator Series Nickel Turkey Load Specifications

Model	Ga.	Length (in.)	Dram Equiv.	Ounces Shot	Standard Shot Sizes	Rnds. Per Box	Rnds. Per Case
P123A	12	3	4	2	4, 6	10	100
P12A	12	2¾	4	1¾	4, 6, 7½	10	100
P12D	12	2¾	4½	1½	4, 6	10	100

All Purpose Field Loads Specifications

Model	Ga.	Length (in.)	Dram Equiv.	Ounces Shot	Standard Shot Sizes	Rnds. Per Box	Rnds. Per Case
G12F	12	2¾	3¼	1¼	6, 7½, 8, 9	25	500
G12GL	12	2¾	3¼	1⅛	6, 7½, 8, 9	25	500
G12H	12	2¾	3¼	1	6, 7½, 8, 9	25	500
G16GL	16	2¾	2¾	1⅛	6, 7½, 8, 9	25	500
G16H	16	2¾	2½	1	6, 7½, 8, 9	25	500
G20H	20	2¾	2½	1	6, 7½, 8, 9	25	500
G20I	20	2¾	2½	⅞	6, 7½, 8, 9	25	500

FEDERAL AMMUNITION

FEDERAL CENTERFIRE RIFLE CARTRIDGES

20 rounds per box, 25 boxes per case. 500 rounds per case.

LOAD NO.	CARTRIDGES	BULLET TYPE	BULLET WEIGHT GRAINS	APPROX. CASE WT. (LBS.)	RETAIL PRICE BOX
222A	222 Remington	Soft Point	50	15	9.38
222B	222 Remington	Metal Case Boat Tail	55	15	9.38
22250A	22-250 Remington	Soft Point	55	22	10.71
22250C	22-250 Remington	BLITZ, Hollow Point	40	21	11.46
223A	223 Remington (5.56 mm)	Soft Point	55	15	10.29
223B	223 Remington (5.56 mm)	Metal Case Boat Tail	55	15	10.29
223C	223 Remington (5.56 mm)	Hollow Point Boat Tail	55	15	11.04
223D	223 Remington (5.56 mm)	BLITZ, Hollow Point	40	14	11.04
6A	6mm Remington	Soft Point	80	26	12.86
6B	6mm Remington	Hi-Shok Soft Point	100	27	12.86
243A	243 Winchester	Soft Point	80	25	12.86
243B	243 Winchester	Hi-Shok Soft Point	100	26	12.86
257A	257 Roberts (High Vel + P)	Hi-Shok Soft Point	117	30	14.36
2506A	25-06 Remington	Hollow Point	90	28	13.94
2506B	25-06 Remington	Hi-Shok Soft Point	117	30	13.94
270A	270 Winchester	Hi-Shok Soft Point	130	31	13.94
270B	270 Winchester	Hi-Shok Soft Point	150	33	13.94
7A	7mm Mauser	Hi-Shok Soft Point	175	33	14.18
7B	7mm Mauser	Hi-Shok Soft Point	140	31	14.18
7RA	7mm Remington Magnum	Hi-Shok Soft Point	150	37	17.26
7RB	7mm Remington Magnum	Hi-Shok Soft Point	175	39	17.26
30CA	30 Carbine	Soft Point	110	16	8.93
730A	7-30 Waters	Boat Tail Soft Point	120	25	13.94
3030A	30-30 Winchester	Hi-Shok Soft Point	150	27	10.95
3030B	30-30 Winchester	Hi-Shok Soft Point	170	28	10.95
3030C	30-30 Winchester	Hollow Point	125	25	10.95

We accept orders for split cases of centerfire – 5 boxes per individual load in increments of 5 boxes.

FEDERAL CENTERFIRE RIFLE CARTRIDGES

20 rounds per box, 25 boxes per case. 500 rounds per case.

LOAD NO.	CARTRIDGES	BULLET TYPE	BULLET WEIGHT GRAINS	APPROX. CASE WT. (LBS.)	RETAIL PRICE BOX
3006A	30-06 Springfield	Hi-Shok Soft Point	150	33	13.94
3006B	30-06 Springfield	Hi-Shok Soft Point	180	35	13.94
3006C	30-06 Springfield	Soft Point	125	31	13.94
3006D	30-06 Springfield	Boat Tail Soft Point	165	34	14.54
3006H	30-06 Springfield	Hi-Shok Soft Point	220	37	13.94
3006J	30-06 Springfield	Round Nose	180	35	13.94
300A	300 Savage	Hi-Shok Soft Point	150	30	14.10
300B	300 Savage	Hi-Shok Soft Point	180	32	14.10
300WB	300 Winchester Magnum	Hi-Shok Soft Point	180	40	18.17
308A	308 Winchester	Hi-Shok Soft Point	150	31	13.94
308B	308 Winchester	Hi-Shok Soft Point	180	32	13.94
308M	308 Winchester (Match)	Boat Tail Hollow Point	168	32	16.91
8A	8mm Mauser	Hi-Shok Soft Point	170	32	14.36
32A	32 Winchester Special	Hi-Shok Soft Point	170	29	11.62
35A	35 Remington	Hi-Shok Soft Point	200	32	12.86
†44A	44 Remington Magnum	Hollow Soft Point	240	29	10.85
4570A	45-70 Government	Hollow Soft Point	300	42	16.67

(New — 308M)

† For Rifle or Pistol.

We accept orders for split cases of centerfire – 5 boxes per individual load in increments of 5 boxes.

FEDERAL AMMUNITION
PREMIUM CENTERFIRE RIFLE CARTRIDGES

	LOAD NO.	CARTRIDGES	BULLET TYPE	BULLET WEIGHT GRAINS	APPROX. CASE WT. (LBS.)	RETAIL PRICE BOX

20 rounds per box, 25 boxes per case. 500 rounds per case.

	LOAD NO.	CARTRIDGES	BULLET TYPE	BULLET WEIGHT GRAINS	APPROX. CASE WT. (LBS.)	RETAIL PRICE BOX
	P22250B	22-250 Remington	Boat Tail Hollow Point	55	22	11.57
	P2506C	25-06 Remington	Boat Tail Soft Point	117	30	15.54
New	P6C	6mm Remington	Nosler Partition	100	27	17.55
	P243C	243 Winchester	Boat Tail Soft Point	100	26	14.28
	P243D	243 Winchester	Boat Tail Hollow Point	85	25	14.28
	P257B	257 Roberts (High Vel + P)	Nosler Partition	120	32	17.55
	P270C	270 Winchester	Boat Tail Soft Point	150	32	15.54
	P270D	270 Winchester	Boat Tail Soft Point	130	31	15.54
	P270E	270 Winchester	Nosler Partition	150	32	19.07
New	P280A	280 Remington	Nosler Partition	150	33	19.07
New	P7C	7mm Mauser	Nosler Partition	140	31	17.55
	P7RD	7mm Remington Magnum	Boat Tail Soft Point	150	37	19.07
	P7RE	7mm Remington Magnum	Boat Tail Soft Point	165	38	19.07
	P7RF	7mm Remington Magnum	Nosler Partition	160	38	22.98
	P7RG	7mm Remington Magnum	Nosler Partition	140	38	22.98
	P3030D	30-30 Winchester	Nosler Partition	170	28	15.88
	P3006D	30-06 Springfield	Boat Tail Soft Point	165	34	15.54
	P3006F	30-06 Springfield	Nosler Partition	180	35	19.07
	P3006G	30-06 Springfield	Boat Tail Soft Point	150	33	15.54
New	P3006L	30-06 Springfield	Boat Tail Soft Point	180	35	15.54
	P300WC	300 Winchester Magnum	Boat Tail Soft Point	200	41	20.02
	P300WD	300 Winchester Magnum	Nosler Partition	180	41	23.77
	P308C	308 Winchester	Boat Tail Soft Point	165	31	15.54
	P338A	338 Winchester Magnum	Nosler Partition	210	42	24.41
	P338B	338 Winchester Magnum	Nosler Partition	250	45	24.41

FEDERAL 22 RIMFIRE CARTRIDGES

	LOAD NO.	CARTRIDGES	BULLET TYPE	BULLET WEIGHT GRAINS	APPROX. CASE WT. (LBS.)	RETAIL PRICE BOX

HI-POWER® 22's – 50 rounds per box, 100 boxes per case. 5000 rounds per case.

	LOAD NO.	CARTRIDGES	BULLET TYPE	BULLET WEIGHT GRAINS	APPROX. CASE WT. (LBS.)	RETAIL PRICE BOX
	701	22 Short	Copper Plated	29	30	1.88
	706	22 Long	Copper Plated	29	32	1.99
New	700CB	22 Long	Lead Lubricated	29	32	1.99
	710	22 Long Rifle	Copper Plated	40	40	1.79
	712	22 Long Rifle	Copper Plated, Hollow Point	38	40	2.07
	716	22 Long Rifle	#12 Shot	#12	34	4.77

HI-POWER® 22's - 100 PACK – 50 boxes per case. 5000 rounds per case.

	LOAD NO.	CARTRIDGES	BULLET TYPE	BULLET WEIGHT GRAINS	APPROX. CASE WT. (LBS.)	RETAIL PRICE BOX
810	22 Long Rifle	Copper Plated	40	45	3.59
812	22 Long Rifle	Copper Plated, Hollow Point	38	45	4.15

MAGNUM 22's – 50 rounds per box, 100 boxes per case. 5000 rounds per case.

	LOAD NO.	CARTRIDGES	BULLET TYPE	BULLET WEIGHT GRAINS	APPROX. CASE WT. (LBS.)	RETAIL PRICE BOX
737	22 Win. Mag.	Full Metal Jacket	40	50	6.33
747	22 Win. Mag.	Jacketed Hollow Point	40	50	6.33

FEDERAL AMMUNITION

FEDERAL CENTERFIRE PISTOL CARTRIDGES

LOAD NO.	CARTRIDGES	BULLET TYPE	BULLET WEIGHT GRAINS	APPROX. CASE WT. (LBS.)	RETAIL PRICE BOX

NYCLAD® PISTOL CARTRIDGES – 50 rounds per box, 20 boxes per case. 1000 rounds per case.

LOAD NO.	CARTRIDGES	BULLET TYPE	GRAINS	CASE WT.	PRICE
N9BP	9mm Luger Auto Pistol	Hollow Point	124	28	19.34
N38A	38 Special	Wadcutter	148	34	16.72
N38B	38 Special	Round Nose	158	35	15.84
N38G	38 Special (High Vel + P)	SW Hollow Point	158	35	18.38
N38M	38 Special	Hollow Point	125	30	18.38
N38N	38 Special (High Vel + P)	Hollow Point	125	30	18.38
N357E	357 Magnum	SW Hollow Point	158	39	20.45

FEDERAL CENTERFIRE PISTOL CARTRIDGES

50 rounds per box, 20 boxes per case. 1000 rounds per case.

LOAD NO.	CARTRIDGES	BULLET TYPE	GRAINS	CASE WT.	PRICE
*25AP	25 Auto Pistol (6.35mm)	Metal Case	50	12	6.89
32AP	32 Auto Pistol (7.65mm)	Metal Case	71	18	15.60
32LA	32 S&W Long	Lead Wadcutter	98	20	14.95
32LB	32 S&W Long	Lead Round Nose	98	20	13.85
32HRA	32 H&R Magnum	Lead Semi-Wadcutter	95	25	15.30
32HRB	32 H&R Magnum	Jacketed Hollow Point	85	21	17.30
380AP	380 Auto Pistol	Metal Case	95	23	15.92
380BP	380 Auto Pistol	Jacketed Hollow Point	90	22	15.92
9AP	9mm Luger Auto Pistol	Metal Case	123	29	19.34
9BP	9mm Luger Auto Pistol	Jacketed Hollow Point	115	28	19.34
9CP	9mm Luger Auto Pistol	Jacketed Soft Point	95	28	19.83
New 9MP	9mm Luger (Match)	Metal Case, S.W.C.	124	30	19.83
38A	38 Special (Match)	Lead Wadcutter	148	34	15.27
38B	38 Special	Lead Round Nose	158	35	14.68
38C	38 Special	Lead Semi-Wadcutter	158	35	15.27
38D	38 Special (High Vel + P)	Lead Round Nose	158	35	16.26
38E	38 Special (High Vel + P)	Jacketed Hollow Point	125	30	18.59
38F	38 Special (High Vel + P)	Jacketed Hollow Point	110	28	18.59
38G	38 Special (High Vel + P)	Lead SW Hollow Point	158	34	15.92
38H	38 Special (High Vel + P)	Lead Semi-Wadcutter	158	35	16.26
38J	38 Special (High Vel + P)	Jacketed Soft Point	125	30	18.59
357A	357 Magnum	Jacketed Soft Point	158	39	20.41
357B	357 Magnum	Jacketed Hollow Point	125	34	20.41
357C	357 Magnum	Lead Semi-Wadcutter	158	38	17.26
357D	357 Magnum	Jacketed Hollow Point	110	30	20.41
357E	357 Magnum	Jacketed Hollow Point	158	39	20.41
357G	357 Magnum	Jacketed Hollow Point	180	44	20.41
41A	41 Remington Magnum	Jacketed Hollow Point	210	54	26.88
44B	44 Remington Magnum	Jacketed Hollow Point	180	50	26.88
**A44B	44 Remington Magnum	Jacketed Hollow Point	180	50	11.04
†44C	44 Remington Magnum	Metal Case Prcfile	220	56	28.56
44SA	44 S & W Special	Lead SW Hollow Point	200	50	20.58
45LCA	45 Colt	Lead SW Hollow Point	225	50	20.90
45A	45 Automatic (Match)	Metal Case	230	49	21.57
45B	45 Automatic (Match)	Metal Case, S.W.C.	185	42	22.40
45C	45 Automatic	Jacketed Hollow Point	185	42	22.40

† For Rifle or Pistol.
 * 25AP packed 25 rounds per box.
** A44B packed 20 rounds per box, 1000 rounds per case.

We accept orders for split cases of centerfire – 5 boxes per individual load in increments of 5 boxes.

FEDERAL AMMUNITION

FEDERAL SHOTSHELLS

LOAD NO.	GAUGE	SHELL LENGTH (INCHES)	POWDER DRAMS EQUIV.	OUNCES SHOT	SHOT SIZES	APPROX. CASE WT. (LBS.)	RETAIL PRICE CASE	RETAIL PRICE BOX

HI-POWER® POWER MAGNUM LOADS – 25 rounds per box, 10 boxes per case. 250 rounds per case.

LOAD NO.	GAUGE	SHELL LENGTH	POWDER DRAMS EQUIV.	OUNCES SHOT	SHOT SIZES	CASE WT.	CASE	BOX
F103	10	3½	4¼	2	BB, 2, 4	44	248.70	24.87
F131	12	3	4	1⅞	BB, 2, 4	39	155.60	15.56
F129	12	3	4	1⅝	2, 4, 6	36	143.90	14.39
F130	12	2¾	3¾	1½	BB, 2, 4,5,6	33	129.40	12.94
F165	16	2¾	3¼	1¼	2, 4, 6	28	127.60	12.76
F207	20	3	3	1¼	2, 4, 6, 7½	27	120.10	12.01
F205	20	2¾	2¾	1⅛	4, 6, 7½	25	106.70	10.67

LIGHT MAGNUM LOADS – 25 rounds per box, 20 boxes per case. 500 rounds per case.

LOAD NO.	GAUGE	SHELL LENGTH	POWDER DRAMS EQUIV.	OUNCES SHOT	SHOT SIZES	CASE WT.	CASE	BOX
F138	12	2¾	4	1⅜	4, 6, 7½	61	242.80	12.14

HI-POWER® LOADS – 25 rounds per box, 20 boxes per case. 500 rounds per case.

LOAD NO.	GAUGE	SHELL LENGTH	POWDER DRAMS EQUIV.	OUNCES SHOT	SHOT SIZES	CASE WT.	CASE	BOX
F127	12	2¾	3¾	1¼	BB, 2, 4,5,6, 7½,8, 9	57	209.60	10.48
F164	16	2¾	3¼	1⅛	4, 6, 7½	52	201.40	10.07
F203	20	2¾	2¾	1	4,5,6, 7½,8	45	184.40	9.22
F413	410	3	Max.	11/16	4,5,6, 7½,8	30	173.20	8.66
F412	410	2½	Max.	½	6, 7½	24	147.20	7.36

STEEL SHOT HI-POWER MAGNUM LOADS – 25 rounds per box, 10 boxes per case. 250 rounds per case.

LOAD NO.	GAUGE	SHELL LENGTH	POWDER DRAMS EQUIV.	OUNCES SHOT	SHOT SIZES	CASE WT.	CASE	BOX
W104	10	3½	Max.	1⅝	F,T,**BBB**,BB, 2	38	223.80	22.38
W149	12	3	Max.	1⅜	F,T,**BBB**,BB,1,2,**3**,4	32	156.50	15.65
W140	12	3	Max.	1¼	BB,1,2,**3**,4	28	143.80	14.38
W148	12	2¾	Max.	1¼	**T,BBB**,BB,1,2,**3**,4	28	143.80	14.38
W168	16	2¾	Max.	15/16	**2, 4**	22	131.90	13.19
W209	20	3	3¼	1	2,**3**,4, 6	22	126.00	12.60

STEEL SHOT HI-POWER® LOADS – 25 rounds per box, 20 boxes per case. 500 rounds per case.

LOAD NO.	GAUGE	SHELL LENGTH	POWDER DRAMS EQUIV.	OUNCES SHOT	SHOT SIZES	CASE WT.	CASE	BOX
W147	12	2¾	3¾	1⅛	BB, 2,**3**,4, 6	54	263.80	13.19
W208	20	2¾	3	¾	4, 6	39	238.00	11.90

FIELD LOADS –

25 rounds per box, 20 boxes per case. 500 rounds per case.

LOAD NO.	GAUGE	SHELL LENGTH	POWDER DRAMS EQUIV.	OUNCES SHOT	SHOT SIZES	CASE WT.	CASE	BOX
*F125	12	2¾	3¼	1¼	7½,8	56	181.80	9.09
F124	12	2¾	3¼	1¼	7½,8, 9	56	177.80	8.89

25 rounds per box, 10 boxes per case. 250 rounds per case.

LOAD NO.	GAUGE	SHELL LENGTH	POWDER DRAMS EQUIV.	OUNCES SHOT	SHOT SIZES	CASE WT.	CASE	BOX
H123	12	2¾	3¼	1⅛	4, 6, 7½,8, 9	26	81.20	8.12
H162	16	2¾	2¾	1⅛	6, 7½,8	26	81.20	8.12
H202	20	2¾	2½	1	6, 7½,8	23	76.10	7.61

*Flyer Load

HI-SHOK® RIFLED SLUGS – 5 rounds per box, 50 boxes per case. 250 rounds per case.

LOAD NO.	GAUGE	SHELL LENGTH	POWDER DRAMS EQUIV.	OUNCES SHOT	SHOT SIZES	CASE WT.	CASE	BOX
F103	10	3½	Mag.	1¾	Rifled Slug	40	303.00	6.06
F131	12	3	Mag.	1¼	Rifled Slug	31	238.50	4.77
F130	12	2¾	Mag.	1¼	Rifled Slug	30	214.00	4.28
F127	12	2¾	Max.	1	Rifled Slug	26	173.00	3.46
F164	16	2¾	Max.	⅘	Rifled Slug	22	173.00	3.46
F203	20	2¾	Max.	¾	Rifled Slug	19	160.50	3.21
F412	410	2½	Max.	⅕	Rifled Slug	9	152.50	3.05

No split case orders accepted for shotshells.   **Bold Face indicates new in 1988.**

FEDERAL AMMUNITION

PREMIUM SHOTSHELLS

LOAD NO.	GAUGE	SHELL LENGTH (INCHES)	POWDER DRAMS EQUIV.	OUNCES SHOT	SHOT SIZES	APPROX. CASE WT. (LBS.)	RETAIL PRICE BOX

MAGNUM LOADS – 25 rounds per box, 10 boxes per case. 250 rounds per case.

LOAD NO.	GAUGE	SHELL LENGTH	POWDER DRAMS	OUNCES SHOT	SHOT SIZES	CASE WT.	PRICE BOX
P109	10	3½	4½	2¼	BB, 2, 4, 6	49	26.47
P159	12	3	4	2	BB, 2, 4, 6	41	18.27
P158	12	3	4	1⅞	BB, 2, 4, 6	40	16.67
P157	12	3	4	1⅝	2, 4, 6	36	15.46
P156	12	2¾	4	1½	BB, 2, 4, 6	34	14.57
P258	20	3	3	1¼	2, 4, 6	27	12.91
P256	20	2¾	2¾	1⅛	4, 6	25	11.42

HI-POWER LOADS – 25 rounds per box, 20 boxes per case. 500 rounds per case.

LOAD NO.	GAUGE	SHELL LENGTH	POWDER DRAMS	OUNCES SHOT	SHOT SIZES	CASE WT.	PRICE BOX
P154	12	2¾	3¾	1¼	4, 6, 7½	58	11.50
P254	20	2¾	2¾	1	6	45	9.97
New P283	28	2¾	2¼	¾	6, 7½,8	37	10.13

FIELD LOADS – 25 rounds per box, 20 boxes per case. 500 rounds per case.

LOAD NO.	GAUGE	SHELL LENGTH	POWDER DRAMS	OUNCES SHOT	SHOT SIZES	CASE WT.	PRICE BOX
P153	12	2¾	3¼	1¼	7½,8	55	10.07
P152	12	2¾	3¼	1⅛	7½	52	9.73
P252	20	2¾	2½	1	7½,8	45	8.79

BUCKSHOT – 10 Gauge: 5 rounds per box. 12 Gauge: 10 rounds per box. 250 rounds per case.

	LOAD NO.	GAUGE	SHELL LENGTH	POWDER DRAMS	SHOT SIZES		CASE WT.	PRICE BOX
New	P108	10	3½	Magnum	00 Buck	18 Pellets	49	6.03
New	P108	10	3½	Magnum	4 Buck	54 Pellets	53	6.03
	P158	12	3	Magnum	000 Buck	10 Pellets	35	9.45
	P158	12	3	Magnum	00 Buck	15 Pellets	40	9.45
	P158	12	3	Magnum	No. 4 Buck	41 Pellets	41	9.45
	P158	12	3	Magnum	1 Buck	24 Pellets	42	9.45
	P156	12	2¾	Magnum	00 Buck	12 Pellets	33	8.28
	P156	12	2¾	Magnum	No. 4 Buck	34 Pellets	34	8.28
	P154	12	2¾	Max	00 Buck	9 Pellets	28	7.58
New	P154	12	2¾	Max	4 Buck	27 Pellets	34	7.58

FEDERAL SHOTSHELLS

LOAD NO.	GAUGE	SHELL LENGTH (INCHES)	POWDER DRAMS EQUIV.	SHOT SIZES	APPROX. CASE WT. (LBS.)	RETAIL PRICE BOX

HI-POWER MAGNUM BUCKSHOT – 5 rounds per box, 50 boxes per case. 250 rounds per case.

LOAD NO.	GAUGE	SHELL LENGTH	POWDER DRAMS	SHOT SIZES		CASE WT.	PRICE BOX
F131	12	3	Mag.	000 Buck	10 Pellets	38	4.31
F131	12	3	Mag.	00 Buck	15 Pellets	39	4.31
F131	12	3	Mag.	No. 1 Buck	24 Pellets	44	4.31
F131	12	3	Mag.	No. 4 Buck	41 Pellets	40	4.31
F130	12	2¾	Mag.	00 Buck	12 Pellets	33	3.72
F130	12	2¾	Mag.	No. 1 Buck	20 Pellets	38	3.72
F130	12	2¾	Mag.	No. 4 Buck	34 Pellets	35	3.72
F207	20	3	Mag.	No. 2 Buck	18 Pellets	30	3.72

HI-POWER BUCKSHOT – 5 rounds per box, 50 boxes per case. 250 rounds per case.

LOAD NO.	GAUGE	SHELL LENGTH	POWDER DRAMS	SHOT SIZES		CASE WT.	PRICE BOX
F127	12	2¾	Max.	000 Buck	8 Pellets	30	3.05
F127	12	2¾	Max.	00 Buck	9 Pellets	27	3.05
F127	12	2¾	Max.	0 Buck	12 Pellets	32	3.05
F127	12	2¾	Max.	No. 1 Buck	16 Pellets	33	3.05
F127	12	2¾	Max.	No. 4 Buck	27 Pellets	30	3.05
F164	16	2¾	Max.	No. 1 Buck	12 Pellets	26	3.05
F203	20	2¾	Max.	No. 3 Buck	20 Pellets	25	3.05

FEDERAL/NORMA

LOAD NO.	CALIBER	BULLET TYPE	BULLET WEIGHT GRAMS	RETAIL BOX

NORMA CENTERFIRE RIFLE CARTRIDGES – Specialty Calibers
20 rounds per box, 10 boxes per case. 200 rounds per case.

	LOAD NO.	CALIBER	BULLET TYPE	BULLET WEIGHT GRAMS	RETAIL BOX
	15701	220 Swift	Soft Point	50	21.43
	15604	22 Savage H.P.	Soft Point	71	22.71
	16531	6.5x50 Japanese	Soft Point Boat Tail	139	22.71
	16532	6.5x50 Japanese	Soft Point	156	22.71
	16535	6.5x52 Carcano	Soft Point	156	22.71
New	16537	6.5x52 Carcano	Soft Point	139	22.71
	16558	6.5x55 Swedish	Protected Power Cavity	139	22.71
	16552	6.5x55 Swedish	Soft Point	156	22.71
	17002	7x57 Mauser	Soft Point	150	21.01
	17005	7x57 R	Soft Point	150	23.81
	17013	7x64 Brenneke	Soft Point	150	23.81
	17511	7.5x55 Swiss	Soft Point Boat Tail	180	23.81
	17634	7.62x54R Russian	Soft Point Boat Tail	180	24.07
New	17637	7.62x54R Russian	Soft Point	150	24.07
	17638	308 Norma Magnum	Dual Core	180	28.76
	17701	7.65x53 Argentine	Soft Point	150	22.71
New	17702	7.65x53 Argentine	Soft Point	180	22.71
	17712	.303 British	Soft Point	150	17.77
	17721	7.7x58 Japanese	Soft Point	130	24.07
	17722	7.7x58 Japanese	Soft Point Boat Tail	180	24.07
	18017	8x57 JS Mauser	Protected Power Cavity	165	22.71
	18003	8x57 JS Mauser	Soft Point	196	22.71
	19303	9.3x57 Mauser	Soft Point	286	27.54
	19315	9.3x62 Mauser	Soft Point	286	27.54

NORMA CENTERFIRE PISTOL CARTRIDGES
50 rounds per box, 20 boxes per case. 1000 rounds per case.

LOAD NO.	CALIBER	BULLET TYPE	BULLET WEIGHT GRAMS	RETAIL BOX
19022	9mm Luger	Full Metal Jacket	116	25.27
19119	38 Special (+P)	Jacketed Hollow Point	110	25.92
19114	38 Special (+P)	Full Metal Jacket	158	25.92
19106	357 Magnum	Full Metal Jacket	158	26.73

20 rounds per box, 25 boxes per case.

LOAD NO.	CALIBER	BULLET TYPE	BULLET WEIGHT GRAMS	RETAIL BOX
11002	10mm Auto	Jacketed Hollow Point	170	14.66
11001	10mm Auto	Full Metal Jacket	200	14.66
11103-5	44 Magnum	Jacketed Soft Point	240	18.14

HORNADY AMMUNITION

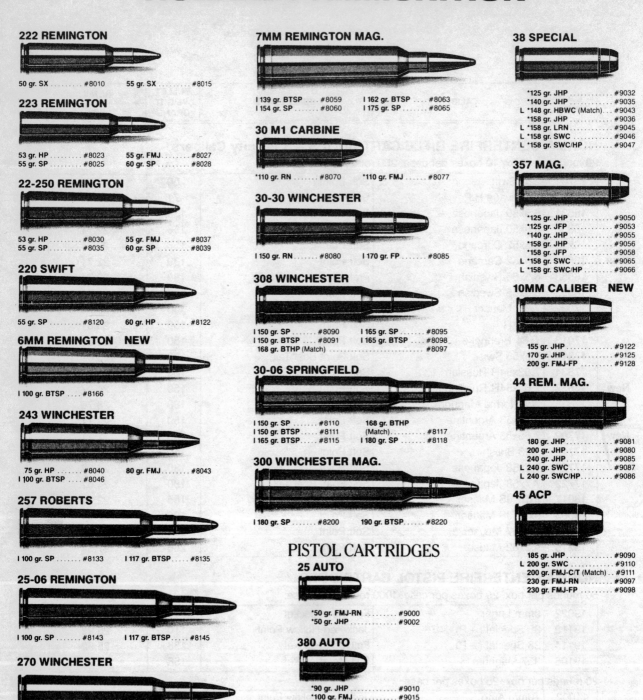

222 REMINGTON

50 gr. SX . . . . #8010   55 gr. SX . . . . . #8015

223 REMINGTON

53 gr. HP . . . . #8023   55 gr. FMJ . . . . #8027
55 gr. SP . . . . #8025   60 gr. SP . . . . . #8028

22-250 REMINGTON

53 gr. HP . . . . #8030   55 gr. FMJ . . . . #8037
55 gr. SP . . . . #8035   60 gr. SP . . . . . #8039

220 SWIFT

55 gr. SP . . . . #8120   60 gr. HP . . . . . #8122

6MM REMINGTON   NEW

I 100 gr. BTSP . . . . #8166

243 WINCHESTER

75 gr. HP . . . . #8040   80 gr. FMJ . . . . #8043
I 100 gr. BTSP . . . #8046

257 ROBERTS

I 100 gr. SP . . . . . . #8133   I 117 gr. BTSP . . . . . #8135

25-06 REMINGTON

I 100 gr. SP . . . . . #8143   I 117 gr. BTSP . . . . . #8145

270 WINCHESTER

I 130 gr. SP . . . . . . #8055   I 140 gr. BTSP . . . . #8056
I 150 gr. SP . . . . . . #8058

7 x 57 MAUSER

I 139 gr. BTSP . . . . #8155   I 154 gr. SP . . . . . #8156

7MM REMINGTON MAG.

I 139 gr. BTSP . . . . #8059   I 162 gr. BTSP . . . . #8063
I 154 gr. SP . . . . . . #8060   I 175 gr. SP . . . . . #8065

30 M1 CARBINE

*110 gr. RN . . . . #8070   *110 gr. FMJ . . . . . . #8077

30-30 WINCHESTER

I 150 gr. RN . . . . . . #8080   I 170 gr. FP . . . . . . #8085

308 WINCHESTER

I 150 gr. SP . . . . . . #8090   I 165 gr. SP . . . . . #8095
I 150 gr. BTSP . . . . #8091   I 165 gr. BTSP . . . . #8098
168 gr. BTHP (Match) . . . . #8097

30-06 SPRINGFIELD

I 150 gr. SP . . . . . . #8110   168 gr. BTHP
I 150 gr. BTSP . . . . #8111   (Match) . . . . #8117
I 165 gr. BTSP . . . . #8115   I 180 gr. SP . . . . #8118

300 WINCHESTER MAG.

I 180 gr. SP . . . . . . #8200   190 gr. BTSP . . . . . #8220

PISTOL CARTRIDGES

25 AUTO

*50 gr. FMJ-RN . . . . . . #9000
*50 gr. JHP . . . . #9002

380 AUTO

*90 gr. JHP . . . . #9010
*100 gr. FMJ . . . . #9015

9MM LUGER

*90 gr. JHP . . . . #9020
*100 gr. FMJ . . . . #9023
*115 gr. JHP . . . . . . #9025
*115 gr. FMJ-RN . . . . . #9026
*124 gr. FMJ-FP . . . . . #9027
*124 gr. FMJ-RN . . . . . #9029

38 SPECIAL

*125 gr. JHP . . . . #9032
*140 gr. JHP . . . . #9035
L *148 gr. HBWC (Match) . . #9043
*158 gr. JHP . . . . #9036
L *158 gr. LRN . . . . #9045
L *158 gr. SWC . . . . #9046
L *158 gr. SWC/HP . . . . . #9047

357 MAG.

*125 gr. JHP . . . #9050
*125 gr. JFP . . . #9053
*140 gr. JHP . . . #9055
*158 gr. JHP . . . #9056
*158 gr. JFP . . . #9058
L *158 gr. SWC . . . #9065
L *158 gr. SWC/HP . . . #9066

10MM CALIBER   NEW

155 gr. JHP . . . . #9122
170 gr. JHP . . . . #9125
200 gr. FMJ-FP . . . . #9128

44 REM. MAG.

180 gr. JHP . . . #9081
200 gr. JHP . . . #9080
240 gr. JHP . . . #9085
L 240 gr. SWC . . . #9087
L 240 gr. SWC/HP . . . #9086

45 ACP

185 gr. JHP . . . . #9090
L 200 gr. SWC . . . . #9110
200 gr. FMJ-C/T (Match) . . #9111
230 gr. FMJ-RN . . . . #9097
230 gr. FMJ-FP . . . . #9098

REMINGTON AMMUNITION

The cartridges pictured below represent the most recent additions to Remington's ammunition lineup. They are being introduced in 1988 and will join the other rifle and handgun cartridges pictured and described on the following pages.

357 MAGNUM - 180-GRAIN
SEMI-JACKETED HOLLOW POINT

41 REMINGTON MAGNUM - 170-GRAIN
SEMI-JACKETED HOLLOW POINT

44 REMINGTON MAGNUM - 210-GRAIN
SEMI-JACKETED HOLLOW POINT

9MM LUGER
88-Gr. Hollow Point

9MM LUGER
115-Gr. METAL CASE

35 WHELEN
(By Remington)
200-Grain Pointed Soft Point

7MM-08 REMINGTON
120-Gr. Pointed Soft Point

280 REMINGTON
120-Gr. Pointed Soft Point

7MM REMINGTON MAGNUM
140-Gr. Pointed Soft Point

35 WHELEN
(By Remington)
250-Grain Soft Point

REMINGTON CENTERFIRE RIFLE CARTRIDGES

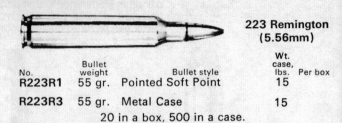

223 Remington (5.56mm)

No.	Bullet weight	Bullet style	Wt. case, lbs.	Per box
R223R1	55 gr.	Pointed Soft Point	15	
R223R3	55 gr.	Metal Case	15	

20 in a box, 500 in a case.

17 Remington

No.	Bullet weight	Bullet style	Wt. case, lbs.	Per box
R17REM	25 gr.	Hollow Point "Power-Lokt"	12	

20 in a box, 500 in a case.

6mm Remington

No.	Bullet weight	Bullet style	Wt. case, lbs.	Per box
R6MM1*	80 gr.	Pointed Soft Point	26	
R6MM2*	80 gr.	Hollow Point "Power-Lokt"	26	
R6MM4	100 gr.	Pointed Soft Point "Core-Lokt"	26	

20 in a box, 500 in a case.

(*) May be used in rifles chambered for .244 Remington.

22 Hornet

No.	Bullet weight	Bullet style	Wt. case, lbs.	Per box
R22HN1	45 gr.	Pointed Soft Point	9	
R22HN2	45 gr.	Hollow Point	9	

50 in a box, 500 in a case.

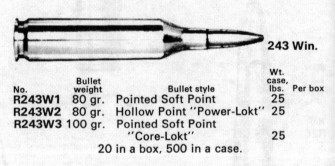

243 Win.

No.	Bullet weight	Bullet style	Wt. case, lbs.	Per box
R243W1	80 gr.	Pointed Soft Point	25	
R243W2	80 gr.	Hollow Point "Power-Lokt"	25	
R243W3	100 gr.	Pointed Soft Point "Core-Lokt"	25	

20 in a box, 500 in a case.

222 Remington

No.	Bullet weight	Bullet style	Wt. case, lbs.	Per box
R222R1	50 gr.	Pointed Soft Point	14	
R222R3	50 gr.	Hollow Point "Power-Lokt"	14	
R222R4	55 gr.	Metal Case	14	

20 in a box, 500 in a case.

222 Remington Magnum

No.	Bullet weight	Bullet style	Wt. case, lbs.	Per box
R222M1	55 gr.	Pointed Soft Point	15	
R222M2	55 gr.	Hollow Point "Power-Lokt"	15	

20 in a box, 500 in a case.

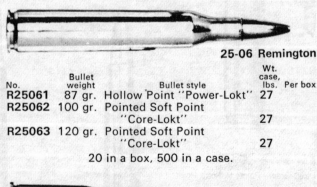

25-06 Remington

No.	Bullet weight	Bullet style	Wt. case, lbs.	Per box
R25061	87 gr.	Hollow Point "Power-Lokt"	27	
R25062	100 gr.	Pointed Soft Point "Core-Lokt"	27	
R25063	120 gr.	Pointed Soft Point "Core-Lokt"	27	

20 in a box, 500 in a case.

22-250 Remington

No.	Bullet weight	Bullet style	Wt. case, lbs.	Per box
R22501	55 gr.	Pointed Soft Point	21	
R22502	55 gr.	Hollow Point "Power-Lokt"	21	

20 in a box, 500 in a case.

25-20 Win.

No.	Bullet weight	Bullet style	Wt. case, lbs.	Per box
R25202	86 gr.	Soft Point	13	

50 in a box, 500 in a case.

REMINGTON CENTERFIRE RIFLE CARTRIDGES

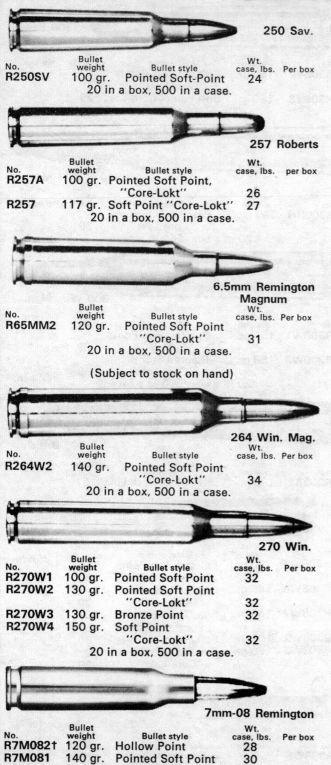

250 Sav.

No.	Bullet weight	Bullet style	Wt. case, lbs.	Per box
R250SV	100 gr.	Pointed Soft-Point	24	

20 in a box, 500 in a case.

257 Roberts

No.	Bullet weight	Bullet style	Wt. case, lbs.	per box
R257A	100 gr.	Pointed Soft Point, "Core-Lokt"	26	
R257	117 gr.	Soft Point "Core-Lokt"	27	

20 in a box, 500 in a case.

6.5mm Remington Magnum

No.	Bullet weight	Bullet style	Wt. case, lbs.	Per box
R65MM2	120 gr.	Pointed Soft Point "Core-Lokt"	31	

20 in a box, 500 in a case.

(Subject to stock on hand)

264 Win. Mag.

No.	Bullet weight	Bullet style	Wt. case, lbs.	Per box
R264W2	140 gr.	Pointed Soft Point "Core-Lokt"	34	

20 in a box, 500 in a case.

270 Win.

No.	Bullet weight	Bullet style	Wt. case, lbs.	Per box
R270W1	100 gr.	Pointed Soft Point	32	
R270W2	130 gr.	Pointed Soft Point "Core-Lokt"	32	
R270W3	130 gr.	Bronze Point	32	
R270W4	150 gr.	Soft Point "Core-Lokt"	32	

20 in a box, 500 in a case.

7mm-08 Remington

No.	Bullet weight	Bullet style	Wt. case, lbs.	Per box
R7M082†	120 gr.	Hollow Point	28	
R7M081	140 gr.	Pointed Soft Point	30	

20 in a box, 500 in a case.

280 Remington ‡

No.	Bullet weight	Bullet style	Wt. case, lbs.	Per box
R280R4†	120 gr.	Hollow Point	32	
R280R3	140 gr.	Pointed Soft Point	33	
R280R1	150 gr.	Pointed Soft Point "Core-Lokt"	33	
R280R2	165 gr.	Soft Point "Core-Lokt"	34	

20 in a box, 500 in a case.
‡ Interchangeable with 7mm "Express" Rem.

7mm Bench Rest Remington

No.	Bullet weight	Bullet style	Wt. case, lbs.	Per box
R7MMBR†	120 gr.	Hollow Point	28	

20 in a box, 500 in a case.

7mm Remington Magnum

No.	Bullet weight	Bullet style	Wt. case, lbs.	Per box
R7MM4†	140 gr.	Pointed Soft Point	36	
R7MM2	150 gr.	Pointed Soft Point "Core-Lokt"	37	
R7MM3	175 gr.	Pointed Soft Point "Core-Lokt"	37	

20 in a box, 500 in a case.

7mm Mauser (7x57)

No.	Bullet weight	Bullet style	Wt. case, lbs.	Per box
R7MSR1	140 gr.	Pointed Soft Point	32	

20 in a box, 500 in a case.

30 Carbine

No.	Bullet weight	Bullet style	Wt. case, lbs.	Per box
R30CAR	110 gr.	Soft Point	15	

50 in a box, 500 in a case.

30 Remington

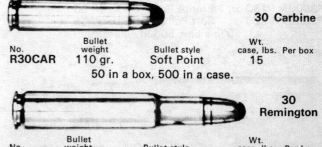

No.	Bullet weight	Bullet style	Wt. case, lbs.	Per box
R30REM	170 gr.	Soft Point "Core-Lokt"	26	

20 in a box, 500 in a case.

REMINGTON CENTERFIRE RIFLE CARTRIDGES

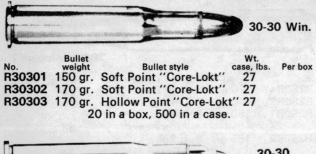

30-30 Win.

No.	Bullet weight	Bullet style	Wt. case, lbs.	Per box
R30301	150 gr.	Soft Point "Core-Lokt"	27	
R30302	170 gr.	Soft Point "Core-Lokt"	27	
R30303	170 gr.	Hollow Point "Core-Lokt"	27	

20 in a box, 500 in a case.

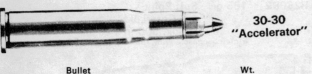

30-30 "Accelerator"

No.	Bullet weight	Bullet style	Wt. case, lbs.	Per box
R3030A	55 gr.	Soft Point	18	

20 in a box, 500 in a case.

30-40 Krag

No.	Bullet weight	Bullet style	Wt. case, lbs.	Per box
R30402	180 gr.	Pointed Soft Point "Core-Lokt"	32	

20 in a box, 500 in a case.

30-06 Spfd.

No.	Bullet weight	Bullet style	Wt. case, lbs.	Per box
R30061	125 gr.	Pointed Soft Point	35	
R30062	150 gr.	Pointed Soft Point "Core-Lokt"	35	
R30063	150 gr.	Bronze Point	35	
R3006B	165 gr.	Pointed Soft Point "Core-Lokt"	35	
R30064	180 gr.	Soft Point "Core-Lokt"	35	
R30065	180 gr.	Pointed Soft Point "Core-Lokt"	35	
R30066	180 gr.	Bronze Point	35	
R30067	220 gr.	Soft Point "Core-Lokt"	35	

20 in a box, 500 in a case.

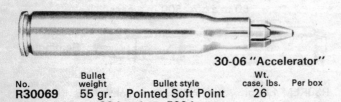

30-06 "Accelerator"

No.	Bullet weight	Bullet style	Wt. case, lbs.	Per box
R30069	55 gr.	Pointed Soft Point	26	

20 in a box, 500 in a case.

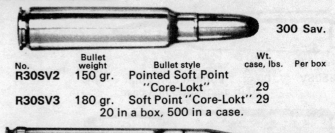

300 Sav.

No.	Bullet weight	Bullet style	Wt. case, lbs.	Per box
R30SV2	150 gr.	Pointed Soft Point "Core-Lokt"	29	
R30SV3	180 gr.	Soft Point "Core-Lokt"	29	

20 in a box, 500 in a case.

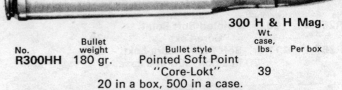

300 H & H Mag.

No.	Bullet weight	Bullet style	Wt. case, lbs.	Per box
R300HH	180 gr.	Pointed Soft Point "Core-Lokt"	39	

20 in a box, 500 in a case.

300 Win. Mag.

No.	Bullet weight	Bullet style	Wt. case, lbs.	Per box
R300W1	150 gr.	Pointed Soft Point "Core-Lokt"	39	
R300W2	180 gr.	Pointed Soft Point "Core-Lokt"	39	

20 in a box, 500 in a case.

303 British

No.	Bullet weight	Bullet style	Wt. case, lbs.	Per box
R303B1	180 gr.	Soft Point "Core-Lokt"	67	

308 Win.

No.	Bullet weight	Bullet style	Wt. case, lbs.	Per box
R308W1	160 gr.	Pointed Soft Point "Core-Lokt"	30	
R308W6	165 gr.	Pointed Soft Point "Core-Lokt"	30	
R308W7†	168 gr.	Boat Tail Hollow Point (Match)	30	
R308W2	180 gr.	Soft Point "Core-Lokt"	30	
R308W3	180 gr.	Pointed Soft Point "Core-Lokt"	30	

.308 Win. "Accelertor"

No.	Bullet weight	Bullet style	Wt. case, lbs.	Per box
R308W5	55 gr.	Pointed Soft Point	26	

20 in a box, 500 in a case.

REMINGTON CENTERFIRE RIFLE CARTRIDGES

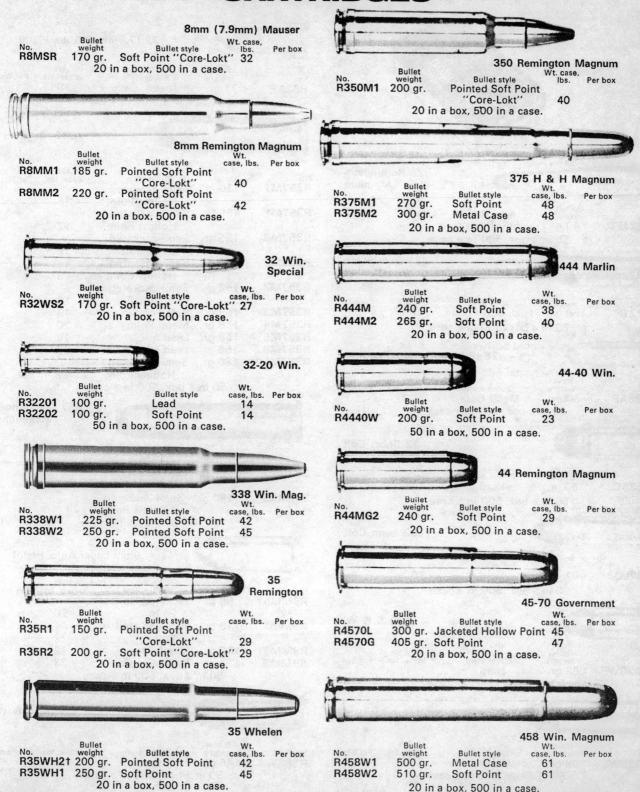

8mm (7.9mm) Mauser

No.	Bullet weight	Bullet style	Wt. case, lbs.	Per box
R8MSR	170 gr.	Soft Point "Core-Lokt"	32	

20 in a box, 500 in a case.

8mm Remington Magnum

No.	Bullet weight	Bullet style	Wt. case, lbs.	Per box
R8MM1	185 gr.	Pointed Soft Point "Core-Lokt"	40	
R8MM2	220 gr.	Pointed Soft Point "Core-Lokt"	42	

20 in a box, 500 in a case.

32 Win. Special

No.	Bullet weight	Bullet style	Wt. case, lbs.	Per box
R32WS2	170 gr.	Soft Point "Core-Lokt"	27	

20 in a box, 500 in a case.

32-20 Win.

No.	Bullet weight	Bullet style	Wt. case, lbs.	Per box
R32201	100 gr.	Lead	14	
R32202	100 gr.	Soft Point	14	

50 in a box, 500 in a case.

338 Win. Mag.

No.	Bullet weight	Bullet style	Wt. case, lbs.	Per box
R338W1	225 gr.	Pointed Soft Point	42	
R338W2	250 gr.	Pointed Soft Point	45	

20 in a box, 500 in a case.

35 Remington

No.	Bullet weight	Bullet style	Wt. case, lbs.	Per box
R35R1	150 gr.	Pointed Soft Point "Core-Lokt"	29	
R35R2	200 gr.	Soft Point "Core-Lokt"	29	

20 in a box, 500 in a case.

35 Whelen

No.	Bullet weight	Bullet style	Wt. case, lbs.	Per box
R35WH2†	200 gr.	Pointed Soft Point	42	
R35WH1	250 gr.	Soft Point	45	

20 in a box, 500 in a case.

350 Remington Magnum

No.	Bullet weight	Bullet style	Wt. case, lbs.	Per box
R350M1	200 gr.	Pointed Soft Point "Core-Lokt"	40	

20 in a box, 500 in a case.

375 H & H Magnum

No.	Bullet weight	Bullet style	Wt. case, lbs.	Per box
R375M1	270 gr.	Soft Point	48	
R375M2	300 gr.	Metal Case	48	

20 in a box, 500 in a case.

444 Marlin

No.	Bullet weight	Bullet style	Wt. case, lbs.	Per box
R444M	240 gr.	Soft Point	38	
R444M2	265 gr.	Soft Point	40	

20 in a box, 500 in a case.

44-40 Win.

No.	Bullet weight	Bullet style	Wt. case, lbs.	Per box
R4440W	200 gr.	Soft Point	23	

50 in a box, 500 in a case.

44 Remington Magnum

No.	Bullet weight	Bullet style	Wt. case, lbs.	Per box
R44MG2	240 gr.	Soft Point	29	

20 in a box, 500 in a case.

45-70 Government

No.	Bullet weight	Bullet style	Wt. case, lbs.	Per box
R4570L	300 gr.	Jacketed Hollow Point	45	
R4570G	405 gr.	Soft Point	47	

20 in a box, 500 in a case.

458 Win. Magnum

No.	Bullet weight	Bullet style	Wt. case, lbs.	Per box
R458W1	500 gr.	Metal Case	61	
R458W2	510 gr.	Soft Point	61	

20 in a box, 500 in a case.

REMINGTON CENTERFIRE PISTOL AND REVOLVER CARTRIDGES

22 Remington "Jet" Magnum

No.	Bullet weight	Bullet style	Wt. case, lbs.	Per box
R22JET	40 gr.	Soft Point	12	

50 in a box, 500 in a case.

221 Remington "Fire Ball"

No.	Bullet weight	Bullet style	Wt. case, lbs.	Per box
R221F	50 gr.	PTd. Soft Point	12	

20 in a box, 500 in a case.

25 (6.35mm) Auto. Pistol

No.	Bullet weight	Bullet style	Wt. case, lbs.	Per box
R25AP	50 gr.	Metal Case	7	

50 in a box, 500 in a case.

32 Short Colt

No.	Bullet weight	Bullet style	Wt. case, lbs.	Per box
R32SC	80 gr.	Lead	10	

50 in a box, 500 in a case.

32 Long Colt

No.	Bullet weight	Bullet style	Wt. case, lbs.	Per box
R32LC	82 gr.	Lead	10	

50 in a box, 500 in a case.

32 S & W

No.	Bullet weight	Bullet style	Wt. case, lbs.	Per box
R32SW	88 gr.	Lead	11	

50 in a box, 500 in a case.

32 S & W Long

No.	Bullet weight	Bullet style	Wt. case, lbs.	Per box
R32SWL	98 gr.	Lead	12	

50 in a box, 500 in a case.

32 (7.65mm) Auto. Pistol

No.	Bullet weight	Bullet style	Wt. case, lbs.	Per box
R32AP	71 gr.	Metal Case	9	

50 in a box, 500 in a case.

357 Magnum

No.	Bullet weight	Bullet style	Wt. case, lbs.	Per box
R357M7	110 gr.	Semi-Jacketed Hollow Point	16	
R357M1	125 gr.	Semi-Jacketed Hollow Point	17	
R357M8	125 gr.	Semi-Jacketed Soft Point	17	
R357M9	140 gr.	Semi-Jacketed Hollow Point	18	
R357M2	158 gr.	Semi-Jacketed Hollow Point	19	
R357M3	158 gr.	Soft Point	19	
R357M4	158 gr.	Metal Point	20	
R357M5	158 gr.	Lead	19	
R357M6	158 gr.	Lead (Brass Case)	20	
R357M10†	180 gr.	Semi-Jacketed Hollow Point	22	

50 in a box, 500 in a case.

357 Remington Maximum

No.	Bullet weight	Bullet style	Wt. case, lbs.	Per box
357MX1	158 gr.	Semi-Jacketed Hollow Point	29	
357MX3	180 gr.	Semi-Jacketed Hollow Point	29	

20 in a box, 500 in a case.

9mm Luger Auto. Pistol

No.	Bullet weight	Bullet style	Wt. case, lbs.	Per box
R9MM5†	88 gr.	Jacketed Hollow Point	20	
R9MM1	115 gr.	Jacketed Hollow Point	22	
R9MM3†	115 gr.	Metal Case	22	
R9MM2	124 gr.	Metal Case	23	

50 in a box, 500 in a case.

38 S & W

No.	Bullet weight	Bullet style	Wt. case, lbs.	Per box
R38SW	146 gr.	Lead	16	

50 in a box, 500 in a case.

REMINGTON CENTERFIRE PISTOL AND REVOLVER CARTRIDGES

38 Special

No.	Bullet weight	Bullet style	Wt. case, lbs.	Per box
R38S1	95 gr.	Semi-Jacketed Hollow Point (+P)	13	
R38S10	110 gr.	Semi-Jacketed Hollow Point (+P)	13	
R38S2	125 gr.	Semi-Jacketed Hollow Point (+P)	17	
R38S13	125 gr.	Semi-Jacketed Soft Point (+P)	17	
R38S3	148 gr.	Targetmaster Lead Wadcutter, brass case	17	
R38S4	158 gr.	Targetmaster Lead Round Nose	18	
R38S5 ..	158 gr.	Lead	18	
R38S6	158 gr.	Lead Semi-Wadcutter	18	
R38S14	158 gr.	Lead Semi-Wadcutter (+P)	18	
R38S7	158 gr.	Metal Point	18	
R38S8	158 gr.	Lead (+P)	18	
R38S12	158 gr.	Jacketed Hollow Point (+P)	18	
R38S9	200 gr.	Lead	21	

50 in a box, 500 in a case.

38 Short Colt

No.	Bullet weight	Bullet style	Wt. case, lbs.	Per box
R38SC	125 gr.	Lead	14	

50 in a box, 500 in a case.

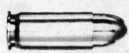

38 Super Auto. Colt Pistol

Adapted only for 38 Colt Super and Colt Commander Automatic Pistols.

No.	Bullet weight	Bullet style	Wt. case, lbs.	Per box
R38SU1	115 gr.	Jacketed Hollow Point (+P)	14	
R38SUP	130 gr.	Metal Case (+P)	16	

50 in a box, 500 in a case.

38 Auto. Colt Pistol

Adapted only for 38 Colt Sporting, Military and Pocket Model Automatic Pistols.

No.	Bullet weight	Bullet style	Wt. case, lbs.	Per box
R38ACP	130 gr.	Metal Case	16	

50 in a box, 500 in a case.
(Subject to stock on hand)

(+P) Ammunition with (+P) on the case headstamp is loaded to higher pressure. Use only in firearms designated for this cartridge and so recommended by the gun manufacturer.

380 Auto. Pistol

No.	Bullet weight	Bullet style	Wt. case, lbs.	Per box
R380A1	88 gr.	Jacketed Hollow Point	12	
R380AP	95 gr.	Metal Case	12	

50 in a box, 500 in a case.

41 Remington Magnum

No.	Bullet weight	Bullet style	Wt. case, lbs.	Per box
R41MG3†	170 gr.	Semi-Jacketed Hollow Point	24	
R41MG1	210 gr.	Soft Point	26	
R41MG2	210 gr.	Lead	26	

50 in a box, 500 in a case.

44 S&W Special

No.	Bullet weight	Bullet style	Wt. case, lbs.	Per box
R44SW1	200 gr.	Lead Semi-Wadcutter	22	
R44SW	246 gr.	Lead	25	

50 in a box, 500 in a case.

44 Remington Magnum

No.	Bullet weight	Bullet style	Wt. case, lbs.	Per box
R44MG5	180 gr.	Semi-Jacketed Hollow Point	29	
R44MG6†	210 gr.	Semi-Jacketed Hollow Point	27	
R44MG1	240 gr.	Lead, Gas-Check	29	
R44MG4	240 gr.	Lead	29	
R44MG2	240 gr.	Soft Point	29	
R44MG3	240 gr.	Semi-Jacketed Hollow Point	29	

20 in a box, 500 in a case.

45 Colt

No.	Bullet weight	Bullet style	Wt. case, lbs.	Per box
R45C1	225 gr.	Lead Semi-Wadcutter	24	
R45C	250 gr.	Lead	26	

50 in a box, 500 in a case.

REMINGTON CENTERFIRE PISTOL AND REVOLVER CARTRIDGES

45 Auto.

No.	Bullet weight	Bullet style	Wt. case, lbs.	Per box
R45AP1	185 gr.	Targetmaster Metal Case Wadcutter	11	
R45AP2	185 gr.	Jacketed Hollow Point	11	
R45AP4	230 gr.	Metal Case	13	

50 in a box, 500 in a case.

45 Auto. Rim

No.	Bullet weight	Bullet style	Wt. case, lbs.	Per box
R45AR	230 gr.	Lead	27	

50 in a box, 500 in a case.

REMINGTON CENTER FIRE BLANK

No.	Caliber	No. in case	Wt. case, lbs.	Per box
R32BLNK	32 S & W	500	4	
R38SWBL	38 S & W	500	7	
R38BLNK	38 Special	500	7	

50 in a box.

.45 Auto Shot Cartridge

No.	Bullet style	Wt. case, lbs.	Per box
R45AP5	650 Pellets—No. 12 Shot	18	

20 in a box, 500 in a case.

REMINGTON RIMFIRE CARTRIDGES

"HIGH VELOCITY" CARTRIDGES with "Golden" Bullets

22 Short

No.	Bullet weight and style	Wt. case, lbs.	Per box
1022	29 gr., Lead	29	
1122	27 gr., Lead, Hollow Point	28	

50 in a box, 5,000 in a case.

22 Long

No.	Bullet weight and style	Wt. case, lbs.	Per box
1322	29 gr., Lead	31	

50 in a box, 5,000 in a case.

22 Long Rifle

No.	Bullet weight and style	Wt. case, lbs.	Per box
1522	40 gr., Lead	40	
1622	36 gr., Lead, Hollow Point	38	

50 in a box, 5,000 in a case.

"TARGET" STANDARD VELOCITY CARTRIDGES

22 Short

No.	Bullet weight and style	Wt. case, lbs.	Per box
5522	29 gr., Lead	29	

50 in a box, 5,000 in a case.

22 Long Rifle

No.	Bullet weight and style	Wt. case, lbs.	Per box
6122	40 gr., Lead	40	

50 in a box, 5,000 in a case.

.22 Long Rifle, Target
100 pack.

No.	Bullet weight and style	Wt. case, lbs.	Per box
6100	40 gr., Lead	40	

100 in a box, 5,000 in a case.

CBee 22 CARTRIDGES†
Low Noise Level

Velocity of 720 f.p.s.; the quietness of an airgun, the impact of a .22 bullet.

22 Short

22 Long

No.	Bullet weight and style	Wt. case, lbs.	Per box
CB-22S Short	30 gr. Lead	29	
CB-22L Long	30 gr. Lead	30	

50 in a box, 5,000 in a case.

"YELLOW JACKET" CARTRIDGES
Hyper-Velocity

22 Long Rifle

No.	Bullet weight and style	Wt. case, lbs.	Per box
1722	33 gr. Truncated Cone, Hollow Point	36	

50 in a box, 5,000 in a case.

"VIPER" CARTRIDGES
Hyper-Velocity

22 Long Rifle

No.	Bullet weight and style	Wt. case, lbs.	Per box
1922	36 gr. Truncated Cone, Solid Point, Copper Plated	38	

50 in a box, 5,000 in a case.

"THUNDERBOLT" CARTRIDGES
Hi-Speed

22 Long Rifle

No.	Bullet weight and style	Wt. case, lbs.	Per box
TB22A	36 gr. Truncated Cone, Solid Point	40	

50 in a box, 5,000 in a case.

REMINGTON SHOTGUN SHELLS

REMINGTON "SPECIAL PURPOSE" MULTIRANGE "DUPLEX" SHOTSHELLS

REMINGTON "DUPLEX" SHOTGUN SHELL

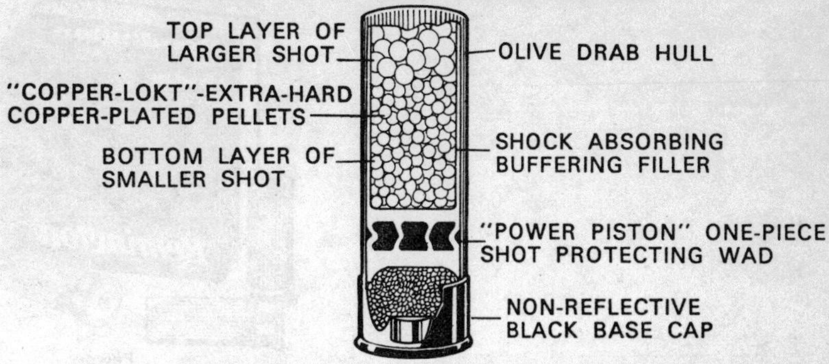

TOP LAYER OF LARGER SHOT — OLIVE DRAB HULL

"COPPER-LOKT"-EXTRA-HARD COPPER-PLATED PELLETS

BOTTOM LAYER OF SMALLER SHOT

SHOCK ABSORBING BUFFERING FILLER

"POWER PISTON" ONE-PIECE SHOT PROTECTING WAD

NON-REFLECTIVE BLACK BASE CAP

Combined large and smaller shot sizes. Available in lead or steel shot magnum loads.

Olive drab hull, non-reflective black base cap. Power-Piston wads. Shock absorbing buffering filler.

	No.	Gauge	Length shell, in.	Powder equiv. drams	Shot, oz.	Size shot	Wt. case, lbs.	Per box
MULTIRANGE DUPLEX MAGNUM COPPER PLATED LEAD SHOT	MRP12S	12	2¾	Max.	1½	BBx4, 2x4†, 2x6 4x6†	35	
	MRP12H	12	3	Max.	1⅞	BBx4, 2x4†, 2x6 4x6†	41	
MULTIRANGE DUPLEX MAGNUM STEEL SHOT	MRS12	12	2¾	Max.	1⅛	BBx1†, BBx2, BBx4, 2x6, 1x3†	29	
	MRS12H	12	3	Max.	1¼	BBx1†, BBx2, BBx4, 2x6, 1x3†	29	

10 in a box, 250 in a case.

REMINGTON "PREMIER" HIGHEST GRADE SHOTSHELLS WITH "COPPER-LOKT" EXTRA HARD PLATED SHOT AND "POWER-PISTON" WADS

	No.	Gauge	Length shell, in.	Powder equiv. drams	Shot, oz.	Size shot		Wt. case, lbs.	Per box
PREMIER™ EXTENDED RANGE BUFFERED MAGNUM LOADS	PR12S Mag.	12	2¾	Max.	1½	BB, 2,	4, 6	34	
	PR12 Mag.	12	3	4	1⅝		4, 6	37	
	PR12H Mag.	12	3	Max.	1⅞	BB, 2,	4	41	
	PR20S Mag.	20	2¾	Max.	1⅛		4, 6	26	
	PR20H Mag.	20	3	Max.	1¼	2,	4, 6	30	
PREMIER™ EXTRA LONG RANGE LOADS	PR12	12	2¾	3¾	1¼	2, 4,	6, 7½	29	
	PR20	20	2¾	2¾	1		4, 6	24	
PREMIER™ "POWER-PATTERN" FIELD LOADS	PR12F	12	2¾	3¼	1⅛		7½, 8	29	
	PR12HF	12	2¾	3¼	1¼		7½, 8	29	
	PR20F	20	2¾	2½	1		7½, 8	23	

25 in a box, 250 in a case.

REMINGTON SHOTGUN SHELLS

REMINGTON "PREMIER" TARGET LOADS

	No.	Gauge	Length shell, in.	Powder equiv. drams	Shot oz.	Size shot	Wt. case, lbs.	Per box
PREMIER TARGET LOADS	RTL12L•	12	2¾	2¾	1⅛	7½, 8, 8½, 9	27	
	RTL12M•	12	2¾	•3	1⅛	7½, 8, 9	27	
	RTL20	20	2¾	2½	⅞	9	41	
SKEET LOADS	SP28	28	2¾	2	¾	9	37	
	SP410	410	2½	Max.	½	9	22	
PREMIER PIGEON LOADS	RTL12P•†	12	2¾	3¼	1¼	7½, 8	27	
	RTL12PN•†	12	2¾	3¼	1¼	7½, 8 (nickel)	27	
PREMIER INTERNATIONAL TARGET LOADS	IRT12†	12	2¾	3¼	1⅛	7½, 8	54	
	NIRT12†	12	2¾	3¼	1⅛	7½, 8 (nickel)	54	

• Packed 25 in a box, 250 per case.

25 in a box, 500 in a case.

REMINGTON PROMOTIONAL SHOTSHELLS

	No.	Gauge	Length shell, in.	Powder equiv. drams	Shot oz.	Size shot	Wt. case, lbs.	Per box
DOVE/QUAIL FIELD LOADS	DQ12	12	2¾	3¼	1	7½, 8	48	
	DQ16	16	2¾	2½	1	7½, 8	47	
	DQ20	20	2¾	2½	⅞	7½, 8	41	
RABBIT/SQUIRREL FIELD LOADS	RS12	12	2¾	3¼	1	6	48	
	RS16	16	2¾	2½	1	6	47	
	RS20	20	2¾	2½	1	6	46	
DUCK/PHEASANT FIELD LOADS	DP12	12	2¾	3¾	1¼	4, 5, 6, 7½	58	
	DP16	16	2¾	3¼	1⅛	4, 6, 7½	52	
	DP20	20	2¾	2⅔	1	4, 6, 7½	46	
SPORT LOADS	SL12†	12	2¾	3¼	1	8	26	
	SL20†	20	2¾	2½	⅞	8	26	

25 in a box, 500 in a case.

REMINGTON SHOTGUN SHELLS

REMINGTON "NITRO MAGNUM," "EXPRESS" AND "SHUR SHOT" SHOTSHELLS

	No.	Gauge	Length shell, in.	Powder equiv. drams	Shot, oz.	Size shot		Wt. case, lbs.
NITRO MAGNUM™	SP12SNM●	12	2¾	Max.	1½	BB, 2, 4, 5, 6		34
EXTENDED RANGE	SP12NM●	12	3	4	1⅝	2, 4, 6		35
BUFFERED	SP12HNM●	12	3	Max.	1⅞	BB, 2, 4		35
MAGNUMS	SP20SNM●	20	2¾	Max.	1⅛	4, 6, 7½		26
	SP20HNM●	20	3	Max.	1¼	2, 4, 6, 7½		30
	SP10MAG	10	3½	Max.	2	BB, 2, 4		72
	SP12	12	2¾	3¾	1¼	BB, 2, 4, 5, 6, 7½,	9	58
"EXPRESS"	SP16	16	2¾	3¼	1⅛	4, 5, 6, 7½,	9	52
LONG RANGE	SP16CMAG	16	2¾	Max.	1¼	2, 4, 6		58
LOADS	SP20	20	2¾	2¾	1	4, 5, 6, 7½,	9	47
	SP28	28	2¾	2¼	¾	6, 7½		36
	SP410	410	2½	Max.	½	4, 6, 7½		23
	SP4103	410	3	Max.	11⁄16	4, 5, 6, 7½,	9	31
	R12H	12	2¾	3¼	1⅛	4, 5, 6,	9	51
"SHUR SHOT"	R12H250CS●	12	2¾	3¼	1⅛	7½, 8		29
FIELD	RP12H250CS●	12	2¾	3¼	1¼	7½, 8		30
LOADS	R16H	16	2¾	2¾	1⅛	4, 6, 7½, 8, 9		51
	R20M	20	2¾	2½	1	4, 5, 6,	9	45
	R20M250CS●	20	2¾	2½	1	7½, 8		23

● Packed 250 per case.

25 in a box, 500 in a case.

REMINGTON STEEL SHOT WATERFOWL LOADS

REMINGTON STEEL SHOT WATERFOWL LOADS

	No.	Gauge	Length shell, in.	Powder equiv. drams	Shot, oz.	Size shot	Wt. case, lbs.
STEEL SHOT	STL10MAG†	10	3½	Max.	1¾	BB, 1, 2, 3	35
WATERFOWL	STL12	12	2¾	Max.	1⅛	BB, 1, 2, 3†, 4, 6	28
LOADS	STL12SMAG	12	2¾	Max.	1¼	1, 2, 3†, 4	30
	STL12MAG	12	3	Max.	1¼	BB, 1, 2, 3†, 4, 6	30
	STL20HMAG	20	3	Max.	1	2, 3†, 4, 6	23

Packed 25 in a box, 250 per case.

REMINGTON SHOTGUN SHELLS

REMINGTON "PREMIER" MAGNUM BUCKSHOT WITH EXTRA HARD NICKEL PLATED SHOT

Nickel plated extra-hard buckshot and granulated polyethylene filler for reduced deformation and improved pattern.

	No.	Gauge	Length shell, in.	Powder equiv. drams	Size shot	Pellets	Wt. case, lbs.	Per box
PREMIER™	P12SN00	12	2¾	4	00	12	29	
MAGNUM	P12SN4	12	2¾	4	4	34	31	
EXTENDED RANGE	P12N000	12	3	4	000	10	40	
BUCKSHOT WITH	P12N00	12	3	4	00	15	40	
NICKEL PLATED	P12N1	12	3	Max.	1	24	40	
SHOT†	P12N4	12	3	4	4	41	42	

Packed 10 in a box, 5 boxes per merchandiser, 250 rds. per case.

REMINGTON "EXPRESS" BUCKSHOT LOADS AND "SLUGGER" RIFLED SLUGS

	No.	Gauge	Length shell, in.	Powder equiv. drams	Shot, oz.	Size shot	Wt. case, lbs.	Per box
	SP12BK	12	2¾	3¾	...	000 Buck—— 8 Pellets	31	
	SP12BK	12	2¾	3¾	...	00 Buck—— 9 Pellets	29	
"Power Pakt"	SP12BK	12	2¾	3¾	...	0 Buck—12 Pellets	32	
"EXPRESS"	SP12BK	12	2¾	3¾	...	1 Buck—16 Pellets	32	
BUCKSHOT LOADS	SP12BK	12	2¾	3¾	...	4 Buck—27 Pellets	31	
	SP16BK	16	2¾	3	...	1 Buck—12 Pellets	26	
	SP20BK	20	2¾	2¾	...	3 Buck—20 Pelelts	24	
"Power Pkt"	SP12SMagBK	12	2¾	4	...	00 Buck—12 Pellets	34	
"EXPRESS"	SP12SMagBK	12	2¾	4	...	1 Buck—20 Pellets	34	
MAGNUM	SP12HMagBK	12	3	4	...	000 Buck—10 Pellets	40	
BUCKSHOT LOADS	SP12HMagBK	12	3	4	...	00 Buck—15 Pellets	40	
	SP12HMagBK	12	3	4	...	1 Buck—24 Pellets	40	
	SP12HMagBK	12	3	4	...	4 Buck—41 Pellets	42	
"SLUGGER" MAGNUM	SP12SMagRS†	12	2¾	Max.	1	Rifled Slug	26	
RIFLED SLUG LOADS	SP12MagRS†	12	3	Max.	1	Rifled Slug	26	
	SP12RS	12	2¾	Max.	1	Rifled Slug H.P.	26	
	SP12SRS	12	2¾	Max.	1	Rifled Slug H.P.	26	
"SLUGGER"	SP12MRS	12	3	Max.	1	Rifled Slug H.P.	26	
RIFLED SLUG	SP16RS	16	2¾	3	⅘	Rifled Slug H.P.	24	
LOADS	SP20RS	20	2¾	2¾	⅝	Rifled Slug H.P.	19	
	SP410RS	410	2½	Max.	⅕	Rifled Slug	8	

Packed 5 in a box, 250 per case.

WINCHESTER AMMUNITION

Centerfire Pistol/Revolver Cartridges
Packaged 50 per Box unless noted—Smokeless Powder—Staynless Non-Corrosive Priming.

WINCHESTER SYMBOL	CARTRIDGE	CASE CONTAINS M'S	BOXES PER CASE	APPROX. CASE WT. LBS.	SUGGESTED RETAIL PRICE PER M	PER CASE	PER BOX
	25 Automatic (6.35mm)						
X25AXP	45 gr. Expanding Point SUPER-X**	2	40	23	276.60	553.20	13.83
X25AP	50 gr. Full Metal Case SUPER-X	2	40	24	255.90	511.80	12.80
	30 Luger (7.65mm)						
X30LP	93 gr. Full Metal Case SUPER-X	½	10	12	465.00	232.50	23.25
	30 Carbine						
X30M1	110 gr. Hollow Soft Point SUPER-X	1	20	29	419.70	419.70	20.98
X30M2	110 gr. Full Metal Case SUPER-X	1	20	29	419.70	419.70	20.98
	32 Smith & Wesson						
X32SWP	85 gr. Lead Round Nose SUPER-X	2	40	39	246.60	493.20	12.33
	32 Smith & Wesson Long (Colt New Police)						
X32SWLP	98 gr. Lead Round Nose SUPER-X	2	40	45	260.40	520.80	13.02
	32 Short Colt						
X32SCP	80 gr. Lead Round Nose SUPER-X	½	10	9	244.80	122.40	12.24
	32 Long Colt						
X32LCP	82 gr. Lead Round Nose SUPER-X	½	10	10	255.90	127.95	12.80
	32 Automatic						
X32ASHP	60 gr. Silvertip Hollow Point SUPER-X	2	40	33	340.50	681.00	17.03
X32AP	71 gr. Full Metal Case SUPER-X	2	40	35	293.40	586.80	14.67
	38 Smith & Wesson						
X38SWP	145 gr. Lead Round Nose SUPER-X	2	40	66	274.50	549.00	13.73
	380 Automatic						
X380ASHP	85 gr. Silvertip Hollow Point SUPER-X	2	40	46	349.50	699.00	17.48
X380AP	95 gr. Full Metal Case SUPER-X	2	40	43	299.40	598.80	14.97
	38 Special						
X38S9HP	110 gr. Silvertip Hollow Point SUPER-X	2	40	57	405.00	810.00	20.25
X38S1P	158 gr. Lead Round Nose SUPER-X	2	40	71	276.00	552.00	13.80
X38WCPSV	158 gr. Lead Semi-Wad Cutter SUPER-X	2	40	72	287.10	574.20	14.36
X38S2P	158 gr. Metal Point SUPER-X	2	40	71	351.00	702.00	17.55
	38 Special+P						
X38SSHP	95 gr. Silvertip Hollow Point SUPER-X+P	2	40	56	405.00	810.00	20.25
X38S6PH	110 gr. Jacketed Hollow Point SUPER-X+P	2	40	62	349.50	699.00	17.48
X38S7PH	125 gr. Jacketed Hollow Point SUPER-X+P	2	40	67	349.50	699.00	17.48
X38S8HP	125 gr. Silvertip Hollow Point SUPER-X+P	2	40	66	405.00	810.00	20.25
X38SPD	158 gr. Lead Hollow Point SUPER-X+P	2	40	74	299.40	598.80	14.97
X38WCP	158 gr. Lead Semi-Wad Cutter SUPER-X+P	2	40	74	305.70	611.40	15.29
	38 Special Match						
X38SMRP	148 gr. Lead Mid-Range (Clean Cutting) Match	2	40	65	287.10	574.20	14.36
	9mm Luger (Parabellum)						
X9LP	115 gr. Full Metal Case SUPER-X	2	40	57	363.60	727.20	18.18
X9MMSHP	115 gr. Silvertip Hollow Point SUPER-X	2	40	56	421.50	843.00	21.08
	38 Super Automatic+P (For use only in 38 Super Automatic Pistols.)						
X38ASHP	125 gr. Silvertip Hollow Point SUPER-X+P	2	40	63	388.50	777.00	19.43
X38A1P	130 gr. Full Metal Case SUPER-X+P	2	40	63	316.80	633.60	15.84
	38 Automatic (For all 38 Automatic Pistols)						
X38A2P	130 gr. Full Metal Case SUPER-X	2	40	62	326.10	652.20	16.31
	357 Magnum						
X3573P	110 gr. Jacketed Hollow Point SUPER-X............	2	40	64	383.70	767.40	19.19
X3576P	125 gr. Jacketed Hollow Point SUPER-X............	2	40	72	383.70	767.40	19.19
X357SHP	145 gr. Silvertip Hollow Point SUPER-X	2	40	75	444.00	888.00	22.20
X3571P	158 gr. Lead Semi-Wad Cutter SUPER-X**	2	40	79	324.60	649.20	16.23
X3574P	158 gr. Jacketed Hollow Point SUPER-X............	2	40	79	383.70	767.40	19.19
X3575P	158 gr. Jacketed Soft Point SUPER-X	2	40	80	383.70	767.40	19.19

**Lubaloy coated
+P = Ammunition with (+P) on the case head stamp is loaded to higher pressure. Use only in firearms designated for this cartridge and so recommended by the gun manufacturer.

WINCHESTER AMMUNITION

Shotshells—Staynless Non-Corrosive Priming.

WINCHESTER SYMBOL	GAUGE	LENGTH OF SHELL INCHES	POWDER DRAM EQUIV.	OZ. SHOT	SHOT SIZES	APPROX. CASE WT. LBS.	CASES PER PALLET	NET WEIGHT PER PALLET	PER M	PER CASE	PER BOX
Super-X Game Loads—Packed 25 per Box, 500 per Case											
X12	12	2¾	3¾	1¼	2,4,5,6,7½,9	56	60	3360	394.20	197.10	9.86
X16H	16	2¾	3¼	1⅛	4,6,7½	49	64	3136	378.60	189.30	9.47
X20	20	2¾	2¾	1	4,5,6,7½,9	44	80	3520	346.80	173.40	8.67
X28	28	2¾	2¼	¾	6,7½	34	90	3060	349.80	174.90	8.75
X41	410	2½	Max.	½	4,6,7½	23	161	3703	276.60	138.30	6.92
X413	410	3	Max.	11/16	4,6,7½	29	108	3132	325.80	162.90	8.15
Double X Magnum Game Loads—Copperplated, Buffered Shot—Packed 25 per Box, 250 per Case unless noted											
X103XC	10	3½	4½	2¼	BB,2,4	47	60	2820	995.40	248.85	24.89
X123XC	12	3	4	1⅞	BB,2,4,6	39	84	3276	621.60	155.40	15.54
•X123XCT	12	3	4	1⅞	4,6	40	84	3318	652.50	163.12	6.53
X12MXC	12	3	4	1⅝	2,4,5,6..........	39	84	3276	574.80	143.70	14.37
•X123MXCT* **NEW**	12	3	Max.	2	4,5,6	40	84	3360	687.00	171.75	6.87
X12XC	12	2¾	Max.	1½	BB,2,4,5,6	32	105	3360	519.60	129.90	12.99
•X12XCT	12	2¾	3¾	1½	4,6	33	84	2730	546.00	136.50	5.46
X16XC	16	2¾	3¼	1¼	2,4,6	27	112	3024	511.20	127.80	12.78
X203XC	20	3	3	1¼	2,4,6	26	84	2184	481.20	120.30	12.03
X20XC	20	2¾	2¾	1⅛	4,6,7½	26	112	2688	426.00	106.50	10.65
Xpert Field Loads—Packed 25 per Box, 500 per Case											
WW12SP	12	2¾	3¼	1¼	6,7½,8	56	60	3360	334.20	167.10	8.36
UWH12	12	2¾	3¼	1⅛	6,7½,8,9	50	60	3000	305.40	152.70	7.64
UWL12	12	2¾	3¼	1	6,7½,8	46	60	2760	272.40	136.20	6.81
UWH16#	16	2¾	2¾	1⅛	6,7½,8	50	64	3200	305.40	152.70	7.64
UWH20#	20	2¾	2½	1	6,7½,8,9	43	80	3440	286.20	143.10	7.16
UWL20	20	2¾	2½	⅞	6,7½,8	40	80	3200	272.40	136.20	6.81
Super-X Buckshot Loads with Buffered Shot—5 Round Pack—Packed 250 Rounds per Case unless noted											
X12000B5	12	2¾	8 Pellets		000 Buck	32	54	1728	573.00	143.25	2.87
X12RB▷	12	2¾	9 Pellets		00 Buck	52	60	3120	572.40	286.20	14.31
X12RB5	12	2¾	9 Pellets		00 Buck	27	54	1458	573.00	143.25	2.87
X120B5	12	2¾	12 Pellets		0 Buck	32	54	1728	573.00	143.25	2.87
X121B5	12	2¾	16 Pellets		1 Buck	33	54	1782	573.00	143.25	2.87
X124B5	12	2¾	27 Pellets		4 Buck	29	54	1566	573.00	143.25	2.87
X16B5	16	2¾	12 Pellets		1 Buck	26	91	2366	573.00	143.25	2.87
X20B5	20	2¾	20 Pellets		3 Buck	24	104	2496	573.00	143.25	2.87
Double X Magnum Buckshot Loads—Copperplated, Buffered Shot—5 Round Pack—Packed 250 Rounds per Case											
X10C4B	10	3½	54 Pellets		4 Buck	51	56	2856	1134.00	283.50	5.67
X123C000B	12	3	10 Pellets		000 Buck	35	54	1890	810.00	202.50	4.05
X12XC3B5	12	3	15 Pellets		00 Buck	39	54	2106	810.00	202.50	4.05
X12XC0B5	12	2¾	12 Pellets		00 Buck	33	54	1782	699.00	174.75	3.50
X12C1B	12	2¾	20 Pellets		1 Buck	38	54	2052	699.00	174.75	3.50
X12XCMB5	12	3	41 Pellets		4 Buck	38	54	2052	810.00	202.50	4.05
X12XC4B5	12	2¾	34 Pellets		4 Buck	33	54	1782	699.00	174.75	3.50
Super-X Hollow Point Rifled Slug Loads—5 Round Pack—Packed 250 Rounds per Case											
X12RS15	12	2¾	Max.	1	Rifled Slug	26	63	1638	651.00	162.75	3.26
X16RS5	16	2¾	Max.	4/5	Rifled Slug	21	117	2457	651.00	162.75	3.26
X20RSM5	20	2¾	Max.	¾	Rifled Slug	19	117	2223	603.00	150.75	3.02
X41RS5	410	2½	Max.	⅕	Rifled Slug	8	198	1584	573.00	143.25	2.87
Super Steel Non-Toxic Game Loads—Packed 25 per Box, 500 per Case—Boldface indicates new shot size for 1988											
W12SD	12	2¾	Max.	1	2,4,6,**7**	46	60	2760	435.00	217.50	10.88
X12SSL	12	2¾	Max.	1⅛	1,2,3,4,**5**,6,**7**	52	60	3120	496.20	248.10	12.41
X20SSL	20	2¾	Max.	¾	4,6,**7**	36	80	2880	447.60	223.80	11.19
Super Steel Non-Toxic Magnum Loads—Packed 25 per Box, 250 per Case—Boldface indicates new shot size for 1988											
X10SSM	10	3½	Max.	1¾	BB,2	39	60	2340	841.80	210.45	21.05
X12SSM	12	3	Max.	1⅜	BB,1,2,3,4	33	84	2772	588.60	147.15	14.72
X123SSM	12	3	Max.	1¼	BB,1,2,3,4,**5**,F...	32	84	2688	540.60	135.15	13.52
X12SSF▷	12	2¾	Max.	1¼	BB,1,2,3,4,**5**,6 ...	56	60	3360	540.60	270.30	13.52
X20SSM	20	3	Max.	1	2,3,4,**5**,6	24	84	2016	474.00	118.50	11.85

#Loads with 7½ or 8 shot recommended for trap shooting   •Packaged in 10 Round Trebark camouflage packaging, 250 per Case
* Available first quarter, 1988   ▷Packed 25 Rounds per Box, 500 Rounds per Case
Applicable Federal Excise Tax Included

Ballistics

FEDERAL BALLISTICS

PREMIUM CENTERFIRE CARTRIDGE BALLISTICS (Approximate)

Federal Load No.	Caliber	Bullet Wgt. in Grains	Bullet Style	Velocity—In Feet Per Second						Energy—In Foot/Pounds					
				Muzzle	100 Yds	200 Yds	300 Yds	400 Yds	500 Yds	Muzzle	100 Yds	200 Yds	300 Yds	400 Yds	500 Yds
P22250B	22-250 Remington	55	Boat-tail H.P.	3680	3280	2920	2590	2280	1990	1655	1315	1040	815	630	480
New P6C	6mm Remington	100	Nosler Partition	3100	2830	2570	2330	2100	1890	2135	1775	1470	1205	985	790
P243C	243 Winchester	100	Boat-tail S.P.	2960	2760	2570	2380	2210	2040	1950	1690	1460	1260	1080	925
P243D	243 Winchester	85	Boat-tail H.P.	3320	3070	2830	2600	2380	2180	2080	1770	1510	1280	1070	890
P257B	257 Roberts (Hi-Vel. + P)	120	Nosler Partition	2780	2560	2360	2160	1970	1790	2060	1750	1480	1240	1030	855
P2506C	25-'06 Remington	117	Boat-tail S.P.	2990	2770	2570	2370	2190	2000	2320	2000	1715	1465	1240	1045
P270C	270 Winchester	150	Boat-tail S.P.	2850	2660	2480	2300	2130	1970	2705	2355	2040	1760	1510	1290
P270D	270 Winchester	130	Boat-tail S.P.	3060	2830	2620	2410	2220	2030	2700	2320	1980	1680	1420	1190
P270E	270 Winchester	150	Nosler Partition	2850	2590	2340	2100	1880	1670	2705	2225	1815	1470	1175	930
New P7C	7mm Mauser	140	Nosler Partition	2660	2450	2260	2070	1890	1730	2200	1865	1585	1330	1110	930
New P280A	280 Remington	150	Nosler Partition	2890	2620	2370	2140	1910	1710	2780	2295	1875	1520	1215	970
P7RD	7mm Remington Magnum	150	Boat-tail S.P.	3110	2920	2750	2580	2410	2250	3220	2850	2510	2210	1930	1690
P7RE	7mm Remington Magnum	165	Boat-tail S.P.	2950	2800	2650	2510	2370	2230	3190	2865	2570	2300	2050	1825
P7RF	7mm Remington Magnum	160	Nosler Partition	2950	2730	2520	2320	2120	1940	3090	2650	2250	1910	1600	1340
P7RG	7mm Remington Magnum	140	Nosler Partition	3150	2920	2700	2500	2300	2110	3085	2650	2270	1940	1640	1380
P3030D	30-30 Winchester	170	Nosler Partition	2200	1900	1620	1380	1190	1060	1830	1355	990	720	535	425
P3006D	30-06 Springfield	165	Boat-tail S.P.	2800	2610	2420	2240	2070	1910	2870	2490	2150	1840	1580	1340
P3006F	30-06 Springfield	180	Nosler Partition	2700	2470	2250	2040	1850	1660	2910	2440	2020	1670	1360	1110
P3006G	30-06 Springfield	150	Boat-tail S.P.	2910	2690	2480	2270	2070	1880	2820	2420	2040	1710	1430	1180
New P3006L	30-06 Springfield	180	Boat-tail S.P.	2700	2540	2380	2220	2080	1930	2915	2570	2260	1975	1720	1495
P308C	308 Winchester	165	Boat-tail S.P.	2700	2520	2330	2160	1990	1830	2670	2310	1990	1700	1450	1230
P300WC	300 Winchester Magnum	200	Boat-tail S.P.	2830	2680	2530	2380	2240	2110	3560	3180	2830	2520	2230	1970
P300WD	300 Winchester Magnum	180	Nosler Partition	2960	2750	2540	2340	2160	1980	3500	3010	2580	2195	1860	1565
P338A	338 Winchester Magnum	210	Nosler Partition	2830	2590	2370	2150	1940	1750	3735	3130	2610	2155	1760	1435
P338B	338 Winchester Magnum	250	Nosler Partition	2660	2400	2150	1910	1690	1500	3925	3185	2555	2025	1590	1245

Ballistic specifications are derived from test barrels 24 inches in length.

SIGHTING-IN INFORMATION (Approximate)

Trajectory figures show the height of bullet impact above or below the line of sight at the indicated yardages. Aim low indicated amount for + figures and high for − figures. Zero ranges indicated by circled crosses.

Bullet Drop — In Inches From Bore Line

Load No.	100 Yds	200 Yds	300 Yds	400 Yds	500 Yds
P22250B	1.4	6.0	14.7	28.7	49.4
P6C	1.9	8.2	19.8	37.7	63.6
P243C	2.0	8.5	20.3	38.2	63.2
P243D	1.6	6.9	16.5	31.2	52.1
P257B	2.4	10.1	24.0	45.5	75.9
P2506C	2.0	8.6	20.5	38.5	63.8
P270C	2.2	9.4	22.3	41.7	68.8
P270D	2.0	8.2	19.6	37.0	61.4
P270E	2.3	9.8	23.7	45.5	77.2
P7C	2.7	10.9	26.3	50.0	81.9
P280A	2.2	9.5	23.0	44.1	74.8
P7RD	1.8	7.6	18.0	33.6	55.2
P7RE	2.1	8.6	20.1	37.1	60.4
P7RF	2.1	8.8	20.9	40.2	66.5
P7RG	1.8	7.8	18.5	34.7	57.6
P3030D	4.0	17.7	44.8	90.3	160.2
P3006D	2.2	9.5	22.7	42.8	71.0
P3006F	2.5	10.8	25.9	49.4	83.2
P3006G	2.0	8.9	21.4	40.7	68.0
P3006L	2.5	10.4	24.5	45.6	74.8
P308C	2.4	10.2	24.5	46.3	76.8
P300WC	2.1	9.0	21.4	39.9	65.3
P300WD	2.1	8.8	20.9	39.4	65.3
P338A	2.3	9.8	23.5	44.8	75.3
P338B	2.6	11.4	27.7	53.6	91.5

Drift in Inches — In 10 mph Crosswind

Load No.	100 Yds	200 Yds	300 Yds	400 Yds	500 Yds
P22250B	0.8	3.6	8.4	15.8	26.3
P6C	0.8	3.3	7.9	14.7	24.1
P243C	0.6	2.6	6.1	11.3	18.4
P243D	0.7	2.7	6.3	11.6	18.8
P257B	0.8	3.3	7.7	14.3	23.5
P2506C	0.7	2.8	6.5	12.0	19.6
P270C	0.7	2.7	6.3	11.6	18.9
P270D	0.7	2.8	6.6	12.1	19.7
P270E	0.9	3.9	9.2	17.3	28.5
P7C	1.3	3.2	8.2	15.4	23.4
P280A	0.9	3.8	9.0	16.8	27.8
P7RD	0.5	2.2	5.1	9.3	15.0
P7RE	0.5	2.0	4.6	8.4	13.5
P7RF	0.8	3.3	7.7	14.1	23.4
P7RG	0.6	2.7	6.2	11.5	18.7
P3030D	1.9	8.0	19.4	36.7	59.8
P3006D	0.7	2.8	6.6	12.3	19.9
P3006F	0.9	3.7	8.8	16.5	27.1
P3006G	0.7	3.0	7.1	13.4	22.0
P3006L	0.6	2.6	6.0	11.0	17.8
P308C	0.7	3.0	7.0	13.0	21.1
P300WC	0.5	2.2	5.0	9.2	14.9
P300WD	0.7	2.8	6.6	12.3	20.0
P338A	0.8	3.5	8.3	15.4	25.4
P338B	1.1	4.5	10.8	20.3	33.6

Short Range

Load No.	50 Yds	100 Yds	150 Yds	200 Yds	250 Yds	300 Yds
P22250B	+0.1	+0.5	⊕	−1.4	−3.8	−7.3
P6C	+0.4	+0.8	⊕	−1.9	−5.2	−9.9
P243C	+0.2	⊕	−0.9	−3.1	−6.5	−11.4
P243D	+0.1	⊕	−0.9	−2.8	−5.8	−9.9
P257B	+0.7	+1.0	⊕	−2.4	−6.4	−12.1
P2506C	+0.5	+0.8	⊕	−2.0	−5.4	−10.1
P270C	+0.6	+0.9	⊕	−2.2	−5.9	−11.0
P270D	+0.4	+0.8	⊕	−1.9	−5.1	−9.7
P270E	+0.6	+1.0	⊕	−2.4	−6.4	−12.2
P7C	+0.4	⊕	−1.5	−4.6	−9.9	−16.4
P280A	+0.6	+0.9	⊕	−2.3	−6.2	−11.8
P7RD	+0.4	+0.7	⊕	−1.8	−4.7	−8.8
P7RE	+0.5	+0.8	⊕	−2.0	−5.2	−9.9
P7RF	+0.5	+0.8	⊕	−2.3	−5.9	−11.1
P7RG	+0.4	+0.7	⊕	−1.8	−4.8	−9.0
P3030D	+0.6	⊕	−3.0	−8.9	−18.0	−31.1
P3006D	+0.5	⊕	−1.1	−4.2	−8.8	−14.3
P3006F	+0.2	⊕	−1.6	−4.8	−9.7	−16.5
P3006G	+0.2	⊕	−1.0	−3.3	−7.0	−12.3
P3006L	+1.3	+2.3	+1.8	⊕	−3.4	−8.4
P308C	+0.1	⊕	−1.3	−4.0	−8.4	−14.4
P300WC	+0.2	+0.7	⊕	−2.0	−5.3	−10.1
P300WD	+0.5	+0.8	⊕	−2.1	−5.5	−10.4
P338A	+0.6	+1.0	⊕	−2.4	−6.3	−11.9
P338B	+0.8	+1.2	⊕	−2.9	−7.6	−14.5

Long Range

Load No.	100 Yds	150 Yds	200 Yds	250 Yds	300 Yds	400 Yds	500 Yds
P22250B	+2.0	+2.3	+1.6	⊕	−2.8	−12.5	−28.9
P6C	+1.7	+1.5	⊕	−2.8	−7.0	−20.4	−41.7
P243C	+1.5	+1.4	⊕	−2.7	−6.8	−19.7	−39.7
P243D	+1.4	+1.2	⊕	−2.3	−5.8	−16.6	−33.6
P257B	+2.2	+1.8	⊕	−3.4	−8.5	−24.5	−49.4
P2506C	+1.8	+1.5	⊕	−2.8	−7.1	−20.4	−40.9
P270C	+2.0	+1.7	⊕	−3.1	−7.7	−22.0	−43.9
P270D	+1.7	+1.4	⊕	−2.7	−6.8	−19.6	−39.5
P270E	+2.2	+1.8	⊕	−3.4	−8.6	−25.0	−51.4
P7C	+2.4	+2.1	⊕	−3.2	−9.6	−27.3	−53.5
P280A	+2.1	+1.7	⊕	−3.3	−8.3	−24.2	−45.7
P7RD	+1.6	+1.3	⊕	−2.5	−6.2	−17.6	−35.0
P7RE	+1.8	+1.5	⊕	−2.7	−6.7	−19.0	−37.5
P7RF	+1.8	+1.6	⊕	−3.1	−7.7	−22.4	−44.5
P7RG	+1.6	+1.3	⊕	−2.5	−6.4	−18.3	−36.8
P3030D	+2.0	⊕	−4.8	−13.0	−25.1	−63.6	−126.7
P3006D	+2.1	+1.8	⊕	−3.0	−8.0	−22.9	−45.9
P3006F	+2.4	+2.0	⊕	−3.7	−9.3	−27.0	−54.9
P3006G	+1.7	+1.5	⊕	−2.9	−7.3	−21.4	−43.6
P3006L	+3.6	+3.9	+2.7	⊕	−4.4	−18.5	−40.7
P308C	+2.0	+1.7	⊕	−3.3	−8.4	−24.3	−48.9
P300WC	+1.7	+1.5	⊕	−2.8	−7.1	−20.3	−40.4
P300WD	+1.9	+1.6	⊕	−2.9	−7.3	−20.9	−41.9
P338A	+2.1	+1.8	⊕	−3.3	−8.4	−24.3	−49.5
P338B	+2.6	+2.1	⊕	−4.0	−10.2	−29.9	−61.8

Note: Ballistic specifications were derived from test barrels 24 inches in length. These trajectory tables were calculated by computer using a modern scientific technique to predict trajectories from available data for each round. Each trajectory is expected to be reasonably representative of the behavior of the ammunition at sea level conditions, but shooters are cautioned that trajectories may differ because of variations in ammunition, rifles, and atmospheric conditions.

FEDERAL BALLISTICS

Automatic Pistol Ballistics (Approximate)

Federal Load No.	Caliber	Bullet Style	Bullet Weight in Grains	Velocity in Feet Per Second Muzzle	50 yds.	Energy in Foot/Lbs. Muzzle	50 yds.	Mid-range Trajectory 50 yds.	Test Barrel Length
25AP	25 Auto Pistol (6.35mm)	Metal Case	50	760	730	64	59	1.8″	2″
32AP	32 Auto Pistol (7.65mm)	Metal Case	71	905	855	129	115	1.4″	4″
380AP	380 Auto Pistol	Metal Case	95	955	865	190	160	1.4″	3¾″
380BP	380 Auto Pistol	Hi-Shok Jacketed Hollow Point	90	1000	890	200	160	1.4″	3¾″
9AP	9mm Luger Auto Pistol	Metal Case	124	1120	1030	345	290	1.0″	4″
9BP	9mm Luger Auto Pistol	Hi-Shok Jacketed Hollow Point	115	1160	1060	345	285	0.9″	4″
9CP	9mm Luger Auto Pistol	Jacketed Soft Point	95	1300	1140	355	275	0.7″	4″
New 9MP	9mm Luger (Match)	Metal Case, S.W.C.	124	1120	1030	345	290	1.0″	4″
45A	45 Automatic (Match)	Metal Case	230	850	810	370	335	1.6″	5″
45B	45 Automatic (Match)	Metal Case, S.W.C.	185	775	695	247	200	2.0″	5″
45C	45 Automatic	Hi-Shok Jacketed Hollow Point	185	950	900	370	335	1.3″	5″

Revolver Ballistics (Approximate)

Federal Load No.	Caliber	Bullet Style	Bullet Weight in Grains	Velocity in Feet Per Second Muzzle	50 yds.	Energy in Foot/Lbs. Muzzle	50 yds.	Mid-range Trajectory 50 yds.	Test Barrel Length*
32LA	32 S & W Long	Lead Wadcutter	98	780	630	130	85	2.2″	4″
32LB	32 S & W Long	Lead Round Nose	98	705	670	115	98	2.3″	4″
32HRA	32 H & R Magnum	Lead Semi-Wadcutter	95	1030	940	225	190	1.1″	4½″
32HRB	32 H & R Magnum	Hi-Shok Jacketed Hollow Point	85	1100	1020	230	195	1.0″	4½″
38A	38 Special (Match)	Lead Wadcutter	148	710	634	166	132	2.4″	4″ -V
38B	38 Special	Lead Round Nose	158	755	723	200	183	2.0″	4″ -V
38C	38 Special	Lead Semi-Wadcutter	158	755	723	200	183	2.0″	4″ -V
▲38D	38 Special (High Velocity + P)	Lead Round Nose	158	890	855	278	257	1.4″	4″ -V
▲38E	38 Special (High Velocity + P)	Hi-Shok Jacketed Hollow Point	125	945	898	248	224	1.3″	4″ -V
▲38F	38 Special (High Velocity + P)	Hi-Shok Jacketed Hollow Point	110	995	926	242	210	1.2″	4″ -V
▲38G	38 Special (High Velocity + P)	Semi-Wadcutter Hollow Point	158	890	855	278	257	1.4″	4″ -V
▲38H	38 Special (High Velocity + P)	Lead Semi-Wadcutter	158	890	855	278	257	1.4″	4″ -V
▲38J	38 Special (High Velocity + P)	Jacketed Soft Point	125	945	898	248	224	1.3″	4″ -V
357A	357 Magnum	Jacketed Soft Point	158	1235	1104	535	428	0.8″	4″ -V
357B	357 Magnum	Hi-Shok Jacketed Hollow Point	125	1450	1240	583	427	0.6″	4″ -V
357C	357 Magnum	Lead Semi-Wadcutter	158	1235	1104	535	428	0.8″	4″ -V
357D	357 Magnum	Hi-Shok Jacketed Hollow Point	110	1295	1094	410	292	0.8″	4″ -V
357E	357 Magnum	Hi-Shok Jacketed Hollow Point	158	1235	1104	535	428	0.8″	4″ -V
357G	357 Magnum	Hi-Shok Jacketed Hollow Point	180	1090	980	475	385	1.0″	4″ -V
41A	41 Rem. Magnum	Hi-Shok Jacketed Hollow Point	210	1300	1130	790	595	0.7″	4″ -V
44SA	44 S & W Special	Semi-Wadcutter Hollow Point	200	900	830	360	305	1.4″	6½″-V
44A	44 Rem. Magnum	Hi-Shok Jacketed Hollow Point	240	1180	1081	741	623	0.9″	6½″-V
44B	44 Rem. Magnum	Hi-Shok Jacketed Hollow Point	180	1610	1365	1045	750	0.5″	6½″-V
A44B	44 Rem. Magnum	Hi-Shok Jacketed Hollow Point	180	1610	1365	1045	750	0.5″	6½″-V
44C	44 Rem. Magnum	Metal Case Profile	220	1390	1260	945	775	0.6″	6½″-V
45LCA	45 Colt	Semi-Wadcutter Hollow Point	225	900	860	405	369	1.6″	5½″

*"V" indicates vented barrels to simulate service conditions.
▲ This " + P" ammunition is loaded to a higher pressure. Use only in firearms so recommended by the manufacturer.
Pistol and revolver cartridges packed 50 rounds per box, 20 boxes per case. Exceptions: 44A and A44B packed 20 rounds per box; 25AP packed 25 rounds per box.

Nyclad Ballistics (Approximate)

Federal Load No.	Caliber	Bullet Style	Bullet Weight in Grains	Muzzle Velocity in Feet Per Second	Muzzle Energy in Foot/Lbs.	Test Barrel Length*
N9BP	9mm Luger Auto Pistol	Hollow Point	124	1120	345	4″
N38A	38 Special	Wadcutter	148	710	166	4″-V
N38B	38 Special	Round Nose	158	755	200	4″-V
▲N38G	38 Special (High Velocity + P)	Semi-Wadcutter Hollow Point	158	915	294	4″-V
N38M	38 Special (Chief's Special)	Hollow Point	125	825	190	2″
▲N38N	38 Special (High Velocity + P)	Hollow Point	125	945	248	4″-V
N357E	357 Magnum	Semi-Wadcutter Hollow Point	158	1235	535	4″-V

* "V" indicates vented barrels to simulate service conditions.
Nyclad cartridges packed 50 rounds per box, 20 boxes (1,000 rounds) per case.

▲This " + P" ammunition is loaded to a higher pressure. Use only in firearms so recommended by the manufacturer.

FEDERAL/NORMA BALLISTICS

Norma Centerfire Rifle Cartridge Ballistics (approximate)
STANDARD CALIBERS

Norma Load No.	Caliber	Bullet Wgt. in Grains	Bullet Style	Velocity In Feet Per Second						Energy In Foot/Pounds					
				Muzzle	100 yds	200 yds	300 yds	400 yds	500 yds	Muzzle	100 yds	200 yds	300 yds	400 yds	500 yds
15711	222 Remington	50	Soft Point	3250	2710	2230	1800	1440	1170	1175	815	555	360	230	155
15733	22-250 Remington	53	Soft Point	3710	3200	2740	2330	1950	1620	1615	1205	885	640	450	310
16003	243 Winchester	100	Soft Point	3100	2830	2570	2330	2090	1880	2135	1775	1465	1200	975	780
16902	270 Winchester	130	Soft Point	3140	2860	2600	2350	2110	1890	2845	2360	1945	1590	1290	1030
16903	270 Winchester	150	Soft Point	2800	2550	2320	2100	1890	1700	2610	2170	1795	1465	1185	955
17050	280 Remington	154	Soft Point	2870	2650	2440	2240	2050	1870	2815	2400	2040	1720	1435	1195
17051	280 Remington	170	Prot'd. Power Cav.	2710	2460	2220	2000	1790	1600	2765	2280	1865	1505	1205	960
17623	308 Winchester	130	Soft Point	2900	2590	2300	2030	1780	1550	2425	1935	1525	1185	910	690
17624	308 Winchester	150	Soft Point	2890	2640	2400	2170	1960	1760	2780	2315	1915	1570	1275	1025
17628	308 Winchester	180	Dual Core	2690	2460	2240	2030	1830	1650	2890	2415	2000	1645	1340	1085
17660	308 Winchester	180	Prot'd. Power Cav.	2690	2400	2140	1880	1650	1450	2890	2310	1820	1415	1095	835
17683	308 Winchester	200	Prot'd. Power Cav.	2460	2220	1980	1770	1570	1400	2690	2180	1750	1390	1100	865
17640	30-'06 Springfield	130	Soft Point	3210	2870	2560	2270	2000	1750	2965	2380	1895	1490	1155	885
17643	30-'06 Springfield	150	Soft Point	2990	2730	2490	2250	2030	1830	2975	2485	2060	1690	1375	1110
17653	30-'06 Springfield	180	Dual Core	2790	2550	2330	2110	1910	1720	3110	2605	2165	1785	1460	1185
17659	30-'06 Springfield	180	Prot'd. Power Cav.	2790	2500	2220	1960	1730	1510	3110	2495	1975	1540	1190	915
17684	30-'06 Springfield	200	Prot'd. Power Cav.	2640	2390	2140	1920	1710	1510	3095	2525	2040	1630	1290	1015
17630	30-30 Winchester	150	Soft Point	2380	2050	1750	1480	1270	1110	1885	1395	1015	730	535	415
17021	7mm Remington Magnum	154	Soft Point	3180	2940	2720	2500	2300	2100	3465	2965	2525	2140	1800	1505
17024	7mm Remington Magnum	170	Prot'd. Power Cav.	3020	2750	2500	2260	2030	1820	3440	2855	2360	1930	1560	1250
17680	300 Winchester Magnum	180	Boat Tail	3020	2800	2590	2380	2190	2010	3645	3125	2670	2270	1915	1605
17679	308 Winchester Match	168	H.P. Boat Tail	2550	2370	2190	2030	1870	1720	2425	2090	1795	1530	1300	1100

Unless otherwise noted, ballistic specifications were derived from test barrels 24 inches in length. Velocity figures rounded off to nearest "10." Energy figures rounded off to nearest "5."

Norma Centerfire Rifle Cartridge Ballistics (approximate)
SPECIALTY CALIBERS

Norma Load No.	Caliber	Bullet Wgt. in Grains	Bullet Style	Velocity In Feet Per Second						Energy In Foot/Pounds					
				Muzzle	100 yds	200 yds	300 yds	400 yds	500 yds	Muzzle	100 yds	200 yds	300 yds	400 yds	500 yds
15701	220 Swift	50	Soft Point	4110	3570	3080	2640	2240	1870	1875	1415	1055	775	555	390
15604	22 Savage H.P.	71	Soft Point	2790	2340	1930	1570	1280	1090	1225	860	585	390	260	190
16531	6.5x50 Japanese	139	Boat Tail	2360	2160	1970	1790	1620	1470	1720	1440	1195	985	810	665
16532	6.5x50 Japanese	156	Alaska	2070	1830	1610	1420	1260	1140	1475	1155	900	695	550	445
16535	6.5x52 Carcano	156	Alaska	2430	2170	1930	1700	1500	1320	2045	1630	1285	1005	780	605
New 16537	6.5x52 Carcano	139	Soft Point	2580	2360	2160	1970	1790	1620	2045	1725	1440	1195	985	810
16558	6.5x55 Swedish	139	Prot'd. Power Cav.	2850	2560	2290	2030	1790	1570	2515	2025	1615	1270	985	760
16552	6.5x55 Swedish	156	Alaska	2650	2370	2110	1870	1650	1450	2425	1950	1550	1215	945	730
17002	7x57 Mauser	154	Soft Point	2690	2490	2300	2120	1940	1780	2475	2120	1810	1530	1285	1080
17005	7x57 R	154	Soft Point	2630	2430	2250	2070	1900	1740	2355	2020	1725	1460	1230	1035
17013	7x64 Brenneke	154	Soft Point	2820	2610	2420	2230	2050	1870	2720	2335	1995	1695	1430	1200
17511	7.5x55 Swiss	180	Boat Tail	2650	2450	2260	2060	1880	1720	2805	2390	2020	1700	1415	1180
17638	308 Norma Magnum	180	Dual Core	3020	2820	2630	2440	2270	2090	3645	3175	2755	2385	2050	1750
17634	7.62x54 R Russian	180	Boat Tail	2580	2370	2180	2000	1820	1660	2650	2250	1900	1590	1325	1100
New 17637	7.62x54 R Russian	150	Soft Point	2950	2700	2450	2220	2000	1800	2905	2420	2005	1645	1335	1075
17701	7.65x53 Argentine	150	Soft Point	2660	2380	2120	1880	1660	1460	2355	1895	1500	1175	915	705
New 17702	7.65x53 Argentine	180	Soft Point	2590	2390	2200	2010	1830	1670	2685	2280	1925	1615	1345	1115
17712	303 British	150	Soft Point	2720	2440	2180	1930	1700	1500	2465	1985	1580	1240	965	745
17721	7.7x58 Japanese	130	Soft Point	2950	2530	2150	1800	1500	1260	2510	1850	1335	935	650	455
17722	7.7x58 Japanese	180	Boat Tail	2500	2300	2100	1920	1750	1590	2490	2105	1770	1475	1225	1015
18017	8x57 JS Mauser	165	Prot'd. Power Cav.	2850	2520	2210	1930	1670	1440	2985	2330	1795	1360	1015	755
18003	8x57 JS Mauser	196	Alaska	2530	2200	1890	1620	1380	1200	2775	2100	1555	1140	830	625
19303	9.3x57 Mauser	286	Alaska	2070	1810	1590	1390	1230	1110	2710	2090	1600	1220	955	780
19315	9.3x62 Mauser	286	Alaska	2360	2090	1840	1610	1410	1240	3535	2770	2145	1645	1255	980

Unless otherwise noted, ballistic specifications were derived from test barrels 24 inches in length. Velocity figures rounded off to nearest "10." Energy figures rounded off to nearest "5."

FEDERAL/NORMA BALLISTICS

Height of Trajectory
Inches above line of sight if sighted in at ⊕ yards. For sights .9" above bore.
Trajectory figures show the height of bullet impact above or below the line of sight at the indicated yardages. Aim low indicated amount for + figures and high for − figures. Zero ranges indicated by circled crosses.

Bullet Drop (In Inches From Bore Line)					Drift (In Inches In 10 mph Crosswind)					Height of Trajectory												
100 yds	200 yds	300 yds	400 yds	500 yds	100 yds	200 yds	300 yds	400 yds	500 yds	50 yds	100 yds	150 yds	200 yds	250 yds	300 yds	100 yds	150 yds	200 yds	250 yds	300 yds	400 yds	500 yds
1.9	8.5	22.2	46.7	87.4	1.5	6.8	16.9	33.5	58.1	0	⊕	−1.2	−3.9	−8.3	−14.9	+1.9	+1.7	⊕	−3.4	−9.0	−28.8	−64.8
1.4	6.2	15.7	31.6	56.6	1.1	4.7	11.3	21.8	37.3	−0.1	⊕	−0.8	−2.5	−5.4	−9.7	+1.3	+1.1	⊕	−2.3	−5.9	−18.2	−39.7
1.9	8.2	19.8	37.8	63.8	0.8	3.4	7.9	14.8	24.4	0	⊕	−1.1	−3.5	−7.1	−12.2	+1.7	+1.5	⊕	−2.8	−7.0	−20.5	−41.9
1.9	8.0	19.3	37.0	62.4	0.8	3.4	7.9	14.8	24.4	0	⊕	−1.1	−3.4	−6.9	−11.9	+1.7	+1.4	⊕	−2.7	−6.9	−20.0	−41.0
2.4	10.1	24.3	46.4	78.3	0.9	3.7	8.8	16.5	27.1	+0.2	⊕	−1.5	−4.4	−9.0	−15.4	+2.2	+1.8	⊕	−3.5	−8.7	−25.3	−51.7
2.2	9.4	22.5	42.4	70.7	0.7	3.1	7.3	13.5	22.1	+0.1	⊕	−1.4	−4.1	−8.2	−14.0	+2.0	+1.7	⊕	−3.1	−7.9	−22.7	−45.8
2.5	10.8	26.2	50.4	85.3	1.0	4.1	9.6	18.1	29.8	+0.2	⊕	−1.6	−4.9	−9.9	−16.8	+2.4	+2.0	⊕	−3.8	−9.5	−27.8	−56.9
2.2	9.7	23.7	46.3	79.9	1.1	4.5	10.7	20.4	34.0	+0.1	⊕	−1.4	−4.3	−8.8	−15.2	+2.2	+1.8	⊕	−3.5	−8.8	−26.0	−54.3
2.2	9.4	22.7	43.4	73.3	0.9	3.6	8.5	15.8	26.1	+0.1	⊕	−1.4	−4.1	−8.4	−14.3	+2.1	+1.7	⊕	−3.2	−8.1	−23.7	−48.3
2.6	10.9	26.2	50.0	84.1	0.9	3.8	8.9	16.7	27.5	+0.2	⊕	−1.6	−4.9	−9.8	−16.7	+2.4	+2.0	⊕	−3.7	−9.4	−27.3	−55.6
2.6	11.2	27.5	53.7	92.5	1.1	4.8	11.5	21.8	36.3	+0.2	⊕	−1.7	−5.1	−10.5	−18.0	+2.6	+2.1	⊕	−4.0	−10.3	−30.3	−63.1
3.1	13.3	32.3	62.5	106.6	1.2	4.9	11.6	21.8	36.0	+0.3	⊕	−2.1	−6.2	−12.5	−21.3	+3.1	+2.5	⊕	−4.8	−12.0	−35.0	−72.1
1.8	7.9	19.3	37.4	64.3	0.9	3.9	9.3	17.6	29.4	0	⊕	−1.1	−3.3	−6.9	−12.0	+1.7	+1.4	⊕	−2.7	−7.0	−20.7	−43.2
2.1	9.9	21.2	40.5	68.2	0.8	3.4	8.1	15.1	24.9	+0.1	⊕	−1.2	−3.8	−7.7	−13.2	+1.9	+1.6	⊕	−3.0	−7.5	−21.9	−44.8
2.4	10.1	24.2	46.2	77.7	0.9	3.6	8.5	15.8	26.0	+0.2	⊕	−1.5	−4.4	−9.0	−15.3	+2.2	+1.8	⊕	−3.4	−8.7	−25.1	−51.1
2.4	10.4	25.5	49.6	85.4	1.1	4.6	10.9	20.7	34.4	+0.2	⊕	−1.6	−4.7	−9.6	−16.5	+2.4	+2.0	⊕	−3.7	−9.4	−27.9	−58.0
2.7	11.5	27.9	53.8	91.6	1.0	4.4	10.5	19.7	32.6	+0.2	⊕	−1.8	−5.2	−10.6	−18.1	+2.6	+2.2	⊕	−4.1	−10.2	−30.0	−61.6
3.4	15.2	38.4	77.2	136.3	1.7	7.5	18.1	34.7	57.2	+0.4	⊕	−2.5	−7.5	−15.3	−26.4	+3.7	+3.1	⊕	−5.9	−15.2	−46.0	−97.0
1.8	7.6	18.2	34.3	57.0	0.7	2.7	6.4	11.9	19.3	0	⊕	−1.0	−3.1	−6.4	−11.0	+1.6	+1.3	⊕	−2.5	−6.3	−18.1	−36.6
2.0	8.7	20.9	40.0	67.4	0.8	3.5	8.2	15.3	25.3	+0.1	⊕	−1.2	−3.7	−7.6	−13.0	+1.9	+1.6	⊕	−3.0	−7.4	−21.7	−44.4
2.0	8.5	20.1	37.9	63.0	0.7	2.8	6.6	12.2	20.0	+0.1	⊕	−1.2	−3.6	−7.2	−12.3	+1.8	+1.5	⊕	−2.8	−7.0	−20.1	−40.5
2.8	11.8	28.1	52.9	87.6	0.8	3.2	7.6	14.0	22.9	+0.3	⊕	−1.8	−5.3	−10.6	−17.9	+2.7	+2.2	⊕	−4.0	−9.9	−28.3	−56.7

NOTE: These trajectory tables were calculated by computer and are given here unaltered. The computer used a standard modern scientific technique to predict trajectories from the best available data for each round. Each trajectory is expected to be reasonably representative of the behavior of the ammunition at sea level conditions, but the shooter is cautioned that trajectories differ because of variations in ammunition, rifles, and atmospheric conditions.

Height of Trajectory
Inches above line of sight if sighted in at ⊕ yards. For sights .9" above bore.
Trajectory figures show the height of bullet impact above or below the line of sight at the indicated yardages. Aim low indicated amount for + figures and high for − figures. Zero ranges indicated by circled crosses.

Bullet Drop (In Inches From Bore Line)					Drift (In Inches In 10 mph Crosswind)					Height of Trajectory												
100 yds	200 yds	300 yds	400 yds	500 yds	100 yds	200 yds	300 yds	400 yds	500 yds	50 yds	100 yds	150 yds	200 yds	250 yds	300 yds	100 yds	150 yds	200 yds	250 yds	300 yds	400 yds	500 yds
1.1	5.0	12.6	25.1	44.7	0.9	4.0	9.7	18.6	31.6	−0.2	⊕	−0.5	−1.8	−4.1	−7.4	+0.9	+0.9	⊕	−1.8	−4.6	−14.2	−30.8
2.5	11.5	29.9	62.4	114.3	1.8	7.7	19.2	37.6	63.6	+0.2	⊕	−1.8	−5.6	−11.6	−20.6	+2.8	+2.4	⊕	−4.7	−12.2	−38.5	−84.3
3.3	14.1	33.9	64.6	108.4	1.0	4.3	10.1	18.8	30.7	+0.4	⊕	−2.3	−6.6	−13.1	−22.2	+3.3	+2.7	⊕	−4.9	−12.3	−35.5	−71.8
4.4	19.3	47.6	92.9	159.0	1.6	6.8	16.2	30.3	49.0	+0.7	⊕	−3.3	−9.6	−19.2	−32.5	+4.9	+3.9	⊕	−7.2	−18.2	−53.4	−109.4
3.2	13.8	33.8	65.8	113.1	1.3	5.4	12.8	24.2	40.0	+0.4	⊕	−2.2	−6.5	−13.2	−22.5	+3.3	+2.7	⊕	−5.0	−12.7	−37.3	−77.3
2.8	11.8	28.3	53.8	90.1	0.9	3.7	8.8	16.5	27.0	+0.3	⊕	−1.8	−5.3	−10.7	−18.2	+2.7	+2.2	⊕	−4.0	−10.1	−29.3	−59.2
2.3	9.9	24.2	47.0	80.7	1.0	4.3	10.4	19.6	32.6	+0.1	⊕	−1.5	−4.4	−9.0	−15.5	+2.2	+1.8	⊕	−3.5	−8.9	−26.3	−54.5
2.7	11.6	28.3	54.9	94.2	1.1	4.7	11.3	21.4	35.5	+0.2	⊕	−1.8	−5.3	−10.8	−18.5	+2.7	+2.2	⊕	−4.1	−10.5	−30.9	−64.0
2.5	10.7	25.4	48.0	79.7	0.8	3.2	7.5	13.9	22.8	+0.2	⊕	−1.6	−4.7	−9.5	−16.0	+2.4	+1.9	⊕	−3.6	−9.0	−25.7	−51.7
2.7	11.2	26.7	50.3	83.6	0.8	3.3	7.6	14.2	23.1	+0.2	⊕	−1.7	−5.0	−10.0	−16.9	+2.5	+2.0	⊕	−3.8	−9.4	−27.0	−54.2
2.3	9.7	23.1	43.5	72.2	0.7	3.0	7.1	13.1	21.3	+0.1	⊕	−1.4	−4.2	−8.5	−14.4	+2.1	+1.7	⊕	−3.2	−8.1	−23.2	−46.6
2.6	11.1	26.4	49.9	83.3	0.8	3.4	8.0	14.9	24.3	+0.2	⊕	−1.7	−4.9	−9.9	−16.8	+2.5	+2.0	⊕	−3.7	−9.4	−26.9	−54.3
2.0	8.4	19.8	37.1	61.1	0.6	2.5	5.9	10.9	17.6	+0.1	⊕	−1.2	−3.5	−7.1	−12.0	+1.7	+1.5	⊕	−2.7	−6.8	−19.4	−38.8
2.8	11.7	28.0	53.1	88.6	0.9	3.6	8.4	15.6	25.4	+0.3	⊕	−1.8	−5.3	−10.6	−17.9	+2.6	+2.2	⊕	−4.0	−10.0	−28.7	−57.9
2.1	9.0	21.8	41.5	70.0	0.8	3.5	8.2	15.4	25.3	+0.1	⊕	−1.3	−3.9	−8.0	−13.6	+1.9	+1.6	⊕	−3.1	−7.7	−22.6	−46.1
2.6	11.4	28.0	54.4	93.5	1.1	4.7	11.3	21.4	35.6	+0.2	⊕	−1.8	−5.3	−10.7	−18.3	+2.6	+2.2	⊕	−4.1	−10.4	−30.6	−63.5
2.7	11.6	27.6	52.4	87.4	0.8	3.5	8.3	15.4	25.2	+0.3	⊕	−1.8	−5.2	−10.4	−17.6	+2.6	+2.1	⊕	−3.9	−9.8	−28.3	−57.1
2.5	10.9	26.7	51.8	88.9	1.1	4.6	10.9	20.7	34.4	+0.2	⊕	−1.7	−5.0	−10.1	−17.3	+2.5	+2.1	⊕	−3.9	−9.9	−29.1	−60.3
2.2	9.9	25.2	51.3	92.5	1.4	6.2	15.1	29.4	50.1	+0.1	⊕	−1.5	−4.6	−9.5	−16.8	+2.3	+1.9	⊕	−3.8	−9.9	−30.6	−66.4
3.0	12.5	30.0	56.9	95.1	0.9	3.8	8.9	16.5	27.0	+0.3	⊕	−2.0	−5.7	−11.5	−19.3	+2.9	+2.3	⊕	−4.3	−10.7	−30.9	−62.4
2.3	10.1	25.1	49.5	86.3	1.2	5.0	12.1	23.1	38.8	+0.2	⊕	−1.5	−4.6	−9.4	−16.3	+2.3	+1.9	⊕	−3.7	−9.4	−28.3	−59.6
3.0	13.3	33.3	66.6	117.5	1.5	6.5	15.8	30.3	50.6	+0.3	⊕	−2.1	−6.4	−13.0	−22.5	+3.2	+2.6	⊕	−5.1	−13.0	−39.2	−83.0
4.5	19.5	48.4	95.0	163.2	1.7	7.3	17.4	32.4	52.3	+0.7	⊕	−3.4	−9.7	−19.5	−33.3	+4.9	+3.9	⊕	−7.4	−18.7	−55.0	−113.1
3.4	14.8	36.5	71.6	123.8	1.4	6.0	14.3	27.1	44.7	+0.4	⊕	−2.4	−7.1	−14.4	−24.6	+3.6	+2.9	⊕	−5.5	−13.9	−41.2	−85.5

NOTE: These trajectory tables were calculated by computer and are given here unaltered. The computer used a standard modern scientific technique to predict trajectories from the best available data for each round. Each trajectory is expected to be reasonably representative of the behavior of the ammunition at sea level conditions, but the shooter is cautioned that trajectories differ because of variations in ammunition, rifles, and atmospheric conditions.

HORNADY BALLISTICS

RIFLE	MUZZLE VELOCITY	VELOCITY FEET PER SECOND					ENERGY FOOT - POUNDS						TRAJECTORY TABLES				
Caliber	Muzzle	100 yds.	200 yds.	300 yds.	400 yds.	500 yds.	Muzzle	100 yds.	200 yds.	300 yds.	400 yds.	500 yds.	100 yds.	200 yds.	300 yds.	400 yds.	500 yds.
222 Rem., 50 gr. SX	3140	2602	2123	1700	1350	1107	1094	752	500	321	302	136	+2.2	0.0	10.0	32.3	73.8
222 Rem., 52 gr. BTHP	3110	2691	2309	1959	1645	1376	1117	836	616	443	313	219	+1.7	0.0	8.4	25.9	56.3
222 Rem., 55 gr. SX	3020	2562	2147	1773	1451	1201	1114	801	563	384	257	176	+2.2	0.0	9.9	31.0	68.7
223 Rem., 53 gr. HP	3330	2882	2477	2106	1710	1475	1305	978	722	522	369	356	+1.7	0.0	7.4	22.7	49.1
223 Rem., 55 gr. SP	3240	2747	2304	1905	1554	1270	1282	921	648	443	295	197	+1.9	0.0	8.5	26.7	59.6
223 Rem., 55 gr. FMJ	3240	2759	2326	1933	1587	1301	1282	929	660	456	307	207	+1.9	0.0	8.4	26.2	57.9
223 Rem., 60 gr. SP	3150	2782	2442	2127	1837	1575	1322	1031	795	603	450	331	+1.6	0.0	7.5	22.5	48.1
22-250 Rem., 53 gr. HP	3680	3185	2743	2341	1974	1646	1594	1194	886	645	459	319	+1.0	-0-	5.7	17.8	38.8
22-250 Rem., 55 gr. SP	3680	3137	2656	2222	1832	1439	1654	1201	861	603	410	272	+1.1	-0-	6.0	19.2	42.6
22-250 Rem., 55 gr. FMJ	3680	3137	2656	2222	1836	1439	1654	1201	861	603	410	273	+1.1	-0-	6.0	19.2	42.6
22-250 Rem., 60 gr. SP	3600	3195	2826	2485	2169	1878	1627	1360	1064	823	627	470	+1.0	-0-	5.4	16.3	34.8
220 Swift, 55 gr. SP	3650	3194	2772	2384	2035	1724	1627	1246	939	694	506	363	+1.0	-0-	-5.6	-17.4	37.5
220 Swift, 60 gr. HP	3600	3199	2824	2475	2156	1868	1727	1364	1063	816	619	465	+1.0	-0-	5.4	16.3	34.8
243 Win., 75 gr. HP	3400	2970	2578	2219	1890	1595	1926	1469	1107	820	595	425	+1.2	-0-	-6.5	20.3	43.8
243 Win., 80 gr. FMJ	3350	2955	2593	2259	1951	1670	1993	1551	1194	906	676	495	+1.2	-0-	6.5	19.9	42.5
243 Win., 87 gr. SP	3300	2992	2705	2435	2181	1943	2104	1730	1414	1146	919	729	+1.2	-0-	6.1	18.0	37.3
243 Win., 100 BTSP	2960	2728	2508	2299	2099	1910	1945	1653	1397	1174	979	810	+1.6	-0-	7.2	-21.0	42.8
6MM Rem., 100 BTSP	3100	2861	2634	2419	2231	2018	2134	1818	1541	1300	1088	904	+1.3	-0-	6.5	18.9	38.5
257 Roberts, 100 SP (+P)	3000	2633	2295	1982	1697	1447	1998	1539	1169	872	639	465	+1.7	-0-	8.5	25.9	55.5
257 Roberts, 117 gr. BTSP (+P)	2780	2587	2402	2225	2055	1893	2008	1739	1499	1286	1097	931	+1.7	-0-	8.0	23.2	46.5
25-06 100 gr. SP	3230	2893	2580	2287	2014	1762	2316	1858	1478	1161	901	689	+1.6	-0-	6.9	20.5	42.7
25-06 117 gr. BTSP	2990	2788	2595	2409	2232	2062	2323	2020	1750	1508	1295	1105	+1.6	-0-	6.6	19.4	39.3
270 Win., 130 gr. SP	3060	2800	2560	2330	2110	1900	2700	2265	1890	1565	1285	1045	+1.8	-0-	7.1	20.6	42.0
270 Win., 140 gr. BTSP	2940	2747	2562	2385	2214	2050	2688	2346	2041	1769	1524	1307	+1.6	-0-	7.0	-20.2	40.3
270 Win., 150 gr. SP	2850	2500	2180	1890	1620	1390	2705	2085	1585	1185	870	640	+2.0	-0-	9.7	-29.2	62.2
7 x 57 Mau., 139 gr. BTSP	2700	2504	2316	2137	1965	1802	2251	1936	1656	1410	1192	1002	+2.0	-0-	-8.5	24.9	50.3
7 x 57 Mau., 154 gr. SP	2600	2400	2208	2025	1852	1689	2312	1970	1668	1403	1173	976	+2.2	-0-	9.5	27.7	-55.8
7MM Rem. Mag., 139 gr. BTSP	3150	2933	2727	2530	2341	2160	3063	2656	2296	1976	1692	1440	+1.2	-0-	6.1	-17.7	35.5
7MM Rem. Mag., 154 gr. SP	3035	2814	2604	2404	2212	2029	3151	2708	2319	1977	1674	1408	+1.3	-0-	6.7	19.3	39.3
7MM Rem. Mag., 162 gr. BTSP	2940	2757	2582	2413	2251	2094	3110	2735	2399	2095	1823	1578	+1.6	-0-	6.7	19.7	39.3
7MM Rem. Mag., 175 gr. SP	2860	2650	2440	2240	2060	1880	3180	2720	2310	1960	1640	1370	+2.0	-0-	7.9	22.7	45.8
30 M1 Carb., 110 gr. RN	1990	1570	1240	1040	920	840	965	600	375	260	210	175	-0-	13.5	49.9		
30 M1 Carb., 110 gr. FMJ	1990	1600	1280	1070	950	870	970	620	400	280	220	185	-0-	7.2	38.7		
30-30 Win., 150 gr. RN	2390	1973	1605	1303	1095	974	1902	1296	858	565	399	316	-0-	8.2	30.0		
30-30 Win., 170 gr. FP	2200	1895	1619	1381	1191	1064	1827	1355	989	720	535	425	-0-	8.9	31.1		
308 Win., 150 gr. SP	2820	2533	2263	2009	1774	1560	2648	2137	1705	1344	1048	810	+2.3	-0-	-9.1	-26.9	55.7
308 Win., 150 gr. BTSP	2820	2560	2315	2084	1866	1644	2649	2183	1785	1447	1160	922	+2.0	-0-	-8.5	-25.2	51.8
308 Win., 165 gr. SP	2700	2440	2194	1963	1748	1551	2670	2180	1763	1411	1119	881	+2.5	-0-	9.7	-28.5	58.8
308 Win., 165 gr. BTSP	2700	2496	2301	2115	1937	1770	2672	2283	1940	1639	1375	1148	+2.0	-0-	8.7	25.2	-51.0
308 Win., 168 gr. BTHP MATCH	2700	2524	2354	2191	2035	1885	2720	2377	2068	1791	1545	1326	+2.0	-0-	8.4	-23.9	-48.0
308 Win., 180 gr. SP	2620	2393	2178	1974	1782	1604	2743	2288	1896	1557	1269	1028	+2.6	-0-	9.9	28.9	-58.8
30-06 150 gr. SP	2910	2617	2342	2083	1843	1622	2820	2281	1827	1445	1131	876	+2.1	-0-	8.5	-25.0	51.8
30-06 150 gr. BTSP	2910	2645	2395	2159	1937	1729	2821	2331	1911	1553	1250	996	+1.7	-0-	-8.0	23.3	-48.1
30-06 150 gr. FMJ BT	2910	2705	2508	2320	2141	1969	2821	2438	2096	1793	1527	1292	+1.6	-0-	-7.2	-20.9	42.3
30-06 165 gr. BTSP	2800	2591	2392	2202	2020	1848	2873	2460	2097	1777	1495	1252	+1.8	-0-	8.0	23.3	47.0
30-06 168 gr. BTHP MATCH	2790	2620	2447	2280	2120	1966	2925	2561	2234	1940	1677	1442	+1.7	-0-	-7.7	-22.2	-44.3
30-06 180 gr. SP	2700	2348	2023	1727	1466	1251	2913	2203	1635	1192	859	625	+2.7	-0-	11.3	34.4	-73.7
300 Win. Mag., 180 SP	2960	2745	2540	2344	2157	1979	3501	3011	2578	2196	1859	1565	+1.9	-0-	7.3	20.9	41.9
300 Win. Mag., 190 BTSP	2900	2711	2529	2355	2187	2026	3549	3101	2699	2340	2018	1732	+1.6	-0-	-7.1		

All 24" barrels except 30 M1 Carbine — 20" barrel.

BARREL LENGTH	PISTOL	MUZZLE VELOCITY	VELOCITY FT. PER SECOND		ENERGY		
	Caliber	Muzzle	50 yds.	100 yds.	Muzzle	50 yds.	100 yds.
2"	25 Auto, 50 gr. FMJ RN	760	707	659	64	56	48
2"	25 Auto, 50 gr. JHP	760	707	659	64	56	48
3¾"	380 Auto, 90 gr. JHP	1000	902	823	200	163	135
3¾"	380 Auto, 100 gr. FMJ	950	875	810	200	170	146
4"	9MM Luger, 90 gr. JHP	1360	1112	978	370	247	191
4"	9MM Luger, 100 gr. FMJ	1220	1059	959	331	249	204
4"	9MM Luger, 115 JHP	1155	1047	971	341	280	241
4"	9MM Luger, 115 gr. FMJ	1155	1047	971	341	280	241
4"	9MM Luger, 124 gr. FMJ/RN	1110	1030	971	339	292	259
4"	9MM Luger, 124 gr. FMJ/FP	1110	1030	971	339	292	259
4"	38 Special, 110 gr. JHP	975	903	841	232	199	173
4"	38 Special, 125 gr. JHP	950	888	834	251	219	193
4"	38 Special, 125 gr. JFP	950	888	834	251	219	193
4"	38 Special, 140 gr. JHP	900	850	806	252	225	202
4"	38 Special, 158 gr. JHP	800	765	731	225	205	188
4"	38 Special, 158 gr. JFP	800	765	731	225	205	188
4"	38 Special, 148 gr. HBWC	710	634	566	166	132	105
4"	38 Special, 158 gr. LRN	755	723	692	200	183	168
4"	38 Special, 158 gr. SWC	755	723	692	200	183	168
4"	38 Special, 158 gr. SWC/HP	755	723	692	200	183	168
4"	357 Mag., 125 gr. JHP	1450	1240	1090	583	427	330
4"	357 Mag., 125 gr. JFP	1450	1240	1090	583	427	330
4"	357 Mag., 140 gr. JHP	1360	1195	1076	575	444	360
4"	357 Mag., 158 gr. JHP	1235	1104	1015	535	428	361
4"	357 Mag., 158 gr. JFP	1235	1104	1015	535	428	361
4"	357 Mag., 158 gr. SWC	1235	1104	1015	535	428	361
4"	357 Mag., 158 gr. SWC HP	1235	1104	1015	535	428	361
7½"	44 Rem. Mag., 180 gr. JHP	1610	1365	1175	1036	745	551
7½"	44 Rem. Mag., 200 gr. JHP	1500	1284	1128	999	732	565
7½"	44 Rem. Mag., 240 gr. JHP	1350	1188	1078	971	753	619
7½"	44 Rem. Mag., 240 gr. SWC	1000	935	879	533	466	412
7½"	44 Rem. Mag., 240 gr. SWC HP	1000	935	879	533	466	412
5"	45 ACP, 185 gr. JHP	950	880	819	371	318	276
5"	45 ACP, 185 gr. JSWC (M)	950	707	650	244	205	174
5"	45 ACP, 200 gr. FMJ C T (M)	1000	938	885	444	391	348
5"	45 ACP, 200 gr. SWC	800	733	671	284	239	200
5"	45 ACP, 230 gr. FMJ RN	850	809	771	369	334	304
5"	45 ACP, 230 gr. FMJ FP	850	809	771	369	334	304

V = Vented   M = Match

REMINGTON PISTOL & REVOLVER BALLISTICS

(1) (2) (3) (4) (5) (6) (7) (8) (9) (10) (11) (12) (13) (14) (15) (16) (17) (18) (19) (20) (21) (22) (23) (23) (24)

Remington Pistol & Revolver Ballistics — CALIBER	Order No.	Primer No.	Wt. Grs.	BULLET Style	VELOCITY (FPS) Muzzle	VELOCITY (FPS) 50 Yds.	VELOCITY (FPS) 100 Yds.	ENERGY (FT-LB) Muzzle	ENERGY (FT-LB) 50 Yds.	ENERGY (FT-LB) 100 Yds.	MID-RANGE TRAJECTORY 50 Yds.	MID-RANGE TRAJECTORY 100 Yds.	BARREL LENGTH
(1) 22 REM. JET® MAG.	R22JET	6½	40*	Soft Point	2100	1790	1510	390	285	200	0.3″	1.4″	8⅜″
(2) 221 REM. FIREBALL®	R221F	7½	50*	Pointed Soft Point	2650	2380	2130	780	630	505	0.2″	0.8″	10½″
(3) 25 (6.35mm) AUTO. PISTOL	R25AP	1½	50*	Metal Case	760	707	659	64	56	48	2.0″	8.7″	2″
(4) 7mm BR	R7MMBR ★	7½	140*	Pointed Soft Point	Refer to page 32 for ballistics.								
(5) 32 S. & W.	R32SW	5½	88*	Lead	680	645	610	90	81	73	2.5″	10.5″	3″
(6) 32 S. & W. LONG	R32SWL	1½	98*	Lead	705	670	635	115	98	88	2.3″	10.5″	4″
(7) 32 SHORT COLT	R32SC	1½	80*	Lead	745	665	590	100	79	62	2.2″	9.9″	4″
(8) 32 LONG COLT	R32LC	1½	82*	Lead	755	715	675	100	93	83	2.0″	8.7″	4″
(9) 32 (7.65mm) AUTO. PISTOL	R32AP	1½	71*	Metal Case	905	855	810	129	115	97	1.4″	5.8″	4″
(10) 357 MAG. Vented Barrel	R357M7	5½	110	Semi-Jacketed H.P.	1295	1094	975	410	292	232	0.8″	3.5″	4″
	R357M1	5½	125	Semi-Jacketed H.P.	1450	1240	1090	583	427	330	0.6″	2.8″	4″
	R357M8	5½	125	Semi-Jacketed S.P.	1450	1240	1090	583	427	330	0.6″	2.8″	4″
	R357M2	5½	158	Semi-Jacketed H.P.	1235	1104	1015	535	428	361	0.8″	3.5″	4″
	R357M3	5½	158	Soft Point	1235	1104	1015	535	428	361	0.8″	3.5″	4″
	R357M4	5½	158	Metal Point	1235	1104	1015	535	428	361	0.8″	3.5″	4″
	R357M5	5½	158	Lead	1235	1104	1015	535	428	361	0.8″	3.5″	4″
	R357M6	5½	158	Lead (Brass Case)	1235	1104	1015	535	428	361	0.8″	3.5″	4″
	R357M9	5½	140	Semi-Jacketed H.P.	1360	1195	1076	575	444	360	0.7″	3.0″	4″
	R357M10 ★	5½	180*	Semi-Jacketed H.P.	1145	1053	985	524	443	388	0.9″	3.9″	8⅜″
(11) 357 REM. MAXIMUM**	357MX1	7½	158*	Semi-Jacketed H.P.	1825	1588	1381	1168	885	669	0.4″	1.7″	10½″
	357MX3	7½	180	Semi-Jacketed H.P.	1555	1328	1154	966	705	532	0.5″	2.5″	10½″
(12) 9mm LUGER AUTO. PISTOL	R9MM1	1½	115	Jacketed H.P.	1155	1047	971	341	280	241	0.9″	3.9″	4″
	R9MM2	1½	124	Metal Case	1110	1030	971	339	292	259	1.0″	4.1″	4″
	R9MM3 ★	1½	115	Metal Case	1135	1041	973	329	277	242	0.9″	4.0″	4″
	R9MM5 ★	1½	88*	Jacketed H.P.	1500	1191	1012	440	277	200	0.6″	3.1″	4″
(13) 380 AUTO. PISTOL	R380AP	1½	95	Metal Case	955	865	785	190	160	130	1.4″	5.9″	4″
	R380A1	1½	88*	Jacketed H.P.	990	920	868	191	165	146	1.2″	5.1″	4″
(14) 38 AUTO. COLT PISTOL (A)	R38ACP	1½	130*	Metal Case	1040	980	925	310	275	245	1.0″	4.7″	4½″
(15) 38 SUPER AUTO. COLT PISTOL (B)	R38SU1	1½	115*	Jacketed H.P. (+P)‡	1300	1147	1041	431	336	277	0.7″	3.3″	5″
	R38SUP	1½	130	Metal Case (+P)‡	1215	1099	1017	426	348	298	0.8″	3.6″	5″
(16) 38 S. & W.	R38SW	1½	146*	Lead	685	650	620	150	135	125	2.4″	10.0″	4″
(17) 38 SPECIAL Vented Barrel	R38S1	1½	95	Semi-Jacketed H.P. (+P)‡	1175	1044	959	291	230	194	0.9″	3.9″	4″
	R38S10	1½	110	Semi-Jacketed H.P. (+P)‡	995	926	871	242	210	185	1.2″	5.1″	4″
	R38S2	1½	125*	Semi-Jacketed H.P. (+P)‡	945	898	858	248	224	204	1.3″	5.4″	4″
	R38S13	1½	125	Semi-Jacketed S.P. (+P)‡	945	908	875	248	229	212	1.3″	5.3″	4″
	R38S3	1½	148	Targetmaster® Lead W.C. Match	710	634	566	166	132	105	2.4″	10.8″	4″
	R38S4	1½	158	Targetmaster Lead	755	723	692	200	183	168	2.0″	8.3″	4″
	R38S5	1½	158	Lead (Round Nose)	755	723	692	200	183	168	2.0″	8.3″	4″
	R38S14	1½	158	Semi-Wadcutter (+P)‡	890	855	823	278	257	238	1.4″	6.0″	4″
	R38S6	1½	158	Semi-Wadcutter	755	723	692	200	183	168	2.0″	8.3″	4″
	R38S7	1½	158	Metal Point	755	723	692	200	183	168	2.0″	8.3″	4″
	R38S8	1½	158	Lead (+P)‡	890	855	823	278	257	238	1.4″	6.0″	4″
	R38S12	1½	158	Lead H.P. (+P)‡	890	855	823	278	257	238	1.4″	6.0″	4″
	R38S9	1½	200	Lead	635	614	594	179	168	157	2.8″	11.5″	4″
(18) 38 SHORT COLT	R38SC	1½	125*	Lead	730	685	645	150	130	115	2.2″	9.4″	6″
(19) 41 REM. MAG. Vented Barrel	R41MG1	2½	210	Soft Point	1300	1162	1062	788	630	526	0.7″	3.2″	4″
	R41MG2	2½	210	Lead	965	898	842	434	376	331	1.3″	5.4″	4″
	R41MG3 ★	2½	170*	Semi-Jacketed H.P.	1420	1166	1014	761	513	388	0.7″	3.2″	4″
(20) 44 REM. MAG. Vented Barrel	R44MG5	2½	180*	Semi-Jacketed H.P.	1610	1365	1175	1036	745	551	0.5″	2.3″	4″
	R44MG1	2½	240	Lead Gas Check	1350	1186	1069	971	749	608	0.7″	3.1″	4″
	R44MG2	2½	240	Soft Point	1180	1081	1010	741	623	543	0.9″	3.7″	4″
	R44MG3	2½	240	Semi-Jacketed H.P.	1180	1081	1010	741	623	543	0.9″	3.7″	4″
	R44MG4	2½	240	Lead (Med. Vel.)	1000	947	902	533	477	433	1.1″	4.8″	6½″
	R44MG6 ★	2½	210	Semi-Jacketed H.P.	1495	1312	1167	1042	803	634	0.6″	2.5″	6½″
(21) 44 S. & W. SPECIAL	R44SW	2½	246	Lead	755	725	695	310	285	265	2.0″	8.3″	6½″
	R44SW1	2½	200*	Semi-Wadcutter	1035	938	866	476	391	333	1.1″	4.9″	6½″
(22) 45 COLT	R45C	2½	250	Lead	860	820	780	410	375	340	1.6″	6.6″	5½″
	R45C1	2½	225*	Semi-Wadcutter (Keith)	960	890	832	460	395	346	1.3″	5.5″	5½″
(23) 45 AUTO.	R45AP1	2½	185	Metal Case Wadcutter Match	770	707	650	244	205	174	2.0″	8.7″	5″
	R45AP2	2½	185*	Jacketed H.P.	940	890	846	363	325	294	1.3″	5.5″	5″
	R45AP4	2½	230	Metal Case	835	800	767	356	326	300	1.6″	6.8″	5″
	R45AP5 ★	2½	Shot*	Shot	Number 12 shot.								
(24) 45 AUTO. RIM	R45AR	2½	230*	Lead	810	770	730	335	305	270	1.8″	7.4″	5½″
38 S. & W.	R38SWBL	1½	– *	Blank	–	–	–	–	–	–	–	–	–
32 S. & W.	R32BLNK	5½	–	Blank	–	–	–	–	–	–	–	–	–
38 SPECIAL	R38BLNK	1½	–	Blank	–	–	–	–	–	–	–	–	–

**Illustrated (not shown in actual size). **Will not chamber in 357 Mag. or 38 Special handguns. ‡Ammunition with (+P) on the case headstamp is loaded to higher pressure. Use only in firearms designated for this cartridge and so recommended by the gun manufacturer. ★ New for 1988. (A) Adapted only for 38 Colt sporting, military and pocket model automatic pistols. These pistols were discontinued after 1928. (B) Adapted only for 38 Colt Super and Colt Commander automatic pistols. Not for use in sporting, military and pocket models.*

REMINGTON BALLISTICS

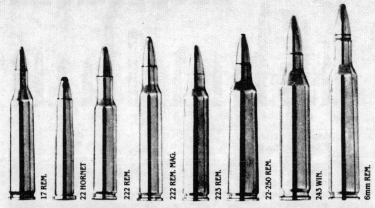

17 REM. | 22 HORNET | 222 REM. | 222 REM. MAG. | 223 REM. | 22-250 REM. | 243 WIN. | 6mm REM.

Remington Ballistics

CALIBERS	REMINGTON Order No.	BULLET			Primer No.
		Wt.-Grs.		Style	
17 REM.	R17REM	25*		Hollow Point Power-Lokt*	7½
22 HORNET	R22HN1	45*		Pointed Soft Point	6½
	R22HN2	45		Hollow Point	6½
222 REM.	R222R1	50		Pointed Soft Point	7½
	R222R3	50*		Hollow Point Power-Lokt	7½
	R222R4	55		Metal Case	7½
222 REM. MAG.	R222M1	55*		Pointed Soft Point	7½
	R222M2	55		Hollow Point Power-Lokt	7½
223 REM.	R223R1	55		Pointed Soft Point	7½
	R223R2	55*		Hollow Point Power-Lokt	7½
	R223R3	55		Metal Case Match	7½
22-250 REM.	R22501	55*		Pointed Soft Point	9½
	R22502	55		Hollow Point Power-Lokt	9½
243 WIN.	R243W1	80		Pointed Soft Point	9½
	R243W2	80*		Hollow Point Power-Lokt	9½
	R243W3	100		Pointed Soft Point Core-Lokt*	9½
6mm REM.	R6MM1	80‡		Pointed Soft Point	9½
	R6MM2	80‡		Hollow Point Power-Lokt	9½
	R6MM4	100*		Pointed Soft Point Core-Lokt	9½
25-20 WIN.	R25202	86*		Soft Point	6½
250 SAV.	R250SV	100*		Pointed Soft Point	9½
257 ROBERTS	R257	117		Soft Point Core-Lokt	9½
	R257A	100*		Pointed Soft Point Core-Lokt	9½
25-06 REM.	R25061	87		Hollow Point Power-Lokt	9½
	R25062	100*		Pointed Soft Point Core-Lokt	9½
	R25063	120		Pointed Soft Point Core-Lokt	9½
6.5mm REM. MAG.	R65MM2	120*		Pointed Soft Point Core-Lokt	9½M
264 WIN. MAG.	R264W2	140*		Pointed Soft Point Core-Lokt	9½M
270 WIN.	R270W1	100		Pointed Soft Point	9½
	R270W2	130*		Pointed Soft Point Core-Lokt	9½
	R270W3	130		Bronze Point	9½
	R270W4	150		Soft Point Core-Lokt	9½
7mm BR ★	R7MMBR ★	140*		Pointed Soft Point	7½
7mm MAUSER (7x57)	R7MSR1	140*		Pointed Soft Point	9½
7mm-08 REM.	R7M081	140		Pointed Soft Point	9½
	R7M083 ★	120*		Hollow Point	9½
280 REM. †	R280R3	140		Pointed Soft Point	9½
	R280R1	150		Pointed Soft Point Core-Lokt	9½
	R280R2	165		Soft Point Core-Lokt	9½
	R280R4 ★	120*		Hollow Point	9½
7mm REM. MAG.	R7MM2	150		Pointed Soft Point Core-Lokt	9½M
	R7MM3	175		Pointed Soft Point Core-Lokt	9½M
	R7MM4 ★	140*		Pointed Soft Point	9½M
30 CARBINE	R30CAR	110*		Soft Point	6½
30 REM.	R30REM	170*		Soft Point Core-Lokt	9½
30-30 WIN. ACCELERATOR'	R3030A	55*		Soft Point	9½
30-30 WIN.	R30301	150*		Soft Point Core-Lokt	9½
	R30302	170		Soft Point Core-Lokt	9½
	R30303	170		Hollow Point Core-Lokt	9½

REMINGTON BALLISTICS

Cartridges (left to right): 250 SAV. · 257 ROBERTS · 25-06 REM. · 6.5mm REM. MAG. · 264 WIN. MAG. · 270 WIN. · 7mm MAUSER · 7mm-08 REM. · 280 REM. · 7mm REM. MAG. · 30 CARBINE · 30 REM. · 30-30 WIN. "ACCELERATOR" · 30-30 WIN.

TRAJECTORY 0.0 indicates yardage at which rifle was sighted in.

SHORT RANGE — Bullet does not rise more than one inch above line of sight from muzzle to sighting-in range.

LONG RANGE — Bullet does not rise more than three inches above line of sight from muzzle to sighting-in range.

VELOCITY FEET PER SECOND						ENERGY FOOT-POUNDS						SHORT RANGE						LONG RANGE							BARREL LENGTH
Muzzle	100 Yds.	200 Yds.	300 Yds.	400 Yds.	500 Yds.	Muzzle	100 Yds.	200 Yds.	300 Yds.	400 Yds.	500 Yds.	50 Yds.	100 Yds.	150 Yds.	200 Yds.	250 Yds.	300 Yds.	100 Yds.	150 Yds.	200 Yds.	250 Yds.	300 Yds.	400 Yds.	500 Yds.	
4040	3284	2644	2086	1606	1235	906	599	388	242	143	85	0.1	0.5	0.0	-1.5	-4.2	-8.5	2.1	2.5	1.9	0.0	-3.4	-17.0	-44.3	24"
2690	2042	1502	1128	948	840	723	417	225	127	90	70	0.3	0.0	-2.4	-7.7	-16.9	-31.3	1.6	0.0	-4.5	-12.8	-26.4	-75.6	-163.4	24"
2690	2042	1502	1128	948	840	723	417	225	127	90	70	0.3	0.0	-2.4	-7.7	-16.9	-31.3	1.6	0.0	-4.5	-12.8	-26.4	-75.6	-163.4	
3140	2602	2123	1700	1350	1107	1094	752	500	321	202	136	0.5	0.9	0.0	-2.5	-6.9	-13.7	2.1	1.9	0.0	-3.8	-10.0	-32.3	-73.8	
3140	2635	2182	1777	1432	1172	1094	771	529	351	228	152	0.5	0.9	0.0	-2.4	-6.6	-13.1	2.1	1.8	0.0	-3.6	-9.5	-30.2	-68.1	24"
3020	2562	2147	1773	1451	1201	1114	801	563	384	257	176	0.6	1.0	0.0	-2.5	-7.0	-13.7	2.2	1.9	0.0	-3.8	-9.9	-31.0	-68.7	
3240	2748	2305	1906	1556	1272	1282	922	649	444	296	198	0.4	0.8	0.0	-2.2	-6.0	-11.8	1.9	1.6	0.0	-3.3	-8.5	-26.7	-59.5	
3240	2773	2352	1969	1627	1341	1282	939	675	473	323	220	0.4	0.8	0.0	-2.1	-5.8	-11.4	1.8	1.6	0.0	-3.2	-8.2	-25.5	-56.0	24"
3240	2747	2304	1905	1554	1270	1282	921	648	443	295	197	0.4	0.8	0.0	-2.2	-6.0	-11.8	1.9	1.6	0.0	-3.3	-8.5	-26.7	-59.6	
3240	2773	2352	1969	1627	1341	1282	939	675	473	323	220	0.4	0.8	0.0	-2.1	-5.8	-11.4	1.8	1.6	0.0	-3.2	-8.2	-25.5	-56.0	24"
3240	2759	2326	1933	1587	1301	1282	929	660	456	307	207	0.4	0.8	0.0	-2.1	-5.9	-11.6	1.9	1.6	0.0	-3.2	-8.4	-26.2	-57.9	
3680	3137	2656	2222	1832	1493	1654	1201	861	603	410	272	0.2	0.5	0.0	-1.6	-4.4	-8.7	2.3	2.6	1.9	0.0	-3.4	-15.9	-38.9	
3680	3209	2785	2400	2046	1725	1654	1257	947	703	511	363	0.2	0.5	0.0	-1.5	-4.1	-8.0	2.1	2.5	1.8	0.0	-3.1	-14.1	-33.4	24"
3350	2955	2593	2259	1951	1670	1993	1551	1194	906	676	495	0.3	0.7	0.0	-1.8	-4.9	-9.4	2.6	2.9	2.1	0.0	-3.6	-16.2	-37.9	
3350	2955	2593	2259	1951	1670	1993	1551	1194	906	676	495	0.3	0.7	0.0	-1.8	-4.9	-9.4	2.6	2.9	2.1	0.0	-3.6	-16.2	-37.9	24"
2960	2697	2449	2215	1993	1786	1945	1615	1332	1089	882	708	0.5	0.9	0.0	-2.2	-5.8	-11.0	1.9	1.6	0.0	-3.1	-7.8	-22.6	-46.3	
3470	3064	2694	2352	2036	1747	2139	1667	1289	982	736	542	0.3	0.6	0.0	-1.6	-4.5	-8.7	2.4	2.7	1.9	0.0	-3.3	-14.9	-35.0	
3470	3064	2694	2352	2036	1747	2139	1667	1289	982	736	542	0.3	0.6	0.0	-1.6	-4.5	-8.7	2.4	2.7	1.9	0.0	-3.3	-14.9	-35.0	24"
3100	2829	2573	2332	2104	1889	2133	1777	1470	1207	983	792	0.4	0.8	0.0	-1.9	-5.2	-9.9	1.7	1.5	0.0	-2.8	-7.0	-20.4	-41.7	
1460	1194	1030	931	858	797	407	272	203	165	141	121	0.0	-4.1	-14.4	-31.8	-57.3	-92.0	0.0	-8.2	-23.5	-47.0	-79.6	-175.9	-319.4	24"
2820	2504	2210	1936	1684	1461	1765	1392	1084	832	630	474	0.2	0.0	-1.6	-4.7	-9.6	-16.5	2.3	2.0	0.0	-3.7	-9.5	-28.3	-59.5	24"
2650	2291	1961	1663	1404	1199	1824	1363	999	718	512	373	0.3	0.0	-1.9	-5.8	-11.9	-20.7	2.9	2.4	0.0	-4.7	-12.0	-36.7	-79.2	
2980	2661	2363	2085	1827	1592	1972	1572	1240	965	741	563	0.1	0.0	-1.3	-4.0	-8.3	-14.3	2.0	1.7	0.0	-3.3	-8.3	-24.6	-51.4	24"
3440	2995	2591	2222	1884	1583	2286	1733	1297	954	686	484	0.3	0.6	0.0	-1.7	-4.8	-9.3	2.5	2.9	2.1	0.0	-3.6	-16.4	-39.1	
3230	2893	2580	2287	2014	1762	2316	1858	1478	1161	901	689	0.4	0.7	0.0	-1.9	-5.0	-9.7	1.6	1.4	0.0	-2.7	-6.9	-20.5	-42.7	24"
2990	2730	2484	2252	2032	1825	2382	1985	1644	1351	1100	887	0.5	0.8	0.0	-2.1	-5.6	-10.7	1.9	1.6	0.0	-3.0	-7.5	-22.0	-44.8	
3210	2905	2621	2353	2102	1867	2745	2248	1830	1475	1177	929	0.4	0.7	0.0	-1.8	-4.9	-9.5	2.7	3.0	2.1	0.0	-3.5	-15.5	-35.3	24"
3030	2782	2548	2326	2114	1914	2854	2406	2018	1682	1389	1139	0.5	0.8	0.0	-2.0	-5.4	-10.2	1.8	1.5	0.0	-2.9	-7.2	-20.8	-42.2	24"
3430	3021	2649	2305	1988	1699	2612	2027	1557	1179	877	641	0.3	0.6	0.0	-1.7	-4.6	-9.0	2.5	2.8	2.0	0.0	-3.4	-15.5	-36.4	
3060	2776	2510	2259	2022	1801	2702	2225	1818	1472	1180	936	0.5	0.8	0.0	-2.0	-5.5	-10.4	1.8	1.5	0.0	-2.9	-7.4	-21.6	-44.3	24"
3060	2802	2559	2329	2110	1904	2702	2267	1890	1565	1285	1046	0.5	0.8	0.0	-2.0	-5.3	-10.1	1.8	1.5	0.0	-2.8	-7.1	-20.6	-42.0	
2850	2504	2183	1886	1618	1385	2705	2087	1587	1185	872	639	0.7	1.0	0.0	-2.6	-7.1	-13.6	2.3	2.0	0.0	-3.8	-9.7	-29.2	-62.2	
2215	2012	1821	1643	1481	1336	1525	1259	1031	839	681	555	0.5	0.0	-2.7	-7.7	-15.4	-25.9	1.8	0.0	-4.1	-10.9	-20.6	-50.0	-95.2	15"
2660	2435	2221	2018	1827	1648	2199	1843	1533	1266	1037	844	0.2	0.0	-1.7	-5.0	-10.0	-17.0	2.5	2.0	0.0	-3.8	-9.6	-27.7	-56.3	24"
2860	2625	2402	2189	1988	1798	2542	2142	1793	1490	1228	1005	0.6	0.9	0.0	-2.3	-6.1	-11.6	2.1	1.7	0.0	-3.2	-8.1	-23.5	-47.7	
3000	2725	2467	2223	1992	1778	2398	1979	1621	1316	1058	842	0.5	0.8	0.0	-2.1	-5.7	-10.8	1.9	1.6	0.0	-3.0	-7.6	-22.3	-45.8	24"
3000	2758	2528	2309	2102	1905	2797	2363	1986	1657	1373	1128	0.5	0.8	0.0	-2.1	-5.5	-10.4	1.8	1.5	0.0	-2.9	-7.3	-21.1	-42.9	
2890	2624	2373	2135	1912	1705	2781	2293	1875	1518	1217	968	0.6	0.9	0.0	-2.3	-6.2	-11.8	2.1	1.7	0.0	-3.3	-8.3	-24.2	-49.7	24"
2820	2510	2220	1950	1701	1479	2913	2308	1805	1393	1060	801	0.2	0.0	-1.5	-4.6	-9.5	-16.4	2.3	1.9	0.0	-3.7	-9.4	-28.1	-58.8	
3150	2866	2599	2348	2110	1887	2643	2188	1800	1468	1186	949	0.4	0.7	0.0	-1.9	-5.1	-9.7	2.8	3.0	2.2	0.0	-3.6	-15.7	-35.6	
3110	2830	2568	2320	2085	1866	3221	2667	2196	1792	1448	1160	0.4	0.8	0.0	-1.9	-5.2	-9.9	1.7	1.5	0.0	-2.8	-7.0	-20.5	-42.1	
2860	2645	2440	2244	2057	1879	3178	2718	2313	1956	1644	1372	0.4	0.9	0.0	-2.3	-5.2	-11.3	2.0	1.7	0.0	-3.2	-7.9	-22.7	-45.8	24"
3175	2923	2684	2458	2243	2039	3133	2655	2240	1878	1564	1292	0.4	0.7	0.0	-1.8	-4.8	-9.1	2.6	2.9	2.0	0.0	-3.4	-14.5	-32.6	
1990	1567	1236	1035	923	842	967	600	373	262	208	173	0.9	0.0	-4.5	-13.5	-28.3	-49.9	0.0	-4.5	-13.5	-28.3	-49.9	-118.6	-228.2	20"
2120	1822	1555	1328	1153	1036	1696	1253	913	666	502	405	0.7	0.0	-3.3	-9.7	-19.6	-33.8	2.2	0.0	-5.3	-14.1	-27.2	-69.0	-136.9	24"
3400	2693	2085	1570	1187	986	1412	886	521	301	172	119	0.4	0.8	0.0	-2.4	-6.7	-13.8	2.0	1.8	0.0	-3.8	-10.2	-35.0	-84.4	24"
2390	1973	1605	1303	1095	974	1902	1296	858	565	399	316	0.5	0.0	-2.7	-8.2	-17.0	-30.0	1.8	0.0	-4.6	-12.5	-24.6	-65.3	-134.9	
2200	1895	1619	1381	1191	1061	1827	1355	989	720	535	425	0.6	0.0	-3.0	-8.9	-18.0	-31.1	2.0	0.0	-4.8	-13.0	-25.1	-63.6	-126.7	24"
2200	1895	1619	1381	1191	1061	1827	1355	989	720	535	425	0.6	0.0	-3.0	-8.9	-18.0	-31.1	2.0	0.0	-4.8	-13.0	-25.1	-63.6	-126.7	

REMINGTON BALLISTICS

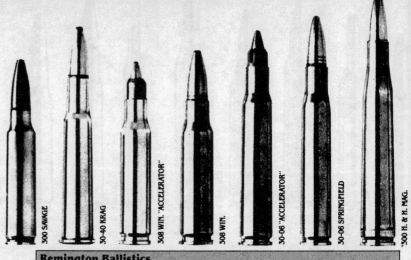

Remington Ballistics				
CALIBERS	**REMINGTON Order No.**	**BULLET**		
		Wt.-Grs.	**Style**	**Primer No.**
300 SAVAGE	R30SV3	180*	Soft Point Core-Lokt*	9½
	R30SV4	180	Pointed Soft Point Core-Lokt	9½
30-40 KRAG	R30402	180*	Pointed Soft Point Core-Lokt	9½
308 WIN. ACCELERATOR'	R308W5	55*	Pointed Soft Point	9½
308 WIN.	R308W1	150	Pointed Soft Point Core-Lokt	9½
	R308W6	165	Pointed Soft Point Core-Lokt	9½
	R308W2	180	Soft Point Core-Lokt	9½
	R308W3	180	Pointed Soft Point Core-Lokt	9½
	R308W7 ★	168*	Boattail H.P. Match	9½
30-06 ACCELERATOR	R30069	55*	Pointed Soft Point	9½
30-06 SPRINGFIELD	R30061	125	Pointed Soft Point	9½
	R30062	150	Pointed Soft Point Core-Lokt	9½
	R30063	150	Bronze Point	9½
	R3006B	165*	Pointed Soft Point Core-Lokt	9½
	R30064	180	Soft Point Core-Lokt	9½
	R30065	180	Pointed Soft Point Core-Lokt	9½
	R30066	180	Bronze Point	9½
	R30067	220	Soft Point Core-Lokt	9½
300 H&H MAG.	R300HH	180*	Pointed Soft Point Core-Lokt	9½M
300 WIN. MAG.	R300W1	150	Pointed Soft Point Core-Lokt	9½M
	R300W2	180*	Pointed Soft Point Core-Lokt	9½M
303 BRITISH	R303B1	180*	Soft Point Core-Lokt	9½
32-20 WIN.	R32201	100	Lead	6½
	R32202	100*	Soft Point	6½
32 WIN. SPECIAL	R32WS2	170*	Soft Point Core-Lokt	9½
8mm MAUSER	R8MSR	170*	Soft Point Core-Lokt	9½
8mm REM. MAG.	R8MM1	185*	Pointed Soft Point Core-Lokt	9½M
	R8MM2	220	Pointed Soft Point Core-Lokt	9½M
338 WIN. MAG.	R338W1	225*	Pointed Soft Point	9½M
	R338W2	250	Pointed Soft Point	9½M
35 REM.	R35R1	150	Pointed Soft Point Core-Lokt	9½
	R35R2	200*	Soft Point Core-Lokt	9½
350 REM. MAG.	R350M1	200*	Pointed Soft Point Core-Lokt	9½M
35 WHELEN	R35WH1 ★	200	Pointed Soft Point	9½M
	R35WH2 ★	250*	Soft Point	9½M
375 H&H MAG.	R375M1	270*	Soft Point	9½M
	R375M2	300	Metal Case	9½M
44-40 WIN.	R4440W	200*	Soft Point	2½
44 REM. MAG.	R44MG2	240	Soft Point	2½
	R44MG3	240	Semi-Jacketed Hollow Point	2½
	R44MG6 ★	210	Semi-Jacketed Hollow Point	2½
444 MAR.	R444M	240	Soft Point	9½
	R444M2	265*	Soft Point	9½
45-70 GOVERNMENT	R4570G	405*	Soft Point	9½
	R4570L	300	Jacketed Hollow Point	9½
458 WIN. MAG.	R458W1	500	Metal Case	9½M
	R458W2	500*	Soft Point	9½M

REMINGTON BALLISTICS

Cartridges shown (left to right): 300 WIN. MAG., 303 BRITISH, 32-20 WIN., 32 WIN. SPECIAL, 8mm MAUSER, 8mm REM. MAG., 35 REM., 350 REM. MAG., 375 H. & H. MAG., 44-40 WIN., 444 MAR., 45-70 GOVERNMENT, 458 WIN. MAG.

| VELOCITY FEET PER SECOND | | | | | | ENERGY FOOT-POUNDS | | | | | | TRAJECTORY** 0.0 indicates yardage at which rifle was sighted in. | | | | | | | | | | | | | BARREL LENGTH |
| | | | | | | | | | | | | SHORT RANGE (Bullet does not rise more than one inch above line of sight from muzzle to sighting-in range.) | | | | | | LONG RANGE (Bullet does not rise more than three inches above line of sight from muzzle to sighting-in range.) | | | | | | | |
Muzzle	100 Yds.	200 Yds.	300 Yds.	400 Yds.	500 Yds.	Muzzle	100 Yds.	200 Yds.	300 Yds.	400 Yds.	500 Yds.	50 Yds.	100 Yds.	150 Yds.	200 Yds.	250 Yds.	300 Yds.	100 Yds.	150 Yds.	200 Yds.	250 Yds.	300 Yds.	400 Yds.	500 Yds.	
2350	2025	1728	1467	1252	1098	2207	1639	1193	860	626	482	0.5	0.0	-2.6	-7.7	-15.6	-27.1	1.7	0.0	-4.2	-11.3	-21.9	-55.8	-112.0	24"
2350	2137	1935	1745	1570	1413	2207	1825	1496	1217	985	798	0.4	0.0	-2.3	-6.7	-13.5	-22.8	1.5	0.0	-3.6	-9.6	-18.2	-44.1	-84.2	
2430	2213	2007	1813	1632	1468	2360	1957	1610	1314	1064	861	0.4	0.0	-2.1	-6.2	-12.5	-21.1	1.4	0.0	-3.4	-8.9	-16.8	-40.9	-78.1	24"
3770	3215	2726	2286	1888	1541	1735	1262	907	638	435	290	0.2	0.5	0.0	-1.5	-4.2	-8.2	2.2	2.5	1.8	0.0	-3.2	-15.0	-36.7	24"
2820	2533	2263	2009	1774	1560	2648	2137	1705	1344	1048	810	0.2	0.0	-1.5	-4.5	-9.3	-15.9	2.3	1.9	0.0	-3.6	-9.1	-26.9	-55.7	24"
2700	2440	2194	1963	1748	1551	2670	2180	1763	1411	1119	881	0.2	0.0	-1.7	-5.0	-10.1	-17.2	2.5	2.1	0.0	-3.9	-9.7	-28.5	-58.8	
2620	2274	1955	1666	1414	1212	2743	2066	1527	1109	799	587	0.3	0.0	-2.0	-5.9	-12.1	-20.9	2.9	2.4	0.0	-4.7	-12.1	-36.9	-79.1	
2620	2393	2178	1974	1782	1604	2743	2288	1896	1557	1269	1028	0.2	0.0	-1.8	-5.2	-10.4	-17.7	2.6	2.1	0.0	-4.0	-9.9	-28.9	-58.8	
2680	2495	2314	2143	1979	1823	2678	2318	1998	1713	1460	1239	0.2	0.0	-1.6	-4.7	-9.4	-15.9	2.4	1.9	0.0	-3.5	-8.9	-25.3	-50.6	
4080	3485	2965	2502	2083	1709	2033	1483	1074	764	530	356	0.4	1.0	0.9	0.0	-1.9	-5.0	1.8	2.1	1.5	0.0	-2.7	-12.5	-30.5	24"
3140	2780	2447	2138	1853	1595	2756	2145	1662	1269	953	706	0.4	0.8	0.0	-2.1	-5.6	-9.7	1.8	1.5	0.0	-3.0	-7.7	-23.0	-48.5	24"
2910	2617	2342	2083	1843	1622	2820	2281	1827	1445	1131	876	0.6	0.9	0.0	-2.3	-6.3	-12.0	2.1	1.8	0.0	-3.5	-8.5	-25.0	-51.8	
2910	2656	2416	2189	1974	1773	2820	2349	1944	1596	1298	1047	0.6	0.9	0.0	-2.2	-6.0	-11.4	2.0	1.7	0.0	-3.2	-8.0	-23.3	-47.5	
2800	2534	2283	2047	1825	1621	2872	2352	1909	1534	1220	963	0.7	1.0	0.0	-2.5	-6.7	-12.7	2.3	1.9	0.0	-3.6	-9.0	-26.3	-54.1	
2700	2348	2023	1727	1466	1251	2913	2203	1635	1192	859	625	0.2	0.0	-1.8	-5.5	-11.2	-19.5	2.7	2.3	0.0	-4.4	-11.3	-34.4	-73.7	
2700	2469	2250	2042	1846	1663	2913	2436	2023	1666	1362	1105	0.2	0.0	-1.6	-4.8	-9.7	-16.5	2.4	2.0	0.0	-3.7	-9.3	-27.0	-54.9	
2700	2485	2280	2084	1899	1725	2913	2468	2077	1736	1441	1189	0.2	0.0	-1.6	-4.7	-9.6	-16.2	2.4	2.0	0.0	-3.6	-9.1	-26.2	-53.0	
2410	2130	1870	1632	1422	1246	2837	2216	1708	1301	988	758	0.4	0.0	-2.3	-6.8	-13.8	-23.6	1.5	0.0	-3.7	-9.9	-19.0	-47.4	-93.1	
2880	2640	2412	2196	1990	1798	3315	2785	2325	1927	1583	1292	0.6	0.9	0.0	-2.3	-6.0	-11.5	2.1	1.7	0.0	-3.2	-8.0	-23.3	-47.4	24"
3290	2951	2636	2342	2068	1813	3605	2900	2314	1827	1424	1095	0.3	0.7	0.0	-1.8	-4.8	-9.3	2.6	2.9	2.1	0.0	-3.5	-15.4	-35.5	24"
2960	2745	2540	2344	2157	1979	3501	3011	2578	2196	1859	1565	0.5	0.8	0.0	-2.1	-5.5	-10.4	1.9	1.6	0.0	-2.9	-7.3	-20.9	-41.9	
2460	2124	1817	1542	1311	1137	2418	1803	1319	950	687	517	0.4	0.0	-2.3	-6.9	-14.1	-24.4	1.5	0.0	-3.8	-10.2	-19.8	-50.5	-101.5	24"
1210	1021	913	834	769	712	325	231	185	154	131	113	0.0	-6.3	-20.9	-44.9	-79.3	-125.1	0.0	-11.5	-32.3	-63.6	-106.3	-230.3	-413.3	24"
1210	1021	913	834	769	712	325	231	185	154	131	113	0.0	-6.3	-20.9	-44.9	-79.3	-125.1	0.0	-11.5	-32.3	-63.6	-106.3	-230.3	-413.3	
2250	1921	1626	1372	1175	1044	1911	1393	998	710	521	411	0.6	0.0	-2.9	-8.6	-17.6	-30.5	1.9	0.0	-4.7	-12.7	-24.7	-63.2	-126.9	24"
2360	1969	1622	1333	1123	997	2102	1463	993	671	476	375	0.5	0.0	-2.7	-8.2	-17.0	-29.8	1.8	0.0	-4.5	-12.4	-24.3	-63.8	-130.7	24"
3080	2761	2464	2186	1927	1688	3896	3131	2494	1963	1525	1170	0.5	0.8	0.0	-2.1	-5.6	-10.7	1.8	1.6	0.0	-3.0	-7.6	-22.5	-46.8	24"
2830	2581	2346	2123	1913	1716	3912	3254	2688	2201	1787	1438	0.6	1.0	0.0	-2.4	-6.4	-12.1	2.2	1.8	0.0	-3.4	-8.5	-24.7	-50.5	
2780	2572	2374	2184	2003	1832	3860	3305	2815	2383	2004	1676	0.6	1.0	0.0	-2.4	-6.3	-12.0	2.2	1.8	0.0	-3.3	-8.4	-24.0	-48.4	24"
2660	2456	2261	2075	1898	1731	3927	3348	2837	2389	1999	1663	0.2	0.0	-1.7	-4.9	-9.8	-16.6	2.4	2.0	0.0	-3.7	-9.3	-26.6	-53.6	
2300	1874	1506	1218	1039	934	1762	1169	755	494	359	291	0.6	0.0	-3.0	-9.2	-19.1	-33.9	2.0	0.0	-5.1	-14.1	-27.8	-74.0	-152.3	24"
2080	1698	1376	1140	1001	911	1921	1280	841	577	445	369	0.8	0.0	-3.8	-11.3	-23.5	-41.2	2.5	0.0	-6.3	-17.1	-33.6	-87.7	-176.4	
2710	2410	2130	1870	1631	1421	3261	2579	2014	1553	1181	897	0.2	0.0	-1.7	-5.1	-10.4	-17.9	2.6	2.1	0.0	-4.0	-10.3	-30.5	-64.0	20"
2675	2378	2100	1842	1606	1399	3177	2510	1958	1506	1145	869	0.2	0.0	-1.8	-5.3	-10.8	-18.5	2.6	2.2	0.0	-4.2	-10.6	-31.5	-65.9	24"
2400	2066	1761	1492	1269	1107	3197	2369	1722	1235	893	680	0.4	0.0	-2.5	-7.3	-15.0	-26.0	1.6	0.0	-4.0	-10.9	-21.0	-53.8	-108.2	24"
2690	2420	2166	1928	1707	1507	4337	3510	2812	2228	1747	1361	0.2	0.0	-1.7	-5.1	-10.3	-17.6	2.5	2.1	0.0	-3.9	-10.0	-29.4	-60.7	24"
2530	2171	1843	1551	1307	1126	4263	3139	2262	1602	1138	844	0.3	0.0	-2.2	-6.5	-13.5	-23.4	1.7	0.0	-3.6	-9.8	-19.1	-49.1	-99.5	
1190	1006	900	822	756	699	629	449	360	300	254	217	0.0	-6.5	-21.6	-46.3	-81.8	-129.1	0.0	-11.8	-33.3	-65.5	-109.5	-237.4	-426.2	24"
1760	1380	1114	970	878	806	1650	1015	661	501	411	346	0.0	-2.7	-10.0	-23.0	-43.0	-71.2	0.0	-5.9	-17.6	-36.3	-63.1	-145.5	-273.0	20"
1760	1380	1114	970	878	806	1650	1015	661	501	411	346	0.0	-2.7	-10.0	-23.0	-43.0	-71.2	0.0	-5.9	-17.6	-36.3	-63.1	-145.5	-273.0	
1920	1477	1155	982	880	802	1719	1017	622	450	361	300	0.0	-2.2	-8.3	-19.7	-37.6	-63.2	0.0	-5.1	-15.4	-32.1	-56.7	-134.0	-256.2	
2350	1815	1377	1087	941	846	2942	1755	1010	630	472	381	0.6	0.0	-3.2	-9.9	-21.3	-38.5	2.1	0.0	-5.6	-15.9	-32.1	-87.8	-182.7	24"
2120	1733	1405	1160	1012	920	2644	1768	1162	791	603	498	0.7	0.0	-3.6	-10.8	-22.5	-39.5	2.4	0.0	-6.0	-16.4	-32.2	-84.3	-170.2	
1330	1168	1055	977	918	869	1590	1227	1001	858	758	679	0.0	-4.7	-15.8	-34.0	-60.0	-94.5	0.0	-8.7	-24.6	-48.2	-80.3	-172.4	-305.9	24"
1810	1497	1244	1073	969	895	2182	1492	1031	767	625	533	0.0	-2.3	-8.5	-19.4	-35.9	-59.0	0.0	-5.0	-14.8	-30.1	-52.1	-119.5	—	
2040	1823	1623	1442	1237	1161	4620	3689	2924	2308	1839	1469	0.7	0.0	-3.3	-9.6	-19.2	-32.5	2.2	0.0	-5.2	-13.6	-25.8	-63.2	-121.7	24"
2040	1770	1527	1319	1157	1046	4712	3547	2640	1970	1516	1239	0.8	0.0	-3.5	-10.3	-20.8	-35.6	2.4	0.0	-5.6	-14.9	-28.5	-71.5	-140.4	

WEATHERBY BALLISTICS

BULLETS		VELOCITY (in Feet per Second)						ENERGY (in Foot Pounds)						BULLET DROP (in Inches From Bore Line)			PATH OF BULLET (Above or below Line-of-sight) For riflescopes mounted 1.5" above bore		
Weight In Grains	Type	Muzzle	100 Yds.	200 Yds.	300 Yds.	400 Yds.	500 Yds.	Muzzle	100 Yds.	200 Yds.	300 Yds.	400 Yds.	500 Yds.	100 Yds.	200 Yds.	300 Yds.	100 Yds.	200 Yds.	300 Yds.
.224 WM																			
55	Pt-Ex	3650	3192	2780	2403	2057	1742	1627	1244	943	705	516	370	−1.4	−6.3	−15.6	2.8	3.6	0
.240 WM																			
87	Pt-Ex	3500	3202	2924	2663	2416	2183	2366	1980	1651	1370	1127	920	−1.5	−6.4	−15.4	2.6	3.4	0
100	Pt-Ex	3395	3106	2835	2581	2339	2112	2559	2142	1785	1478	1215	990	−1.6	−6.8	−16.4	2.9	3.6	0
100	Partition	3395	3069	2766	2483	2216	1966	2559	2091	1698	1368	1091	859	−1.6	−6.9	−16.8	3.0	3.8	0
.257 WM																			
87	Pt-Ex	3825	3456	3118	2805	2513	2239	2826	2308	1878	1520	1220	969	−1.3	−5.5	−13.2	2.1	2.9	0
100	Pt-Ex	3555	3237	2941	2665	2404	2159	2806	2326	1920	1576	1283	1035	−1.5	−6.2	−15.1	2.6	3.3	0
100	Partition	3555	3292	3044	2810	2589	2377	2806	2406	2058	1754	1488	1254	−1.4	−6.1	−14.5	2.4	3.1	0
117	Semi Pt-Ex	3300	2882	2502	2152	1830	1547	2829	2158	1626	1203	870	621	−1.7	−7.7	−19.3	3.7	4.6	0
117	Partition	3300	2998	2717	2452	2202	1967	2829	2335	1917	1561	1260	1005	−1.7	−7.3	−17.6	3.2	3.9	0
120	Partition	3290	3074	2869	2673	2486	2306	2884	2518	2193	1904	1646	1416	−1.7	−7.0	−16.7	2.9	3.6	0
.270 WM																			
100	Pt-Ex	3760	3380	3033	2712	2412	2133	3139	2537	2042	1633	1292	1010	−1.3	−5.7	−13.9	2.3	3.0	0
130	Pt-Ex	3375	3100	2842	2598	2366	2148	3287	2773	2330	1948	1616	1331	−1.6	−6.9	−16.4	2.9	3.6	0
130	Partition	3375	3119	2878	2649	2432	2225	3287	2808	2390	2026	1707	1429	−1.6	−6.8	−16.2	2.8	3.5	0
150	Pt-Ex	3245	3019	2803	2598	2402	2215	3507	3034	2617	2248	1922	1634	−1.7	−7.3	−17.3	3.0	3.8	0
150	Partition	3245	3036	2837	2647	2465	2290	3507	3070	2681	2334	2023	1746	−1.7	−7.2	−17.1	3.0	3.7	0
7mm WM																			
139	Pt-Ex	3400	3138	2892	2659	2437	2226	3567	3039	2580	2181	1832	1529	−1.6	−6.7	−16.0	2.7	3.5	0
140	Partition	3400	3163	2939	2726	2522	2328	3593	3110	2684	2309	1978	1684	−1.6	−6.6	−15.7	2.7	3.4	0
150	Pt-Ex	3260	3023	2799	2586	2382	2188	3539	3044	2609	2227	1890	1595	−1.7	−7.2	−17.2	3.0	3.8	0
160	Partition	3200	3004	2816	2637	2464	2297	3637	3205	2817	2469	2156	1875	−1.8	−7.4	−17.4	3.0	3.7	0
175	Pt-Ex	3070	2879	2696	2520	2351	2189	3662	3220	2824	2467	2147	1861	−1.9	−8.0	−19.0	3.4	4.1	0
.300 WM																			
110	Pt-Ex	3900	3441	3028	2652	2305	1985	3714	2891	2239	1717	1297	962	−1.2	−5.4	−13.5	2.2	3.0	0
150	Pt-Ex	3600	3297	3015	2751	2502	2266	4316	3621	3028	2520	2084	1709	−1.4	−6.0	−14.5	2.4	3.1	0
150	Partition	3600	3307	3033	2776	2533	2303	4316	3642	3064	2566	2137	1766	−1.4	−6.0	−14.4	2.4	3.1	0
180	Pt-Ex	3300	3064	2841	2629	2426	2233	4352	3753	3226	2762	2352	1992	−1.7	−7.1	−16.8	2.9	3.6	0
180	Partition	3300	3077	2865	2663	2470	2285	4352	3784	3280	2834	2438	2086	−1.7	−7.0	−16.6	2.9	3.6	0
220	Semi Pt-Ex	2905	2498	2126	1787	1490	1250	4122	3047	2207	1560	1085	763	−2.3	−10.2	−25.8	5.3	6.5	0
.340 WM																			
200	Pt-Ex	3260	3011	2775	2552	2339	2137	4719	4025	3420	2892	2429	2027	−1.7	−7.3	−17.4	3.1	3.8	0
210	Partition	3250	2991	2746	2515	2295	2086	4924	4170	3516	2948	2455	2029	−1.7	−7.4	−17.6	3.1	3.9	0
250	Semi Pt-Ex	3000	2670	2363	2078	1812	1574	4995	3958	3100	2396	1823	1375	−2.1	−9.1	−22.4	1.7	0	−8.0
250	Partition	3000	2806	2621	2443	2272	2108	4995	4371	3812	3311	2864	2465	−2.0	−8.5	−19.9	1.5	0	−6.5
																	3.6	4.3	0
.378 WM																			
270	Pt-Ex	3180	2976	2781	2594	2415	2243	6062	5308	4635	4034	3495	3015	−1.8	−7.5	−17.8	1.2	0	−5.8
																	3.1	3.8	0
300	RN	2925	2576	2252	1952	1680	1439	5698	4419	3379	2538	1881	1379	−2.2	−9.7	−24.0	1.9	0	−8.7
																	4.8	5.8	0
.460 WM																			
500	RN	2700	2404	2128	1869	1635	1425	8092	6416	5026	3878	2969	2254	−2.6	−11.2	−27.4	2.3	0	−9.8
																	5.6	6.6	0
500	FMJ	2700	2425	2166	1923	1700	1497	8092	6526	5210	4105	3209	2488	−2.5	−11.1	−26.9	2.2	0	−9.5
																	5.4	6.3	0

NOTE: These tables were calculated by computer using a standard modern scientific technique to predict trajectories from the best available data for each cartridge. The figures shown are expected to be reasonably accurate of ammunition behavior under standard conditions. However, the shooter is cautioned that performance will vary because of variations in rifle, ammunition and atmospheric conditions. BALLISTIC COEFFICIENTS used for these tables are as published by Hornady and Nosler ballistic data compiled using 26" barrels.

WINCHESTER BALLISTICS
CENTERFIRE PISTOL AND REVOLVER

Cartridge	Symbol	Bullet Wt. Grs.	Type	Velocity (fps)			Energy (ft-lbs.)			Mid Range Traj. (in.)		Barrel Length Inches
				Muzzle	50 Yds.	100 Yds.	Muzzle	50 Yds.	100 Yds.	50 Yds.	100 Yds.	
25 Automatic (6.35mm) Expanding Point Super-X	X25AXP	45	XP**	815	729	655	66	53	42	1.8	7.7	2
25 Automatic (6.35mm) Full Metal Case Super-X	X25AP	50	FMC	760	707	659	64	56	48	2.0	8.7	2
# 30 Luger (7.65mm) Full Metal Case Super-X	X30LP	93	FMC	1220	1110	1040	305	255	225	0.9	3.5	4½
# 30 Carbine Hollow Soft Point Super-X	X30M1	110	HSP	1790	1601	1430	783	626	500	0.4	1.7	10
# 30 Carbine Full Metal Case Super-X	X30M2	110	FMC	1740	1552	1384	740	588	468	0.4	1.8	10
32 Smith & Wesson Lead Round Nose Super-X (Inside Lubricated)	X32SWP	85	Lead-RN	680	645	610	90	81	73	2.5	10.5	3
32 Smith & Wesson Long (Colt New Police) Lead Round Nose Super-X (Inside Lubricated)	X32SWLP	98	Lead-RN	705	670	635	115	98	88	2.3	10.5	4
32 Short Colt Lead Round Nose Super-X (Greased)	X32SCP	80	Lead-RN	745	665	590	100	79	62	2.2	9.9	4
32 Long Colt Lead Round Nose Super-X (Inside Lubricated)	X32LCP	82	Lead-RN	755	715	675	105	93	83	2.0	8.7	4
32 Automatic Silvertip Hollow Point Super-X	X32ASHP	60	STHP	970	895	835	125	107	93	1.3	5.4	4
32 Automatic Full Metal Case Super-X	X32AP	71	FMC	905	855	810	129	115	97	1.4	5.8	4
38 Smith & Wesson Lead Round Nose Super-X (Inside Lubricated)	X38SWP	145	Lead-RN	685	650	620	150	135	125	2.4	10.0	4
380 Automatic Silvertip Hollow Point Super-X	X380ASHP	85	STHP	1000	921	860	189	160	140	1.2	5.1	3¾
380 Automatic Full Metal Case Super-X	X380AP	95	FMC	955	865	785	190	160	130	1.4	5.9	3¾
38 Special Silvertip Hollow Point Super-X	X38S9HP	110	STHP	945	894	850	218	195	176	1.3	5.4	4V
38 Special Lead Round Nose Super-X (Inside Lubricated)	X38S1P	158	Lead-RN	755	723	693	200	183	168	2.0	8.3	4V
38 Special Lead Semi-Wad Cutter Super-X (Inside Lubricated)	X38WCPSV	158	Lead-SWC	755	721	689	200	182	167	2.0	8.4	4V
38 Special Metal Point Super-X (Inside Lubricated) (Lead Bearing)	X38S2P	158	Met. Pt.	755	723	693	200	183	168	2.0	8.3	4V
38 Special Silvertip Hollow Point + P Super-X	X38SSHP	95	STHP	1100	1002	932	255	212	183	1.0	4.3	4V
# 38 Special Jacketed Hollow Point + P Super-X	X38S6PH	110	JHP	995	926	871	242	210	185	1.2	5.1	4V
38 Special Jacketed Hollow Point + P Super-X	X38S7PH	125	JHP	945	898	858	248	224	204	1.3	5.4	4V
# 38 Special Silvertip Hollow Point + P Super-X	X38S8HP	125	STHP	945	898	858	248	224	204	1.3	5.4	4V
38 Special Lead Hollow Point + P Super-X (Inside Lubricated)	X38SPD	158	Lead-HP	890	855	823	278	257	238	1.4	6.0	4V
38 Special Lead Semi-Wad Cutter + P Super-X (Inside Lubricated)	X38WCP	158	Lead-SWC	890	855	823	278	257	238	1.4	6.0	4V
38 Special Lead Mid-Range (Clean Cutting) Match (Inside Lubricated)	X38SMRP	148	Lead-WC	710	634	566	166	132	105	2.4	10.8	4V
9mm Luger (Parabellum) Full Metal Case Super-X	X9LP	115	FMC	1155	1047	971	341	280	241	0.9	3.9	4
9mm Luger (Parabellum) Silvertip Hollow Point Super-X	X9MMSHP	115	STHP	1225	1095	1007	383	306	259	0.8	3.6	4
* 38 Super Automatic Silvertip Hollow Point + P Super-X	X38ASHP	125	STHP	1240	1130	1050	427	354	306	0.8	3.4	5
* 38 Super Automatic Full Metal Case + P Super-X	X38A1P	130	FMC	1215	1099	1017	426	348	298	0.8	3.6	5
# 38 Automatic (For all 38 Automatic Pistols) Full Metal Case Super-X	X38A2P	130	FMC	1040	980	925	310	275	245	1.0	4.7	4½
# 357 Magnum Jacketed Hollow Point Super-X	X3573P	110	JHP	1295	1095	975	410	292	232	0.8	3.5	4V
# 357 Magnum Jacketed Hollow Point Super-X	X3576P	125	JHP	1450	1240	1090	583	427	330	0.6	2.8	4V
# 357 Magnum Silvertip Hollow Point Super-X	X3575HP	145	STHP	1290	1155	1060	535	428	361	0.8	3.5	4V
# 357 Magnum Lead Semi-Wad Cutter Super-X (Inside Lubricated)	X3571P	158	Lead-SWC**	1235	1104	1015	535	428	361	0.8	3.5	4V
# 357 Magnum Jacketed Hollow Point Super-X	X3574P	158	JHP	1235	1104	1015	535	428	361	0.8	3.5	4V
# 357 Magnum Jacketed Soft Point Super-X	X3575P	158	JSP	1235	1104	1015	535	428	361	0.8	3.5	4V
# 9mm Winchester Magnum Full Metal Case Super-X	X9MMWM	115	FMC	1475	1264	1109	555	408	314	0.6	2.7	5
# 41 Remington Magnum Silvertip Hollow Point Super-X	X41MSTHP	175	STHP	1250	1120	1029	607	488	412	0.8	3.4	4V
# 41 Remington Magnum Lead Semi-Wad Cutter Super-X	X41MP	210	Lead-SWC	965	898	842	434	376	331	1.3	5.4	4V
# 41 Remington Magnum Jacketed Soft Point Super-X	X41MJSP	210	JSP	1300	1162	1062	788	630	526	0.7	3.2	4V
# 41 Remington Magnum Jacketed Hollow Point Super-X	X41MHP	210	JHP	1300	1162	1062	788	630	526	0.7	3.2	4V
# 44 Smith & Wesson Special Silvertip Hollow Point Super-X	X44STHPS	200	STHP	900	860	822	360	328	300	1.4	5.9	6½
# 44 Smith & Wesson Special Lead Round Nose Super-X (Inside Lubricated)	X44SP	246	Lead-RN	755	725	695	310	285	265	2.0	8.3	6½
# 44 Remington Magnum Silvertip Hollow Point Super-X	X44MSTHP	210	STHP	1250	1106	1010	729	570	475	0.8	3.5	4V
# 44 Remington Magnum Lead Semi-Wad Cutter (Med. Vel.) Super-X (Inside Lubricated)	X44MWCP	240	Lead-SWC	1000	937	885	533	468	417	1.2	4.9	6½V
44 Remington Magnum Lead Semi-Wad Cutter (Gas Check) Super-X	X44MP	240	Lead-SWC	1350	1186	1069	971	749	608	0.7	3.1	4V
45 Automatic Silvertip Hollow Point Super-X	X45ASHP5	185	STHP	1000	938	888	411	362	324	1.2	4.9	5
45 Automatic Full Metal Case Super-X	X45A1P	230	FMC	810	776	745	335	308	284	1.7	7.2	5
45 Automatic Super-Match Full Metal Case Semi-Wad Cutter	X45AWCP	185	FMC-SWC	770	707	650	244	205	174	2.0	8.7	5
# 45 Colt Silvertip Hollow Point Super-X	X45CSHP	225	STHP	920	877	839	423	384	352	1.4	5.6	5½
# 45 Colt Lead Round Nose Super-X (Inside Lubricated)	X45CP	255	Lead-RN	860	820	780	420	380	345	1.5	6.1	5½
# 45 Winchester Magnum Full Metal Case Super-X (Not for Arms Chambered for Standard 45 Automatic)	X45WM	230	FMC	1400	1232	1107	1001	775	636	0.6	2.8	5
CENTERFIRE BLANK CARTRIDGES												
32 Smith & Wesson Black Powder	32BL2P		Black Powder	—	—	—	—	—	—	—	—	—
38 Smith & Wesson Smokeless Powder	38BLP		Smokeless Powder	—	—	—	—	—	—	—	—	—
38 Special Smokeless Powder	38SBLP		Smokeless Powder	—	—	—	—	—	—	—	—	—

+ P Ammunition with (+ P) on the case head stamp is loaded to higher pressure. Use only in firearms designated for this cartridge and so recommended by the gun manufacturer.

V-Data is based on velocity obtained from 4" vented test barrels for revolver cartridges (38 Special, 357 Magnum, 41 Rem. Mag. and 44 Rem. Mag.)

*For use only in 38 Super Automatic Pistols.

#Acceptable for use in rifles also.

Specifications are nominal. Test barrels are used to determine ballistics figures. Individual firearms may differ from test barrel statistics. Specifications subject to change without notice

FMC-Full Metal Case ● JHP-Jacketed Hollow Point ● JSP-Jacketed Soft Point
LHP-Lubaloy Hollow Point ● RN-Round Nose
Met. Pt.-Metal Point ● XP-Expanding Point ● WC-Wad Cutter ● SWC-Semi Wad Cutter
STHP-Silvertip Hollow Point ● HP-Hollow Point
L-Lubaloy ● **-Wax Coated
HSP - Hollow Soft Point

WINCHESTER BALLISTICS CENTERFIRE RIFLE

Cartridge	Symbol	Game Selector Guide	Bullet Wt. Grs.	Bullet Type	Barrel Length Inches	Velocity In Feet Per Second (fps) Muzzle	100	200	300	400	500
218 Bee Super-X	X218B	V	46	HP	24	2760	2102	1550	1155	961	850
22 Hornet Super-X	X22H1	V	45	SP	24	2690	2042	1502	1128	948	840
22 Hornet Super-X	X22H2	V	46	HP	24	2690	2042	1502	1128	948	841
22-250 Remington Super-X	X222501	V	55	PSP	24	3680	3137	2656	2222	1832	1493
222 Remington Super-X	X222R	V	50	PSP	24	3140	2602	2123	1700	1350	1107
222 Remington Super-X	X222R1	V	55	FMC	24	3020	2675	2355	2057	1783	1537
223 Remington Super-X	X223RH	V	53	HP	24	3330	2882	2477	2106	1770	1475
223 Remington Super-X	X223R	V	55	PSP	24	3240	2747	2304	1905	1554	1270
223 Remington Super-X	X223R1	V	55	FMC	24	3240	2877	2543	2232	1943	1679
225 Winchester Super-X	X2251	V	55	PSP	24	3570	3066	2616	2208	1838	1514
243 Winchester Super-X	X2431	V	80	PSP	24	3350	2955	2593	2259	1951	1670
243 Winchester Super-X	X2432	D,O/P	100	PP	24	2960	2697	2449	2215	1993	1786
6mm Remington Super-X	X6MMR1	V	80	PSP	24	3470	3064	2694	2352	2036	1747
6mm Remington Super-X	X6MMR2	D,O/P	100	PP	24	3100	2829	2573	2332	2104	1889
25-06 Remington Super-X	X25061	V	90	PEP	24	3440	3043	2680	2344	2034	1749
25-06 Remington Super-X	X25062	D,O/P	120	PEP	24	2990	2730	2484	2252	2032	1825
# 25-20 Winchester Super-X	X25202	V	86	SP	24	1460	1194	1030	931	858	798
25-35 Winchester Super-X	X2535	D	117	SP	24	2230	1866	1545	1282	1097	984
† 250 Savage Super-X	X2501	V	87	PSP	24	3030	2673	2342	2036	1755	1504
250 Savage Super-X	X2503	D,O/P	100	ST	24	2820	2467	2140	1839	1569	1339
† # 256 Winchester Mag. Super-X	X2561P	V	60	HP	24	2760	2097	1542	1149	957	846
257 Roberts + P Super-X	X257P2	D,O/P	100	ST	24	3000	2633	2295	1982	1697	1447
257 Roberts + P Super-X	X257P3	D,O/P	117	PP	24	2780	2411	2071	1761	1488	1263
† 264 Winchester Mag. Super-X	X2641	V	100	PSP	24	3320	2926	2565	2231	1923	1644
264 Winchester Mag. Super-X	X2642	D,O/P	140	PP	24	3030	2782	2548	2326	2114	1914
270 Winchester Super-X	X2701	V	100	PSP	24	3430	3021	2649	2305	1988	1699
270 Winchester Super-X	X2705	D,O/P	130	PP	24	3060	2802	2559	2329	2110	1904
270 Winchester Super-X	X2703	D,O/P	130	ST	24	3060	2776	2510	2259	2022	1801
270 Winchester Super-X	X2704	O,M	150	PP	24	2850	2585	2336	2100	1879	1673
284 Winchester Super-X	X2841	D,O/P	125	PP	24	3140	2829	2538	2265	2010	1772
284 Winchester Super-X	X2842	D,O/P,M	150	PP	24	2860	2595	2344	2108	1886	1680
7mm Mauser (7 × 57) Super-X	X7MM	D	175	SP	24	2440	2137	1857	1603	1382	1204
7mm Remington Mag. Super-X	X7MMR1	D,O/P,M	150	PP	24	3110	2830	2568	2320	2085	1866
7mm Remington Mag. Super-X	X7MMR2	D,O/P,M	175	PP	24	2860	2645	2440	2244	2057	1879
# 30 Carbine Super-X	X30M1	V	110	HSP	20	1990	1567	1236	1035	923	842
# 30 Carbine Super-X	X30M2	V	110	FMC	20	1990	1596	1278	1070	952	870
30-30 Winchester Super-X	X30301	D	150	HP	24	2390	2018	1684	1398	1177	1036
30-30 Winchester Super-X	X30306	D	150	PP	24	2390	2018	1684	1398	1177	1036
30-30 Winchester Super-X	X30302	D	150	ST	24	2390	2018	1684	1398	1177	1036
30-30 Winchester Super-X	X30303	D	170	PP	24	2200	1895	1619	1381	1191	1061
30-30 Winchester Super-X	X30304	D	170	ST	24	2200	1895	1619	1381	1191	1061
30-06 Springfield Super-X	X30062	V	125	PSP	24	3140	2780	2447	2138	1853	1595
30-06 Springfield Super-X	X30061	D,O/P	150	PP	24	2920	2580	2265	1972	1704	1466
30-06 Springfield Super-X	X30063	D,O/P	150	ST	24	2910	2617	2342	2083	1843	1622
30-06 Springfield Super-X	X30065	D,O/P,M	165	SP	24	2800	2573	2357	2151	1956	1772
30-06 Springfield Super-X	X30064	D,O/P,M,L	180	PP	24	2700	2348	2023	1727	1466	1251
30-06 Springfield Super-X	X30066	D,O/P,M,L	180	ST	24	2700	2469	2250	2042	1846	1663
30-06 Springfield Super-X	X30069	M,L	220	ST	24	2410	2192	1985	1791	1611	1448
30-40 Krag Super-X	X30401	D	180	PP	24	2430	2099	1795	1525	1298	1128

TRAJECTORY Inches above (+) or below (−) line of sight. 0 = yardage at which rifle is sighted in.

Specifications are nominal. Test barrels are used to determine ballistics figures. Individual firearms may differ from these test barrels statistics. Specifications subject to change without notice.

#Acceptable for use in pistols and revolvers also. †These items will be obsolete subject to existing inventories.
HSP-Hollow Soft Point, PEP-Positive Expanding Point, PSP-Pointed Soft Point, PP-Power-Point®, FMC-Full Metal Case, SP-Soft Point, HP-Hollow Point, ST-Silvertip®, JHP-Jacketed Hollow Point, STHP-Silvertip Hollow Point

GAME SELECTOR CODE

| V = Varmint | D = Deer | M = Medium Game (i.e. Elk) | L = Large Game (i.e. Moose) | O/P = Open or Plains shooting (i.e. Antelope, Deer) | XL = Extra Large Game (i.e. Kodiak Bear) |

WINCHESTER BALLISTICS
CENTERFIRE RIFLE

Energy In Foot-Pounds (ft.-lbs.)						Trajectory, Short Range						Trajectory, Long Range						
Muzzle	100	200	300	400	500	50	100	150	200	250	300	100	150	200	250	300	400	500
								Yards							Yards			
778	451	245	136	94	74	0.3	0	-2.3	-7.2	-15.8	-29.4	1.5	0	-4.2	-12.0	-24.8	-71.4	-155.6
723	417	225	127	90	70	0.3	0	-2.4	-7.7	-16.9	-31.3	1.6	0	-4.5	-12.8	-26.4	-75.6	-163.4
739	426	230	130	92	72	0.3	0	-2.4	-7.7	-16.9	-31.3	1.6	0	-4.5	-12.8	-26.4	-75.5	-163.3
1654	1201	861	603	410	272	0.2	0.5	0	-1.6	-4.4	-8.7	2.3	2.6	1.9	0	-3.4	-15.9	-38.9
1094	752	500	321	202	136	0.5	0.9	0	-2.5	-6.9	-13.7	2.2	1.9	0	-3.8	-10.0	-32.3	-73.8
1114	874	677	517	388	288	0.5	0.9	0	-2.2	-6.1	-11.7	2.0	1.7	0	-3.3	-8.3	-24.9	-52.5
1305	978	722	522	369	256	0.3	0.7	0	-1.9	-5.3	-10.3	1.7	1.4	0	-2.9	-7.4	-22.7	-49.1
1282	921	648	443	295	197	0.4	0.8	0	-2.2	-6.0	-11.8	1.9	1.6	0	-3.3	-8.5	-26.7	-59.6
1282	1011	790	608	461	344	0.4	0.7	0	-1.9	-5.1	-9.9	1.7	1.4	0	-2.8	-7.1	-21.2	-44.6
1556	1148	836	595	412	280	0.2	0.6	0	-1.7	-4.6	-9.0	2.4	2.8	2.0	0	-3.5	-16.3	-39.5
1993	1551	1194	906	676	495	0.3	0.7	0	-1.8	-4.9	-9.4	2.6	2.9	2.1	0	-3.6	-16.2	-37.9
1945	1615	1332	1089	882	708	0.5	0.9	0	-2.2	-5.8	-11.0	1.9	1.6	0	-3.1	-7.8	-22.6	-46.3
2139	1667	1289	982	736	542	0.3	0.6	0	-1.6	-4.5	-8.7	2.4	2.7	1.9	0	-3.3	-14.9	-35.0
2133	1777	1470	1207	983	792	0.4	0.8	0	-1.9	-5.2	-9.9	1.7	1.5	0	-2.8	-7.0	-20.4	-41.7
2364	1850	1435	1098	827	611	0.3	0.6	0	-1.7	-4.5	-8.8	2.4	2.7	2.0	0	-3.4	-15.0	-35.2
2382	1985	1644	1351	1100	887	0.5	0.8	0	-2.1	-5.6	-10.7	1.9	1.6	0	-3.0	-7.5	-22.0	-44.8
407	272	203	165	141	122	0	-4.1	-14.4	-31.8	-57.3	-92.0	0	-8.2	-23.5	-47.0	-79.6	-175.9	-319.4
1292	904	620	427	313	252	0.6	0	-3.1	-9.2	-19.0	-33.1	2.1	0	-5.1	-13.8	-27.0	-70.1	-142.0
1773	1380	1059	801	595	437	0.5	0.9	0	-2.3	-6.1	-11.8	2.0	1.7	0	-3.3	-8.4	-25.2	-53.4
1765	1351	1017	751	547	398	0.2	0	-1.6	-4.9	-10.0	-17.4	2.4	2.0	0	-3.9	-10.1	-30.5	-65.2
1015	586	317	176	122	95	0.3	0	-2.3	-7.3	-15.9	-29.6	1.5	0	-4.2	-12.1	-25.0	-72.1	-157.2
1998	1539	1169	872	639	465	0.5	0.9	0	-2.4	-6.4	-12.3	2.9	3.0	1.6	0	-6.4	-23.2	-51.2
2009	1511	1115	806	576	415	0.8	1.1	0	-2.9	-7.8	-15.1	2.6	2.2	0	-4.2	-10.8	-33.0	-70.0
2447	1901	1461	1105	821	600	0.3	0.7	0	-1.8	-5.0	-9.7	2.7	3.0	2.2	0	-3.7	-16.6	-38.9
2854	2406	2018	1682	1389	1139	0.5	0.8	0	-2.0	-5.4	-10.2	1.8	1.5	0	-2.9	-7.2	-20.8	-42.2
2612	2027	1557	1179	877	641	0.3	0.6	0	-1.7	-4.6	-9.0	2.5	2.8	2.0	0	-3.4	-15.5	-36.4
2702	2267	1890	1565	1285	1046	0.4	0.8	0	-2.0	-5.3	-10.1	1.8	1.5	0	-2.8	-7.1	-20.6	-42.0
2702	2225	1818	1472	1180	936	0.5	0.8	0	-2.0	-5.5	-10.4	1.8	1.5	0	-2.9	-7.4	-21.6	-44.3
2705	2226	1817	1468	1175	932	0.6	1.0	0	-2.4	-6.4	-12.2	2.2	1.8	0	-3.4	-8.6	-25.0	-51.4
2736	2221	1788	1424	1121	871	0.4	0.8	0	-2.0	-5.4	-10.1	1.7	1.5	0	-2.8	-7.2	-21.1	-43.7
2724	2243	1830	1480	1185	940	0.6	1.0	0	-2.4	-6.3	-12.1	2.1	1.8	0	-3.4	-8.5	-24.8	-51.0
2313	1774	1340	998	742	563	0.4	0	-2.3	-6.8	-13.8	-23.7	1.5	0	-3.7	-10.0	-19.1	-48.1	-95.4
3221	2667	2196	1792	1448	1160	0.4	0.8	0	-1.9	-5.2	-9.9	1.7	1.5	0	-2.8	-7.0	-20.5	-42.1
3178	2718	2313	1956	1644	1372	0.6	0.9	0	-2.3	-6.0	-11.3	2.0	1.7	0	-3.2	-7.9	-22.7	-45.8
967	600	373	262	208	173	0.9	0	-4.5	-13.5	-28.3	-49.9	0	-4.5	-13.5	-28.3	-49.9	-118.6	-228.2
967	622	399	280	221	185	0.9	0	-4.3	-13.0	-26.9	-47.4	2.9	0	-7.2	-19.7	-38.7	-100.4	-200.5
1902	1356	944	651	461	357	0.5	0	-2.6	-7.7	-16.0	-27.9	1.7	0	-4.3	-11.6	-22.7	-59.1	-120.5
1902	1356	944	651	461	357	0.5	0	-2.6	-7.7	-16.0	-27.9	1.7	0	-4.3	-11.6	-22.7	-59.1	-120.5
1902	1356	944	651	461	357	0.5	0	-2.6	-7.7	-16.0	-27.9	1.7	0	-4.3	-11.6	-22.7	-59.1	-120.5
1827	1355	989	720	535	425	0.6	0	-3.0	-8.9	-18.0	-31.1	2.0	0	-4.8	-13.0	-25.1	-63.6	-126.7
1827	1355	989	720	535	425	0.6	0	-3.0	-8.9	-18.0	-31.1	2.0	0	-4.8	-13.0	-25.1	-63.6	-126.7
2736	2145	1662	1269	953	706	0.4	0.8	0	-2.1	-5.6	-10.7	1.8	1.5	0	-3.0	-7.7	-23.0	-48.5
2839	2217	1708	1295	967	716	0.6	1.0	0	-2.4	-6.6	-12.7	2.2	1.8	0	-3.5	-9.0	-27.0	-57.1
2820	2281	1827	1445	1131	876	0.6	0.9	0	-2.3	-6.3	-12.0	2.1	1.8	0	-3.3	-8.5	-25.0	-51.8
2873	2426	2036	1696	1402	1151	0.7	1.0	0	-2.5	-6.5	-12.2	2.2	1.9	0	-3.6	-8.4	-24.4	-49.6
2913	2003	1635	1192	859	625	0.2	0	-1.8	-5.5	-11.2	-19.5	2.7	2.3	0	-4.4	-11.3	-34.4	-73.7
2913	2436	2023	1666	1362	1105	0.2	0	-1.6	-4.8	-9.7	-16.5	2.4	2.0	0	-3.7	-9.3	-27.0	-54.9
2837	2347	1924	1567	1268	1024	0.4	0	-2.2	-6.4	-12.7	-21.6	1.5	0	-3.5	-9.1	-17.2	-41.8	-79.9
2360	1761	1288	929	673	508	0.4	0	-2.4	-7.1	-14.5	-25.0	1.6	0	-3.9	-10.5	-20.3	-51.7	-103.9

WINCHESTER BALLISTICS
CENTERFIRE RIFLE

Cartridge	Symbol	Game Selector Guide	Wt. Grs.	Bullet Type	Barrel Length Inches	Muzzle	Velocity In Feet Per Second (fps)				
							100	200	300	400	500
300 Winchester Mag. Super-X	X30WM1	D,O/P	150	PP	24	3290	2951	2636	2342	2068	1813
300 Winchester Mag. Super-X	X30WM2	O/P,M,L	180	PP	24	2960	2745	2540	2344	2157	1979
300 Winchester Mag. Super-X	X30WM3	M,L,XL	220	ST	24	2680	2448	2228	2020	1823	1640
300 H. & H. Magnum Super-X	X300H2	O/P,M,L	180	ST	24	2880	2640	2412	2196	1991	1798
300 Savage Super-X	X3001	D,O/P	150	PP	24	2630	2311	2015	1743	1500	1295
300 Savage Super-X	X3003	D,O/P	150	ST	24	2630	2354	2095	1853	1631	1434
300 Savage Super-X	X3004	D	180	PP	24	2350	2025	1728	1467	1252	1098
303 Savage Super-X	X3032	D	190	ST	24	1890	1612	1372	1183	1055	970
303 British Super-X	X303B1	D	180	PP	24	2460	2233	2018	1816	1629	1459
307 Winchester Super-X	X3075	D	150	PP	24	2760	2321	1924	1575	1289	1091
† 307 Winchester Super-X	X3076	D,M	180	PP	24	2510	2179	1874	1599	1362	1177
† 308 Winchester Super-X	X3087	V	125	PSP	24	3050	2697	2370	2067	1788	1537
308 Winchester Super-X	X3085	D,O/P	150	PP	24	2820	2488	2179	1893	1633	1405
308 Winchester Super-X	X3082	D,O/P	150	ST	24	2820	2533	2263	2009	1774	1560
308 Winchester Super-X	X3086	D,O/P,M	180	PP	24	2620	2274	1955	1666	1414	1212
308 Winchester Super-X	X3083	D,O/P,M	180	ST	24	2620	2393	2178	1974	1782	1604
32 Win. Special Super-X	X32WS2	D	170	PP	24	2250	1870	1537	1267	1082	971
32 Win. Special Super-X	X32WS3	D	170	ST	24	2250	1870	1537	1267	1082	971
# 32-20 Winchester Super-X	X32202	V	100	SP	24	1210	1021	913	834	769	712
# 32-20 Winchester Super-X	X32201	V	100	Lead	24	1210	1021	913	834	769	712
8mm Mauser (8 × 57) Super-X	X8MM	D	170	PP	24	2360	1969	1622	1333	1123	997
338 Winchester Mag. Super-X	X3381	D,O/P,M	200	PP	24	2960	2658	2375	2110	1862	1635
338 Winchester Mag. Super-X	X3383	M,L,XL	225	SP	24	2780	2572	2374	2184	2003	1832
348 Winchester Super-X	X3482	D,M	200	ST	24	2520	2215	1931	1672	1443	1253
35 Remington Super-X	X35R1	D	200	PP	24	2020	1646	1335	1114	985	901
35 Remington Super-X	X35R3	D	200	ST	24	2020	1646	1335	1114	985	901
351 Winchester S.L. Super-X	X351SL2	D	180	SP	20	1850	1556	1310	1128	1012	933
356 Winchester Super-X	X3561	D,M	200	PP	24	2460	2114	1797	1517	1284	1113
† 356 Winchester Super-X	X3563	M,L	250	PP	24	2160	1911	1682	1476	1299	1158
357 Magnum Super-X	X3574P	V,D	158	JHP	20	1810	1408	1125	972	877	803
357 Magnum Super-X	X3575P	V,D	158	JSP	20	1830	1427	1138	980	883	809
358 Winchester 8.8mm Super-X	X3581	D,M	200	ST	24	2490	2171	1876	1610	1379	1194
375 Winchester Super-X	X375W	D,M	200	PP	24	2200	1841	1526	1268	1089	980
375 Winchester Super-X	X375W1	D,M	250	PP	24	1900	1647	1424	1239	1103	1011
375 H. & H. Magnum Super-X	X375H1	M,L,XL	270	PP	24	2690	2420	2166	1928	1707	1507
375 H. & H. Magnum Super-X	X375H2	M,L,XL	300	ST	24	2530	2268	2022	1793	1583	1397
375 H. & H. Magnum Super-X	X375H3	XL	300	FMC	24	2530	2171	1843	1551	1307	1126
# 38-40 Winchester Super-X	X3840	D	180	SP	24	1160	999	901	827	764	710
38-55 Winchester Super-X	X3855	D	255	SP	24	1320	1190	1091	1018	963	917
# 44 Remington Magnum Super-X	X44MSTHP	V,D	210	STHP	20	1580	1198	993	879	795	725
# 44 Remington Magnum Super-X	X44MHSP5	D	240	HSP	20	1760	1362	1094	953	861	789
# 44-40 Winchester Super-X	X4440	D	200	SP	24	1190	1006	900	822	756	699
45-70 Government Super-X	X4570H	D,M	300	JHP	24	1880	1650	1425	1235	1105	1010
458 Winchester Mag. Super-X	X4580	XL	500	FMC	24	2040	1823	1623	1442	1287	1161
458 Winchester Mag. Super-X	X4581	L,XL	510	SP	24	2040	1770	1527	1319	1157	1046

WINCHESTER BALLISTICS
CENTERFIRE RIFLE

Energy In Foot-Pounds (ft.-lbs.)						Trajectory, Short Range						Trajectory, Long Range						
Muzzle	100	200	300	400	500	50	100	150	200 (Yards)	250	300	100	150	200	250 (Yards)	300	400	500
3605	2900	2314	1827	1424	1095	0.3	0.7	0	-1.8	-4.8	-9.3	2.6	2.9	2.1	0	-3.5	-15.4	-35.5
3501	3011	2578	2196	1859	1565	0.5	0.8	0	-2.1	-5.5	-10.4	1.9	1.6	0	-2.9	-7.3	-20.9	-41.9
3508	2927	2424	1993	1623	1314	0.2	0	-1.7	-4.9	-9.9	-16.9	2.5	2.0	0	-3.8	-9.5	-27.5	-56.1
3315	2785	2325	1927	1584	1292	0.6	0.9	0	-2.3	-6.0	-11.5	2.1	1.7	0	-3.2	-8.0	-23.3	-47.4
2303	1779	1352	1012	749	558	0.3	0	-1.9	-5.7	-11.6	-19.9	2.8	2.3	0	-4.5	-11.5	-34.4	-73.0
2303	1845	1462	1143	886	685	0.3	0	-1.8	-5.4	-11.0	-18.8	2.7	2.2	0	-4.2	-10.7	-31.5	-65.5
2207	1639	1193	860	626	482	0.5	0	-2.6	-7.7	-15.6	-27.1	1.7	0	-4.2	-11.3	-21.9	-55.8	-112.0
1507	1096	794	591	469	397	1.0	0	-4.3	-12.6	-25.5	-43.7	2.9	0	-6.8	-18.3	-35.1	-88.2	-172.5
2418	1993	1627	1318	1060	851	0.3	0	-2.1	-6.1	-12.2	-20.8	1.4	0	-3.3	-8.8	-16.6	-40.4	-77.4
2538	1795	1233	826	554	397	0.2	0	-1.9	-5.6	-11.8	-20.8	1.2	0	-3.2	-8.7	-17.1	-44.9	-92.2
2519	1898	1404	1022	742	554	0.3	0	-2.2	-6.5	-13.3	-22.9	1.5	0	-3.6	-9.6	-18.6	-47.1	-93.7
2582	2019	1559	1186	887	656	0.5	0.8	0	-2.2	-6.0	-11.5	2.0	1.7	0	-3.2	-8.2	-24.6	-51.9
2648	2061	1581	1193	888	657	0.2	0	-1.6	-4.8	-9.8	-16.9	2.4	2.0	0	-3.8	-9.8	-29.3	-62.0
2648	2137	1705	1344	1048	810	0.2	0	-1.5	-4.5	-9.3	-15.9	2.3	1.9	0	-3.6	-9.1	-26.9	-55.7
2743	2066	1527	1109	799	587	0.3	0	-2.0	-5.9	-12.1	-20.9	2.9	2.4	0	-4.7	-12.1	-36.9	-79.1
2743	2288	1896	1557	1269	1028	0.2	0	-1.8	-5.2	-10.4	-17.7	2.6	2.1	0	-4.0	-9.9	-28.9	-58.8
1911	1320	892	606	442	356	0.6	0	-3.1	-9.2	-19.0	-33.2	2.0	0	-5.1	-13.8	-27.1	-70.9	-144.3
1911	1320	892	606	442	356	0.6	0	-3.1	-9.2	-19.0	-33.2	2.0	0	-5.1	-13.8	-27.1	-70.9	-144.3
325	231	185	154	131	113	0	-6.3	-20.9	-44.9	-79.3	-125.1	0	-11.5	-32.3	-63.6	-106.3	-230.3	-413.3
325	231	185	154	131	113	0	-6.3	-20.9	-44.9	-79.3	-125.1	0	-11.5	-32.3	-63.6	-106.3	-230.3	-413.3
2102	1463	993	671	476	375	0.5	0	-2.7	-8.2	-17.0	-29.8	1.8	0	-4.5	-12.4	-24.3	-63.8	-130.7
3890	3137	2505	1977	1539	1187	0.5	0.9	0	-2.3	-6.1	-11.6	2.0	1.7	0	-3.2	-8.2	-24.3	-50.4
3862	3306	2816	2384	2005	1677	1.2	1.3	0	-2.7	-7.1	-12.9	2.7	2.1	0	-3.6	-9.4	-25.0	-49.9
2820	2178	1656	1241	925	697	0.3	0	-2.1	-6.2	-12.7	-21.9	1.4	0	-3.4	-9.2	-17.7	-44.4	-87.9
1812	1203	791	551	431	360	0.9	0	-4.1	-12.1	-25.1	-43.9	2.7	0	-6.7	-18.3	-35.8	-92.8	-185.5
1812	1203	791	551	431	360	0.9	0	-4.1	-12.1	-25.1	-43.9	2.7	0	-6.7	-18.3	-35.8	-92.8	-185.5
1368	968	686	508	409	348	0	-2.1	-7.8	-17.8	-32.9	-53.9	0	-4.7	-13.6	-27.6	-47.5	-108.8	-203.9
2688	1985	1434	1022	732	550	0.4	0	-2.3	-7.0	-14.3	-24.7	1.6	0	-3.8	-10.4	-20.1	-51.2	-102.3
2591	2028	1571	1210	937	745	0.6	0	-3.0	-8.7	-17.4	-30.0	2.0	0	-4.7	-12.4	-23.7	-58.4	-112.9
1150	696	444	332	270	226	0	-2.5	-9.4	-21.6	-40.2	-65.8	0	-5.6	-16.6	-33.9	-58.3	-131.0	-240.5
1175	715	454	337	274	229	0	-2.4	-9.1	-21.0	-39.2	-64.3	0	-5.5	-16.2	-33.1	-57.0	-128.3	-235.8
2753	2093	1563	1151	844	633	0.4	0		-6.5	-13.3	-23.0	1.5	0	-3.6	-9.7	-18.6	-47.2	-94.1
2150	1506	1034	714	527	427	0.6	0	-3.2	-9.5	-19.5	-33.8	2.1	0	-5.2	-14.1	-27.4	-70.1	-138.1
2005	1506	1126	852	676	568	0.9	0	-4.1	-12.0	-24.0	-40.9	2.7	0	-6.5	-17.2	-32.7	-80.6	-154.1
4337	3510	2812	2228	1747	1361	0.2	0	-1.7	-5.1	-10.3	-17.6	2.5	2.1	0	-3.9	-10.0	-29.4	-60.7
4263	3426	2723	2141	1669	1300	0.3	0	-2.0	-5.9	-11.9	-20.3	2.9	2.4	0	-4.5	-11.5	-33.8	-70.1
4263	3139	2262	1602	1138	844	0.3	0	-2.2	-6.5	-13.5	-23.4	1.5	0	-3.6	-9.8	-19.1	-49.1	-99.5
538	399	324	273	233	201	0	-6.7	-22.2	-47.3	-83.2	-130.8	0	-12.1	-33.9	-66.4	-110.6	-238.3	-425.6
987	802	674	587	525	476	0	-4.7	-15.4	-32.7	-57.2	-89.3	0	-8.4	-23.4	-45.6	-75.2	-158.8	-277.4
1164	670	460	361	295	245	0	-3.7	-13.3	-29.8	-54.2	-87.3	0	-7.7	-22.4	-44.9	-76.1	-168.0	-305.8
1650	988	638	484	395	332	0	-2.7	-10.2	-23.6	-44.2	-73.3	0	-6.1	-18.1	-37.4	-65.1	-150.3	-282.5
629	449	360	300	254	217	0	-6.5	-21.6	-46.3	-81.8	-129.1	0	-11.8	-33.3	-65.5	-109.5	-237.4	-426.2
2355	1815	1355	1015	810	680	0	-2.4	-8.2	-17.6	-31.4	-51.5	0	-4.6	-12.8	-25.4	-44.3	-95.5	—
4620	3689	2924	2308	1839	1496	0.7	0	-3.3	-9.6	-19.2	-32.5	2.2	0	-5.2	-13.6	-25.8	-63.2	-121.7
4712	3547	2640	1970	1516	1239	0.8	0	-3.5	-10.3	-20.8	-35.6	2.4	0	-5.6	-14.9	-28.5	-71.5	-140.4

CONVERSION FACTORS

Common inch calibers converted to metric
.25   inch = 6.35mm
.256 inch = 6.5mm
.270 inch = 6.858mm
.280 inch = 7.11mm
.297 inch = 7.54mm
.300 inch = 7.62mm
.301 inch = 7.62mm
.303 inch = 7.696mm
.308 inch = 7.82mm
.311 inch = 7.899mm
.312 inch = 7.925mm
.380 inch = 9.65mm
.400 inch = 10.16mm
.402 inch = 10.21mm
.450 inch = 11.43mm
.455 inch = 11.557mm
.500 inch = 12.7mm
.550 inch = 13.97mm
.577 inch = 14.65mm
.600 inch = 15.24mm
.661 inch = 16.79mm

Pressure

1 kg per sq cm = 14.223 lb per sq inch
1 kg per sq cm =   0.0063493 tons per sq inch
1 kg per sq cm =   0.968 Atmospheres
1 Atmosphere = 14.7 lb. per sq inch
1 Atmosphere =   0.00655 tons per sq inch

1 ton per sq inch = 152.0 Atmospheres
1 lb   per sq inch =   0.0680 Atmospheres
1 Atmosphere   =   1.03 kg per sq cm
1 lb   per sq inch =   0.070309 kg per sq cm
1 ton per sq inch = 157.49 kg per sq cm

Energy
1 m.kg = 7.2331 foot lb
1 foot lb = 0.13825 m.kg

Velocity
1 meter per second = 3.2809 feet per second
1 foot   per second = 0.30479 meters per second

Weight

1 gram =   15.432 grains
1 grain =   0.0648 grams
1 oz   = 28.349 grams

Linear
1 meter = 1.0936 yards
1 meter = 3.2808 feet
1 yard = 0.91438 meters
1 foot = 0.30479 meters
1 inch = 25.4mm
$1/4$ inch =   6.35mm
$1/2$ inch =   12.7mm
$3/4$ inch = 19.05mm
$1/8$ inch =   3.175mm
$3/8$ inch =   9.525mm
$5/8$ inch = 15.875mm
$7/8$ inch = 22.225mm
$1/16$ inch =   1.5875mm
$3/16$ inch =   4.7625mm
$5/16$ inch =   7.9375mm
$7/16$ inch = 11.1125mm
$9/16$ inch = 14.2875mm
$11/16$ inch = 17.4625mm
$13/16$ inch = 20.6375mm
$15/16$ inch = 23.8125mm

Reloading

FOR ADDRESSES AND PHONE
NUMBERS OF MANUFACTURERS AND
DISTRIBUTORS INCLUDED IN THIS
SECTION, SEE *DIRECTORY OF
MANUFACTURERS AND SUPPLIERS*

REMINGTON BULLETS

REMINGTON RIFLE BULLETS

Remington component rifle bullets bring the renown performance of "Core-Lokt", "Power-Lokt" and "Bronze Point" to reloaders.

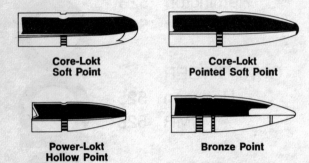

Core-Lokt Soft Point

Core-Lokt Pointed Soft Point

Power-Lokt Hollow Point

Bronze Point

"Core-Lokt" Pointed Soft Point and Soft Point bullets for controlled expansion and high weight retention—ideal for medium and big game.

"Power-Lokt" hollow points for pin point accuracy on targets, small game and varmints.

"Bronze Point" for flat trajectory and excellent accuracy at extended ranges.

Order No.	Caliber	Bullet weight	Bullet style	Boxes per case*	Case wt., lbs.
B1705	17 Cal	25 gr.	Hollow Point "Power-Lokt"	40	
B2240	22 Cal	50 gr.	Hollow Point "Power-Lokt"	40	
B2265	22 Cal	55 gr.	Hollow Point "Power-Lokt"	40	
B2430	6mm	80 gr.	Hollow Point "Power-Lokt"	24	
B2460	6mm	100 gr.	Pointed Soft Point "Core-Lokt"	24	
B2510	25 Cal	87 gr.	Hollow Point "Power-Lokt"	24	
B2540	25 Cal	120 gr.	Pointed Soft Point "Core-Lokt"	24	
B2720	270	130 gr.	Pointed Soft Point "Core-Lokt"	24	
B2730	270	130 gr.	"Bronze Point"	20	
B2830	7mm	150 gr.	Pointed Soft Point "Core-Lokt"	20	
B2850	7mm	175 gr.	Pointed Soft Point "Core-Lokt"	20	
B3020	30 Cal	150 gr.	"Bronze Point"	20	
B3030	30 Cal	150 gr.	Pointed Soft Point "Core-Lokt"	20	
B3060	30 Cal	180 gr.	"Bronze Point"	20	
B3080	30 Cal	180 gr.	Pointed Soft Point "Core-Lokt"	20	

*Packed 100 per box.

REMINGTON HANDGUN BULLETS

The Choice of Champions

Semi-Jacketed Hollow Point
Scalloped jacket delivers maximum expansion and stopping power, with controlled expansion even at high velocities.

Soft Point
Delivers deeper penetration than the semi-jacketed hollow point.

Metal Case
Helps ensure positive functioning in autoloaders.

Jacketed Hollow Point
Controlled expansion with no exposed lead to impair functioning in autoloaders.

Wadcutter
Solid lead for precision target shooting. Leave an easy-to-see hole in the target.

Lead Round Nose
A general purpose bullet and standard for law enforcement.

Order No.	Caliber	Bullet weight	Bullet style	Boxes per case*	Case wt., lbs.
B2525	25	50 gr.	Metal Case	40	
B3550	9mm	115 gr.	Jacketed Hollow Point	24	
B3552	9mm	124 gr.	Metal Case	24	
B3572	357	125 gr.	Semi-Jacketed Hollow Point	24	
B3576	357	158 gr.	Semi-Jacketed Hollow Point	20	
B3578	357	158 gr.	Lead	20	
B3810	38	95 gr.	Semi-Jacketed Hollow Point	24	
B3830D	38	148 gr.	Wadcutter	20*	
B4110	41 Mag	210 gr.	Soft Point	20	
B4120	41 Mag	210 gr.	Lead	20	
B4410	44 Mag	240 gr.	Soft Point	20	
B4420	44 Mag	240 gr.	Semi-Jacketed Hollow Point	20	
B4405	44 Mag	180 gr.	Semi-Jacketed Hollow Point	20	
B4520	45	185 gr.	Jacketed Hollow Point	20	
B4530	45	230 gr.	Metal Case	20	

*Packed 100 per box except B3830D, 500 per box.

SIERRA BULLETS

RIFLE

.22 Caliber Hornet
(.223/5.66MM Diameter)

40 gr. Hornet
Varminter #1100

45 gr. Hornet
Varminter #1110

.22 Caliber Hornet
(.224/5.69MM Diameter)

40 gr. Hornet
Varminter #1200

45 gr. Hornet
Varminter #1210

.22 Caliber
(.224/5.69MM Diameter)
High Velocity

40 gr. HP
Varminter #1385

45 gr. SMP
Varminter #1300

45 gr. SPT
Varminter #1310

50 gr. SMP
Varminter #1320

50 gr. SPT
Varminter #1330

50 gr. Blitz
Varminter #1340

52 gr. HPBT
MatchKing #1410

53 gr. HP
MatchKing #1400

55 gr. Blitz
Varminter #1345

55 gr. SMP
Varminter #1350

55 gr. FMJBT
GameKing #1355

55 gr. SPT
Varminter #1360

55 gr. SBT
GameKing #1365

55 gr. HPBT
GameKing #1390

60 gr. HP
Varminter #1375

63 gr. SMP
Varminter #1370

69 gr. HPBT
MatchKing #1380

6MM .243 Caliber
(.243/6.17MM Diameter)

60 gr. HP
Varminter #1500

70 gr. HPBT
MatchKing #1505

75 gr. HP
Varminter #1510

85 gr. SPT
Varminter #1520

85 gr. HPBT
GameKing # 1530

90 gr. FMJBT
GameKing #1535

100 gr. SPT
Pro-Hunter #1540

100 gr. SMP
Pro-Hunter #1550

100 gr. SBT
GameKing #1560

.25 Caliber
(.257/6.53MM Diameter)

75 gr. HP
Varminter #1600

87 gr. SPT
Varminter #1610

90 gr. HPBT
GameKing #1615

100 gr. SPT
Pro-Hunter #1620

100 gr. SBT
GameKing #1625

117 gr. SBT
GameKing #1630

117 gr. SPT
Pro-Hunter #1640

120 gr. HPBT
GameKing #1650

6.5MM .264 Caliber
(.264/6.71MM Diameter)

85 gr. HP
Varminter #1700

100 gr. HP
Varminter #1710

120 gr. SPT
Pro-Hunter #1720

140 gr. SBT
GameKing #1730

140 gr. HPBT
MatchKing #1740

.270 Caliber
(.227/7.04MM Diameter)

90 gr. HP
Varminter #1800

110 gr. SPT
Pro-Hunter #1810

130 gr. SBT
GameKing #1820

130 gr. SPT
Pro-Hunter #1830

140 gr. HPBT
GameKing #1835

140 gr. SBT
GameKing #1845

150 gr. SBT
GameKing #1840

150 gr. RN
Pro-Hunter #1850

7MM .284 Caliber
(.284/7.21MM Diameter)

NEW 100 gr. HP
Varminter #1895

120 gr. SPT
Pro-Hunter #1900

140 gr. SBT
GameKing #1905

140 gr. SPT
Pro-Hunter #1910

150 gr. SBT
GameKing #1913

150 gr. HPBT
MatchKing #1915

160 gr. SBT
GameKing #1920

NEW 160 gr. HPBT
GameKing #1925

168 gr. HPBT
MatchKing #1930

170 gr. RN
Pro-Hunter #1950

SIERRA BULLETS

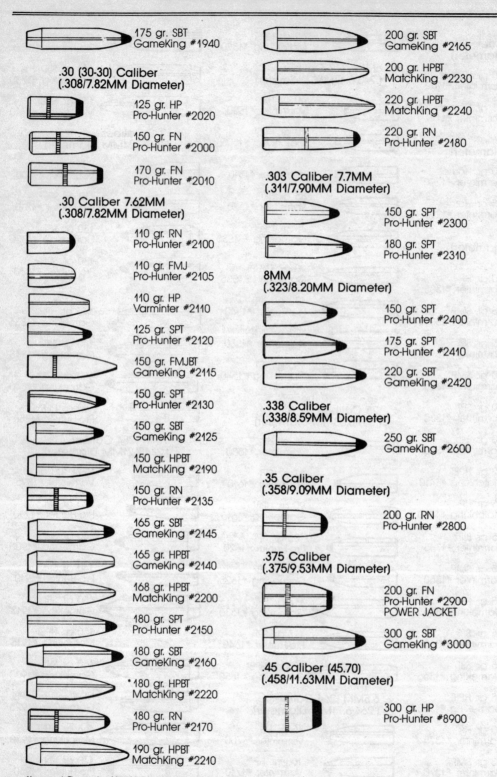

175 gr. SBT
GameKing #1940

.30 (30-30) Caliber
(.308/7.82MM Diameter)

125 gr. HP
Pro-Hunter #2020

150 gr. FN
Pro-Hunter #2000

170 gr. FN
Pro-Hunter #2010

.30 Caliber 7.62MM
(.308/7.82MM Diameter)

110 gr. RN
Pro-Hunter #2100

110 gr. FMJ
Pro-Hunter #2105

110 gr. HP
Varminter #2110

125 gr. SPT
Pro-Hunter #2120

150 gr. FMJBT
GameKing #2115

150 gr. SPT
Pro-Hunter #2130

150 gr. SBT
GameKing #2125

150 gr. HPBT
MatchKing #2190

150 gr. RN
Pro-Hunter #2135

165 gr. SBT
GameKing #2145

165 gr. HPBT
GameKing #2140

168 gr. HPBT
MatchKing #2200

180 gr. SPT
Pro-Hunter #2150

180 gr. SBT
GameKing #2160

* 180 gr. HPBT
MatchKing #2220

180 gr. RN
Pro-Hunter #2170

190 gr. HPBT
MatchKing #2210

200 gr. SBT
GameKing #2165

200 gr. HPBT
MatchKing #2230

220 gr. HPBT
MatchKing #2240

220 gr. RN
Pro-Hunter #2180

.303 Caliber 7.7MM
(.311/7.90MM Diameter)

150 gr. SPT
Pro-Hunter #2300

180 gr. SPT
Pro-Hunter #2310

8MM
(.323/8.20MM Diameter)

150 gr. SPT
Pro-Hunter #2400

175 gr. SPT
Pro-Hunter #2410

220 gr. SBT
GameKing #2420

.338 Caliber
(.338/8.59MM Diameter)

250 gr. SBT
GameKing #2600

.35 Caliber
(.358/9.09MM Diameter)

200 gr. RN
Pro-Hunter #2800

.375 Caliber
(.375/9.53MM Diameter)

200 gr. FN
Pro-Hunter #2900
POWER JACKET

300 gr. SBT
GameKing #3000

.45 Caliber (45.70)
(.458/11.63MM Diameter)

300 gr. HP
Pro-Hunter #8900

*Improved. The angle of boat tail has been increased to allow more bearing surface, providing substantial improvement to bullet accuracy. Now one of the most accurate in the Sierra line.

SIERRA BULLETS

HANDGUN

Single Shot Pistol Bullets

6MM .243 Dia. 80 gr. SPT
Pro-Hunter #7150

7MM .284 Dia. 130 gr. SPT
Pro-Hunter #7250

.30 cal. .308 Dia. 135 gr. SPT
Pro-Hunter #7350

.25 Caliber (.251/6.38MM Diameter)

50 gr. FMJ
Tournament Master #8000

.32 Caliber 7.65MM (.312/7.92MM Diameter)

71 gr. FMJ
Tournament Master #8010

.32 Mag. .312/7.92MM Diameter

90 gr. JHC
Sports Master #8030
POWER JACKET

9MM .355 Caliber (.355/9.02MM Diameter)

90 gr. JHP
Sports Master #8100
POWER JACKET

95 gr. FMJ
Tournament Master #8105

115 gr. JHP
Sports Master #8110
POWER JACKET

115 gr. FMJ
Tournament Master #8115

125 gr. FMJ
Tournament Master #8120

130 gr. FMJ
Tournament Master #8345

.38 Caliber (.357/9.07MM Diameter)

110 gr. JHC Blitz
Sports Master #8300
POWER JACKET

125 gr. JSP
Sports Master #8310

125 gr. JHC
Sports Master #8320
POWER JACKET

140 gr. JHC
Sports Master #8325
POWER JACKET

158 gr. JHC
Sports Master #8360
POWER JACKET

158 gr. JSP
Sports Master #8340

170 gr. JHC
Sports Master #8365
POWER JACKET

170 gr. FMJ Match
Tournament Master #8350

180 gr. FPJ Match
Tournament Master #8370

10MM .400 Caliber (.400/10.16MM Diameter)

NEW 150 gr. JHP
Sports Master #8430
POWER JACKET

NEW 180 gr. JHP
Sports Master #8460

.41 Caliber (.410/10.41MM Diameter)

170 gr. JHC
Sports Master #8500
POWER JACKET

210 gr. JHC
Sports Master #8520
POWER JACKET

220 gr. FPJ Match
Tournament Master #8530

.44 Magnum (.4295/10.91MM Diameter)

180 gr. JHC
Sports Master #8600
POWER JACKET

210 gr. JHC
Sports Master #8620
POWER JACKET

220 gr. FPJ Match
Tournament Master #8605

240 gr. JHC
Sports Master #8610
POWER JACKET

250 gr. FPJ Match
Tournament Master #8615

.45 Caliber (.4515/11.47MM Diameter)

185 gr. JHP
Sports Master #8800
POWER JACKET

185 gr. FPJ Match
Tournament Master #8810

200 gr. FPJ Match
Tournament Master #8825

230 gr. FMJ Match
Tournament Master #8815

240 gr. JHC
Sports Master #8820
POWER JACKET

Abbreviations: SBT — Spitzer Boat Tail, **SPT** — Spitzer, **HP** — Hollow Point, **JHP** — Jacketed Hollow Point, **JHC** — Jacketed Hollow Cavity, **JSP** — Jacketed Soft Point, **FN** — Flat Nose, **RN** — Round Nose, **FMJ** — Full Metal Jacket, **HPBT** — Hollow Point Boat Tail, **SMP** — Semi-Pointed, **FPJ** — Full Profile Jacket, **FMJBT** — Full Metal Jacket Boat Tail.

SPEER BULLETS

HANDGUN BULLETS

CALIBER & TYPE	25 FMJ+	9mm HP	9mm FMJ+	9mm HP	9mm FMJ+	9mm HP	9mm FMJ+	9mm SP	38 HP	38 SP	38 HP	38 HP	38 HP	38 FMJ+
WEIGHT (GRS.)	50	88	95	100	115	115	124	125	110	125	125	140	146	150
DIAMETER	.251"	.355"	.355"	.355"	.355"	.355"	.355"	.355"	.357"	.357"	.357"	.357"	.357"	.357"
USE	P	P,V	P	P,V	P,T,V	P,V	P,T,V	P,V	P,V	P,V	P,V	P,V	P,V	P,T,V
PART NUMBER	3982	4000	4001	3983	3995*	3996	4004	4005	4007	4011	4013	4203	4205	4207

	38 HP	38 SP	38 SP	38 FMJ+ Sil.	38 FMJ+ Sil.	41 HP	41 SP	44 Mag. HP	44 HP	44 SP	44 Mag. HP	44 Mag. SP	44 FMJ+ Sil.	45 HP
	158	158	160	180	200	200	220	200	225	240	240	240	240	200
	.357"	.357"	.357"	.357"	.357"	.410"	.410"	.429"	.429"	.429"	.429"	.429"	.429"	.451"
	P,V,S	P,V,S	P,V,S	P,S	P,S	P,V,SG,S	P,V,S,D	P,V,SG,S	P,V,SG,S,D	P,V,SG,S,D	P,V,SG,S,D	P,V,SG,S,D	P,V,S	P,V,SG
	4211	4217	4223	4229*	4231*	4405	4417	4425	4435	4447	4453	4457	4459*	4477

	45 Mag. HP	45 FMJ+	45 HP	32 HB WC	9mm Round Nose	38 BB WC	38 HB WC	38 SWC HP	38 SWC	38 Round Nose	44 SWC	45 SWC	45 Round Nose	45 SWC
	225	230	260	98	125	148	148	158	158	158	240	200	230	250
	.451"	.451"	.451"	.314"	.356"	.358"	.358"	.358"	.358"	.358"	.430"	.452"	.452"	.452"
	P,V,SG,S	P,T,S	P,V,SG,D	P,T,M	P,T	P,T	P,T,M	P,T,V,SG	P,T,V,SG	P,T	P,T,V,SG,D	P,T,M	P,T	P,T,V,SG,D
	4479	4480*	4481	4600**	4601*	4605*	4617*	4623*	4627*	4647*	4660*	4677*	4690*	4683*

PLASTIC SHOT CAPSULES

CALIBER	38	44
NO. PER BOX	50	50
PART NUMBER	8780	8782

PLASTIC INDOOR AMMO

	BULLETS	CASES
NO. PER BOX	50	50
38 CAL.	8510	8515
44 CAL.	8520	8525
45 CAL.	8530	See Note

NOTE: Shown are 44 bullet and 44 case. 45 bullet is used with regular brass case.

Abbreviation Guide: HP–Hollow Point; FMJ–Full Metal Jacket; SP–Soft Point; Sil.–Silhouette; WC–Wadcutter; SWC–Semi-Wadcutter; HB–Hollow Base; BB–Bevel Base.

Usage Codes: P–Plinking; T–Target; V–Varmint; SG–Small Game; S–Silhouette; D–Deer; M–Match.

+ TMJ™ = Totally Metal Jacketed™
* Also available in 500-bullet Bulk-Pak.
** Available in bulk quantities only.

LEAD BALLS

WT. (GRS)	64	80	120	128	133	138	141	144	177	182	224	230	278
DIAMETER	.350"	.375"	.433"	.440"	.445"	.451"	.454"	.457"	.490"	.495"	.530"	.535"	.570"
PART #	5110	5113	5127	5129	5131	5133	5135	5137	5139	5140	5142	5150	5180
GUN TYPE	Some 36 Pistols & Rifles	36 Sheriffs Revolver / 36 Leech & Rigdon Revolver / 36 Navy Revolver	45 Hawken / 45 Kentucky / 45 Percussion Pistols	45 Thompson Center Rifle / Seneca / Hawken	45 Kentucky (F&P) / 45 Mountain / 45 Springfield / 45 Yorkshire / 45 Michigan Carbine / 45 Morse Navy / 45 Huntsman	44 Revolvers / 44 Percussion Revolving Carb. / 44 Ballister Revolver	44 Percussion Revolving Carb.	Ruger New Old Army	50 Thompson Center Hawken	50 Douglas / 50 Sharon / 50 Morse Navy	54 Thompson Center Renegade	54 Douglas / 54 Sharon / 54 Mountain	58 Morse Navy / 58 Harpers Ferry Pistol

SPEER BULLETS

RIFLE BULLETS

BULLET CALIBER AND TYPE	22 Spire Soft Point	22 Spitzer Soft Point	22 Spire Soft Point	22 Spitzer Soft Point	22 Spitzer Soft Point	22 Hollow Point	22 Full Metal Jacket	22 Spitzer Soft Point	22 Spitzer S.P. w/ Cannelure	22 Semi-Spitzer Soft Point	6mm Hollow Point	6mm Spitzer Soft Point*	6mm Spitzer Soft Point B.T.	6mm Full Metal Jacket
DIAMETER	.223″	.223″	.224″	.224″	.224″	.224″	.224″	.224″	.224″	.224″	.243″	.243″	.243″	.243″
WEIGHT (GRS.)	40	45	40	45	50	52	55	55	55	70	75	80	85	90
USE	V	V	V	V	V	V,M	V	V	V	BG	V	V	V,BG	V
PART NUMBER	1005	1011	1017	1023	1029	1035	1045	1047	1049	1053	1205	1211	1213	1215

CAL. & TYPE	270 Spitzer Soft Point B.T.	270 Spitzer Soft Point*	7mm Hollow Point	7mm Spitzer Soft Point*	7mm Spitzer Soft Point B.T.	7mm Spitzer Soft Point B.T.	7mm Spitzer Soft Point*	7mm Match B.T.	7mm Spitzer Soft Point B.T.	7mm Spitzer Soft Point*	7mm Mag-Tip Soft Point*	7mm Mag-Tip Soft Point*	30 Round Soft Point Plinker®	30 Hollow Point	30 Round Soft Point*
DIA.	.277″	.277″	.284″	.284″	.284″	.284″	.284″	.284″	.284″	.284″	.284″	.284″	.308″	.308″	.308″
WT.	150	150	115	130	130	145	145	145	160	160	160	175	100	110	110
USE	BG	BG	V	V,BG	V,BG	BG	BG	M	BG	BG	BG	BG	V	V	V
PART #	1604	1605	1617	1623	1624	1628	1629	1631	1634	1635	1637	1641	1805	1835	1845

CAL. & TYPE	30 Mag-Tip Soft Point*	30 Match B.T.	30 Spitzer Soft Point*	303 Spitzer Soft Point*	303 Round Soft Point*	32 Flat Soft Point*	8mm Spitzer Soft Point*	8mm Semi-Spitzer Soft Point*	8mm Spitzer Soft Point*	338 Spitzer Soft Point*	338 Semi-Spitzer Soft Point*	35 Flat Soft Point*	35 Flat Soft Point*	35 Spitzer Soft Point*	9.3mm Semi-Spitzer Soft Point*
DIA.	.308″	.308″	.308″	.311″	.311″	.321″	.323″	.323″	.323″	.338″	.338″	.358″	.358″	.358″	.366″
WT.	180	190	200	150	180	170	150	170	200	200	275	180	220	250	270
USE	BG	M	BG	BG	BG	BG	BG	BG	BG	BG	BG	BG	BG	BG	BG
PART #	2059	2080	2211	2217	2223	2259	2277	2283	2285	2405	2411	2435	2439	2453	2459

V-Varmint; BG-Big Game; M-Match. ★ Hot-Cor.

SPEER BULLETS

6mm Spitzer Soft Point*	6mm Spitzer Soft Point B.T.	6mm Round Soft Point*	6mm Spitzer Soft Point*	25 Spitzer Soft Point*	25 Spitzer Soft Point*	25 Hollow Point	25 Spitzer Soft Point*	25 Spitzer Soft Point B.T.	25 Spitzer Soft Point*	6.5mm Spitzer Soft Point*	6.5mm Spitzer Soft Point*	270 Hollow Point	270 Spitzer Soft Point*	270 Spitzer Soft Point B.T.	270 Spitzer Soft Point*
.243"	.243"	.243"	.243"	.257"	.257"	.257"	.257"	.257"	.257"	.263"	.263"	.277"	.277"	.277"	.277"
90	100	105	105	87	100	100	100	120	120	120	140	100	100	130	130
V,BG	V,BG	BG	BG	V	V,BG	V	V,BG	BG	BG	V,BG	BG	V	V	BG	BG
1217	1220	1223	1229	1241	1405	1407	1408	1410	1411	1435	1441	1447	1453	1458	1459

30 Spire Soft Point*	30 Hollow Point	30 Flat Soft Point*	30 Flat Soft Point*	30 Round Soft Point*	30 Spitzer Soft Point B.T.	30 Spitzer Soft Point*	30 Mag-Tip Soft Point*	30 Round Soft Point*	30 Spitzer Soft Point B.T.	30 Spitzer Soft Point*	30 Match B.T.	30 Flat Soft Point*	30 Round Soft Point*	30 Spitzer Soft Point B.T.	30 Spitzer Soft Point*
.308"	.308"	.308"	.308"	.308"	.308"	.308"	.308"	.308"	.308"	.308"	.308"	.308"	.308"	.308"	.308"
110	130	130	150	150	150	150	150	165	165	165	168	170	180	180	180
V	V	V,BG	BG	BG	BG	BG	BG	BG	BG	BG	M	BG	BG	BG	BG
1855	2005	2007	2011	2017	2022	2023	2025	2029	2034	2035	2040	2041	2047	2052	2053

GRAND SLAM™

375 Semi-Spitzer Soft Point*	45 Flat Soft Point	BULLET CALIBER AND TYPE	270 G.S. Soft Point*	270 G.S. Soft Point*	7mm G.S. Soft Point*	7mm G.S. Soft Point*	30 G.S. Soft Point*	30 G.S. Soft Point*	338 G.S. Soft Point*	375 G.S. Soft Point*
.375"	.458"	DIAMETER	.277"	.277"	.284"	.284"	.308"	.308"	.338"	.375"
235	400	WEIGHT (GRS.)	130	150	160	175	165	180	250	285
BG	BG	USE	BG	BG	BG	BG	BG	BG	BG	BG
2471	2479	PART NUMBER	1465	1608	1638	1643	2038	2063	2408	2473

REMINGTON CASES & PRIMERS

Remington brass cases with 5% more brass for extra strength in head section—annealed neck section for longer reloading life—primer pocket dimension controlled to .0005 inch to assure precise primer fit—heavier bridge and sidewalls—formed and machined to exacting tolerances for consistent powder capacity—

Rifle Cases (Unprimed)

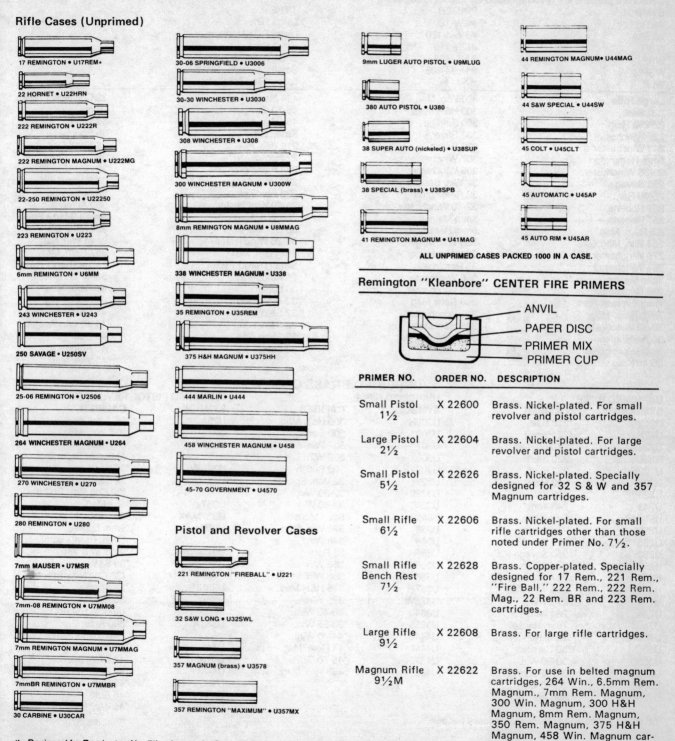

17 REMINGTON • U17REM *

22 HORNET • U22HRN

222 REMINGTON • U222R

222 REMINGTON MAGNUM • U222MG

22-250 REMINGTON • U22250

223 REMINGTON • U223

6mm REMINGTON • U6MM

243 WINCHESTER • U243

250 SAVAGE • U250SV

25-06 REMINGTON • U2506

264 WINCHESTER MAGNUM • U264

270 WINCHESTER • U270

280 REMINGTON • U280

7mm MAUSER • U7MSR

7mm-08 REMINGTON • U7MM08

7mm REMINGTON MAGNUM • U7MMAG

7mmBR REMINGTON • U7MMBR

30 CARBINE • U30CAR

30-06 SPRINGFIELD • U3006

30-30 WINCHESTER • U3030

308 WINCHESTER • U308

300 WINCHESTER MAGNUM • U300W

8mm REMINGTON MAGNUM • U8MMAG

338 WINCHESTER MAGNUM • U338

35 REMINGTON • U35REM

375 H&H MAGNUM • U375HH

444 MARLIN • U444

458 WINCHESTER MAGNUM • U458

45-70 GOVERNMENT • U4570

Pistol and Revolver Cases

221 REMINGTON "FIREBALL" • U221

32 S&W LONG • U32SWL

357 MAGNUM (brass) • U3578

357 REMINGTON "MAXIMUM" • U357MX

9mm LUGER AUTO PISTOL • U9MLUG

380 AUTO PISTOL • U380

38 SUPER AUTO (nickeled) • U38SUP

38 SPECIAL (brass) • U38SPB

41 REMINGTON MAGNUM • U41MAG

44 REMINGTON MAGNUM • U44MAG

44 S&W SPECIAL • U44SW

45 COLT • U45CLT

45 AUTOMATIC • U45AP

45 AUTO RIM • U45AR

ALL UNPRIMED CASES PACKED 1000 IN A CASE.

Remington "Kleanbore" CENTER FIRE PRIMERS

- ANVIL
- PAPER DISC
- PRIMER MIX
- PRIMER CUP

PRIMER NO.	ORDER NO.	DESCRIPTION
Small Pistol 1½	X 22600	Brass. Nickel-plated. For small revolver and pistol cartridges.
Large Pistol 2½	X 22604	Brass. Nickel-plated. For large revolver and pistol cartridges.
Small Pistol 5½	X 22626	Brass. Nickel-plated. Specially designed for 32 S & W and 357 Magnum cartridges.
Small Rifle 6½	X 22606	Brass. Nickel-plated. For small rifle cartridges other than those noted under Primer No. 7½.
Small Rifle Bench Rest 7½	X 22628	Brass. Copper-plated. Specially designed for 17 Rem., 221 Rem., "Fire Ball," 222 Rem., 222 Rem. Mag., 22 Rem. BR and 223 Rem. cartridges.
Large Rifle 9½	X 22608	Brass. For large rifle cartridges.
Magnum Rifle 9½M	X 22622	Brass. For use in belted magnum cartridges, 264 Win., 6.5mm Rem. Magnum., 7mm Rem. Magnum, 300 Win. Magnum, 300 H&H Magnum, 8mm Rem. Magnum, 350 Rem. Magnum, 375 H&H Magnum, 458 Win. Magnum cartridges.

* Designed for Remington No. 7½ primer only. Substitutions not recommended. U number is unprimed.

WINCHESTER PRIMERS & UNPRIMED CASES

CENTERFIRE PRIMERS

Centerfire primers are recommended for use as follows:

SYMBOL	PRIMER	TYPE
WLR	#8½-120	Large Rifle
WLRM	#8½M-120	Large Rifle Magnum
WSR	#6½-116	Small Rifle
WSP	#1½-108	Small (Regular) Pistol
WSPM	#1½M-108	Small (Magnum) Pistol
WLP	#7-111	Large (Regular Pistol)

Large Rifle
220 Swift
22-250 Rem.
225 Winchester
243 Winchester
6mm Remington
25-35 Winchester
250 Savage
25-06 Rem.
257 Roberts
257 Roberts + P
6.5 Rem. Mag.
264 Win. Mag.
270 Winchester
284 Winchester
7mm Mauser
280 Remington
7mm Express Rem.
7mm Rem. Mag.
30-30 Winchester
30 Remington
30-06 Springfield
30-40 Krag

300 Win. Mag.
300 H&H Mag.
300 Savage
303 Savage
303 British
307 Winchester
308 Winchester
32 Win. Special
32 Remington
32-40 Winchester
8mm Mauser
8mm Rem. Mag.
338 Win. Mag.
348 Winchester
35 Remington
356 Winchester
358 Winchester
350 Rem. Mag.
375 Winchester
375 H&H Mag.
38-55 Winchester

444 Marlin
45-70 Gov.
458 Win. Mag.
Small Rifle
218 Bee
22 Hornet
222 Remington
222 Rem. Mag.
223 Remington
25-20 Winchester
256 Win. Mag.
30 Carbine
32-20 Winchester
357 Rem. Max.
Small (Reg.) Pistol
25 Automatic
30 Luger
32 Automatic
32 S&W
32 S&W Long
32 Short Colt
32 Long Colt

32 Colt New Police
9mm Luger
38 S&W
38 Special
38 Short Colt
38 Long Colt
38 Colt New Police
38 Super-Auto
38 Automatic
380 Automatic
Small (Mag.) Pistol
357 Magnum
9mm Win. Mag.
357 Rem. Max.
Large (Reg.) Pistol
38-40 Winchester
41 Rem. Mag.
44 Rem. Mag.
44 S&W Special
44-40 Winchester
45 Colt
45 Automatic
45 Win. Mag.

UNPRIMED BRASS CASES

UNPRIMED RIFLE SYMBOL	CALIBER	UNPRIMED RIFLE SYMBOL	CALIBER	UNPRIMED PISTOL/REVOLVER SYMBOL	CALIBER
U218	*218 Bee	U300H	300 H&H Mag.	U25A	*25 Auto.
U22H	*22 Hornet	U300	300 Savage	U256	*256 Win. Mag.
U22250	22-250 Rem.	U307	307 Win.	U32A	*32 Auto. (7.65mm Browning)
U22OS	220 Swift	U308	308 Win.		
U222R	222 Rem.	U303	303 British	U32SW	*32 S&W
U223R	223 Rem.	U32W	32 Win. Special	U32SWL	*32 S&W Long (32 Colt New Police)
U225	225 Win.	U3220	*32-20 Win.		
U243	243 Win.	U3240	32-40 Win.	U357	*357 Mag.
U6MMR	6mm Rem.	U8MM	8mm Mauser	U357MAX	*357 Rem. Max.
U2520	25-20 Win.	U338	338 Win. Mag.	U9MM	*9mm Luger (9mm Parabellum)
U256	*256 Win. Mag.	U348	348 Win.		
U250	250 Savage	U35R	35 Rem.	U9MMWM	*9mm Win. Mag.
U2506	25-06 Rem.	U356	356 Win.	U38SW	*38 S&W (38 Colt New Police)
U257P	257 Roberts + P	U358	358 Win.		
U264	264 Win. Mag.	U357H	375 H&H Mag.	U38SP	*38 Special
U270	270 Win.	U375W	375 Win.	U38A	*38 Auto (and 38 Super)
U284	284 Win.	U3840	38-40 Win.		
U7MM	7mm Mauser	U3855	*38-55 Win.	U380A	*380 Auto (9mm Short-9mm Corto)
U7MAG.	7mm Rem. Mag.	U4440	*44-40 Win.		
U30C	*30 Carbine	U44M	*44 Rem. Mag.	U41	*41 Rem. Mag.
U3030	30-30 Win.	U4570	*45-70 Govt.	U44S	*44 S&W Special
U3006	30-06 Springfield	U458	458 Win. Mag.	U44M	*44 Rem. Mag.
U3040	30-40 Krag			U45C	*45 Colt
U300WM	300 Win. Mag.			U45A	*45 Auto
				U45WM	*45 Win. Mag.

*50 cases per box—all others are 20 cases per box.

HODGDON SMOKELESS POWDER

RIFLE POWDER

H4227 AND H4198
$14.98/lb.

H4227 is the fastest burning of the IMR series. Well adapted to Hornet, light bullets in 222 and all bullets in 357 and 44 Magnum pistols. Cuts leading with lead bullets. H4198 was developed especially for small and medium capacity cartridges.

H322
$14.98/lb.

A new extruded bench rest powder which has proved to be capable of producing fine accuracy in the 22 and 308 bench rest guns. This powder fills the gap between H4198 and BL-C(2). Performs best in small to medium capacity cases.

SPHERICAL BL-C®, Lot No. 2
$14.98/lb.

A highly popular favorite of the bench rest shooters. Best performance is in the 222, and in other cases smaller than 30/06.

SHOTGUN AND PISTOL POWDER

HP38
$13.65/lb.

A fast pistol powder for most pistol loading. Especially recommended for mid-range 38 specials.

TRAP 100
$12.80/lb.

Trap 100 is a spherical trap and light field load powder, also excellent for target loads in centerfire pistols. Mild recoil.

SPHERICAL H335®
$14.98/lb.

Similar to BL-C(2), H335 is popular for its performance in medium capacity cases, especially in 222 and 308 Winchester.

H4895®
$14.98/lb.

4895 may well be considered the most versatile of all propellants. It gives desirable performance in almost all cases from 222 Rem. to 458 Win. Reduced loads, to as low as 3/5 of maximum, still give target accuracy.

SPHERICAL H380®
$14.98/lb.

This number fills a gap between 4320 and 4350. It is excellent in 22/250, 220 Swift, the 6mm's, 257 and 30/06.

#25 DATA MANUAL (544 pp.)
$14.95

HS-6 and HS-7
$13.65/lb.

HS-6 and HS-7 for Magnum field loads are unsurpassed, since they do not pack in the measure. They deliver uniform charges and are dense to allow sufficient wad column for best patterns.

H110
$14.65/lb.

A spherical powder made especially for the 30 M1 carbine. H110 also does very well in 357, 44 Spec., 44 Mag. or .410 ga. shotshell. Magnum primers are recommended for consistent ignition.

SPHERICAL H414®
$7.99/lb.

A new development in spherical powder. In many popular medium to medium-large calibers, pressure velocity relationship is better.

SPHERICAL H870®
$7.99/lb.

Very slow burning rate adaptable to overbore capacity Magnum cases such as 257, 264, 270 and 300 Mags with heavy bullets.

H4350
$14.98/lb.

This powder gives superb accuracy at optimum velocity for many large capacity metallic rifle cartridges.

H4831®
$14.98/lb.

The most popular of all powders. Outstanding performance with medium and heavy bullets in the 6mm's, 25/06, 270 and Magnum calibers.

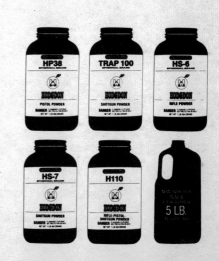

IMR SMOKELESS POWDERS

SHOTSHELL POWDER

Hi-Skor 700-X Double-Base Shotshell Powder. Specifically designed for today's 12-gauge components. Developed to give optimum ballistics at minimum charge weight (means more reloads per pound of powder). 700-X is dense, easy to load, clean to handle, and loads uniformly.

PB Shotshell Powder. Produces exceptional 20- and 28-gauge skeet reloads; preferred by many in 12-gauge target loads, it gives 3-dram equivalent velocity at relatively low chamber pressures.

Hi-Skor 800-X Shotshell Powder. An excellent powder for 12-gauge field loads and 20- and 28-gauge loads.

SR-4756 Powder. Great all-around powder for target and field loads.

SR-7625 Powder. A fast growing "favorite" for reloading target as well as light and heavy field loads in 4 gauges. Excellent velocity-chamber pressure.

IMR-4227 Powder. Can be used effectively for reloading .410-gauge shotshell ammunition.

RIFLE POWDER

IMR-3031 Rifle Powder. Specifically recommended for medium-capacity cartridges.

IMR-4064 Rifle Powder. Has exceptionally uniform burning qualities when used in medium- and large-capacity cartridges.

IMR-4198. Made the Remington 222 cartridge famous. Developed for small- and medium-capacity cartridges.

IMR-4227 Rifle Powder. Fastest burning of the IMR Series. Specifically designed for the 22 Hornet class of cartridges.

SR-4759. Brought back by shooter demand. Available for cast bullet loads.

IMR-4320. Recommended for high-velocity cartridges.

IMR-4350 Rifle Powder. Gives unusually uniform results when loaded in Magnum cartridges. Slowest burning powder of the IMR series.

IMR-4831. Produced as a canister-grade handloading powder. Packaged in 1 lb. canister, 8 lb. caddy and 20 lb. kegs.

IMR-4895 Rifle Powder. The time-tested standard for caliber 30 military ammunition; slightly faster than IMR-4320. Loads uniformly in all powder measures. One of the country's favorite powders.

IMR-7828 Rifle Powder. The slowest-burning DuPont IMR cannister powder, intended for large capacity and magnum-type cases with heavy bullets.

PISTOL POWDER

PB Powder. Another powder for reloading a wide variety of centerfire handgun ammunition.

IMR-4227 Powder. Can be used effectively for reloading "Magnum" handgun ammunition.

"Hi-Skor" 700-X Powder. The same qualities that make it a superior powder contribute to its exellent performance in all the popular handguns.

SR-7625 Powder. For reloading a wide variety of centerfire handgun ammunition.

SR-4756, IMR-3031 and IMR-4198. Three more powders in a good selection—all clean burning and with uniform performance.

BONANZA RELOADING TOOLS

CO-AX® BENCH REST® RIFLE DIES

Bench Rest Rifle Dies are glass hard for long wear and minimum friction. Interiors are polished mirror smooth. Special attention is given to headspace, tapers and diameters so that brass will not be overworked when resized. Our sizing die has an elevated expander button which is drawn through the neck of the case at the moment of the greatest mechanical advantage of the press. Since most of the case neck is still in the die when expanding begins, better alignment of case and neck is obtained. **Bench Rest® Seating Die** is of the chamber type. The bullet is held in alignment in a close-fitting channel. The case is held in a tight-fitting chamber. Both bullet and case are held in alignment while the bullet is being seated. Cross-bolt lock ring included at no charge.

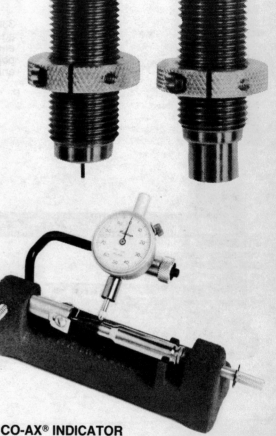

Bench Rest® Die Set 48.00
Full Length Sizer 20.00
Bench Rest Seating Die 29.00

PRIMER SEATER
with "E-Z-Just" Shellholder

The Bonanza Primer Seater is designed so that primers are seated Co-Axially (primer in line with primer pocket). Mechanical leverage allows primers to be seated fully without crushing. With the addition of one extra set of Disc Shell Holders and one extra Primer Unit, all modern cases, rim or rimless, from 222 up to 458 Magnum, can be primed. Shell holders are easily adjusted to any case by rotating to contact rim or cannelure of the case.

Primer Seater $45.00
Primer Tube 3.25

PRIMER SEATER

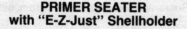

CO-AX® INDICATOR

Bullets will not leave a rifle barrel at a uniform angle unless they are started uniformly. The Co-Ax Indicator provides a reading of how closely the axis of the bullet corresponds to the axis of the cartridge case. The Indicator features a spring-loaded plunger to hold cartridges against a recessed, adjustable rod while the cartridge is supported in a "V" block. To operate, simply rotate the cartridge with the fingers; the degree of misalignment is transferred to an indicator which measures in one-thousandths.

Price without dial $39.00
with Indicator Dial 45.00

BONANZA RELOADING TOOLS

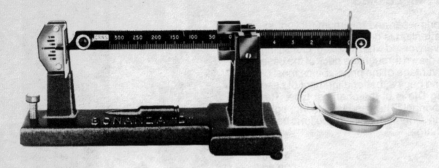

POWDER AND BULLET SCALE
MODEL "D"™ $44.00

330-grain capacity, tempered stainless steel right-hand poise, diamond-polished agate "V" bearings, non-glare white markings. Die cast aluminum base, strengthened beam at pivot points, powder pan for right or left pouring. Easy to read pointer and reference point. Guaranteed accurate to ¹/₁₀ grain; sensitivity guaranteed to ¹/₂₀ grain.

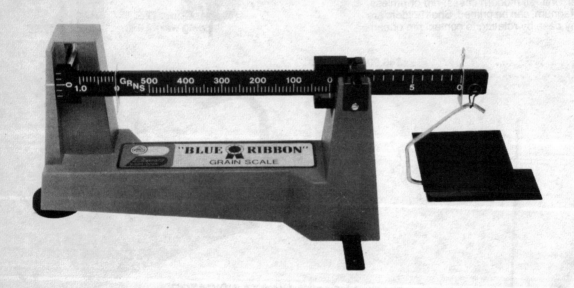

BLUE RIBBON GRAIN SCALE

511-grain capacity for ease of weighing powder. "Blue Ribbon" scales have three poises for better accuracy and convenience. White markings on non-glare enhance reading with less eye strain. Comparator scale and resting point locator lie in the same plane, which eliminates errors in reading due to parallax. Base has three point suspension, eliminating rocking. Guaranteed accurate to ¹/₁₀ grain. Sensitivity to ¹/₂₀ grain.

"Blue Ribbon"™ Magnetic Dampened Grain Scale $59.90

C-H RELOADING ACCESSORIES

ZINC BASE SWAGE DIE

- Maximum Energy
- 100% expansion, every time
- Zinc Base coats the bore with every shot
- Actually cleans the bore as you shoot
- No leading, even using maximum loads
- Perfect gas seal
- Use with any standard loading press
- Simple to use—one stroke of the handle and tap the finished bullet out.
- The perfect lubricating qualities of zinc combined with the perfect expansion

of pure lead produce outstanding, accurate bullets and will appreciably increase bore life.

No. 105-Z Zinc Base Swage Dies, 38/357 SWC
Shipping weight, 1 lb. $29.95
No. 105 Z1 Nose Punch, SWC, caliber 38/357 . . . . 4.00
38/357 caliber Zinc Base Washer, per 1000 (shipping weight per M, 1 lb.) 23.20

308 WINCHESTER AND 223 REMINGTON TAPER CRIMP DIE

- No longer necessary to have perfect trimmed cases
- Use as a separate die to form a perfect taper crimp each time
- Eliminates time-consuming trimming
- Produces Match Grade ammo
- Perfect feeding in semiauto rifles
- Load your ammo just like the factory does

Taper Crimp Die
Shipping weight 1 lb. $17.00

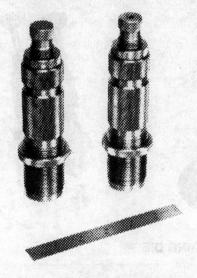

50 CALIBER BMG LOADING DIES

With **50 BMG Priming Accessories** the priming post and the shell holder can be used as is with any Hollywood tool. With the addition of the shell holder die, the priming can be accomplished with any existing loading tool with 7/8-inch top threads. The shell holder die screws into the top of the tool and the threaded shell holder is screwed into this. By adding the priming post you have a complete separate priming system.

Priming Post complete $11.95
Shell Holder Die 9.95
Shell Holder with lock ring 17.95

50 BMG DIE SET

C-H offers a die set for loading 50 caliber BMG. To give you an idea of the massive size of these dies they are shown with a 6-inch steel rule alongside a standard 308 Win. die and cartridge. They are threaded 1 1/2 × 12.

50 BMG Die set (full-length sizer and crimp seater) $275.00

DEBURRING/CHAMFERING TOOL

Standard size: Bevels both the inside and outside of the case mouth for easy bullet insertion. Hardened for long life. Extra sharp cutters. Fits 17 to 45 calibers.
Magnum size: For those who load 45 caliber and over, a Magnum Deburring Tool is available from C-H. Fits all cases from 45 to 60 caliber.

Standard Deburring Tool . . . . $ 8.95
Magnum Deburring Tool 14.95

C-H RELOADING TOOLS

Available for 38 Special/357, 45 ACP, 44 Mag. and 9mm Luger. Features reloading capability of 500 rounds per hour. Fully progressive loading. Powder measure cam allows you to "jog" the machine without dispensing powder. Simple powder measure emptying device included with each unit. Tungsten-carbide sizing die at no extra cost. Unit comes with your choice of powder bushing and seating stem (round nose, wadcutter or semi-wadcutter). Seating die cavity tapered for automatic alignment of the bullet. One 100-capacity primer tube, two 15-capacity case tubes and tube coupling also included at no extra cost $699.00

AUTO CHAMPION MARK V-a PROGRESSIVE RELOADING PRESS

MODEL 444 "H" PRESS

Offers 4-station versatility—two, three or four-piece die sets may be used. New casting design offers increased strength, and there is sufficient room for the longest magnum cases.

Model 444 4-Station "H" Press (includes 4 rams, 4 shell-holders, primer arm, and primer catcher **$158.00**
Same model but with one standard caliber die set **176.00**

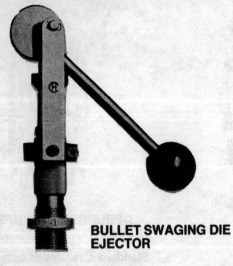

BULLET SWAGING DIE EJECTOR

A helpful accessory for use with the new C-H jacketed bullet swaging dies. The ejector attaches easily to the swaging die body with one screw. Can be used with either the core seating die or the swage die. Ejects the seated core or finished bullet with ease. No more tapping the top of the die.

Price $24.65

¾ JACKETED PISTOL BULLET SWAGING DIES

- Any bullet weight from 110 gr. to 250 gr. with same set of dies
- Can be used in any good ⅞" × 14 loading tool
- Absolutely no leading
- Complete no extras to buy
- Increased velocity
- Solid nose or hollow point
- Available in 38/357, 41 S & W, 44 Mag. and 45 Colt calibers

Price: $44.45

CANNELURE TOOL

- Solid steel
- Will work on all sizes of bullets, from 17 to 45
- Completely adjustable for depth and height
- One set will process thousands of bullets
- Necessary for rolling in grooves on bullets prior to crimping
- Hardened cutting wheel, precision-machined throughout

Price: $34.95

C-H RELOADING ACCESSORIES

NO. 725 POWDER and BULLET SCALE

Chrome-plated, brass beam. Graduated in 10 gr., 1 gr. and 1/10th gr. increments. Convenient pouring spout on pan. Leveling screw on base. All metal construction. 360 gr. capacity.

Price. **$35.95**

C-HAMPION PRESS

Compound leverage press for all phases of reloading. Heavyweight (26#) C-Hampion comes complete with primer arms, $7/8 \times 14$ bushing for use with all reloading dies. Spent primers fall through back of press into waste basket. 'O' frame design will not spring under any conditions. Ideal press for swaging bullets. Top of frame bored $1^1/4 \times 18$ for use with special dies and shotshell dies.

C-Hampion Press **$199.50**

NO. 301 CASE TRIMMER

This design features a unique clamp to lock case holder in position. Ensures perfect uniformity from 22 through 45 caliber whether rifle or pistol cases. Complete including hardened case holder.

No. 301 Case Trimmer **$21.95**
Extra case holders (hardened & hand-lapped) **3.50**

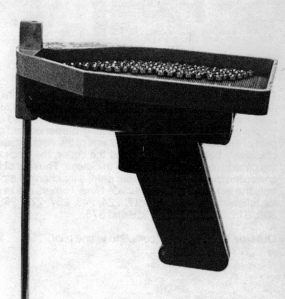

PRIMER TUBE FILLER

Fills a primer tube with 100 primers in seconds. Adjustable gate prevents upside-down primers from entering tube. Filler comes with three tubes and tube rack.

Model L (Large Primers) **$39.95**
Model S (Small Primers) **39.95**

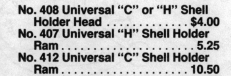

UNIVERSAL SHELL HOLDERS

Up to now, shell holders came in one piece—you needed as many shell holders as the calibers you wished to reload. With the C-H Universal Shell Holder all the reloader needs is the Shell Holder ram.

**No. 408 Universal "C" or "H" Shell
Holder Head** **$4.00**
**No. 407 Universal "H" Shell Holder
Ram** **5.25**
**No. 412 Universal "C" Shell Holder
Ram** **10.50**

FORSTER RELOADING TOOLS

CASE TRIMMER

The Forster Case Trimmer trims all cases from 17 cal. to 458 Winchester. Its shell holder is a Brown & Sharpe type collet, which closes on the case rim without pulling the case back, thus insuring uniform case length (even when there is variation in rim diameter).

Case Trimmer (less collet and pilot) $39.00
Case Trimmer Pilot 1.98
Case Trimmer Collet 6.00

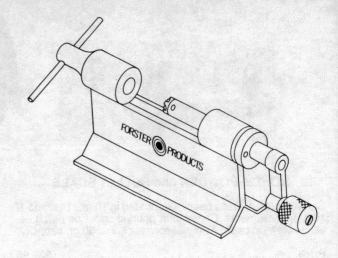

OUTSIDE NECK TURNER
(Shown on Forster Case Trimmer)

The Outside Neck Turner consists of a cutter head which carries an adjustable circular carbide cutter. The tool will turn any diameter between .170 and .375. The short pilot used in case trimming is replaced with an extra long, hardened and ground pilot of the desired caliber. As the wall of the neck passes progressively between the pilot and the cutter, the neck wall of the case is reduced to a uniform thickness. The rate of feed is controlled by rotating the feeder cam; a mechanical stop controls the length of the cut. Outside Neck Turners are available for following caliber sizes: 17, 224, 243, 257, 277, 263, 284, 308, 311, 323, 333, 338, 358 and 375.

Outside Neck Turner (complete w/one pilot) $27.00

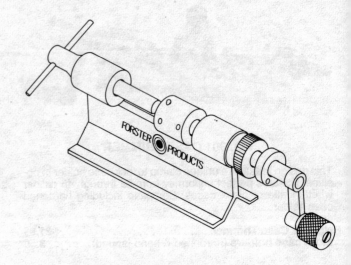

POWER CASE TRIMMER

Can be used with any standard drill press. Case length is controlled by the stop on drill press spindle. A line-up bar aligns the trimmer and drill press spindle. The threaded lever for opening and closing the Brown & Sharpe collet can be removed easily. The cutter shaft is made with a 1/4″ shank and has four staggered cutting edges for chatterless trimming of cases.

Power Case Trimmer (less collet and pilot) $39.00

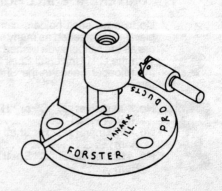

HORNADY

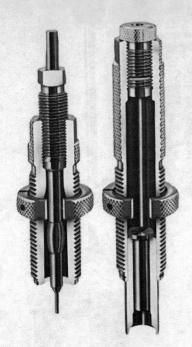

NEW DIMENSION RELOADING DIES

Features an Elliptical Expander that minimizes friction and reduces case neck stretch, plus the need for a tapered expander for "necking up" to the next larger caliber. Other recent design changes include a hardened steel decap pin that will not break, bend or crack even when depriming stubborn military cases. A bullet seater alignment sleeve guides the bullet and case neck into the die for in-line benchrest alignment. All New Dimension Reloading Dies include collar and collar lock to center expander precisely; one-piece expander spindle with tapered bottom for easy cartridge insertion; wrench flats on die body, Sure-Loc™ lock rings and collar lock for easy tightening; and built-in crimper.

New Dimension Reloading Dies
Two-die Set $23.50
Three-die Set 36.00

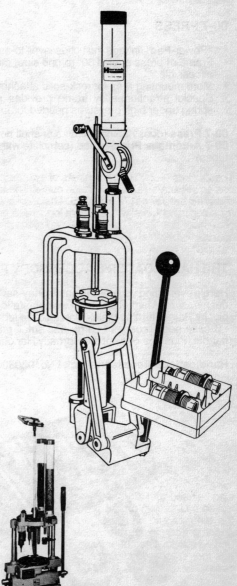

PRO-JECTOR PRESS PACKAGE

- Includes Pro-Jector Press, set of dies, automatic primer feed, brass kicker, primer catcher, shell plate, and automatic primer shut-off
- Just place case in shell plate, start bullet, pull lever and drop powder. Automatic rotation of shell plate prepares next round.
- Fast inexpensive changeover requires only shell plate and set of standard ⁷/₈ × 14 threaded dies.
- Primes automatically.
- Power-Pac Linkage assures high-volume production even when full-length sizing.
- Uses standard powder measures and dies.

Series I $342.50
Series II 354.25
Extra Shell Plates 21.50

MODEL 366 AUTO SHOTSHELL RELOADER

The 366 Auto features full-length resizing with each stroke, automatic primer feed, swing-out wad guide, three-stage crimping featuring Taper-Loc for factory tapered crimp, automatic advance to the next station and automatic ejection. The turntable holds 8 shells for 8 operations with each stroke. The primer tube filler is fast. The automatic charge bar loads shot and powder. Right- or left-hand operation; interchangeable charge bushings, die sets and Magnum dies and crimp starters for 6 point, 8 point and paper crimps.

Model 366 Auto Shotshell Reloader
12, 20 or 28 Gauge $450.00
.410 Bore 470.00
Model 366 Auto Die Set 90.00
Auto Advance 43.85
Swing-out Wad Guide 74.55

HORNADY

THE 00-7 PRESS PACKAGE
A reloading press complete with dies and shell holder

Expanded and improved to include Automatic Primer Feed. It sets you up to load any caliber in the list below and includes: Choice of a basic 00-7 complete with • Set of Durachrome Dies • Primer catcher • Removable head shell holder • Positive Priming System • Automatic Primer Feed.

00-7 Package (13 lbs.) $139.35
00-7 Package Series II Titanium Nitride (13 lbs.). 161.15

00-7 PRESS

- "Power-Pac" linkage multiplies lever-to-arm power.
- Frame of press angled 30° to one side, making the "O" area of press totally accessible.
- More mounting area for rock-solid attachment to bench.
- Special strontium-alloy frame provides greater stress, resistance. Won't spring under high pressures needed for full-length resizing.

00-7 Press (does not include dies or shell holder) $106.00
00-7 Automatic Primer Feed (complete with large and small primer
tubes) 12.75

THE HANDLOADER'S ACCESSORY PACK I

Here's everything you need in one money-saving pack. It includes: • Deluxe powder measure • Magnetic scale • Two non-static powder funnels • Universal loading block • Primer turning plate • Unique case lube • Chambering and deburring tool • 3 case neck brushes • Large and small primer pocket cleaners • Accessory handle. Plus one copy of the Hornady Handbook of Cartridge Reloading.

Handloader's Accessory Pack I No. 030300 . . . . $146.95

HORNADY

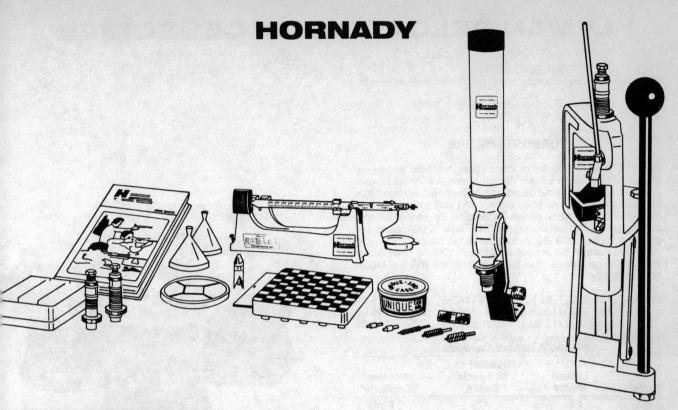

THE HORNADY RELOADING KIT

The Hornady Reloading Kit is ideal for any reloader who wants to start from scratch with a complete outfit. It includes your choice of a basic 00-7 or PRO-Jector press, completely equipped with: Set of Dies • Primer catcher • Removable shell holder • Positive Priming System • Automatic Primer Feed.

Plus, all these bench accessories: Deluxe powder measure • Magnetic scale • 2 static-resistant powder funnels • Primer turning plate • Universal reloading block • Unique case lube.

In addition, we include these case care accessories: Chamfering and deburring tool • Large and small primer pocket cleaners • 3 case neck brushes and accessory handle. Also, a copy of the Hornady Handbook. The Hornady Kit provides substantial savings over all these items if purchased separately.

00-7 Kit.	$284.40
00-7 Kit Series II Titanium Nitride	306.25
PRO-Jector Kit	444.45
PRO-Jector Kit Series II Titanium Nitride	456.25

Hornady Reloading Kits are available in these calibers . . .

SERIES I Cartridge	Pro-Jector Order No.	00-7 Order No.
222 Rem.	090200	080020
223 Rem.	090205	080025
22/250	090210	080030
243 Win.	090215	080040
270 Win.	090225	080065
7MM Rem. Mag.	090235	080075
30/30 Win.	090245	080090
308 Win.	090250	080105
30/06	090255	080115
300 Win. Mag.	090260	080365

SERIES II TITANIUM NITRIDE Cartridge	Pro-Jector Order No.	00-7 Order No.
9MM Luger	090400	080400
38-357-357 Max.	090405	080405
44 Spl. 44 Mag.	090420	080420
45 ACP	090430	080430
10MM Auto	090345	—

LYMAN RELOADING ACCESSORIES

TURBO TUMBLERS

Lyman's Turbo Tumblers process cases twice as fast as old style tumblers. Their unique design allows the media to swirl around totally immersed cases in a high-speed, agitated motion that cleans and polishes interior and exterior surfaces simultaneously; it also allows inspection of cases without stopping the polishing operation. The Turbo 3200 cleans and polishes up to 1,000 .38 Special cartridge cases. The Turbo 1200 can handle the equivalent of over 300 .38 Specials or 100 .30/06 cartridges. The Turbo 600 cleans half the Model 1200 capacity.

Price:
Turbo 600 (7 lbs.)	110V	$114.95	220V	$115.00
Turbo 1200 (10 lbs.)	110V	144.95	220V	145.00
Turbo 3200 (13 lbs.)	110V	209.95	220V	210.00

Turbo™ Tumbler Capacities

Model	Lyman Media	Number of .38 Special Cases	Nominal Capacity*
600	1 lb.	175	3 Pints
1200	2 lbs.	350	4 Quarts
3200	5 lbs.	1000	2.2 Gallons

*Refer to product instructions for suggested operating procedures and weight guidelines for best results.

TURBO SIFTER & MEDIA

Lyman's Turbo Sifter allows easy separation of cleaned and polished cases from the Turbo Tumbler media. Its diameter of 14″ allows the sifter to fit the mouth of most household buckets. Open grate bottom allows media to pass into recepticle while stopping the bases.
Price: $7.95

Turbo Media produces a "factory finish" and eliminates abrasive and wax films.
Prices:
1 lb. can .... $ 3.95
2 lb. box 6.95
10 lb. box 19.95

LYMAN RELOADING TOOLS

UNIVERSAL DRILL PRESS CASE TRIMMER

Intended for competitive shooters, varmint hunters, and other sportsmen who use large amounts of reloaded ammunition, this new drill press case trimmer consists of the Universal™ Chuck Head, a cutter shaft adapted for use in a drill press, and two quick-change cutter heads. Its two major advantages are speed and accuracy. An experienced operator can trim several hundred cases in a hour, and each will be trimmed to a precise length.

Price: **$39.95**

UNIVERSAL TRIMMER WITH NINE PILOT MULTI-PACK

This trimmer with patented chuck head accepts all metallic rifle or pistol cases, regardless of rim thickness. To change calibers, simply change the case head pilot. Other features include coarse and fine cutter adjustments, an oil-impregnated bronze bearing, and a rugged cast base to assure precision alignment and years of service. Optional carbide cutter available. Trimmer Stop Ring includes 20 indicators as reference marks.

Trimmer less pilots **$57.95**
Extra pilot (state caliber) 2.95
Replacement carbide cutter 39.95
Trimmer Multi-Pack (incl. 9 pilots: 22, 24, 27, 28/7mm,
    30, 9mm, 35, 44 and 45A 62.95
Nine Pilot Multi-Pack 9.95

ACCUTRIMMER

Lyman's new AccuTrimmer can be used for all rifle and pistol cases from 22 to 458 Winchester Magnum. Standard shellholders are used to position the case, and the trimmer incorporates standard Lyman cutter heads and pilots. Mounting options include bolting to a bench, C-clamp or vise.

AccuTrimmer **$29.95**
    With 9-pilot multi-pak 34.95

LYMAN RELOADING TOOLS

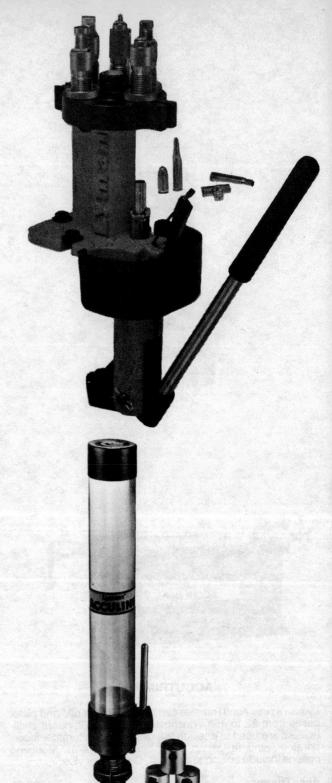

T-MAG TURRET RELOADING PRESS

With the T-Mag you can mount up to six different reloading dies on our turret. This means you can have all your dies set up, precisely mounted, locked in and ready to reload at all times. The T-Mag works with all $7/8 \times 14$ dies. The T-Mag turret with its quick-disconnect release system is held in rock-solid alignment by a $3/4$-inch steel stud.

Also featured is Lyman's Orange Crusher compound leverage system. It has a longer handle with a ball-type knob that mounts easily for right- or left-handed operation.

T-Mag Press w/Priming Arm & Catcher **$129.95**

ACCULINE POWDER MEASURE

Lyman's Pistol AccuMeasure uses changeable brass rotors pre-drilled to drop precise charges of ball and flake pistol propellants (the tool is not intended for use with long grain IMR-type powders). Most of the rotors are drilled with two cavities for maximum accuracy and consistency. The brass operating handle, which can be shifted for left or right hand operation, can be removed. The Pistol AccuMeasure can be mounted on all turret and single station presses; it can also be hand held with no loss of accuracy.

Pistol AccuMeasure **$19.95**
With 3-rotor starter kit 28.95

LYMAN BULLET SIZING EQUIPMENT

MAG 20 ELECTRIC FURNACE

The MAG 20 is a new furnace offering several advantages to cast bullet enthusiasts. It features a steel crucible of 20-pound capacity and incorporates a proven bottom-pour valve system and a fully adjustable mould guide. The improved design of the MAG 20 makes it equally convenient to use the bottom-pour valve, or a ladle. A new heating coil design reduces the likelihood of pour spout "freeze." Heat is controlled from "Off" to nominally 825° F by a calibrated thermostat which automatically increases temperature output when alloy is added to the crucible. A pre-heat shelf for moulds is attached to the back of the crucible. Availalbe for 100 V and 200 V systems.

Price: 110 V $214.95
220 V 215.00

UNIVERSAL DECAPPING DIE

Covers all calibers .22 through .45 (except .378 and .460 Weatherby). Can be used before cases are cleaned or lubricated. Requires no adjustment when changing calibers; fits all popular makes of $7/8 \times 14$ presses, single station or progressive, and is packaged with 10 replacement pins.

Universal Decapping Die $10.95

Deburring Tool
Lyman's deburring tool can be used for chamfering or deburring of cases up to 45 caliber. For precise bullet seating, use the pointed end of the tool to bevel the inside of new or trimmed cases. To remove burrs left by trimming, place the other end of the deburring tool over the mouth of the case and twist. The tool's centering pin will keep the case aligned **$10.95**

Mould Handles
These large hardwood handles are available in three sizes single-, double- and four-cavity.
Single-cavity handles (for small block, black powder and specialty moulds; 12 oz.) **$18.95**
Double-cavity handles (for two-cavity and large-block single-cavity moulds; 12 oz.) **18.95**
Four-cavity handles (1 lb.) **21.95**

Rifle Moulds
All Lyman rifle moulds are available in double cavity only, except those moulds where the size of the bullet necessitates a single cavity (12 oz.) **$43.95**

Hollow-Point Bullet Moulds
Hollow-point moulds are cut in single-cavity blocks only and require single-cavity handles (9 oz.) **$43.95**

Shotgun Slug Moulds
Available in 12 or 20 gauge; do not require rifling. Moulds are single cavity only, cut on the larger double-cavity block and require double-cavity handles (14 oz.) **$43.95**

Pistols Moulds
Cover all popular calibers and bullet designs in double-cavity blocks and, on a limited basis, four-cavity blocks.
Double-cavity mould block **$43.95**
Four-cavity mould block **72.95**

Lead Casting Dipper
Dipper with cast-iron head. The spout is shaped for easy, accurate pouring that prevents air pockets in the finished bullet. **$9.95**

Gas Checks
Gas checks are gilding metal caps which fit to the base of cast bullets. These caps protect the bullet base from the burning effect of hot powder gases and permit higher velocities. Easily seated during the bullet sizing operation. Only Lyman gas checks should be used with Lyman cast bullets.

22 through 35 caliber (per 1000) **$19.95**
375 through 45 caliber (per 1000) **21.95**

Lead Pot
Cast-iron pot allows bullet caster to any source of heat. Pot capacity is 8 pounds of alloy. The flat bottom prevents tipping. **$9.95**

LYMAN RELOADING TOOLS
FOR RIFLE OR PISTOL CARTRIDGES

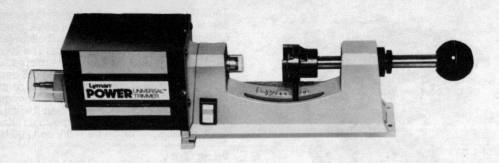

POWERED CASE TRIMMER

The new Lyman Power Trimmer is powered by a fan-cooled electric motor designed to withstand the severe demands of case trimming. The unit, which features the Universal™ Chuckhead, allows cases to be positioned for trimming or removed with fingertip ease. The Power Trimmer package includes Nine Pilot Multi-Pack. In addition to two cutter heads, a pair of wire end brushes for cleaning primer pockets are included. Other features include safety guards, on-off rocker switch, heavy cast base with receptacles for nine pilots, and bolt holes for mounting on a work bench. Available for 110 V or 220 V systems.

Prices: 110 V Model **$179.95**
           220 V Model **180.00**

ACCULINE OUTSIDE NECK TURNER

To obtain perfectly concentric case necks, Lyman's Outside Neck Turner assures reloaders of uniform neck wall thickness and outside neck diameter. The unit fits Lyman's Universal Trimmer and AccuTrimmer. In use, each case is run over a mandrel, which centers the case for the turning operation. The cutter is carefully adjusted to remove a minimum amount of brass. Rate of feed is adjustable and a mechanical stop controls length of cut. Mandrels are available for calibers from .17 to .375; cutter blade can be adjusted for any diameter from .195″ to .405″.

Outside Neck Turner w/extra blade, 6 mandrels . . . **$27.95**
Outside Neck Turner only **19.95**
Individual Mandrels **4.00**

LYMAN "ORANGE CRUSHER" RELOADING PRESS

The only press for rifle or pistol cartridges that offers the advantage of powerful compound leverage combined with a true magnum press opening. A unique handle design transfers power easily where you want it to the center of the ram. A 4¹/₂-inch press opening accommodates even the largest cartridges.

"Orange Crusher" Press
With Priming Arm and
Catcher **$89.95**

MTM

CASE-GARD PISTOL AMMO WALLET
CASE-GARD 6, 12 AND 18

MTM offers 3 different models of varying capacity. All share common design features:
- Textured finish looks like leather, and provides good gripping surface, even when wet.
- Snap-lok latch protects contents from damage, even if unit is dropped.
- Integral hinge.
- Contents are protected from dust and moisture.
- Each round is carried securely in its own individual rattle-proof recess.
- Available in dark brown.

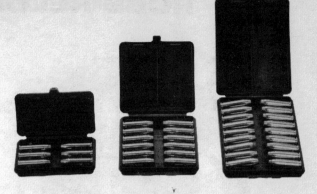

Capacity	380 Auto & 9mm	38 & 357 Mag	41 Mag	44 Mag	45 Auto
6 Round		W6-38/$2.83		W6-44/$2.83	
12 Round	W12-9/$3.05	W12-38/$3.05		W12-44/$3.05	W12-45/$3.05
18 Round	18-9/$3.60	18-38/$3.60	18-41/$3.60	18-44/$3.60	18-45/$3.60

CASE-GARD AMMO WALLET
FOR 22's

Special **Case-Gard Ammo Wallet** carrier holds 30 rounds, 22 Longs or 22 Mags . . . a convenient way to carry ammo to the range or field. Design features are:
- Leather-like finish available in dark brown.
- Snap-lok latch protects case against inadvertent opening, even if dropped.
- Each round is carried securely in its own recess.
- Virtually indestructible hinge.

30-22M . . . . ea. **$3.25**

MTM HANDLOADER'S LOG

Space is provided for 1,000 entries covering date, range, group size or score, components, and conditions. Book is heavy-duty vinyl, reinforced 3-ring binder.

HL-74 . . . . **$8.75**
HL-50 extra pages **3.75**

CASE-GARD 100 AMMO CARRIER
FOR SKEET AND TRAP

The MTM™ Case-Gard® 100-round shotshell case carries 100 rounds in 2 trays; or 50 rounds plus 2 boxes of factory ammo; or 50 rounds plus sandwiches and insulated liquid container; or 50 round with room left for fired hulls. Features include:
- Recessed top handle for easy storage.
- High-impact material supports 300 pounds, and will not warp, split, expand or contract.
- Dustproof and rainproof.
- Living hinge guaranteed 3 years.
- Available in deep forest green.

SF-100-12 (12 gauge) **$14.45**
SF-100-20 (20 gauge) **14.45**

FUNNELS

MTM Benchrest Funnel Set is designed specifically for the bench-rest shooter. One fits 222 and 243 cases only; the other 7mm and 308 cases. Both can be used with pharmaceutical vials popular with bench-rest competitors for storage of pre-weighed charges. Funnel design prevents their rolling off the bench.

MTM Universal Funnel fits all calibers from 222 to 45.
UF-1 . . . . **$1.99**
Patented MTM Adapt 5-in-1 Funnel Kit includes funnel, adapters for 17 Rem., 222 Rem. and 30 through 45. Long drop tube facilitates loading of maximum charges: 222 to 45.
AF-5 . . . . **$3.67**

RCBS RELOADING TOOLS

SIDEWINDER CASE TUMBLER

This RCBS case tumbler cleans cases inside and out and was designed exclusively for handloaders. Instead of just vibrating, the tilted easy-access drum rotates for fast, thorough cleaning. Its built-in timer adjusts for automatic shut-offs from five minutes to 12 hours. A perforated cap doubles as a screen to separate either liquid or dry RCBS cleaning medium from cleaned cases. Capacity is up to 300 38 Special cases or 150 30-06 cases. Available in 120 or 240 volt models. An 8-ounce bottle of Liquid Case Cleaner is included.

Sidewinder Case Tumbler
120 V $185.00
240 V 195.00

ROTARY CASE TRIMMER-2

Much like a miniature lathe, this Precisioneer® tool is the ideal way to trim stretched cases, shorten a quantity of them to the same exact length, or correct slightly uneven case mouths. This improved model has been redesigned for absolute case length control. Adjustments have been simplified and refined for near-perfect precision in trimming fired cases.

Case is locked into trimmer collet, the cutting blade is adjusted to desired case length, the handle is turned a few times, and it's done. You then bevel and deburr the trimmed case, and it's ready to reload.

The interchangeable collets are available for all popular calibers (17 to 45) and are designed to lock cases securely for accurate trimming. Special trimmer pilots come in 20 sizes to fit 17 to 45 caliber cases. Each is Precisioneered®, and locks into the cutter with set screw. This type of lock ensures perfect case alignment, both vertically and horizontally.

The cutting assembly features a lock ring so that any quantity of cases can be trimmed to the exact same length with a single adjustment. Cutter blades are made of hardened steel for prolonged service life. Case trimmer also has sockets for holding extra collets and pilots and holes for screwing base to bench.

Rotary Case Trimmer-2 .... $49.50
Kit 78.00

CASE TRIMMER PILOT $2.60			
PART NO.	PILOT CAL.	PART NO.	PILOT CAL.
09377	17	09387	33
09378	22	09388	34
09379	24	09389	35
09380	25	09390	36
09381	26	09391	37
09382	27	09392	40
09383	28	09393	41
09384	30	09394	44
09385	31	09395	45
09386	32	09396	.45-R

This tool is used to: (1) trim to standard length those cases which have stretched after repeated firings; (2) trim a quantity of cases to the same length for uniform bullet seating; (3) correct uneven case mouths.

CASE TRIMMER COLLET $6.50			
PART NO.	COLLET NO.	PART NO.	COLLET NO.
09371	1	09373	3
09372	2	09374	4

RCBS RELOADING TOOLS

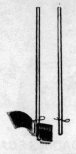

UNIVERSAL PRIMER ARM-2

RCBS primer arms are designed for fast, accurate seating of all primers. Interchangeable primer plugs and sleeves eliminate necessity of having to buy a completely new primer arm for each primer size. Primer plugs and sleeves furnished for large and small primers. Body cast of rust-resistant zinc alloy. The Universal Primer Arm-2 is designed for use with RCBS Rock Chucker and J.R. as well as most "C" type presses.

Universal Primer Arm-2 . . . . . . $9.00
Plug and Sleeve (sm. or lg.) 2.50

PRIMER TRAY

For fast, easy handling of primers and loading automatic primer feed tubes, place primers in this tray, shake tray horizontally, and primers will automatically position themselves anvil side up. Sturdy plastic case.

Primer Tray $2.40

PRIMER POCKET BRUSH COMBO

A slight twist of this tool thoroughly cleans residue out of primer pockets. Interchangeable stainless steel brushes for large and small primer pockets attach easily to accessory handle.

Primer Pocket Brush Combo: $11.00

AUTOMATIC PRIMING TOOL

Precision-engineered to provide fast, accurate and uniform seating of primers in one simple step. Single-stage leverage system is so sensitive it enables you actually to "feel" the primer being seated to the bottom of the primer pocket. This priming tool permits you to check visually each primer pocket before seating the primer, thus eliminating wasted motion or slowing down the reloading process.

Primers are released one at a time through the RCBS automatic primer feed, eliminating contamination caused by handling primers with oily fingers. Both primer rod assemblies furnished with this tool will handle all large and small American-made Boxer-type rifle and pistol primers.

Economy Features: If you already have RCBS automatic primer feed tubes and RCBS shell holders, they will fit this RCBS Priming Tool, thus eliminating the need to buy extras.

Berdan Primer Rod Assemblies: Optional Berdan Primer Rod Assemblies are available in three sizes and are interchangeable with the American Boxer-type Primer Rod Assemblies, furnished with the Priming Tool.

Priming Tool (less shell holder). $57.00

AUTOMATIC PRIMER FEED

Stop misfires greasy hands never need to touch primers. Automatically drops primers one at a time into the primer plug and sleeve of the primer arm. Adjustable primer stop pin eliminates jamming found in other automatic primer feeds. Easily mounted on RCBS and most "C" type presses. The primer tubes for large and small primers are completely interchangeable with the body.

Automatic Primer
Feed $17.50

PRIMER POCKET SWAGER COMBO

For fast, precision removal of primer pocket crimp from military cases. Leaves primer pocket perfectly rounded and with correct dimensions for seating of American Boxer-type primers. Will not leave oval-shaped primer pocket that reaming produces. Swager Head Assemblies furnished for large and small primer pockets no need to buy a complete unit for each primer size. For use with all presses with standard $7/8$-inch $\times$ 14 top thread, except RCBS "A-3" Press. The RCBS "A-2" Press requires the optional Case Stripper Washer.

Pocket
Swager Combo $21.00

RCBS RELOADING TOOLS

RELOADER SPECIAL-3

This RCBS Reloader Special-3 Press is the ideal setup to get started reloading your own rifle and pistol ammo from 12 gauge shotshells and the largest Magnums down to 22 Hornets. This press develops ample leverage and pressure to perform all reloading tasks including: (1) resizing cases their full length; (2) forming cases from one caliber into another; (3) making bullets. Rugged Block "O" Frame, designed by RCBS, prevents press from springing out of alignment even under tons of pressure. Frame is offset 30° for unobstructed front access, and is made of 48,000 psi aluminum alloy. Compound leverage system allows you to swage bullets, full-length resize cases, form 30-06 cases into other calibers. Counter-balanced handle prevents accidental drop. Extra-long ram-bearing surface minimizes wobble and side play. Standard 7/8-inch-14 thread accepts all popular dies and reloading accessories.

Reloader Special
  (Less dies) . . . . $ 93.00
Reloader Special-3 Combo,
  Rifle 109.00
Reloader Special-3 Combo,
  Pistol 111.00

RELOADING SCALE MODEL 5-0-5

This 511-grain capacity scale has a three-poise system with widely spaced, deep beam notches to keep them in place. Two smaller poises on right side adjust from 0.1 to 10 grains, larger one on left side adjusts in full 10-grain steps. The first scale to use magnetic dampening to eliminate beam oscillation, the 5-0-5 also has a sturdy die-cast base with large leveling legs for stability. Self-aligning agate bearings support the hardened steel beam pivots for a guaranteed sensitivity to 0.1 grains.

Model 5-0-5	09071	1½ lbs.	$69.00

ROCK CHUCKER "COMBO"

The Rock Chucker Press, with patented RCBS compound leverage system, delivers up to 200% more leverage than most presses for heavy-duty reloading of even the largest rifle and pistol cases. Rugged, Block "O" Frame prevents press from springing out of alignment even under the most strenuous operations. It case-forms as easily as most presses full-length size; it full-length sizes and makes bullets with equal ease. Shell holders snap into sturdy, all-purpose shell holder ram. Non-slip handle with convenient grip. Operates on downstroke for increased leverage. Standard 7/8-inch × 14 thread.

Rock Chucker Press
  (Less dies) $129.00
Rock Chucker Combo, Rifle . . 151.00
Rock Chucker Combo,
  Pistol 153.00

Combos include interchangeable primer plugs and sleeves for seating large and small rifle and pistol primers, shell holder, and primer catcher.

RELOADING SCALE MODEL 10-10

Up to 1010 Grain Capacity
Normal capacity is 510 grains, which can be increased, without loss in sensitivity, by attaching the included extra weight.

Features include micrometer poise for quick, precise weighing, special approach-to-weight indicator, easy-to-read graduations, magnetic dampener, agate bearings, anti-tip pan, and dust-proof lid snaps on to cover scale for storage. Sensitivity is guaranteed to 0.1 grains.

Model 10-10 Scale	09073	3 lbs.	$102.50

REDDING RELOADING TOOLS

MATCH GRADE POWDER MEASURE MODEL 3BR

Designed for the most demanding reloaders—bench rest, silhouette and varmint shooters. The Model 3BR is unmatched for its precision and repeatability. Its special features include a powder baffle and zero backlash micrometer.

No. 3BR with Universal or Pistol
Metering Chamber . . . . **$ 98.00**
No. 3 BRK includes both metering
chambers **124.95**
No. 3-30 Benchrest metering
chambers (fit only 3BR) **28.50**

MASTER POWDER MEASURE MODEL 3

Universal- or pistol-metering chambers interchange in seconds. Measures charges from 1/2 to 100 grains. Unit is fitted with lock ring for fast dump with large "clear" plastic reservoir. "See-thru" drop tube accepts all calibers from 22 to 600. Precision-fitted rotating drum is critically honed to prevent powder escape. Knife-edged powder chamber shears coarse-grained powders with ease, ensuring accurate charges.

No. 3 Master Powder Measure
(specify Universal- or Pistol-
Metering chamber) **$79.95**
No. 3K Kit Form, includes both
Universal and Pistol
chambers **98.00**
No. 3-12 Universal or Pistol
chamber **19.95**

POWDER TRICKLER MODEL 5

Brings underweight charges up to accurate reading, adding powder to scale pan a granule or two at a time by rotating knob. Speeds weighing of each charge. Solid steel, low center of gravity. "Companion" height to all reloading scales; weighs a full pound.

No. 5 Powder Trickler **$13.95**

MASTER CASE TRIMMER MODEL 1400

This unit features a universal collet that accepts all rifle and pistol cases. The frame is solid cast iron with storage holes in the base for extra pilots. Both coarse and fine adjustments are provided for case length.

The case-neck cleaning brush and primer pocket cleaners attached to the frame of this tool make it a very handy addition to the reloading bench. Trimmer comes complete with:
• New speed cutter shaft
• Two pilots (22 and 30 cal.)
• Universal collet
• Two neck cleaning brushes (22 thru 30 cal.)
• Two primer pocket cleaners (large and small)

No. 1400 Master Case Trimmer complete **$62.95**
No. 1500 Pilots **2.50**

STANDARD POWDER AND BULLET SCALE MODEL RS-1

For the beginner or veteran reloader. Only two counterpoises need to be moved to obtain the full capacity range of 1/10 grain to 380 grains. Clearly graduated with white numerals and lines on a black background. Total capacity of this scale is 380 grains. An over-and-under plate graduate in 10th grains allows checking of variations in powder charges or bullets without further adjustments.

Model No. RS-1 . . . . **$48.00**

REDDING RELOADING TOOLS

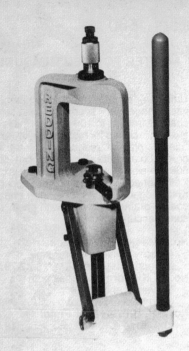

MODEL 721
"THE BOSS" PRESS

This "O" type reloading press features a rigid cast iron frame whose 36° offset provides the best visibility and access of comparable presses. Its "Smart" primer arm moves in and out of position automatically with ram travel. The priming arm is positioned at the bottom of ram travel for lowest leverage and best feel. Model 721 accepts all standard 7/8-14 threaded dies and universal shell holders.

Model 721 "The Boss" $84.95

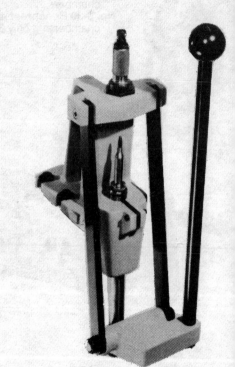

ULTRAMAG MODEL 700

Unlike other reloading presses that connect the linkage to the lower half of the press, the Ultramag's compound leverage system is connected at the top of the press frame. This allows the reloader to develop tons of pressure without the usual concern about press frame deflection. Huge frame opening will handle 50 × 3 1/4-inch Sharps with ease.

No. 700 Press, complete $192.00
No. 700K Kit, includes shell holder and one set of dies 219.50

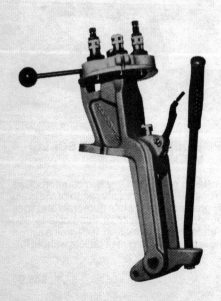

TURRET RELOADING PRESS
MODEL 25

Extremely rugged, ideal for production reloading. No need to move shell, just rotate turret head to positive alignment. Ram accepts any standard snap-in shell holder. Includes primer arm for seating both small and large primers.

No. 25 Press, complete $219.95
No. 25K Kit, includes press, shell holder, and one set of dies 247.50
No. 25T Extra Turret (6 Station). 50.00
No. 19T Automatic Primer Feeder 16.00

Reference

THE SHOOTER'S BOOKSHELF

An up-to-date listing of book titles, old and new, of interest to shooters and gun enthusiasts. Most of these books can be found at your local library, bookstore, or gun shop. If not available, contact the publisher. Names and addresses of leading publishers in the field are listed at the end of this section.

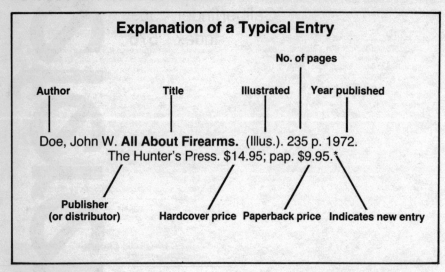

Explanation of a Typical Entry

Author — Title — Illustrated — No. of pages — Year published

Doe, John W. **All About Firearms.** (Illus.). 235 p. 1972.
The Hunter's Press. $14.95; pap. $9.95.*

Publisher (or distributor) — Hardcover price — Paperback price — Indicates new entry

AIR GUNS
Churchill, Bob & Davies, Granville. **Modern Airweapon Shooting,** (Illus.), 1981. David & Charles. $25.95.

AMMUNITION
Brown, Ronald. **Homemade Guns & Homemade Ammo.** 191 p. 1986. Loompanics. pap. text ed. $9.95.
Donnelly, John J. **Handloader's Manual of Cartridge Conversions.** (Illus.) 1056 p. 1987. Stoeger Pub. Co. pap. $24.95; spiral bound $29.95; hardcover $34.95.
Evaluation of Police Handgun Ammunition. (Law Enforcement Series) 1986. Gordon Press. $79.95 (lib. bdg.).
Geary, Don. **The Reloader's Bible: The Complete Guide to Making Ammunition at Home.** (Illus.) 256 p. 1986. Prentice-Hall. $17.95.
Goad, K.J. & Halsey, D. H. **Ammunition, Grenades & Mines.** 1982. Pergamon Press. $39.00; pap. $21.00.
Hogg, Ian V. **Jane's Directory of Military Small Arms Ammunition.** (Illus.). 160 p. 1985. Jane's Pub. Inc. $24.95.
Long, Duncan. **Combat Ammunition: Everything You Need to Know.** (Illus.) 136 p. 1986. Palladin Pr. text. ed. $19.95.
Matunas, Edward. **American Ammunition and Ballistics.** (Illus.). 1979. Winchester Press. $18.95.
Parkerson, Codman. **A Brief History of Bullet Moulds.** Pioneer Press. $1.75.
Sears & Roebuck 1910 **Ammunition Catalog** (Illus.). pap. Sand Pond $2.00.
Stegen, Arthur E. **Biathlon.** (Illus.). 144 p. National Rifle Assn. $30.00.
Steindler, R. A. **Reloader's Guide.** 3rd ed. (Illus.). 1975. softbound. Stoeger. $9.95.
Trzoniec, Stanley W. **Handloader's Guide.** (Illus.). 256 p. pap. 1985. Stoeger. $11.95.
Withers, John. **Precision Handloading.** (Illus.). 224 p. 1985. Stoeger Pub. Co. pap. $11.95.

ARCHERY (see also Bow and Arrow)
Ascham, Roger. **Toxophilius, 1545.** Arber, Edward ed. 1971 Repr. of 1895 ed. Scholarly Press. $29.00.
Athletic Institute, ed. **Archery: A Sport for Everyone.** (Illus.). 96 p. 1984. Athletic Inst. pap. $6.95.
Barrett, Jean. **Archery.** 3rd ed. 1980. Scott, Foresman & Co. $6.95.
Bear, Fred. **Archer's Bible.** (Illus.). 1980. pap. Doubleday, $6.95.
Bow & Arrow Magazine Staff, ed. **Archery Equipment Illustrated.** (Illus.). 256 p. (Orig.). 1984. pap. DBI. $10.95.

Burke, Edmund H. **History of Archery.** 1971. Repr. of 1957. Greenwood Press, $22.50.
Combs, Roger. **Archers Digest,** 4th ed. (Illus.) 256 p. 1986. DBI. pap. $12.95.
Cub Scouts Sports Archery. (Illus.). 32 p. 1985. BSA. pap. $0.95.
Gillelan. G. Howard. **Complete Book of the Bow and Arrow.** rev. ed. 1981. Stackpole Books. $11.95.
Glogan, Joseph. **Sportsman's Book of U.S. Records.** (Illus.). 1980. pap. text ed. NY Outdoor Guide. $4.95.
Henderson, Al. **Understanding Winning Archery.** Helgeland, G., ed. (Illus.). 114 p. 1983. Target Comm. pap. $8.95.
Johnson, Dewayne J. & Oliver, Robert A. **Archery.** 1980. pap. American Press. $2.95.
Klann, Margaret L. **Target Archery.** 1970. pap. Addison-W. $7.95.
Latham, J. D. ed. **Saracen Archery.** (Illus.). Albert Saifer, pub. $35.00.
Laubin, Reginald & Laubin, Gladys. **American Indian Archery.** (Illus.). 1980. University of Oklahoma Press. $18.95.
McKinney, Wayne C. & McKinney, Mike W. **Archery.** 5th ed. (Illus.). 176 p. 1985. Wm. C. Brown. Price on request.
Markham, Gervase. **The Art of Archerie.** facs. ed. 1968. Repr. of 1634 ed. George Shumway Publisher. $15.00.
Mosley, Walter M. **An Essay on Archery.** 1976. Charles River Books. $17.50.
Neade, William. **The Double Armed Man.** facs. ed. (Illus.). 1971. George Shumway Publisher. $10.00.
Odums, R.I. & Allen, D.G. **Career Guide to Officiating Archery & Riflery.** Tessman, Rita, ed. (Illus.) 150 p. 1986. Guideposts Pub. Dists. $12.95.
Pszczola, Lorraine. **Archery.** 2nd ed. (Illus.). 1976. pap. Holt, Rinehart & Winston. $3.95.
Wood, William. **The Bowman's Glory, or, Archery Revived.** 1976. Charles River Books. $7.50

ARMS AND ARMOR (see also Firearms)
Albion, Robert G. **Introduction to Military History.** (Illus.). 1971. Repr. of 1929 ed. AMS Press. $29.00.
American Machines & Foundry Co. **Silencers: Patterns & Principles, Vol. 2.** (Illus.). 1972. pap. Paladin Enterprises. $12.95.
Beckett, Brian. **Weapons of Tomorrow.** 160 p. 1983. Plenum Pub. $14.95.
Bivens, John. **Art of the Fire-Lock, Twentieth Century: Being a Discourse Upon the Present and Past Practices of Stocking and Mounting the Sporting**

Fire-Lock Rifle Gun. 1982. Shumway. $40.00.
Blair, Claude. **Arms, Armour & Base Metalwork.** (Illus.). 532 p. 1985. Sotheby Pubns. text ed. $45.00.
Collier, Basil. **Arms and the Men: The Arms Trade and Governments.** (Illus.). 1980. (Pub. by Hamish Hamilton England). David & Charles. $27.50.
Constant, James N. **Fundamentals of Strategic Weapons.** 940 p. 1981. Sijthoff & Nordoff. $140.00.
Curtis, Anthony. **The Lyle Offical Arms & Armour Review.** 416 p. 1983. Apollo. $24.95.
—**Lyle Official Arms & Armour Review** (Illus.). 415 p. 1982. Apollo. $24.95.
Daniel, Larry J. & Gunter, Riley W. **Confederate Cannon Foundries.** Pioneer Press. ed. Pioneer Press. $17.95.
Diagram Group. **Weapons** (Illus.). 1980. St. Martin's Press. $27.50.
Dunnigan, James F. **How to Make War: A Comprehensive Guide to Modern Warfare.** (Illus.). 416 p. 1981. Morrow $14.50.
Dupuy, Trevor N. **The Evolution of Weapons & Warfare.** (Illus.). 360 p. 1984. Repr. of 1980 ed. Hero Bks. text ed. $19.95.
Ezell, Edward C. **Small Arms Today: Latest Reports on the World's Weapons & Ammunition.** 256 p. (Orig.). 1984. pap. Stackpole. $16.95.
Fadala, Sam. **Black Powder Handgun.** 288 p. 1981. DBI. pap. $11.95.
Foss, Christopher F., ed. **Jane's Armour & Artillery** 1985–1986. 6th ed. (Jane's Yearbooks) 900 p. 1985. Jane's Pub. Inc. $125.00.
—**Jane's Armour & Artillery,** 1986–1987, 7th ed. (Jane's Yearbooks) 930 p. 1986. Jane's Pub. Inc. $137.50.
Frost, H. Gordon. **Blades and Barrels: Six Centuries of Combination Weapons.** Walloon Press. $16.95. deluxe ed. $25.00; presentation ed. $50.00.
Funcken, Lilane & Funcken, Fred. **Arms & Uniforms: The Second World War,** vols. I, III & IV. 120 p. 1984. P-H. $17.95 (ea.).
Gambordella, Ted. **Weapons of the Street.** (Illus.). 80 p. (Orig.). 1984. pap. Paladin Pr. $8.00.
Gordon, Don E. **Electronic Warfare: Element of Strategy & Multiplier of Combat Power.** (Illus.). 200 p. 1982. Pergamon Press. $17.50.
Gruzanski, C. V. **Spike and Chain.** Wehman Brothers, Inc. $7.50.
Guthman, William, ed. **Guns and Other Arms.** (Illus.). 1980. pap. Mayflower Books. $7.95.
Hamilton, T. M. **Firearms on the Frontier: Guns at Fort Michilimackinac 1715–1781.** Armour, David A., ed. (Illus.). 1976. pap. Mackinac Island State Park Commission. $3.00.
Hart, Harold H. **Weapons & Armor: A Pictorial Archive of Woodcuts & Engravings.** 1983. Peter Smith. $14.50.
Hogg, Ian, ed. **Jane's Infantry Weapons 1986–1987,** (Illus.). 950 p. Jane's Pub. Inc. $136.00.
—**The Weapons That Changed The World.** (Illus.). 1986. Arbor House. $22.95.
Hoy, M. **Exotic Weapons: An Access Book:** 200 Different Weapons Described & Analyzed with Dealer Listings for All. 1986. Gordon Pr. $90.00 (lib. bdg.).
Johnson, Thomas M. **Collecting the Edged Weapons of the Third Reich.** 4 vols. Bradach, Wilfrid, tr. (Illus.). T. M. Johnson. Vol. 1: $18.50; pap. $10.00. Vol. 2: $18.50. Vol. 3; $20.00; Vol. 4: $25.00.
Journal of the Arms and Armour Society. Vol. 1. (Illus.). 1970. George Shumway Publisher. $12.00.
Klare, Michael T. **American Arms Supermarket.** (Illus.). 336 p. 1985. pap. U. of Texas Pr. $10.95.
Knife World Publications Staff. **Best of Knife World,** vol. 2. (Illus.). 224 p. 1984. Knife World. pap. $6.95.
Kozan, S. **Manufacture of Armour and Helmets in Sixteenth Century Japan.** Albert Saifer, Publisher. $35.00.
Laking, Guy F. **A Record of European Armour and Arms Through Seven Centuries.** 5 vols. (Illus.). Repr. AMS Press. set $295.00.
Long, Duncan. **Modern Ballistic Armor: Clothing, Bomb Blankets, Shields, Vehicle Protection. . . . Everything You Need To Know.** (Illus.). 104 p. 1986. Paladin Press. pap. $8.00.

McAulay, John D. **Carbines of the Civil War, 1861–1865.** 1981. Pioneer Press. $7.95.

Macksey, Kenneth. **Technology in War:** The Impact on Science of Weapon Development & Modern Battles. (Illus.) 224 p. 1986. Arco. $19.95.

Marchant-Smith, D. J. & Haslem, P. R. **Small Arms & Cannons.** (Brassey's Battlefield Weapons System & Technology: Vol. 5) 160 p. 1982. Pergamon. $26.00.

Matunas, Edward. **Handbook of Metallic Cartridge Reloading.** (Illus.) 272 p. 1981. New Century. $12.95.

Mowbray, E. Andrew, ed. **Arms-Armor: From the Atelier of Ernst Schmidt, Munich.** (Illus.) 1967. Mowbray Co. $15.00.

Moyer, Frank, A. **Special Forces Foreign Weapons Handbook.** (Illus.) 1970. Paladin Enterprises. (OP).

Owen, J. I. ed. **Brassey's Infantry Weapons of the World.** (Illus.). 2nd ed. 1979. Pergamon Press. $61.00.

—**Infantry Weapons of the Armies of Africa, the Orient and Latin America.** 1980. pap. Pergamon Press. $24.00.

—**Infantry Weapons of the NATO Armies.** 2nd ed. 1980. pap. Pergamon Press. $24.00.

—**Infantry Weapons of the Warsaw Pact Armies.** 2nd ed. 1979. Pergamon Press. $28.50.

Peterson, Harold L. **The American Sword. 1775–1945.** (Illus.). 1977. Riling, Ray, Arms Books. $25.00.

Pierre, Andrew, J. **The Global Politics of Arms Sales.** 1981. Princeton University Press. $20.00; pap. $5.95.

Pretty, Ronald T., ed. **Jane's Weapon Systems 1986–1987.** 17th ed. (Illus.) 1060 p. Jane's Pub. Inc. $145.00.

Rossner-Owen, Davais. **Vietnam Weapons Handbook.** (Illus.) 128 p. 1986. Sterling. pap. $6.95.

Royal United Service Institute for Defense Studies, ed. **International Weapon Developments: A Survey of Current Developments in Weapons Systems,** 4th ed. (Illus.). 1980. pap. Pergamon Press $14.25.

Schuyler-Hartley-Graham Military Furnishers. **Illustrated Catalog Arms and Military Goods.** facs. ed. (Illus.). 1864. Flayderman, N. & Co. $9.50.

Seaton, Lionel. **The International Arms Review,** Vol. I. (Illus.). 1977. Jolex. $6.95.

Seaton, Lionel, tr. **The International Arms Review,** Vol. II. (Illus.). 1979. Jolex. $6.95.

Smith, W. H. **Small Arms of the World: A Basic Manual of Small Arms,** 12 ed. 1042 p. 1983. Stackpole, $59.95.

Snodgrass, A. M. **Arms and Armour of the Greeks.** (Illus.). 1967. Cornell University Press. $25.00.

Suenaga, M. **Pictorial History of Ancient Japanese Weapons, Armour & Artifacts.** (Illus.). 100 p. 1983. pap. Saifer. $12.95.

Traister, John. **Learn Gunsmithing: The Troubleshooting Method.** (Illus.) 1980. Winchester Press. $16.95.

Truby, J. David. **Quiet Killers, Vol. 1.** (Illus.). 1972. pap. Paladin Enterprises. $8.00.

—**Quiet Killers II: Silencer Update** (Illus.) 1979. pap. Paladin Enterprises. $8.00.

Warry, John. **Warfare in the Classical World: An Illustrated Encyclopedia of Weapons, Warriors and Warfare in the Ancient Civilizations of Greece and Rome.** 1981. St. Martin. $19.95.

Whisker, James B. **Arms Makers of Pennsylvania.** (Illus.). 1988. Susquehanna U. Press. $60.00.*

Wintringham, Thomas H. **Story of Weapons and Tactics.** facs. ed. 1943. Arno Press. $16.00.

Wright, James & Rossi, Peter. **Under the Gun: Weapons, Crime & Violence in America.** 360 p. 1983. Aldine Pub. $24.95.

Zaloga, Stephen J. & Grandsen, James. **The Eastern Front.** 96 p. 1983. Squad Sig. Pubns. $7.95.

ARTILLERY

Bidwell, Shefford, ed. **Brassey's Artillery of the World.** 2nd rev. ed. 1981. Pergamon Press. $49.50.

Foss, Christopher. **Artillery of the World.** 2nd ed. (Illus.). 1976. Scribner's. $8.95.

Foss, Christopher F., ed. **Jane's Armour & Artillery 1985–86.** 6th ed. (Illus.). 900 p. 1985. Jane's Pub. Inc. $125.00.

Gander, Terry. **Artillery** (Modern Military Techniques Service). (Illus.). 48 p. (gr. 5 up). 1987. Lerner Publications. $9.95*

Macchiavelli, Nicolo. **The Arte of Warre (Certain Wales of the Orderyng of Souldiours).** Whitehorne, P., tr. 1969. Repr. of 1562 ed. W. J. Johnson. $42.00.

Manucy, Albert. **Artillery through the Ages:** A Short Illus.

History of Cannon Emphasizing Types Used in America. (Illus.) 96 p. 1985. Govt. Ptg. Off. pap. $2.75.

Rogers. H. B. **A History of Artillery.** (Illus.). 230 p. 1974. Lyle Stuart. $7.95.

Rogers, H. C. **A History of Artillery.** (Illus.). 1977. Citadel Press. pap. $4.95.

Simienowicz, Casimir. **The Great Art of Artillery.** 1976. Charles River Books. $20.00.

BALLISTICS

Farrar, C. L. & Leeming, D. W. **Military Ballistics: A Basic Manual.** 225 p. 1983. Pergamon Press. $27.00.

Krier, Herman & Summerfield, Martin, eds. **Interior Ballistics of Guns.** 385 p. 1979. AIAA. $69.00.

Laible, Roy C. **Ballistic Materials & Penetration Mechanics.** 1980. Elsevier. $70.00

Mann, Franklin W. **The Bullet's Flight to Target From Powder: The Ballistics of Small Arms.** 391 p. 1980. Wolfe Pub. Co. Repr. text ed. $22.50.

Mannes, Philip. **Tables of Bullet Performance.** Wolfe, Dave, ed. 407 p. (Orig.) 1980. pap. text ed. Wolfe Pub. Co. $17.50.

Matunas, Edward. **American Ammunition and Ballistics.** (Illus.). 1979. Winchester Press. $18.95.

Wilber, Charles G. **Ballistic Science for the Law Enforcement Officer.** (Illus.) 1977. C. C. Thomas. $30.75.

—**Forensic Biology for the Law Enforcement Officer.** (Illus.). 1974. C. C. Thomas. $25.75.

Williams, M. **Practical Handgun Ballistics.** 1980. C. C. Thomas. $17.50.

Wolfe, Dave, ed. **The Art of Bullet Casting.** (Illus.). 258 p. pap. 1981. Wolfe Pub. Co. pap. $12.95.

—**Propellant Profiles.** (Illus.) 158 p. 1982. Wolfe Pub. Co. pap. text ed. $12.95.

BIRD DOGS

Falk, John R. **The Complete Guide to Bird Dog Training.** 1976. Winchester Press. $14.95.

Rafe, Stephen C. **Training Your Dog For Birdwork.** (Illus.). 96 p. 1987. Denlingers. pap. $16.95.*

Stuart, Jack. **Bird Dogs and Upland Game Birds.** (Illus.) 1983. Denlingers. $24.95.

Waterman, Charles F. **Gun Dogs & Bird Guns: A Charley Waterman Reader.** (Illus.). 244 p. 1987. GSJ Press (South Hamilton, Mass.). text ed $25.00.*

BLACK POWDER GUNS (see also Firearms)

Bridges, Toby. **Advanced Muzzeloader's Guide.** (Illus.). 256 p. 1985. pap. Stoeger. $11.95.

Elliot, Brook. **Complete Smoothbore Hunter.** (Illus.) 240 p. 1986. New Century. $16.95.

Fadala, Sam. **The Black Powder Handgun.** 1981. pap. DBI Book. $9.95.

—**Gun Digest Black Powder Loading Manual.** (Illus.). 224 p. 1982. pap. DBI Books. $9.95.

—**The Complete Black Powder Handbook.** (Illus.). 224 p. 1983. DBI. pap. $11.95.

Lewis, Jack. **Black Powder Gun Digest,** 3rd ed. 256 p. 1982. pap. DBI Books $10.95.

Nonte, George C. Jr., **Black Powder Guide.** (Illus.). 256 p. pap. Stoeger Pub. Co. $9.95.

BOW AND ARROW (see also Archery)

Adams, Chuck. **Bowhunter's Digest.** 2nd ed. pap. 1981. DBI Books. $12.95.

Bear, Fred. **The Archer's Bible.** rev. ed. (Illus.). 1980. Doubleday. pap. $5.95.

Bowring, Dave. **Bowhunting for Whitetails: Your Best Methods for Taking North America's Favorite Deer.** (Illus.) 320 p. 1985. Stackpole. $24.95.

Elliot, Cheri, ed. **Digest Book of Bowhunting.** 96 p. DBI. pap. $3.95.

Helgeland, G. **Archery World's Complete Guide to Bow Hunting.** 1975. P-H. pap. $5.95.

James, M. R. **Bowhunting for Whitetail and Mule Deer.** rev. ed. 224 p. 1976. pap. Jolex. $6.95.

Kinton, Tony. **The Beginning Bowhunter.** 128 p. 1985. ICS Books. pap. $9.95.

Maynard, Roger. **Advanced Bowhunting Guide.** (Illus.) 224 p. 1984. Stoeger Pub. Co. pap. $11.95.

Schuh, Dwight. **Bowhunting for Mule Deer.** 1986. Stoneydale Press Pub. $14.95. pap. $9.95.

Schuyler, Keith C. **Bowhunting for Big Game.** 224 p. 1977. pap. Stackpole, $7.95.

Smythe, John. **Bow Versus Gun.** 1974. Repr. of 1590 ed. text ed. British Book Center (OP).

Thayer, Dixon. **Bow Hunting Basics: Fundamentals for Successful Hunting.** (Illus.). 32 p. 1985. Blue Sky. pap. $2.95.

BOWHUNTING (see Bow and Arrow)

CARTRIDGES

Bartlett, W. A. & Gallatin, D. B. **B and G Cartridge Manual,** Pioneer Press. $2.00.

Datig, Fred A. **Cartridges for Collectors,** 3 vols. Borden, $8.95 ea.

Donnelly, John J. **Handloader's Manual of Cartridge Conversions.** (Illus.) 1056 p. 1987. Stoeger Pub. Co. pap. $24.95; spiral bound $29.95; hardcover $34.95.*

Harvey, Clay. **Popular Sporting Rifle Cartridges.** 320 p., 1984. pap. DBI. $12.95.

Keith, Elmer. **Sixgun Cartridges & Loads.** 1985. Repr. of 1936 ed. Gun Room. $19.95.

Manual of Pistol & Revolver Cartridges. 2 vols. 1987. Gordon Press. lib. bdg. $79.75.*

Matthews, Charles. **Shoot Better With Centerfire Rifle Cartridges-Ballistics Tables.** (Illus.) 560 p. 1984. Matthews Inc. pap. $16.45.

Nonte, George. **The Home Guide to Cartridge Conversions.** rev. ed. Gun Room Press. rev. ed. $19.95.

Suydam, Charles R. **American Cartridge.** Borden. $10.95.

Thomas, Gough. **Shotguns and Cartridges for Game and Clays.** 3rd ed. (Illus.). 1976. Transatlantic Arts, Inc. $25.00.

COLLECTING (see Firearms—Collectors and Collecting)

COLT REVOLVERS

Bady, Donald B. **Colt Automatic Pistols,** rev. ed. 1973. Borden. $16.50.

Cochran, Keith. **Colt Peacemaker Ready-Reference Handbook.** (Illus.) 76 p. 1985. Cochran Pub. pap. $12.95.*

—**Colt Peacemaker Encyclopedia.** (Illus.). 434 p. 1986. Cochran Pub. $59.95.

—**Colt Peacemaker Yearly Variations.** (Illus.) 96 p. 1987. Cochran Pub. $17.95. pap. $12.95.*

The Colt Point Forty-Five Auto Pistol. 1986. Gordon Pr. $79.95.

The Colt .45 Exotic Weapons System. (Illus.). 88 p. 1984. Paladin Pr. pap. $12.00.

Graham, Ron, et al. **A Study of the Colt Single Action Army Revolver.** (Illus.) 523 p. 1985. Repr. of 1976 ed. Kopec Pubns. $69.95.

Moore, C. Kenneth. **Colt Revolvers & the U.S. Navy 1865–1888.** (Illus.) 144 p. 1986. Dorrance. $29.95.*

Shumaker, P. L. **Colt's Variations of the Old Model Pocket Pistol.** 1957. Borden. $8.95.

Whittington, Robert D. III. **The Colt Whitneyville-Walker Pistol.** (Illus.). 96 p. 1984. Brownlee Books. $20.00.

Wilkerson, Don. **The Post-War Colt Single-Action Revolver, 1976–1986.** (Illus.). 324 p. 1986. Cherokee Pub. $100.00.

CROSSBOWS

Combs, Roger, ed. **Crossbows.** (Illus.). 192 p. 1987. DBI. $10.95.*

Payne-Gallwey, Ralph. **Cross-Bow, Medieval and Modern.** Saifer, Albert, Pub. $55.00.

Wilbur, C. Martin. **History of the Crossbow.** (Illus.). Repr. of 1936 ed. pap. Shorey. $2.95.

DECOYS (see also Duck Shooting)

Barber, Joel. **Wild Fowl Decoys.** (Illus.). pap. Dover. $6.95.

—**Wild Fowl Decoys.** (Illus.). Peter Smith. $13.50.

Berkey, Barry R., et al. **Pioneer Decoy Carvers: A Biography of Lemuel and Stephen Ward.** (Illus.). 1977. Tidewater. $17.50.

Bridenhagen, Keith. **Decoy Pattern Book.** (Illus.). 224 p. (Orig.). 1985. Sterling. $9.95.

—**Realistic Decoys.** 224 p. 1985. Stoeger Pub. Co. pap. $14.95.

Bridenhagen, Keith & Spielman, Patrick. **Realistic Decoys: Carving, Texturing, Painting & Finishing.** (Illus.). 224 p. (Orig.). 1984. Stoeger Pub. Co. pap. $14.95.

Buckwalter, Harold R. **Susquehanna River Decoys.** (Illus.). 1978. Schiffer. $12.95.

Burk, Bruce. **Game Bird Carving.** 2nd ed. (Illus.). 304 p. 1982. Winchester Press. $24.95.

Carpenter, Pearl E. **The Duck Book One & Two:** Basics for Painting Wood-Carved Ducks & Birds. (Illus.) 1984. Shades Mother Nature wkbk. $12.75.

Chapell, Carl & Sullivan, Clark. **Wildlife Woodcarvers:** A Complete How-to-do-it Book for Carving & Painting Wildfowl. (Illus.) 216 p. 1986. Stackpole. $39.95.

Chitwood, Henry C., et al. **Connecticut Decoys.** (Illus.). 256 p. 1987. Schiffer. $45.00.*

Connett, Eugene. **Duck Decoys.** 1980. Durrell. $12.50.

Coykendall, Ralf, Sr. **Duck Decoys & How To Rig Them.** Coykendall, Ralf, Jr., ed. (Illus.). 135 p. 1987. New Century. pap. $14.95.*

Delph, John and Delph, Shirley. **Factory Decoys of Mason Stevens.** (Illus.). Schiffer. $35.00.

Earnest, Adele. **The Art of the Decoy: American Bird Carvings.** (Illus.). 1982. pap. Schiffer. $14.95.

Frank, Chas. W., Jr. **Wetland Heritage: The Louisiana Duck Decoy.** 192 p. 1985. Pelican. $49.95.

Johnsgard, Paul A. ed. **The Bird Decoy: An American Art Form.** (Illus.). 1976. University of Nebraska Press. $17.95.

Luckey, Carl F. **Collecting Antique American Bird Decoys: An Identification and Value Guide.** (Illus.). 208 p. 1983. pap. Books Americana. $14.95.

Mackey, William J., Jr. **American Bird Decoys.** (Illus.). 256 p. 1987. Dutton. $22.50.*

Mackey, William F., Jr. & Colio, Quinton. **American Bird Decoys.** (Illus.). 1979. Repr. of 1965 ed. Schiffer. $19.95.

Murphy, Charles F. **Working Plans for Working Decoys.** (Illus.). 1979. Winchester Press. $21.95.

Parmalee, Paul W. & Loomis, Forrest D. **Decoys and Decoy Carvers of Illinois.** 1969. pap. Northern Illinois University Press. $25.00.

Reiger, George. **Floaters & Stick-Ups.** 208 p. 1986. Godine. $40.00.

Schroeder, Roger. **How To Carve Wildfowl: Nine North American Masters Reveal the Carving and Painting Techniques That Win Them International Blue Ribbons.** 256 p. 1984. Stackpole. $34.95.

Shourds, Harry V. & Hillman, Anthony. **Carving Duck Decoys.** 1981. pap. Dover. $4.95.

Spielman, Patrick. **Making Wood Decoys.** 1982. Sterling. $16.95; lib. bdg. $18.95; pap. $8.95.

Starr, George R., Jr. **How to Make Working Decoys.** (Illus.). 1978. Winchester Press. $21.95.

Veasey, William. **Head Patterns.** (Illus.). 58 p. 1983. pap. Schiffer. $14.95.

—**Making Hunting Decoys.** (Illus.). 256 p. 1986. Schiffer. $45.00.

—**Miniature Decoy Patterns.** (Illus.). 58 p. 1983. pap. $14.95.

Veasey, William & Hull, Cary S. **Waterfowl Carving: Blue Ribbon Techniques.** (Illus.). 1982. Schiffer. $35.00.

Walsh, Clune, Jr. & Jackson, Lowell G., eds. **Waterfowl Decoys of Michigan and the Lake St. Clair Region.** (Illus.). 175 p. 1983. Gale. $50.00.

DEER HUNTING (see also Hunting)

Adams, Chuck. **Complete Guide to Bowhunting Deer.** 256 p. 1984. pap. DBI. $10.95.

Bauer, Erwin. A. **Digest Book of Deer Hunting.** pap. DBI Books. $2.95.

Bowring, Dave. **Bowhunting for Whitetails: Your Best Methods for Taking North America's Favorite Deer.** (Illus.) 304 p. 1985. Stackpole. $24.95.

Cameron, Donald. **Among The Red Deer: The Stalking Portfolio of Henry Hope Creslock.** 1985. State Mutual Bks. $300.00.

Chalmers, Patrick R. **Deer-Stalking.** 256 p. 1985. State Mutual Bks. $60.00.

Conway, Bryant W. **Successful Hints on Hunting White Tail Deer.** 2nd ed. 1967. pap. Claitors. $1.98.

Dalrymple, Bryon W. **The Complete Book of Deer Hunting.** 256 p. pap. Stoeger. $8.95.

—**Deer Hunting with Dalrymple: A Lifetime of Lore on The Whitetail and Mule Deer.** 256 p. 1983. pap. Arco. $7.95.

Darner, Kirt. **How To Find Giant Bucks.** (Illus.). 283 p. 1984. Walsworth's. $20.00.

Deer Hunter's Guide. (Illus.). 160 p. Nat'l Rifle Assn. $4.95.

Elman, Robert, ed. **All About Deer Hunting in America.** 1976. New Century. $16.95.

Fadala, Sam. **Successful Deer Hunting.** 288 p. 1983. pap. DBI Books. $10.95.

Guide to Deer Hunting in the Catskill Mountains. pap. Outdoor Pubns. $1.75.

Hayes, Tom. **How to Hunt the White Tail Deer.** A. S. Barnes, rev. ed. pap. $6.95.

Horner, Kent. **Art & Science of Whitetail Hunting:** How to Interpret the Facts & Find the Deer. (Illus.) 192 p. 1986. Stackpole. pap. $11.95.

James, M. P. **Bowhunting for Whitetail and Mule Deer.** new ed. 224 p. 1976. Joles. pap. $6.95.

Laycock, George. **Deer Hunter's Bible.** rev. ed. (Illus.). 1971. pap. Doubleday. $3.95.

Nelson, Norm. **Mule Deer: How To Bring Home North America's Big Deer of the West.** (Illus.). 208 p. 1987. Stackpole. $16.95.*

Sell, Francis E. **Art of Successful Deer Hunting.** 1980. pap. Willow Creek. $5.95.

Sisley, Nick. **Deer Hunting Across North America.** (Illus.). 1975. Freshet Press. $12.95.

Smith, Richard P. **Deer Hunting.** rev. ed. (Illus.). 1981. pap. Stackpole Books. $9.95.

Wegner, Robert. **Deer & Deer Hunting:** The Serious Hunter's Guide. 324 p. 1984. Stackpole. $24.95.

Weiss, John. **The Whitetail Deer Hunter's Handbook.** (Illus.). 1979. pap. Winchester Press. $11.95.

Whitehead, Kenneth. **Hunting and Stalking Deer Throughout the Ages.** (Illus.). 1980. David & Charles. $45.00.

Wolff, Ed. **Taking Big Bucks: Solving the Whitetail Riddle.** (Illus.). 176 p. 1987. Stoneydale Pr. Pub. pap. $9.95.*

Wooters, John. **Hunting Trophy Deer.** rev. ed. (Illus.). 265 p. 1983. pap. New Century. $12.95.

Zumbo, Jim & Elman, Robert. **All-American Deer Hunter's Guide.** (Illus.). 320 p. 1983. New Century. $29.95.

DUCK & GEESE SHOOTING (see also Decoys)

Adams, Chuck. **The Digest Book of Duck and Goose Hunting.** (Illus.). pap. DBI Books. $3.95.

Cadieux, Charles L. **Successful Goose Hunting.** (Illus.). 240 p. 1986. Stone Wall Press. $24.95.

Hinman, Bob. **The Duck Hunter's Handbook.** (Illus.). 1976. softbound. Stoeger. $9.95.

—**The Duck Hunter's Handbook,** rev. ed. 288 p. 1985. New Century. $15.95.

Jordan, James M. & Alcorn, George T., eds. **The Wildfowler's Heritage.** (Illus.). 120 p. 1984. JCP Corp. Va. $46.50.

MacQuarrie, Gordon. **The Last Stories of the Old Duck Hunters.** (Illus.). 204 p. 1985. Willow Creek. $15.00.

—**Stories of the Old Duck Hunters & Other Drivel.** repr. of 1967 ed. Willow Creek. $15.00.

Milner, Robert. **Retriever Training for the Duck Hunter.** (Illus.) 150 p. 1985. Repr. of 1983 ed. Junction Press. $18.95.

Smith, Steve. **Hunting Ducks & Geese: Hard Facts, Good Bets and Serious Advice From a Duck Hunter You Can Trust.** 160 p. 1984. Stackpole. $14.95.

FALCONRY (see also Fowling)

Beebe, Frank L. **A Falconry Manual.** (Illus.). 128 p. 1983. pap. Hancock House. $12.95.

Bert, Edmund. **An Approved Treatise of Hawkes and Hawking Divided into Three Bookes.** 1968. Repr. of 1619 ed. W. J. Johnson. $16.00.

Fisher, Charles H. **Falconry Reminiscences.** 1972. Falcon Head Press. $15.00; deluxe ed. $25.00.

Ford, Emma. **Falconry in News and Field.** (Illus.). 1982. Branford. $32.50.

Fox, David G. **Garden of Eagles: The Life & Times of a Falconer.** (Illus.). 216 p. 1984. Merrimack Pub. Cir. $16.95.

Frederick II of Hohenstaufen. **The Art of Falconry.** Wood, Casey A. & Fyfe, F. Marjorie, eds. (Illus.). 1943. Stanford University Press. $39.50.

Freeman, Gage E. & Salvin, Francis H. **Falconry: Its Claims, History and Practice.** 1972. Falcon Head Press. $12.50; deluxe ed. $25.00.

Gryndall, William. **Hawking, Hunting, Fouling and Fishing;** Newly Corrected by W. Gryndall Faulkener. 1972. Repr. of 1596 ed. Walter J. Johnson, Inc. $13.00.

Harting, J. E. **Hints on the Management of Hawks and Practical Falconry.** 1982. (Pub. by Saiga). State Mutual Book & Periodical Service. $50.00.

Harting, James E. **Bibliotheca Accipitraria, a Catalogue of Books Ancient and Modern Relating to Falconry.** 1977. Repr. of 1963 ed. Oak Knoll Books. $45.00.

Jameson, Everett W., Jr. **The Hawking of Japan, the History and Development of Japanese Falconry.** (Illus.). Repr. of 1962 ed. Jameson & Peeters. $24.50.

Jameson, E. W. Jr. & Peeters, Hans J. **Introduction to Hawking.** 2nd ed. (Illus.). 1977. pap. E. W. Jameson, Jr. $8.85.

Lascelles, Gerald. **Art of Falconry.** (Illus.). Saifer. $12.50.

Latham, Simon. **Lathams Falconry, 2 pts.** 1977. Repr. of 1615 ed. Walter J. Johnson, Inc. $32.50.

Madden, D. H. **Chapter of Medieval History.** 1969. Repr. of 1924 ed. Kennikat. $15.00.

Mellor, J. E. **Falconry Notes by Mellor.** 1972. Falcon Head Press. $8.50.

Mitchell, E. B. **Art & Practice of Falconry.** (Illus.). 303 p. 1981. State Mutual Book Svce. $15.00.

Oswald, Allan. **The History & Practice of Falconry.** 128 p. 1981. State Mutual Book Svce. $25.00.

Phillott, D. C. & Harcourt, E. S., trs. from Persian Urdu. **Falconry—Two Treatises.** 1968. text ed. Falcon Head Press. $30.00.

Rowley, Sam R. **Discovering Falconry: A Comprehensive Guide to Contemporary Falconry.** (Illus.). 160 p. 1985. New Dawn. pap. $11.95.

Samson, Jack. **Modern Falconry: Your Illustrated Guide To The Art & Sport of Hunting With North American Hawks.** 160 p.

Schlegel, H. & Verster De Wulverhorst, J. A. **The World of Falconry.** 1980. Vendome Press. $60.00.

Schlegel, H. & Wulverhorst, A. H. **Traite De Fauconnerie: Treatise of Falconry.** Hanlon, Thomas, tr. (Illus.). 1973. Chasse Pubns. $32.50.

FIREARMS (see also Arms and Armor, Pistols, Revolvers, Rifles, Shotguns)

Ackley, Parker O. **Home Gun Care and Repair.** (Illus.). 1974. pap. Stackpole Books. $6.95.

Akehurst, Richard. **Game Guns & Rifles:** From Percussion to Hammerless Ejector in Britain. (Illus.) 192 p. 1985. Sterling. $19.95.

Anderson, Robert S. **Metallic Cartridge Reloading.** (Illus.). 1982. pap. DBI Books. $10.95.

Anderson, Robert S., ed. **Gun Digest Hunting Annual,** 1988. 5th ed. (Illus.). 256 p. 1987. DBI. pap. $13.95.*

Askins, Charles. **Askins on Pistols and Revolvers.** Bryant, Ted & Askins, Bill. eds., 1980. National Rifle Association, $25.00; pap. $8.95.

Automatic and Concealable Firearms: Design Book, 3 vols. 1986. Gordon Pr. $299.00 (lib. bdg.).

Barwick, Humphrey. **Concerning the Force and Effect of Manual Weapons of Fire.** 1974. Repr. of 1594 ed. W. J. Johnson. $8.00.

Bell, Bob. **Scopes & Mounts: Gun Digest Book.** 224 p. 1983. pap. DBI Books. $9.95.

Berger, Robert J. **Know Your Broomhandle Mausers.** (Illus.). 96 p. 1985. Blacksmith Corp. pap. $6.95.

Bodio, Stephen. **Good Guns.** 128 p. 1986. N. Lyons Bks. $14.95.

Bridges, Toby. **Advanced Muzzleloader's Guide.** 256 p. 1985. Stoeger Pub. Co. pap. $11.95.

Brown, Ronald. **Homemade Guns & Homemade Ammo.** 191 p. 1986. Loompanics. pap. text ed. $9.95.

Browne, Bellmore H. **Guns and Gunning.** (Illus.). Repr. of 1908 ed. pap. Shorey. $4.95.

The Browning Hi-Power Exotic Weapons System. (Illus.). 72 p. 1985. Paladin Pr. pap. $12.00.

Cameron, Frank & Campione, Frank. **Micro Guns.** (Illus.). 48 p. 1982. Mosaic Press, OH. $24.00.

Chant, Chris. **Armed Forces of the United Kingdom.** (Illus.). 1980. David & Charles. $14.95.

Clede, Bill. **Police Handgun Manual: How To Get Street-Smart Survival Habits.** (Illus.). 128 p. Stackpole. $11.95.

Combs, Roger. **Holsters and Other Gun Leather: Gun Digest Book.** 256 p. 1983. pap. DBI Books. $9.95.

Cromwell, Giles. **The Virginia Manufactory of Arms.** 1975. University Press of Virginia. $20.00.

Davis, John E. **Introduction to Tool Marks, Firearms and the Striagraph.** (Illus.). 1958. C. C. Thomas. $24.50.

Daw, George. **Gun Patents 1864.** 1982. Saifer. $15.00.

Donnelly, John. **Handloader's Manual of Cartridge Conversions.** (Illus.). 1056 p. 1987. Stoeger Pub. $34.95. sp. bd. $29.95. pap. $24.95.*

Edsall, James. **Volcanic Firearms and Their Successors.** Pioneer Press. $2.50.

Educational Research Council of America. **Firearms Examiner.** Ferris, Theodore N. & Marchak, John P., eds. (Illus.). 1977. Changing Times Education Service. $2.25.

Erickson, Wayne R. & Pate, Charles E. **The Broomhandle Pistol: 1896–1936.** 300 p. E&P Enter. $49.95.

Ezell, Edward C. **Handguns of the World.** (Illus.). 1981. Stackpole Books. $39.95.

—**Small Arms Today: Latest Reports on the World's Weapons & Ammunition.** 256 p. (Orig.). 1984. pap. Stackpole. $16.95.

Fadala, Sam. **The Complete Shooter.** (Illus.). 480 p. (Orig.). 1984. pap. DBI. $15.95.

Farnum, John. **The Street Smart Gun Book.** Police Bookshelf. pap. $11.95.

Flayderman, Norm. **Flayderman's Guide to Antique American Firearms & Their Values,** 4th ed. (Illus.). 624 p. 1987. DBI. pap. $22.95*

Flores, Eliezer, ed. **How To Make Disposable Silencers,** Vol. II. (Illus.). 120 p. 1985. J.O. Flores. pap. $12.00.

Gambordella, Ted. **Weapons of the Street.** (Illus.). 80 p. 1984. Paladin Pr. pap. $8.00.

George, John N. **English Pistols and Revolvers.** Albert Saifer, Pub. $20.00.

Grennell, Dean A. **ABC's of Reloading.** 2nd ed. (Illus.). 1980. pap. DBI Books. $9.95.

—**Gun Digest Book of 9MM Handguns.** (Illus.) 256 p. 1986. DBI. pap. $12.95.

—**Handgun Digest.** (Illus.). 256 p. 1987. DBI. pap. $12.95.*

Hamilton, T. M. **Early Indian Trade Guns: 1625–1775.** (Contributions of the Museum of the Great Plains Ser.: No. 3). (Illus.). 1968. pap. Museum of the Great Plains Pubns. Dept. $4.00.

Hatcher. **The Book of the Garand.** Gun Room Press. $15.00.

Hatcher, Julian S. **Hatcher's Notebook.** rev. ed. (Illus.). 1962. Stackpole Books. $19.95.

Hoffschmidt, Edward J. **Know Your Gun, Incl. Know Your .45 Auto Pistols; Know Your Walther P. .38 Pistols; Know Your Walther P. P. and P. P. K. Pistols; Know Your M1 Garand Rifles; Know Your Mauser Broomhandle Pistol; Know Your Anti-Tank Rifle.** 1976. Borden pap. $5.95. ea.

Hogg, Brig., fwrd. by **The Compleat Gunner.** (Illus.). 1976. Repr. Charles River Books. $10.50.

Hogg, Ian V. **Guns and How They Work.** (Illus.). 1979. Everest House. $16.95.

Home Workshop Silencers 1. 1980. pap. Paladin Enterprises. $12.00.

Huebner, Siegfried. **Silencers for Hand Firearms.** Schreier, Konrad & Lund, Peter C., eds. 1976. pap. Paladin Enterprises. $11.95.

Huntington, R. T. **Hall's Breechloaders: John H. Hall's Invention and Development of a Breechloading Rifle with Precision-Made Interchangeable Parts, and Its Introduction Into the United States Service.** (Illus.). 1972. pap. George Shumway Publisher. $20.00.

Jackson & Whitelaw. **European Hand Firearms.** 1978. Albert Saifer, Pub. $22.50.

James, Garry, ed. **Guns for Home Defense.** (Illus.). 1975. pap. Petersen Publishing. $3.95.

Kelly, Palo. **An American Tradition: Handguns.** (Illus.) 250 p. 1986. Tarantula Press. pap. $9.95.

Kennedy, Monty. **Checkering and Carving of Gunstocks.** rev. ed. (Illus.). 1952. Stackpole Books. $27.95.

King, Peter. **The Shooting Field: One Hundred Fifty Years with Holland & Holland.** (Illus.). 176 p. 1985. Blacksmith. $39.95.

Kukla, Robert J. **Gun Control.** 449 p. Nat'l Rifle Assn. pap. $4.95.

Larson, E. Dixon. **Remington Tips.** Pioneer Press. $4.95.

Lauber, George. **How to Build Your Own Flintlock Rifle or Pistol.** Seaton. Lionel tr. from Ger. (Illus.). 1976. pap. Jolex. $6.95.

—**How To Build Your Own Wheellock Rifle or Pistol.** Seaton, Lionel, tr. from Ger. (Illus.). 1976. pap. Jolex. $6.95.

Laycock, George. **Shotgunner's Bible.** (Illus.). 176 p. 1987. Doubleday. pap. $7.95.*

—**Black Powder Gun Digest.** 3rd ed. 256 p. pap. 1982. DBI. $10.95.

—**Gun Digest Book of Modern Gun Values,** 5th ed. (Illus.). 432 p. 1985. DBI. pap. $14.95.

Lindsay, Merrill. **Twenty Great American Guns.** (Illus.). 1976. Repr. pap. Arma Press. $1.75.

Long, Duncan. **Automatics: Fast Firepower, Tactical Superiority.** (Illus.). 144 p. 1986. Paladin Pr. pap. text ed. $14.95.

Miller, Martin. **Collector's Illustrated Guide to Firearms.** (Illus.). 1978. Mayflower Books. $24.95.

Murtz, Harold A., ed. **Gun Digest Book of Exploded Firearms Drawings.** 3rd ed. 1982. pap. DBI Books. $14.95.

—**Guns Illustrated.** 1987. (Illus.) 320 p. 1986. DBI. pap. $14.95.

Myatt, F. **An Illustrated Guide to Rifles and Automatic Weapons.** (Illus.). 1981. Arco. $9.95.

National Muzzle Loading Rifle Association. Muzzle Blasts: Early Years Plus Vol. I and II 1939–41. 1974. pap. George Shumway Publisher. $18.00.

Nonte, George C., Jr. **Handgun Competition.** (Illus.). 1978. Winchester Press. $16.95.

Nonte, George C., Jr. **Combat Handguns.** Jurras, Lee F., ed. (Illus.). 1980. Stackpole Books. $19.95.

Norton (R. W.) Art Gallery. **E. C. Prudhomme: Master Gun Engraver.** (Illus.). 1973. pap. Norton Art Gallery. $3.00.

NRA Gun Collectors Guide. 336 p. Nat'l Rifle Assn. $4.50.

Olson, John. **Olson's Encyclopedia of Small Arms.** (Illus.). 1985. New Century. $22.95.

Painter, Doug. **Hunting & Firearms Safety Primer.** 128 p. 1986. N. Lyons Bks. pap. $8.95.

Pollard, Hugh B. **The History of Firearms.** 1974. Burt Franklin, Pub. $29.50; pap. $8.95.

Price, Robert M. **Firearms Self-Defense: An Introductory Guide.** (Illus.) 1981. Paladin Enterprises. $19.95.

Rees, Clair. **Sportsman's Handgunning Bible.** (Illus.). 336 p. 1985. New Century. $22.95.

—**Matching The Gun To The Game.** (Illus.). 272 p. 1982. New Century. $17.95.

Reese, Michael, II. **Nineteen Hundred Luger—U.S. Test Trials.** 2nd rev. ed. Pioneer Press, ed. (Illus.). Pioneer Press. $4.95.

Reilly, Robert M. **United States Military Small Arms, 1816–1865.** 1983. Gun Room. $35.00.

Riling, Ray. **Guns and Shooting: A Bibliography.** (Illus.). 1981. Ray Riling. $75.00.

Riviere, Bill. **The Gunner's Bible.** rev. ed. 1973. pap. Doubleday. $3.95.

The Ruger Exotic Weapons System. (Illus.). 96 p. (Orig.). 1984. pap. Paladin Pr. $12.00.

Rutherford, Ken. **Collecting Shotgun Cartridges.** (Illus.). 126 p. 1988. David & Charles. $45.00.*

Shelsby, Earl, ed. **NRA Gunsmithing Guide:** Updated rev. ed. (Illus.). 336 p. (Orig.). 1980. pap. Nat'l Rifle Assn. $11.95.

Shooter's Bible 1988. Vol. 79. (Illus.) 576 p. 1987. Stoeger Pub. Co. $14.95.

Shooter's Bible 1989. Vol. 80. (Illus.). 576 p. 1988. Stoeger Pub. Co. $14.95.*

Smythe, John & Barwick, Humphrey. **Bow vs. Gun.** 1976. Repr. Charles River Books. $15.00.

Steindler, R. A. **Reloader's Guide.** (Illus.). 3rd ed. 1975. softbound. Stoeger. $9.95.

—**Steindler's New Firearms Dictionary.** (Illus.). 320 p. 1985. Stackpole. $24.95.

Steiner, Bradley. **The Death Dealer's Manual.** (Illus.). 120 p. 1982. pap. Paladin Press. $10.00.

Stockbridge, V. D. **Digest of U.S. Patents Relating to Breech-loading & Magazine Small Arms, 1836–1873.** (Illus.). 1963. N. Flayderman & Co. $12.50.

Sybertz, Gustav. **Technical Dictionary for Weaponry.** (Ger.-Eng.). 1969. pap. French & European Pubns. Inc. $120.00.

Taylor, Chuck. **The Combat Shotgun & Submachine Gun: A Special Weapons Analysis.** 176 p. 1985. Paladin Pr. pap. $14.95.

Thielen, Thomas W. **The Complete Guide to Gun Shows.** 1980. pap. Loompanics Unlimited. $6.95.

Thomas, Donald G. **Silencer Patents, Vol. III: European Patents 1901–1978.** (Illus.). 1978. Paladin Enterprises. $15.00.

—**Complete Book of Thompson Patents.** 1985. Gun Room. pap. $15.95.

Traister, John E. **How To Buy and Sell Used Guns.** (Illus.). 1982. softbound. Stoeger. $10.95.

—**Gunsmithing at Home.** (Illus.). 256 p. pap. (Orig.). 1985. Stoeger. $11.95.

—**Professional Care & Finishing of Gun Stocks.** (Illus.). 208 p. 1985. TAB Bks. $21.95; pap. $15.95.

Trzoniec, Stanley. **Handloader's Guide.** 256 p. 1985. Stoeger Pub. Co. pap. $11.95.

Van Rensselaer, S. **American Firearms.** (Illus.). 1948. pap. Century House. $10.00.

Waite, Malden & Ernst, Bernard. **Trapdoor Springfield.** 1985. Gun Room. $29.95.

Walsh, J. H. **The Modern Sportsman's Gun & Rifle.** Vol I & II. (Illus.). 536 p. 1986. Wolfe Pub. Co. Price on request.

Walter, John. **The Luger Book.** (Illus.). 288 p. 1987. Sterling. $40.00.*

Warner, Ken, ed. **Handloader's Digest.** 10th ed. 1984. DBI Books. $12.95.

—**Gun Digest, 1988,** 42nd ed. (Illus.). 496 p. 1987. DBI. pap. $14.95.

West, Bill. **Winchester Encyclopedia.** (Illus.). B. West. $15.00.

—**Winchester Lever-Action Handbook.** (Illus.). B. West. $25.00.

—**The Winchester Single Shot.** (Illus.). B. West. $15.00.

Weston, Paul B. **The New Handbook of Handgunning.** (Illus.). 1980. C. C. Thomas $12.95.

Williams, John J. **Survival Guns and Ammo: Raw Meat** (Illus.) 1979. pap. Consumertronics. $19.00.

Williams, Mason. **The Law Enforcement Book of Weapons, Ammunition & Training Procedures: Handguns, Rifles and Shotguns.** (Illus.). 1977. C. C. Thomas. $35.75.

Wirnsberger, Gerhard. **Standard Directory of Proof Marks.** Steindler, R. A. tr. from Ger. (Illus.). 1976. pap. Jolex. $5.95.

Withers, John. **Precision Handloading.** 224 p. 1985. Stoeger Pub. Co. pap. $11.95.

Wood, J. B. **Gun Digest Book of Firearm Assembly-Disassembly: Law Enforcement Weapons, Pt. VI** (Illus.). 1981. pap. DBI Books. $12.95.

—**Gun Digest Book of Gun Care, Cleaning & Refinishing. Book I: Handguns.** (Illus.). 192 p. 1984. pap. DBI. $8.95.

—**Gun Digest Book of Gun Care, Cleaning & Refinishing. Book 2: Long Guns.** (Illus.). 192 p. (Orig.) 1984. pap. DBI. $8.95.

Zellman, Aaron & Neuens, Michael L. **Consumer's Guide to Handguns.** (Illus.). 208 p. 1986. Stackpole. pap. $16.95.

Zhuk, A. B. **Revolvers & Pistols.** 304 p. 1987. State Mutual Bks. $40.00.*

FIREARMS—CATALOGS

Barnes, Frank L. **Cartridges of the World,** 5th ed. (Illus.). 416 p. 1985. DBI. pap. $15.95.

Catalogue of Rim Fire and Center Fire Pistol, Rifle & Military Cartridges, U.S. Cartridge Co. 1881. 116 p. 1984. Rolling Block. pap. $8.00.

E. Remington & Son's Sporting Arms & Ammunition, 1887, Revised Price List. 36 p. 1984. Rolling Block. pap. $5.00.

Hogg, Ian V. **Jane's Infantry Weapons 1985–86.** 11th ed. (Illus.). 975 p. 1985. Jane's Pub. Inc. $125.00.

Murtz, Harold, ed. **Guns Illustrated 1986.** 18th ed. (Illus.). 320 p. 1985. DBI. pap. $13.95.

Remington Gun Catalog 1877. Pioneer Press. $1.50.

Sears & Roebuck c1910 Ammunition Catalog. (Illus.). pap. Sand Pond. $2.00.

Tarassuk, Leonid, ed. **Antique European and American Firearms at the Hermitage Museum.** (Illus., Eng. & Rus.). 1976. Arma Press. ltd. ed. $40.00.

Tinkham, Sandra S., ed. **Catalog of Tools, Hardware, Firearms, and Vehicles.** 1979. Somerset House. pap. incl. color microfiche. $260.00.

United States Cartridge Co.-Lowell, Mass. 1891 Catalog. (Illus.). Sand Pond. $2.50.

Wahl, Paul. **Gun Trader's Guide.** 12th ed. 464 p. 1986. Stoeger Pub. Co. pap. $13.95.*

West, Bill. **Remington Arms Catalogues, 1877–1899.** 1st ed. (Illus.). 1971. B. West. $8.00.

Winchester Shotshell Catalog 1897. (Illus.). pap. Sand Pond. $1.50.

FIREARMS—COLLECTORS AND COLLECTING

Chapel, Charles E. **The Gun Collector's Handbook of Values.** 14th ed. (Illus.). 523 p. 1983. Putnam Pub. Group. $19.95.

—**Gun Collector's Handbook of Values.** 1984. Putnam Pub. Gp. pap. $11.95.

Dicarpegna, N. **Firearms in the Princes Odescalchi Collection in Rome.** (Illus.). 1976. Repr. of 1969 ed. Arma Press. $20.00.

Dixie Gun Works Antique Arms Catalog. Pioneer Press. $1.50.

Flayderman, Norm. **Flayderman's Guide to Antique American Firearms and Their Values.** 4th ed. (Illus.). 1983. pap. DBI Books. $22.95.

Frith, James & Andrews, Ronald. **Antique Pistols Collection 1400–1860.** Saifer. $25.00.

Gusler, Wallace B. & Lavin, James D. **Decorated Firearms 1540–1870, from the Collection of Clay P. Bedford.** 1977. University Press of Virginia. $25.00.

Madaus, H. Michael. **The Warner Collector's Guide to American Long Arms.** 1981. pap. Warner Books. $9.95.

Quertermous, Russel & Quertermous, Steve. **Modern Guns, Identification and Values.** 4th ed. 1980. pap. Wallace-Homestead. $11.95.

Serven, James. **Rare and Valuable Antique Arms.** 1976. Pioneer Press. $4.95.

Shumaker, P. L. **Colt's Variations of the Old Model Pocket Pistol.** 1957. Borden. $8.95.

Stevenson, Jan. **Modern Sporting Guns.** 1988. Doubleday. $19.95.*

Traister, John E. **How To Buy and Sell Used Guns.** (Illus.). 1982. softbound. Stoeger. $10.95.

Wahl, Paul. **Gun Trader's Guide.** 12th ed. (Illus.). softbound. Stoeger. $13.95.

Wilson, R. L. **Colt—Christie's Rare and Historic Firearms Auction Catalogue.** (Illus.). 1981. Arma Press. $25.00.

FIREARMS—HISTORY

Ayalon, David. **Gunpowder and Firearms in the Mamluk Kingdom: A Challenge to Medieval Society.** 2nd ed. 1978. Biblio Distribution Centre. $22.50.

Barnes, Duncan. **History of Winchester Firearms 1866–1980.** 5th ed. rev. (Illus.). 256 p. New Century. $16.95.

Blanch, H. J. A. **A Century of Guns: A Sketch of the Leading Types of Sporting and Military Small Arms.** (Illus.). 1977. Repr. of 1909 ed. Charles River Books. $25.00.

Brown, M. L. **Firearms in Colonial America: The Impact of History and Technology 1492–1792.** 1980. Smithsonian Institution Press. $45.00.

Buchele, W. & Shumway, G. **Recreating the American Long Rifle.** Orig. Title: **Recreating the Kentucky Rifle.** (Illus.). 1973. pap. George Shumway Publisher. $16.00.

Cooper, Jeff. **Fireworks: A Gunsite Anthology.** 1981. Janus Press. $19.95.

Fuller, Claude E. **Breech-Loader in the Service 1816–1917.** (Illus.). 1965. Flayderman, N. & Co. $14.50.

Fuller, Claude E. & Stewart, Richard D. **Firearms of the Confederacy.** 1977. Reprint of 1944 ed. Quarterman. $25.00.

Garavaglia, Louis A. & Worman, Charles G. **Firearms of the American West, 1803–1865.** (Illus.). 1983. U of NM Press. $35.00.

—**Firearms of the American West,** 1866–1894. (Illus.). 423 p. 1983. U. of N. Mex. Press. $40.00.

Greener, W. W. **The Gun & Its Development.** (Illus.). 423 p. 1987. Sterling. $35.00.*

Gusler, Wallace B. & Lavin, James D. **Decorated Firearms, 1540–1870 from the Collection of Clay P. Bedford.** 1977. (Colonial Williamburg Foundation). University Press of Virginia. $25.00.

Hackley, F. W. et al. **History of Modern U.S. Military Small Arms Ammunition: Vol. 2, 1940–1945.** Gun Room Press. $25.00.

Hamilton, T. M. ed. **Indian Trade Guns.** 1983. Pioneer Press. $10.95.

Helmer, William J. **The Gun That Made the Twenties Roar.** Gun Room Press. $16.95.

Hetrick, Calvin. **The Bedford County Rifle and Its Makers.** (Illus.). 1975. pap. George Shumway Publisher. (OP).

Holme, N. & Kirby, E. L. **Medal Rolls: Twenty-Third Foot Royal Welch Fusiliers, Napoleonic Period.** 1979. S. J. Durst. $39.00.

Hutslar, Donald A. **Gunsmiths of Ohio: 18th and 19th Centuries.** Vol. I. (Illus.). casebound. George Shumway Publisher. $35.00.

Jackson, Melvin H. & De Beer, Charles. **Eighteenth Century Gunfounding.** (Illus.). 1974. Smithsonian Institution Press. $19.95.

Kennett, Lee & Anderson, James L. **The Gun in America: The Origins of a National Dilemma.** (Illus., Orig). 1975. Greenwood Press. $22.50; pap. $3.95.

Lindsay, Merrill. **The New England Gun: The First 200 Years.** (Illus.). 1976. Arma Press. $20.00. pap. $12.50.

Nonte, George C., Jr. **Black Powder Guide.** 2nd ed. (Illus.). pap. Stoeger, $9.95.

North & North. **Simeon North: First Official Pistol Maker of the United States.** Repr. Gun Room Press. $9.95.

Peterson, Harold. **Historical Treasury of American Guns.** Benjamin Co. pap. $2.95.

Pollard, Hugh B. **History of Firearms.** (Illus.). 1974. B. Franklin. $29.50; pap. $8.95.

Reese, Michael II. **Nineteen-hundred Luger-U.S. Test Trials.** 2nd rev. ed. (Illus.). pap. Pioneer Press. $4.95.

Rosebush, Waldo E. **American Firearms and the Changing Frontier.** 1962. pap. Eastern Washington State Historical Society. $3.00.

Rywell, Martin. **American Antique Pistols.** Pioneer Press. $2.00.

—**Confederate Guns.** Pioneer Press. $2.00.

Schreier, Konrad F., Jr. **Remington Rolling Block Firearms.** (Illus.). pap. Pioneer Press. $3.95.

Sellers, Frank M. **Sharps Firearms.** (Illus.). 1982. Sellers Pubns. $39.95.

Shelton, Lawrence P. **California Gunsmiths.** (Illus.). 302 p. 1977. casebound. George Shumway Publisher. $29.95.

Tonso, William R. **Gun & Society: The Social and Existential Roots of the American Attachment to Firearms.** 1982. U Press of America. pap. $14.25 lib bdg. $26.50.

West, Bill. **Marlin and Ballard, Arms and History, 1861–1978.** (Illus.). 1978. B. West. $36.00.

—**Savage & Stevens, Arms and History, 1849–1971.** (Illus.). 1971. B. West. $29.00.

FIREARMS—IDENTIFICATION

Anti-Tank Rifle. (Illus.). 12 p. 1983. pap. Ide House. $2.95.

Baer, Larry L. **The Parker Gun.** Gun Room. $29.95.

Brophy, Williams S. **The Krag Rifle.** Gun Room. $29.95.

—**L.C. Smith Shotguns.** Gun Room. $29.95.

Garton, George. **Colt's SAA Post-War Models.** Gun Room. $21.95.

Madaus, H. Michael. **The Warner Collector's Guide to American Long Arms.** 1981. pap. Warner Books. $9.95.

Matthews, J. Howard. **Firearms Identification: Original Photographs and Other Illustrations of Hand Guns, Vol. 2.** 1973. Repr. of 1962 ed. C. C. Thomas. $56.75.

—**Firearms Identification Original Photographs and Other Illustrations of Hand Guns, Data on Rifling Characteristics of Hand Guns & Rifles, Vol. 3.** Wilimovsky, Allan E., ed. (Illus.). 1973. C. C. Thomas. $88.00.

—**Firearms Identification: The Laboratory Examination of Small Arms, Rifling Characteristics in Hand Guns, and Notes on Automatic Pistols, Vol. 1.** 1973. Repr. of 1962 ed. C. C. Thomas. $56.75.

Nelson, Thomas B. & Lockhaven, Hans B. **The World's Submachine Guns: Developments from 1915 to 1963.** Vol. I rev. ed. 1980. TBN Ent. $29.95.

Ruth, Larry. **M-1 Carbine.** pap. Gun Room. $17.95.

Small Arms Training: Sten Machine Carbine, Vol. I. 1983. pap. Ide House $2.95.

Wilber, Charles G. **Ballistic Science for the Law Enforcement Officer.** (Illus.). 1977. C. C. Thomas. $30.75.

FIREARMS—INDUSTRY AND TRADE

Grancsay, Stephen V. & Lindsay, Merrill. **Illustrated British Firearms Patents 1718–1853.** limited ed. (Illus.). Arma Press. $75.00.

Hartzler, Daniel D. **Arms Makers of Maryland.** 1975. George Shumway Publisher. $35.00.

Kirkland, Turner. **Southern Derringers of the Mississippi Valley.** Pioneer Press. $2.00.

Noel-Baker, Phillip. **The Private Manufacture of Armaments.** 1971. pap. Dover. $6.00.

Russell, Carl P. **Guns on the Early Frontiers: A History of Firearms from Colonial Times through the Years of the Western Fur Trade.** 1980. University of Nebraska Press. $27.95. pap. $10.95.

Stiefel, Ludwig, ed. **Gun Proportion Technology.** 500 p. 1987. AJAA. $79.00.*

Stockholm International Peace Research Institute (SIPRI). **The Arms Trade Registers.** 1975. MIT Press. $18.00.

West, Bill. **Browning Arms and History, 1842–1973.** (Illus.). 1972. B. West. $29.00.

FIREARMS—LAWS AND REGULATIONS

Cook, Phillip J. & Lambert, Richard D., eds. **Gun Control.** 1981. American Academy of Political and Social Science. $7.50. pap. $6.00.

Cruit, Ronald L. **Intruder in Your Home: How to Defend Yourself Legally with a Firearm.** 288 p. 1983. Stein & Day. $17.95.

Foster, Carol D., et al. **Gun Control: Restricting Rights or Protecting People?** 104 p. 1987. Info Aids. pap. $14.95.*

Garrison, William L. **Women's Views on Guns & Self-Defense.** 114 p. (Orig.). 1983. pap. Second Amend. $5.50.

Gottlieb, Alan. **The Rights of Gun Owners.** 216 p. 1981. Green Hill. pap. $6.95.

Gun Control. 1976. pap. American Enterprise Institute for Public Policy Research. $3.75.

Halbrook, Stephen P. **That Every Man Be Armed: An Evolution of a Constitutional Right.** 240 p. 1984. U of N Mex. pap. $19.95.

Hardy, David T. **Origins & Development of the 2nd Amendment.** 96 p. 1986. Blacksmith Corp. $11.95.

Kates, Don B., ed. **Firearms & Violence: Issues of Public Policy.** 475 p. 1983. pap. Pacific Inst. Pub. $12.95.

Kennett, Lee & Anderson, James L. **The Gun in America.** (Illus.). text ed. pap. Greenwood Press. $22.50; pap. $3.95.

Krema, Vaclav. **Identification and Registration of Firearms.** (Illus.). 1971. C. C. Thomas. $19.75.

Kruschke, Earl R. **The Right To Keep and Bear Arms.** 230 p. 1985. C.C. Thomas. $24.50.

Kukla, Robert J. **Gun Control: A Written Record of Efforts to Eliminate the Private Possession of Firearms in America.** Orig. Title: Other Side of Gun Control. 1973. pap. Stackpole Books. $4.95.

Leddy, Edward B. **Magnum Force Lobby: The NRA Fights Gun Control.** 1987. U. Pr. of Amer. $28.50.*

The Right To Keep & Bear Arms: A Presentation of Both Sides. 1986. Gordon Pr. $79.95 (lib. bdg.).*

Stewart, Alva W. **Gun Control: Its Pros & Cons. A Checklist.** 12 p. 1986. Vance Biblios. $3.75.

Whisker, James B. **The Citizen Soldier and U.S. Military Policy.** 1979. North River Press. $7.50; pap. $4.50.

Zimring, Franklin E. & Hawkins, Gordon. **The Citizen's Guide to Gun Control.** 224 p. 1987. Macmillan. $17.95.*

FOWLING (see also Decoys, Duck & Geese Shooting, Falconry)

Bauer, Erwin A. **Duck Hunter's Bible.** pap. Doubleday. $3.95.

Begbie, Eric. **Modern Waterfowling.** (Illus.). 190 p. 1980. Saiga. $14.95.

Bell, Bob. **Hunting the Long Tailed Bird.** (Illus.). 1975. Freshet Press. $14.95.

Dalrymple, Byron W. **Bird Hunting with Dalrymple:** The Rewards of Shotgunning Across North America. (Illus.) 288 p. 1987. Stackpole. $29.95.*

Dickey, Charley. **Quail Hunting.** (Illus.). 1975. softbound. Stoeger. $3.95.

Elliot, Charles. **Turkey Hunting With Charlie Elliot.** 288 p. Arco. $14.95; pap. $8.95.

Gryndall, William. **Hawking, Hunting, Fowling and Fishing; Newly Corrected by W. Gryndall Faulkner.** 1972. Repr. of 1596 ed. W. J. Johnson. $13.00.

Johnson, A. E. **Shooting Woodpigeon.** (Illus.). 126 p. 1980. Longwood Pub. Gp. $14.95.

Norman, Geoffrey. **The Orvis Book of Upland Bird Shooting.** 160 p. 1985. New Century. $14.95.

Smith, Steve. **Hunting Ducks & Geese: Hard Facts, Good Bets and Serious Advice From a Duck Hunter You Can Trust.** 160 p. 1984. Stackpole. $14.95.

Woolmer, Frank. **Grouse & Grouse Hunting.** (Illus.). 192 p. Repr. of 1970 ed. N Lyons Bks. $18.95.

Zutz, Don. **Modern Waterfowl Guns & Gunning.** 288 p. 1985. Stoeger Pub. Co. pap. $11.95.

GAME AND GAME BIRDS (see also Duck & Geese Hunting, Fowling, Hunting)

Beasom, Sam L. & Roberson, Sheila F., eds. **Game Harvest Management.** (Illus.). 300 p. 1985. CK Wildlife Res. $20.00; pap. $15.00.

Billmeyer, Patricia. **The Encyclopedia of Wild Game and Fish Cleaning and Cooking.** Yeshaby Pubs. $3.95.

Blair, Gerry. **Predator Caller's Companion.** 1981. Winchester Press. $15.95.

Candy, Robert. **Getting The Most From Your Game & Fish.** (Illus.). 278 p. (Orig.). 1984. pap. A. C. Hood Pub. $12.95.

Grooms, Steve. **Modern Pheasant Hunting.** (Illus.). 224 p. 1984. pap. Stackpole. $8.95.

Hagerbaumer, David. **Selected American Game Birds.** 1972. Caxton. $30.00.

Harbour, Dave. **Advanced Wild Turkey Hunting & World Records.** (Illus.). 264 p. 1983. New Century. $19.95.

McDaniel, John M. **Spring Turkey Hunting:** The Serious Hunter's Guide. (Illus.) 224 p. 1986. Stackpole. $21.95.

McKelvie, Colin. **A Future for Game?** (Illus.) 240 p. 1985. Allen & Unwin. $15.95.

Marchington, John **The Natural History of Game.** (Illus.) 256 p. 1984. Longwood Publ. Gp. $25.00.

Nesbitt, W. H., ed. **Eighteenth Boone & Crockett Big Game Awards, 1980–82.** (Illus.). 250 p. 1983. Boone & Crockett. $19.50.

Nesbitt, W. H. & Wright, Phillip L., eds. **Records at North American Big Game.** 8th ed. 412 p. 1981, Boone & Crockett. $195.00.

Oldham, J. **The West of England Flying Tumbler.** 1981. State Mutual Book & Periodical Service, Ltd. $25.00.

Robbins, Charles T., ed. **Wildlife Feeding and Nutrition.** 1983. Academic Press. $31.50.

Sherwood, Morgan. **Big Game in Alaska.** 1981. Yale University Press. $27.50.

Stuart, Jack. **Bird Dogs & Upland Game Birds.** (Illus.). 1983. Denlinger. $24.95.

GAME AND GAME BIRDS—NORTH AMERICA

Bent, Arthur C. **Life Histories of North American Wild Fowl.** 685 p. 1987. Dover. pap. $12.95.*

Foster. **New England Grouse Shooting.** 1983. Willow Creek. $45.00.

Leopold, A. Starker, et al. **North American Game Birds and Mammals.** (Illus.). 224 p. 1981. Scribner. $19.95.

Leopold, A. Starker & Gutierrez, Ralph J. **North American Game Birds and Mammals.** (Illus.). 208 p. 1984. pap. Scribner. $14.95.

Nesbitt, W. H. & Wright, Phillip L., eds. **Records of North American Big Game.** 8th ed. 1981. Boone & Crockett Club. $29.50.

Phillips, John C. **American Game Mammals and Birds: A Catalog of Books, Sports, Natural History and Conservation. 1582–1925.** 1978. Repr. of 1930 ed. Arno Press. $37.00.

Sanderson, Glen C., ed. **Management of Migratory Shore & Upland Game Birds in North America.** 1980. pap. University of Nebraska Press. $10.95.

Tinsley, Russell, ed. **All About Small-Game Hunting in America.** 1976. Winchester Press. $14.95.

Walsh, Harry M. **The Outlaw Gunner.** 1971. Cornell Maritime Press. $12.50.

Walsh, Roy. **Gunning the Chesapeake.** 1960. Cornell Maritime. $10.00

GAME COOKERY (see also Outdoor Cookery)

Barbour, Judy. **Elegant Elk: Delicious Deer.** 3rd ed. (Illus.). 196 p. 1983 reprint of 1978 ed. Peters Studio. $12.95.

Beard, James. **Fowl & Game Bird Cookery.** 1983. Peter Smith. $11.75.

Billmeyer, Patricia. **The Encyclopedia of Wild Game and Fish Cleaning and Cooking.** pap. Yesnaby Pubs. $3.95.

Bryant, Jim. **The Wild Game & Fish Cookbook.** (Illus.). 224 p. 1983. Little. $14.95.

Cameron, Angus & Jones, Judith. **The L. L. Bean Game & Fish Cookbook.** 1983. Random. $19.95.

Canino, Thomas L. **Mountain Man Cookbook: Venison & Other Recipes.** 85 p. 1985. TLC Enterprises. pap. $7.95.

Chicken and Game Hen Menus. 1983. Silver. $15.95.

Cone, Joan. **Fish and Game Cooking.** 1981. pap. EPM Publications. $7.95.

De Gouy, Louis V. **The Derrydak Game Cookbook,** Vol. I. repr. of 1937 ed. 308 p. 1987. Willow Creek Pr. $25.00.*

Del Guidice, Paula J. **Microwave Game & Fish Cookbook.** (Illus.) 160 p. 1985. Stackpole. pap. $12.95.*

D'Ermo. Dominique. **Dominique's Famous Fish, Game & Meat Recipes.** 1981. pap. Acropolis. $8.95.

Duffala, Sharon L. **Rocky Mountain Cache: Western Wild Game Cookbook.** (Illus.). 72 p. 1982. pap. Pruett. $5.95.

Fadala, Sam. **Complete Guide to Game Care & Cookery.** 288 p. DBI. pap. $12.95.*

French, Jack. **Pioneer Heritage Wild Game Cookbook.** (Illus.). 416 p. 1987. Realco Pub. pap. $14.95.*

Goolsby, Sam. **Great Southern Wild Game Cookbook.** 193 p. 1980. Pelican. $13.95.

Gorton, Audrey A. **Venison Book: How to Dress, Cut Up and Cook Your Deer.** 1957. pap. Greene. $4.95.

Gray, Rebecca & Reeve, Cintra. **Gray's Wild Game Cookbook: A Menu Cookbook.** (Illus.). 220 p. 1983. Grays Sporting. $25.00.

Hibler, Jane. **Fair Game: A Hunter's Cookbook.** Lawrence, Betsy, ed. 1983. pap. Chalmers. $5.95.

Humphreys, Angela. **Game Cookery.** (Illus.) 144 p. 1986. David & Charles. $19.95.*

Jaxson, Jay. **Wild Country All Game & Fish Recipes.** (Illus.). 81 p. 1982. pap. Jackson G. B. $7.95.

Johnson, L. W., ed. **Wild Game Cookbook: A Remington Sportsmen's Library Bk.** pap. Benjamin Co. $3.95.

Knight, Jacqueline E. **The Hunter's Game Cookbook.** (Illus.). 1978. Winchester Press. $12.95.

Lamagna, Joseph. **Wild Game Cookbook for Beginner and Expert.** J. Lamagna. $6.95.

Mabbutt, Bill & Mabbutt, Anita: **North American Wild Game Cookbook.** 216 p. 1982. NC Book Exp. $9.95.

Mabbutt, Bill, et al. **North American Game Fish Cookbook.** 192 p. 1983. NC Bk. pap. $9.95.

MacIlquham, Frances. **Complete Fish & Game Cookery of North America.** (Illus.). 304 p. 1983. Winchester Press. $29.95.

Manion, Timothy E. **The Game & Fish Menu Cookbook.** (Illus.). 320 p. 1987. Weidenfeld. $19.95.*

—**Wild Game & Country Cooking.** 200 p. 1983. Manion Outdoors Co. 5 p. bd. $9.95.

Marsh, Judy and Dyer, Carole, eds. **The Maine Way—A Collection of Maine Fish and Game Recipes.** (Illus.). 1978. DeLorme Pub. $3.95.

Michigan United Conservation Clubs. **The Wildlife Chef.** new ed. 1977. pap. Mich United Conserv. $3.95.

Oakland, Ann. **Buffalo at Steak.** 32 p. 1983. pap. One Percent. $3.95.

Obern, Jane & Waldron, Valerie, eds. **NAHC Wild Game Cookbook.** (Illus.). 192 p. 1987. N. Am. Hunt Club. pap. $14.95.*

Orcutt, Georgia and Taylor, Sandra, eds **Poultry and Game Birds.** 1982. pap. Yankee Books. $8.95.

Pederson, Rolf A. **Rolf's Collection of Wild Game Recipes:** Vol. I: Upland Game Birds. 174 p. 1982. pap. Rolf's Gallery. $9.95.

—**Waterfowl,** Vol. II. 1983. pap. Rolf's Gallery. $9.95.

Perkins, Roni. **Game in Season: The Orvis Cookbook.** (Illus.) 224 p. 1986. New Century. $19.95.*

Rojas-Lombardi, Felipe. **Game Cookery.** (Illus.). 1973. Livingston, dura. $2.95.

—**Game Cookery.** (Illus.). 1973. plastic bdg. Harrowood Books. $2.95.

Rywell, Martin. **Wild Game Cook Book.** 1952. pap. Buck Hill. $4.95.

Sagstetter, Brad. **The Venison Handbook.** (Illus.). 80 p. 1981. Larksdale. $6.95.

Smith, Capt. James A. **Dress 'Em Out.** 256 p. pap. (Orig.). Stoeger. $12.95.

Smith, John A. **Wild Game Cookbook.** 64 p. 1986. Dover. pap. $4.95.*

Steindler, Geraldine. **Game Cookbook.** New Revised Edition. 1985. softbound. Stoeger. $12.95.

Turkey, Duck & Goose Menus. 1985. (Pub. by Time-Life) Silver. $15.94.

Upland Game Birds, Vol. I. (Illus.). 174 p. pap. Rolf's Gallery. $9.95.

Wary, Carol. **Wild Game Cookery: The Hunter's Home Companion.** (Illus.). 1984. pap. (Orig.). Countryman. $8.95.

Willard, John. **Game Is Good Eating.** 4th rev. ed. (Illus.). 111 p. repr. of 1954 ed. J.A. Willard. $6.95.

Wongrey, Jan. **Southern Wildfowl and Wildgame Cookbook.** 1976. Sandlapper Store. $5.95.

Zumbo, Jim & Zumbo, Lois. **The Venison Cookbook.** (Illus.) 208 p. 1986. P-H. $17.45.*

GUNPOWDER (see Black Powder Guns, Ammunition)

GUNS (see Firearms, Pistols, Revolvers, Rifles, Shotguns)

GUNSMITHING

Angier, R. H. **Firearms Blueing and Browning.** 1936. Stackpole Books. $12.95.

Baker, Clyde. **Modern Gunsmithing.** (Illus.). 605 p. 1981. Stackpole. $24.95.

Bish, Tommy L. **Home Gunsmithing Digest,** 3rd ed. 256 p. 1984. pap. DBI. $10.95.

Demeritt, Dwight B., Jr. **Maine Made Guns and Their Makers.** (Illus.). Maine State Museum Pubns. $22.00.

Dunlap, Roy F. **Gunsmithing.** 1963. Stackpole Books. $24.95.

Hartzler, Daniel D. **Arms Makers of Maryland.** (Illus.). 1977. George Shumway Publisher. $35.00.

Hutslar, Donald A. **Gunsmiths of Ohio: 18th and 19th Centuries.** Vol. 1. (Illus.). 1973. George Shumway Publisher. $35.00.

Mills, Desmond & Barnes, Mike. **Amateur Gunsmithing.** 1987. Longwood Pub. Group. $35.00.*

Mitchell, Jack. **Gun Digest Book of Pistolsmithing.** 1980. pap. DBI Books. $9.95.

—**Gun Digest Book of Riflesmithing.** 256 p. 1982. pap. DBI Books. $11.95.

Newell, A. Donald. **Gunstock Finishing and Care.** (Illus.). 1949. Stackpole Books. $22.95.

Norton Art Gallery. **Artistry in Arms: The Art of Gunsmithing and Gun Engraving.** (Illus.). 1971. pap. Norton Art Gallery. $2.50.

NRA Gunsmithing Guide. 336 p. Natl Rifle Assn. $9.95.

Sellers, Frank M. **American Gunsmiths: A Source Book.** 1983. Gun Room. $39.95.

Shelsby, Earl, ed. **NRA Gunsmithing Guide: Updated.** rev. ed. (Illus.). 336 p. 1980. pap. Natl. Rifle Assn. $11.95.

Shelton, Lawrence P. **California Gunsmiths.** (Illus.). 1977. George Shumway Publisher. $29.65.

Spearing, O.W. **The Craft of the Gunsmith.** (illus.) 144 p. 1987. Sterling. $14.95.*

Stelle & Harrison. **The Gunsmith's Manual: A Complete Handbook for the American Gunsmith.** (Illus.). Repr. of 1883 ed. Gun Room Press. $12.95.

Traister, John. **Gun Digest Book of Gunsmithing Tools & Their Uses.** 256 p. 1980. DBI. pap. $10.95.

—**Gunsmithing at Home.** (Illus.). 256 p. pap. (Orig.). Stoeger. $11.95.

Walker, Ralph. **Shotgun Gunsmithing: Gun Digest Book.** 256 p. 1983. pap. DBI. $9.95.

Wood, J. B. **Gunsmithing: Tricks of the Trade.** (Illus.). 1982. pap. DBI Books. $11.95.

HAWKEN RIFLES

Baird, John D. **Fifteen Years in the Hawken Lode.** (Illus.). Gun Room Press. $17.95.

—**Hawken Rifles. The Mountain Man's Choice.** Gun Room Press. $17.95.

HUNTING (see also Bird Dogs, Decoys, Deer Hunting, Duck & Geese Shooting, Fowling, Hunting Dogs)

Acerrano, Anthony J. **The Practical Hunter's Handbook.** (Illus.). 1978. pap. Winchester Press. $9.95.

Anderson, Luther A. **Hunting the Woodlands for Small and Big Game.** (Illus.). 1980. A. S. Barnes. $12.00.

Bashline, L. James. ed. **The Eastern Trail.** (Illus.). 1972. Freshet Press. $8.95.

Begbie, Eric. **Sportsman's Companion.** 266 p. 1981. Saiga. $14.95.

Bell, Bob. **Digest Book of Upland Game Hunting.** 96 p. pap. DBI. $2.95.

Bland, Dwain. **Turkey Hunter's Digest.** (Illus.) 256 p. 1986. DBI. pap. $12.95.*

Bourjaily, Vance. **Country Matters: Collected Reports from the Fields and Streams of Iowa and Other Places.** 1973. Dial Press. $8.95.

Brister, Bob. **Shotgunning: The Art and the Science.** 1976. Winchester Press. $15.95.

Burnham, Murry & Tinsley, Russell. **Murry Burnham's Hunting Secrets.** (Illus.). 244 p. 1983. New Century. $17.95.

Cadieux, Charles L. **Goose Hunting.** 208 p. 1983. Stoeger. $9.95.

Camp, Doug. **Turkey Hunting: Spring & Fall.** (Illus.). 176 p. 1984. pap. Outdoor Skills. $12.95.

Capossela, Jim. **How to Turn Your Fishing-Hunting Experiences Into Cash: Twenty-Five Ways to Earn Cash from Your Hobbies.** 1982. pap. Northeast Sportsmans. $3.50.

Coon, Carlton. **The Hunting Peoples.** 423 p. 1987. N Lyons Bks. $15.95.*

Douglas, James. **The Sporting Gun.** (Illus.) 240 p. 1983. David & Charles. $23.50.

Elliott, William. **Carolina Sports by Land and Water: Incidents of Devil-Fishing. Wild-Cat, Deer and Bear Hunting.** (Illus.) 1978. Repr. of 1859 ed. Attic Press. $10.00.

Elman, Robert. **The Hunter's Field Guide to the Game Birds and Animals of North America.** 1982. Knopf. $12.95.

—**One Thousand One Hunting Tips.** rev. ed. 1983. pap. New Century. $14.95.

Fears, J. Wayne. **Successful Turkey Hunting.** 92 p. 1984. Target Comm. pap. $4.95.

Fergus, Charles, et al. **Rabbit Hunting.** 1985. Allegheny. pap. $7.95.

Field & Stream. **Field and Stream Reader.** facs. ed. 1946. Arno. $19.50.

Fischl, Josef & Rue, Leonard Lee, III. **After Your Deer is Down.** 1981. pap. Winchester Press. $9.95.

Geer, Galen. **Meat On The Table: Modern Small-Game Hunting.** (Illus.). 216 p. 1985. Paladin Pr. $14.95.

Gilsvik, Bob. **The Guide to Good Cheap Hunting.** (Illus.). 1979. Stein & Day. pap. $5.95.

Grinnell, George B. & Sheldon, Charles, eds. **Hunting and Conservation.** 1970. Repr. of 1925 ed. Arno. $25.00.

Gryndall, William. **Hawking, Hunting, Fouling and Fishing: Newly Corrected by W. Gryndall Faulkener.** 1972. Repr. of 1596 ed. W. J. Johnson. $13.00.

Hagel, Bob. **Game Loads and Practical Ballistics for the American Hunter.** (Illus.). 1978. Knopf. $13.95.

—**Guns, Loads & Hunting Tips.** Wolfe, Dave, ed. (Illus.) 536 p. 1986. Wolfe Pub. Co. $19.50.

Hammond, Samuel H. **Wild Northern Scenes or Sporting Adventures with Rifle and Rod.** (Illus.). 1979. Repr. of 1857 ed. Harbor Hill Books. $12.50.

Harbour, Dave. **Advanced Wild Turkey Hunting & World Records.** (Illus.) 264 p. 1983. New Century. $19.95.

Henckel, Mark. **Hunter's Guide to Montana.** (Illus.). 224 p. 1985. Falcon Pr. MT. pap. $8.95.

Hill, Gene. **A Hunter's Fireside Book: Tales of Dogs, Ducks, Birds and Guns.** (Illus.) 1972. Winchester Press. $12.95.

—**Mostly Tailfeathers.** 1975. Winchester Press. $12.95.

Hill, Gene & Smith, Steve. **Outdoor Yarns & Outright Lies.** 168 p. 1983. Stackpole. $12.95.

Humphreys, John. **The Do-It-Yourself Game Shoot.** (Illus.). 144 p. 1983. David & Charles. $18.95.

James, David & Stephens, Wilson, eds. **In Praise of Hunting.** (Illus.). 1961. Devin-Adair Co. $10.00.

Janes, Edward C. **Ringneck! Pheasants and Pheasant Hunting.** (Illus.). 1975. Crown. $8.95.

Johnson, et al. **Outdoor Tips.** pap. Benjamin Co. $2.95.

Keith, Elmer. **Keith's Rifles for Large Game.** (Illus.). 424 p. 1987. Repr. of 1946 ed. Wolfe Pub. Co. $54.00.*

Knap, Jerome J. **Digest Book of Hunting Tips.** pap. DBI Books. $2.95.

Laycock, George. **Shotgunner's Bible.** (Illus.) 1969. pap. Doubleday. $3.95.

Lindner, Kurt. **The Second Hunting Book of Wolfgang Birkner.** (Illus.). 1976. Ltd. ed. Arma Press. $175.00.

Liu, Allan J. **The American Sporting Collector's Handbook.** (Illus.). pap. Stoeger. $5.95.

McClane, A. J., ed. **McClane's Great Fishing & Hunting Lodges of North America.** 176 p. 1984. HR&W. $29.95.

Madden, D. H. **Chapter of Mediaeval History.** 1969. Repr. of 1924 ed. Kennikat Press. $15.00.

Madden, Dodgson H. **Diary of Master William Silence: A Study of Shakespeare and Elizabethan Sport.** 1970. Repr. of 1897. ed. Haskell Booksellers. $51.95.

Merrill, Wm. & Rees, Clair. **Hunter's Bible,** rev. ed. (Illus.) 192 p. 1986. Doubleday. pap. $6.95.

Meyer, Jerry. **Bear Hunting.** 224 p. 1983. Stackpole. $14.95.

Money, Albert W. **Pigeon Shooting.** Gould, A. C., ed. (Illus.). 109 p. 1987. Repr. of 1896 ed. Gunnerman Pr. $19.95.*

NRA Guidebook for Hunters. 144 p. Nat'l Rifle Assn. $5.00.

Ortega y Gasset, Jose. **Meditations on Hunting.** 144 p. 1986. Scribner. pap. $7.95.

Painter, Doug. **Hunting & Firearms Safety Primer.** 128 p. 1986. N. Lyons Bks. pap. $8.95.

Pyle, Wilf E. **Hunting Predators for Hides & Profit.** 224 p. Stoeger Pub. Co. pap. $11.95.

Ricketts, Mitchell S. **Bobcat Trapper's Guide.** (Illus.). 116 p. 1987. Elk River Pr. pap. $7.95.*

Schwenk, Sigrid, et al. eds. **Multum et Multa: Beitraege zur Literatur, Geschichte und Kultur der Jagd.** (Illus.). 1971. De Gruyter. $75.00.

Shelsby, Earl & Gilford, James eds. **Basic Hunter's Guide,** rev. ed. (Illus.). 280 p. 1982. pap. Nat'l Rifle Assn. $14.95.

Shooter's Bible 1988. (Illus.) 576 p. 1987. Stoeger Pub. Co. pap. $14.95.

Shooter's Bible 1989. Vol. 80. (Illus.). 576 p. 1988. Stoeger Pub. Co. pap. $14.95.*

Smith, James A. **Dress 'Em Out.** (Illus.). 1982. pap. Stoeger. $11.95.

Smith, Steve. **More & Better Pheasant Hunting.** (Illus.). 192 p. 1987. New Century. $15.95.*

Stehsel, Donald. L. **Hunting the California Black Bear.** (Illus.). pap. Donald Stehsel. $7.00.

Strong, Norman. **The Art of Hunting.** (Illus.). 160 p. 1984. Cy De Cosse. $16.95.

Walrod, Dennis. **More Than a Trophy.** (Illus.). 256 p. 1983. pap. Stackpole. $12.95.

—**Grouse Hunter's Guide.** 192 p. 1985. Stackpole. $16.95.

Washburn, O. A. **General Red.** (Illus.). Jenkins. $5.50.

Waterman, C. F. **The Hunter's World.** (Illus.). 250 p. 1983. reprint of 1973 ed. New Century. $29.95.

Whelen, Townsend. **The Hunting Rifle.** 464 p. 1984. Repr. of 1924 ed. Wolfe Pub. Co. $39.00.

Whisker, James B. **The Right to Hunt.** 1981. North River Press. $8.95.

Wolff, Ed. **Elk Hunting in the Northern Rockies.** 164 p. 1984. pap. Stoneydale Pr. Pub. $8.95.

Young, Ralph. W. **Grizzlies Don't Come Easy.** (Illus.). 1981. Winchester Press. $15.95.

—**My Lost Wilderness.** (Illus.). 196 p. 1984. New Century. $15.95.

Zern, Ed. **Fishing & Hunting From A to Zern.** 288 p. 1985. New Century. $17.95.

Zumbo, Jim. **Hunting America's Mule Deer.** 1981. Winchester Press. $14.95.

HUNTING—DICTIONARIES

Burnand, Tony. **Dictionnaire de la Chasse.** 250 p. (Fr.) 1970. pap. French & European Pubns. Inc. $7.50.

Frevert, W. **Woerterbuch der Jaegerei.** 4th ed. (Ger.) 1975. French & European Pubns. Inc. $12.00.

Kehrein, Franz. **Woerterbuch der Weidmannssprache.** (Ger.) 1969. French & European Pubns. Inc. $36.00.

Kirchoff, Anne. **Woerterbuch der Jagel. (Ger., Eng. & Fr. Dictionary of Hunting.)** 1976. French & European Pubns. Inc. $27.50.

Sisley, Nick. **All about Varmint Hunting.** (Illus.). 1982. pap. Stone Wall Press. $8.95.

Wisconsin Hunting Encyclopedia. 1976. pap. Wisconsin Sportsman. $2.95.

HUNTING—HISTORY

Greene, Robert. **The Third and Last Part of Conny-Catching.** 1923. Arden Library. $12.50.

Harding, Robert S. ed. **Omnivorous Primates: Gathering and Hunting in Human Evolution.** Teleki, Geza P. (Illus.). 1981. Columbia University Press. $45.00.

Petersen, Eugene T. **Hunters' Heritage: A History of Hunting in Michigan.** Lowe, Kenneth S. ed. (Illus.). 1979. Michigan United Conservation Clubs. $4.65.

Rick, John W. **Prehistoric Hunters of the High Andes.** (Studies in Archaeology Ser.). 1980. Academic Press. $27.50.

Speth, John D. **Bison Kills and Bone Counts: Decision Making by Ancient Hunters.** 272 p. 1983. pap. U of Chicago. $9.00.

Spiess, Arthur E. **Reindeer and Caribou Hunters: An Archaeological Study.** (Studies in Archaeology Ser.). 1979. Academic Press. $30.00.

HUNTING—AFRICA

Capstick, Peter H. **Death in the Long Grass.** (Illus.). 1978. St. Martin's Press. $11.95.

—**Death in the Dark Continent.** (Illus.) 320 p. 1983. St. Martin. $14.95.

Cloudsley-Thompson, J. L. **Animal Twilight, Man and Game in Eastern Africa.** (Illus.). 1967. Dufour Editions, Inc. $12.00.

Findlay, Frederick R. N. & Croonwright-Schreiner, S. C. **Big Game Shooting and Travel in Southeast Africa: Account of Shooting Trips in the Cheringoma and Gorongoza Divisions of Portuguese South-East Africa and in Zululand.** Repr. of 1903 ed. Arno. $40.25.

Gilmore, Parker. **Days and Nights by the Desert.** Repr. of 1888 ed. Arno. $20.50.

Hemingway, Ernest. **Green Hills of Africa.** 1935. Scribner's. $17.50. pap. $5.95.

Holub, Emil. **Seven Years in South Africa.** 2 vols. 1881. Set. Scholarly Press. $45.00.

Lyell, Denis D. **Memories of an African Hunter.** (Illus.). 288 p. 1987. St. Martin. $15.95.*

MacQueen, Peter. **In Wildest Africa.** 1909. Scholarly Press. $29.00.

Selous, Frederick. **Hunter's Wanderings in Africa.** 526 p. 1986. repr. of 1920 ed. Wolfe Pub. Co. $47.00.*

Stigand, Chauncey H. **Hunting the Elephant in Africa.** (Illus.) 400 p. 1985. St. Martin. $14.95.*

White, S. E. **Lions in the Path.** (Illus.). 352 p. 1987. Repr. of 1926 ed. Wolfe Pub. Co. $25.00.*

—**African Campfires.** (Illus.). 456 p. 1987. Repr. of 1910 ed. Wolfe Pub. Co. $25.00.*

HUNTING—ALASKA

Batin, Christopher M. **Hunting in Alaska.** (Illus.). 416 p. 1987. Alaska Angler. pap. $24.95.*

Keim, Charles J. **Alaska Game Trails with a Master Guide.** pap. Alaska Northwest. $6.95.

HUNTING—GREAT BRITAIN

Edward of Norwich. **Master of Game: Oldest English Book on Hunting.** Baillie-Grohman. William A. & Baillie-Grohman, F. eds. (Illus.). Repr. of 1909 ed. AMS Press. $45.00.

Jeffries, Richard. **The Gamekeeper at Home and the Amateur Poacher.** 1978. pap. Oxford University Press. $5.95.

Thomas, William B. **Hunting England: A Survey of the Sport and of its Chief Grounds.** 1978. Repr. of 1936 ed. R. West. $30.00.

Watson, J. N. **British and Irish Hunts and Huntsmen: Vols. I & II.** (Illus.). 1981. David & Charles. Set. $50.00 ea; set $85.00.

HUNTING—NORTH AMERICA

Dalrymple, Byron W. **Bird Hunting with Dalrymple:** The Rewards of Shotgunning Across North America. (Illus.) 288 p. 1987. Stackpole. $29.95.*

Leopold, Luna. B., ed. **Round River: From the Journals of Aldo Leopold.** (Illus.). 1972. pap. Oxford University Press. $3.95.

HUNTING—U.S.

Abbott, Henry. **Birch Bark Books of Henry Abbott: Sporting Adventures and Nature Observations in the Adirondacks in the Early 1900s).** Illus., Repr. of 1914 & 1932 eds.). 1980. Harbor Hill Books. $19.95.

Baily's Hunting Directory. 1978–79. (Illus.). 1978. J. A. Allen. $36.00.

Baker, Ron. **The American Hunting Myth.** 287 p. 1985. Vantage. $10.95.

Barsness, John. **Hunting the Great Plains.** 164 p. 1979. pap. Mountain Press. $6.95.

Cadbury, Warder, intro by. **Journal of a Hunting Excursion to Louis Lake, 1851.** (Illus.). 1961. Syracuse University Press. $8.95.

Catsis, John R., ed. **Hunter's Handbook:** Western Edition. 526 p. 1986. Sabio Pub. pap. $12.95.*

Cory, Charles B. **Hunting and Fishing in Florida, Including a Key to the Water Birds.** 1970. Repr. of 1896 ed. Arno. $14.00.

Dahl, Ruby W., et al. **Lander: One-Shot Antelope Hunt.** 129 p. 1986. $19.95; leather bound lmtd. ed. $50.00.

Elman, Robert, ed. **All About Deer Hunting in America 1976.** New Century. $16.95.

Hirsch, Bob. **Outdoors in Arizona: A Guide to Fishing & Hunting.** 192 p. 1986. Arizona Highway. pap. $12.95.*

Huggler, Tom. **Hunt Michigan: How to, Where to, When to.** (Illus.). 1985. Mich. United Conserv. pap. $12.95.

Kozickey, Edward L. **Hunting Preserves for Sport or Profit.** 250 p. 1987. CK Wildlife Res. $24.95.*

Lang, Varley. **Follow the Water.** (Illus.). 1961. John F. Blair. $6.95.

Lapinski, Mike, et al. **All About Elk.** Miller, Bill, ed. 253 p. 1987. N Amer. Hunt Club. text ed. $15.95.*

Lowenstein, Bill. **Hunting in Michigan: The Early 80's.** Arnold, David A., ed. 1981. pap. Michigan Natural Resources Michigan. $6.95.

Mitchell, John G. **The Hunt.** 1980. Knopf. $11.95.

—**The Hunt.** 1981. pap. Penguin. $4.95.

Murray, William H. **Adventures in the Wilderness.** Verner, William K., ed. (Illus.). 1970. Repr. Syracuse University Press. $10.50.

Roosevelt, Theodore. **Hunting Trips of a Ranchman.** Repr. of 1885 ed. Irvington, $17.50.

—**Outdoor Pastimes of an American Hunter.** 1970. Repr. of 1905 ed. Arno Press. $24.00.

—**Ranch Life and the Hunting-Trail.** 1985. Repr. of 1901 ed. Hippocrene. pap. $8.95.

—**Ranch Life.** 210 p. 1983 pap. University of Nebraska. $8.95.

—**Theodore Roosevelt's America.** Wiley, Farida, ed. (Illus.). 1955. Devin-Adair Co. $10.00.

—**Wilderness Hunter.** 1970. Repr. of 1900 ed. Irvington, $16.00.

Sandoz, Mari. **The Buffalo-Hunters: The Story of the Hide Men.** 1978. pap. University of Nebraska Press. $6.50.

Tome, Philip. **Pioneer Life or Thirty Years a Hunter: Being Scenes and Adventures in the Life of Philip Tome.** (Illus.). 1971. Repr. of 1854 ed. Arno Press. $15.00.

Wootters, John. **A Guide to Hunting in Texas.** 1979. pap. Pacesetter Press. $5.95.

Zumbo, Jim. **Hunt Elk.** 256 p. 1985. New Century. $17.95.

HUNTING DOGS (see also Bird Dogs)

Bernard, Art. **Dog Days.** 1969. Caxton. $5.95.

Detert, Herman. **Heartbeat of a Hunter.** (Illus.). 63 p. 1986. Carlton. $7.00.

Duffey, David M. **Hunting Dog Know-How** (Illus.). 1972. Winchester Press. pap. $8.95.

Falk, John R. **The Practical Hunter's Dog Book.** (Illus.). 1984. pap. New Century. $11.95.

Goodall, Charles. **How to Train Your Own Gun Dog.** (Illus.). 1978. Howell Book House, Inc. $10.95.

Hartley, Oliver. **Hunting Dogs.** pap. A. R. Harding Pub. $3.00.

Irving, Joe. **Training Spaniels.** (Illus.). 1980. David & Charles. $16.95.

—**Gun Dogs: Their Learning Chain.** 231 p. 1983. State Mutual Bks. $35.00.

Knap, Jerome. **Digest Book of Hunting Dogs.** 96 p. DBI. pap. $3.95.*

Lent, Patricia A. **Sport with Terriers.** (Illus.). 1973. Arner Publications, $9.95.

Roebuck, Kenneth C. **Gun-Dog Training Spaniels and Retrievers.** 1982. Stackpole. $12.95.

—**Gun-Dog Training Pointing Dogs.** 192 p. 1983. Stackpole. $12.95.

Salmon, H. M. **Gazehounds and Coursing.** (Illus.). 1977. North Star Press. $18.50.

Smith, Guy N. **Sporting and Working Dogs.** 1981. (Pub. by Saiga). State Mutual Book and Periodical Service. $40.00.

Tarrant, Bill. **Best Way to Train Your Gun Dog: The Dalmar Smith Method.** 1977. David McKay Co. $10.95.

Waterman, Charles F. **Gun Dogs & Bird Guns: A Charley Waterman Reader.** (Illus.). 244 p. 1987. GSJ Press. text ed. $25.00.*

Wehle, Robert G. **Wing and Shot.** 1964. Country Press NY. $12.00.

Whitney, Leon F. & Underwood, Acil B. **Coon Hunter's Handbook.** Hart, Ernest, ed. 1952. Holt, Rinehart & Winston. $5.95.

Wolters, Richard A. **Gun Dog. Revolutionary Rapid Training Method.** (Illus.). 1961. Dutton. $12.50.

HUNTING STORIES

Hill, Gene. **Hill Country: Stories About Hunting and Fishing and Dogs and Such.** (Illus.). 198. Dutton. $13.50.

McManus, Patrick. **They Shoot Canoes, Don't They?** 1981. Holt, Rinehart & Winston. $10.95.

MacQuarrie. Gordon. **Stories of the Old Duck Hunters.** 1979. pap. Willow Creek Press. $5.95.

—**More Stories of the Old Duck Hunters.** 1983. Willow Creek. $15.00.

—**Stories of the Old Duck Hunters & Other Drivel.** 228 p. 1985. repr. of 1967 ed. Willow Creek. $15.00.

Sassoon, Siegfried. **Memoirs of a Fox-Hunting Man.** 320 p. 1960. pap. Faber & Faber. $6.95.

Smith, Steve. **Picking Your Shots & Other Stories of Dogs & Birds & Guns & Days Afield.** (Illus.). 160 p. 1986. Stackpole. $16.95.

Sobol, Donald. **Encyclopedia Brown's Book of the Wacky Outdoors.** (gr. 5 up). 1988. Bantam. pap. $2.50.*

Sparano, Vin., ed. **Hunting Tales,** Vol. II. 256 p. 1987. Beaufort Bks. NY. $18.95.*

HUNTING WITH BOW AND ARROW (see Bow and Arrow)

KNIVES

Berner, Douglas C. **Survival Knife Reference Guide.** (Illus.) 207 p. 1986. Bee Tree. pap. $12.95.*

Blade Magazine Staff. **American Blades 1986.** Am. Blade Bk. Svce. $11.95.*

Brewster, Melvyn & Hoyem, George. **Remington Bullet Knives.** (Illus.). 60 p. 1985. Armory Pubns. (price on request).

Combs, Roger & Lewis, Jack, ed. **Gun Digest Book of Knives,** 2d ed. 288 p. 1982. DBI. $10.95.

Erhardt, Roy & Ferrell, J. **Encyclopedia of Pocket Knives: Book One and Book Two Price Guide.** rev. ed. (Illus.). 1977. Heart of America Press. $6.95.

Goins, John E. **Pocketknives—Markings, Manufacturers & Dealers.** 2d ed. 280 p. 1982. pap. Knife World. $8.95.

Hardin, Albert N., Jr. & Hedden, Robert W. **Light but Efficient: A Study of the M1880 Hunting and M1890 Intrenching Knives and Scabbards.** (Illus.). 1973. Albert N. Hardin. $7.95.

Hughes, B. R. **Modern Hand-Made Knives.** Pioneer Press. $9.95.

Latham, Sid. **Knives and Knifemakers.** (Illus.). 1974. pap. Macmillan. $7.95.

Levine, Bernard R. **The Knife Identification & Value Guide.** (Illus.). 184 p. 1981. Knife World. $7.95.

—**Levine's Guide to Knife Values.** (Illus.). 480 p. 1985. DBI. pap. $19.95.

Loveless, R. W. **Contemporary Knifemaking.** 1986. Am Blade Bk. Svce. $18.95.*

McCreight, Tim. **Custom Knifemaking: 10 Projects from a Master Craftsman.** (Illus.). 234 p. 1985. Stackpole. pap. $14.95.

Paul, Don. **Everybody's Knife Bible.** (Illus.). 128 p. 1987. Pathfinder. pap. $9.95.*

Peterson, Harold L. **American Knives.** 1980. Gun Room. $17.95.

Sanchez, John. **Blade Master: Advanced Survival Skills for the Knife Fighter.** (Illus.). 96 p. 1982. pap. Paladin Press. $8.00.

Stephens, Frederick J. **Fighting Knives.** 144 p. 1985. Arco. pap. $11.95.

Tappan, Mel. ed. **A Guide to Handmade Knives and the Official Directory of the Knifemaker's Guild.** (Illus.). 1977. Janus Press. $9.95.

Warner, Ken. **Practical Book of Knives.** (Illus.). 1976. softbound. Stoeger. $9.95.

Warner, Ken, ed. **Knives Eighty Six,** 6th ed. 256 p. 1985. pap. DBI. $11.95.

NATURAL HISTORY—OUTDOOR BOOKS

Barrus, Clara, ed. **The Heart of Burrough's Journals.** 1979. Repr. of 1928 ed. Arden Lib. $30.00.

Bedichek, Roy. **Adventures with a Texas Naturalist.** (Illus.). 1961. pap. University of Texas Press. $8.95.

Errington, Paul L. **The Red Gods Call.** (Illus.). 1973. Iowa State University Press. $6.95.

Fuller, Raymond T. **Now That We Have to Walk: Exploring the Out-of-Doors.** facsimile ed. Repr. of 1943 ed. Arno Press. $17.00.

Godfrey, Michael A. **A Sierra Club Naturalist's Guide to the Piedmont of Eastern North America.** (Illus.). 432 p. 1980. pap. Sierra. $9.95.

Jefferies, Richard. **Old House at Coate.** 1948. Arno Press. $16.00.

Kieran, John F. **Nature Notes.** facs. ed. 1941. Arno Press. $14.50.

Leopold, Aldo. **Sand County Almanac: With Other Essays on Conservation from Round River.** (Illus.). 1966. Oxford University Press. $15.95.

—**Sand County Almanac Illustrated.** new ed. 1977. Tamarack Press. $25.00.

Olson, Sigurd F. **Listening Point.** (Illus.). 1958. Knopf. $13.45.

—**Sigurd Olson's Wilderness Days.** 1972. Knopf. $22.95.

Pearson, Haydn S. **Sea Flavor.** facs. ed. 1948. Arno Press. $15.00.

Rowlands, John J. **Cache Lake County.** (Illus.). 1959. W. W. Norton & Co. $12.95.

Sharp, Dallas L. **Face of the Fields.** facs. ed. 1911. Arno Press. $15.00.

—**Sanctuary! Sanctuary!** facs. ed. 1926. Arno Press. $10.00.

Sharp, William. **Where the Forest Murmurs.** 1906. Arno Press. $19.50.

Shepard, Odell. **Harvest of a Quiet Eye: A Book of Digressions.** facs. ed. Repr. of 1927 ed. Arno Press. $19.50.

Wiley, Farida, ed. **John Burroughs' America.** (Illus.). Devin-Adair Co. $10.50; pap. $5.25.

ORDNANCE (see also Ballistics)

Colby, C. B. **Civil War Weapons: Small Arms and Artillery of the Blue and Gray.** (Illus.). 1962. Coward, McCann & Geoghegan. $5.29.

Derby, Harry L. **The Hand Cannons of Imperial Japan.** Reidy, John and Welge, Albert, eds., 1981. Derby Publishing Co. $37.95.

Lewis, Ernest A. **The Fremont Cannon: High Up and Far Back.** 1981. Arthur H. Clark. $32.50.

Marchant-Smith, D. J. & Haslem, P. R. **Small Arms and Cannons.** 1982. Pergamon Press. $26.00; pap. $13.00.

Norton, Robert. **The Gunner, Shewing the Whole Practise of Artillerie.** 1973. Repr. of 1628 ed. W. J. Johnson. $40.00.

Tomlinson, Howard. **Guns and Government: The Ordnance Office Under the Later Stuarts.** 1979. Humanities Press. $42.50.

ORIENTATION

Burton, Maurice. **The Sixth Sense of Animals.** (Illus.). 192 p. 1973. Taplinger. $7.95.

Henley, B. M. **Orienteering.** (Illus.). 1976. Charles River Books. $6.95.

Kals, W. S. **Land Navigation Handbook: The Sierra Club Guide to Map & Compass.** (Illus.). 288 p. 1983. pap. Sierra. $8.95.

Lynn, R. **Attention, Arousal & The Orientation Reaction.** 1966. ed. pap. Pergamon. $10.25.

Ratliff, Donald E. **Map Compass and Campfire.** (Illus.). 1970. Binford & Mort Pubs. pap. $2.50.

Vassilevsky, B. **Where is the North?** 1977. pap. Imported Pubns. $3.95.

Watson, J. D. **Orienteering.** (Illus.). 1975. Charles River Books, pap. $2.50.

OUTDOOR COOKERY (see also Game Cookery)

Anderson, Beverly M. & Hamilton, Donna M. **The New High Altitude Cookbook.** (Illus.). 1980. Random House. $14.95.

Antell, Steven. **Backpacker's Recipe Book.** (Illus.). 1980. pap. Pruett. $5.50.

Banks, James E. **Alfred Packer's Wilderness Cookbook.** (Illus.). 1969. Filter Press. $7.00. pap. $1.50.

Barker, Harriett. **The One-Burner Gourmet.** rev. ed. 1981. pap. Contemporary Books. $8.95.

Bock, Richard. **Camper Cookery.** 1977. pap. Lorenz Press. $5.95.

Brent, Carol D., ed. **Barbecue: The Fine Art of Charcoal, Gas and Hibachi Outdoor Cooking.** (Illus.). 1971. Doubleday. (OP).

Bunnelle, Hasse. **Food for Knapsackers: And Other Trail Travelers.** 1971. pap. Sierra Club Books. $4.95.

Bunnelle, Hasse & Sarvis, Shirley. **Cooking for Camp and Trail.** 1972. pap. Sierra Club. $4.95.

Christensen, Lillian & Smith, Carol S. **Outdoor Cookbook.** 192 p. 1984. Walker & Co. pap. $5.95.

Drew, Edwin P. **The Complete Light-Pack Camping and Trail-Food Cookbook.** 1977. pap. McGraw-Hill. $3.95.

Farm Journal's Food Editors. **Farm Journal's Picnic and Barbecue Cookbook.** Ward, Patricia, ed. (Illus.). 1982. Farm Journal. $13.95.

Fears, J. Wayne. **Backcountry Cooking.** (Illus.). 1980. East Woods Press. $11.95; pap. $7.95.

Fleming, June. **The Well-Fed Backpacker.** (Illus.). 1981, pap. Random House. $3.95.

Heffron, Lauren. **Cycle Food: A Guide to Satisfying Your Inner Tube.** (Illus.). 96 p. 1983. pap. Ten Speed Press. $4.95.

Hemingway, Joan & Maricich, Connie. **The Picnic Gourmet.** (Illus.). 1978. pap. Random House. $7.95.

Holm, Don. **Old-Fashioned Dutch Oven Cookbook.** 1969. pap. Caxton Printers. $5.95.

Hughes, Stella. **Chuck Wagon Cookin'.** 1974. pap. University of Arizona Press. $8.50.

Krenzel, Kathleen & Heckendorf, Robyn. **The Sporting Life Gourmet.** (Illus.). 74 p. 1980. R. Louis Pub. $9.95.

Lund, Duane R. **Camp Cooking . . . Made Easy and Kind of Fun.** Adventure Publications. 1978. $4.45.

McElfresh, Beth. **Chuck Wagon Cookbook.** pap. Swallow Press. 72 p. 1960. $4.95.

McHugh, Gretchen. **The Hungry Hiker's Book of Good Cooking.** (Illus.). 1982. Alfred A. Knopf. $17.50. pap. $7.95.

Macmillan, Diane D. **The Portable Feast.** (Illus.). 1973. 101 Productions. pap. $4.95.

Maurer, Stephen G. **The Bannock Book: Food for the Outdoors.** (Illus.) 64 p. 1986. Heritage Assn. pap. $6.95.*

Mendenhall, Ruth D. **Backpack Cookery.** (Illus.). 1974. pap. La Siesta. $1.95.

Miller, Dorcas S. **The Healthy Trail Food Book.** rev. ed. (Illus.). 1980. pap. East Woods Press. $3.95.

Nagy, Jean. **Brown Bagging It: A Guide to Fresh Food Cooking in the Wilderness.** 1976 pap. Marty-Nagy Bookworks. $2.50.

Outdoor Cooking. (Illus.). 176 p. 1983. Time Life. $14.95.

Picnic and Outdoor Menus. 1984. Silver. $15.94.

Prater, Yvonne & Mendenhall, Ruth D. **Gorp, Glop and Glue Stew: Favorite Foods from 165 Outdoor Experts.** (Illus.). 1981. pap. Mountaineers. $6.95.

Raup, Lucy G. **Camper's Cookbook.** 1967. pap. C. E. Tuttle. $3.75.

Roden, Claudia. **Picnic.** 1981. State Mutual Book & Periodical Service. $40.00.

Schultz, Philip S. **Cooking with Fire and Smoke.** 273 p. 1986. S&S. $17.95.

Tarr, Yvonne Y. **The Complete Outdoor Cookbook.** (Illus.). 1973. Times Books. $8.95.

Thomas, Dian. **Roughing It Easy: A Unique Ideabook on Camping and Cooking.** (Illus.). 1974. pap. Brigham Young University Press. $8.95. pap. $6.95.

Wood, Jane. **Elegant Fare from the Weber Kettle.** (Illus.). 1977. Western Publishing. $6.95.

Woodall's Campsite Cookbook. Woodall. pap. $4.95.

Woodruff, Leroy L. **Cooking the Dutch Oven Way.** (Illus.). 1980. pap. ICS Books. $6.95.

OUTDOOR LIFE

Acerrano, Anthony. **The Outdoorsman's Emergency Manual.** 1976. 352 p. softbound. Stoeger. $9.95.

Anderson, Steve. **The Orienteering Book.** (Illus.). 1980. pap. Anderson World. $3.95.

Angier, Bradford. **How to Stay Alive in the Woods.** Orig. Title: **Living off the Country.** 1962. pap. Macmillan. $2.95.

—**The Master Backwoodsman.** 1979. pap. Fawcett Book Group. $4.95.

—**The Master Backwoodsman.** 1978. Stackpole Books. $10.95.

Brown, Vinson. **Reading the Outdoors at Night.** (Illus.). 1982. pap. Stackpole Books. $9.95.

Camazine, Scott. **The Naturalist's Year: Twenty-Six Outdoor Explorations.** 1987. Wiley. Aug. $14.95.*

Douglas & McIntyre. **Outdoor Safety & Survival.** (Illus.). 154 p. 1986. Salem Hse Pub. $4.95.

Eastman, P. F. **Advanced First Aid for All Outdoors.** 1976. pap. Cornell Maritime Press. $6.00.

Fear, Gene. **Fundamentals of Outdoor Enjoyment.** (Illus.). 1976. pap. Survival Ed. Assoc. $5.00.

Green, Paul. **The Outdoor Leadership Handbook.** 42 p. 1982. pap. Survival Ed. Assoc. (write for info).

Grow, Laurence. **The Old House Book of Outdoor Living Places.** (Illus.). 1981. Warner Books. $15.00; pap. $8.95.

Hamper, Stanley R. **Wilderness Survival.** 3rd ed. 1975. Repr. of 1963 ed. Peddlers Wagon. $1.79.

Hanley, Wayne. **A Life Outdoors: A Curmudgeon Looks at the Natural World.** (Illus.) 1980. Stephen Greene Press. pap. $5.95.

Hickin, Norman. **Beachcombing for Beginners.** 1976. pap. Wilshire Book Co. $2.00.

Johnson, et al. **Outdoor Tips: A Remington Sportsman's Library Book.** pap. Benjamin Co. $2.95.

Kodet, E. Russell & Angier, Bradford. **Being Your Own Wilderness Doctor.** (Illus.). 1975. Stackpole Books. $7.95.

Lund, Duane R. Nature's **Bounty for Your Table.** 1982. Adventure Pubns. $4.95.

Maguire, Jack. **Outdoor Spaces.** 1987. H. Holt. $19.95.*

Olsen, Larry D. **Outdoor Survival Skills.** rev. ed. 1973. Brigham Young University Press. $7.95.

Olson, Sigurd F. **Olson's Wilderness Days.** (Illus.) 1972. Knopf. $22.95.

Outdoor Living Skills Instructor's Manual. 1979. pap. American Camping Association. $5.00.

Owings, Loren C., ed. **Environmental Values, 1860–1972: A Guide to Information Sources.** 1976. Gale Research Co. $40.00.

Patmore, J. Allan. **Land and Leisure in England and Wales.** 1971. Fairleigh Dickinson. $27.50.

Paul, Don, ed. **Great Livin' in Grubby Times.** (Illus.) 140 p. 1986. Pathfinder HL. pap. $12.95.*

—**Green Beret's Guide to Outdoor Survival.** (Illus.) 134 p. 1986. Pathfinder HL. pap. $12.95.*

Platten, David. **The Outdoor Survival Handbook.** David & Charles. $6.95.

Rae, William E., ed. **A Treasury of Outdoor Life.** (Illus.). 520 p. 1983. Stackpole. $24.95.

Rafferty, Milton D. **The Ozarks Outdoors:** A Guide for Fishermen, Hunters & Tourists. (Illus.) 408 p. 1985. U of Okla. Press. $24.95.*

Rawick, George P. **From Sundown to Sunup.** 1972. pap. Greenwood Press. $15.00; pap. $4.45.

Risk, Paul H. **Outdoor Safety and Survival.** 300 p. 1983. Wiley. $15.95; pap. text ed. $11.00.

Roberts, Harry. **Keeping Warm and Dry.** 1982. pap. Stone Wall Press. $7.95.

Rutstrum, Calvin. **New Way of the Wilderness.** (Illus.) 1966. pap. Macmillan. $2.95.

—**Once Upon a Wilderness.** (Illus.). 1973. Macmillan. $10.95.

Shepherd, Laurie. **A Dreamer's Log Cabin: A Woman's Walden.** (Illus.). 1981. Dembner Books. $8.95.

Van De Smissen, Betty, et al. **Leader's Guide to Nature-Oriented Activities.** 3rd ed. (Illus.). 1977. pap. Iowa State University Press. $7.95.

Wood, Dave. **Wisconsin Life Trip.** 1982. Adventure Pubns. $4.95.

Wurman, Richard S. et al. **The Nature of Recreation: A Handbook in Honor of Frederick Law Olmstead.** 1972. pap. MIT Press. $5.95.

PISTOL SHOOTING

Antal, Laslo. **Competitive Pistol Shooting.** 190 p. 1982. State Mutual Bks. $30.00.

Duncan, Mark. **On Target with Mark Duncan:** An Illustrated Pocket Guide to Handgun Accuracy. (Illus.). 52 p. 1984. Duncan Gun. pap. $4.95.

Given, T. **Survival Shooting: Handguns & Shotguns.** 1986. Gordon Pr. $79.95 (lib. bdg.).*

Mason, James D. **Combat Handgun Shooting.** (Illus.) 286 p. 1980. C. C. Thomas. $28.50.

Taylor, C. **The Complete Book of Combat Handgunning.** 1986. Gordon Press. $79.905 (lib. bdg.).*

PISTOLS

American Historical Foundation Staff, ed. **M1911A1 Automatic Pistol:Proud American Legend.** (Illus.) 1985. Am. Hist. Found. pap. $8.95.*

Askins, Charles. **Askins on Pistols and Revolvers.** Bryant, Ted & Askins, Bill, eds. 1980. National Rifle Association. $25.00; pap. $8.95.

Blackmore, Howard L. **English Pistols.** (Illus.) 64 p. 1985. Sterling. $12.95.*

Buxton, Warren H. **The P-38 Pistol,** Vol. 2. 1940–1945. (Illus.). 256 p. 1985. Ucross Bks. $45.50.

Catalogue of Rim Fire & Center Fire Pistol, Rifle & Military Cartridges, U.S. Cartridge Company, 1881. 116 p. 1984. Rolling Block. pap. $8.00.

Datig, Fred A. **Luger Pistol.** rev. ed. Borden, $12.50.

Dixon, Norman. **Georgian Pistols: The Art and Craft of the Flintlock Pistol, 1715–1840.** 1972. George Shumway Publisher. $22.50.

Dyke, S. E. **Thoughts on the American Flintlock Pistol.** (Illus.). 1974. George Shumway Publisher. $6.50.

Erickson, Wayne & Pate, Charles E. **The Broomhandle Pistol, 1896 to 1936.** 300 p. 1985. E&P Enter. $49.95.

Gould, A. C. **Modern American Pistols & Revolvers.** (Illus.). 244 p. 1987. Repr. of 1888 ed. Wolfe Pub. Co. $37.00.*

Grennel, Dean, ed. **Pistol and Revolver Digest.** 3rd ed. (Illus.). 1982. pap. DBI Books. $10.95.

Grennell, Dean. **Autoloading Pistols: Gun Digest Book.** 288 p. 1983. pap. DBI. $10.95.

Hoffschmidt, E. J. **Know Your Forty-Five Caliber Auto Pistols.** (Illus.). 1973. pap. Blacksmith Corp. $5.95.

—**Know Your Walther PP and PPK Pistols.** (Illus.). 1975. pap. Blacksmith Corp. $5.95.

—**Know Your Walther P. 38 Pistols.** (Illus.). pap. 1974. Blacksmith Corp. $5.95.

Horlacher, R., ed. **The Famous Automatic Pistols of Europe.** Seaton, L. & Steindler, R. A. trs. from Ger. (Illus.). 1976. pap. Jolex. $6.95.

Kirkland, Turner. **Southern Derringers of the Mississippi Valley.** Pioneer Press. $2.00.

Klay, Frank. **The Sammuel E. Dyke Collection of Kentucky Pistols.** 1980. Gun Room Press. $2.00.

Landskron, Jerry. **Remington Rolling Block Pistols.** (Illus.). 1981. Rolling Block Press. $34.95; deluxe ed. $39.95.

Long, Duncan. **Assault Pistols, Rifle & Submachine Guns.** 1986. Gordon Pr. $79.95 (lib. bdg.).*

Manual of Pistol & Revolver Cartridges, Vols 1 & 2. 1987. Gordon Pr. lib. bdg. $79.75.*

Mitchell, Jack. **The Gun Digest of Pistolsmithing.** 1980. pap. DBI Books. $9.95.

Myatt, F. **An Illustrated Guide to Pistols and Revolvers.** 1981. Arco. $8.95.

Nonte, George C. Jr. **Pistol Guide.** (Illus.). 1980. Stoeger. $10.95.

—**Pistol Guide.** (Illus.) 280 p. Stoeger Pub. Co. pap. $10.95.

—**Pistolsmithing.** (Illus.). 1974. Stackpole. $19.95.

North & North. **Simeon North: First Official Pistol Maker of the United States.** Repr. Gun Room Press. $9.95.

The Parabellum Automatic Pistol. 1986. Gordon Pr. $79.95 (lib. bdg.).*

Reese, Michael. **Collector's Guide to Luger Values.** 1972. pap. Pelican. $1.95.

Reese, Michael, II. **Luger Tips.** 1976. Pioneer Press. $6.95.

The Ruger Pistol Exotic Weapon System. 1986. Gordon Pr. $79.95 (lib. bdg.).*

Seaton, Lionel, tr. **Famous Auto Pistols and Revolvers, Vol. II.** (Illus.). 1971. Jolex. $6.95.

Van Der Mark, Kist & Van Der Sloot, Puype. **Dutch Muskets and Pistols.** (Illus.). 1974. George Shumway Publisher. $25.00.

Wallack, L. R. **American Pistol and Revolver Design and Performance.** 1978. Winchester Press. $16.95.

Walther P-38 Auto Pistol Caliber 9mm Parabellum. 1986. Gordon Pr. lib. bdg. $79.95.

Weeks, John & Hogg, Ian. **Pistols of the World.** rev. ed. 306 p. 1982. DBI. $12.95.

Whittington, Robert D. **German Pistols and Holsters, 1943–45: Military-Police-NSDAP.** (Illus.). Gun Room Press. $15.00.

Whittington, Robert D. III. **The Colt Whitneyville-Walker Pistol.** 96 p. 1984. Brownlee Books. $20.00.

Williams, Mason. **The Sporting Use of the Handgun.** (Illus.). 1979. C. C. Thomas. $14.75.

Wood, J. B. **Gun Digest Book of Firearms Assembly-Disassembly. Pt. 1: Automatic Pistols.** (Illus.). 1979. pap. DBI Books. $9.95.

—**Beretta Automatic Pistols: The Collector's & Shooter's Comprehensive Guide.** (Illus.). 192 p. 1985. Stackpole. $19.95.

RELOADING

Anderson, Robert S., ed. **Reloading for Shotgunners.** 1981. pap. DBI Books. $8.95.

Donnelly, John J. **Handloader's Manual of Cartridge Conversions.** (Illus.) 1056 p. 1987. Stoeger Pub. Co. pap. $24.95; spiral bound $29.95; hardcover $34.95.*

Matunas, Edward. **Handbook of Metallic Cartridge Reloading.** (Illus.). 1981. Winchester Press. $15.95.

Steindler, R. A. **Reloader's Guide.** 3rd ed. (Illus.). 1975. softbound. Stoeger. $9.95.

REVOLVERS (see also Colt Revolvers)

Askins, Charles. **Askins on Pistols and Revolvers.** Bryant, Ted & Askins, Bill, eds. 1980. National Rifle Association. $25.00; pap. $8.95.

Dougan, John C. **Know Your Ruger Single Action Revolvers: 1953–1963.** Amber, John T., ed. 1981. Blacksmith Corp. $35.00.

Hogg, Ian V. **Revolvers.** (Illus.). 1984. Stackpole. $12.95.

Lewis, Jack. **Gun Digest Book of Single-Action Revolvers.** (Illus.). 1982. pap. DBI Books. $9.95.

Munnell, J. C. **A Blacksmith Guide to Ruger Rimfire Revolvers.** (Illus.). 56 p. 1982. pap. Blacksmith Corp. $7.50.

Myatt, F. **An Illustrated Guide to Pistols & Revolvers.** 160 p. 1981. Arco. (Illus.). 1980. Stoeger. $8.95.

Nonte, George C. Jr. **Revolver Guide.** (Illus.). 1980. Stoeger. $10.95.

Ross, H. W. **A Blacksmith Guide to Ruger Flattops & Super Blackhawks.** (Illus). 96 p. 1982. pap. Blacksmith Corp. $9.95.

Seaton, Lionel, tr. **Famous Auto Pistols and Revolvers, Vol. II.** (Illus.). 1979. Jolex. $6.95.

Williams, Mason. **The Sporting Use of the Handgun.** (Illus.). 1979. C. C. Thomas. $14.75.

Wood, J. B. **Gun Digest Book of Firearms Assembly-Disassembly: Part II: Revolvers.** (Illus.). 320 p. 1979. pap. DBI. $10.95.

RIFLES (see also Firearms, Hawken Rifles, Sharps Rifles, Winchester Rifles)

Bridges, Toby. **Custom Muzzleloading Rifles:** An Illustrated Guide to Building or Buying a Handcrafted Muzzleloader. (Illus.) 224 p. 1986. Stackpole. pap. $16.95.*

Buchele, William and Shumway, George. **Recreating the American Longrifle.** Orig. Title: **Recreating the Kentucky Rifle.** (Illus.). 1973. pap. George Shumway Publisher. $16.00.

Clayton, Joseph D. **The Ruger Number One Rifle.** (Illus.). 212 p. 1982. Blacksmith Corp. $39.95.

Colvin & Viall. **The Manufacture of Model 1903 Springfield Service Rifle.** 392 p. 1984. repr. of 1917 ed. Wolfe Pub. Co. $19.50.

Davis, Henry. **A Forgotten Heritage: The Story of the Early American Rifle.** 1976. Repr. of 1941 ed. Gun Room Press. $9.95.

DeHaas, Frank. **Bolt Action Rifle.** rev. ed. 448 p. 1984. DBI. pap. $14.95.

—**Single Shot's Gunsmithing Idea Book.** (Illus.) 176 p. 1983. TAB Bks. $13.50.

Ezell, Edw. C. **The Great Rifle Controversy: Search for The Ultimate Infantry Weapon From World War II Through Vietnam & Beyond.** 352 p. 1984. Stackpole. $29.95.

—**The AK47 Story: Evolution of the Kalishnokov Weapons.** (Illus.). 256 p. 1986. Stackpole. $29.95.

Fadala, Sam. **Rifleman's Bible.** (Illus.). 192 p. 1987. Doubleday. pap. $7.95.*

Fremantle, J. F. **The Book of the Rifle.** (Illus.). 576 p. 1985. repr. of 1901 ed. Wolfe Pub. Co. $54.00.

Grant James J. **More Single Shot Rifles.** (Illus.). Gun Room Press. $25.00.

—**Single-Shot Rifles.** Gun Room Press. $25.00.

—**Still More Single Shot Rifles.** 1979. Pioneer Press. $17.50.

Grissom, Ken. **Buckskins & Black Powder: A Mountain Man's Guide to Muzzle Loading.** (Illus.). 224 p. New Century. $15.95.

Hanson. **The Plains Rifle.** Gun Room Press. $15.00.

Hoffschmidt, E. J. **Know Your M-1 Garand Rifles.** 1976. pap. Blacksmith Corp. $5.95.

Hoyem, George. **The History & Development of Small Arms: British Sporting Rifle,** vol. 3. 236 p. 1985. Armory Pubns. $39.50.

Huddleston, Joe D. **Colonial Riflemen in the American Revolution.** (Illus.). 1978. George Shumway Publisher. $18.00.

Keith, Elmer. **Big Game Rifles & Cartridges.** 176 p. 1985. repr. of 1936 ed. Gun Room. $19.95.

—**Big Game Rifles & Cartridges.** (Illus.). 176 p. 1984. Deluxe ed. Wolfe Pub. Co. $30.00.

—**Keith's Rifles for Large Game.** (Illus.). 424 p. 1987. Repr. of 1946 ed. Wolfe Pub. Co. $54.00.*

Kindig, Joe, Jr. **Thoughts on the Kentucky Rifle in Its Golden Age.** annotated 2nd ed. (Illus.). 1982. George Shumway Publisher. $75.00.

Kirton, Jonathan G. **British Falling Block Breechloading Rifles From 1865.** (Illus.). 250 p. 1985. Armory Pubns. $39.95.

Klinger, Bernd., ed. **Rifle Shooting As a Sport.** 1981. A. S. Barnes. $15.00.

Lewis, Jack. **The Hunting Rifle: A Gun Digest Book.** 356 p. 1983. pap. DBI. $10.95.

Long, Duncan. **Assault Pistols, Rifles & Submachine Guns.** (Illus.). 152 p. 1986. Paladin Pr. text ed. $19.95.

—**The Mini-14: The Plinker, Hunter, Assault & Everything Else Rifle.** (Illus.).120 p. 1987. Paladin Pr. pap. text ed. $10.00.*

McAulay, John D. **Carbines of the Civil War, 1861–1865.** 1981. Pioneer Press. $7.95.

Mallory, Franklin B. & Olson, Ludwig. **The Krag Rifle Story.** 1980. Springfield Research Service. $20.00.

Matthews, Charles W. **Shoot Better With Centerfire Rifle Cartridges-Ballistic Tables.** (Illus.). 560 p. 1984. Matthews Inc. pap. $16.45.

Myatt, F. **An Illustrated Guide to Rifles and Automatic Weapons.** (Illus.). 1981. Arco. $8.95.

O'Connor, Jack, **The Rifle Book.** 3rd ed. (Illus.). 1978. Knopf. $13.95; pap. $10.95.

Otteson, Stuart. **The Bolt Action.** 2 vols. rev. ed. 1984. Wolfe Pub. Co. cased set $39.00.

—**Benchrest Actions & Triggers.** (Illus.). 61 p. 1983. Wolfe Pub. Co. pap. $8.50.

Page, Warren. **The Accurate Rifle.** (Illus.). 1975. softbound. Stoeger. $8.95.

Rywell, Martin. **American Antique Rifles.** Pioneer Press. $2.00.

Sharpe, Philip. **The Rifle in America.** (Illus.). 726 p. 1987. Repr. of 1938 ed. Wolfe Pub. Co. $59.00.*

Shelsby, Earl, ed. **NRA Gunsmithing Guide.** Updated rev. ed. (Illus.). 336 p. (Orig.). 1980. pap. Nat'l Rifle Assn. $11.95.

Shumway, George. **Pennsylvania Longrifles of Note.** (Illus.). 1977. pap. George Shumway Publisher. $7.50.

—**Rifles of Colonial America.** 2 vols. incl. Vol. 1; Vol. 2. (Illus.). 1980. casebound. George Shumway Publisher. ea. $49.50.

Steindler, R. A. **Rifle Guide.** 1978. softbound. Stoeger. $9.95.

Taylor, C. **African Rifles and Cartridges.** Gun Room Press. $16.95.

—**The Fighting Rifles.** 1986. Gordon Pr. $79.95 (lib. bdg.).*

U.S. Rifle Caliber .30 Model 1903. Pioneer Press. $2.00.

U.S. Rifle Model 1866 Springfield. Pioneer Press. $0.75.

U.S. Rifle Model 1870 Remington. Pioneer Press. $0.75.

Walsh, J. H. **The Modern Sportsman's Gun & Rifle.** Vol. I & II. (Illus.). 536 p. 1986. Wolfe Pub. Co. price on request.

Whelen, Townsend. **The Hunting Rifle.** 464 p. 1984. Repr. of 1924 ed. Wolfe Pub. Co. $39.00.

White, S. E. **The Long Rifle.** (Illus.). 544 p. 1987. Repr. of 1930 ed. Wolfe Pub. Co. $25.00.*

Womack, Lester. **The Commercial Mauser Ninety Eight Sporting Rifle.** Angevine, Jay B., Jr., ed. (Illus.). 1981. Womack Assoc. $20.00.

Wood, J. B. **Gun Digest Book of Firearms Assembly/Disassembly. Pt. III: Rimfire Rifles.** (Illus.). 1980. pap. DBI Books. $8.95.

—**Gun Digest Book of Firearms Assembly/Disassembly. Part IV: Centerfire Rifles.** (Illus.). 1979. pap. $12.95.

Workman, William E. **Know Your Ruger 10-22 Carbine.** (Illus.) 96 p. 1986. Blacksmith Corp. pap. $9.95.*

SHARPS RIFLES

Manual of Arms for the Sharps Rifle. Pioneer Press. $1.50.

Rywell, Martin. **Sharps Rifle: The Gun That Shaped American Destiny.** Pioneer Press. $5.00.

SHOOTING (see also Firearms, Trap & Skeet Shooting)

Berger, Robert J. **Know Your Broomhandle Mauser.** (Illus.) 96 p. 1985. Blacksmith Corp. pap. $6.95.*

Bowles, Bruce. **The Orvis Wing Shooting Handbook.** 96 p. 1985. N Lyons Bks. pap. $8.95.

Brister, Bob. **Shotgunning: The Art and the Science.** (Illus.). 1976. Winchester Press. $15.95.

Crossman, Jim. **Olympic Shooting.** (Illus.). 144 p. Natl Rifle Assn. $12.95.

Day, J. Wentworth. **The Modern Shooter.** 1976. Repr. of 1952 ed. Charles River Books. $15.00.

Farrow, W. M. **How I Became a Crack Shot With Hints to Beginners.** (Illus.). 204 p. Wolfe Pub. Co. $16.50.

Gates, Elgin. **Gun Digest Book of Metallic Silhouette Shooting.** 1979. pap. DBI Books. $7.95.

Hagel, Bob. **Guns, Loads & Hunting Tips.** Wolfe, Dave, ed. (Illus.). 536 p. 1986. Wolfe Pub. Co. $19.50.

Humphreys, John. **Learning To Shoot.** (Illus.). 192 p. 1985. David & Charles. $16.95.

Jarrett, William S., ed. **Shooter's Bible 1988.** 79th ed. (Illus.). 576 p. 1987. Stoeger Pub. Co. pap. $14.95.

—**Shooter's Bible 1989.** 80th ed. (Illus.). 576 p. 1988. Stoeger Pub. Co. $14.95.*

King, Peter. **The Shooting Field: 150 Years With Holland & Holland.** (Illus.). 176 p. 1985. Blacksmith. $39.95.

Klinger, Bernd, ed. **Rifle Shooting as a Sport.** (Illus.). 186 p. 1981. A. S. Barnes. $15.00.

Lind, Ernie. **Complete Book of Trick and Fancy Shooting.** (Illus.). 1977. pap. Citadel Press. $3.95.

McGivern, Ed. **Fast and Fancy Revolver Shooting.** New Century. $14.95.

Marchington, John. **Shooting: A Complete Guide for Beginners.** (Illus.). 1982. pap. Faber & Faber. $6.95.

Merkley, Jay P. **Marksmanship with Rifles: A Basic Guide.** (Illus.). pap. American Press. $2.95.

Rees, Clair. **Be An Expert Shot: With Rifle, Handgun, or Shotgun.** (Illus.). 192 p. 1984. New Century. $19.95.

Reynolds, Mike & Barnes, Mike. **Shooting Made Easy.** (Illus.) 144 p. 1986. Longwood Pub. Gp. $17.95.*

Riling, Ray. **Guns and Shooting: A Bibliography.** (Illus.). 1981. Ray Riling. $75.00.

Ruffer, J. E. **Good Shooting.** (Illus.). 1980. David & Charles. $22.50.

Set Your Sights: A Guide to Handgun Basics. (Illus.). 1982. Outdoor Empire. $1.95.

Slabor, Stephen, et al. **Shooting Guide for Beginners.** (Illus.). 144 p. 1986. Allegheny. pap. $7.95.

Weston, Paul B. **Combat Shooting for Police.** 2nd ed. (Illus.). 1978. C. C. Thomas. $12.75.

Willock, Colin. **The ABC of Shooting.** (Illus.). 353 p. 1975. Andre Deutsch. $18.95.

—**Duck Shooting.** (Illus.). 144 p. 1981. Andre Deutsch. $14.95.

Yochem, Barbara. **Barbara Yochem's Inner Shooting.** 1981. By By Productions. $6.95; pap. $3.95.

SHOTGUNS

Anderson, Robert S., ed. **Reloading for Shotgunners.** (Illus.). 224 p. 1981. pap. DBI. $9.95.

Askins, Charles. **The American Shotgun.** (Illus.). 336 p. 1987. Repr. of 1910 ed. Wolfe Pub. Co. $39.00.*

Bowlen, Bruce. **The Orvis Wing Shooting Handbook.** 96 p. 1985. N. Lyons Bks. pap. $8.95.*

Brockway, William R. **Recreating the Double Barrel Muzzleloading Shotgun.** (Illus.). 1985. Shumway. $27.50; pap. $20.00.

Burch, Monte. **Shotgunner's Guide.** (Illus.). 1980. Winchester Press. $15.95.

Elliott, Robert W. & Cobb, Jim. **Lefevre: Guns of Lasting Fame.** 174 p. 1987. R. W. Elliott. $29.95.*

Grozik, Richard S. **Game Gun.** (Illus.) 160 p. 1986. Willow Creek. $39.00.*

Hastings, Macdonald. **The Shotgun: A Social History.** 1981. David & Charles. $29.95.

Hinman, Bob. **The Golden Age of Shotgunning,** 2nd ed. Wolfe, Dave, ed. (Illus.). 175 p. Wolfe Pub. Co. $17.95.

Johnson, Peter H. Parker, **America's First Shotgun.** (Illus.). 272 p. Stackpole. $17.95.

Laycock, George. **Shotgunner's Bible.** (Illus.). 1969. pap. Doubleday. $3.95.

Lewis, Jack & Mitchell, Jack. **Shotgun Digest.** 2nd ed. 1980. pap. DBI Books. $9.95.

McIntosh, Michael. **The Best Shotguns Ever Made in America: Seven Vintage Doubles to Shoot and to Treasure.** 1981. Scribner's. $17.95.

Marshall-Ball, Robin. **The Sporting Shotgun.** 1981. Saiga. $14.95.

O'Connor, Jack, **The Shotgun Book,** 2nd ed. rev. (Illus.). 1978. Knopf. pap. $9.95.

Robinson, Roger H. **The Police Shotgun Manual.** (Illus.). 1973. C. C. Thomas. $14.75.

Skillen, Charles R. **Combat Shotgun Training.** (Illus.). 1982. C. C. Thomas. $26.75.

Swearengen, Thomas F. **World's Fighting Shotguns.** 1978. TBN Ent. $29.95.

Thomas, Gough. **Shotguns and Cartridges for Game and Clays.** 3rd ed. (Illus.). 1976. Transatlantic Arts, Inc. $25.00.

Wallack, L. R. **American Shotgun Design and Performance.** 1977. Winchester Press. $16.95.

Zutz, Don. **The Double Shotgun,** rev. ed. 304 p. (Illus.). 1985. New Century. $19.95.

SURVIVAL (see also Outdoor Life)

Angier, Bradford. **How to Stay Alive in the Woods.** Orig. Title: **Living Off the Country.** 1962. pap. Macmillan. $2.95.

Benson, Ragnar. **Live Off the Land in The City and Country.** (Illus.). 1981. Paladin Enterprises. $16.95.

Canadian Government. **Never Say Die: The Canadian Air Force Survival Manual.** (Illus.). 208 p. 1979. Paladin Pr. pap. $8.00.

Clayton, Bruce D. **Life After Doomsday: A Survivalist Guide to Nuclear War and Other Disasters.** (Illus.). 1981. pap. Dial Press. $8.95.

Dennis, Lawrence. **Operational Thinking for Survival.** 1969. R. Myles. $5.95.

Dept. of the Air Force. **Survival: Air Force Manual 64–5.** (Illus.). 1976. pap. Paladin Enterprises. $8.00.

Fear, Daniel E., ed. **Surviving the Unexpected: A Curriculum Guide for Wilderness Survival and Survival from Natural and Man Made Disasters.** (Illus.). rev. ed. 1974. Survival Education Association. $5.00.

Fear, Eugene H. **Surviving the Unexpected Wilderness Emergency.** 6th ed. (Illus.). 1979. pap. Survival Education Association. $5.00.

Freeman, Daniel B. **Speaking of Survival.** (Illus.). pap. Oxford University Press. $5.95.

Olsen, Larry D. **Outdoor Survival Skills.** 4th rev. ed. 1973. Brigham Young University Press. $7.95.

—**Outdoor Survival Skills.** 1984. pap. Pocket Books. $3.95.

Read, Piers Paul. **Alive: The Story of the Andes Survivors.** (Illus.). 1974. pap. Harper & Row. $12.50.

Survival Improvised Weapons. 1986. Gordon Press. $79.95 (lib. bdg.).*

Thygerson, Alton L. **Disaster Survival Handbook.** (Illus.). 1979. pap. Brigham Young University Press. $7.95.

Wiseman, John. **Survive Safely Anywhere:** The SAS Survival Manual. (Illus.) 1986. Crown. $24.95.*

TAXIDERMY

Farnham, Albert B. **Home Taxidermy for Pleasure and Profit.** (Illus.). pap. A. R. Harding Publishing. $3.00.

Grantz, Gerald J. **Home Book of Taxidermy and Tanning.** (Illus.). 1985. Stackpole. pap. $8.95.

Harrison, James M. **Bird Taxidermy.** (Illus.). 1977. David & Charles. $12.50.

McFall, Waddy F. **Taxidermy Step by Step.** (Illus.). 1975. Winchester Press. $12.95.

Metcalf, John C. **Taxidermy: A Computer Manual.** (Illus.). 166 p. 1981. pap. Biblio Dist. $15.00.

Moyer, John W. **Practical Taxidermy.** 2nd ed. 1979. Wiley. $15.95.

Pray, Leon L. **Taxidermy.** (Illus.). 1943. Macmillan. $9.95.

Smith, Capt. James A. **Dress 'Em Out, Vol. 1.** (Illus.). 1982. softbound. Stoeger. $11.95.

Tinsley, Russell. **Taxidermy Guide.** 2nd ed. (Illus.). 1977. softbound. Stoeger. $9.95.

TRAP AND SKEET SHOOTING

Blatt, Art. **Gun Digest Book of Trap & Skeet Shooting.** 256 p. 1984. pap. DBI. $10.95.

Campbell, Robert, ed. **Trapshooting with D. Lee Braun and the Remington Pros.** pap. Benjamin Co. $5.95.

—**Skeet Shooting with D. Lee Braun:** A Remington Sportsman's Library Book. Benjamin Co. $4.95.

Cradock, Chris. **Manual of Clayshooting.** (Illus.) 192 p. 1986. David & Charles. $29.95.*

National Skeet Shooting Association Record Annual. 320 p. Natl. Skeet Shoot. Assn. $7.00.

TRAPPING

Errington, Paul L. **Muskrats and Marsh Management.** (Illus.). 1978. University of Nebraska Press. $13.50; pap. $3.25.

Geary, Steven. **Fur Trapping in North America.** (Illus.). 384 p. 1985. Stackpole. $44.95.

Gertsell, Richard. **The Steel Trap in North America.** (Illus.). 384 p. 1985. Stackpole. $44.95.

Get Set To Trap. (Illus.). 1982. Outdoor Empire. $1.95.

Gilsvik, Bob. **The Modern Trapline: Methods and Materials.** 1980. Chilton Book Co. $12.50.

Harding, A. R. **Deadfalls and Snares.** (Illus.). pap. A. R. Harding Publishing. $3.00.

—**Fox Trapping.** (Illus.). pap. A. R. Harding Publishing. $3.00.

—**Mink Trapping.** (Illus.). pap. A. R. Harding Publishing. $3.00.

—**Trappers' Handbook.** 1975. pap. A. R. Harding Publishing. $1.50.

—**Trapping as a Profession.** 1975. pap. A. R. Harding Publishing. $1.50.

—**Wolf & Coyote Trapping.** (Illus.) 252 p. A. R. Harding Pub. pap. $3.50.*

Jamison, Rick. **Trapper's Handbook.** 224 p. 1983. pap. DBI. $10.95.

Kreps, E. **Science of Trappings.** (Illus.). pap. A. R. Harding Publishing. $3.00.

Lindsey, Neil M. **Tales of A Wilderness Trapper.** 1973. pap. A. R. Harding Publishing. $1.50.

Lynch, V. E. **Trails to Successful Trapping.** pap. A. R. Harding Publishing. $3.00.

McCracken, Harold & Van Cleve, Harry. **Trapping.** (Illus.). 1974. A. S. Barnes. $8.95.

Mascall, Leonard. **A Booke of Fishing with Hooke and Line.** 1973. Repr. of 1590 ed. Walter J. Johnson. $9.50.

Montgomery, David. **Mountain Man Crafts & Skills.** (Illus.). 1981. Horizon Utah. $9.95.

Musgrove, Bill & Blair, Gerry. **Fur Trapping.** (Illus.). 1984. New Century. $13.95.

Russell, Andy. **Trails of a Wilderness Wanderer.** 1975. Knopf. $10.95.

Sandoz, Mari. **The Beaver Men: Spearheads of Empire.** (Illus.). 1978. pap. University of Nebraska Press. $5.95.

Simms, Jeptha R. **Trappers of New York.** 1980. Repr. of 1871 ed. Harbor Hill Books. $15.00.

Smith, Guy N. **Ferreting and Trapping for Amateur Game Keepers.** 1981. (Pub. by Saiga). State Mutual Book & Periodical Service. $25.00.

The Trapper's Companion. (Illus.). pap. A. R. Harding Publishing. $2.00.

Walters, Keith. **The Book of the Free Trapper.** 1981. Pioneer Press. $7.95.

Woodcock, E. N. **Fifty Years a Hunter and Trapper.** pap. A. R. Harding Publishing. $3.00.

WINCHESTER RIFLES

Fadala, Sam. **Winchester's 30-30, Model 94:** The Rifle America Loves. (Illus.) 224 p. 1986. Stackpole. $24.95.*

Madis, George. **The Winchester Model Twelve.** (Illus.). 1982. Art & Ref. $14.95.

—**The Winchester Book.** 3rd ed. (Illus.). 1979. Art & Reference House. $39.50.

—**The Winchester Handbook.** (Illus.). 1981. Art & Reference House. $19.50.

Twesten, Gary. **Winchester 1894 Carbine: A 90-Year History of the Variations of the Winchester Carbine 1894–1984.** (Illus.). 1984. G. Twesten. $20.00; pap. $10.00.

—**Winchester Model 1892 Carbine.** 1985. G. Tuesten. Pap. $10.00.*

West, Bill. **Winchester Encyclopedia.** (Illus.). B. West. $15.00.

—**Winchester Lever-Action Handbook.** (Illus.). B. West. $25.00.

—**Winchester Single Shot.** (Illus.). B. West. $15.00.

—**Winchesters, Cartridges and History.** (Illus.). B. West. $29.00.

Winchester—Complete Volume I: All Early Winchester Arms 1849–1919. (Illus.) 1981. B. West. $36.00

Winchester—Complete Volume II: All Winchester Arms 1920–1982. 1981. B. West. $36.00.

Names and Addresses of Leading Gun Book Publishers

ARCO PUBLISHING INC.
(see Prentice-Hall Inc.)

ARMORY PUBLICATIONS
P.O. Box 44372
Tacoma, Washington 98444

BLACKSMITH CORP.
P.O. Box 424
Southport, Ct. 06490

DAVID & CHARLES INC.
P.O. Box 57
Pomfret, Vermont 05053

DBI BOOKS, INC.
4092 Commercial Avenue
Northbrook, Illinois 60062

DENLINGER'S PUBLISHERS LTD.
P.O. Box 76
Fairfax, Virginia 22030

E & P ENTERPRISES
P.O. Box 2116
San Antonio, Texas 78297-2116

GUN ROOM PRESS
127 Raritan Avenue
Highland Park, N.J. 08904

HOUSE OF COLLECTIBLES
1904 Premier Row
Orlando, Florida 32809

JANE'S PUBLISHING INC.
c/o International Thomson Organisation Inc.
135 W. 50 Street
New York, N.Y. 10020

ALFRED A. KNOPF, INC.
201 E. 50 Street
New York, N.Y. 10022

LONGWOOD PUBLISHING GROUP INC.
51 Washington Street
Dover, New Hampshire 03820

NATIONAL RIFLE ASSOCIATION
1600 Rhode Island Avenue NW
Washington, D.C. 20036

NEW CENTURY PUBLICATIONS, INC.
220 Old New Brunswick Road
Piscataway, N.J. 08854
(also handles titles published under Winchester
Press imprint)

PALADIN PRESS
P.O. Box 1307
Boulder, Colorado 80306

PRENTICE-HALL
Englewood Cliffs, N.J. 07632

ROLLING BLOCK PRESS
P.O. Box 5357
Buena Park, California 90622

ALBERT SAIFER, PUBLISHERS
P.O. Box 239
West Orange, N.J. 07052

SAIGA PUBLISHING CO. LTD.
(see under Longwood Pub. Group Inc.)

GEORGE SHUMWAY PUBLISHERS
RD 7, P.O. Box 388B
York, Pennsylvania 17402

STACKPOLE BOOKS
P.O. Box 1831
Harrisburg, Pennsylvania 17105

STEIN & DAY
Scarborough House
Briarcliff Manor, N.Y. 10510

STERLING PUBLISHING CO., INC.
2 Park Avenue
New York, N.Y. 10016

STOEGER PUBLISHING COMPANY
55 Ruta Court
South Hackensack, N.J. 07606

TAB BOOKS INC.
Blue Ridge Summit
Pennsylvania 17214

TARGET COMMUNICATIONS CORP.
7626 West Donges Bay Road
P.O. Box 188
Mequon, Wisconsin 53092

WILLOW CREEK PRESS
Div. of Wisconsin Sportsman
P.O. Box 2266
Oshkosh, Wisconsin 54903

WOLFE PUBLISHING COMPANY, INC.
P.O. Box 3030
Prescott, Arizona 86302

Directory of Manufacturers and Suppliers

Action Arms, Ltd. (UZI, Galil paramilitary)
P.O. Box 9573
Philadelphia, Pennsylvania 19124
(215) 744-0100

Aimpoint (sights, mounts)
203 Eldin Street, Suite 302
Herndon, Virginia 22070
(703) 471-6828

American Arms (shotguns)
715 E. Armour Road
N. Kansas City, Missouri 64116
(816) 474-3161

American Derringer Corp. (handguns)
127 North Lacy Drive
Waco, Texas 76705
(817) 799-9111

American Industries (Calico paramilitary)
405 E. 19th Street
Bakersfield, California 93305
(805) 323-1327

American Military Arms Corp. (AMAC paramilitary)
See Iver Johnson/AMAC

Anschutz (rifles)
Available through Precision Sales International

Arcadia Machine & Tool Inc. (AMT handguns)
6226 Santos Diaz Street
Irwindale, California 91706
(818) 334-6629

Armes de Chasse (Gamba and Merkel shotguns)
P.O. Box 827
Chadds Ford, Pennsylvania 19317
(215) 388-1146

Armsport, Inc. (shotguns, black powder)
3590 NW 49th Street
Miami, Florida 33142
(305) 635-7850

Astra (handguns)
Available through Interarms

Auto-Ordnance Corp. (paramilitary)
West Hurley, N.Y. 12491
(914) 679-7225

Barrett Firearms Mfg. Co., Inc. (paramilitary)
Route 1, Box 645
Murfreesboro, Tennessee 37130
(615) 896-2938

Bausch & Lomb (scopes)
See Bushnell (Division of)

Beeman Precision Arms, Inc. (imported handguns, rifles, scopes)
3440-SBL Airway Drive
Santa Rosa, California 95403
(707) 578-7900

Benelli (shotguns)
Available through Heckler & Koch

Benson Firearms (Uberti black powder, rifles, revolvers)
P.O. Box 30137
Seattle, Washington 98103
(206) 361-2595

Beretta U.S.A. Corp. (handguns, shotguns, paramilitary)
17601 Indian Head Highway
Accokeek, Maryland 20607
(301) 283-2191
See also under Uberti, USA

Bernardelli (shotguns)
Available through Quality Arms

Bersa (handguns)
Available through Outdoor Sports Headquarters

Blaser USA, Inc. (rifles)
c/o Autumn Sales, Inc.
1320 Lake Street
Fort Worth, Texas 76102
(817) 335-1634

Bonanza (reloading tools)
See Forster Products

Brno (handguns, rifles)
Available through Saki International

Browning (handguns, rifles, shotguns)
Route One
Morgan, Utah 84050
(801) 987-2711

B-Square Company (scope mounts)
P.O. Box 11281
Fort Worth, Texas 76109
(817) 923-0964

Maynard P. Buehler, Inc. (mounts)
17 Orinda Highway
Orinda, California 94563
(415) 254-3201

Burris Company, Inc. (scopes, sights, mounts)
311 East Eighth Street
Greeley, Colorado 80634
(303) 356-1670

Bushnell (scopes)
Division of Bausch & Lomb
2828 East Foothill Boulevard
Pasadena, California 91107
(818) 577-1500

CCI (ammunition, primers)
Available through Omark Industries, Inc.

C-H Tool & Die Corp. (reloading)
P.O. Box L
Owen, Wisconsin 54460
(715) 229-2146

CVA (black powder guns)
5988 Peachtree Corners East
Norcross, Georgia 30071
(404) 449-4687

Charter Arms Corp. (handguns)
430 Sniffens Lane
Stratford, Connecticut 06497
(203) 377-8080

Churchill (shotguns)
Available through Kassnar Imports

Classic Doubles (shotguns)
1001 Craig Road, Suite 353
St. Louis, Missouri 63146
(314) 997-7281

Classic Rifles Co. (rifles)
P.O. Box 321
Rodgers Lane
Charleroi, Pennsylvania 15022
(412) 483-6358

Colt Industries Firearms Division (handguns, paramilitary)
150 Huyshope Avenue, Box 1868
Hartford, Connecticut 06102
(203) 236-6311

Competition Arms, Inc. (Erma target handguns)
1010 S. Plumer Avenue
Tucson, Arizona 85719
(602) 792-1075

Coonan Arms, Inc. (handguns)
830 Hampden Ave.
St. Paul, Minnesota 55114
(612) 328-6795

Dakota (handguns)
Available through E.M.F. Co., Inc.

Charles Daly (shotguns)
Available through Outdoor Sports Headquarters Inc.

Davis Industries (handguns)
13748 Arapahoe Place
Chino, California 91710
(714) 591-4727

Defense Systems International (M.A.C. paramilitary)
Dallas Road
Powder Springs, Georgia 30073
(404) 422-5731

Detonics (handguns)
See under New Detonics Manufacturing Corp.

Dixie Gun Works (black powder guns)
Reelfoot Avenue, P.O. Box 130
Union City, Tennessee 38261
(901) 885-0561

DuPont (gunpowder)
See under IMR Powder Company

Dynamit Nobel of America, Inc. (Rottweil shotguns)
105 Stonehurst Court
Northvale, New Jersey 07647
(201) 767-1660

E.M.F. Company, Inc. (Dakota handguns, rifles, paramilitary, black powder)
1900 East Warner Avenue
Santa Ana, California 92705
(714) 261-6611

Erma (handguns)
Available through Competition Arms (target guns only)

Euroarms of America Inc. (black powder guns)
1501 Lenoir Drive, P.O. Box 3277
Winchester, Virginia 22601
(703) 662-1863

Excam (Targa and Tanarmi pistols, shotguns)
4480 E. 11th Avenue
Hialeah, Florida 33013
(305) 681-4661-2

Fabrique Nationale (paramilitary)
Available through Gun South Inc.

Federal Cartridge Corporation (Federal and Norma ammunition, bullets, primers, cases)
900 Ehlen Drive
Anoka, Minnesota 55303-7503
(612) 422-2840

Ferlib (shotguns)
Available through W. L. Moore & Co.

FFV Norma, Inc. (Norma ammunition, gunpowder, reloading cases)
See under Federal Cartridge Corp.

FIE Corporation (pistols, black powder guns, Franchi shotguns)
P.O. Box 4866
Hialeah, Florida 33014
(305) 685-5966

Forster Products (Bonanza and Forster reloading)
82 East Lanark Avenue
Lanark, Illinois 61046
(815) 493-6360

Franchi (shotguns, paramilitary)
Available through FIE Corp.

Freedom Arms (handguns)
One Freedom Lane, P.O. Box 1776
Freedom, Wyoming 83120
(307) 883-2468

Galil (paramilitary)
Available through Action Arms, Ltd.

Gamba (shotguns)
Available through Armes de Chasse

Garbi (shotguns)
Available through W. L. Moore & Co.

Griffin & Howe, Inc. (sights, mounts)
36 W. 44th Street
New York, New York 10036
(212) 921-0980

Gun South Inc. (Fabrique Nationale, Steyr, Steyr Mannlicher rifles, paramilitary)
P.O. Box 129
Trussville, Alabama 35173
(205) 655-8299

Hammerli (handguns)
Available through Beeman's Precision Arms

Heckler & Koch (handguns, rifles, paramilitary)
14601 Lee Road
Chantilly, Virginia 22021
(703) 631-2800

Heym (rifles, shotguns)
Available through Paul Jaeger, Inc.

Hodgdon Powder Co., Inc. (gunpowder)
6231 Robinson, P.O. Box 2932
Shawnee Mission, Kansas 66202
(913) 362-9455

Hopkins & Allen Arms (black powder guns)
3 Ethel Avenue, P.O. Box 217
Hawthorne, New Jersey 07507
(201) 427-1165

Hornady Manufacturing Company (reloading, ammunition)
P.O. Box 1848
Grand Island, Nebraska 68802-1848
(308) 382-1390

Howa (rifles)
Available through Interarms

IMR Powder Company (gunpowder; formerly DuPont gunpowder)
R.D. 5, Box 247E
Plattsburgh, New York 12901
(518) 582-7407

Interarms (handguns, shotguns and rifles, including Astra, Howa, Mark X, Rossi, Star, Walther, Whitworth)
10 Prince Street
Alexandria, Virginia 22313
(703) 548-1400

Intratec U.S.A. Inc. (paramilitary)
11990 S.W. 128th Street
Miami, Florida 33186
(305) 232-1821

Ithaca Acquisition Corp. (Ithaca shotguns)
123 Lake Street
Ithaca, New York 14850
(607) 273-0200

Iver Johnson/AMAC (handguns, rifles, paramilitary)
Division of American Military Arms Corp.
2202 Redmond Road
Jacksonville, Arkansas 72076
(501) 982-1633

Paul Jaeger, Inc. (Heym rifles, shotguns, Schmidt & Bender scopes, mounts)
P.O. Box 449
1 Madison Ave.
Grand Junction, Tennessee 38039
(901) 764-6909

K.D.F. Inc. (rifles)
2485 Highway North
Seguin, Texas 78155
(512) 379-8141

Kassnar Imports (Churchill shotguns, Omega shotguns)
P.O. Box 6097
Harrisburg, Pennsylvania 17112
(717) 652-6101

Kimber (rifles, scopes)
9039 S.E. Jannsen Road
Clackamas, Oregon 97015
(503) 656-1704

Krico (rifles)
Available through Beeman Precision Arms

Krieghoff International Inc. (shotguns, Shotguns of Ulm)
P.O. Box 549
Ottsville, Pennsylvania 18942
(215) 847-5173 (telex: 140914 DK USA)

L.A.R. Manufacturing, Inc. (Grizzly handguns)
4133 West Farm Road
West Jordan, Utah 84084
(307) 883-2468

Lebeau-Courally (shotguns)
Available through W. L. Moore & Co.

Leupold & Stevens, Inc. (scopes, mounts)
P.O. Box 688
Beaverton, Oregon 97075
(503) 646-9171

Llama (handguns)
Available through Stoeger Industries

Lyman Products Corp. (black powder guns, sights, scopes, reloading tools)
Route 147
Middlefield, Connecticut 06455
(203) 349-3421

M.A.C. (paramilitary)
See Defense Systems International

M.O.A. Corp. (handguns)
7996 Brookville-Salem Road
Brookville, Ohio 45309
(513) 833-5559

MTM Molded Products Co. (reloading tools)
5680 Webster Street
Dayton, Ohio 45414
(513) 890-7461

Magnum Research Inc. (handguns, paramilitary,
Victory Arms handguns)
7271 Commerce Circle West
Minneapolis, Minnesota 55432
(612) 574-1868

Marlin Firearms Company (rifles, shotguns)
100 Kenna Drive
North Haven, Connecticut 06473
(203) 239-5621

Merit Corporation (sights, optical aids)
Box 9044
Schenectady, New York 12309
(518) 346-1420

Merkel (shotguns)
Available through Armes de Chasse

Michigan Arms Corp. (handguns, paramilitary)
363 Elmwood
Troy, Michigan 48082
(313) 583-1518

Millett Sights (sights and mounts)
16131 Gothard Street
Huntington Beach, California 92647
(714) 847-5245

Mitchell Arms (handguns, paramilitary)
19007 South Reyes Avenue
Compton, California 90221
(213) 603-0465

Modern Muzzle Loaders Inc. (black powder guns)
Highway 136 East, P.O. Box 130
Lancaster, Missouri 63548
(816) 457-2125

William L. Moore & Co. (Garbi, Ferlib, Lebeau-
Courally, and Piotti shotguns)
31360 Via Colinas, No. 109
Westlake Village, California 91361
(818) 889-4160

O.F. Mossberg & Sons, Inc. (shotguns)
7 Grasso Avenue
North Haven, Connecticut 06473
(203) 288-6491

Navy Arms Company, Inc. (shotguns, black powder
guns, replicas)
689 Bergen Boulevard
Ridgefield, New Jersey 07657
(201) 945-2500

New Detonics Manufacturing Corp. (handguns)
13456 Southeast 27th Place
Bellevue, Washington 98005
(206) 747-2100

New England Firearms Company (shotguns)
Industrial Rowe
Gardner, Massachusetts 01440
(617) 632-9393

Norma (ammunition, gunpowder, reloading cases)
Available through Federal Cartridge Corp.

North American Arms (handguns)
1800 North 300 West
P.O. Box 707
Spanish Fork, Utah 84660   O 8 (/(/(/))
(801) 798-7401

Olin/Winchester (ammunition, primers, cases)
East Alton, Illinois 62024
(618) 258-2000
Shotguns now available Classic Doubles

Omark Industries, Inc. (CCI ammunition, Shotguns
available through Classic Doubles RCBS reloading
tools, Speer bullets, Weaver mount rings)
Box 856
Lewiston, Idaho 83501
(208) 746-2351

Omega (shotguns)
Available through Kassnar Imports

Outdoor Sports Headquarters, Inc. (Bersa
handguns, Charles Daly shotguns)
P.O. Box 1327
967 Watertower Lane
Dayton, Ohio 45401
(513) 865-5855

Parker Hale (rifles, shotguns)
Available through Precision Sports

Parker Reproduction (shotguns)
124 River Road
Middlesex, New Jersey 08846
(201) 469-0100

Perazzi (shotguns)
206 South George Street
Rome, New York 13440
(315) 337-8566

Piotti (shotguns)
Available through W.L. Moore & Co.

Precision Sales International (Anschutz pistols,
rifles)
P.O. Box 1776
Westfield, Massachusetts 01086
(413) 562-5055

Precision Sports (Parker-Hale rifles, shotguns)
P.O. Box 5588, Kellogg Road
Cortland, New York 13045-5588
(607) 756-2851

RCBS, Inc. (reloading tools)
See Omark Industries, Inc.

Redding-Hunter, Inc. (reloading tools)
114 Starr Road
Cortland, New York 13045
(607) 753-3331

Redfield (sights, scopes)
5800 East Jewell Avenue
Denver, Colorado 80224
(303) 757-6411

Remington Arms Company, Inc. (rifles, shotguns,
ammunition, primers)
939 Barnum Avenue
Bridgeport, Connecticut 06601
(203) 333-1112

Rossi (handguns, rifles, shotguns)
Available through Interarms

Rottweil (shotguns)
Available through Dynamit Nobel of America, Inc.

Ruger (handguns, rifles, shotguns, black powder
guns)
See Sturm, Ruger & Company, Inc.

Saki International (Brno handguns, rifles)
19800 Center Ridge Road
P.O. Box 16189
Rocky River, Ohio 44116
(216) 331-3533

Sako (rifles, actions, scope mounts)
Available through Stoeger Industries

Sauer (rifles)
Available through Sigarms, Inc.

Savage Arms (rifles, shotguns, Stevens & Fox)
Springdale Road
Westfield, Massachusetts 01085
(413) 562-2361

Schmidt and Bender (scopes)
Available through Paul Jaeger, Inc.

C. Sharps Arms Co., Inc. (Shiloh Sharps black
powder rifles)
P.O. Box 885
Big Timber, Montana 59011
(406) 932-4353

Shotguns of Ulm (shotguns)
Available through Krieghoff International

Sierra Bullets (bullets)
10537 S. Painter Avenue
Santa Fe Springs, California 90670
(213) 941-0251

Sigarms Inc. (Sig paramilitary, Sauer rifles)
8330 Old Courthouse Road, Suite 885
Tyson's Corner, Virginia 22180
(703) 893-1940

Sig-Sauer (handguns)
Available through Sigarms Inc.

Simmons Outdoor Corp. (scopes)
14205 SW 119th Ave.
Miami, Florida 33186
(305) 252-0477

SKB Shotguns (shotguns)
c/o Ernie Simmons Enterprises
719 Highland Avenue
Lancaster, Pennsylvania 17603
(717) 392-0021

Smith & Wesson (handguns)
2100 Roosevelt Avenue
Springfield, Massachusetts 01101
(413) 781-8300

Southern Gun Distributors (Sovereign shotguns,
Tanarmi and Targa handguns)
13490 N.W. 45th Avenue
Opa-Locke (Miami), Florida 33054-0025
1-800-327-8500

Sovereign (shotguns)
Available through Southern Gun Distributors

Speer (bullets)
See Omark Industries, Inc.

Springfield Armory (handguns, paramilitary)
420 West Main Street
Geneseo, Illinois 61254
(309) 944-5138

Star (handguns)
Available through Interarms

Stevens & Fox (shotguns)
Available through Savage Arms

Steyr (handguns, paramilitary)
Available through Gun South Inc.

Steyr Mannlicher (rifles, paramilitary)
Available through Gun South Inc.

Stoeger Industries (Sako rifles, Llama handguns,
Stoeger shotguns, Sako-Valmet rifles, shotguns,
paramilitary; scopes, mounts, actions)
55 Ruta Court
South Hackensack, New Jersey 07606
(201) 440-2700

Sturm, Ruger and Company, Inc. (Ruger handguns,
rifles, shotguns)
Lacey Place
Southport, Connecticut 06490
(203) 259-7843

Swarovski Optik (scopes)
1 Kenney Drive
Cranston, Rhode Island 02920
(401) 463-6400

Tanarmi and Targa (pistols)
Available through Southern Gun Distributors

Tasco (scopes)
7600 N.W. 26th Street
Miami, Florida 33122
(305) 591-3670

Taurus International, Inc. (Taurus handguns)
4563 Southwest 71st Street
Miami, Florida 33155
(305) 662-2529

Thompson/Center Arms (handguns, black powder
guns, paramilitary)
Farmington Road, P.O. Box 2426
Rochester, New Hampshire 03867
(603) 332-2333

Tikka (rifles, shotguns)
SF-41160
Tikkakoski, Finland

Traditions, Inc. (black powder)
Saybrook Road
Haddam, Connecticut 06438
(203) 345-8561

Uberti USA, Inc. (black powder rifles, revolvers)
41 Church Street
New Milford, Connecticut 06776
(203) 355-8827
See also under Benson Firearms

Ultra Light Arms Company (rifles)
P.O. Box 1270
Granville, West Virginia 26534
(304) 599-5687

U.S. Repeating Arms Co. (Winchester rifles,
shotguns)
275 Winchester Avenue
New Haven, Connecticut 06504
(203) 789-5000

UZI (paramilitary)
Available through Action Arms Ltd.

Valmet, Inc. (rifles, shotguns, paramilitary)
Available through Stoeger Industries

Varner Sporting Arms (rifles)
1004F Cobb Parkway, N.E.
Marietta, Georgia 30062
(404) 422-5468

Victory Arms (handguns)
See under Magnum Research

Walther (handguns)
Available through Interarms

Weatherby, Inc. (rifles, shotguns, scopes,
ammunition)
2781 Firestone Boulevard
South Gate, California 90280
(213) 569-7186

Weaver (mount rings)
See Omark Industries

Dan Wesson Arms, Inc. (handguns)
293 Main Street
Monson, Massachusetts 01057
(413) 267-4081

Whitworth (rifles)
Available through Interarms

Williams Gun Sight Co. (sights, scopes, mounts)
7389 Lapeer Road
Davison, Michigan 48423
(313) 653-2131

Winchester (ammunition, primers, cases)
See Olin/Winchester

Winchester (domestic rifles, shotguns)
See U.S. Repeating Arms Co.

Winslow Arms Co. (rifles)
P.O. Box 783
Camden, South Carolina 29020
(803) 432-2938

Zeiss Optical, Inc. (scopes)
P.O. Box 2010
Petersburg, Virginia 23804
(800) 446-1807

GUNFINDER

To help you find the model of your choice, the following list includes each gun found in the catalog section of **Shooter's Bible 1989**. A supplemental listing of **Discontinued Models** and the **Caliberfinder** follow immediately after this section.

BLACK POWDER GUNS
MUSKETS AND RIFLES

Armsport
Tryon Trailblazer	366
Model 5110 Kentucky rifle	366
Hawken Model 5101–5104	367

CVA
Squirrel	371
Blazer & Blazer II	371
St. Louis Hawken	371
Missouri Ranger	372
Hawken	372
Kentucky	372
Pennsylvania Long	374
Express Double Barrel	374
Double Barrel Carbine	373
Mountain	373
Frontier	374

Dixie
Second Model Brown Bess	379
Kentuckian Flintlock/Perc.	379
Hawken	380
Tennessee Mountain	380
Tennessee Squirrel	380
Lancaster Co., Pennsylvania	380
Mississippi Rifle	381
Winchester '73 Carbine	381
Wesson	381
1862 Three-Band Enfield	382
1858 Two-Band Enfield	382
1863 Springfield Civil War	382

Euroarms
Hawken	386
London Armory Company 3-Band	387
Cook & Brother Confederate Carbine	386
London Armory Company (two-band)	387
London Armory Company Enfield Musketoon	387

Hopkins & Allen
Brush Rifle Model 345	388
Underhammer Model 32	389
Pennsylvania Hawken Model 29	389

Lyman
Great Plains	390
Trade	390

Michigan Arms
Wolverine	391
Silverwolf	391
Friendship Special Match	391

Navy Arms
Parker-Hale Whitworth Military Target	397
Parker-Hale 451 Volunteer	397
Ithaca/Navy Hawken	397
#2 Creedmoor Target	398
Rolling Block Buffalo	398
Country Boy	398
1853 Enfield	399
1858 Enfield	399
1861 Enfield Musketoon	399
1863 Springfield	399
Mississippi Model 1841	400
Rigby-Style Target	400
Henry Military	401
Iron Frame Henry	401
Henry Trapper	401
Henry Carbine	401

Henry Carbine Engraved	401

Shiloh Sharps
Model 1874 Business	402
Model 1874 Military	402
Model 1874 Carbine	402
Model 1874 Sporting #1	403
Model 1874 Sporting #3	403
Model 1863 Sporting	403

Thompson/Center
Pennsylvania Hunter	404
Hawken	404
New Englander	404
Renegade	405
Renegade Hunter	405
Cherokee	405

Traditions
Frontier Scout	406
Hunter	406
Hawken	406
Hawken Woodsman	407
Pennsylvania	407
Shenandoah	407
Frontier	408
Trapper	408

A. Uberti
1858 New Army Target Revolving Carbine	409
Santa Fe Hawken	409

PISTOLS

CVA
Kentucky	376
Colonial	376
Philadelphia Derringer	376

Dixie
Screw Barrel Derringer	378
French Charleville Flint	378
"Hideout" Derringer	378
Lincoln Derringer	378
Pennsylvania	378
Abilene Derringer	378

Hopkins & Allen
Model 10	388
Boot Pistol	388

Lyman
Plains Pistol	390

Navy Arms
LePage Flintlock	395
LePage Percussion	395
LePage Double Cased Set	395
Kentucky	396
Harper's Ferry	396
Elgin Cutlass	396

Thompson/Center
Patriot	403

Traditions
Trapper	408

REVOLVERS

Armsport
Models 5133/5136/5138/5120/5139	368
Models 5152/5153/5154	369

CVA
1861 Colt Navy	375
1851 Colt Navy	375
Colt Sheriff's Model	375

1858 Remington Army	370
1860 Colt Army	375
Colt Walker	370
New Model Pocket Remington	370
Remington Bison	376
Third Model Colt Dragoon	376

Dixie
1860 Army	377
Navy Revolver	377
Spiller & Burr	377
Wyatt Earp	377
Walker	378
Third Model Dragoon	378

EMF
Sheriff's Model 1851	383
Model 1860 Army	383
Model 1862 Police	383
Model 1851 Steel Navy	383

Euroarms
Rogers & Spencer	384
Rogers & Spencer Army	384
Rogers & Spencer Model 1007	384
New Model Army Model 1020	384
New Model Army Model 1034	384
Remington 1858 New Model Army Engraved	384
New Model Army Target	384
Remington 1858 Model 1045	385
Schneider & Glassick 1851 Navy Sheriff	385
Schneider & Glassick 1851 Navy	385
Schneider & Glassick 1851 Navy Confederate	385

Navy Arms
Lemat	392
Colt Walker 1847	392
1862 Police	392
Reb Model 1860	393
Colt Army 1860	393
1851 Navy Yank	393
Rogers & Spencer Navy	393
Stainless Steel 1858 Remington	394
Target Model Remington	394
Deluxe 1858 Remington-Style	394
Remington New Model Army	394
Army 60 Sheriff's	394

A. Uberti
1st, 2nd & 3rd Model Dragoons	409
1861 Navy	409

SHOTGUNS

Armsport
Models 5124 & 5125	367

CVA
Brittany 12 Ga. Percussion Trapper	373

Dixie
Double Barrel Magnum	379

Euroarms
Magnum Cape Gun	386

Navy Arms
Model T&T	400

Thompson/Center
New Englander	404

RIFLE/SHOTGUN COMBINATION

DISCONTINUED MODELS

The following models, all of which appeared in the 1988 edition of Shooter's Bible, have been discontinued by their manufacturers and/or distributors and therefore do not appear in this year's edition.

BLACK POWDER

CVA
Brittany 12 ga. percussion shotgun
Prospector pistol
Hawken pistol

DIXIE
Buffalo Hunter rifle

EUROARMS
Remington 1858 New Model rifle

HOPKINS & ALLEN
Schuetzen rifle

IVER JOHNSON
Model BP .50HB rifle

NAVY ARMS
Swiss Federal Target rifle
Morse Muzzleloading rifle

THOMPSON/CENTER
Patriot pistol
Cougar Hawken Model rifle

TRADITIONS
Single Barrel Fowler

HANDGUNS

BEEMAN
SP Deluxe Metallic Silhouette
FAS Models 601 & 602

BERETTA
Model 86
Model 71

BERSA
Model 383SA

IVER JOHNSON
380 Pony
9mm DA Auto
Trailsman

MAUSER
Lugers (can still be ordered direct from German manufacturer)

NAVY ARMS
Luger

RUGER
Speed Six
Service Six DA

STEYR
Model GB Semiauto pistol

TANARMI
Model TA385B Derringer

RIFLES

ALPHA ARMS
Custom
Alaskan
Jaguar

ANSCHUTZ
Models 1807, 1810, 1811, 1813 (replaced by 1900 Series)
The Kadett 22LR
Model 1803D Match

BEEMAN/KRICO
Model 640 Standard Sniper

BROWNING
Model 92
Model 71 Grade I Carbine
Model 71 High Grade Carbine

COLT SAUER
Sporting Rifle
Short Action Rifle
Safari

HEYM
Model 55BF Double Rifle
Models 88B & 88B SS

MARLIN
Golden 39M
Models 336TS & 336ER
Model 70
Model 990

MAUSER
Model 66SM Bolt Action
Model 77 Bolt Action
Model 83 Sporting Rifle

MOSSBERG
Model 1500 Mountaineer Grade I
Model 1700LS Classic Hunter

REMINGTON
Sportsman 74 Autoloader
Model 581 Sportsman Bolt Action
Sportsman 76 Pump Action
Model Four
Model Six
Model 552A Speedmaster
Model 572A Fieldmaster

SAVAGE
Models 110-DL, 110-K, 110-V

SOVEREIGN
"Little Joe" 22 Single Shot
Model TD22 Semiauto Takedown

WHITWORTH
Mannlicher-Style Carbine

SHOTGUNS & PARAMILITARY

BERETTA
MODEL A302

BERNARDELLI
Orione O/U
Model 120 O/U (shotgun-rifle combo)
Model 190 O/U
Model 115L O/U

DIARM (see also American Arms for models still available)
Excelsior
Model FS200
AYA Model 2

EMF
Model AP74 (Commando & Assault models)

EXEL (see also under New England Firearms for models still available)
Models 101, 102, 103, 106, 107 (Series 100)
Series 300

FRANCHI
Standard Automatic (w/vent. ribs)
Magnum Automatic (w/vent. ribs)

GAMBA
Grifone O/U
Model 2100 Riot Gun

HEYM
Model 55BF Shotgun-Rifle Combo

NAVY ARMS
Models 100 & 150 Field Hunter

OLIN/WINCHESTER (see Classic Doubles in Shotgun Section for models still available)

PERUGINI-VISINI
Liberty Side-by-Side
Classic Side-by-Side

ROTTWEIL
International Trap
Supreme Field O/U

CALIBERFINDER

How to use this guide: To find a 22LR handgun, look under that heading below. You'll find several models of that description, including Beretta Model 21. Turn next to the **Gunfinder** section and locate the heading for **Beretta** (pistols, in this case). Beretta's **Model 21,** as indicated, appears on p. 99.

BLACK POWDER

HANDGUNS

31

CVA Pocket Remington

36

Armsport Models 5133, 5135
CVA 1851 & 1861 Colt Navy Revolvers, Sheriff's Model
Dixie Navy Revolver, Spiller & Burr Revolver
Euroarms Schneider & Glassick 1851 Navy & Navy Sheriff, Schneider & Glassick 1851 Navy Confederate revolver
Navy Arms 1862 Police Revolver, Reb Model 1860, Army 60 Sheriff's Model, "Yank" Revolver, 1851 Navy Yank, Remington New Model Army
Traditions Trapper pistol
A. Uberti 1861 Navy

41

Dixie Abilene & Lincoln Derringers

44

Armsport Models 5138, 5120, 5134, 5136, 5139, 5152, 5135, 5136
CVA 1861 Colt Navy, 1860 Colt Army Revolvers, Colt Walker Third Model Colt Dragoon, Remington Bison, 1858 Remington Army Steel Frame Revolver (also Brass Frame)
Dixie Walker Revolver, Pennsylvania Pistol, Third Model Dragoon, Wyatt Earp Revolver
Euroarms Rogers & Spencer Models 1005 & 1006, Remington 1858 New Model Army (and Target) 1851 Navy Sheriff, Schneider & Glassick 1851 Navy Sheriff Revolver, Schneider & Glassick 1851 Navy Confederate Revolver
Hopkins & Allen Model 10, Yank Revolver
Navy Arms Colt Walker 1847, Reb Model 1860 Revolver, Colt Army 1860 Revolver, Rogers & Spencer Navy Revolver, Target Model Remington Revolver, Army 60 Sheriff's Model, Stainless Steel 1858 Remington, Remington New Model Army, LeMat Revolvers, 1851 Navy Yank Revolver, LePage Dueling Pistol, Deluxe 1858 Remington-Style Revolver

45

CVA Kentucky, Colonial, Philadelphia Derringer
Hopkins & Allen Boot Pistol Model 13
Navy Arms LePage Perc. & Flint Pistols, Moore & Patrick English Pistols, Double Cased LePage Pistols
Traditions Trapper Pistol

50

Lyman Plains Pistol
Traditions Trapper

54

Lyman Plains Pistol

58

Navy Arms Harper's Ferry Pistols

RIFLES (Black Powder)

32

CVA Squirrel
Dixie Tennessee Squirrel
Navy Arms Country Boy

36

Armsport Model 5108
Hopkins & Allen Brush Rifle, Model 32
Navy Arms Country Boy
Traditions Trapper

44

Navy Arms Henry Carbine Military, Iron Frame

44-40

Dixie Winchester '73 Carbine
Navy Arms Henry Carbine, Henry Trapper, Military, Iron Frame

45

Armsport Models 5108, 5110, 5111, 5101
CVA Kentucky, Frontier (kit)
Dixie Kentuckian, Hawken
Hopkins & Allen Brush Rifle, Schuetzen, Model 32
Michigan Arms Wolverine, Silverwolf
Navy Arms Kentucky, Country Boy
Thompson/Center Cougar, Hawken, Cherokee
Traditions Frontier, Frontier Scout, Hawken, Pennsylvania, Kentucky Scout, Trapper

451

Navy Arms Rigby-Style Target Rifle, Parker-Hale Whitworth Military Target, Parker-Hale 451 Volunteer

45-70

Navy Arms Rolling Block Buffalo Rifle

50

Armsport Models 5109, 5110A, 5102, 5104
CVA Frontier, Blazer II, St. Louis Hawken, Pennsylvania Long Rifle, Missouri Ranger, Hawken, Express Double Rifle & Carbine
Dixie Hawken, Tennessee Mountain, Wesson
Euroarms Model 2210A Hawken
Hopkins & Allen Model 32, 29
Lyman Great Plains, Trade Rifle
Michigan Arms Wolverine, Silverwolf, Knight MK 85 Hunter
Navy Arms Kentucky, Ithaca-Navy Hawken, Country Boy
Thompson/Center Renegade, Renegade Hunter, Cougar Hawken, Hawken, New Englander, Pennsylvania Hunter
Traditions Frontier Scout, Hunter, Hawken, Pennsylvania, Kentucky Scout, Shenandoah, Hawken Woodsman, Trapper

54

Armsport Model 5103, 5204B
CVA Hawken, Mountain
Dixie Hawken
Lyman Great Plains, Trade Rifle

Michigan Arms Wolverine, Silverwolf, Knight MK 85 Hunter
Navy Arms Ithaca-Navy Hawken
Shiloh Sharps Model 1863, Military Carbine
Thompson, Center Renegade, Hawken, New Englander
Traditions Hunter
A. Uberti Sante Fe Hawken

56

Thompson, Center Renegade

58

Dixie Hawken, Mississippi, 1863 Springfield Civil War Musket
Euroarms Model 2260 London Armory Company Enfield Rifled Musket, Models 2270 and 2280 London Armory Company Enfield Rifled Muskets, Model 2300 Cook & Brother Confederate Carbine
Hopkins & Allen Model 32
Navy Arms 1863 Springfield, Mississippi Model 1841
Traditions Hawken

74

Dixie Second Model Brown Bess Musket

75

Navy Arms Second Model Brown Bess Musket

557

Navy Arms 1853 Enfield Rifle Musket, 1858 Enfield, 1861 Enfield Musketoon

SHOTGUNS (Black Powder)

Armsport Models 5115, 5124, 5125
CVA Trapper (12 ga.)
Dixie Double Barrel Magnum 12-Gauge
Euroarms Model 2290 12-Gauge, Model 2295 Magnum Cape
Navy Arms Model T&T
Thompson/Center New Englander

HANDGUNS

22LR

American Derringer Model 1, Model 7
Anschutz Exemplar XIV
Beeman FAS 602, Beeman/Korth, Unique 69 Target, Model PO8
Beretta Model 21
Bersa Model 224DA
Browning Buck Mark 22
Charter Arms Pathfinder, Off-Duty
Dakota Model 1873, Dakota Target, 1894 Bisley
Davis Model D-22
Erma ESP 85A Sporting Pistol, Model 772 Match Revolver
F.I.E. Arminius, Titan II
Freedom Arms FA-S
Hammerli Models 150, 152, 208, 215 Target
Iver Johnson Pocket Model
Llama Automatic (Small Frame)

Mitchell Arms SA Army Model (revolvers)
New England Firearms DA Revolvers
North American Arms Mini-Revolvers
Rossi Model 511
Ruger New Model Single-Six, Mark II Pistols
Sako Olympic Triace
Smith & Wesson Models 17, 34, 63, 41, 422
Tanarmi Model TA76M
Targa Model GT22T
Thompson/Center Contender
A. Uberti DA Automatics (Models PP, P-38, TPH, GSP Match, GSP Jr., UIT-BV)
Walther Model P-38, Model TPH DA, Models OSP & GSP, Model FP (Free Pistol), Model U.I.T.-BV

22 Rimfire Magnum

American Derringer Model 1
Anschutz Exemplar XIV
Ruger Government Target Model
Smith & Wesson Model 650
Tanarmi Model TA76M
Dan Wesson 22 Rimfire Magnum

22 Short

Beeman FAS 601, Unique 2000-U
Beretta Model 950
F.I.E. Arminius DA
Hammerli Model 232
North American Arms Mini-Revolvers
Ruger New Model Single-Six Revolver
Sako Olympic Triace

22 Hornet

American Derringer Model 1
MOA Maximum
Thompson/Center Contender

22 Win. Mag.

Dakota Model 1873
Davis Model D-22
F.I.E. Arminius
Freedom Arms FA-S
North American Mini-Revolvers
Ruger New Model Single-Six
Thompson/Center Contender

221 Fireball

Kimber Predator

223 Remington

Kimber Predator
Remington Model XP-100
Thompson/Center Contender

223 Rem. Comm. Auto

American Derringer Model 1
Thompson/Center Contender

25 Auto

Beretta Model 21, Model 950BS
Davis Model D-22 Derringer
F.I.E. Model A27BW, Titan 25
Iver Johnson Pocket
Targa Model GT26S

7mm TCU

Kimber Predator
Thompson/Center Contender

7mm BR

Remington Model XP-100

7-30 Water

Thompson/Center Contender

30 Luger

American Derringer Model 1

30 Carbine

Dakota Model 1873
Ruger Model BN-31, Blackhawk SA
Thompson/Center Contender

30 Mauser (7.62 Tokarev)

American Derringer Model 1

30-30 Win.

American Derringer Model 1
Thompson/Center Contender

32 Mag.

American Derringer Models 1 and 7
Dan Wesson 32 Mag. Six-Shot

32 Auto

Davis Models D-22 and P-32
F.I.E. Titan and Super Titan II
Llama Auto (Small Frame)

32 H&R

Charter Arms Police Bulldog, Police Undercover
New England Firearms DA Revolvers
Ruger New Model Single-Six SSM
Thompson/Center Contender

32 S&W Long

American Derringer Model 7
Charter Arms Undercover
F.I.E. Arminius
Ruger New Model Single-Six SSM
Sako Olympic Triace
Smith & Wesson Model 31
Taurus Model 73
Walther Model GSP-C

32 S&W Wadcutter

Erma ESP 85A Sporting Pistol, Model 773 Match Revolver

32-20

American Derringer Model 1
Dakota Model 1873

35 Remington

Remington Model XP-100
Thompson/Center Contender

357 Mag.

American Derringer Model 1
Astra 357 Mag.
Beeman Korth
Charter Arms Bulldog Tracker
Colt King Cobra, Python
Coonan Arms Model B
Dakota Target, 1894 Bisley, 1875 Outlaw, Model 1873
Erma Model 777 Sporting Revolver
F.I.E. Arminius
L.A.R. Grizzly Mark I
Llama Super Comanche, Comanche III
Magnum Research Desert Eagle
Ruger Model GP-100, New Model Bisley, Blackhawk SA

(continued)

Smith & Wesson Models 13, 19, 27, 65, 66, 586
Taurus Models 65, 66, 669
Thompson/Center Contender
A. Uberti 1875 Remington Army Outlaw
Dan Wesson 357 Mag., 357 Super Mag.

357 Maximum

American Derringer Model 1
Thompson/Center Contender

358 Winchester

MOA Maximum

38 Special

American Derringer Models 1, 3, 7, 11
Charter Arms Police Undercover, Police Bulldog, Off-Duty
Colt Combat Commander, Government Model
F.I.E. Derringer D-86, Titan Tiger, Arminius
Rossi Models 68, M88, 851, M951, 971
Smith & Wesson Models 10, 15, 64, 66, 67, 649
Taurus Models 66, 80, 82, 83, 85, 86, 669
A. Uberti 1873 Cattleman Quick Draw
Dan Wesson 38 Special Revolvers

380 Auto

American Derringer Models 1 and 7
Astra Constable
Beeman Model Mini-PO8
Beretta Models 84 and 85
Bersa Model 383 DA
Browning Model BDA-380
Colt Government Model, Mustang, Mustang Plus II
F.I.E. Titan II, Super Titan II
Heckler & Koch Model P7K3
Llama Automatic (Small Frame)
Sig Sauer Model 230
Targa Model GT380XE
Taurus Model PT 58
Walther Model PPK/S American

38 Super

American Derringer Model 7
Colt Combat Commander, Government Model
Sig Sauer Model 220
Springfield Armory Omega
Victory Arms Model MC5

38 S&W

American Derringer Model 7
Smith & Wesson Models 13, 36, 38, 49, 52, 60, 65

38-40

Dakota Model 1873

41 Action Express

Action Arms AT-84 and AT-84P
American Derringer Model 1
F.I.E. Model TZ75
Victory Arms Model MC5

41 Mag.

American Derringer Model 1
Ruger Redhawk, New Model Bisley, Blackhawk SA
Smith & Wesson Models 57, 657
Thompson/Center Contender
Dan Wesson 41 Mag. Revolvers

.410

American Derringer Models 1, 4, 6

9mm Federal

American Derringer Model 1

9mm Luger

American Derringer Model 1
Colt Combat Commander, Government Model
Heckler & Koch Model P7 Pistol, Model P9S
   Auto Pistol, Model VP702
Smith & Wesson Models 438, 459, 469, 639, 659
Thompson/Center Contender

9mm Parabellum

Action Arms Models AT-84 and AT-84P
American Derringer Semmerling LM-4
Astra Model A-90
Beretta Model 92F
Brno Model CZ75
Browning 9mm Hi-Power
F.I.E. Model TZ75
Glock Models 17, 19, 17L Competition
Llama Automatics (Compact Frame), Model M-82
Ruger Model P-85
Sig Sauer Models P210, 220, 225, 226
Springfield Armory Model 1911-A1 Standard
Star Models BKM & BM, 30M & 30PK
Steyr Model GB Semiauto
Tanarmi Models BTA90B and BTA90C
Targa Models 92 and 99
Taurus Models PT92 and PT99
Victory Arms Model MC5
Walther Models P-38, P-88DA, P-5DA

10mm

Colt Delta Elite
Springfield Armory Omega

44 Magnum

American Derringer Model 1
Astra Model 44
Freedom Arms Model FA-454AS
Llama Super Comanche IV
Magnum Research Desert Eagle
Mitchell Arms SA Army Model Revolvers
Ruger Redhawk, New Model Bisley, Blackhawk
   SA, Super Blackhawk, Super Redhawk DA
Smith & Wesson Model 29
Thompson/Center Contender
Dan Wesson 44 Mag. Revolvers

44 Special

American Derringer Models 1 and 7
Charter Arms Bulldog
Ruger Super Blackhawk

44-40

American Derringer Model 1
Dakota Models 1873, 1875 Outlaw, Bisley
A. Uberti 1873 Cattleman Quick Draw, 1875
   Remington Army Outlaw

45 Auto

American Derringer Models 1, 10, Semmerling
   LM-4
Astra Model A-90
Colt Combat Commander, Lightweight
   Commander, Gold Cup National Match,
   Officer's ACP, Combat Elite, Government
   Model
Detonics Combat Master, Servicemaster II,
   Scoremaster, Janus Scoremaster
Heckler & Koch Model P9S
L.A.R. Grizzly Mark I

Llama Automatics (Large and Compact Frame)
Sig Sauer Model 220
Smith & Wesson Models 645 and 745
Springfield Armory Model 1911-A1 Standard,
   Omega
Star Model PD
Victory Arms Model MC5

45 Colt

American Derringer Models 1, 4, 6, 10
Astra Model 45
Dakota Target Model 1873, 1875 Outlaw, Bisley
Freedom Arms Model FA-454AS
Mitchell Arms SA Army Model Revolvers
Ruger New Model Bisley, Blackhawk SA
Smith & Wesson Model 25
Thompson/Center Contender
A. Uberti 1873 Cattleman Quick Draw, 1875
   Remington Army
Dan Wesson 45 Colt DA

45 Win. Mag.

American Derringer Model 1
L.A.R. Grizzly Mark I

451 Detonics Magnum

Detonics Scoremaster

454 Casull

Freedom Arms Model FA-454AS

RIFLES

CENTERFIRE BOLT ACTION

Standard Calibers

17 Rem.

Kimber Model 84
Sako Fiberclass, Hunter, Deluxe
Tikka Model M55
Ultra Light Model 20

222 Rem.

Beeman/Krico Varmint, Super Sniper, Model 640
Brno Models ZKK 600, 601, 602
Churchill Regent, Highlander
Kimber Model 84
Sako Varmint, Fiberclass, Hunter, Deluxe
Steyr-Mannlicher Model ST
Tikka Model M55
Ultra Light Model 20
Winslow Varmint

223 Rem.

Beeman/Krico Varmint, Super Sniper, Model 640
Brno Model ZKK601
Browning A-Bolt
Heckler & Koch Models 630, SL6
Howa Sporting, Varmint
Kimber Model 84
Mark X Mini
Remington Models 700, 7, Sportsman 78
Sako Fiberclass, Hunter, Varmint, Deluxe
Savage Model 110E
Steyr-Mannlicher Model SL
Tikka Model M55
Ultra Light Model 20
Weatherby Vanguard VGL, Fiberguard
Winchester Models 70XTR Featherweight,
   Sporter Varmint, Lightweight Carbine

Winslow Varmint

22-250

Beeman/Krico Model 640, Varmint
Blaser Models R 84, Ultimate
Browning Short Action A-Bolt
Howa Sporting, Varmint
Mark X American Field Sporting Series
Parker-Hale Models M81, 1000, 1200, 2100,
   1100
Remington Model 700
Ruger Models M-77RL, M-77RSI International,
   M-77V Varmint, M-77R
Sako Mannlicher-Style, Deluxe, Varminter,
   Carbine, Hunter, Fiberclass
Savage Model 110E
Steyr-Mannlicher Model L
Tikka Model M55
Ultra Light Model 20
Weatherby Vanguard VGS, Lazermark, Deluxe
Winchester Model 70 XTRFeatherweight,
   Lightweight, VGX

224

Weatherby Mark V Lazermark, Deluxe

240

Weatherby Mark V Lazermark, Deluxe,
   Fibermark, Euromark

243 Win.

Beeman/Krico Models 600, 700
Blaser Models R 84, Ultimate
Brno Models ZKK, 601
Browning Short Action A-Bolt
Churchill Regent, Highlander
Heym Models SR20, 22S
Howa Sporting
K.D.F. Model K-15
Mark X American Field Series
Mauser Model 66
Parker-Hale Models M81, 1000, 1200, 1100,
   2100, M87
Remington Models 700, 78, 7400
Ruger Models M-77RL, RS, RSI International,
   M-77V Varmint
Sako Carbine, Varminter, Fiberclass, Hunter,
   Deluxe
Sauer Models 200, 90
Savage Models 110E
Steyr-Mannlicher Models L, SSG Marksman,
   Match UIT, Luxus
Tikka Model M55
Ultra Light Model 20
Weatherby Vanguard VGS, VGL, VGX
Winchester Models 70XTR Featherweight,
   Lightweight, Carbine, Varmint, Ranger Youth
Winslow Basic, Grade Crown

6mm Rem.

Blaser Model R 84
Parker-Hale Models M81, 1000, 1100, 1200,
   2100
Remington Model 7
Ruger Model M-77
Ultra Light Model 20
Steyr-Mannlicher Model L

250-3000 Savage

Ultra Light Model 20

257

Weatherby Mark V Lazermark, Deluxe,
   Fibermark, Euromark

25-06

Blaser Models R 84, Ultimate
Browning A-Bolt Action
Churchill Regent, Highlander
K.D.F. Model K-15
Mark X American Field Sporting Series
Remington Model 700 ADL
Ruger Models M-77V Varmint, 77RS
Sako Fiberclass, Hunter, Carbine, Deluxe
Sauer Models 90, 200
Steyr-Mannlicher Model M
Weatherby Vanguard VGS, VGX
Winchester Models 70XTR Featherweight, Sporter
Winslow Basic, Grade Crown

257 Roberts

Browning A-Bolt Short Action
Dakota Arms Model 76
Ultra Light Model 20

270 Win.

Beeman/Krico Model 600
Blaser Models R 84, Ultimate
Brno Model ZKK 600
Browning A-Bolt Action
Churchill Regent, Highlander
Dakota Arms Model 76
Heym Model SR20
Howa Sporting, Lightning
Kimber Big Game
Mark X LTW, American Field Sporting Series
Mauser Model 66
Parker-Hale Models M81, 1000, 1100, 1200, 2100
Remington Models 78, 700, 7400, 7600
Ruger Model M-77 RLS
Sako Deluxe, Carbine, Fiberclass, Hunter
Sauer Models 90, 200
Savage Model 110E
Steyr-Mannlicher Model M
Tikka Model M65
Weatherby Models Mark V Lazermark, Deluxe, Fibermark, Vanguard VGS, VGL, VGX
Winchester Models 70XTR, Lightweight, Featherweight, Ranger
Winslow Basic, Grade Crown

280 Rem.

Blaser Models R 84, Ultimate
Browning A-Bolt Action
Dakota Arms Model 76
Kimber Big Game
Winchester Models 70 Lightweight, 7400, 7600
Winslow Basic, Grade Crown

284 Win.

Ultra Light Model 20

7mm-08

Browning A-Bolt Short Action
Remington Model Seven
Sako Fiberclass, Hunter, Deluxe
Ultra Light Model 20

30-06

Beeman/Krico Model 700
Blaser Models R 84, Ultimate
Brno Model ZKK 600
Browning A-Bolt Action
Churchill Regent, Highlander
Dakota Arms Model 76
Howa Sporting, Lightning

Heckler & Koch Model 940
K.D.F. Model K-15
Kimber Big Game
Krieghoff Models Ulm, Teck
Mark X American Field Sporting Series, LTW Sporter
Mauser Model 66
Parker-Hale Models M81 Classic, 1100 Lightweight, 1000, 1200 Super, 2100 Midland, M87
Remington Models 78, 700, 7400
Ruger Models M-77RS, 77RL
Sako Carbine, Fiberclass, Hunter, Deluxe
Sauer Models 90, 200
Savage Model 110E
Steyr-Mannlicher Model M
Tikka Model M65
Weatherby Mark V. Fibermark, Lazermark, Euromark, Deluxe, Vanguard VGS, VGL, VGX
Winchester Models 70XTR Featherweight, Winlite, Sporter, Lightweight Carbine, Ranger
Winslow Basic, Grade Crown

30-06 Carbine

Remington Model 7400

300 Savage

Ultra Light Model 20

308 Win.

Beeman/Krico Models 600, 640
Blaser Ultimate
Brno Model ZKK 601
Browning A-Bolt Short Action
Churchill Regent, Highlander
Heckler & Koch Models HK PSG-1, 770
Heym Model 66
Howa Sporting
K.D.F. Model K-15
Krieghoff Ulm, Teck
Mark X American Field Sporting Series
Mauser Model 66
Parker-Hale Models M81, 1000, 1100, 1200, 2100, M87
Remington Models Seven, 83, 700, 78, 7400
Ruger Models M-77RS, 77RL, 77RSI International, 77V Varmint
Sako Carbine, Varminter, Fiberclass, Hunter, Deluxe
Sauer Models 90, 200
Savage Model 99-C
Steyr-Mannlicher Models L, SSG Marksman, Match UIT
Tikka Models M55, M65
Ultra Light Model 20
Weatherby Vanguard VGL
Winchester Model 70XTR Lightweight, Featherweight (Short Action)
Winslow Basic, Grade Crown

35 Whelen

Remington Models 700 CL, 7600

358 Win.

Ultra Light Model 20

MAGNUM CALIBERS

222 Rem. Mag.

Kimber Model 84 Sporter

257 Weatherby

Blaser Model R 84

K.D.F. Model K-15
Steyr-Mannlicher Model S

264 Win. Mag.

Blaser Models R 84, Ultimate
Steyr-Mannlicher Model S

270 Weatherby Mag.

K.D.F. Model K-15

270 Win. Mag.

Sako Carbine

7mm Rem. Mag.

Blaser Models R 84, Ultimate
Browning A-Bolt Action
Churchill Regent, Highlander
Dakota Arms Model 76
Heym Model SR20
Howa Lightning
K.D.F. Model K-15
Kimber Big Game
Mark X American Field Sporting Series, LTW Sporter
Parker-Hale Model M81 Classic
Remington Model 700
Ruger Models M-77RS, 77RL
Sako Fiberclass, Hunter, Carbine, Deluxe
Sauer Model 90
Savage Model 110E
Steyr-Mannlicher Models S, T
Tikka Model M65
Weatherby Mark V Fibermark, Deluxe, Lazermark, Vanguard VGL, VGX
Winslow Basic, Grade Crown

300 Weatherby

Blaser Models R 84, Ultimate
K.D.F. Model K-15
Sako Hunter, Deluxe

300 Win. Mag.

Blaser Models R 84, Ultimate
Brno Model ZKK 602
Browning A-Bolt Action
Churchill Regent, Highlander
Dakota Arms Model 76
Heym Model SR20
K.D.F. Model K-15
Kimber Big Game
Krieghoff Ulm, Teck
Mark X American Field Sporting Series
Parker-Hale Models M81 Classic, M87
Ruger Models M-77RS, 77RL
Sako Safari Grade, Fiberclass, Hunter, Deluxe, Carbine
Sauer Model 90
Steyr-Mannlicher Models S, T Magnum, Luxus
Weatherby Mark V Fibermark, Euromark, Lazermark, Vanguard VGS, VGX
Winchester Model 70XTR Sporter Magnum
Winslow Basic, Grade Crown

338 Win. Mag.

Blaser Models R 84, Ultimate
Browning A-Bolt Action
Dakota Arms Model 76
Kimber Big Game
Ruger Models M-77RS, 77R, 77RL
Sako Safari Grade, Hunter, Carbine, Deluxe, Fiberclass
Steyr-Mannlicher Models S, T
Tikka Model M65

Winchester Model 70 Win-lite
Winslow Basic, Grade Crown

340 Win. Mag.

Weatherby Mark V Lazermark, Euromark

375 H&H

Browning A-Bolt Gold Medallion
Dakota Arms Model 76
Heym Models SR20, 88 Safari
K.D.F. Model K-15
Kimber Big Game
Krieghoff Ulm, Teck
Parker-Hale Model M81 African
Sako Safari Grade, Carbine, Fiberclass, Hunter, Deluxe
Sauer Model 90
Steyr-Mannlicher Models S, T
Whitworth Safari Grade Express
Winchester Model 70XTR Super Express (standard)
Winslow Basic, Grade Crown

378 Win. Mag.

Weatherby Mark V Lazermark, Euromark

458 Win. Mag.

Brno Model ZKK 602
Dakota Arms Model 76
Heym Model 88 Safari
Krieghoff Ulm, Teck
Ruger Models M-77RS, Tropical
Sauer Model S-90 Safari
Steyr-Mannlicher Models S, T
Whitworth Safari Grade
Winchester Model 70XTR Super Express (standard)
Winslow Basic, Grade Crown

460 Win. Mag.

Weatherby Lazermark, Euromark

470 Nitro Express

Heym Model 88 Safari

CENTERFIRE LEVER ACTION

222 Rem./223 Rem.

Browning Models 81BLR, 1885

22-250

Browning Models 81BLR, 1885

25-20 Win.

Marlin Model 1894 Classic

257 Roberts

Browning Model 81BLR

243 Win.

Browning Model 81 BLR
Ruger Model No. 1 International
Savage Model 99-C

270

Browning Model 1885
Ruger Model No. 1 International

7mm-08

Browning Model 81BLR

307 Win.

Winchester Model 94

308 Win.

Browning Model 81BLR
Savage Model 99-C

30-30 Win.

Marlin Models 336CS, 336 LTS, 30AS
Winchester Models 94 Standard, 70XTR, Trapper, Ranger

30-06

Browning Model 1885
Ruger Model No. 1 International

32-20 Win.

Marlin Model 1894 Classic

358 Win.

Browning Model 81BLR

35 Rem.

Marlin Model 336CS

356 Win.

Winchester Model 94

357 Win.

Winchester Model 94

357 Mag.

Marlin Model 1894CS
Rossi Puma

358 Win.

Browning Model 81BLR

375 Win.

Marlin Model 336CS

38 Special

Marlin Model 1894S
Rossi Puma
A. Uberti 1866 Sporting, 1873 Carbine

41 Mag.

Marlin Model 1894S

44 Special

Marlin Model 1894S

44 Rem. Mag.

Browning Model 92
Marlin Model 1894S
Winchester Model 94 Standard

444 Marlin

Marlin Model 444SS

45 Colt

Marlin Model 1894S, 45-70 Government
Browning Models 1885, 81BLR
Marlin Model 1895SS

7mm Rem. Mag.

Browning Models 1885, 81BLR

SLIDE ACTION

22 LR

Rossi Model M62SA

6mm Rem.

Remington Model 7600

243 Win.

Remington Model 7600

270 Win.

Remington Model 7600

30-06/30-06 Accelerator

Remington Model 7600

SINGLE SHOT

22S,L,LR

Iver Johnson L'il Champ
Varner Favorite Model
Walther Running Boar, Model GX-1, UIT Match, Model KK/MS

22 PPC

Sako Varminter

222 Rem.

Remington Models 40-XB, 40XB-BR
Thompson/Center Hunter

220 Swift

Ruger No. 1 Special Varminter

223

Ruger No. 1 Special Varminter, Standard

22-250 Rem.

Blaser Model K 77A
Remington Model 40-XB
Ruger No. 1 Standard, Special Varminter
Thompson/Center Hunter

243 Win.

Blaser Model K 77A
Remington Model 40-XB
Ruger No. 1 Light Sporter, Standard, RSI International

25-06

Remington Model 40-XB
Ruger Special Varminter, Standard

6mm Rem.

Remington Model 40-XB
Ruger No. 1 International, Special Varminter, Standard

6mm PC

Sako Varminter

257 Roberts

Ruger No. 1 Standard

270 Win.

Blaser Model K 77A
Ruger No. 1 Light Sporter, Standard, RSI International

280 Rem.

Blaser Model K 77A
Ruger No. 1 Standard

30-06

Blaser Model K 77A
Remington Model 40/XB
Ruger No. 1 Light Sporter, Standard, RSI
    International
Thompson/Center Hunter

300 Win. Mag.

Blaser Model K 77A
Remington Model 40-XB, 40XB-BR
Ruger No. 1 Medium Sporter, Standard

7mm Rem. Mag.

Blaser Model K 77A
Remington Models 40XB, 40XB-BR
Ruger No. 1 Medium Sporter, Standard

300 Weath. Mag.

Blaser Model K 77A

338 Win. Mag.

Ruger No. 1 Medium Sporter

375 H&H

Ruger No. 1 Tropical

375 Win.

Marlin Model 336CS

458 Win. Mag.

Ruger No. 1 Tropical

AUTOLOADING

222 Rem.

Thompson/Center Contender

223 Rem.

Ruger Mini-14, Mini-14 Ranch, Mini-30

Thompson/Center Contender

243 Win.

Browning Grades I, III, IV

30-06

Browning BAR Standard

30-30 Win.

Thompson/Center Contender

300 Win. Mag.

Browning BAR Standard

308 Win.

Browning BAR Standard
Ruger Model XG1

44 Mag.

Thompson/Center Contender

45 Auto

Marlin Model 45

7mm Rem. Mag.

Browning BAR Standard

9mm

Marlin Model 9 Camp

RIMFIRE BOLT ACTION

218 Bee

Kimber Model 82B Classic

22S,L,LR

Anschutz Models Mark 2000MK, 1403D, 1803D,
    64MS, 54.18MS, 1913, 1911, 1910, 1907,
    1808, 1422D, 1522D, 525, Achiever
Beeman/Weirauch Model HW60 Smallbore
Beeman/FWB Models 2000, 2600
Beeman/Krico Models 320 Sporter, 340
Browning Model A-Bolt 22
K.D.F. Model K-22

Kimber Model 82 Classic
Marlin Models 15, 15Y, 780
Remington Models 40-XR, 40-XC, 541-T
Rossi Gallery Rifles
Ruger Models 77, 22RS

22 Hornet

Anschutz Bavarian 1422D, 1522D
Beeman/Krico Models 400, 420

22 WMR

Heckler & Koch Model 300
Marlin Models 25M, 783

22 Mag.

Anschutz Bavarian 1422D, 1522D
K.D.F. Model K-22

222 Rem.

Anschutz Bavarian 1422D, 1522D

RIMFIRE AUTOLOADING

22S,L,LR

Anschutz Model 525
Browning Model 22 (Grades I, VI)
Iver Johnson U.S. Carbine .22
Marlin Models 70P, 70HC, 75C, 60, 995
Remington Models 552BDL, 572BDL Fieldmaster
Ruger Model 10/22
Weatherby Mark XXII

25-20

Kimber Model 82B Classic

RIMFIRE LEVER ACTION

22S,L,LR

Browning Model BL-22 (Grades I, II)
Iver Johnson Wagonmaster
Marlin Models 39TD, Golden 39AS

444 Marlin

Marlin Model 444SS

INDEX